Disrupting Pedagogies in the Knowledge Society:

Countering Conservative Norms with Creative Approaches

Julie Faulkner
RMIT University, Australia

Managing Director:	Lindsay Johnston
Senior Editorial Director:	Heather Probst
Book Production Manager:	Sean Woznicki
Development Manager:	Joel Gamon
Development Editor:	Michael Killian
Acquisitions Editor:	Erika Gallagher
Typesetters:	Adrienne Freeland
Print Coordinator:	Jamie Snavely
Cover Design:	Nick Newcomer, Greg Snader

Published in the United States of America by
Information Science Reference (an imprint of IGI Global)
701 E. Chocolate Avenue
Hershey PA 17033
Tel: 717-533-8845
Fax: 717-533-8661
E-mail: cust@igi-global.com
Web site: http://www.igi-global.com

Library of Congress Cataloging-in-Publication Data

Disrupting pedagogies in the knowledge society: countering conservative norms with creative approaches / Julie Faulkner, editor.
     p. cm.
  Includes bibliographical references and index.
  Summary: "This book examines a range of 'disruptive' approaches, exploring how challenge, dissonance, and discomfort might be mobilized in educational contexts in order to shift taken-for-granted attitudes and beliefs held by both educators and learners"--Provided by publisher.
  ISBN 978-1-61350-495-6 (hardcover) -- ISBN 978-1-61350-496-3 (ebook) -- ISBN 978-1-61350-497-0 (print & perpetual access) 1. Critical pedagogy. 2. Critical thinking--Study and teaching. 3. Educational change. I. Faulkner, Julie, 1952-
  LC196.D57 2012
  370.11'5--dc23
                                        2011036893

British Cataloguing in Publication Data
A Cataloguing in Publication record for this book is available from the British Library.

Table of Contents

Detailed Table of Contents

Chapter 1
Locating and Loving the Personal: Risk and Vulnerability in a Secondary English Language Arts
Methods Course 1
> *Suzanne Knight, University of Michigan—Flint, USA*

Exploring vulnerability and risk taking as disruptive behaviour, Knight looks into competing expectations on the part of teachers and students through narrative analyses and affirms the value of building a connected knowing group.

Chapter 2
Disrupting Relationships: A Catalyst for Growth 16
> *Vicki Stieha, University of Cincinnati, USA*
> *Miriam Raider-Roth, University of Cincinnati, USA*

The authors examine partnered teacher work through 'relational rupture'. Exploring the complex development procedure of 'unlearning' through Hevruta, or traditional Jewish text study, they observe how shared exploration strengthens deeper understanding.

Chapter 3
"Critical Friendship" and Sustainable Change: Creating Liminal Spaces to Experience Discomfort
Together 32
> *Susan R. Adams, Butler University, USA*
> *Ross Peterson-Veatch, Goshen College, USA*

This chapter details the role of collaborative learning in supporting change, wherein the authors underline the value of willing professional learning communities, suggesting protocols to maintain a critical focus.

The author uses the Interactive Learning Model to examine the role of retrospective sense making to enable more effective learning.

The author deconstructs the power of metaphor in shaping rhetoric in university composition courses. Examining the agendas and tropes of scholarly writing, Ellis argues for more diverse forms of inquiry and writing to embrace, rather than fear, the irreducibility of the conversation metaphor.

The chapter analyses composition's dependence on critical pedagogies. Constructing students as incomplete and in need of transformation, a trope which can arguably be taken too far, teachers concerned with social change represent students as 'other', thus limiting agency and complexity in student identity.

This chapter takes the Freirean concept conscientização, or consciousness of consciousness. Linking discomfort to the notion of aporia, Harris argues that educators can no longer continue to privilege print-based texts in the face of a generation who work differently. We need to teach critical thinking within digital contexts.

The authors collaborate on a cross-cultural project involving Australian and American students exploring a satirical television series. In this case, parody is the vehicle for demonstrating that normative cultural patterns have no necessity; we are amused partly because our culture has taught us how to laugh.

The author notes that disruptive pedagogies could spark resistance in students who might well feel protective over family and community loyalties. Beginning college students leave behind comforting certainties, and the author asks whether they might see disruptive approaches as a form of indoctrination to liberal politics. Knoblauch builds a case for invitational rhetoric to encourage stronger questioning of students' deeply held beliefs.

This chapter focuses on art, particularly the visual arts, an area which can offer fertile spaces for moving away from "safe" thinking in schools. It asks how students use bodies and sexualities as a medium for disruption, and what kinds of emotions are evoked around this process.

The authors of this chapter bring drama techniques into the professional writing classroom. Compressing the space between the workplace and classroom, students are required to resist familiar patterns of learner interaction and assume professional identities.

This chapter further explores questions of identity in the process of becoming a teacher. In the arguably daunting areas of mathematics and the arts, they look at how student discomfort might be managed by experiential learning and specifically designed assessment. Their focus is on teacher education pedagogies in conjunction with pre-service learning, and the relationship of these processes to teacher identity formation.

Chapter 13

The author examines how mathematics positions pre-service teachers. Arguing that the language of mathematics is neither context-free nor ahistorical, she analyses ways that language connects to power in the classroom. Teachers of mathematics need to experience more ambiguity and understand the microdynamics of the classroom in order to more deeply control learning and teaching processes.

Chapter 14

The author writes from an ESL context where heterosexuality is presumed as part of the normative expectations of classrooms. This chapter examines sensitive issues around sexuality and explores ways that disruption might productively play out when supported by an aware and reflective teacher.

This chapter provides a critical methodology to interrogate received notions of self, opening avenues of inquiry and transformation. Challenging binary thinking complicates either/or approaches, enabling expanded ways of knowing and being in the world.

The author asks 'proprioceptive' questions to challenge taken-for-granted ways of thinking and writing. Highlighting and calling into question one's own words, phrases and images, this kind of question breaks up the rhythm of the writing by asking 'what do I mean by ...?', thus calling attention to language and meaning.

Chapter 17

This chapter begins with a theoretical exploration of the concept and process of disruption. Focussing on rhetorical inquiry processes, The author examines the rising complexity of performative and dialogic encounters within increasingly unfamiliar and complex contexts, in order to 'willingly embrace' discomfort, and enrich our experience of the world.

In Early Childhood Education, the authors demonstrate how Socratic questioning can serve as a pedagogy to create new perspectives. They ask how students can question and resist habituated assumptions around issues of academic pushdown, teacher identity, standardization and developmentally appropriate practice.

Chapter 19

Pre-service teachers are placed in a virtual school, where they experience surprise and dislocation as they attempt to negotiate the environment without a site map. The process invites critical reflection of normative schooled practices – practices strongly embedded in .. pasts – which contain ways beginning teachers might imagine the future.

Chapter 20

Working within a real and already disrupted environment, cross-cultural (mis)understandings provide the impetus for this chapter. Building social work curriculum with health care refugee workers on the Thailand Burmese border, the author encounters a range of unshared cultural concepts. Her chapter narrates six stories from her research which discuss the impact of Boal's theatre of the oppressed strategies to promote alternative thinking.

Chapter 21

Theorising disruption in terms of current political ideologies, the chapter examines the New Public Management in the United Kingdom. Using Foucault's concept of genealogy, the author invites readers to critically examine new university pedagogies' claims to grant learners agency within the 'normalizing' powers of the knowledge economy.

Chapter 22

Exploring tensions linked to disruption and contemporary political conditions, the author calls for teachers to become 'curriculum workers' in challenging top-down curriculum planning and standardized testing. Identifying reflection, transformative learning, and affect as pathways for teacher change, Joseph's curriculum workers question and modify mandated curriculum.

Foreword

"We return to our special problem, which is how the rigid character of past custom has unfavorably influenced beliefs, emotions and purposes having to do with morals" (Dewey, 1922).

"How do you un-think something you considered fact? Or, a question could be, 'What does it mean to know something?'" (Adler & Iorio).

This collection offers an invaluable contribution to the field of pedagogical studies and the exploration of social and cultural transformation. Each chapter offers careful analyses of particular educational settings, dilemmas, and challenges, while each is also rooted in a thoughtful and rigorous theoretical framework. The result is a one-of-a-kind collection that maps different understandings of "disruptive pedagogies" for educators and scholars in almost every conceivable type of educational space. The chapters reflect diverse international and cultural contexts, a range of formal and informal educational sites, and educational settings from early childhood to higher education, as well as dilemmas across sites of contestation—from personal identities in negotiation of classroom relations, to questions of educational policies and curricula that shape educational spaces.

During the 1980s when I first began looking for accounts of how emotion shapes and is shaped by educational dynamics and environments, the few scholars and theorists who recognized emotions in their social context were those writing about "feminist pedagogies." Since 1999, when I first articulated "pedagogy of discomfort," studies of affect and emotion have become increasingly popular within scholarly circles outside of education. Not surprisingly—as I will show here - neither education nor emotion has traditionally been considered a "sexy" area of study. In this brief foreword, I offer a broader context of how Western dualistic thought has structured our modes of thought and our lived experience of affect, emotion, and the habituated "common sense" beliefs that can be understood as the reproduction of hegemony or dominant cultural values. Two key and related "sites" where shared cultural values are produced are (1) education/schools, and (2) individual and collective consciousness/habituated ways of being and doing. While critical analysis of the sites of hegemonic reproduction is assisted by philosophies of feminist thought, Marxism, or post-structuralism, one need not identify with these theories to recognize that education and schools, and the terrain of habituated emotions, are "sites" where cultural values are systematically engrained and inscribed.

DISRUPTING COMMON SENSE

When considering the disruption of habits and emotions as the foundation for social change, a central concern is how social custom shapes and molds cultural and individual beliefs and values, and how critical reflexivity can be introduced to "interrupt" what seems given or natural; "That's just how things are!" is the status quo response to those questioning the order of the world. How do we disrupt what are called by some "hegemonic" or "dominant" cultural beliefs and values that work against practices of social change, freedom, and justice? Hegemony can be understood as the coercive control of norms and assumptions through inculcation and reinscription of so-called "common sense"—the unquestioned assumptions and myths that drive and uphold particular cultures, values, and hierarchies. To discover "hegemony" one need only examine the givens, the common-sensically accepted, popular, and ingrained truths about what is "normal," "true," and accepted simply as "how things are."

These codifications of "common sense" present dilemmas and challenges to transformative education. To disrupt "common sense" is to challenge that which is taken for granted, that which is unnoticed like the air we breathe. The aim of "disruptive pedagogies," it can be argued, is for all involved to develop the capacity to uncover the hidden implications of unquestioned codifications of "common sense." More often than not, throwing into question our common sense views can be a deeply unsettling experience. "Being 'uncomfortable'," writes Adams in this volume (in press), "is a crucial part of setting the stage for change." It is a fundamental inclination of human beings to form potent affective attachments to structures of belief and a corresponding reluctance to disrupt the comfort of that which is taken for granted. So-called teachable moments might well be defined as the moments in which learning and/or education and emotion powerfully intersect and clash.

Crucially, there is no one prescriptive mode of a "disruptive pedagogy," in part because any given situation/relationship requires distinct and differentiated sensitivity and nuance; because the cultural differences and identities of those engaged complicate the entire enterprise of "transforming"—who gets to determine what counts as "transformative"? Who designs educational aims, values, and goals? As Costello notes in this collection (in press), "Where people's lives are disrupted by their past, present, and unknown futures, educators need to be wary of inflicting additional risks and pressures by imposing Western concepts and teaching methods. Deeply held culturally prescribed beliefs and assumptions are not easily challenged or changed, for neither the outsider teacher nor the host country learners."

THE GENDERED CONSTRUCTION OF SCHOOLING AND EMOTIONS

Both education and emotion have historically been associated with women and with gendered forms of labor. Within Western cultural histories, persistent binaries inscribe misleading dualisms that powerfully define our thinking, values, cultural norms and social hierarchies, and resulting internalized sense of worth. These oft-cited dualisms include male/female, public/private, and rational/emotional. Across history and cultures, women are traditionally assigned as caretakers of the private sphere, which includes the domestic realm of reproduction of daily life and family. While men are expected/permitted to take up authoritative roles within the political and public sphere, women are held responsible for the quality of society's next generation by ensuring that children—both in the home and in schools—adopt appropriate social values, roles, and norms.

Despite being expected to fulfill these crucial social duties of "raising society's children," to this day women are not rewarded for educational and emotional labor they perform: to point, every society across history and culture values and rewards men's labor more than women's. In the rare instances where men are responsible for schooling, in an "about face," schooling is automatically more highly valued and better paid.

If the domestic sphere were masculine and not as thoroughly feminized as it is in most cultures, wages for housework and parenting might well be a *fait accompli*. Similarly, were it the case that men performed the *emotional* labor within sites of families or education, emotion would not have had the "bad rap" it has received over these many centuries under the gaze of Western Enlightenment traditions, values, science, and philosophies, as polluting truth with subjective and skewing bias.

It is noteworthy that the pioneering scholars and theorists of emotion have, by and large, been women. While progressive, radical, and critical pedagogies have long valued variations of what in this collection are called "disruptive pedagogies," such pedagogies—whether rooted in the American traditions founded by John Dewey or the critical and/or Marxist pedagogical traditions inspired by Paolo Freire—have not dwelled on the centrality of emotion and affect as an integral and inseparable aspect of the subject and her processes of learning and inquiry. It has been largely feminist theories—and as mentioned above, feminist pedagogies--that have recognized and brought to the foreground the necessity of understanding emotion's value in knowledge and learning. Much of the work on emotion and affect can be traced, in this sense, to social movements.

Feminist scholars also insisted that we understand affect not solely as an individual, private, or internal experience. The most radical development has been to show that emotion and affect are not merely private and internally experienced, but rather circulate much the way that Foucault shows us power circulates. Thus, emotions can be understood in part as socially-constructed rules and learned modes of expression that maintain existing gender roles and social order. These cultural myths about emotion rules include, "Boys shouldn't cry; angry black women are dangerous; women are hysterical; men are naturally rational, et cetera." In this sense, emotions and emotional expression and rules are intertwined with hierarchies of power. As well, in feminist accounts, affect and emotion are not defined as obstacles to thought, as our inherited Cartesian binaries would have it, but rather as valued sources of knowledge, aspects of perception and epistemology that need not be denied or siphoned off in fear of it polluting "Truth." Emotions are understood as having a collective presence and circulation, rather than simply residing in a person.

Thus, to foreground the implications of emotion as part of the disruption of habits and dominant cultural norms reflects certain courage: the courage to associate oneself or one's practices with a "contagious pollutant"—namely, emotion-- that dirties the "pure" waters of knowledge, truth, and scholarship. This bifurcation of emotion and reason that has long defined projects of knowledge and schooling perpetuates myths such as the idea of a neutral curriculum. This powerful myth of neutral curricula ensures hegemony." Yet *no curriculum is neutral*: any educational project has an agenda, and what is not taught or discussed is as potent as what is. Absence and silence are in no way synonymous with neutrality. For example, a homophobic remark by a student in a classroom left unaddressed by the teacher is tantamount to approving homophobia. As Brunskell-Evans writes in this collection (in press), "I understand my ethical task as examining those aspects of teaching and learning that appear to be both neutral and independent so that the powers that are exercised obscurely are unmasked."

What are we taught to care about, what are we schooled to value? When and how are we invited to reflect on the source of one's aims and aspirations, to question what counts as socially-condoned, valued, and accepted? What "matters" to us, and how do we recognize the source and implication of our investments in what matters? Dissidence requires dissonance, not just letting everything sail smoothly by; it's disquieting. Dissidents sit not in objective relationship to the regimes they oppose; on the contrary, they are subjectively engaged; they resist because what occurs disturbs - it matters to them…. Within the privacy of thought, democratic citizens will self-regulate, censor, and conform.

For these reasons, this collection offers a bold invitation to educators and scholars across the disciplines. The range of approaches to the question of "disruptive pedagogies"—pedagogies that seek to question cherished values and beliefs—creating space and opening for seeing how diverse educational settings provide opportunities to invite teachers and students to see the world differently. These are opportunities to disrupt habit, as Dewey would have it; to replace outmoded and even harmful tradition and custom with fresh insight and curiosity reflective of willingness to transform oneself and the worlds one inhabits in the cause of a more just and equitable world.

The taken-for-granted cultural conception that education and curricula are neutral is slowly being replaced with recognition of the ideological nature of any given schooling particularly formal schooling. How does one know one is not indoctrinating? Dewey responded that it is not possible to indoctrinate people about actual democracy, because the process of democracy would necessitate questioning all habits and directives.

The emotionally fraught instances of teachable moments exemplify the slogan of the women's liberation movement: "the personal is political." As Carpenter writes in this collection (in press), "In my own teaching experience, students and teachers alike find a critical interrogation of romantic love to be even more discomforting than questions of race and sexuality…" Engaging the private can be uncomfortable enough; critiquing the personal can be downright disturbing, and no wonder.

The tight bond between habit and emotion has long been recognized not only by those seeking a more equitable social structuring, but as well by the most conservative interests of those invested in maintaining political and/or economic power. Shaping "desire"—indeed, manufacturing and creating "desires"--is a key aim of capitalism, advertising, and elite political interests. Such elite interests have indeed successfully shaped and produced the desires of masses of humanity for the past century, profiting on produced desires at the cost of human and environmental well-being and sustainability. Our task of disruption is in some sense more challenging than ever as we face the infinite resources of these dominant interests, who can afford to pay billions of dollars to public relations, advertising, and lobbyists. Such institutions are able to shape public opinion through complex and carefully designed orchestration informed by the best psychologists, sociologists, and political scientists working hand in glove with corporate and partisan political interests.

Yet at the same time, the work of disruption perhaps becomes increasingly viable and feasible, as the common-sense, mystification, and hidden truths and costs of dominant corporate and power interests become increasingly revealed appear as the emperor with no clothes. At the time of this writing, the Occupy Movement has become global—people around the world representing the 99% are protesting corporate greed, the bankruptcy of democracy, and demanding new and sustainable solutions to economic injustice. As Brunskell-Evans again writes, "Human beings cannot escape power, but what they can do is weigh up the costs and benefits of particular forms of subjectivity and decide collectively how to act at 'the limits of the self' or even transgress these limits at local sites of power" (in press). Indeed, the global disruptions and transformations underway in their commitment to a vision of a different and sustainable economy, environment, and forms of governance are changes far from cosmetic but radical—and the practices of participatory, grassroots, and leaderless movement are indeed a call for a collective reevaluation of power.

Clearly, the publication of this publication is timely and apt. Given the disruption of dominant economic and political narratives currently underway around the globe, we are fortunate to have on hand an unusually thoughtful set of careful studies of the complex, yet inspiring challenges of disruption and transformation within educational spaces.

Megan Boler
University of Toronto

Megan Boler *is Professor and Associate Chair of the Department of Theory and Policy Studies at the Ontario Institute of Studies in Education at the University of Toronto. She is Associate Faculty of the Center for the Study of United States and the Knowledge Media Design Institute also at UT. Her books include Feeling Power: Emotions and Education (NY: Routledge 1999); Democratic Dialogue in Education: Troubling Speech, Disturbing Silences (M. Boler, ed., Peter Lang, 2004); and Digital Media and Democracy: Tactics in Hard Times (Cambridge: MIT Press, 2008). She is currently completing a three-year funded research project, "Rethinking Media, Citizenship and Democracy: Digital Dissent after 9/11," through interviews and surveys examining the motivations of producers of "digital dissent"–practices of digital media to counter mainstream media. Her Web-based productions include a study guide to accompany the documentary The Corporation (dirs. Achbar and Abbott 2003) and the multimedia website Critical Media Literacy in Times of War. Boler's essays have been published in such journals as Educational Theory, Cultural Studies, and Women's Studies Quarterly; recent publications include M. Boler, Guest Editor with Ted Gournelos, "Irony and Politics: User-Producers, Parody, and Digital Publics," Electronic Journal of Communication (September 2008), and M. Boler, "The Politics of Making Truth Claims: The Responsibilities of Qualitative Research," in Methodological Dilemmas of Qualitative Research, ed. Kathleen Gallagher (Routledge 2008). She teaches Philosophy, Cultural Studies, Feminist Theory, Media Studies, and Social Equity courses in the Teacher Education program and Media Studies at the Knowledge Media Design Institute at University of Toronto.*

REFERENCES

Adams, S. (in press). Critical friendship and sustainable change: Creating liminal spaces to experience discomfort together. In Faulkner, J. (Ed.), *Disrupting pedagogies in the knowledge society: Countering conservative norms with creative approaches*. Hershey, PA: IGI Global.

Brunskell-Evans, H. (in press). The new public management of higher education: Teaching and learning. In Faulkner, J. (Ed.), *Disrupting pedagogies in the knowledge society: Countering conservative norms with creative approaches*. Hershey, PA: IGI Global.

Carpenter, R. (in press). Disruptive relation(ship)s: Romantic love as critical praxis. In Faulkner, J. (Ed.), *Disrupting pedagogies in the knowledge society: Countering conservative norms with creative approaches*. Hershey, PA: IGI Global.

Costello, S. (in press). Coevolving through disrupted discussions on critical thinking, human rights and empathy. In Faulkner, J. (Ed.), *Disrupting pedagogies in the knowledge society: Countering conservative norms with creative approaches*. Hershey, PA: IGI Global.

Dewey, J. (1922). *Human nature and conduct* (pp. 63–64). New York, NY: Holt Publishing.

Preface

Schools and universities are traditionally spaces where skills are learned and, in some cases, knowledge gained. However, they are also places defined by norms and the need to conform. As a result they often reproduce, rather than interrogate, those power and cultural relations. Risk taking in classrooms is increasingly curtailed by emphasis on high stakes testing and policy pressures. Habituated practices, combined with common sense approaches, have tended to reinforce outmoded beliefs and assumptions, with such beliefs being deeply connected to identity formations around teaching and learning.

To animate change in ways that we can reconfigure what we know, there is a need to critically reflect on personal and cultural identities built up over time. Such an interrogation may lead to disruption, and disruption may produce a sense of unease. Learners often resist tension and discomfort which might emerge from confrontation with the unknown, and the fallout from this can land heavily on teachers. Ethical questions arise around responsibility for shaking presumptions learners hold dear, and educators need to become mindful of the complex power relationships in and outside the classroom. Nevertheless, failing to interrogate routine or habituated thinking leads to no change at all. In times of increasing governmental control and regulatory compliance, critical exploration of new paradigms is now a pressing educational issue. In some cases, pushing boundaries and agitating for change are essential to challenge questionable policy and argue future directions. Moreover, robust debate serves also to enlarge and enrich the cultural contexts in which people work.

In *Feeling Power* (1999), Megan Boler coined the phrase "pedagogy of discomfort," or critical enquiry into one's own values and beliefs by recognizing how thinking and seeing is culturally constructed. Disruptive pedagogies enable educators and students to understand their own reflexivity more deeply, "learn[ing] to trace how one's subjectivities are shifting and contingent" (Zembylas & Boler 2002. p. 3). The chapters in this book examine a range of disruptive approaches: attempts to shift taken-for-granted attitudes and beliefs held by both educators and learners to redesign current practices. Australian and international contributors investigate the origins and frameworks of such initiatives, seeking to understand how they are realized across various learning settings.

The questions for critical educators centre on how challenge, dissonance, and disruption might be mobilized in educational contexts to bring about constructive change. Educators might value resistant thinking, but often the concept remains elusive, an abstraction, perhaps even an impossibility to teach and enact. However, the writers in this collection have entered the debate with philosophical and strategic deliberation. They consider the nature of disruption and wrestle with questions interrogating the rationale, ethics and responsibilities of implementing related pedagogies. How might disruption be defined and negotiated? How might disruption break habitual cycles and foster the unlearning of conservative norms? What forms might such pedagogies take and among what kinds of disciplinary areas? Can disruption become synonymous with indoctrination or develop its own orthodoxy?

Critical responses range across sites such as college composition courses, a virtual school, and the Thailand Burmese border. Concepts such as humor, heteronormativity, and feminism are interrogated, while romantic love is positioned as a site for critical praxis. Mathematics, art, traditional Jewish text study, ESL, and digital classrooms are examined for their potential to shift traditional thinking. Gentle approaches sit beside more deliberate ruptures in contested ideological and political contexts. Inhabiting different roles, learners and teachers occupy dialogical spaces of possibility for change. Although all contributions are from English-speaking countries, they range across three continents, and early childhood, secondary, tertiary, and adult learners are considered, as writers question their own practices, asking how learning and teaching might be challenged and reinvigorated.

To theorize disruptive pedagogies, critical literacy traditions have been drawn upon from the work of Foucault, Freire, Habermas, and Giroux. Resisting dominant ideologies to liberate thinking from hegemonic structures has long been a feature of critical, radical liberatory pedagogies. Foucault's (1980) concept of governmentality explains how we are produced by power even as we resist it; power and resistance are mutually constituted. Freire's (1970) emphasis on dialogue as a way of learning and knowing emerges in this collection as significant to the role of collegial encounters with critical thinking. Reflection and disruption are linked by Habermas in relation to reflection as a form of self construction that emancipates as it releases the subject from dysfunctional beliefs (Habermas cited in Mezirow, 2000). Moreover, self-understanding enables "full potential as active, reflective scholars and practitioners" for Giroux (1985/2010, p. 202), while critical reflection around liminal spaces and praxis disrupt the "quest for certainty" (Dewey, 1929). Zembylas and Boler (2002); meanwhile, in their study of disruptive pedagogy as a methodology to reframe post 9/11 patriotism, emphasize the power and complexity of emotional investments in critiquing ideology. Their recognition of emotions as discursive practices differentiates pedagogies of discomfort from critical media literacy, as they argue for "a collectivized engagement in learning to see, feel, and act differently" (p. 4).

Adding their voices to Zembylas and Boler are a number of writers who examine disruption in the context of research-based diverse practices of community building. Assumptions inherent in teaching and learning practice that remain unexamined are highlighted in Suzanne Knight's chapter, "Locating and loving the personal: Risk and vulnerability in a secondary English language and Arts methods course." Exploring vulnerability and risk taking as disruptive behaviour, Knight looks into competing expectations on the part of teachers and students through narrative analyses and affirms the value of building a connected knowing group.

Also supporting collective ways of knowing, Vicki Stieha and Miriam Raider-Roth examine partnered teacher work through "relational rupture." Examining the complex development procedure of unlearning through *Hevruta*, or traditional Jewish text study, they observe how shared exploration strengthens deeper understanding in "Disrupting relationships: A catalyst for growth." It is in the liminal spaces where collegial questioning can function to move educators to more transformative possibilities, claim Susan Adams and Ross Peterson-Veatch in "'Critical friendship' and sustainable change: Creating liminal spaces to experience discomfort together." The authors underline the value of willing professional learning communities, suggesting protocols to maintain a critical focus.

Also investigating the role of collaborative learning in supporting change, Edith Rusch describes her work with educational leaders. "Smart people learning: Self-knowledge that disrupts practice in meaningful ways" uses the Interactive Learning Model to examine the role of retrospective sense making to enable more effective learning.

Rhetoric and composition studies prove a rich area for contributions to the disruptive pedagogies conversation. Erik Ellis deconstructs the power of metaphor in shaping rhetoric in university composition courses. Examining the agendas and tropes of scholarly writing, "Shushes in the parlor: Reclaiming the 'conversation' metaphor" argues for more diverse forms of inquiry and writing to embrace, rather than fear, the irreducibility of the conversation metaphor. In "Tracing the trope of teaching as transformation," Julie Myatt Barger also examines composition's dependence on critical pedagogies. Constructing students as incomplete and in need of transformation, a trope she argues can be taken too far, teachers concerned with social change represent students as "other," thus limiting agency and complexity in student identity.

Heidi Skurat Harris takes the Freirean concept *conscientização*, consciousness of consciousness. Linking discomfort of aporia, she argues in "Web 2.0 and *conscientização*: Digital students and critical reflection on and in multimedia" that educators can longer continue to privilege print-based texts in the face of a generation who work differently. Educators need to teach critical thinking within digital contexts. Also exploring young people's preferred media modes and texts, Julie Faulkner and Bronwyn Williams collaborate on a cross-cultural project involving Australian and American students exploring a satirical television series. In the case of "'I'm not always laughing at the jokes': Humor as a force for disruption," parody is the vehicle for demonstrating that normative cultural patterns have no necessity; people are amused partly because their culture has taught them *how* to laugh.

Abby Knoblauch notes that disruptive pedagogies could spark resistance in students who might well feel protective over family and community loyalties. "Disrupting disruption: Invitational pedagogy as a response to student resistance" looks carefully at students leaving behind comforting certainties and asks whether they might see disruptive approaches as a form of indoctrination to liberal politics. Knoblauch builds a case for invitational rhetoric to encourage stronger questioning of students' deeply held beliefs, especially when those students find themselves distanced from supportive contexts.

Jennifer Elsden-Clifton's "Negotiating disruption in visual arts education" focuses on art, particularly the visual arts, an area which can offer fertile spaces for moving away from safe thinking in schools. She asks how students use bodies and sexualities as a medium for disruption, and what kinds of emotions are evoked around this process. Her chapter picks up Zembylas and Boler's argument that paraphrase effective analysis of ideology requires not only rational inquiry and dialogue but also excavation of emotional investments (2002, p. 2).

"Setting the stage for professionalism: Disrupting the student identity" by Lynn Hanson and Meredith A. Love brings drama techniques into the professional writing classroom. Compressing the space between the workplace and classroom, students are required to resist familiar patterns of learner interaction and assume professional identities.

Mia O'Brien and Shelley Dole further explore questions of identity in the process of becoming a teacher in "Pre-service learning and the (gentle) disruption of emerging teacher identity." In the conceivably daunting areas of mathematics and the arts, they look at how student discomfort might be managed by experiential learning and specifically designed assessment. Their focus is on teacher education pedagogies in conjunction with pre-service learning, and the relationship of these processes to teacher identity formation.

In "The emotional labor of imagining otherwise: Undoing the mastery model of mathematics teacher identity," Elizabeth de Freitas also examines how mathematics positioning pre-service teachers. Arguing that the language of mathematics is neither context-free nor ahistorical, she analyses ways that language connects to power in the classroom. Teachers of mathematics need to experience more ambiguity and understand the microdynamics of the classroom, she argues, in order to more deeply control learning and teaching processes.

Greg Curran writes from an ESL context where heterosexuality is presumed as part of the normative expectations of classrooms. Conscious and respectful of cultural difference, "Are you married: Exploring the boundaries of sexual taboos in the ESL classroom" examines sensitive issues around sexuality and explores ways that disruption might productively play out when supported by an aware and reflective teacher. Also exploring boundaries between the personal and social, Rick Carpenter in "Disruptive Relation(ship)s: Romantic love as critical praxis" problematizes romantic love. He provides a critical methodology to interrogate received notions of self, opening avenues of inquiry and transformation. Challenging binary thinking complicates either/or approaches, enabling expanded ways of knowing and being in the world.

Kaitlin Briggs' chapter disrupts the very form of the conventional academic chapter. She asks "proprioceptive" questions to challenge taken-for-granted ways of thinking and writing. Highlighting and calling into question one's own words, phrases, and images, this kind of question breaks up the rhythm of the writing by asking "what do I mean by ...?," thus calling attention to language and meaning. "Performing dissident thinking through writing: Using the proprioceptive question to break out of the classroom" explores this method of unpacking thinking as a political intervention.

Drew Kopp begins with a theoretical exploration of the concept and process of disruption. Also focussing on rhetorical inquiry processes, Drew Kopp's detailed analysis in "The risk of rhetorical Inquiry: Practical conditions for a disruptive pedagogy" critiques the teacher's role. He examines the increasing complexity of performative and dialogic encounters within increasingly unfamiliar and complex contexts in order to willingly embrace discomfort and enrich people's experience of the world.

In Early Childhood Education, Susan Matoba Adler and Jeanne Marie Iorio demonstrate how Socratic questioning can serve as a pedagogy to create new perspectives. Through blogs and discussion board postings, pre-service teachers move toward more critical positions in relation to young learners. "Teachers of young children: Moving students from agents of surveillance to agents of change" asks how students can question and resist habituated assumptions around issues of academic pushdown, teacher identity, standardization, and developmentally appropriate practice.

A virtual school is the site for Gloria Latham's provocation in "Creating tension: Orchestrating disruptive pedagogies in a virtual school environment." Pre-service teachers placed in this school experience surprise and dislocation as they attempt to negotiate the environment without a site map. The process invites critical reflection of normative school practices, practices strongly embedded in students' schooled pasts and which constrain ways beginning teachers might imagine the future.

Working within a real and already disrupted environment, cross-cultural (mis)understandings provide the impetus for Susie Costello in "Coevolving through disrupted discussions on critical thinking, human rights and empathy." Building social work curriculum with health care refugee workers on the Thailand-Burmese border, she encounters a range of unshared cultural concepts. Her chapter narrates six stories from her research which discuss the impact of Boal's theatre of the oppressed strategies to promote alternative thinking.

Theorising disruption in terms of current political ideologies, Heather Brunskell-Evans examines the New Public Management in the United Kingdom ("The new public management of higher education: Teaching and Learning"). Using Foucault's concept of genealogy, Brunskell-Evans invites readers to critically examine new university pedagogies' claims to grant learners agency within the normalizing powers of the knowledge economy. Similarly exploring tensions linked to disruption and contemporary political conditions, Pamela Bolotin Joseph analyses the power of utilitarian discourse to enculturate educational thinking. Her chapter, "Disrupting the utilitarian paradigm: Teachers doing curriculum inquiry," calls for teachers to become curriculum workers in challenging "top down" curriculum planning and standardized testing. Identifying reflection, transformative learning, and affect as pathways for teacher change, Joseph's curriculum workers question and modify mandated curriculum.

At the time of writing (November, 2011), significant political shifts are occurring in the Middle East. Hosni Mubarak's thirty- nine year dictatorship in Egypt has ended, while Libya's political control has finally shifted hands. Twitter and Linkedin because of their role in organizing anti-government demonstrations. Digital technologies and social networking have changed the face of political resistance, and the imperative to think critically is now more urgent than ever. This book offers a range of philosophical and strategic approaches to explore dimensions of belief systems and their relationships to social hierarchies and technologies. It explores articulations and change within feelings of entrenchment and vulnerability. The authors scrutinize the social and political relations in which individuals are positioned, asking how such relations influence values and practices. The contributors speculate on the boundaries between risk taking and the need to conform, framed by inevitable complications of culture and power.

In this collection, these tensions emerge at different stages of learning and teaching. For some writers, the aim of shifting learners' beliefs and attitudes is the motivating force for pedagogical design. Others begin with the idea of disruption, then pause at points in the process to question the implications of what they have embarked upon. Yet other authors are almost caught by surprise by dislocation and find that conceptualizing practice then serves to enable deeper understanding.

The chapters that follow offer a spectrum of possibilities for practitioners to explore their capacity to challenge and transform learner perceptions. These forms of critical inquiry encourage readers to explore the limits and possibilities of disruption, comprehensively examining the teacher's role and offering a range of creative, philosophical, and social approaches. At the core of the authors' various responses, however, lies the vital, transformative challenge from Zembylas and Boler. A pedagogy of discomfort is an invitation not only to challenge our thinking but to re-invent ourselves (2002, p. 14).

REFERENCES

Boler, M. (1999). *Feeling power: Emotions and education*. New York, NY: Routledge.

Dewey, J. (1929, 1960). *The quest for certainty*. New York, NY: Capricorn.

Foucault, M. (1980). *Power/knowledge: Selected interviews and other writings, 1972-1977* (Gordon, C. (Trans. Eds.) New York, NY: Pantheon Books.

Freire, P. (1970). *Pedagogy of the oppressed* (2008 30th anniversary edition, M. B. Ramos, Trans.) New York, NY: The Continuum International Publishing Group.

Freire, P., & Macedo, D. (1995). A dialogue: Culture, language, and race. *Harvard Educational Review*, 65(3), 377–402.

Giroux, H. (1985/2010). Teacher as transformative intellectuals. In Canestrari, A., & Marlow, B. (Eds.), *Education foundations: An anthology of critical readings* (pp. 197–204). Thousand Oaks, CA: Sage Publications.

Mezirow, J. (2000). *Learning as transformation: Critical perspectives in theory as progress* (1st ed.). San Francisco, CA: Jossey-Bass.

Zembylas, M., & Boler, M. (2002). *On the spirit of patriotisim: Challenges of a "pedagogy of discomfort"*. Retrieved January 6, 2010, from http://www.tcrecord.org/library

Acknowledgment

My warm thanks in particular to Gloria Latham and Jennifer Elsden-Clifton for many encouraging conversations around the idea of writing about discomfort and change. Moving from ideas to something more tangible was further enabled through the invaluable support of Gloria, Jennifer, Ilana Snyder, Michael Crowhurst, Catherine Beavis, Kate Lovig and Mary Hanrahan. Above all, I want to thank the writers in this volume, who share their enthusiasm and determination to continually rethink learning.

Julie Faulkner
RMIT University, Australia

Chapter 1
Locating and Loving the Personal:
Risk and Vulnerability in a Secondary English Language Arts Methods Course

Suzanne Knight
University of Michigan—Flint, USA

ABSTRACT

In this chapter the author takes up the use of narrative inquiry within a secondary English language arts methods course. She focuses on two discrete moments that took place during one class session, where she and her students shared and discussed personal narratives. In particular, she explores the pedagogy that might be required to support a group of pre-service teachers' work to become a connected knowing group, including the disruptive nature of vulnerability and risk taking.

INTRODUCTION

For my teaching purposes, I define narrative inquiry as a pedagogy designed to support prospective teachers' work toward greater self-awareness and self-understanding. Its purpose is to systematically draw teacher candidates' attention to the ways they understand their world and to examine how those understandings then impact them in the classroom. The assumption behind such an inquiry is that prospective teachers enter their teacher preparation coursework already holding experiential knowledge that is often tacit (Clandinin, 1985; Johnson, 1989; Willinsky, 1989). If the knowledge itself is tacit, it also stands to reason that how this knowledge then shapes individuals as teachers is also tacit.

One goal of narrative inquiry as pedagogy, therefore, is to make this tacit knowledge visible. Toward this end this pedagogy begins with

DOI: 10.4018/978-1-61350-495-6.ch001

the act of "telling stories," initially the writing of personal narratives. Some researchers, such as Villegas and Lucas (2002) refer to this telling as autobiographical writing (which I argue may be understood as personal narrative and thus, consistent with narrative inquiry) and argue that in addition to helping teacher candidates to better understand their worldviews, it can also provide a means through which they might examine their teaching practices, specifically the extent to which they equitably treat and respond to all students.

However, this aim of interrogating worldviews cannot be reached solely through the individual writing of narratives. The distinctive quality of narrative inquiry comes from its more collective nature (Conle, 2003); collaboration is essential (Bruner, 1996). Deeper and more complicated understandings of the self and how that self is then located in a classroom occur through dialogue (Witherell & Noddings, 1992). That said, then, another essential component of narrative inquiry is candidates' sharing their narratives with each other and discussing the salient issues the written narratives raise, most specifically in relation to teaching practice.

Narrative inquiry, as I have described it above, holds the potential to disrupt future teachers' misinformed perceptions of students (often shaped by embedded and invisible worldviews) and creates a space where they can interrogate the instructional choices they make based on those perceptions. Complicating this further, however, is that the pedagogy required in order to create such a space may—at the same time--disrupt students' notions about the roles of teachers and students. Resting on my conviction of the potential of narrative inquiry, I explored the pedagogy involved in facilitating students' discussions of their own written personal narratives, the collective feature of narrative inquiry.

My students were enrolled in a year long, masters-level secondary English language arts methods course while simultaneously completing a year of student teaching (post BA) in order

to receive certification. At two points during the second semester of this year-long course, my students and I wrote a narrative piece, after which we identified the salient societal issue(s) that we believed had shaped us, such as race, social class or gender. For example, one student took up how being raised in a White, upper middle class home may have provided the types of experiences and knowledge that led to greater academic success. After identifying the issue(s) suggested in each narrative, we located an outside text that spoke to that issue. For example, the student mentioned above selected *Lives on the Boundary: A Moving Account of the Struggles and Achievements of America's Educationally Underprepared* (1989) and *Savage Inequalities: Children in America's Schools* by Jonathan Kozol (1991) to help her make sense of and better understand the significance of her personal knowledge and experiences in light of her teaching practice.

For each of the narratives, the students and I composed an accompanying reflective piece that explored the following: 1) how the narrative, combined with the outside text, informed our thinking about ourselves and our students; and 2) what we learned about ourselves through this process and how we might apply this knowledge to our teaching practice. At two different times during the semester, my students and I shared our writing with each other and discussed our learning. The rest of this chapter is devoted to examining this collective work of the narrative inquiry, evidenced in classroom moments.

BACKGROUND

What Does Examining Classroom Moments Tell Us?

Examining teaching practice is the "systematic, intentional inquiry by teachers about their own school and classroom work [that]….stems from or generates questions and reflects teachers' desire to make sense of their experiences…" (Cochran-Smith & Lytle, 1993, pp. 22, 24). Making sense of experience is a very personal - and perhaps idiosyncratic - goal. However, examining classroom moments works to "illuminate pedagogical acts by researching experience … [and making] visible the knowledge that teachers often implicitly employ" (Burton & Seidl, 2002, p. 226).

Cochran-Smith and Lytle (1993) further assert that neither theory nor practice generate the questions that inform teacher research but "critical reflection on the intersection of the two" (p. 15). Though teacher researchers attend to the nature of these questions that constitute teacher research and thus frame inquiry, they also concern themselves with the methods of inquiry that result in systematic and intentional examination of teaching practice. Burton and Seidl (2002) argue that teacher research "provides valuable theoretical and practical knowledge to the educational community in general" (p. 229). Beyond its power to inform more personal questions related to teaching practice then, teacher research also adds to the public knowledge of teaching.

Toward these ends of teacher research, I drew on the constructs of Belenky, Clinchy, Goldberger, and Tarule (1997) to help me gain deeper insights into the pedagogy that might support the collective work of narrative inquiry, particularly how they explicate the concept of connected knowing and a connected knowing group. For instance, they characterize connected knowing as rooted in personal experience but also focused on relationship with others in order to access other people's experiences and ways of thinking and knowing. Such access, they claim, allows learners to extend their understanding to reach the strange and unfamiliar. Members of a connected knowing group will put forth incomplete ideas, counting on others to help them further develop those ideas. Therefore, exploratory talk or rough draft speech (Barnes, 1979) is prevalent in a connected knowing group as members jointly explore ideas and

concepts. In addition, members understand that each person adds to the whole group's understandings and work to share each others' perspectives. Finally, such a group will identify problems and pose questions for further inquiry.

Despite this characterization of a connected knowing group, the requisite pedagogy for a group of students (or students and instructor) to interact together in such a way within a university methods course remains somewhat ambiguous. That said, this chapter seeks to explore what that pedagogy might look like and will focus on the moves (and mis-moves) one teacher educator made in her teaching practice: moves that demonstrate the importance of a teacher's being genuine and honest, moves that reflect varying levels of vulnerability (and resistance to being vulnerable), and moves that worked to either support students' efforts or in some cases to undermine or squelch their efforts to move toward becoming a connected knowing group.

Striving Toward Connected Knowing

When students (regardless of their age) enter the classroom, they come with a set of expectations about their, as well as the teacher's, roles and responsibilities in that classroom. Teachers enter the classroom with a similar set of expectations. Therefore, when teachers attempt to develop teaching practices that may seem new to both them and their students, they run the risk of disrupting the cultural norms of classroom life to which both they and students have grown accustomed. For my purposes here, the teaching practice that is most significant is where the teacher locates herself with respect to her students, her "self." One conservative cultural norm would be for the teacher to approach instruction based on the banking model, depositing knowledge into students (Freire, 1993). However, in narrative inquiry this norm is disrupted as "…both teacher and students engage in the process of thinking, and they talk out what they are thinking in a public dialogue. As they think and talk together, their roles merge" (Belenky et al., 1997, p. 219).

The merging of roles, however, is disruptive to both teachers and students. Teachers come to instruction with agendas, sometimes explicit, other times implicit. Further, students come to instruction with their agendas as well: interest in the course content, inclination to take the course, motivation to succeed in the course, conviction (or lack thereof) of the course's merit. These respective agendas then collide with the conservative expectations of what it means to be teacher and student.

In the narrative inquiry I designed, my agenda was clear to me (if not always clear to my students). Fuller's (1969) and Kennedy's (2006) work suggests the persistence of the agendas with which pre-service teachers enter their teacher preparation coursework, particularly their methods courses. Understanding how a positioned self shapes teaching practice (my agenda) does not necessarily match with learning how to maintain classroom control or how to manage day-to-day survival in the classroom (student agenda). This suggests that my agenda would disrupt my students' expectations for what the content of this course might entail. Complicating this is the disruption of the expected norms around what it means to be a teacher and a student in a classroom. The narrative inquiry I designed was therefore potentially disruptive to students in the content with which I asked students to grapple, as well as in my attempts to shift—and to have them shift - the roles that we played in the classroom.

Asking students to reflect on a point of view that is outside the familiar will prove disruptive for them, as interrogating worldviews and perhaps stretching and shifting perspective is inherently uncomfortable and disconcerting. However, what I could not make claims about was the extent to which I was engaged in connected teaching or whether and to what extent my pedagogical choices effectively supported our efforts to form a connected knowing group. I tended to *assume* that I took risks alongside my students, acted in ways that revealed my vulnerability, and communicated my belief in the legitimacy of their knowledge because of my *desire* to do so. However, such an assumption was problematic because I never systematically examined my practice; I really did not know the extent to which these practices were evident in my teaching.

What I describe in the next section of this chapter is representative of how I went about examining one aspect of my teaching practice in a deliberate and systematic way.

I present concrete examples in the form of two discrete moments that took place during one class session. In my analysis and discussion of these moments, I have located what I understood as the procedures of a connected knowing group, procedures supported by connected teaching. Further, I worked to determine the extent to which my facilitation of the discussions around my students' and my narratives might be considered an example of "connected teaching."

My analysis of these discussions is framed more particularly by an examination of how genuineness and honesty might support and sustain relationship and connection, as well as an examination of the nature of my own risk-taking and vulnerability. Therefore, while this analysis included the nature of the content that formed the basis of the discussions at key moments, it concentrated more on the processes shaping those moments, including: how (and for what purposes) questions were posed and working to understand the nature of what it means to take risks and remain vulnerable. A way to engage in such an examination of whether and to what extent I was able to demonstrate the stance I desired to take, as well as to form a connected knowing group with and among my students, therefore, was to investigate both my moves as a member of the group and the group processes as a whole. Therefore, this analysis focused on the procedures of a connected knowing group and what either encourages or impedes such a group.

A NARRATIVE ANALYSIS: SHARING AND DISCUSSING

Context and Overview of the Session

The second day of sharing narratives and reflections took place during the second to last class session in mid to late April, after I had spent an entire academic year with this group of students. For the most part the students were finished with their student teaching, though they were still involved at their schools to varying degrees, whether it was observing other teachers in the building or at other schools or grading student work. They were also in the midst of preparing their portfolios and completing all of their university coursework.

This day of sharing was not always as focused as the first day for perhaps various reasons (which could be attributed to both my students and me): a "senioritis" type of phenomenon; a more relaxed feeling since we all had a better idea of what we might expect during the discussion, having already shared and discussed the first narratives; a general preoccupation with end-of-the-year events; or perhaps exhaustion. Despite this, the narratives and discussion covered a wide range of topics and issues:

- Parental involvement
- Teacher/parent relationships
- Teachers' attitudes as they progress through their careers
- Dismissing or "writing off" students
- "Saving" students
- Teachers' perceptions of students and students' perceptions of teachers
- Parental access to the education "system"
- Teachers' vulnerability in the classroom
- The "power hierarchy" that reflects students' varying degrees of status among their peers
- Relationship between students' social lives and academic lives

- Differences between public and private schools
- Classroom discussions around uncomfortable issues
- Competition between and among students (school as the "real world" as opposed to an isolated world)
- Connections between school curricula and students' lived experiences

Rather than talk about the entire discussion, or about any specific ideas raised during the discussion, I have chosen two significant moments, both of which focus on moves that the students and I made.

The two moments took place within a time frame of roughly 150 minutes. Throughout the duration of these two moments, nine students (approximately one half of the class) participated, sharing their narratives and/or responding to others. Of these nine students, only one of them is a participant in both moments. My description of these moments follows a chronological pattern, interwoven with what I was thinking at the time (taken from a journal that I kept throughout the semester) and my interpretations of what was taking place.

I chose the first moment, which took place during the first fifteen minutes of the session, to show how genuineness and honesty can implicitly communicate a desire for connection. Like the first time we shared and discussed our narratives, I read mine first; the first moment occurred immediately after I shared my narrative. The second moment took place approximately one quarter of the way through the session. I have included the second moment as it reflects the students' attempts to become a more connected knowing group as they took risks and became vulnerable. However, I made moves that got in their way. It is a moment that reveals how a teacher's failure to engage in connected teaching can impede the development of a connected knowing group.

Moment One: Trying to be Honest

This analysis starts with what took place after I read my narrative (being the first reader). It demonstrates how my motivation, particularly my need to tell my story, might have created a more hospitable space for connected knowing. It also demonstrates how my primary concern with process, in this instance the act of "telling," opened the door for all of us - my students and I - to connect in meaningful ways.

A Parent's Story

I read first, a narrative about my oldest son, his experiences in middle and high school, and my experiences as a parent trying to access—and communicate with—his teachers and school counselor. Part of that experience was my feelings of frustration about the assumptions that some teachers, counselors, and administrators made about both my son and me. I had always been a teacher in public schools, an "insider." However, I was no longer a public school teacher; instead, I was an "outsider," trying to access a public school.

I had heard many of my previous students say on many occasions that their own students' parents were uninterested in their child's education because the parents did not behave in ways that fit their notions of the "norm" for parental involvement. My perceptions of my students' idea of "norms" - based on what they said - was how *their* parents had been involved in *their* education. As they had described the parents of their students, I often felt as if they were describing *me*; and I knew that my attitude as a parent was not what they thought it was. Therefore, I wanted to disrupt some of their perceptions about parents, as well as their interpretations of parental actions and decisions. Mainly, though, I think I wanted my students to hear my story, perhaps in defense of my own parental choices or perhaps for them to see that sometimes situations are not what they might seem.

Genuinely desiring to do nothing more than share my story and not concerned so much about what happened after I told my story (the direction of the discussion or the topics my students discussed), my agenda in that moment was to vent some of that frustration and perhaps gain a little sympathy. I was a frustrated mom at that point in my life and feeling sorry for myself. Though perhaps a pathetic reason to share, it was genuine and honest.

After I finished reading, one of the students, Dana, immediately jumped in and stated: "I am glad that you read that and that we had the opportunity to hear it. Because most of us do not yet have children, we don't necessarily understand the parental perspective, which is unique." Looking at this moment with fresh - and perhaps more distanced - eyes, it now seems that my motivation altered the nature of what took place. Though perhaps a bit defensive and self-serving, it was honest. As a result, Dana could simply respond to the story and in turn, respond to me.

However, her response also suggests that she gained a new insight by extending her understanding to include my perspective. Though I do not know what her previous notions of her students' parents might have been, it seems that those notions had been disrupted to some extent, as her responses suggest that her thoughts had changed or were complicated.

After she responded, then Darian and Erica responded. Darian talked about her own family, about how she and her sister did well in school while her brother struggled. In looking at her parents' experiences with her brothers' teachers, she identified a new understanding: perhaps those teachers made some incorrect assumptions about *her* parents. She then claimed that she did not want to be that kind of teacher; instead, she wanted to be the one trying to reach out to each of her students, free of assumptions.

When Erica spoke after Darian, she - like Dana - responded to me:

I believe the real problem your narrative brought to the surface was that you were a parent who really wanted to get involved and who wanted to have lots of communication with your son's teachers, but his teachers were an obstruction. Not only did they not initiate communication with you, but they actually got in the way of that process. I felt frustrated while I listened to your narrative.

All three of these students' responses reveal how they worked to stretch their perspective to include mine. Even though none was a parent, each worked to weave my parental point of view with her own. In turn, they raised new issues, such as teachers obstructing or perhaps eliminating the possibility for honest communication with parents and the unique qualities of individual students. By the same token, they did not seem to be trying to solve any particular problem or trying to identify any particular strategy to use. Instead, they identified some issues my narrative had raised for them, thus allowing them to develop new understandings, all of which reflect the procedures of a connected knowing group.

What is also telling about this moment, however, is that these students did not really disrupt anything for me. Though I did want to share my story and was, at the moment of telling, frustrated and convinced I was being genuine and authentic, perhaps that was not the case. After all, when I wrote the narrative, I recalled what these - and past - students had said about parents. Their words were not the reason I told the story, but their words were not absent from my mind either. I must admit that I expected my students to sympathize with me, and I must admit that I knew that sympathizing with me would mean their re-considering some of their assumptions. To that extent, this might be considered a "successful" moment. On the other hand, the notion of my authority had not been disrupted at all; as a result, this moment did not yield the sort of connection that marks a connected knowing group. More accurately, I was still the instructor; they were still the students. We were not equal members of a connected knowing group in the way that I sought.

The second moment reveals in a much more painful way how difficult it is to truly step out of the conservative role of "teacher" in order to reach a place of connected knowing. This moment is significant in that it illuminates what it might mean to trust both ourselves and our students, as well as what taking risks and being vulnerable might entail. It also further elucidates the importance of authenticity and genuineness in connected knowing groups, as it suggests the necessity of taking risks and explores what those risks might entail.

Moment Two: Trying to be Vulnerable

After a brief conversation around what it means to "save" kids or what that looks like, Steve came into the conversation and raised the issue of students' perceptions of teachers. He asserted that until teachers are able to connect with their students, those students will not see their teachers as "people." He further asserted that once students see teachers as people, then teachers "have them;" and he shared two anecdotes of how he has tried to reveal his humanity to his students, also stating that he never perceived his own teachers this way (as people). He concluded with: "Being a person means being able to say you are sorry or being able to say you are wrong."

It is here that Lisa spoke for the first time, and her response to Steve indicated that she was responding to what he said and working to extend it. However, she worked to connect with what Steve was saying not through her own narrative but through the text she located to inform her narrative: *Teaching to Transgress* by bell hooks (1994). She said:

One of hooks's arguments is that teachers need to make themselves vulnerable in the classroom, which is probably the scariest thing in the entire world. *But if students see the teacher as vulnerable, then they will be more willing to be vulnerable as well and be willing to take risks with the teacher and see that the teacher is not perfect.*

Not everyone possesses necessarily the same understanding of concepts such as honesty or vulnerability. Therefore, raising those issues implies some kind of question or the need for some kind of exploration. This seems consistent with the procedures for connected knowing. In addition, this procedure moves students toward positing new questions and holds the potential for students to extend their initial understandings of the concepts beyond what they perhaps have previously thought.

Understanding Vulnerability

At this point I encouraged Lisa to read her narrative, where she had described an extremely personal tragedy, the death of her boyfriend of three years and who she would - in all likelihood - have married. Her voice shook throughout her reading of the narrative, and many of the students and I cried while she read. After she finished, she talked about how she utilized it with her own students, which was what she described in her reflection. She told us about what happened when she shared this with her students: how her classroom changed for the rest of the year, how her students perceived her differently, how her views of her students changed because of what they were then willing to share. She described her choice to share this with her students as "probably the best decision" she made that year. When Lisa finished, a long moment of silence ensued.

Kathy was the first student who responded to Lisa's narrative, and she began by simply thanking Lisa for sharing and for being vulnerable with all of us. She also told Lisa that she liked the connections she made to the classroom, but that even more, "I want to call everyone I love and tell them

how much I love them." What I found interesting in Kathy's response is that just as Lisa became vulnerable, so did Kathy, in that she was willing to share her feelings with all of us. It was as if Lisa had invited all of us to join her.

I, on the other hand, *wanted* to respond as Kathy had responded but did not. I was too busy trying to control my own emotions and feeling like I could not let myself just "go with it." In retrospect, I wish I had done that or could have done that, but going with it required a level of vulnerability that I could just not get to. I had not expected my students to show such raw emotion, and in that terrifying moment I realized that I too held norms about what it meant to be a teacher that I had not acknowledged. And there I was in front of my students, completely torn and not knowing what to do. I had not anticipated this, had not planned for it. I could not trust myself to speak for fear of the rush of emotion that might escape, and so I remained silent. Choosing how and when to be vulnerable - as well as having control over the *level* of vulnerability - is very different than being vulnerable in response to someone else where there is no expectation of choice. Therefore, my silence was not my giving all of us time to connect on a deeper level; it was not a "relishing" of this powerful moment. Instead, it was an uncomfortable and tense moment, where my mind raced to try and figure out how to get back to some sense of equilibrium and to restore some type of control or order. I now wish I had taken bigger risks and had not lost that chance to connect with my students in a deep and powerful way.

Lost Opportunity to Connect out of Fear of Losing Control

The conversation took an interesting twist at this juncture. Wanda asked Lisa if she had cried when she shared this story with her own students. Lisa answered that she had shared it on four different occasions with various classes and that while she shook badly (as she did when she read it to us), she did not cry (as she did when she read it to us). It seems that perhaps Wanda was feeling as I did, that we should not cry in front of our students. I had worked to keep a tight rein on my emotions in order to not cry, though not very successfully. While Wanda was asking her question, I was asking myself: What is it about crying? Why are we so afraid to let someone see us cry?

But instead of asking that question - the *real, genuine* question that was in my mind - I asked a more "teacherly," distanced question: "What made you decide to take this stance, to share this with your students, and to set yourself up (in a sense) to be this vulnerable? Even though at the time I thought this was an important question, one that would get behind her thinking and encompass the complexities of teacher practice, it now seems like my question diminished this entire moment. Because I was not honest with my students about what I was really thinking and how I was really feeling and because I resisted exposing my own tattered emotions, I missed the opportunity to truly connect. My students were sincerely struggling to do that, and I did not support them in that effort like I could have. As a result, this particular moment in time, the one moment where we could have all *really* "connected" as we considered fear and loss and sadness, vanished.

Lisa did try to bring us back to that level when she said: "I felt I would be lying if I didn't choose to share this particular story. When I think personal narrative I think that this is the story of my life so far." And then once again, I tried to create some distance and asked the class what is scary about doing this, about opening yourself up to your students like this. I asked them to consider themselves and why or how that would be frightening for them. So instead of *living* this with my students, I retreated and made it a more "academic" exercise.

What is painfully ironic about this is that the very question I was posing to my students was the one I refused to answer for myself in that very

moment. What makes it even more ironic is that the idea of being vulnerable with students - and perhaps working to shift some of the "traditional" boundaries between teacher and student - was one of the more theoretical ideas that informed this inquiry and what I hoped informed my teaching practice. However, when the time came to put that to the test, I failed miserably.

Diane then answered my question (a disingenuous one at that since I already knew the answer) that teachers want to be in control or at least to feel like they are in control. She stated: "When you share something about yourself, you equate pain with weakness or tears with weakness. When you share that side of yourself, it's almost like you're out of control and that you're not sure you want your students to see you in that state." At that point two other students, Erica and Karen, began to talk about what happens when we ask students to share personal parts of their lives, thus making students uncomfortable. Though the moment may not have been lost, in that moment I felt like it had been lost, like I could not recapture it. As hard as some of my students tried to work as a connected knowing group, it seems I worked just as hard to undermine them, thus eliminating that opportunity in order to protect myself.

Though I had started this class session with sincerity and authenticity (or what I thought was sincerity and authenticity), I was unable to maintain any semblance of either in this moment. In order to redeem this situation, I might have owned up to that and admitted my struggles to my students. However, like many teachers, I got caught up in the need to look good to my students, to preserve some modicum of control or what some might perceive as dignity, and to convince them of my authority. I had reverted back to the conservative norms of what it traditionally means to be "the teacher," making it next to impossible to gain back the authenticity I sought to embody.

When my control was gone, when being vulnerable meant responding to a student in a way that revealed a deep and personal part of myself,

I balked. As much as I wanted to disrupt my students' notions, I seemed unable to disrupt my own. This kind of reverting back to conservative norms might be inevitable to the process of undergoing disruption. Every moment of disruption is (perhaps necessarily) followed by moves that return the situation to "normalcy," at least what feels normal at that moment. Similar to our inability to be in a state of cognitive dissonance for an extended period of time, we perhaps cannot tolerate moments of disruption indefinitely before we have to return to what is familiar. Or perhaps we cannot tolerate them too often before we feel some type of compulsion to restore what might feel like a sense of order and thus, maintain control.

Solutions and Recommendations

Asking genuine questions seems critical. The tension in this is that sometimes the relationship between our learning goals and our most genuine questions is not readily apparent. Further, our students make statements or assertions that we may see as problematic, disagreeable, or perhaps even offensive. Therefore, posing genuine questions may seem to take us away from the learning that we would like our students to acquire and develop. However, these questions - and the motivation behind them - communicate a desire to understand experiences that are unlike our own as a way of gaining insights into other people's ways of thinking. It is only through this connection with those whose experiences are unlike our own that we can then begin to gain richer understandings of ourselves, despite the discomfort (even pain) and disruption that this might cause. Encouraging this, however, lets students know that we value all of them as knowers and as thinkers.

Related to this is the idea of vulnerability. A willingness to be vulnerable may be preferable to a response, question, or statement that is offered in order to ease the tension. In fact, vulnerability may be necessary for powerful connections to oc-

cur within a group. Revealing deep-set emotions could be indicative of - and requisite for - a group working to become more connected and may be the only way that we can truly absorb another's story, understand another's feelings, or extend ourselves into an experience unlike our own.

This process requires time, perhaps time for quietude and reflection. But it also requires discomfort and a willingness to take in and *feel* the emotions of others, a willingness to be in awe of the myriad experiences of those with whom we come in contact every day. Yes, some members of the group may not speak out of a sense of discomfort; on the other hand, we too often speak *because* it feels awkward and because we are hesitant to *un*-comfortably dwell in the realm of emotion.

Finally, it seems that being genuine and valuing emotions reflect one central goal that all teacher educators might set for themselves: a sincere desire for relationship, which is disruptive in that it means pushing at the relational boundaries that we often erect between ourselves and our students. A desire for relationship seems to set a somewhat different tone and encourage a more connected orientation both between teacher and student and among students. A primary concern with process: the telling, or need for the telling, the providing of space to share feelings and emotions, and the willingness to also remain silent may open the door for teachers and students to all connect in ways that perhaps were not previously possible. It seems that the basic human need to connect with others (in this instance through story) communicates to students that the classroom space is safe, a place where ideas, thoughts, and feelings can be shared openly and with the certainty that no one will be harmed in any way. It is only in such an environment that students will be willing to interrogate and challenge the beliefs and values that shape their notions of what should and could be their realities as secondary English language arts teachers.

FUTURE RESEARCH DIRECTIONS

One direction for future research that seems salient is whether students' learning through narrative inquiry such as this impacts their teaching practices. Further, if we were to work from the assumption that narrative inquiry does shape (or re-shape) their teaching, the question then becomes where and how it shapes their teaching. Perhaps even more complicated is how do epistemological beliefs, such as acknowledging and appreciating our students as knowers and thinkers, manifest themselves in teaching practice? Or what constitutes risk-taking and vulnerability? Moreover, given the fact that the nature and extent of the risk can change across situations, how do we determine the extent to which an action is truly an example of risk-taking?

Another direction for future research would be to look more into the pedagogy(ies) for secondary English language arts methods courses. The pedagogy I have already described is not without its challenges and also merits further investigation. Considering my students' responses, as well as my own fears, it seems that perhaps safety and trust are the primary challenges inherent in the pedagogy for narrative inquiry. It seems impossible to engage in a project such as this without safety. While students might seemingly appear to feel safe, that may not truly be the case.

This suggests to me that perhaps some other "bridging" pedagogies need to be created and systematically examined, pedagogies that help students feel safe and that work to develop trust between teacher and students and among students. Again, these pedagogies need to present themselves as processes, as opposed to activities such as ice breakers or problem-solving tasks. While such exercises can be beneficial and worthwhile, they will not generate the assurance of safety and level of trust that the vulnerable nature of sharing stories requires.

How to accomplish these goals (or similar ones) given the constraints of time many, often conflicting, curricular demands, remains to be seen. What I have briefly described constituted two weeks of one 16-week semester, the second semester of a year-long methods course. My students had already worked with each other over the course of one semester, and many of them had shared undergraduate work. However, this was a somewhat unique situation. Many students enter a methods course never having met each other before, which can be especially problematic if a course only meets for 13 or 14 weeks, much less during a more abbreviated session. Whether a narrative inquiry such as this would be effective, much less possible, under those circumstances is doubtful. However, if we are convinced of its value, then how to make it an integral part of methods course curricula requires additional research. Or perhaps another way to look at this would be more investigation into how to develop a sequence of curricular segments that will connect conceptually as well as prepare students for and build on the processes that are requisite to connected knowing and forming a connected knowing group. Related to this is additional research into practices that are consistent with the notion of connected teaching. These areas could extend into other content areas beyond teacher education and carry implications across various levels of education.

CONCLUSION

I cannot - and refuse to - ignore how and why the personal, in the form of story, always remains important to me. Frederick Buechner (1983) helps me to explain this when he talks about why he decided to write his autobiography:

I do it because it seems to me that no matter who you are, and no matter how eloquent or otherwise, if you tell your own story with sufficient candor and concreteness, it will be an interesting story and in some sense a universal story. I do it also in the hopes of encouraging others to do the same

- at least to look back...as I have looked back... for certain themes and patterns and signals that are so easy to miss when you're caught up in the process of living them" (pp. 2-3).

Found in narrative inquiry I have discussed was the beginning of my own journey of learning how to teach teachers with its success and failures, fears and uncertainties, tears and laughter. It could be argued that it is *just* story. I believe, though, that story still holds the power and the potential to provide others with insights into their own lives and experiences or to think about their own lives and experiences in some new way. If nothing else, I believe, like Buechner, that story might encourage someone else to stop and think about her life, in particular her teaching life, and try to pick up on what she may have lost along the way - and in the middle - of her living it.

This narrative inquiry also reflects my beginning to understand my students' learning, as well as explicates and ultimately complicates, my understanding of my own pedagogy. However, it encompasses my students' stories, as interestingly enough, I cannot tell my story without weaving it with theirs, as they are such an integral part of my story. Furthermore, it was the process of working with narrative inquiry that brought my intuitions to a conscious level. It was through writing that I began to learn who I was in my classroom, what I believed and deemed valuable, as well as some ideas about the source(s) of those beliefs and values. In addition, writing gave me further insights into what my students were saying and doing as I tried to reveal who they were and what they learned through the stories *they* told. It allowed me to examine what we all gained, what we found challenging, even frightening. Perhaps more importantly, I learned why my students and I might be hesitant or resistant, as well as why despite those feelings, we nevertheless felt compelled to tell our stories.

I have a great empathy for my students who may feel lost or silenced. Therefore, I seek to create opportunities for my students so that their learning might lead to the same sense of empowerment that I have felt. Perhaps if I am able to give them opportunities to realize this, despite the seemingly inevitable landmines, they will reach the same conclusions I have and will then work to create the same opportunities for *their* students.

REFERENCES

Barnes, D. (1979). *From communication to curriculum*. New York, NY: Penguin Books.

Belenky, M. F., Clinchy, B. M., Goldberger, N. R., & Tarule, J. M. (1997). *Women's ways of knowing: The development of self, voice, and mind*. New York, NY: Basic Books.

Bruner, J. (1996). *The culture of education*. Cambridge, MA: Harvard University Press.

Buechner, F. (1983). *Now and then: A memoir of vocation*. San Francisco, CA: Harper.

Burton, F. R., & Seidl, B. (2002). Teacher researcher projects: From the elementary school teacher's perspective. In Flood, J., Lapp, D., Squire, J., & Jensen, J. M. (Eds.), *Handbook of research on teaching the English language arts* (2nd ed., pp. 225–231). Mahweh, NJ: Lawrence Erlbaum Associates.

Clandinin, D. J. (1985). Personal practical knowledge: A study of teachers' classroom images. *Curriculum Inquiry*, *15*(4), 361–385. doi:10.2307/1179683

Cochran-Smith, M., & Lytle, S. L. (1999). Relationships of knowledge and practice: Teacher learning in communities. *Review of Research in Education*, *24*, 249–305.

Conle, C. (2003). An anatomy of narrative curricula. *Educational Researcher, 32*(3), 3–15. doi:10.3102/0013189X032003003

Connelly, F. M., & Clandinin, D. J. (1990). Stories of experience and narrative inquiry. *Educational Researcher, 19*(5), 2–14.

Freire, P. (1993). *Pedagogy of the oppressed.* New York, NY: Continuum.

Fuller, F. F. (1969). Concerns of teachers: A developmental conceptualization. *American Educational Research Journal, 6*(2), 207–226.

hooks, b. (1994). *Teaching to transgress—Education as the practice of freedom.* New York, NY: Routledge.

Johnson, M. (1989). Embodied knowledge. *Curriculum Inquiry, 19*(4), 361–377. doi:10.2307/1179358

Kennedy, M. M. (2006). Knowledge and vision in teaching. *Journal of Teacher Education, 57*(3), 205–211. doi:10.1177/0022487105285639

Kozol, J. (1991). *Savage inequalities: Children in America's schools.* New York, NY: Crown Publishers.

Lortie, D. C. (1975). *Schoolteacher: A sociological study.* Chicago, IL: University of Chicago Press.

Maher, F., & Thompson Tetreault, M. (2001). *The feminist classroom: Dynamics of gender, race, and privilege.* New York, NY: Rowman & Littlefield Publishers, Inc.

Rose, M. (1989). *Lives on the boundary: A moving account of the struggles and the achievements of America's educational underclass.* New York, NY: Penguin Books.

Villegas, A. M., & Lucas, T. (2002). *Educating culturally responsive teachers: A coherent approach.* Albany, NY: State University of New York Press.

Willinsky, J. (1989). Getting personal and practical with personal practical knowledge. *Curriculum Inquiry, 19*(3), 247–264. doi:10.2307/1179416

Wilson, D. E., & Ritchie, J. S. (1994). Resistance, revision, and representation: Narrative in teacher education. *English Education, 26*(3), 177–188.

Witherell, C., & Noddings, N. (1991). Prologue: An invitation to our readers. In Witherell, C., & Noddings, N. (Eds.), *Stories lives tell: Narrative and dialogue in education* (pp. 1–12). New York, NY: Teachers College Press.

ADDITIONAL READING

Carter, K. (1993). The place of story in the study of teaching and teacher education. *Educational Researcher, 22* (1), 5-12+18.

Casey, K. (1995-1996). The new narrative research in education. *Review of Research in Education, 21*, 211–253.

Cochran-Smith, M., & Lytle, S. L. (1999). Relationships of knowledge and practice: teacher learning in communities. *Review of Research in Education, 24*, 249–305.

Conle, C. (1999). Why narrative? which narrative? struggling with time and place in life and research. *Curriculum Inquiry, 29*(1), 7–32. doi:10.1111/0362-6784.00111

Cooper, J. E. (1991). Telling our own stories: The reading and writing of journals or diaries. In Witherell, C., & Noddings, N. (Eds.), *Stories lives tell: Narrative and dialogue in education* (pp. 96–112). New York: Teachers College Press.

Dewey, J. (1938). *Experience and education.* New York: Macmillan.

Ellsworth, E. (1994). Why doesn't this feel empowering? Working through the repressive myths of critical pedagogy. In Luke, C., & Gore, J. (Eds.), *Feminisms and Critical Pedagogy* (pp. 90–119). New York: Routledge.

Floden, R., & Buchmann, M. (1993). Between routines and anarchy: Preparing teachers for uncertainty. *Oxford Review of Education, 19*(3), 373–382. doi:10.1080/0305498930190308

Florio-Ruane, S. (2001). *Teacher Education and the Cultural Imagination: Autobiography, Conversation, and Narrative*. Mahwah: Lawrence Erlbaum Associates.

Fried, R. L. (1995). *The Passionate Teacher: A Practical Guide*. Boston: Beacon Hill.

Gilligan, C. (1993). *In a Different Voice: Psychological Theory and Women's Development*. Cambridge: Harvard University Press.

Greene, M. (1995). *Releasing the Imagination: Essays on Education, the Arts, and Social Change*. San Francisco: Jossey-Bass.

Grumet, M. R. (1988). *Bitter Milk: Women and Teaching*. Amherst: University of Massachusetts Press.

Hollingsworth, S. (1992). Learning to Teach through Collaborative Conversation: A Feminist Approach. *American Educational Research Journal, 29*(2), 373–404.

Jackson, P. W. (1986). *The Practice of Teaching*. New York: Teachers College Press.

Laird, S. (1988). Reforming "woman's true profession": A Case for "feminist pedagogy" in teacher education? *Harvard Educational Review, 58*(4), 449–463.

Lampert, M. (1985). How do Teachers Manage to Teach? Perspectives on Problems in Practice. *Harvard Educational Review, 55*(2), 178–194.

Lampert, M. (2001). *Teaching Problems and the Problems of Teaching*. New Haven: Yale University Press.

Lewis, M. (1994). Interrupting Patriarchy: Politics, Resistance and Transformation in the Feminist Classroom. In Luke, C., & Gore, J. (Eds.), *Feminisms and Critical Pedagogy* (pp. 167–191). New York: Routledge.

MacDonald, J. (1992). *Teaching: Making Sense of an Uncertain Craft*. New York: Teachers College Press.

Meyer, T., & Sawyer, M. (2006). Cultivating an Inquiry Stance in English Education: Rethinking the Student Teaching Seminar. *English Education, 39*(1), 46–71.

Nespor, J., & Barylske, J. (1991). Narrative Discourse and Teacher Knowledge. *American Educational Research Journal, 28*(4), 805–823.

Noblit, G. W. (1993). Power and Caring. *American Educational Research Journal, 30*(1), 23–38.

Schafsma, D., Pagnucci, G., Wallace, R., & Stock, P. (2007). Composing Storied Ground: Four Generations of Narrative Inquiry. *English Education, 39*(4), 282–306.

Schafsma, D., & Vinz, R. (2007). Composing Narratives for Inquiry. *English Education, 39*(4), 77–81.

Scholes, R. (1981). Language, Narrative, and Anti-narrative. In Mitchell, W. J. T. (Ed.), *On Narrative* (pp. 200–208). Chicago: University of Chicago Press.

Smith, K., & Lambert Stock, P. (2002). Trends and Issues in Research in the Teaching of the English Language Arts. In Flood, J., Lapp, D., Squire, J., & Jensen, J. M. (Eds.), *Handbook of Research on Teaching the English Language Arts* (2nd ed., pp. 114–130). Mahweh: Lawrence Erlbaum Associates.

Wortham, S. (2001). *Narratives in Action: A strategy for Research and Analysis*. New York: Teachers College Press.

KEY TERMS AND DEFINITIONS

Connected Knowing: A way of knowing that is focused on relationship; concerned with understanding, particularly extending understanding to positions that seem strange and unfamiliar; drawn on personal experience; and concerned with accessing other people's experiences, ways of thinking, and knowledge.

Connected Teaching: A way of teaching where teachers think aloud with their students in a public dialogue, where teachers embrace uncertainty and work to develop a community or practice, where teachers value students on their own terms, where the role of student and teacher begin to merge.

Narrative Inquiry: A pedagogical approach where students use written personal narratives to focus their attention on the way they understand the world around them, to bring that knowledge to the surface, and to illuminate how that knowledge impacts them in the classroom.

Story: A construction of an event or series of events connected by the element of time and tied together by subject matter.

Chapter 2
Disrupting Relationships:
A Catalyst for Growth

Vicki Stieha
University of Cincinnati, USA

Miriam Raider-Roth
University of Cincinnati, USA

ABSTRACT

Can the disruption of teachers' relationships with themselves, as both teachers and learners, be a source for professional growth? In this chapter the authors explore teachers' professional development experiences as a source for disrupting relationships with the "self-as-teacher" and "self-as-learner" and the way this process can facilitate innovative changes in their teaching practices. While some may view "disrupting relationships" as a negative move, the chapter will frame a view of such relational ruptures with subsequent repair as potentially growth fostering. In contrast to a view that sees disrupting relationships as a negative move, this work provides a view of reconciliation and repair as one that propels the individual forward – a move that is steeped in learning about self and about other. Developmentally, the authors understand the sense of disconnection, or rupture, as an essential "evolutionary" step as individuals continue to move beyond their mental and emotional boundaries increasing growth and learning (Kegan, 1982, 1994). In seeking to understand the teachers' experiences, this work provides an intimate and descriptive picture of the negotiations participants made during and after an extended professional development seminar vis-à-vis their learning and teaching practice. In doing so, the authors make visible the complicated processes involved as teachers question conventional practices and invite innovation into their classrooms.

DOI: 10.4018/978-1-61350-495-6.ch002

THE SUMMER TEACHERS INSTITUTE

This chapter focuses on the experiences of veteran teachers who participated in an intense week-long professional development Summer Teachers Institute (the Institute), focusing on the study of Jewish history, culture and civilization. The goal of the Institute was to help teachers who are responsible for teaching about Judaism (in public and private non-sectarian and Jewish schools) deepen their subject matter knowledge through first-hand experiences. At the center of this experience was a close examination of collaborative text study, how it could be incorporated into teachers' practice and students' learning, and the study. One of the curricular assumptions was that text study itself was an important form of professional development because of the dispositions it requires of the learner. In particular, we asked the participants to engage in *Hevruta* study, a form of collaborative text study drawing from ancient Jewish traditions involving pairs of learners who remain partners throughout the Institute. This form of study asks participants to engage in practices that sharpen their capacity for active listening, attentive questioning, voicing, and challenging (Holzer, 2002, 2006; Raider-Roth & Holzer, 2009). Additionally, participants investigated archival documents drawn from the American Jewish Archives, artifacts, portraits, and film through a historiographic approach, asking participants to "read" the texts for meaning, association, historical context, and interpretation (Raider, in progress). This immersion experience embodies Boler's (1999) charge to "challenge rigid patterns of thinking" by placing participants in a learning context in which they begin to "self-reflectively evaluate the complex relations of power and emotion" (p. 157). Throughout the Institute the teachers were prompted to consider their thought patterns through written reflections, their consideration of prior knowledge, their processes for making meaning, and the ways they were engaging with the texts, with Institute facilitators, and with their peers. Additionally, this process of self-reflection opened spaces for them to understand themselves (cognitively and emotionally) and provided an opportunity for growth—learning we see as transformational (Mezirow, 2000).

The teacher participants have described the "fluid" experience of shifting roles (from teacher to learner and back again) that they experienced during the Institute, noting how the week differed dramatically from the typical professional development experience. As one participant reflected, "everybody had the opportunity to be the guy in charge" during their learning and that gave her a sense that she could "take up space" (Hadassah, personal communication, August 2007). In short, the Institute provides a "counter-story" of teaching-learning relationships in professional development (Raider-Roth & Holzer, 2009) and challenged them to integrate this experience into their teaching lives as they returned to their own classrooms and students.

THEORETICAL LENSES FOR THIS WORK

We find that identifying how people "unlearn" conventional practices - a complex developmental process - is best approached through three theoretical lenses. First we turn to David Hawkins' (2002/1974) model of the "I, Thou, It" triangle, which captures the essential relationships of classroom life. Second we examine relational theories (e.g. Gilligan, 1982; Jordan, 2004; Miller, 1976; Miller & Stiver, 1997) to help us understand how these essential learning relationships support and impede learning. Third, we add understandings gleaned from human developmental theory, particularly focusing on adult developmental theory (Kegan, 1982, 1994). Each of these lenses helps us take into consideration the emotional, cognitive, interpersonal, and intrapersonal facets of this developmental move.

The Relational Triangle

Hawkins (2002/1974) conceptualizes the fundamental relationships in learning between I, thou, and it—the teacher, student, and subject matter. This model demonstrates the potential of rebalancing the ubiquitous hierarchies of teaching (normatively placing the teacher above student) by emphasizing the essential roles of each player in a triarchic figure. In Hawkins' model of the triangle, the teacher brings the subject matter ("it") into the room, facilitates the students' relationship with the subject matter, and provides the "external" loop of feedback to help the student move forward. The teacher retreats toward the periphery as the learners negotiate with the text: questioning, challenging, and voicing their thinking in a mutually empathetic relationship. Others (Cohen, Raudenbush, & Ball, 2003) have referred to Hawkins' "I, Thou, It" model as an "instructional triangle." However, we argue that the term "instructional" is inadequate to describe what we see happening in the dynamic three-way interchanges at the Institute.

Rather, we have conceptualized Hawkins' triangle for adult collaborative learning as a *relational triangle* (see Raider-Roth & Holzer, 2009). In constructing the relational triangle, "I" and "thou" are co-learners in relationship to one another and with the text. Each corner has a key role in learning, and the "legs," or the relationship between each angle, is central in sustaining the triangular nature of this learning gestalt. Our own research indicates that the strength of relationship represented by each leg plays into the resilience of the learner as each relationship can strengthen (or weaken) the other (Raider-Roth, Stieha, & Hensley, 2010b).

Relational-Cultural Theory

The relational theorists help us better understand why structuring adult learning with great attention to the relational dynamics in this triangle is so critical. Establishing the essential human need for connection, researchers on human development have taught us that relationships are rooted in a life-long mutual regulation cycle, where communication of needs and desires is foundational, and where reciprocity, and mutual empathy are central processes (Miller & Stiver, 1997; Tronick & Weinberg, 1997). Further, it is within these mutually empathic relationships that "relational confidence" - a confidence that is found not only in self worth, but in knowing that one has something to offer in a mutually sustaining relationship - is found (Jordan, 2004).

The relational theorists hold that disconnections are inevitable and expected. Further, these disconnections can be triggered by the images that an individual carries of herself in one relationship, which she then applies to another. This type of disconnection, which Sarah Lawrence-Lightfoot (2003) vividly describes through her portraits of teacher-parent conferences, can be built on either party's past school experiences and not necessarily on the relationship at hand. In general, disconnections can compromise authentic connection in favor of a connection that may appear to be "acceptable." However, disconnections that are transformed and renewed through the repair cycle can be brought back into mutually empathic relationships fostering profound human growth (which we also understand as learning).

Applied to learning, relational theory has contributed our understandings of how mutually empathic relationships are linked to students' and teachers' trust of their knowledge (Raider-Roth, 2005; Raider-Roth, Albert, Bircann-Barkley, Gidseg, & Murray, 2008); students' reading of the cultural climate of a university (Hensley, 2009); teachers' negotiations of teaching practice in light of the web of relationships within a school context (Stieha, 2010); and teachers' understandings of gender equity in schools (Spencer, Porche, & Tolman, 2003) to name a few. In short, the idea that human relationships in schooling are central to students' capacity to learn well and teachers' capacities to teach well is now convincingly argued in the fields of educational research, educational psychology and relational psychology.

Adult Learning and Developmental Theory

A third lens expands our understanding of adult development through the lifespan and offers powerful explanations for individual responses to learning at the Institute. Like others who resist the separation of cognition from emotion (e.g. Boler, 1999; Gilligan, 1982, 1996; Mezirow, 2000; Miller & Stiver, 1997), the constructive developmental model (Kegan, 1982, 1994) is not limited to either cognitive or affective domains; it illuminates adults' life-long development. Human development, according to Kegan, "involves a succession of renegotiated balances" which are "intrinsically cognitive, but [...] no less affective; we are this activity and we experience it" (1982, p. 80). By positioning developmental processes as "evolutionary" he captures the dynamic nature of individuals' responses to the world and to others in it, suggesting, "In considering where a person is in his or her evolutionary balancing we are looking not only at how meaning is made; we are looking, too, at the possibility of the person losing this balance" (Kegan, 1982, p. 114). Thus, a "loss" of balance can be an *asset* rather than a deficit if we see it as necessary for finding new meaning.

This view of adult human development provides a useful perspective on the psychological "disequilibrium" experienced as an old self is released and a new self is constructed when faced with the realization that "how we know" is not sufficient for the demand we are facing (Kegan, 1982). In other words, a loss of balance in this sense is attributed less to *what* we know than it is to the way in which we make meaning or *how* we think. In our own research of teachers' professional development experiences, we have noted multiple disruptions in relationships with the self, with others (facilitators or learning partners), and with the text (Raider-Roth, Stieha, & Hensley, 2010a; Stieha, 2010). We have found the process of disconnection and repair often results in strengthened relationships and the construction of new knowledge. The movement from disconnection, through repair, and to renewed connection can be experienced in as a sense of "felt difficulty"—the recognition of a "perplexity" that has been "felt (directly experienced)" which moves the individual to seek an answer (Dewey, 1933/1989, p. 200).

Extending Kegan's work to our understandings of the necessarily conditions for adult learning helps us consider the importance of our participants taking educative "risks" through "supported vulnerability" (Jordan, 2004, 2008). The ideas undergirding Kegan's work are consistent with the expectations for transformational learning (see Drago-Severson, 2009; Mezirow, 2000; Raider-Roth & Holzer, 2009) which best describes the learning at the Summer Teachers Institute.

THE STUDY

When we began our inquiry with the 2007 cohort we did so as an inquiry action research study (Cochran-Smith & Lytle, 2009); as we designed the curriculum for the Institute we simultaneously designed a research study hoping to inform our own teacher professional development practice. We planned interviews, reflective writing, essays and observations with an intention to inform the continuous development of the Institute. Additionally, we kept our own journals to record our observations, responses, questions, and confusions during the Institute and wrote research memos continuously through the analysis of data. These journals assisted us in looking at our end of the relational dynamics and how our teaching of -

and learning from - the participants shaped our thinking as well as the relational dimensions of the Institute.

This chapter is built upon prior analysis of data collected from two participant cohorts attending the Summer Teachers Institute (2007 and 2009). Our analysis is informed by the Listening Guide (Brown & Gilligan, 1992; Gilligan, Spencer, Weinberg, & Bertsch, 2003) and feminist grounded theory (Clarke, 2007). Throughout our processes we mined our own associative thinking (Raider-Roth, 2010) to complicate rather than oversimplify our reading of the data. Using a recursive process as data were collected, we continuously wrote memos documenting our questions, and inviting contemplation of the voices that did not seem to fit "neatly" into our developing theories. These processes mark our analysis as particularly feminist and push against facets of grounded theory that have been deemed problematic by some feminist critics (Clarke, 2007). We did not seek a single "Truth" but rather to understand the multiple experiences of our participants as adult learners during and after these professional development experiences.

The Institute participants (15 teachers in 2007 & 13 teachers in 2009) were educators coming from diverse suburban and urban schools. They ranged widely in age and experience - from their early 20's into their 60's. They taught in public and private schools (including religiously based schools) as well as informal educational settings. While some enrolled in the Institute to earn continuing educational credit for professional development, or for university credit, others cited "personal growth" as their motivation. The widely varying perspectives and teaching contexts added a rich backdrop to our learning communities during each Institute. We did not differentiate teachers or privilege any career path over another; we take the position that education takes place in many forms and in multiple venues - education is more than "schooling."

DISRUPTING RELATIONSHIPS

As we consider the trajectory of participants' experiences, we are careful not to homogenize their stories, or confine their narratives of learning and practice into a singular standard. At the same time, from our analysis, a pattern has emerged which points to phases of engagement in innovative classroom pedagogies following our participants' Institute experiences. In the following section we will detail these phases which take place in two micro-cultures: the Summer Teacher's Institute and the teachers' school contexts. These phases include (1) disrupting relationships, particularly the relationship to self as learner and teacher; (2) evaluating and assimilating new ways of knowing and finding relational confidence; and, (3) upon return to their school context, new ways of knowing are read against this environment as teachers negotiate integrating innovative practices into their teaching.

Disrupting Relationships with the Self

Throughout participants' interviews we heard stories indicating disruption in the relationship with self which took place early in the Institute. For example, during a post-Institute interview, Naomi (a veteran K-2 teacher at a private Jewish day school) shares her journal entry about being "physically, intellectually, and emotionally exhausted" at the beginning of the Institute. She continues, describing "something that is brewing" and a "heaviness of my chest, and I feel like it's an explosion in my heart." These feelings leave her with "uncertainty" about what is to come, yet a certainty that the "transformation [is] strong." She continues, "I had a revelation about myself and my learning style. I realized that much of the disequilibrium caused by experiential coursework is because I was never exposed to this kind of learning as a student." Closing her journal, Naomi reflects, "It was so foreign to me, it was not the kind of learning I did when I was - I was a rote learner. I was a great student, but I never had to think. You know, it was memorize, memorize" (Interview, 10/2007).

Naomi's description of the "disequilibrium" she experienced at the Institute poignantly captures a disconnection with her learner-self and illustrates her need to "think" with a partner. Her words suggest she struggles to maintain a commitment to the image she carries of herself as a good student ("I was a great student, but I never had to think"), although she does not feel like a "great student" when faced with experiential learning. As we move through her interview, Naomi contrasts this moment of disruption, faced with a need to *know* in a different manner, to the experience she has turning to her learning partner at the Institute (activating the relational triangle), finding repair, and thereby growing in "relational confidence" (Jordan, 2004).

Similarly, Sarah describes how she had to confront her own "inhibitions about learning" during the Institute when she was asked to write reflectively after each session. Sarah, a veteran teacher with 30 years experience teaching Judaic Studies and Hebrew at a Jewish day school, reveled in the process of text study - working through a text with her partner and emerging from that work with great confidence. Shifting to reflective writing (a solitary act), however, caused a disconnection for her. Sarah clearly expresses that "on the level of learning and knowing that I know things, that I can put them together" and yet she encountered the reflective writing as "a shortcoming." She explains her ability to reflect, saying, "I saw, as if I needed proof, that my shortcomings - it's almost, I consider it, a learning disability" (Interview, 10/2007).

Sarah's realization that she "knows things" and "can put them together" points to her comfort with informational learning. Essentially, Sarah is expressing her confidence in being able to draw from the vast resources of content knowledge she has and to apply it to a new task. The require-

ment to reflect on the lesson and her learning process, however, asks something entirely different of Sarah. The act of reflecting on learning is a transformational learning task; it draws upon cognitive, emotional, and intrapersonal ways of knowing (Mezirow, 2000). The move into transformational learning requirements raises a "felt difficulty" (Dewey, 1933/1989) for Sarah in her relationship with self as a learner since she has little experience of competence with reflective writing. Sarah ultimately turned to trusted peers to continue developing her reflective capacities at the Institute and then later upon her return to her own school.

Evaluating and Assimilating New Ways of Knowing

In many participants' narratives we noted moments of disconnection as discrete and clearly articulated. In other cases, however, participants described momentary ruptures when faced with the learning challenge followed quickly by a story of assimilating new ways of knowing. This finding reminds us that disconnections are often opportunities for learning as individuals experience repair and emerge with a stronger, mutually empathic relationship (Jordan, 2004; Miller & Stiver, 1997).

As we discussed above, applying constructive-developmental theory and relational theory with an understanding of repair to this phase, we can see that in a state of destabilization an individual is poised for a transformation in her learning. In our discussions of Sarah and Naomi's experiences we noted that they turn to trusted others in order to repair their relationship with self and to continue their learning. An example of this phase is clear as we listen to Amy, a mid-career primary grade school teacher. In her narrative we hear a brief disconnection as she confronts her tendency to bring her "own prejudices" to reading. Her realization that she reads with "a single lens" is something that she "hadn't really ever thought about" until the Institute when she read Hawkins' (2002/1974) "I, Thou, and It" and then discussed it as a group. In addition to Amy's sense that she wanted to be "more open" and questioning by saying, "how would somebody else read this?" she comes to understand that working in collaboration with another adult she has a "feeling like, um, somebody is in this with me. I am not trying to figure this out alone" (Interview, 10/2007).

In her written Institute evaluation, Amy elaborated on her experience in collaborative text study as "powerful." In the follow up interview, Miriam asked her to explain what she meant by "powerful" learning. Amy responded that it had to do with "being focused on something" in contrast to other times when adults work together and they talk about "kids or mates or, you know, gripes." Rather, she paints a picture of a mutually empathic learning partnership, saying, "It's like we had a task, we understood what we were supposed to do, we did it together and it was SO interesting that we didn't need to digress." Then, Amy goes on to explain how she and her partner built a relationship as learners through the process of challenging one another:

She's got a lot to say, she's a thinker and she's very specific sometimes, like, "well, what do you mean by that," which is part of what you wanted us to do. Where I'm a little, I'm less, more tentative, I guess, about challenging people's thinking. Um, and knowing that she was doing that gave me permission within my value system to kinda do that back, it was going to be safe, if she could do it, then I could do it. (Interview, 10/2007; L. 66-75)

In Amy's story we can trace the progression from a moment of disconnection that is found in her realization about herself as a learner (bringing her own "prejudices" and being "tentative") and then her moves to assimilate key ideas from the Institute (e.g. challenging interpretations of texts together). In the process she learns that there may

be multiple interpretations of a single text, and working collaboratively, she and her partner can help one another learn more deeply from text. Additionally, Amy evaluates her experiences against her "value system" through reflection - a marker of her transformative learning.

Other participants had similar stories of assimilating ideas and practices from the Institute which they found unfamiliar and initially uncomfortable. One said, "I had to get comfortable with the idea of challenging" in a manner that mirrors Amy's sentiments. Paul (who teaches English in a public high school) admitted to feeling "trepidation" when he walked into the Institute on the first day. In particular, he saw himself as a "solo learner" and worried about working collaboratively. His fears were short lived; in his post-Institute interview he narrates the process of coming into a relationship with his partner, Sonia, who he had initially expected to "take the lead." Rather, "the tables kind of got turned. And she was kind of following my lead, which made me, then, want, you know, really want to praise her and do the same for her" (Interview, 12/2009).

In each of the narratives above, it was the mutually empathic relationships the teachers were able to form with their learning partners that serve as one of the first keys to reconnecting the rupture with the self-as-learner at the Institute. In the teachers' narratives, their reflective writing, and open ended post-Institute evaluations we trace a pattern of their references linking, "safety," and "trust," as descriptions of the conditions they need to take a "risk" as a learner. For instance, Sonia (who teaches middle school art in a religious school) says that the idea of "challenging [became] a growth and positive word as opposed to an obstacle word" in the community of learners because "we were very supportive of each other. It was a very safe environment" (Interview, 12/2009). As they share stories of themselves as learners, we hear the powerful connections they make between emotional and cognitive expressions about learning. Understanding these descriptions of what they needed for learning as a "healthy relational context" we see these criteria as critical supports for the cycle they experienced moving from destabilization through repair and to new learning during the Institute.

Back to School: Transferring Learning to Teaching

One challenge facing professional development is to understand how teachers transfer their learning back to the classroom environment and assimilate pedagogical approaches into their teaching practices. Above we traced a pattern of learning at the Institute that is characterized by encountering a destabilization when faced with a "felt difficulty" (Dewey, 1933/1989), finding "repair" through relational confidence, and moving to assimilate new knowledge. We noted that building relational confidence and sensing a "healthy relational context" at the Institute (one that is rich

in trust, community, and support for vulnerability) facilitated the participants' movement through this cycle. We have found that a similar pattern that plays into teachers' negotiation of innovative practices following the Institute as well. In Figure 1, we trace the patterns of disconnection through new learning at the Institute and then show how this cycle plays out for the teachers upon return to their own schools.

As we have discussed, these data are drawn from two Institute cohorts. The 2007 Institute participants included a team of eight teachers from one private Jewish day school (which we call Meir School), as well as six advanced rabbinical students and one additional graduate student from a local university. Although the interviews with the rabbinical students and the graduate student were compelling, in our data analysis we have focused on the experiences of those who were actively teaching. Unlike the 2007 cohort, all of the participants attending the 2009 Institute did so independently and returned separately to their

Figure 1. Model of teacher learning at the Institute and subsequent return to the school context

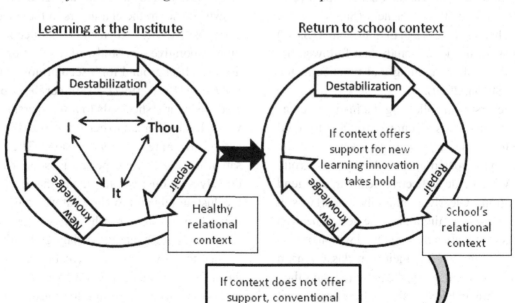

respective schools and organizations. Because we know that that the contexts for teaching are important in terms of the teachers' application of their newly learned pedagogical and content knowledge (Stieha, 2010), we will discuss the 2007 cohort first and then move to the 2009 cohort.

2007 Cohort Teachers Return to School

For the Meir School teachers, attending the Institute was part of a movement at the school to transform its culture. That transformation included a more integrated approach to disciplinary content, including weaving cultural content into the curriculum and helping students connect intellectually, culturally, and emotionally with their Jewish identities. There was also an effort to shift the school away from conventional teaching as the norm. Therefore, the relational model of teaching as well as the content of the Institute was very consistent with the direction the school hoped to take. As we explained, the teachers from the school attended as a "team" and that team spirit continued upon return to their school for several months. Four of these teachers (Sarah, Tamar, Hadassah, and Nancy) and their principal (Sally) participated in a longer study that followed the trajectory of their learning and practice at the school (Stieha, 2010).

In the first year following the Institute it was clear that there was a communal effort to build on the teachers' learning. In fact, several of the teachers participated in a teacher inquiry group led by Miriam, the Reflective Seminar, to extend their learning. Clearly, community support was an important key in minimizing the destabilization teachers faced when they wrestled with integrating new pedagogies into their own classrooms in this school context. Sally, the principal, says they were "willing to take risks" and there was a spirit of experimenting with new practices together (In-

terview, 3/2009). Nancy, a social studies teacher with over thirty years in the classroom, echoed Sally's assessment saying, "It just, it has a feel of, of, um, working together as a community which we're trying to build, you know, and increase that" (Interview, 10/2007).

The trajectory that traces the phases of initial uncertainty, looking for relational confidence, and integration of new learning into practice is reflected in a post-Institute essay written by Tamar, a mid-career language arts teacher. Opening her essay, Tamar wrote that the first challenge she faced when returning to her school was to "figure out how I would apply graduate level lessons" to a middle school class. Important elements involved in negotiating this challenge include the Reflective Seminar and Sally's support. Tamar makes it clear that these sources of relational support play into her efforts for pedagogical innovation.

Tamar writes, "studying with a hevruta partner was definitely an experience that I wanted to provide for my own students." Writing reflectively about the way these methods shifted her pedagogy, Tamar shares that she noticed students reaching "more abstract and interesting thoughts" and being drawn "closer to the characters in the novel in a very positive way" when she integrated hevruta, or collaborative text study, of a selection of the Torah as background for a secular novel, *Out of the Dust* (Hesse, 1997). As Tamar describes the students' work, she shifts to a first person plural voice, linking herself to her students as they were actively learning together. She says, "The conversation then led to an unexpected question. We asked ourselves, if dust is what made them, what did the dust turn them into? In what way did the dust make them different from how they were before?" Tamar concludes that the pedagogy led them all to "see the novel as a new creation experience, an angle that I had not previously considered and one I found truly surprising for a group of sixth-graders" (Post-institute essay, 2007).

Tamar's essay provides compelling evidence about the powerful learning that she experienced at the Institute and its inspiration for her pedagogical goals. Further, it illuminates the way that she was encouraged to assimilate her learning into her classroom pedagogies based on her reading of the cultural context of the school as the "team" attempted to transform the conventional norms for teaching and to integrate more innovative practices.

Indeed, Tamar was joined by the other teachers who attended the Institute as they enacted their learning in interesting and innovative ways in the year following the Institute. For example, Amy, whose initial Institute experience was discussed earlier, returned to her primary classroom with a desire to slow down the learning for her students. One of the practices that the Institute introduced was to conduct multiple readings and consider alternative meanings for a short selection of text. Relating the ways the Institute shifted her pedagogical approach, Amy tells us:

I found myself thinking, now, my first grader sits down and reads this book, are they really going to be able to understand it or are they going to be so busy decoding…. You know, how many times do you need to go through it before they can get to a level of fluency and then we can start digging into why do you think she did that? Why did this happen? (Interview, 10/2007; L. 144-148)

Amy concluded that she was "really trying to […] give them a chance to dig deeper." She transferred her Institute learning about the importance of connecting emotionally and relationally to other learners into her approach with her own students. She shifted from "always being so task oriented" and focusing on "skills" to an empowering perspective, explaining her desire to "get them to a place where they'll say, wow, I can read this, I can understand it and I have something to say about it" (Interview, 10/2007).

2009 Cohort Teachers Return to Their Schools

Unlike the Meir School teachers in 2007, the 2009 participants were recruited to attend the Institute from a wide variety of public and private, secular and religious, elementary through secondary schools. Ruth, who teaches high school English at a Catholic parochial school, attended the Institute on her own. After the Institute she returned to the school to find that a new principal was hired and "they fired all of the [administrative staff], all of the assistants" because "they wanted a new team." As tumultuous as this "welcome back" was, it is not surprising that Ruth's reading of the relational scene at her school was, "you do it our way or it's the highway." Even though Ruth referred to her Institute experience as "absolutely precious to me," she was reluctant to bring these pedagogical innovations to her classroom. Despite experiencing relational learning, referring to her own students she says, "I realized that for my particular situation right now, I don't want that kind of relationship building" (12/2009). Ruth noted that she has her students "work in groups all the time," although it is not the same as the collaborative text study at the Institute because "they don't stay with the same person." We understand that empowering students in a true *hevruta* learning partnership shifts the hierarchy in the classroom from teacher to a shared dynamic (Raider-Roth & Holzer, 2009) and we also understand there may be a reluctance to relinquish teacher-control in school contexts in which teachers feel vulnerable (Stieha, 2010). Ruth's claim that she went into "survival mode" in her teaching context makes it clear that she is not in a place that fosters taking a teaching risk, which is required if teachers are to abandon conventional teaching practices.

While far less destabilizing than Ruth's return to school, other teachers also shared stories indicating a need to rebalance their Institute learning in their own context. For Marie (who teaches 6th grade Language Arts and Science in a Catholic parochial school), learning about listening and challenging moved her personally and professionally. She explained that she began relating to others differently as a result of her learning and now, finds herself questioning others more. She said, "I feel like if they say something to me, or even with my husband, I need to ask them, well, where is that coming from? Or what evidence do you have of that, or why are you bringing that up now?" However, questioning is complicated for Marie in her parochial school setting. She explains:

M: *But I am finding that to be much more…I mean, even in my religion, I am questioning more now.*
V: *How does that feel?*
M: *Scary. Yeah. It feels scary.*
V: *Because…*
M: *Um. I don't know if I want to get into that. (Interview, 12/2009)*

We hear the way Marie silences herself signaling discomfort with the idea of challenging her religion, particularly in her Catholic school. Yet, as destabilizing as the notion of "challenging" some ideas is for Marie, she explains to us that she was compelled to bring pedagogies she learned at the Institute back to her classroom. Connecting her own powerful learning to the experiences she wants to create for her students, Marie says, "I've been to other workshops where I come away with, 'what am I supposed to do with that?' And…but if it is going to be something that changes me, I don't feel that way. You know, because I feel like then I *have* to find a way to use it with the kids" (Interview, 12/2009).

Despite her realization that learning to "challenge" poses an emotional balancing act for her, it is clear that she finds a way to transfer this important learning to her teaching. In her post-Institute essay Marie confirms that she does find ways to weave her learning into her teaching as she writes about shifting a previously held conventional notion of teaching:

By encouraging - even requiring - group consensus, I often times discouraged the challenging of teammates in the false promise of group harmony. I now see it differently. Students are *obligated* to challenge each other, so that in considering the other's point of view, both are strengthened. Because each voicing of an idea involves the risk of challenge from their partner, students are required to provide more powerful evidence for their stance. (Post-institute essay, 2/2010)

In her explanation we have evidence that Marie is able to reconcile her tension around the idea of challenge enough to move her toward integrating it into her pedagogy, a point that we will return to in our closing comments.

Other participants' essays and narratives point to the experience of disconnections, minor and major, when they returned to their own context. Each had his or her own negotiation of minor or more significant disconnections requiring repair in order to move forward with innovations in their teaching practice. Space limitations preclude us from detailing more of these experiences. However, we have clear indications that the trajectory which we have described above for several of the teachers has played out along similar lines in our participants' practice. Stories that come back to us in their essays about creative application of their Institute learning strengthen our conviction that the model for adult learning at the Institute is powerful. Further, these stories reaffirm that the relational and cultural contexts for teaching and learning at their schools are critical for the teachers' continued exploration of their new knowledge and for altering conventional pedagogies.

CONCLUSION AND IMPLICATIONS

"Unlearning" conventional practices, as we suggest at the beginning of this chapter, is a complicated process. It requires a kind of cognitive and emotional destabilization or disequilibrium that most of us try to avoid. And yet, the evidence in our study suggests that it is this very state of unease that is a prerequisite for transformative learning. Our research also teaches us that the repair, or integration, of the disconnections is a necessary step in this learning process.

In order to make this kind of repair, our participants tell us that "trust," "safety," and "community" are necessary conditions for their learning. They also refer to the relational practices of "challenging" and "voicing" ideas without fear as important contextual features of their learning. These conditions are important in creating a micro-culture that bolsters learners' efforts to reconnect or rebalance as they come to new knowledge. They also tell us that, positioned as learners, they came to understand the essential nature of a healthy relational environment to foster the practices of challenging and voicing - essential to the collaborative text practices at the Institute. They share with us powerful stories of teaching and learning that they have transferred from the Institute into their own schools.

Upon returning to their own school micro-cultures, they are leaving behind the laboratory-like learning environment of the Institute to face the realities of their own school cultures. As they return to their classrooms, the teachers share stories of stepping back to assess the conditions there and negotiate whether or how to integrate their new knowledge into their teaching practice. This negotiation often includes a momentary (or extended) rupture in the relationship the teachers have with the school itself (Stieha, 2010). If the conditions are conducive, the teachers can move forward to integrate their new learning into their teaching.

Indeed, the teachers reported powerful stories of teaching and learning following their Institute experiences. Although Marie had a somewhat more pronounced moment of disconnection, she found a commitment that seems to be deeply rooted in her relationship to self that made bringing the idea of "challenging" to her students too compelling to abandon. She was supported by the important relationship with "self-as-learner." In this relationship Marie found repair and moved forward, shifting from a stance of consensus to one that celebrates multiple voices. In her voice we heard the fear ("it's scary") and we noted the silence around ideas that may be "unspeakable" which are associated with this transformation for Marie. For Ruth, however, her relational reading of a new school administration and subsequent air of vulnerability at the school proved insurmountable. In her painful story, we can see the profound impact of a school climate. We can see how destabilization without repair can stunt growth, leading to the withering of innovation and creativity.

Through the stories told in this chapter, we learn that the cycle of rupture (destabilization, disequilibrium, disconnection) followed by repair (reintegration) leading toward action is a powerful description of an adult learning process in professional development settings. We learn not only to tolerate the moments of "felt difficulty" but to highlight them for our participants as profound moments of opportunity for growth, change, and new possibility. Finally, as our work continues, we welcome opportunities to engage with teachers in diverse settings from primary grades through higher education to understanding how teachers' transformative learning experience can foster profound pedagogical shifts.

REFERENCES

Boler, M. (1999). *Feeling power: Emotions and education*. New York, NY: Routledge.

Brown, L. M., & Gilligan, C. (1992). *Meeting at the crossroads: Women's psychology and girls' development*. New York, NY: Ballantine.

Clarke, A. E. (2007). Feminisms, grounded theory, and situational analysis. In Hesse-Beber, S. (Ed.), *Handbook of feminist research: Theory and praxis* (pp. 345–370). Thousand Oaks, CA: Sage.

Cochran-Smith, M., & Lytle, S. L. (2009). *Inquiry as stance: Practitioner research for the next generation.* New York, NY: Teachers College Press.

Cohen, D. K., Raudenbush, S. W., & Ball, D. L. (2003). Resources, instruction and research. *Educational Evaluation and Policy Analysis, 25*(2), 119–142. doi:10.3102/01623737025002119

Dewey, J. (1989). How we think. In Boydston, J. A. (Ed.), *John Dewey: The later works, 1925-1933* (*Vol. 8*, pp. 107–352). Carbondale, IL: Southern Illinois University Press. (Original work published 1933)

Drago-Severson, E. (2009). *Leading adult learning: Supporting adult development in our schools.* Thousand Oaks, CA: Corwin.

Feiman-Nemser, S. (2006). Beit Midrash for teachers: An experiment in teacher preparation. *Journal of Jewish Education, 72*(3), 161–181. doi:10.1080/15244110600990148

Gilligan, C. (1982). *In a different voice: Psychological theory and women's development.* Cambridge, MA: Harvard University Press.

Gilligan, C. (1996). The centrality of relationship in human development: A puzzle, some evidence, and a theory. In Noam, G. G., & Fischer, K. W. (Eds.), *Development and vulnerability in close relationships* (pp. 237–261). Mahwah, NJ: Lawrence Erlbaum Associates.

Gilligan, C., Spencer, R., Weinberg, M. K., & Bertsch, T. (2003). On the listening guide: A voice centered relational method. In Camic, P. M., Rhodes, J. E., & Yardley, L. (Eds.), *Qualitative research in psychology: Expanding perspectives in methodology and design* (pp. 157–172). Washington, DC: American Psychological Association. doi:10.1037/10595-009

Hawkins, D. (1974/2002). I, thou, and it. In Hawkins, D. (Ed.), *The informed vision: Essays on learning and human nature* (pp. 48–62). New York, NY: Agathon Press.

Hensley, B. (2009). *Seeking safe spaces: The impact of campus climate on college choice.* Ph.D. dissertation, University of Cincinnati, United States -- Ohio. Retrieved February 25, 2011, from Dissertations & Theses @ University of Cincinnati. (Publication No. AAT 3371013).

Hesse, K. (1997). *Out of the dust.* New York, NY: Scholastic.

Holzer, E. (2002). Conceptions of the study of Jewish texts in teachers' professional development. *Religious Education (Chicago, Ill.), 97*(4), 377. doi:10.1080/00344080214723

Holzer, E. (2006). What connects "good" teaching, text study and Hevruta LEARNING? A conceptual argument. *Journal of Jewish Education, 72*(3), 183–204. doi:10.1080/15244110600990163

Jordan, J. V. (2004). Relational resilience. In Jordan, J. V., Walker, M., & Hartling, L. (Eds.), *The complexity of connection: Writings from the Stone Center's Jean Baker Miller Training Institute* (pp. 28–46). New York, NY: Guilford Press.

Jordan, J. V. (2008). Learning at the margin: New models of strength. *Women & Therapy, 31*(2-4), 189–208. doi:10.1080/02703140802146365

Kegan, R. (1982). *The evolving self.* Cambridge, MA: Harvard University Press.

Kegan, R. (1994). *In over our heads: The mental demands of modern life.* Cambridge, MA: Harvard University Press.

Kent, O. (2008). *Interactive text study and the co-construction of meaning: Hevruta in the DeLeT Beit Midrash.* Boston: Brandeis University.

Lawrence-Lightfoot, S. (2003). *The essential conversation: What parents and teachers can learn from each other.* New York: Ballantine Books.

Maxwell, J. (2005). *Qualitative research design: An interactive approach* (2nd ed.). Thousand Oaks, CA: Sage.

Mezirow, J. (2000). Learning to think like an adult: Core concepts of transformation theory. In J. Mezirow & Assoc. (Eds.), *Learning as transformation: Critical perspectives on a theory in progress* (pp. 3-33). San Francisco, CA: Jossey-Bass.

Miller, J. B. (1976). *Toward a new psychology of women*. Boston, MA: Beacon Press.

Miller, J. B., & Stiver, I. P. (1997). *The healing connection: How women form relationships in therapy and in life*. Boston, MA: Beacon.

Raider-Roth, M. B. (2005). *Trusting what you know: The high stakes of classroom relationships*. San Francisco, CA: Jossey-Bass.

Raider-Roth, M. B. (2010). Listening to the heartbeat of the classroom: Bringing the listening guide to teaching and learning. In Davis, P. C. (Ed.), *Enacting pleasure*. London, UK: Seagull Books.

Raider-Roth, M. B., Albert, M. K., Bircann-Barkley, I., Gidseg, E., & Murray, T. (2008). Teaching boys: A relational puzzle. *Teachers College Record, 110*(2), 443–481.

Raider-Roth, M. B., & Holzer, E. (2009). Learning to be present: How *Hevruta* learning can activate teachers' relationships to self, other and text. *Journal of Jewish Education, 75*(3), 216–239. doi:10.1080/15244110903079045

Raider-Roth, M. B., Stieha, V., & Hensley, B. (2010a). *Rupture and repair in the relational triangle: Veteran teachers, professional development and collaborative text study*. Manuscript under review.

Raider-Roth, M. B., Stieha, V., & Hensley, B. (2010b). *Rupture and repair: Episodes of resistance and resilience in teachers' learning*. Paper presented at the 31st Annual Ethnography in Education Research Forum.

Spencer, R., Porche, M. V., & Tolman, D. L. (2003). We've come a long way -- Maybe: New challenges for gender equity in education. *Teachers College Record, 105*(9), 1774–1807. doi:10.1046/j.1467-9620.2003.00309.x

Stieha, V. (2010). *The relational Web in teaching and learning: Connections, disconnections and the central relational paradox in s*chools. Ph.D. dissertation, University of Cincinnati, United States -- Ohio. Retrieved February 25, 2011, from Dissertations & Theses @ University of Cincinnati. (Publication No. AAT 3419997).

Tappan, M. B. (2001). Interpretive psychology: Stories, circles and understanding lived experience. In Tolman, D. L., & Brydon-Miller, M. (Eds.), *From subjects to subjectivities: A Handbook of interpretive and participatory methods* (pp. 45–56). New York, NY: New York University Press. doi:10.1111/j.1540-4560.1997.tb02453.x

Tronick, E. Z., & Weinberg, M. K. (1997). Depressed mothers and infants: Failure to form dyadic states of consciousness. In Murray, L., & Cooper, P. (Eds.), *Postpartum depression and child development*. New York, NY: Guilford Press.

ADDITIONAL READING

Brookfield, S. (1995). *Becoming a Critically Reflective Teacher*. San Francisco: Jossey-Bass.

Cochran-Smith, M., & Lytle, S. L. (2009). *Inquiry as Stance: Practitioner Research for the Next Generation*. New York: Teachers College Press.

Dewey, J. (1989). How We Think. In Boydston, J. A. (Ed.), *John Dewey: The Later Works, 1925-1933* (*Vol. 8*, pp. 107–352). Carbondale, IL: Southern Illinois University Press. (Original work published 1933)

Drago-Severson, E. (2009). *Leading Adult Learning: Supporting Adult Development in our Schools*. Thousand Oaks, CA: Corwin.

Fink, D. (2003). *Creating Significant Learning Experiences*. San Francisco: Jossey-Bass.

Gilligan, C. (2003). *The Birth of Pleasure*. New York: Vintage.

Guskey, T. R. (2000). *Evaluating Professional Development*. Thousand Oaks, CA: Corwin Press.

Hawkins, D. (2002). I, Thou, and It. In Hawkins, D. (Ed.), *The Informed Vision: Essays on Learning and Human Nature* (pp. 48–62). New York: Agathon Press.

Holzer, E. (2002). Conceptions of the Study of Jewish Texts in Teachers' Professional Development. *Religious Education (Chicago, Ill.)*, *97*(4), 377. doi:10.1080/00344080214723

Holzer, E. (2007). Ethical Dispositions in Text Study: a Conceptual Argument. *Journal of Moral Education*, *36*(1), 37–49. doi:10.1080/03057240601185455

Kegan, R. (1994). *In Over our Heads: The Mental Demands of Modern Life*. Cambridge, MA: Harvard University Press.

Kegan, R., & Lahey, L. (2001). *How the Way We Talk Can Change the Way We Work: Seven Languages for Transformation*. San Francisco: Jossey-Bass.

Mezirow, J. (2000). Learning to Think Like an Adult: Core Concepts of Transformation Theory. In J. Mezirow & Assoc. (Eds.), *Learning as Transformation: Critical Perspectives on a Theory in Progress*. (pp. 3-33). San Francisco: Jossey-Bass.

Miller, J. B., & Stiver, I. P. (1997). *The Healing Connection: How Women Form Relationships in Therapy and in Life*. Boston, MA: Beacon.

Raider-Roth, M. B. (2005). *Trusting What you Know: The High Stakes of Classroom Relationships*. San Francisco, CA: Jossey-Bass.

KEY TERMS AND DEFINITIONS

Evolutionary Development: A concept developed by Kegan (1982) to describe the challenges to development that trigger growth. Kegan suggests that disequilibrium is a necessary state towards growth. This term reminds us of Dewey's (1933) notion of "felt difficulty." Disequilibrium has been described in our work as destabilization (Stieha 2010) and disconnection (Raider-Roth, 2005).

Hevruta (hev root ah): Hebrew term to describe a tradition form of Jewish text study involving partners who study intensively together a given text. The goal of this kind of study is not to arrive at one interpretation of the text, but rather to study many interpretations, and challenge one another to understand the most compelling or convincing interpretation. The model of Hevruta study implemented at the Institute was developed the Brandeis University Mandel Center for Studies in Jewish Education. For further reading about the Mandel Center model see (Feiman-Nemser, 2006; Holzer, 2002; Kent, 2008).

Historiographic Inquiry Method: An approach to investigating a variety of texts, asking participants to "read" the texts for meaning, association, historical context, and interpretation (For further explanation see Raider, in progress).

Interpretive Community: As Tappan (2001) explains, "the process of interpretation is, inescapably, a relational enterprise" (p. 46). We operationalize the work of interpretation in community by bringing multiple voices to bear on our analysis in search of "interpretive agreement." In our work this has included other action researchers (Dr. Billy Hensley, Dr. Elie Holzer, Carrie Turpin, & Mark Kohan) to deepen our understandings of these data. We also include our participants in a member checking process (Maxwell, 2005)

Mutual Empathy: From the relational-cultural theorists, this notion blends empathy (thinking and feeling with the other) and mutuality. In this sense mutual empathy has a reciprocity that is not necessarily equal, but offers an intention to be present to the other cognitively and affectively.

Mutual Regulation Cycle: A concept developed by Tronick & Weinberg (1997) to describe the communication cycle between parents and infants. Key to our discussion is their notion of "repair," where parents or infants may misread the other's cues and momentarily disconnect. It is the process of repairing the disconnection that builds a stronger bond between care-giver and infant, where communication pathways are developed, strengthened, and sense of self is enhanced.

Public Education: For our international readers we note that in the United States public education is secular and largely governed by each individual state. The separation of religiously based content is mandated by the U.S. Constitution. Private and parochial schools are not held to the requirement to separate religious from secular content.

Relational Trust: A trust that is built in mutual and reciprocal relationships in which one is free to know what she knows as a basis for learning. In this light, trust is built when one is given the opportunity to draw upon what she or he knows, and is fostered when people act in their roles as we would hope one would act in that role.

Chapter 3
"Critical Friendship" and Sustainable Change:
Creating Liminal Spaces to Experience Discomfort Together

Susan R. Adams
Butler University, USA

Ross Peterson-Veatch
Goshen College, USA

ABSTRACT

The central focus of this chapter will be to describe the theory and practice of critical friendship in teacher professional development, paying special attention to the ways in which participants in small professional learning communities (PLCs) create spaces in which to experience discomfort together for the purpose of sustaining their own transformation as practitioners. Using protocols (prescribed turn-taking mechanisms) as social processes to negotiate and then arrive at explicitly named norms and agreements, PLCs that use critical friendship as their goal aim to create the conditions for personal and communal transformation of both their members and their institutional contexts.

INTRODUCTION

Opening the Door

Susan's House

Every few years I have a recurring dream that is so compelling I literally walk around in a fog the following day as I wonder about its implications for my life. In the dream, I am walking around in the small house that has been my home for more than 22 years and as I walk, I discover doors I did not know existed. In the dream, I open the doors only to find whole rooms I had simply overlooked or somehow forgotten all these years. I am delighted to see spaces that would allow my family to play, work and rest more creatively than we are able to now in our modest home. I begin to re-imagine where I will put furniture, how I could create a quiet study for myself, places where we could joyfully and graciously share our home with friends and neighbors.

DOI: 10.4018/978-1-61350-495-6.ch003

As I dream, I feel my heart quicken and a new energy fire my creative spirits and inevitably, this is where I awaken. For a split second, I forget that it was only a dream, and I am briefly suspended in that moment of possibility. Even as I realize I am back to the reality of my unpretentious home, even as I rise and go about my day, I am consumed by the meaning of the dream. What is my subconscious mind trying to tell me? What does the dream mean? While it is true that there are not new rooms waiting to be found in my house, I begin to wonder: what unexplored spaces might be waiting for me in my life, in my work, in my teaching practice?

Just as in Susan's dream, there are spaces of almost limitless possibility for teachers to explore together. At different points in our teaching careers, both of us opened a door and quite unexpectedly stepped into a space we had not suspected existed: the space of critical friendship. What we found in that space revolutionized our teaching, our professional relationships, our friendships, our parenting of our own children and our individual understandings of ourselves. We have experienced this space in small groups of educators which we first encountered under the name "Critical Friends Groups," but our exploration of critical friendship extends beyond the boundaries of these groups. In that sense, the group processes and "social technologies" we practice in these groups, serve not only to bond the group's members to one another, but serve to create a commitment to one another and one another's students that invites us to dive deeply to those places in ourselves that we rarely visit, places where our assumptions live and rest unexamined, protecting us from whatever forces might (dis)integrate us.

In critical friendship, we have been able to open ourselves to one another as professionals in ways we could not imagine – our groups aim to become places in which we can critically examine

instructional decisions to surface assumptions that influence instructional design. Indeed, the longer we work with one another using the lens of critical friendship, the more deeply we enter into what Zembylas and Boler (2002) refer to as a *pedagogy of discomfort:*

...[a] pedagogy of discomfort creates the spaces to move beyond inquiry as an individualized process and raises issues of collective accountability by exploring the possibilities to embrace discomfort, establish alliances and come out of this process enriched with new emotional discursive practices. (Zembylas & Boler, 2002, Patriotism Interrupted section, para. 18)

What Zembylas and Boler describe can be transferred into our classrooms only after we invite *our colleagues* to share that space of discomfort with us, where we thoughtfully examine our students' responses to our assignments, tests, and assessments. We literally teach one another how to improve as teachers using our students' work and observations of one another. This chapter, then, is about how we foster and sustain critical friendship in professional learning communities as a pedagogy of discomfort that supports our learning as educators.

The Beginning of the Journey

We first met at a breakout workshop during a teaching conference in 2003. Susan recalls a scene that calls to mind her recurring dream. She approached the room, the door opened and a man with a friendly, bearded face grinned and said, "Come in."

Stepping through this doorway and accepting this invitation into a new space proved to be life-altering. The experience of that week revolutionized her and the group's understandings of teaching, of learning, and of collaborating with colleagues. Their minds were delighted by the new possibilities they had discovered, and unlike Susan's dream, the spaces created by these possibilities were real. When school resumed, the participants returned to their teaching renewed and reborn, filled with a fierce determination to teach with intentionality. Susan was, however, concerned that she was the only teacher from her high school that had participated in the coaches seminar. Where would she find colleagues with whom she could collaborate? How would she sustain this energy and excitement alone?

Do you believe in coincidence? We don't! Ross was abruptly and unexpectedly assigned to Susan's high school as an external instructional coach. For the following two academic years, we were able to continue creating and holding space for their critical friendship to grow, develop and extend to others in the building in small, but significant ways.

Critical Friendship: A Light in Dark Times

We found that changing a school is difficult, even dangerous work. Interrupting the status quo, even in schools where failure is almost universally acknowledged, is slow and requires tenacity. The need is urgent, as bell hooks claims,

There is a serious crisis in education. Students often do not want to learn and teachers do not want to teach...[E]ducators are compelled to confront the biases that have shaped teaching practices in our society and to create new ways of knowing, different strategies for the sharing of knowledge...[to] celebrate teaching that enables transgressions-a movement against and beyond boundaries." (1994, p. 12)

As educators, we have often felt overwhelmed. What do to? How to begin? In our education programs, we were prepared to teach in isolation and behind closed doors. Opening the door, talking to colleagues, and speaking truthfully about what is happening in our classrooms are risky decisions, but as Huebner (1987) says,

Teachers must act in an imperfect world. We have no choice but to risk ourselves. The choice is to consider the risk private or to build a community that accepts vulnerability and shares risks. Vulnerability is endurable in a community of care and support - a community in which members take time telling and listening to the stories of each other's journey...We need people who listen to us and to whom we listen, who help in the narration of our story, so we can more readily recognize our changing values and meanings...We must begin to scrutinize and become intentional about the communities within which we teach. We must seek out new coalitions and work intentionally at the social fabric that surrounds those of us who are called to be teachers. (1987, pp. 26-27)

Over the next two years, we spent many hours talking about what was possible and how to continue to work with intentionality to disrupt what had been and to move toward creating strong, supportive relationships between teachers. We were confident that critical friendship would provide the structure needed to disrupt the culture of expected failure that permeated Susan's school.

The "Critical Friends Group" or CFG is one model of a professional learning community, or PLC, that uses critical friendship as a focus. As practiced in these groups, critical friendship is expected to function as a "cultural context" in which professional transformation is expected of group members. Gene Thomson-Grove, one of the initial developers of the CFG model explained these expectations in a keynote address to practitioners at a 2005 gathering:

We work together, over time, so we can move with patient urgency into the risk zone, our most fertile place for learning - the place where we can open

up to others with curiosity and interest, where we can consider options or ideas we hadn't thought of before, where we can have the courage to identify and explicitly work on the questions that matter most to our students - the questions or aspects of our practice that perhaps make us the most uncomfortable (January 2005, emphasis added).

Indeed, "patient urgency" (Thompson-Grove, January 2005) was our mindset as we strengthened our mutual resolve to examine our own professional practice before asking others to change theirs. Over sack lunches, in the hallways, and even in the parking lot in the rain, we kept talking and listening to one another, asking hard questions and respectfully, but firmly, insisting on truthful answers.

Being "uncomfortable" is a crucial part of setting the stage for change. From Jack Mezirow's "transformative" learning (1991) to the most recent work by Kegan and Lahey on the "immunity" to change that we experience personally and in so many organizations (2009), experiencing discomfort is widely posited to be a necessary step in any process by which adult learners change and grow. CFGs are typically constructed to provide participants a place to experience discomfort with an eye towards examining the issues involved in changing professional practice. Since we do our jobs in the "regular flow of time," we generally experience critical friends groups as a different kind of space; a slower, safer, more nurturing space than the one that exists for us in that regular flow.

But how can creating a "safe place to experience discomfort" really work to provide the necessary conditions for supporting a change? We have found Turner's concept of "liminoid" spaces to be particularly helpful in understanding how this move toward change can unfold. The idea of liminal or threshold-like spaces (Van Gennep, 1909) inspired cultural anthropologist Victor Turner to build on Van Gennep's notion, pushing it outward from rites of passage, to other types of rituals, festivals, and different forms of cultural performances. Turner's

conception (1986) of "liminoid" spaces – spaces in which ritual play and cultural performance make possible the conceptualization and negotiation of new cultural forms and new cultural agreements – provides a platform for further development of the notion of liminal spaces that make possible the transformation of individuals, communities, organizations, and institutions.

In traditional forms of teacher professional development, improvement is driven by accumulating new "tools" or "processes" with which to better accomplish one's goals. A great deal of this "filling the toolbox" happens through workshops or other methods of instruction in which the teacher learns from an expert about something new. To return to the metaphor of the house which appears in Susan's dream, this "additive" approach emerges from a deficit perspective, one in which you "build on" to the house you believe is "not big enough." In a critical friends group, on the other hand, improvement is driven by "holding space" or "creating space" in which critical reflection on one's assumptions, expectations and habits is the focus. The power of this space is that it holds great possibility for perspective shift, something Mezirow posits as the foundational beginning of "transformative learning":

Perspective transformation is the process of becoming critically aware of how and why our assumptions have come to constrain the way we perceive, understand, and feel about our world; changing these structures of habitual expectation to make possible a more inclusive, discriminating, and integrating perspective; and, finally, making choices or otherwise acting upon these new understandings. (1991, p. 167)

This approach is more of a "structural remodeling" approach – not one in which all you do is address the "finishes" (the paint, the carpet, etc.), but rather an asset-based approach in which you reorganize the rooms of your mental "house." Critical friends groups operate within the liminoid

(Turner, 1986) space as communities of disruption, of trust, of risk-taking, of changing perspectives, of changing practice, and as enactors of the pedagogy of discomfort as collegial friends, allies, and co-conspirators across time, distance, and work contexts as an example of what is possible.

What Exactly *Is* Critical Friendship?

A typical critical friends group is a group of 6-10 educators that meets regularly (often monthly) for an extended block of time (preferably 2-3 hours of uninterrupted time) to talk, listen, ask questions, examine teacher and student work, and share new texts that spark in-depth discussions. Contrary to popular misconception, *critical* does not mean members are cruel, harsh, or that members practice criticizing one another; on the contrary, the atmosphere in critical friendship is one of support, careful listening, and valuing the input of each member. In this case we choose the word critical to indicate that these friendships are indispensable, crucial, and essential, and that the work done in these groups creates conditions in which we can each take a critical, thoughtful look at our beliefs, practices and underlying assumptions. The word *friendship* reveals a level of collegiality and cooperation that create the conditions for this necessary work to be accomplished.

This work is accomplished under the leadership of a *facilitator,* a person who has been trained and has experienced the processes used in this model of professional learning community. The facilitator has an important role in creating and supporting a successful group, but the work of maintaining and developing the group is shared by the members. While each group is unique, in general groups hold in common some critical precepts and practices. We will now examine these tenets in light of their contribution to the life of the critical friends group and in relation to the pedagogy of disruption.

Voluntary Membership

It is currently common in our region of the United States for teachers to be assigned to a professional learning community (PLC) in which membership is not optional. The PLC meetings are conducted during the school day and attendance is mandatory and recorded as evidence of compliance. Teachers are assigned to each group based upon the content they teach, the grade level of the students they teach, or sometimes are simply composed of teachers who all have the same preparatory period each day.

During these PLC meetings, it can be difficult to detect anything that feels remotely like "learning" or "community." Frequently teachers are frustrated by the coercive nature of the groupings and the mandatory attendance and often complain about the misuse and waste of their time. Teachers who miss PLC meetings face unpleasant consequences, including written reprimands and possible dismissal. Because teachers are required to attend, some are visibly disengaged, bored, angry or frustrated.

PLCs that use a critical friendship frame, on the other hand, are small groups of educators who choose to be group members, who decide when and where they will meet, and who decide what the content of their meetings will be. This decision most often means that the group will meet outside the contract time of the school day, usually without compensation. Many find the freedoms associated with meeting voluntarily outside of the school day is worth the investment of the time, even when participants do not receive payment. One group Susan works with is a group of educators from three distinct school districts and a university. This group meets one Saturday morning a month of their own volition - a serious indication of the value they place upon the relationships and what is accomplished during those meetings.

Flattening the Hierarchy

As we noted earlier, each group has a facilitator, but the facilitator does not direct the activity of the critical friends group. Instead, the facilitator merely serves the group as an organizer, making sure that meetings are scheduled, meeting locations secured, refreshments planned for (a necessary component!), a tentative agenda is created and supplies are organized. This work is not generally done by the facilitator alone since distributed responsibility is an important component of the group's development and maintenance. The role of facilitator may rotate from one member to another or the group may choose to have one person assume this role indefinitely.

Deep Trust and Confidentiality

We have learned that building trust within the critical friends group is absolutely essential; without trust, members will generally withhold thoughts, ideas, practices and beliefs and will not submit them to the scrutiny of the group. We believe the honest and transparent practices and processes of a critical friends group may well be the most disruptive element of a group within a larger school culture that actively encourages educators to hide struggles, problems, and imperfections. We have been shaped by our own school experiences, by the

... [d]ominator culture [that] has tried to keep us all afraid, to make us choose safety instead of risk, sameness instead of diversity. Moving through that fear, finding out what connects us, reveling in our differences; this is the process that brings us closer, that gives us a world of shared values, of meaningful community." (hooks, 2003, p. 197)

In our own professional friendship, we learned that the investment in truthfully sharing our experiences, our fears, and our wonderings was an investment in our future capacity to work together. Just as Miller recounts:

We needed to tell our own stories first, in order not only to establish our individual interests within our explorations but also to develop the trust... to develop an awareness of and respect for one another's struggles. As we invited each other to listen and respond to our individual stories, we also began to develop a trust in the accepting and supportive nature of our meetings...[creating] necessary foundations for establishing collaborative approaches to examining the relationships among our personal perspectives, our situations, and both the diminishing and enabling dynamics of the contexts in which we work. (1990, p. 63)

It is not sufficient, however, to merely state that what happens within a critical friends group meeting will be confidential. It takes time for members to see that they can trust one another to respect confidentiality agreements and the risk involved must not be underestimated. In the "dominator culture" hooks (2003) described, speaking truthfully is a legitimately precarious position in which to put oneself. Imagine divulging and describing a teaching practice or attitude only to find days later that one's supervisor and colleagues are all now openly discussing the matter. Now imagine the same scenario, but one in which your colleagues listen with empathy, understanding and encouragement and out of respect for your courage, they maintain absolute confidentiality.

As Miller (1990) noted, we have found that trust builds upon trust and deepens with time. It has been our experience that educators are often skeptical of the group's ability to maintain confidentiality because they have seldom experienced a professional context in which confidence was reliably maintained. As members take small steps toward trust, this prepares them for the deeper, more dangerous conversations few professional groups have the will, skill or capacity in which to engage.

As we have grown in our own understandings of how schools, curricula, and systems create and maintain inequitable practices and outcomes for students of color and for language minority students, we have found teachers are more willing to examine their individual biases, prejudices, and unquestioned teaching practices when an environment of deep trust is developed and maintained vigorously. Recently a teacher described the experience of speaking truthfully about the impact of race and culture as "just sort of cleansing to let those things off my chest because I knew I wasn't being judged…I was free to speak my truth [after] I watched other people be willing to take a step and be vulnerable. That opened the pathway for me."

De-Privatizing the Practice

In very close alignment with trust, the decision to open the doors into our practice takes courage and confidence in the members of the critical friends group. In our experience with these groups, we have found that it is common for teachers to be uncomfortable, reluctant and often unwilling to share examples of student work or teacher-created assignments with their colleagues. Many teachers secretly harbor fears of inadequacy or incompetence, while others have learned to jealously guard their curricular materials for fear others will "steal" and implement them. This "private" practice of secrecy and self-protection generally goes unquestioned, unacknowledged and unchallenged in the schools with which we are familiar.

Following a critical friendship meeting, a seasoned high school teacher wrote:

If I look back to my pre-service teacher preparation, I remember explicitly and deliberately being taught to heed my own counsel while pretending to listen, to shut my classroom door and do whatever I thought was right. No one questioned my right to do that; in fact, it was celebrated and applauded. What have I missed while my door was closed? What did my students lose because I was too proud to learn from them and from my colleagues? Now

my door is open, my heart and mind are opening to the new possibilities we create when we speak our truth to one another.

This practice of closing classroom doors may in fact be an unstated norm of the school, a part of the "hidden curriculum" (Pinar, 2004) that is only discovered when one accidentally violates it by asking to visit a classroom or when one has students read a text which "belongs" to another teacher. To return once more to the earlier quotation, in opposition to this culture of competition and fear, critical friends groups practice,

…[a] pedagogy of discomfort [which] creates the spaces to move beyond inquiry as an individualized process and raises issues of collective accountability by exploring the possibilities to embrace discomfort, establish alliances and come out of this process enriched with new emotional discursive practices. (Zembylas & Boler, 2002, Patriotism Interrupted section, para. 18, emphasis added)

Zembylas and Boler (2002) conclude by noting that embracing these new discursive practices effectively opens new doors, doors which had gone unopened and unexplored previously. Teachers are amazed to learn that sharing teaching ideas and dilemmas results in new respect from their colleagues and not the scorn or harsh rejection they feared. They find that by listening deeply, through asking carefully constructed questions and by taking the time necessary to adequately describe their work, new ideas are generated and shared freely by the members of the group. When asked about discomfort, a teacher responded, "Being disturbed helps me see what I believe," which confirms Zembylas and Boler's contention that,

…effective analysis of ideology requires not only rational inquiry and dialogue but also excavation of the emotional investments that underlie any ideological commitment …A pedagogy of

discomfort invites [participants] to leave behind learned beliefs and habits, and enter the risky areas of contradictory and ambiguous ethical and moral differences. (Zembylas & Boler, 2002, Introduction section, para. 5)

Within communities of critical friendship, this "risky area" is the same risk zone described earlier by Thompson Grove (January 2005) as the place where the seeming paradox of creating both a hospitable and charged atmosphere is possible and where participants, "…feel the risks inherent in pursuing the deep things of the world or of the soul" (Palmer, 2007, p. 78). If members are too comfortable or too uneasy, our best work and learning cannot take place. The pedagogy of discomfort (Zembylas & Boler, 2002) pushes members to take a hard, potentially painful look at previously unquestioned beliefs and unexamined practices; this is best accomplished within the bounds of critical friendship relationships.

Balancing the Tensions

Faithfulness to this tenet is critical to the long-term survival and success of a critical friends group, but maintaining the balance between the personal and the professional is a tenuous balance of competing needs. Skilled facilitators understand and take seriously the needs of adult learners resulting in meetings that are productive, respectful of the time of the members and that result in discussions that stimulate new ideas and new connections to teaching and learning. Yet most new critical friends group members are surprised by the profoundly personal nature of the work and by the strong bonds that develop between group members who engage in critical friendship practices together. They are often startled to notice that the time passes swiftly and pleasantly.

Somehow, the work of critical friends groups feels less like "work" and more like pleasurable learning. How is this accomplished? In the written

reflections collected and analyzed following each meeting, teachers routinely point to 3 elements of critical friendship they find essential in making these groups work:

1. Members learn about the work of their colleagues, going beyond shallow strategies and into underlying beliefs, experiences, and philosophies. Even teachers who have taught next door to one another for many years are amazed at what they learn about each other in a group in which critical friendship is operating.

2. As individuals share their work, the other members learn to listen intently and to ask thoughtful, carefully constructed questions. Many participants report that being listened to by their colleagues is deeply touching and creates a strong bond between members.

3. Members refrain from attempting to "fix" one another or from offering advice. This is difficult at first since teachers often instinctively want to tell one another what to do or how to solve a problem. In a critical friends group, a liminoid space (Turner, 1986) is created in which members can re-imagine professional dilemmas from fresh, creative perspectives.

Many participants look up in surprise at the close of a session, shocked at how quickly and pleasantly the time flew by. One participant wryly quipped, "Why wasn't I bored today?" after having devoted an entire summer day to learning and working within a critical friendship group. Few teachers would relinquish a vacation day with such gratification in a traditional professional development paradigm.

Fay (1977) reminds us,

Coming to a radical new self-conception is hardly ever a process that occurs simply by reading some theoretical work; rather, it requires an environment of trust, openness, and support in which one's own perceptions and feelings can be made properly conscious to oneself... (p. 232, emphasis added)

While it is true that the meetings are professional, and that often members expose their vulnerabilities, critical friendship meetings are not gloom and doom; on the contrary, it is common to hear much laughter and voices full of excitement and energy! Participants find much to celebrate as they share their practice with one another. Explicit inclusion of openness and support is a stark contrast to the usual culture of faculty meetings, where it is business as usual, or of PLCs where false community is imposed, and is a change new members find refreshing and empowering.

Focusing on the Work

Freire insisted that "dialogue characterizes an epistemological relationship...dialogue is a way of knowing...[we] engage in dialogue because [we] recognize the social and not merely the individualistic character of the process of knowing... dialogue [is] an indispensible component of the process of both learning and knowing" (Freire & Macedo, 1995, p. 379). In critical friends groups, learning is dialogic and requires the active engagement of each member. This dialogue is most often done by talking with the use of protocols, but sometimes is done in writing, through graphic organizers, or with symbols or art.

An important component of most critical friends group meeting agendas is examining some kind of student or teacher work. For example, a member may be puzzled by an assignment turned in by a particular student. Instead of failing the student or sinking into self-flagellation, group members ask the group to examine the work and to try to see the work from the perspective of the student -a radical departure from and a disruption of the common practice of pretending that teachers are capable of evaluating student work from an ob-

jective position. As members ask themselves what the student was working on, hidden assumptions about the assignment, the student, and the quality of the work emerge. The teacher often realizes that she was unclear in some component of the lesson or the directions; the members each take away questions about their own assumptions; a new respect for what the student has accomplished bubbles to the surface.

It takes courage to make oneself vulnerable to colleagues. The first time Ross asked Susan to present some student work, there was simply no time to create an impressive assignment to "wow" the rest of the group. She reluctantly shared the index cards upon which her English language learners (ELLs) had transferred important sentences, phrases, and words from a chapter in a paperback novel as she used a simple text-based strategy known as a The Text Rendering Experience (http://schoolreforminitiative.org/protocol/doc/text_rendering.pdf) in her classroom.

Susan was worried her colleagues would find the work disappointing and shallow. To her amazement, her colleagues were impressed with how the strategy got the students talking to one another and at how the process engaged students in all four language domains: speaking, listening, reading and writing-no easy feat for ELLs. Over the next few weeks group members came back to report that they had not only tried The Text Rendering Experience, but they had found success and even made some adaptations for their content area subjects. The ice was broken and now others were more willing to bring work from their classrooms.

Co-Negotiated Agendas

Creating an agenda is not a neutral act. In schools, teachers regularly have curriculum decisions, policies, and meetings imposed upon them with little or no explanation. As Miller points out, in schools,

...expectations and difficulties are shaped by the complex relationships among the forces of power, control, prediction and accountability that drive much of current educational research and practice. We also try to see the spaces within and among these relationships where we can take action to change the inequitable or silencing effects of those forces on ourselves and on the students and colleagues with whom we work (Miller, 1990, p. 73, emphasis added).

Within critical friendship, there is space to attend to the needs and interests of the members, instead of merely presenting the agenda as a *fait accompli* to a passive audience. Taking control of the agenda is a small, but mighty shifting of the power back to the teachers. In turn, when teachers notice how important it is for them to manage the agenda, they frequently begin to notice their own stranglehold on classroom agendas and they begin to wonder how their classroom agendas might have "silencing effects" (Miller, 1990) or perpetuate inequities upon students.

Norms and Agreements

Just as creating and negotiating meeting agendas empowers the group to do the work it needs to do, deciding *how* the work will be done is liberating. We have found that asking participants a simple question, "Under what conditions do you do your best work?" allows participants to generate a list of agreements that reflects the goals, personalities, and needs of the individuals in balance with the needs of the group.

Each group negotiates its own unique list of agreements and the list changes as the group becomes comfortable with one another and as the members internalize the reality of the freedom they have truly been given to determine their own working conditions. Teachers have generally been conformed to obey the norms or rules imposed by an administrator or a chairperson, so deter-

mining group norms is a radical departure from daily school practices. One of the most startling agreements may include something as simple as granting permission to leave the meeting briefly to visit the restroom-a practice no classroom teacher takes for granted.

We have found that some groups are so unaccustomed to creating norms that we have to give them a general "starter" list of agreements upon which to build. It is only when the group understands that the facilitator sincerely is ready to be flexible to the needs of the individuals that the group takes ownership and begins altering and adapting the starter agreements. This practice is critical to the group's ability to address complex, painful, or uncomfortable subjects. Indeed, as Shohat (1995) inquires,

Rather than ask who can speak, then, we should ask how we can speak together, and more important, how we can move the dialogue forward. How can diverse communities speak in concert? How might we interweave our voices, whether in chorus, in antiphony, in call and response, or in polyphony? What are the modes of collective speech? (p. 177)

A representative set of beginning agreements might look something like this:

- Be fully present
- Support each other's learning
- Take responsibility for your own learning
- Take care of your own needs
- Content of the meetings is anonymous, not confidential
- Give "gentle reminders" to one another when we stray from these agreements

As the group becomes more confident, the agreements will reflect the "personality" of the group. For example, one group Susan works with added "Dream" to their list to remind them that in this context, dreaming is not only permissible, but it is requested. Another added "Ecstatic engagement" to serve as a cue to enter into the work with joy.

Each member is aware that they have a responsibility to themselves and to the group to monitor the extent to which the group has honored their agreements and each member is empowered to point it out gently when discussions veer off course or when a member seems distracted. Rather than attacking one another for noncompliance, this practice creates an opportunity to discuss whether the norms need adjustment or if something is troubling a member. At the beginning and end of each session, members evaluate both the group's and their individual alignment with the agreements. The group may well determine that "Be fully present" needs to be more specific and include mention of silencing electronic devices or the elimination of sidebar conversations.

It is traditional to post the group's agreements on a chart where all can see them. As the group's ownership, confidence and trust develop over time, many groups feel fondness and connection to the bedraggled, curled, and marked up chart since the chart is a historical artifact which connects members to their past and reminds them of all they have accomplished together. As a participant left a critical friendship meeting, she turned with wide eyes and asked, "What if school were like this every day?"

Responsive Facilitation

Gathering feedback from members opens the door to constantly fine-tune agendas, agreements, and facilitation styles. Feedback is requested at the conclusion of nearly every agenda activity and most importantly, at the conclusion of each meeting. We take seriously Freire's reminder that, "[a]t the point of encounter there are neither utter ignoramuses nor perfect sages; there are only people who are attempting, together, to learn more

than they now know" (1970, p. 90). We believe we can always learn from today's work, that each element will have strong features and that no approach will suit every person or every situation.

Feedback is requested so that future agendas will reflect changes requested by the members. This is especially important in the early days of a new group. If the facilitator requests feedback, but ignores requests, the members will not feel their opinions or needs are valued. It is common, for example, for a member to find a meeting location unsuitable due to temperature, noise, lack of privacy or lack of windows. This observation should be shared with the group to see what additional space options exist for future meetings. Members are frequently awed to see that they were taken seriously; responsive facilitation is the hallmark of a skilled facilitator.

Protocols as Disruptive Pedagogy

Palmer encourages teachers induce the "creative tension" produced by paradoxes and then exhorts us to resist the urge to reduce the tensions of those paradoxes (Palmer, 2007). Palmer urges us to see the learning space as both "bounded and open" (2007) We need enough structure and enough freedom to be "...open to the many paths that always come with real learning...[and] [t]he openness of a learning space reminds us that the destination we plotted at the outset of the journey may not be the one that we will reach..." (2007, p. 77). Creating an environment of trust, where intensive and often deeply personal work can be addressed, requires careful attention to the processes the group will use.

The structures we find most productive are called *protocols*. A protocol is an activity or a conversation structured by an agreement to talk or work in a particular order, by taking turns, and by honoring processes that ensure everyone participates evenly. A protocol may seem to restrict one's speech or activity, but it restricts one aspect in order to emphasize another. Miller (1990) describes her conception of the dissonance we might experience in a group of professionals:

Points of dissonance are pinpricks in our consciousness; they sometimes sting at inopportune moments when we are most concerned with maintaining a smooth and unruffled countenance. We become adept at brushing away the annoyance, shooing the discrepancy from our line of vision, as we wave away a fly... Only when the buzzing becomes too persistent, when the sting finally penetrates beneath surface awareness, are we forced to directly confront the sources of dissonance that disrupt our equilibrium, our sense of balance in the world (p. 85).

As we have indicated several times now, we believe *how* we talk is as important as what we talk about. The use of protocols allows the group to approach "difficult knowledge" (Britzman, 1998) without descending into arguments, silencing behaviors, withdrawal, or aggression.

A typical protocol focuses on a text, a piece of student work, a lesson plan, or a project brought by a member. The protocol will provide enough structure to allow the discussion to be "bounded," yet enough space for the participants to be "open" to seeing, hearing, considering, imagining and speaking new learning. The protocol may prescribe limited amounts of time for each person to speak and may require different kinds of talking and questioning at each round. One round may ask participants to listen intently to a description in round 1, ask clarifying questions only in round 2, and then ask open-ended, probing questions during round 3. The facilitator will gently remind participants of the structure as needed in order to ensure that the goals of the presenter are met.

While many new members initially find using protocols to be rigid or restrictive, most ultimately find the process forces them to think deeply before speaking; what results is that members do not issue judgments, advice, or harsh criticism, but

instead offer questions and wonderings intended to help the presenter examine the work in a fresh light. Indeed, we have found that learning to talk to one another through the use of protocols has caused each of us to become better listeners and more thoughtful responders in our personal, as well as our professional, lives. One participant wrote that the group strengthens him to resist conformity and "...to find a way like water to erode traditional roadblocks and to question assumptions...It means not giving up!"

It is during protocol work that the resolve of the group is tested and where the investment in group agreements and trust-building inevitably pays off. Opening a lesson plan for the scrutiny of colleagues is an act of courage that must be acknowledged and honored by the group. The respect and care shown by the members liberates the presenting teacher to speak truthfully about the struggles, fears, and failures that lie underneath what is visible. Faithfulness to the protocol keeps the group from straying off into unrelated topics and creates opportunity to ask hard questions, challenge their own assumptions, and wonder about new ideas. One of the most exciting outcomes is the shared interest and collective investment in what had previously been the private work of one individual teacher. The group members leave the session with new energy to apply what was shared in their individual teaching contexts. The presenting member leaves affirmed in her creative capacity to transform her teaching with the support of her colleagues.

CONCLUSION

In this chapter, we have shared what we have learned together in our exploration of liminoid (Turner, 1986) spaces created when educators work together toward and within a culture of critical friendship. We have not intended to proscribe or impose concrete practices as if we had discovered a "surefire" way to create and sustain significant transformation in schools. Instead we have chosen to align our thinking, our practices and our friendship more closely to the radical invitation into uncertainty of Paulo Freire (1970):

The radical, committed to human liberation, does not become the prisoner of a "circle of certainty" within which reality is also imprisoned. On the contrary, the more radical the person is, the more fully he or she enters into reality so that, knowing it better, he or she can better transform it. This individual is not afraid to confront, to listen, to see the world unveiled. This person is not afraid to meet people or enter into dialogue with them. (p. 39)

We propose that critical friendship is just this kind of radical invitation – a practice of unveiling our assumptions so that we can support one another to see the world more clearly. And in order to shed our fears and "see the world unveiled," we need an intermediate space – a liminoid space – between our "circles of certainty" and a world of overwhelming complexity, a space where we are in a "...constant state of revision" as one member states it. Critical friendship groups have three important elements of social structure that bound them and allow for "safe passage" between the members' closed circles and an unbounded world:

1. Agreements – the foundation of the group's trust
2. Protocols – the "social technology" that helps to re-culture the group and
   a. supports members in drilling down to their assumptions and then surfacing them
   b. for public examination
3. An emotional commitment to one another's success and improvement – either
   a. incremental or revolutionary

Absent any of these, a traditional PLC may appear to offer an on-going effort at improvement, but may also serve inadvertently to reinforce our own cherished positions, personal interests,

hidden biases, and to concretize our misconceptions, rather than give us a place to challenge one another's views of the schools in which we work. As one member eloquently writes,

I once was lost, but now I am not just found, but am uplifted and supported. I am no longer lonely and too tired to fight for all students. The trust and respect we have developed is vital to me and was very much missing in my professional life. I don't feel so alone anymore.

Our own story has taken us both on unexpected journeys into innovative roles, fresh teaching positions, and even to new communities. Ross's family moved to a different town and an exciting new university job several hours away, but our friendship, collaboration, and mutual encouragement not only survived, but matured. Susan accepted a university teaching position and began pursuit of a PhD, but we continue to find opportunities to collaborate through the use of technology and meeting face to face when possible. We have found that our early investment in shared risk-taking, daring to interrupt and disrupt the status quo, and embracing the pedagogy of discomfort (Zembylas & Boler, 2002) created the capacity for our story to continue across time, distance and changing work contexts.

Indeed, we have learned that the more we listen and talk openly and honestly with one another, the more we long to deepen our dialogue and to delve into previously unexplored spaces. Now when we talk, we are eager to hear about one another's work in our separate locations and we continue to ask the questions in our pursuit to mine our current work for new wisdom. Just as in Susan's dream, there are whole rooms, buildings and worlds waiting for us to discover and to seek to understand what we might learn within the community of critical friendship. Having allies, co-conspirators, and collegial friends for company strengthens us for the journey into transformation. We invite you to open the door.

REFERENCES

Britzman, D. (1998). *Lost subjects, contested objects: Toward a psychoanalytic inquiry of learning.* Albany, NY: State University of New York Press.

Freire, P. (1970). *Pedagogy of the oppressed* (2008 30th Anniversary Edition ed.). (M. B. Ramos, Trans.) New York, NY: The Continuum International Publishing Group.

Freire, P., & Macedo, D. (1995). A dialogue: Culture, language, and race. *Harvard Educational Review, 65*(3), 377–402.

hooks, b. (1994). *Teaching to transgress: Education as the practice of freedom.* London, UK: Routledge.

hooks, b. (2003). *Teaching community: A pedagogy of hope.* New York, NY: Routledge.

Huebner, D. (1987). The vocation of teaching. In Bolin, F., & Falk, J. M. (Eds.), *Teacher renewal: Professional issues, personal choices* (pp. 17–29). New York, NY: Teachers College Press.

Kegan, R., & Lahey, L. L. (2009). *Immunity to change: How to overcome it and unlock the potential in yourself and your organization.* Cambridge, MA: Harvard Business Press.

Mezirow, J. (1990). *Fostering critical reflection in adulthood: A guide to transformational and emancipatory practice.* San Francisco, CA: Jossey-Bass.

Mezirow, J. (1991). *Transformative dimensions of adult learning.* San Francisco, CA: Jossey-Bass.

Miller, J. L. (1990). *Creating spaces and finding voices: Teachers collaborating for empowerment.* Albany, NY: State University of New York Press.

Nieto, S. (2008). Nice is not enough: Defining caring for students of color. In Pollock, M. (Ed.), *Everyday antiracism: Getting real about change in school* (pp. 28–31). New York, NY: The New Press.

Palmer, P. J. (2007). *The courage to teach: Exploring the inner landscape of a teacher's life.* San Francisco, CA: Jossey-Bass.

Pinar, W. F. (2004). *What is curriculum theory?* Mahwah, NJ: Lawrence Erlbaum Associates.

School Reform Initiative. (2009). Retrieved December 5, 2009, from www.schoolreforminitiative.org

Shohat, E. (1995). The struggle over representation: Casting, coalitions, and the politics of identification. In de la Campa, R., Kaplan, E. A., & Sprinkler, M. (Eds.), *Late emperial culture.* New York, NY: Vetso.

Thompson-Grove, G. (January 2005). *A call to action.* Keynote Address (abridged) The 9th Annual NSRF Winter Meeting. Cambridge, MA.

Turner, V. (1986). *The anthropology of performance.* Baltimore, MD: PAJ Publications.

Van Gennep, A. (1909). *The rites of passage* (2004th ed.). London, UK: Routledge.

Zembylas, M., & Boler, M. (2002). *On the spirit of patriotism: Challenges of a pedagogy of discomfort.* Retrieved January 6, 2010, from http://www.tcrecord.org/library

Chapter 4
Smart People Learning:
Self-Knowledge that Disrupts Practice in Meaningful Ways

Edith A. Rusch
University of Nevada, Las Vegas, USA

ABSTRACT

This chapter highlights instructional practices informed by an Interactive Learning Model (Johnston & Dainton, 1996) that fosters retrospective sensemaking (Weick, 1995) and heightens reflective practice (Osterman & Kottkamp, 2004; Schon, 1987). This disruptive pedagogy reveals the symbiotic nature of theory and practice and teaches aspiring and practicing leaders that effective leadership is all about learning.

INTRODUCTION

Today, *learning* has a central role in conversations and research about quality leadership of organizations (Collinson & Cook, 2007; Crispeels, 2004; Senge, Cambron-McCabe, Lucas, Smith Dutton, & Kleiner, 2000). In fact, Silverburg and Kottkamp (2006), in the premier issue of the *Journal of Research on Leadership Education*, argued that an essential skill for today's leaders was "behaving as

learners". This view has also been fostered by the National College for School Leadership (NCSL) under the auspices of the Collaborative Leadership Learning project. The intent of the project is to engage Collaborative Leadership Learning Groups (CLLG) in collective learning that eventually leads to discussions about the actual experience of engaging in collective learning, an example of reflection on action. According to James, Mann, & Creasy (2007), the learning "design implicitly

DOI: 10.4018/978-1-61350-495-6.ch004

and explicitly parallels the elements of distributive leadership that top leaders are required to address in their own organizations" (p. 91) as they lead change efforts.

The CLLG project is one of very few examples of instructional approaches to collective leadership that engage students in sensemaking activities focused on learning. This chapter highlights pedagogical practices that are grounded in similar perspectives, practices that enlist the symbiotic nature of theory and practice to foster disruption that enhances collective learning. In this case, the instructional approaches connect to Weick's notions of sensemaking (1995), Johnston's Interactive Learning Model (1996), and Mezirow's adult learning theories (2000; 2000a). Thus far, these classroom practices heighten reflective practice (Osterman & Kottkamp, 2004; Schon, 1987) and foster more sophisticated sensemaking. A decade of findings from action research (Rusch & Horsford, 2008; Rusch, 2005; 2004, 2004a) indicate that a process of retrospective sensemaking (Weick, 1995), coupled with knowledge about individual learning processes and skills of reflective discourse, fosters qualitatively different responses and in some cases, deep and transformative insights into beliefs and actions of educators who want to be viewed as change agents.

BACKGROUND

My professional life has been devoted to learning. Early stages of my career were dedicated to helping children learn about long division, the difference between latitude and longitude, and important facts like what three U. S. rivers meet in Pittsburgh! As I pursued a Ph.D, my most thrilling discovery was that academics actually were paid to engage in learning. During both stages of my career, I truly believed a teacher's role was to share everything I had learned and I worked hard to present all my knowledge in creative,

provocative, and disruptive ways. I have fond memories of a 4th grade lesson on giving directions that led to total class disruption when I put a large glob of peanut butter on my nose because I rigidly followed student instructions for making a peanut butter sandwich! Once I became a university professor, I gained a reputation for disruptive assignments, the kind that invited student-designed approaches or sketched, rather than written products; most of my assignments lacked rigid instructions and encouraged student inventions. My all-time favorite assignment provided small groups of doctoral students with garbage bags filled with identical assortments of children's outdoor game objects (e.g. balls, hula hoops, bats, frisbees) followed by instructions to invent a game that they could teach to the other groups the next day. The planning process, and the field event that followed, became a yearlong textbook on organizational development, team building, and group dynamics. The point of this brief recap of my teaching career is that there came a very disruptive moment when I realized, much to my dismay, that my teaching did not always lead to learning, that in fact, my creative approaches to sharing all I had learned actually inhibited learning for some of my students. In other words, my versions of disruption did not support the reflective outcomes I wanted for many of my students. The outcomes of my own reflections indicated I had to learn new approaches that fostered learning rather than just continuing to share my knowledge. My own learning, detailed in the sections that follow, was guided by an interesting symbiosis of theory and practice.

SENSEMAKING

Karl Weick (1969), in his seminal treatise on *The Social Psychology of Organizing,* highlighted the critical importance of *affect* in-group functions. In the case of problem solving or decision-making,

Weick noted, "affective distinctions (i.e. feelings of like and dislike) develop before the ability to make cognitive distinctions" (p. 14). Drawing from the work of sociologist, George Simmel, Weick concluded that the prominence of affect among individuals in groups led people to "like and interact with those who are most similar to them" (p. 14), fostering groups that are connected more by emotions and feelings than intellectual or cognitive elements. As Weick continued to develop his concepts related to human endeavors of organizing, he introduced the notion of *sensemaking*, the process of forming "unconscious and conscious anticipations and assumptions, which serve as predictions about future events" (Weick, 1995, p. 4). Pointing out that sensemaking is something more than mere interpretation of the moment or situation, Weick posited that sensemaking also involved "authoring" (p. 8), that is to say, individual sensemaking involved "creation, as well as, discovery" (p.8). He then connected his concept to Schön's views of problem setting, a process that limits what will be attended to, depending on what any one individual senses or gives meaning to. Sensemaking then, Weick argued, "is about ways people generate what they interpret" (p. 13).

As Weick delineated the actual processes of sensemaking, he identified the construction of personal identity, the definition of self, as a key factor. Two points, among the various interpretations of identity construction, offer a framework for this discussion of leaders who aspire to foster change by acting as learners. First, Weick describes "a complex mixture of proaction and reaction" (p. 23) that individuals engage in as they interpret the behavior of others and then intentionally try to influence that behavior. Secondly, and most importantly, Weick argues, "the idea that sensemaking is self-referential suggests that the self, rather than the environment, may be the text in need of interpretation" (p. 23).

Classroom Sensemaking

Classroom settings are vivid examples of individual sensemaking that, in turn, inform group interactions. As any class begins, both students and instructors filter classroom environments through a complex screen of personal assumptions, values, beliefs, and past experiences (Cranton, 2000). According to Mezirow (2000), frames of reference always involve cognitive, conative, and affective dimensions. For example, when learning takes place, the brain becomes very active, sensing surroundings, communicating, and processing previous experiences in an attempt to make sense of people, a situation or an assignment. Cognitively, the moment is vetted through files of past experience, looking for a personal rubric that best fits what individuals see or feel. That mental rubric, which some call a mental model (Senge, et al. 2000) is usually based on long-held assumptions. Additionally, multiple factors such as culture, heritage, class structures, gender, race, and life experience influence an individual's sensemaking of the moment. If an individual's background includes a value for male dominance or White privilege, she/he has a rubric that informs how or what is seen or felt when gender is part of the dynamic. For example, some religious ideologies do not accept women in leadership roles and male members of those particular religious groups, who aspire to become educational leaders, sometimes struggle with the fact that their classmates include women who behave as equals. Even if someone has a value for gender equity, because cognitive and affective processing are simultaneous, memories of a vividly embarrassing past experience with gender dynamics can overshadow a stated commitment.

The importance of past experience in sensemaking cannot be overstated. If the mental file of the past experience (cognitive) is about an encounter that led to conflict or failure, an individual's affect will instantly inform the present encounter.

Argyris (1993) describes this moment as walking up a ladder of inference, noting that once a memory is triggered, individuals "impose their meaning on the actions they believe the other person intends" (p. 57) and even go so far as to evaluate the actions and the person, and predetermine a response based on the memory, not on the actual behavior occurring at the moment. In other words, stored feelings about a previous experience may shape a lifetime of actions.

Conation, the actions or volition of learning, are the most visible elements of sensemaking in any situation. In fact, according to Johnston (1996), our conative processing compels us to act in a certain manner. That is, when individuals encounter people or situations, cognition reveals the assumptive rubrics, which translate to affect and affect, in turn, translates to conation or actions. At times, conative responses or the actions of sensemaking are less than tactful. Examples that are visible in classrooms or school organizations include individuals who easily respond to new ideas becoming impatient with peers who ask persistent and repetitive questions and appear to resist any new ideas. Working groups also include people who seemed compelled to offer lengthy explanations, even in response to direct questions. We also encounter students and professional colleagues who never contribute anything to a discussion. All of these varied behaviors lend themselves to overt and covert reactions, which often disrupt or prevent quality collective learning among classmates or a workgroup. When these sensemaking interactions are confounded by race, gender, sexual orientation, or some other form of difference, the affective responses can lead to subtle and not-so subtle intra and interpersonal dynamics. Eventually, these dynamics deter or thwart individual and/or group potential to practice the skills critical to the success of school leaders who wish to engage an organization in learning that leads to change.

Sensemaking That Transforms

The sensemaking action needed to overcome the scene just narrated above is described as transformative learning, which according to Mezirow (2000) "is at the heart of significant adult learning" (p. xv). Mezirow grounds his transformative learning theory in Habermas' view of "reflection as a form of self-formation that emancipates as it releases one from the constraints of dysfunctional beliefs (p. xiii). Self-formation requires "communicative competence" (Habermas cited in Mezirow, 2000, p. xiii) because it is "a process of examining, questioning, validating and revising those perceptions" (Cranton, 1994, p. 26). Mezirow argues that if perspectives really transform, the individual must modify a personal paradigm, reject a habit of mind, or reorder assumptions, which Brookfield (2000) suggests, can lead to epiphany of cataclysmic proportions. In his critique of transformative learning and critical reflection, Brookfield (2000) cautioned that perspective transformation that actually leads to action is no simple task. In other words, if adult learners are going to challenge their deepest-held meanings, they have to experience disruption.

Brookfield's cautions are worthy of attention, particularly among higher education faculty whose tenure is informed by student evaluations. Higher education classrooms are bounded experiences with limited opportunities for engagement and disruptive pedagogies can lead to individual and collective dissatisfaction with an instructor that may harm one's future. As I examined increasingly negative teaching evaluations that documented my less than successful practices, I wondered if students would benefit more from a disruptive pedagogy that had a deep connection to their identity. The Interactive Learning Model© (ILM) seemed to offer a new pathway.

Learning about the Learning Self

Leadership classrooms have the potential to serve as a practice field for managing inter and intrapersonal differences, but the practice is enriched if individuals have a clear sense of their own and others' approaches to sensemaking or learning. The Learning Connections Inventory© (LCI) is one tool that disrupts assumptions about the self and others in a profound way. The inventory, though developed around sound scientific principles, is not complex or lengthy, thus allowing students to continue use, reflection, and transformative action over time.

Recognizing the limitations of a psychological approach that informs learning styles inventories, Johnston and Dainton (1987)) drew from cognitive science to develop an advanced learning system, the Interactive Learning Model© (ILM. A 28-item Learning Connections Inventory© (LCI) captures the degree to which an individual uses each of four learning patterns (Sequential, Precise, Technical, and Confluent). Johnston (1998, 1996) posited that the interactions of an individual's patterns represent how any learner sees the world, internalizes stimuli, integrates stimuli, and formulates a response. The LCI© includes three opened ended questions that triangulate responses to the other 28 forced choice questions. Three ranges of use emerge from the scored inventory: Use first (25-35); Use as Needed (17-24); and Avoid this Pattern (7-16).

The theoretical base of the inventory and the LML process is an Interactive Learning Model that depicts the simultaneous interactions of cognition, conation, and affectation (noted earlier as related to Mezirow's work on adult learning). Operationalized, individual learning is governed by the strength and interactions of four synchronous patterns that Johnston and Dainton (1987) called sequence, precision, technical, and confluence. The researchers point out that any learner uses all four processes, but to different degrees and in different order; thus the system avoids the label-

ing that often comes with styles inventories. The interacting patterns represent how the learner sees the world, takes in stimuli, integrates the stimuli, and formulates a response. An individual typically begins his or her learning with a preferred pattern or interaction of patterns, uses as needed patterns in a secondary response, and rarely engages in avoid patterns. A learners preferred, or Use First patterns always govern initial approaches to any learning task. For example, someone who leads with confluence sees multiple approaches to any classroom assignment and will often defy directions in order to satisfy her/his need for creativity. If confluent and precise patterns are equally strong, a need to have an abundance of information becomes an added force that can interfere with timely completion of tasks. That learner will get caught up in acquiring vast amounts of knowledge and, at the last minute, may develop a creative product that lacks quality. If forced to work in an avoid pattern, a learner experiences serious frustration. Table 1 offers some brief examples of patterns in action at the cognitive, affective and conative levels. A reader can get a sense of their most or least preferred patterns just by reading these brief examples. The scoring system noted above, allows a learner to understand more about how the patterns actually interact for one's self and others. Nationally and internationally validated, the LCI© has test-retest reliability as well as content, construct, and predictive validity. Used both in educational and industrial settings in the United States and abroad, the process has proved to be an effective tool for learning and team building because, unlike typical styles inventories, the LCI© fosters understanding of how the patterns interact and govern sensemaking actions.

Over a decade ago, I introduced the learning inventory as tool for enhancing organizational learning. The inventory and (ILM) (Johnston, 1996), used in conjunction with retrospective sensemaking activities (Weick, 1995) helped individuals connect their *learning self* to actions that constructed their personal identity (Weick,

Table 1. Cognitive, conative and affective experiences of dominant learning patterns

	Cognitively	**Conatively**	**Affectively**
Sequential Processing	• Organize information • Mentally analyze data • Break tasks down into steps	• Make lists • Organize • Plan first, *then* act	• Thrive on consistency and dependability • Need things to be tidy and organized • Feel frustrated when the game plan keeps changing • Feel frustrated when rushed
Precise Processing	• Research information • Ask *lots* of questions • Always want to know more	• Challenge statements and ideas that I doubt • Prove I am right • Document my research and findings • Write things down • Write long e-mail messages and leave long voice mail messages	• Thrive on knowledge • Feel good when I am correct • Feel frustrated when incorrect information is accepted as valid • Feel frustrated when people do not share information with me
Technical Processing	• Seek concrete relevance – what does this mean in the real world? • Only want as much information as I need – nothing extraneous	• Hands on • Tinker • Solve the problem • Do	• Enjoy knowing how things work • Feel good that I am self sufficient • Feel frustrated when the task has no real world relevance • Enjoy knowing things, but I do not feel the need to share that knowledge
Confluent Processing	• Read between the lines • Think outside the box • Brainstorm • Make obscure connections between things that are seemingly unrelated	• Takes risks • Not afraid to fail • Talk about things – a lot • Start things and not finish them • Start a task first – *then* ask for directions	• Enjoy energy • Feel comfortable with failure • Do not enjoy having ideas criticized • Feel frustrated by people who are not open to new ideas • Enjoy a challenge • Feel frustrated by repeating a task over and over

1995). Individual knowledge of learning pattern interactions opened a window of understanding into seemingly intuitive leadership actions. For example, one educator described the knowledge gained from the inventory as "the most influential activity I did in this course", noting that the knowledge of his learning patterns "helped me to realize why I excel in certain environments and why I try to hide in others". Tables 2 and 3 show almost oppositional pattern sets between two individuals in the same class. The information on the tables is an example of how the inventory results allow for individual or group analyses of the inventory. When small groups of students, with similar patterns, develop these analyses, the entire class can predict the interpersonal dynamics that might interfere with learning or productive work. Essentially, the data themselves offer a teachable moment that leads to individual and group sensemaking.

The key principle of Johnston's Interactive Learning Model© is that every individual's combination of learning patterns is unique, *and* that all have a unique approach to learning that is interconnected with the way one thinks and feels during a task. Researchers have demonstrated that this advanced learning system gives people the means to understand who they are as learners so they can articulate that awareness to others in important relationships. In both educational and workplace settings, researchers find (1) heightened awareness of learning orientations in self and others; (2) a change in the assumptions of individuals who learn and teach within a given context; (3) lowering of bias toward those individuals whose learning patterns are different from oneself;

Table 2. Student who leads with sequence and precision avoids technical and confluence

LCI Score	I connect with-	I get annoyed with-
Sequence 32; Precise 34; Technical 8; Confluent 8	•Gives clear directions •Neat •Organized •Factual •Detailed	•Haphazard •Creative •Unorganized [sic] •Project-oriented •No clear plan •Messy

Table 3. Student who leads with confluence and avoids sequence and technical

LCI Score	I connect with-	I get annoyed with-
Sequence 11 Precise 17; Technical 11; Confluent 30	•Creative •One who discusses concepts/higher order thinking •Willing to compromise and tease out ideas •Wants to work together	•Short and to the point •Too concrete in their thinking •Everything is black and white •Hates group work •Thinks activities are stupid

and (4) increased awareness of embedded stereotypes of successful and unsuccessful learners (Johnston, 1998). Equally important, the effectiveness of this advanced learning system is predicated on reflective practice being used *with intention* to increase the conscious understanding of every individual's unique actions, thoughts, and feelings (Brookfield, 1995; Osterman & Kottkamp, 2004). The intention was clear for a school leader who realized how his overwhelming need for sequence and order led him to shut down when situations were unclear or ambiguous. The new awareness led to an observation that "while I found my reaction unacceptable, it was an enlightening moment for me ... it made me think about how I can approach similar situations in the future so that I can learn to overcome my 'Sequential Disability' in less structured settings". In truth, no one can ever overcome his/her interactive learning patterns, but actual knowledge of the cognition, conation, and affectation does support intentional management of personal patterns in ways that contribute to relearning and identity reconstruction.

A CLOSER LOOK AT CLASSROOM DYNAMICS

Over the decade, I documented a variety of emotional responses among school leaders as they encountered fellow educators who were either comfortably similar or represented diametrically opposed patterns of learning (Rusch, 2005, 2004, 2004a). For example, graduate students in educational leadership classrooms talked openly about preferring to work only with people who are "like me," and they described frustrations when forced to engage in group work with individuals who represented mismatches, verifying Weick's (1969) observations that affect is the most prominent determiner of group dynamics in organizations. Educators related stories about their work settings, describing colleagues or superiors who displayed behaviors that "aggravate me to no end". Highly organized individuals frequently described a peer whose room "always looks like a pigpen ... I don't know how the kids can learn in that room". Individuals also lamented peers or superiors "who focus so much on procedures and paperwork that any good ideas are completely blocked ... if we can't try new ideas, how will we ever help kids?". Individuals frequently admitted that they were appalled by the *opposite other* despite the fact that, as colleagues, they had similar goals and intentions. Early on, I discovered that when students and the instructor had a common language related to learning, the differences became easier to confront, communicative competence increased, and educators reported intentionally different actions in their work settings (Rusch, 2004; 2005). Our common language also led to deeper and more informed conversations about the responsibilities of school leaders to work with a wide range of adult learners, leading to important reflections about the kinds of skills individuals needed to acquire to be an effective leader. The information from the learning inventory appeared to be a tool that allowed individuals to engage in a new kind of sensemaking, with the self actually becoming a text (Weick, 1995).

Retrospective Sensemaking

Retrospective sensemaking (Weick, 1995), using the *data* from the learning inventory, proved to be the most potent activity for transformational learning. Learning from the past is a relatively common endeavor in the education of leaders. However, most often the lessons are focused on historical accounts of issues, processes, and organizations or cynical observations of the cyclical nature of issues, couched in the phrase, *what goes around, comes around.* Weick's version of retrospect centers around the concept "that people can know what they are doing only after they have done it" (p. 24) and "we are always a little behind or our actions are always a bit ahead of us" (p.26). When retrospective sensemaking is clearly focused on an individual's learning process, the origins of actions become crystal clear.

A Learning History

I introduce students to retrospective sensemaking by asking them to develop a learning history based on memories of experiences rooted primarily in childhood. Once completed, the history is shared in a group of no more than four students. Beginning with a collection of artifacts (real or reconstructed) that depict important learning benchmarks or turning points in an individual's life (e.g. report cards, photos, and school projects), individuals explain to their group how each artifact was pivotal to their learning history.

The presentation of learning histories is a particularly powerful experience; typically one brave individual in each group breaks an awkward silence and struggles through being the first to share a personal world with strangers. Then slowly, each group comes to life, with laughter or tears accompanying the story telling. Follow-up discussions reveal that individuals shared far more than they had intended and describe an increased sense of connection among group members. Many express surprise at the number of peers who overcame extremely difficult experiences as young learners. For example, one educator told her group about racing through homework so she could help her dad fix things that were broken. Several artifacts from elementary school spoke to her artistic talent and a need for perfection. She reported an unsuccessful struggle to obtain grades of A, describing her need for hands-on work and her extreme dislike of reading. Her efforts seldom resulted in good grades or encouragement to aspire to college, a story heard often from high technical processors with low sequence and precision. Yet here she was, an advanced degree candidate and an aspiring school leader who now understood that she made sense of the world through a technical processor and that highly technical approach to learning had nothing to do with her potential or intelligence. However, that journey to further education only began later in midlife, after a friend convinced her she was smart. Her story, and others like it, lead to critical discussions about the school structures that encourage and discourage learners; more often than not, the reflections are highly personal and about family members, or current students.

The learning history assignment and knowledge of the interaction of learning patterns also can lead to instant awareness of how particular actions (conative responses) lead to stereotyping. One prominent example involved an observation from a group of Black women about a very vocal White male classmate, that they had labeled "a typical White male know-it all" (student journal entry). After the learning history experience, one of the women wrote,

I guess I really stereotyped Jack. All that talk all the time, sharing everything he thinks he knows - that's just his confluence showing. I couldn't believe the story of his background, coming from a family on welfare. After tonight, I think I can tell him that his 'smarts' inhibit me. (Student reflective paper)

During the next class meeting, three Black women initiated a discussion about the learning history experience, shared their carpool conversation, and revealed how a tall, verbal, and very well read White administrator had triggered every embedded stereotype of domineering and know-it-all White men. Jack, in turn, shared an ongoing internal struggle; for weeks he had been trying to understand why he couldn't find any kind of communication link with two of the three women, revealing that he'd concluded it was a gender issue. Several students pointed out the visibility of the discomfort and obvious tensions among the peers, but the discussion quickly moved on to the differences in learning patterns among the group. All concluded that the tensions actually were far more about very oppositional approaches to learning than gender or race. More importantly, this teachable moment opened the door to an open and honest discussion of how easily gender and race stereotypes created impassable barriers and limited the knowing of *others* in organizational settings, a discussion that typically is filled with tension, discomfort, and exquisite relief when concluded. The degree to which learning patterns drove sensemaking and framed actions was a surprise, even a shock, to advanced graduate educators who occasionally were very experienced school leaders. This form of disruption seemed to foster increased comfort with the discussion and a deeper and more complex probing of issues related to gender and race. The next step was retrospective examination of individual experiences with profound change.

A Change History

A third instructional approach that fosters a disruption that leads to transformative learning is a written retrospective sensemaking assignment that requires individuals to revisit three or four profound professional changes that had been mandated and imposed on them. Learners are instructed to recall any and all personal and organizational reactions, their own degree of involvement, and any personal overt and covert actions during the change process. One example might be a reassignment that involuntarily moved an individual from a highly individualized and traditional classroom setting to an open classroom, team-teaching setting. Once students have written the stories connected to their retrospective sensemaking, they are required to use the stories as a data set, looking for any patterns of actions or reactions that connect with how, in their current professional roles, they lead change efforts. As individuals connect their recollections to the knowledge of their learning patterns, new understandings abound. For example, individuals who are highly confluent realize why they so eagerly embrace new ideas. "Does change really bother people?" one highly confluent principal mused. Once again, the change history papers become a qualitative data set with students connecting complex change theories to their experiences (e.g. institutional theory; dialectical theory, Marris's (1975) change and loss theory. Similar to the Learning History lesson, students engage in a paired discussion of the change history in order to unpack the experience.

Reflective Discourse

The Change History is examined using reflective discourse, a process that requires generative listening and invited inquiry between pairs. During a two hour session, partners take turns talking through one of their change experiences, describing any sensemaking that has occurred during the previous learning activities and exploring any new questions or insights they have about their approaches to leading change. The listening partner can *only* contribute questions that support deeper inquiry into the partner's reasoning. Once both partners have completed the reflective discourse, they work together to deepen their sensemaking about the connections between and among their personal experiences, their interactive learning processes, their current change agent practices, and the theoretical perspective under study. The change history lesson concludes with partner presentations of personal insights for fellow learners.

Sensemaking Lessons

The poignant and significant student reflections that occur during the reflective discourse conversations (e.g. "what Linda helped me see") continue to occur during presentations (e.g. I'm just thinking about this right now because you are asking me about this again—I can see now how my learning curve contributed to the mess), and expanded even further as additional pairs present their own versions of analyses (e.g. I'm having an aha moment too), verifying Weick's (1995) observations about the importance of after-the-fact sensemaking one

more time. One educator described insights from her Reflective Discourse, stating,

When I started looking back, I didn't really understand. I tried to explain everything as an ego thing. I had no idea what I didn't know! I'm getting mad about what I see now, but mad is a stage of grief. This exercise was not comfortable to do, but thank you very much!

Another principal who had written and talked about a frustrating experience with a successful accreditation process that never really changed anything in the school, explained his sensemaking as realizing his approach had gotten the job done, but he had "missed the boat - I was missing the people. I turned practical too soon ... my approach got the job done, but I robbed others of the process". His highly technical learning pattern led him to value problem solving, but his preference was to always work alone – a strategy not conducive to organizational learning. He concluded, "I've moved from modern to post-modern perspective overnight ... I'm going back home and train the people in the process". He also connected accreditation to mimetic isomorphism, but understood that the fundamental attributes of the process were the very things his faculty needed to work on continuously. Recently, a former student who is now a long-term superintendent, recounted his experience with the change history as the "most profound experience I've ever had". In his view, the awareness of his learning patterns (high confluence and equally high sequence) led him understand why he easily took risks and never feared mistakes, yet supported skilled and detailed planning. Knowledge about his learning patterns gave him the incentive to study of the learning approaches of people around him in order to enhance the success of change efforts. He intentionally began to withhold the grandiose visions that came so easily to him and stopped labelling people as *resistors* when they asked unending questions or appeared fearful of new ideas. He described his new and very intentional practice of engaging with people with diametrically opposed sensemaking patterns, noting, "I've never had so much fun as a school leader".

The statements above are only a few examples of the vivid reordering of assumptions that take place when retrospective sensemaking is coupled with knowledge of learning processes. As each educator revealed thought patterns, new or troubling questions, or discovered deeply embedded assumptions that drove actions, the learning interactions between and among members only deepened. Reference to complex theories flowed easily as individuals attached them to personal experiences. In many ways, it was as though each learner was a new kind of *textbook about change* and could choose to keep turning pages so everyone could learn.

Critical Reflection in Practice

Mastering disruptive classroom practices that lead to critical reflection is no simple task. Instructors find multiple strategies to create comfortable, seemingly risk-free classroom spaces, mediate traditional power relationships between students and teachers, and work to reveal a more authentic self in the classroom. None of these actions guarantee that students will engage in or become skilled at "critically reflect[ing] on ... sacred truths" (Mezirow, 2000) or engage in unlearning and relearning experiences" (Kreisburg, 1992).

Graduate level learners, in this case educators, are a unique lot. Many students pursue advanced degrees to insure their professional certification or advance their salaries. Many are highly skilled at completing course requirements and posturing intellectual discourse without ever connecting the ideas to daily practice. These individuals have mastered the standard processes and practices of schooling and become skilled at engaging without

disrupting any of their deepest-held meanings. Essentially, many adult learners in graduate education programs will complete assigned critical reflection activities but complete the activity only as an assignment, not as a reflection that might disrupt their belief sets or practices.

The strength of the LML inventory is that it provides a productive disruption that fosters "authoring" (Weick, 1995, p. 8), that combination of discovery and creation. For some individuals, the self-knowledge explains everything they experience as a habit or a label. They walk away with insights and language that support a more sophisticated understanding of self and others. In many cases, assumptions and mental models are replaced by intentional managing of self and interpretation of others. Most importantly, LML is not a bounded activity that anticipates deep understanding in a short time frame (e g. a 15-week semester) (Boud, 1998). The knowledge of learning processes in action unfolds overtime and becomes visible in unpredictable and very teachable moments. During a term, students return to class with new stories. One student found how her sequence worked when she shopped for groceries, another reported on a breakthrough with a challenging learner in his classroom, and yet another had new insights into his very diverse sons. In each case, the emergent discussion led to deeper questioning of the embedded notions of *normal* learners and the hegemonic designs of and practices in schooling. In that particular class, students' fluency in the discourse of hegemony increased dramatically because they personalized the concept in a unique way. More importantly, the power to instruct the lesson became highly dispersed. Overtime, my students and I have discovered that we had a *life textbook* (Weick, 1995) to examine in order to increase our understanding of self and the interaction of our self with others. We also have discovered that the *textbook* has new pages every day, thus supporting the growth of "reflection in action" (Argyris & Schon, 1978).

CONCLUSION

Many academics work in education-related programs with stated missions to develop transformational leaders. We work hard to facilitate disruptive and reflective processes that support individual growth and development, as well as increase understanding of group growth and development. The ILM© process, when used intentionally, not only enhances self-awareness in a recursive manner, it also supports reflective inquiry about the values, knowledge, and actions that undergird transformative leadership behaviors. In this instructor's view, intentional use of the LML process helps students and the instructor to not only reflect on, but to deconstruct and act on intrapersonal and interpersonal dynamics in a multitude of educational settings. Knowledge of pattern interaction also helps all participants to decode daily encounters, to use a common vocabulary that supports increased communicative competence, and to devise strategies that help individuals and groups to engage in organizational learning. In the words of a student,

It was not until I took this course that I realized that I had simply moved from the idea of dispensing knowledge to students to the idea of dispensing knowledge to teachers. No wonder I could not effect change in the alternative program! I had not realized that, while [sic] the only way to be a teacher was to be a learner, the only way to be a leader was to be a learner. While I could administrate without being a learner, I cannot lead without being a learner. (emphasis added)

His view is supported by Schein, who says, "unless leaders become learners themselves - unless they can acknowledge vulnerabilities and uncertainties - then transformational learning will never take place" (cited in Cuoto, 2002, p. 6).

The ILM© process is not a panacea. Although the learning inventory provides unique insights into the self and interaction with others, quality sensemaking still requires learning experiences that allow students to integrate the knowledge with theory and practice. Weick's sensemaking, the construction and reconstruction of the personal self, takes an inordinate amount of time, patience and persistence (Weick, 1995). The good news is that the ILM© process is not finite; once you have the basic knowledge and information, the work consists of long-term intentional attention to practice; the abundance of stories from former students suggest the knowledge base supports ongoing reflection on action. The evidence so far suggests that transformational learning is feasible, as long as learners have quality self-knowledge that transfers easily to daily experience.

Note: The author has no paid affiliation with Learning Connections Resources and does not benefit monetarily from the sale of the inventories.

REFERENCES

Argyris, C. (1993). *On organizational learning.* Cambridge, MA: Addison Wesley.

Argyris, C., & Schön, E. (1978). *Organizational learning.* Reading, MA: Addison Wesley.

Boud, D., & Walker, D. (1998). Promoting reflection in professional courses: The challenge of context. *Studies in Higher Education, 23*(2), 191–207. doi:10.1080/03075079812331380384

Brookfield, S. (1995). *On becoming a critically reflective teacher.* San Francisco, CA: Jossey Bass.

Brookfield, S. (2000). Transformative learning as ideology critique. In Mezirow, J. (Ed.), *Learning as transformation: Critical perspectives on theory as progress* (pp. 125–150). San Francisco, CA: Jossey Bass.

Collinson, V., & Cook, T. F. (2007). *Organizational learning: Improving learning, teaching, and leading in school systems.* Thousand Oaks, CA: Sage Publications.

Cranton, P. (1994). *Understanding and promoting transformative learning*. San Francisco, CA: Jossey Bass.

Cranton, P. (2000). Individual differences and transformative learning. In Mezirow, J. (Ed.), *Learning as transformation* (pp. 181–204). San Francisco, CA: Jossey Bass.

Crispeels, J. H. (Ed.). (2004). *Learning to lead together: The promise and challenge of sharing leadership*. Thousand Oaks, CA: Sage.

Cuoto, D. (2002). The anxiety of learning. *Harvard Business Review, 80*(3), 100–107.

James, K., Mann, J., & Creasy, J. (2007). Leaders as learners: A case example of facilitating collaborative leadership learning for school leaders. *Management Learning, 38*(1), 79–94. doi:10.1177/1350507607073026

Johnston, C. (1996). *Unlocking the will to learn*. Thousand Oaks, CA: Corwin Press, Sage Publications.

Johnston, C. (1998). *Accountability that counts: Making a difference for learners*. Retrieved on February 15, 2005, from http://www.letmelearn.org

Johnston, C., & Dainton, G. (1987). *Learning connections inventory*. Turnersville, NJ: Learning Connections Resources. Retrieved from http://lcrinfo.con/index/shtml

Kreisburg, S. (1992). *Transforming power: Domination, empowerment, and education*. Albany, NY: SUNY Press.

Marris, P. (1975). *Loss & change*. New York, NY: Doubleday.

Mezirow, J. (2000). *Learning as transformation: Critical perspectives on a theory in progress* (1st ed.). San Francisco: Jossey-Bass.

Mezirow, J. (2000a). Learning to think like an adult. In Mezirow, J. (Ed.), *Learning as transformation* (pp. 3–34). San Francisco, CA: Jossey Bass.

Osterman, K. F., & Kottkamp, R. B. (2004). *Reflective practice for educators: Professional development to improve student learning* (2nd ed.). Thousand Oaks, CA: Corwin Press.

Rusch, E. (2004a, November). *Transformative learning: The foundation to transformative leadership*. Paper presented as part of symposium with D. Miller, K. Sernak, M. Scherr. University Council for Educational Administration, Fall Convention, Kansas City, MO.

Rusch, E. (2005, April). *Self knowledge that transforms*. Paper presented to the Annual Meeting of the American Educational Research Association. Montreal, CA.

Rusch, E., & Horsford, S. (2008, November). Unifying messy communities: Learning social justice in educational leadership classrooms. *Teacher Development, 12*(4), 353–367. doi:10.1080/13664530802579934

Rusch, E. A. (2004). Gender and race in leadership preparation: A constrained discourse. *Educational Administration Quarterly, 40*(1), 16–48. doi:10.1177/0013161X03259110

Schön, D. (1983). *The reflective practitioner. City*. Basic Books.

Schön, E. (1987). *Educating the reflective practitioner*. San Francisco, CA: Jossey Bass.

Senge, P., Cambron-McCabe, N., Lucas, T., Smith, B., Dutton, J., & Kleiner, A. (2000). *Schools that learn: A fifth discipline fieldbook for educators, parents, and everyone who cares about education*. New York, NY: Doubleday.

Silverburg, R., & Kottkamp, R. (2006). Language matters. *Journal of Research on Leadership Education, 1*(1). Retrieved on April 4, 2010 from http://www.ucea.org/jrle

Weick, K. E. (1969). *The social psychology of organizing*. Reading, MA: Addison-Wesley Pub. Co.

Weick, K. E. (1995). *Sensemaking in organizations*. Thousand Oaks, CA: Sage.

KEY TERMS AND DEFINITIONS

Collective Leadership: Group engagement in retrospective sensemaking and reflection, with a goal of transformative learning.

Interactive Learning Model©: An advanced learning system that depicts the simultaneous interactions of cognition, conation, and affectation (Johnston & Dainton, 1987).

Learning Patterns: An individual's approaches to sensemaking governed how one takes in stimuli, integrates stimuli, and formulates a response.

Reflective Practice: Deliberate examination of actions and the thinking that guides actions.

Retrospective Sensemaking: A precurser to reflective practice; an after-the-fact examination of actions.

Sensemaking: The formation of personal perspectives based implicit or explicit assumptions that guide action and reaction (Weick, 1995).

Transformative Learning: Deliberate examination and modification of assumptions that guide actions and reactions (Mezirow, 2000).

Chapter 5
Shushes in the Parlor:
Reclaiming the "Conversation" Metaphor

Erik Ellis
Stanford University, USA

ABSTRACT

In The Philosophy of Literary Form, Kenneth Burke compares scholars to the participants in an unending conversation in a parlor. Although the famous passage in which Burke expresses this metaphor highlights the need for would-be participants to familiarize themselves with a conversation before joining it, scholars in rhetoric and composition have often used the metaphor to insist that participants in academic conversations must follow particular written conventions—conventions that are often at odds with the concept of conversation. In doing so, scholars overlook or conceal their ideological agendas and serve as de facto guardians of the parlor, etiquette police who shush even the most knowledgeable would-be participants—both students and scholars—who seek to join academic conversations in "inappropriate" ways. This chapter analyzes representative misappropriations of the conversation metaphor, including Graff & Birkenstein's best-selling composition textbook They Say/I Say: The Moves that Matter in Academic Writing, and argues for a more egalitarian interpretation and application of the metaphor. By acknowledging the inadequacy of how we typically present the conversation metaphor to students and emerging scholars, we can begin to reclaim the metaphor as one that cultivates more diverse forms of inquiry and writing. Such diversity disrupts comfortable assumptions about "stable" genres and predictable pedagogies. As Boler (1999) reminded us, "Learning to live with ambiguity, discomfort, and uncertainty is a worthy educational ideal" (p.198). Educators should model this ideal in teaching and scholarship, and should cultivate it in students. To this end, we should embrace rather than fear the complexity and irreducibility of the conversation metaphor, and should write and invite students to write intellectually rigorous yet structurally flexible essays in the exploratory tradition of Montaigne. In other words, we should disrupt the notion that there is only one way to join an ongoing conversation, and should create and take advantage of opportunities to join such conversations in conversational ways.

DOI: 10.4018/978-1-61350-495-6.ch005

INTRODUCTION

Even seemingly "neutral" metaphors have ideological ramifications.— Philip Eubanks (1999, p. 437)

While holding office hours one day as a graduate student at the University of Arizona, I overheard the graduate instructor in the cubicle next to me conferencing with his students, and at first I couldn't believe my ears. No, he didn't say anything offensive or inappropriate per se. In fact, he spoke amiably and seemed eager to help his students. But I couldn't get over the way he kept asking them to think of the argumentative essay they were writing as "a persuasion machine." How ludicrous, I thought. How crude and mechanistic and dehumanizing. How macho. "It doesn't have to be a Ferrari," he said, "but it must be a Yugo." To a more ambitious student he counseled, "It's a little go-cartish, but it's moving toward Lexus." I cringed at each new twist on the metaphor.

This instructor was no more enlightened, I reasoned, than the other male instructor I had seen, earlier that day, wheel his female student down the long hallway, full speed, in his office chair, her squeals and giggles as socially conditioned as his masculine presumption of authority. Would he, as an undergraduate, have welcomed such a gesture by his female counterpart? Both he and Mr. Lexus were firmly in the pedagogical "driver's seat." As Mr. Lexus continued his "Car Talk" monologue, I felt a twinkling of self-righteous pride for knowing that I would never reduce writing to such simplistic, capitalistic terms.

Yet in the days afterward, while conferencing with my own students, I found myself envying my colleague's metaphor - not his particular metaphor but the mere fact that he had one, that he had developed and articulated a memorable way to help students think about academic writing. Of course, all faculty use metaphors when communicating with students about their writ-

ing, albeit unconsciously. Those of us who teach writing suggest ways to fix a structural problem, to weave in a quotation, or to recast a sentence so that it will flow better. These metaphors, and countless others, arise constantly and inevitably in daily discourse. According to Ungerer and Schmid (1996), "everyday language is rife with metaphorical expressions" (p. 116). What difference does it make, then, if Mr. Lexus chose to map his metaphor from the source domain of automobile to the target domain of essay? Why should educators even bother to think about metaphors, other than to help students get their writing into running condition—or whatever metaphors we prefer?

Far more influential than individual pedagogical metaphors are the metaphors at the heart of a discipline. As Ungerer and Schmid have pointed out, "the metaphors that have unconsciously been built into the language by long-established conventions are the most important ones" (p. 119), because their linguistic invisibility often shields them from scrutiny. But what happens when we fail to scrutinize these metaphors? What happens, for example, when rhetoric and composition - a discipline intent on situating discourse and identity within the context of social construction - fails to examine the educational assumptions and implications of its key metaphors? What are the risks of failing to think meta-metaphorically?

CONCEPTUAL METAPHOR

The notion of conceptual metaphor, as articulated by Lakoff and Johnson (1980), is important here, although it offers a mixed blessing for metaphor analysis. Lakoff and Turner (1989) made the important distinction between linguistic expressions of metaphors and metaphors themselves. They argued that "metaphor resides in thought, not just in words" (p. 2). Moreover, according to Stockwell (2002), "much work in cognitive science has demonstrated that metaphor is a basic pattern in the way the human mind works" (p.

105). As a result, any analysis of metaphors should consider them holistically rather than inflate or otherwise distort their importance as isolated uses of language.

By the same token, it would be wrong to decontextualize metaphors and to assume that if they are widely accepted as apt, they must necessarily resonate with timeless inevitability. Eubanks (1999) noted, "Conceptual metaphors are inseparable from the circumstances in which they are uttered, and thus they are always inflected by discursive conventions and ideological commitments" (p. 422). We can perhaps gain the most constructive insight into metaphors by regarding them as both conceptual - embedded in our thinking - and situated - embedded in our thinking in particular ways, for particular reasons that are subject to change. As Goatly (2007) observed, "[. . .] the influence of language upon our thought and perception of reality is most powerful when we are unaware of it, when it expresses hidden or, technically, latent ideology" (p. 27). In other words, the more natural a metaphor seems to us, the less likely we are to recognize, let alone question and disrupt, the values and assumptions underlying its construction and use. In this light, I will examine one of the central, recurring metaphors in rhetoric and composition: writing as entering an ongoing conversation.

BURKE'S CONVERSATION METAPHOR

Many scholars have cited or alluded to this passage from Burke's (1941) *The Philosophy of Literary Form*:

Imagine that you enter a parlor. You come late. When you arrive, others have long preceded you, and they are engaged in a heated discussion, a discussion too heated for them to pause and tell you exactly what it is about. In fact, the discussion had already begun long before any of them got there, so that no one present is qualified to retrace for you all the steps that had gone before. You listen for a while, until you decide that you have caught the tenor of the argument; then you put in your oar. Someone answers; you answer him; another comes to your defense; another aligns himself against you, to either the embarrassment or gratification of your opponent, depending upon the quality of your ally's assistance. However, the discussion is interminable. The hour grows late, you must depart. And you do depart, with the discussion still vigorously in progress. (pp. 110-11)

This passage, inspired by philosopher George Herbert Mead's notion of "unending conversation," surfaces again and again in composition books, journals, conferences, and literal conversations with colleagues and especially students. Considering how paramount this metaphor seems to our disciplinary identity, it deserves critical scrutiny. "It is not enough," insisted Eubanks (2001), "that we recognize, in a general way, the substantive ramifications of metaphor, not if we misunderstand the particular metaphors we encounter. As writing scholars, we need to be especially concerned about metaphors for language and writing" (p. 93). Indeed, the more widely and univocally the conversation metaphor circulates, the more deeply its ideological undercurrents escape us and the greater the potential that the unending conversation about conversation will degenerate into a monologue.

Scholars typically cite Burke's passage in two contexts, for two audiences: textbooks designed to introduce undergraduates to academic writing, and books and articles designed to introduce aspiring academics to scholarly writing. In both cases the purpose seems fundamentally the same - to orient readers to the world of academic discourse. Although composition textbooks aimed at undergraduates clearly have more immediate pedagogical impact than texts aimed at novice scholars, the latter texts are no less important, to the extent that they shape the discipline and influence the thinking of future generations of composition teachers and writing program administrators. I will turn first to how a popular college composition textbook uses the conversation metaphor to disguise its authors' conservative ideological values and to constrain possibilities for student writing.

PREPARING STUDENTS FOR THE PARLOR

One of the most widely adopted college composition textbooks today is Gerald Graff and Cathy Birkenstein's (2010)*They Say/I Say: The Moves that Matter in Academic Writing*. As the authors noted in the preface to the second edition, their book "is being used" in more than a thousand colleges and universities in the United States (p. xiii). That's nearly one fourth of U.S. institutions of higher learning (Snyder & Dillow, 2010, p. 287). Of course, *They Say/I Say* isn't required reading in all sections of all writing courses at all of these schools. Still, its influence is enormous. Because the conversation metaphor frames the whole book, *They Say/I Say* may represent the most prominent use of the metaphor in U.S. higher education today. Freshmen across the country are reading Burke's famous "parlor" passage, which Graff and Birkenstein quote early and allude to often. Because the authors' voice in the meta-conversation is disproportionately loud, and because their book's popularity suggests that their take on the conversation metaphor will be amplified for many years to come, how the authors interpret and apply the metaphor has significant implications for teaching and learning.

Having devoted my own teaching career to helping students write exploratory, idea-driven essays that embody what Spigelman (2004) has called "personal academic argument" (p. 14), and having read scathing critiques on the Writing Program Administrator's Listserv of Graff and Birkenstein's fill-in-the-blanks, template-based approach to helping students enter academic conversations, I have to admit I read the book with a skeptical eye. Far from being completely turned off, I was in fact impressed not just by the authors' good intentions in using the conversation metaphor and by their frequently excellent, practical advice about writing but also by the fact that they encourage students to embrace ambivalence, to welcome rather than shun the use of "I," to adopt colloquial language, and generally to think about academic writing in sophisticated, ethical ways. I frequently wrote "Yes!" and "Good example" in the margins. I'm thinking of assigning the book in my first-year writing seminar next semester.

Unfortunately, I do think Graff and Birkenstein overreach in their application of the conversation metaphor. They should have used it simply to establish the unending nature of academic conversations and to highlight the need for students to familiarize themselves with other voices before entering a conversation. They do this and they do it well, but they go on to insist that writers must join a given conversation "by stating clearly whether you agree, disagree, or both, using a direct, no-nonsense formula such as 'I agree,' 'I disagree,' or 'I am of two minds. I agree that _____, but I cannot agree that _____'" (p. 57). We can see this same insistence on directness in Graff's *Clueless in Academe: How Schooling Obscures the Life of the Mind* (2003), which also makes ample use of the conversation metaphor. In the epigraph to Clueless, entitled "How to Write an Argument: What Students and Teachers Really Need to Know," Graff wrote, "Make a claim, the sooner the better, preferably flagged for the reader by a phrase like 'My claim here is that. [sic] . . .'" (p. 275). Whatever the merits of this "sooner the better" approach to academic writing, it does not stem logically from the conversation metaphor, which suggests no clear limitations on how one can enter a conversation. Graff and Birkenstein thus piggy-back on Burke's passage to make a point that the metaphor itself doesn't imply.

In *They Say/I Say*, Graff and Birkenstein have insisted that "all writers need to answer the 'so what?' and 'who cares?' questions up front" - advice that Burke himself could hardly be said to have followed in his own prolific writing (p. 93). According to Warnock (1986), "Burke's meaning is not only in what he says but in what he does: the roundabout approach, as the reader learns to cope with it, provides an attitude, which in turn allows a 'way in,' a positive identification with Burke, until the negative sets in and the cycling begins again" (p. 72). In other words, Burke creates meaning not by bonking readers over the head ASAP with thesis statements but by inviting and challenging readers to experience his dynamic texts in all their unfolding, suggestive complexity. Burke's "indirectness is a way of avoiding oversimplification" (Warnock, 1986, p. 70). According to Elbow (2006), "Successful writers lead us on a journey to satisfaction by way of expectations, frustrations, half-satisfactions, and temporary satisfactions: a well-planned sequence of yearnings and reliefs, itches and scratches. This is a central insight from Burke" (p. 626). Granted, few of us would cheer if *They Say/I Say* were to teach students to write like Burke, even if such a task were possible in 243 pages. Still, Graff and Birkenstein seem to conflate two distinct claims: 1) the need to familiarize oneself with an ongoing conversation before joining it, and 2) the need to enter a conversation in a particular way. The conversation metaphor implies the former but not the latter. If anything, asking students to enter a conversation would seem to invite a more leisurely, dialogic, narrative structure - a point I will address later.

That said, I can't really blame Graff and Birkenstein for hyperextending Burke's metaphor as they have. Not only have other scholars applied the metaphor similarly in the past, but much of Burke's own language in the "parlor" passage suggests a more expeditious, agonistic approach to conversation than his philosophy warrants.

Such complexity should not be unexpected. As Ritchie (2003) noted,

When a term such as 'attack,' 'defend,' or 'strategy' appears in a discussion of an argument, we cannot be sure whether any particular person will associate the term with chess, boxing, or all-out war - or with nothing beyond an abstract concept. How any particular speaker intends a metaphor to be interpreted, and how any particular hearer does interpret the metaphor, can never be absolutely determined. (p. 138)

Although metaphors have this inherently ambiguous quality, we can consider their rhetorical contexts to help find plausible interpretations of their meaning. For example, Joseph Harris (2006), in his own impressive if similarly restrictive composition textbook *Rewriting: How to Do Things with Texts*, acknowledged the irony of Burke's language, noting that his famous passage "fails to suggest the larger aim of Burke's writing, which was to theorize a 'rhetoric of courtship,' a discourse that strives for agreement rather than confrontation, identification rather than division" (p. 35). He went on to note that "despite Burke's somewhat militarist talk of allies and opponents, the metaphor also hints at the more civil tone of much academic work. [. . .] The arts of conversation are subtler than those of debate; they join our need to articulate the differences among us with our need to keep talking with one another" (p. 36). Brummet (1995) offered an even more nuanced reading of Burke, noting that

the passage moves from conflict through exchange to progress. Note that when one arrives, the discussion is heated; we are told so twice. But soon there appears a "tenor" to the argument, tenor defined as "the flow of meaning apparent in something written or spoken." [. . .] Tenor is a word of concord, of shared purpose and goals, in other words. Neither a shouting match nor a brawl has a tenor. [. . .] By the time one leaves the parlor, what started as "heated" has turned into a "discussion still vigorously in progress," in other words, a dialogue that is getting somewhere. (p. 224)

Of course, the dialogue never does arrive at a final destination. If it did, the conversation would hardly be "unending." But it is important, as Harris and Brummet remind us, to read Burke's metaphor in the context of his philosophy.

To be sure, Graff and Birkenstein are hardly unique in asking students to get to the point in their academic writing. Demands for hasty declarations of certitude pervade most composition textbooks. Heilker (1996) noted that his survey of 29 textbooks and rhetorics "reveals a litany consistently intoning that the thesis statement is a necessary part of the ritual, an indispensable part of effective writing [. . .]" (p. 1). By wedding this insistence on haste with the conversation metaphor, Graff and Birkenstein offer students what amounts to a polite invitation punctuated by a fist-slamming demand: "Listen thoughtfully and then join the conversation - pronto!"

Such worship of efficiency contradicts the advice of the Writing Study Group of the NCTE Executive Committee. In their 2004 statement "NCTE Beliefs about the Teaching of Writing," the group noted that "[w]hen writers actually write, they think of things that they did not have in mind before they began writing. The act of writing generates ideas" (para. 16). ("Writing to learn" pedagogies take this insight to heart, albeit within the limited confines, often, of short, low-stakes writing tasks.) The more we pressure students to hurry up and develop a thesis, the less incentive they have to discover ideas as they write, let alone to provide in their final drafts what Hoy (2001a) has called "one of the cherished gifts afforded to reader and writer alike: a picture of a mind thinking" (p. 45). Warnock (1986) noted that "[t]he reader experiences Burke's mind at work [. . .]" (p. 72), making it that much harder to imagine him applauding the reduction of his metaphor

to an "academic version of Madlibs" (Arthur & Case-Halferty, 2008). According to Winterowd (1983), "Put into the admonitory terms of the composition handbook, Burke's ideas might read something like this: Find a representative anecdote (instead of a thesis or enthymeme), and follow its implications as far as you can, dramatistically" (p. 585). Winterowd's suspicion "that Burke's tacit advice and its concomitant method have kept him outside the traditional mainstream" (p. 586) seems especially ironic in light of the success of *They Say/I Say*. By asking students to invoke an impatient reader and by offering them one choice of how to enter an academic conversation, Graff & Birkenstein - and the thousands of writing instructors who assign their book, presuming they don't add the kind of disruptive caveat I'm adding here - serve as guardians of the parlor, etiquette police who shush even the most knowledgeable would-be participants who seek to join academic conversations in "inappropriate" ways.

To be fair, Graff and Birkenstein have noted that "listening closely to others and summarizing what they have to say can help writers generate their own ideas," and they do advocate a kinder, gentler form of academic writing (p. xx). They urge students to consider others' voices and perspectives with an open mind, and they even encourage students to value ambivalence - an almost sacrilegious notion in most composition textbooks. At the same time, Graff and Birkenstein tend to oversimplify things, not only by insisting that academic conversationalists cut to the chase but also by asking students to "plant a naysayer in the text" - a concept that, in these words, all but invites students to insert precisely the sorts of disingenuous, token nods to opposing views that the authors elsewhere wisely caution students to avoid.

Unfortunately, even their encouragement of ambivalence feels half-hearted. Consider the following template, which is supposed to illustrate how "the 'they say/i say' format also works to both agree and disagree at the same time" (p. 8): "He claims that _____, and I have mixed feelings about it. On the one hand, I agree that _____. On the other hand, I still insist that _____" (p. 9). The phrase "I still insist" in this thesis statement lingers as the author's "main point" and thus precludes real, persistent ambivalence. A nearly identical template appears under the anti-ambivalence subheading "Templates for Making Concessions While Still Standing Your Ground": "On the one hand, I agree with X that _____. But on the other hand, I still insist that _____" (p. 89). Only two of the book's 163 templates encourage lasting ambivalence (p. 66). Such restrictions stifle genuine inquiry and work against the open-minded spirit of the conversation metaphor. Real conversations accommodate inquiry and ambivalence, and they evolve in countless ways. Although the pedagogical implications of this insight for those who use the conversation metaphor may cause discomfort, we do ourselves and our students a disservice by denying it. As Burdick and Sandlin (2010) argued, "Resolving anti-institutional discourse into the language of the institution recasts the colonial project as described by Willinsky (1999) and Bhabba (1992, 2004) and reduces the possibility of the unknown, the new, and the Other/wise to rigid, static categories" (p. 357).

DISCIPLINE AND PUBLISH

Because prevailing attitudes about the conversation metaphor in most college composition textbooks, including *They Say/I Say*, derive from rhetoric and composition, how the discipline trains new scholars to think about the metaphor has enormous implications for pedagogy. I will examine Gary A. Olson's (1997) "Publishing Scholarship in Rhetoric and Composition: Joining the Conversation" - an important, representative work explicitly designed to shape the future of the discipline at a crucial stage of its development. Olson's text, which appears in the book he co-edited *Publish-*

ing in Rhetoric and Composition, aims to teach new scholars in rhetoric and composition what it means to join an ongoing scholarly conversation.

Olson draws heavily on Burke's metaphor to explain why and how new scholars should follow the conventions of academic discourse if they want to publish in scholarly journals. He advised newcomers to "acquire a sense of the larger conversation" before "rushing into print about this or that subject." He argued that this conversational awareness is a way of "preventing you from tackling an issue that has long been laid to rest" (p. 21).

But if scholarship is so dynamic, how can it lay anything to rest? When one theory gains prominence in a field, does that mean that counter-theories have been laid to rest? As Brummett (1995) observed, in Burke's parlor scholars cannot lay any issue to rest. He wrote, "It is the fact of turn-taking and not of victory or superiority that is featured in this vision of 'argument'; notice we never discover who 'wins.' Winning would tragically end the conversation" (p. 223). If the scholarly conversation never ends, how can anyone presume to bury an issue, let alone know "where each conversation is leading," as Olson suggested savvy scholars should (p. 21)?

Olson explained that "the scholarly article has changed drastically" in the last 20 years from "a kind of leisurely 'journey' through a subject, meandering from point to point, often reserving its thesis for the very end of the article" to a succinct, direct argument that "is more a kind of technical writing in your given field than a leisurely and entertaining sojourn." To illustrate the implications of this transformation, Olson quoted one editor's dictum: "I can't afford an article that meanders." He added that the editor's "concerns are fairly representative of those of all editors" (p. 25). In other words, anyone who wants to enter a scholarly conversation in rhetoric and composition should engage in a technical transaction of information rather than in a leisurely and entertaining sojourn that meanders toward cumulative insight.

But isn't a conversation in fact more like a leisurely and entertaining sojourn - in other words, more like an essay - than a technical transaction? Experience suggests so, and scholars emphasize the informality and structural flexibility of conversations. For example, Thornbury and Slade (2006) noted that "conversation is characterized by an informal style" (p. 20), and they defined conversation as "the informal, interactive talk between two or more people, which happens in real time, is spontaneous, has a largely interpersonal function, and in which participants share symmetrical rights" (p. 25). Sawyer (2001) maintained that "all conversations are improvised and creative" (P. 3). He pointed out that "[a]nthropologists have studied just about every world language, and no matter where you go, people are creative in conversations [. . .]" (p. 62). Based on the way scholars in rhetoric and composition highlight the importance of conventional "moves" when invoking the conversation metaphor, you would never guess that creativity is an essential component of conversation.

Similarly, you would never guess that a conversation is often precisely like what Olson suggested it is unlike: "a kind of leisurely 'journey' through a subject, meandering from point to point" (Olson, p. 25). According to Rundell (2002), "As corpus data shows, we frequently see conversations and discussions as a sort of journey, with the speakers going from one place to another. Conversations drift, move from point to point, and sometimes take unexpected turns" (P. 21). The very etymology of converse reveals its earliest meanings to include "to move to and fro" and "to move about" (Converse). So it seems that, in fact, writing a scholarly journal article using established conventions is extremely unlike participating in a conversation. To be ethical and precise, those who would invite new scholars or students to join an ongoing conversation in writing should acknowledge where the metaphor's logic ends and their own disciplinary or pedagogical agenda begins.

Again, to argue that one must become familiar with other participants' contributions to an ongoing conversation before joining that conversation is a perfectly reasonable expectation. This is true of spoken conversations as well. "To join a conversation," Sawyer noted, "we have to pay particularly close attention to its flow, and wait for an opportunity to join in" (p. 54). It is an entirely separate demand, however, to insist that only writers who "get to the point" fast, who write explicit thesis statements, and who view communication as a sender-receiver transaction, are authorized to enter the parlor and make a contribution. A discourse community's conventions should not be confused with its conversations.

To emphasize his point that journal editors demand efficiency, Olson quoted William Van Til, "author of over 250 scholarly publications," on the proper way to conduct a conversation in a scholarly journal: "In writing for your fellow scholars, tell them in your opening precisely and sharply what your article will be about" (p. 25). This demand to sharpen one's rhetoric blends well with Olson's view that "[u]nderstanding the nature of scholarship is half the battle" when trying to get published (p. 20). Graff, too, has repeatedly praised student texts that are "sharply argued" (p. 164) and "more pointed" (p. 166) by "forceful arguers" (p. 172). Graff and Birkenstein tend to avoid such phrases in They Say/I Say, and they include Deborah Tannen's excellent essay "Agonism in the Academy: Surviving the Argument Culture" at the end of their book. But Tannen has the feeling of a "naysayer" that Graff and Birkenstein have planted to win over skeptical readers. The implicit message remains: Sharpen your rhetoric, if not for battle, then for readers who must know your "point" right away.

Of course, there are all kinds of conversations, and they vary by culture and context. I don't mean to suggest that journal editors should publish or that students should write rambling pieces that read like transcripts of trivial conversations over breakfast. Still, the notion that conversations, unlike debates, are often like informal journeys, raises doubts about Olson's appropriation of the metaphor. He wrote:

The fact that the modern scholarly article is streamlined and to the point is in keeping with our conversation metaphor. If you really do want to make a true contribution to an ongoing conversation, you certainly are not going to risk being interrupted or abandoned before you get to your point; rather, you're going to make your point immediately and then provide the appropriate evidence and examples to support it. The same is true of the contemporary scholarly article. (p. 25)

Olson here assumes that rhetoric and composition as a field has unanimously agreed to view conversation as a series of terse, trenchant exchanges. "Editors of scholarly journals," he wrote, "agree that one of the most common and frustrating problems with submitted articles is a failure on the part of authors to express their thesis clearly and early in the article. [. . .] It is extremely frustrating to be reading page after page of a submitted article and still find yourself questioning, 'What is this author's point, anyway?'" (p. 25) Presumably readers who, like Graff and Birkenstein, continually ask (and require their students to ask one another of their academic writing) "So what?" and "Who cares?" see value in literature and in essays of the sort that routinely appear in *The Best American Essays*, despite their authors' consistent failure to answer these questions upfront. Why the impatience with student writers and aspiring scholars? We should disrupt the assumption that such writers deserve fewer creative options, fewer means of persuasion.

According to Robert Atwan (1998), series editor of *The Best American Essays*, "What was especially maddening about the typical five-paragraph theme had less to do with its tedious structure than with its implicit message that writing should be the end product of thought and not the enactment of its process" (p. xi). He

has called the five-paragraph essay "a charade. It not only paraded relentlessly to its conclusion; it began with its conclusion. It was all about its conclusion. Its structure permitted no change of direction, no reconsideration, no wrestling with ideas. It was - and still is - the perfect vehicle for the sort of reader who likes to ask: 'And your point is . . .?'" (p. xii). In other words, it - or, rather, its glorified non-five-paragraph contemporary counterpart - is the perfect vehicle for readers like Graff and Birkenstein.

BRUFFEE, CONVERSATION, AND GENRE

I fear that if the prevailing application of the conversation metaphor continues to go unchallenged, it will be invoked in increasingly hegemonic ways. As Semino (2008) pointed out, "[. . .] when particular uses of metaphor become the dominant way of talking about a particular aspect of reality within a particular discourse, they may be extremely difficult to perceive and challenge, since they come to represent the 'commonsense' or 'natural' view of things" (p.33). By tracing the conversation metaphor over time, we can see how it has continued to circulate yet also disappear, much as a pebble tossed into a pond forms concentric circles whose ripples gradually vanish.

In his influential essay "Collaborative Learning and the 'Conversation of Mankind,'" Kenneth A. Bruffee (1984) created a ripple by arguing that allegiance to a discourse community's prevailing discourse conventions should serve as a prerequisite for contributing to that community's conversations. "Mastery of a knowledge community's normal discourse," he wrote, "is the basic qualification for acceptance into that community." What is *normal discourse*? According to Bruffee, "Normal discourse is pointed; it is explanatory and argumentative. Its purpose is to justify belief to the satisfaction of other people within the author's community of knowledgeable peers" ("Collaborative," p. 643). Although the title of his article alludes to Michael Oakeshott's 1959 essay "The Voice of Poetry in the Conversation of Mankind," Bruffee hardly shares the late philosopher's understanding of what a conversation means. Oakeshott (1962) considered a conversation "an unrehearsed intellectual adventure" in which "there is no 'truth' to be discovered, no proposition to be proved, no conclusion sought. [Participants] are not concerned to inform, to persuade, or to refute one another, and therefore the cogency of their utterances does not depend upon their all speaking in the same idiom" (p. 197). Seen in this light, conversation is pretty much the opposite of "normal discourse."

To his credit, Bruffee did acknowledge that abnormal discourse is also "necessary to learning," but he added that "ironically, abnormal discourse cannot be directly taught." He explained, "We must teach practical rhetoric and critical analysis in such a way that, when necessary, students can turn to abnormal discourse in order to undermine their own and other people's reliance on the canonical conventions and vocabulary of normal discourse." In a class where students systematically learn to write normal discourse, complete with its "canonical conventions," and where they are graded on their ability to practice this discourse, it is hard to imagine why students would dare to engage in abnormal discourse - let alone how. Bruffee simply stated that we should teach discourse conventions "in such a way that students can set them aside, if only momentarily, for the purpose of reconstituting knowledge communities in more satisfactory ways" ("Collaborative" p.648). The significant caveat "if only momentarily" hints at the apparent disingenuousness of his concession. A more direct statement of Bruffee's (1986) ideology appears in his claim that "the purpose of education - hence the job teachers are hired to do - is to induct people into the mores and values of the 'state,' that is, the prevailing culture" ("Kenneth" p. 77). This statement is a much clearer, more direct, and more disturbing expression of Bruffee's values than his

feel-good pronouncements about "collaborative learning" or his stumbling concessions to would-be practitioners of "abnormal discourse."

Petraglia (1991) noted that "social constructionists do not explain how a minority's knowledge can exist in the face of consensus, much less alter that knowledge. From where do individuals derive unconventional ideas, and how can the expression of this 'abnormal' discourse be tolerated?" (para. 38). Other critics of Bruffee have observed that he uses the conversation metaphor in a very restricted way. France (1994), for example, argued that "the conversation metaphor disguises not only who may speak but also what may be spoken" (p. 102). He observed,

If all knowledge is composed of 'community-generated, community-maintaining symbolic artifacts' ['Social Construction,' p. 777], the language of each community becomes a solipsistic circle of self-referentiality. [...] To equate knowledge with conformity to an institutional discourse is ideological as well as epistemological, and the rhetoric of consensus is most handy to those whose oxen are not being gored. (p. 104)

As Charteris-Black (2004) argued, "The advantage of using metaphors - especially those that have become the conventional ways of expressing certain points of view - is that this taps into an accepted communal system of values" (pp. 11-12). Unfortunately, the conversation metaphor seems especially handy to those who promote the rhetoric of consensus.

Indeed, most uses of the conversation metaphor have a calm, reassuring tone. Trimbur (1997) pinpointed the problem beneath such ho-hum reassurances:

"This," we tell students, "is the way we [English teachers, biologists, lawyers, chemical engineers, social workers, whatever] do things around here. There's nothing magical about it. It's just the way we talk to each other." The problem is

that invoking the "real world" authority of such consensual practices neutralizes the critical and transformative project of collaborative learning, depoliticizes it, and reduces it to an acculturative technique. (p. 450)

Rather than brand unconventional approaches to writing (and thus thinking) "abnormal" and shush their practitioners out of the parlor, we should invite more heterogeneous voices and forms of discourse into the parlor. As Zembylas & Boler (2002) argued, "A pedagogy of discomfort requires that individuals step outside of their comfort zones and recognize what and how one has been taught to see (or not see)." It may not be feasible to reappropriate the term abnormal discourse - to transform it from a derogatory term into a point of pride, à la queer theory - but we should disrupt the notion of normal discourse, lest the Burkean parlor become an echo chamber of textual normativity.

IMPLICATIONS FOR PEDAGOGY

My title announces that I want to "reclaim" the conversation metaphor, but I don't presume to claim its meaning in any pure, final sense. What I really want to do is encourage critical reflection about conceptual metaphors related to teaching and learning. Rather than abandon and struggle to replace potentially insightful conceptual metaphors that are conventional - yet not so conventional that they cease to be recognizable as metaphors - it may be more constructive to point out the ways in which these metaphors' contextual uses can undermine the concepts they illustrate. In the case of the conversation metaphor, Newkirk (1989) posed one of the most relevant yet least asked pedagogical questions in composition studies: "Do current approaches to teaching expository writing promote or do they actually foreclose possibilities for open-ended, conversation-like, exploration?" (p. 6). I don't have space to analyze the metaphor

argument is exploration or to detail a disruptive pedagogy that promotes authentically conversational academic writing (see Elbow, 1987, 2006; Ellis, 2012; Heilker, 1996, 2006; Hoy, 2001a, 2001b, 2001c, 2005, 2009; Spigelman, 2004), but I will argue that the exploratory essay, not the thesis-driven article, is the genre most reminiscent of conversation.

According to Lopate (1997), "The conversational dynamic - the desire for contact - is ingrained in the [essay] form and serves to establish a quick emotional intimacy with the audience" (p. xxv). Newkirk (2005) argued, "The reader of the essay, like the participants in a good conversation, did not seek to carry away precepts or conclusions. Montaigne claimed that he was more concerned with the 'manner' of speaking than the 'matter,' the 'form' as much as the 'substance' [...]." Indeed, Newkirk continued, "The manner of seeking, the wondering was more important than the truthfulness of that which was found - because any truth was provisional, sure to be undone or revised by subsequent inquiries" (p. 12). Montaigne's epistemological skepticism should strike contemporary readers as virtually post-modern, and considering his engagement with an exceptional array of thinkers and texts and ideas, he can hardly be written off as a solipsist. He may have written his essays in his chateau tower, but his writing continues to resound in the Burkean parlor.

Anyone who wants student to join academic conversations in conversational ways should invite students to explore their own ideas. The essay provides the perfect genre. According to Kirklighter (2002), "Instead of working toward definitive conclusions, as in an article, the essay's spontaneity allows the writer to wander, to make connections in unusual places, to emphasize discoveries instead of conclusions" (p. 6). Teaching this kind of essay successfully is hard but rewarding. Pat C. Hoy II (2009), who directs the Expository Writing Program at New York University, has devoted his career to teaching the essay in precisely this way via progressions, each of which is "a series of reading, writing, thinking, and imagining exercises that lead to an essay" (p. 305). Hoy (2001c) wants students to develop "a supple idea, something more akin to notion than to thesis. Not a simple declarative sentence promising proof but a more digressive invitation to the reader to participate in an excursion, an exploration, an inquiry" (p. 23) - in short, a conversation. Students move "from evidence to idea to essay" (Hoy, 2009, p. 307) - an inductive process that challenges students' preconceptions of good academic writing and that also challenges instructors, who must help students develop ideas and craft their writing exercises into complex but coherent essays that become journeys toward cumulative insight. As Hoy (2009) has explained,

[...] inductive reasoning does not lead to certainty, to a thesis that can be "proved"; it leads instead to discovery, to the rigorous combination and application of analysis and imagination, to ideas that must, like the evidence itself, be continually reassessed and reconceptualized to represent more accurately whatever truth the evidence suggests to [students]. [...] This inductive process is, of course, the same process that leads to discovery in science or in any other academic discipline. (p. 307)

Essays that emerge inductively from progressions may annoy impatient readers skimming for thesis statements and topic sentences, and they will never conform to fill-in-the-blanks formulas, but they do offer patient, curious readers rewarding contributions to ongoing conversations. As Barnard (2010) wondered in "The Ruse of Clarity," "Surely inexpert complexity is preferable to expert simplicity if it is indicative of intellectual wrestling and scholarly ambition rather than the complacency of comfort?" (p. 446).

In my own composition courses, I teach progressions ranging from a reflective analysis of personal food choices - an assignment that asks students to explore the ethical, environmental,

and health implications of what they eat, in light of works by Michael Pollan, Eric Schlosser, and others - to an ambivalence-based research argument. The latter assignment invites and challenges students to embrace uncertainty, which, according to Recchio (1994), is "a fundamental quality of the essay form" (p. 272). Students first choose a controversial issue about which they feel ambivalent - no easy task in itself - and then explore that controversy not only in their research but also in their writing. If their inquiry persuades them to hold a particular position on the controversy, then I ask them to write their final essay for their previous, ambivalent selves - the side of them that recently saw merit in opposing views. By drawing upon their annotated sources and their reflective, exploratory writing, including their idea maps, their dialogues with themselves (useful as an early exercise to test the sincerity of their ambivalence - and fun to have them perform in class), and their letters to a friend (talk about a conversational genre), students can retrace the rhetorical paths that shaped their beliefs and structure their essays to persuade skeptical readers accordingly. If students remain ambivalent, they need not pretend otherwise and can frame their lack of conviction as a reasonable compromise amid swirls of extremism. Such progressions honor the spirit of inquiry so central to ongoing conversations. As Seitz (1991) pointed out, "The story of acquiring more power as a writer is not, as composition often implies, simply that of gaining greater control over language, but also a story of *seeing where a lack of control will take you*" (p. 292).

As first-year writing faces increasing scrutiny about its relevance beyond itself (Bawarshi, 2003; Devitt, 2007; Downs & Wardle, 2007; Smit, 2004; Wardle, 2007), the essay offers the potential to give students a valuable ability to think not only critically but originally. Whereas students who write academic "papers" must follow a formula and construct good thesis statements - which may or may not contain original ideas - students who compose essays must contemplate how to join conversations by developing original ideas in interesting ways.

In "An Immodest Proposal for Connecting High School and College," Graff and Birkenstein (2009) cited David Bartholomae's (1985) influential article "Inventing the University," as well as work by Irene Clark and Joseph Harris, as "evidence of an emerging consensus on the conversational nature of academic discourse" (p. W416). I hope they're wrong. Nothing stifles an ongoing conversation like consensus, especially when the consensus involves a metaphor that offers so much unexplored pedagogical potential. As the hour grows late, will the meta-conversation still be vigorously in progress?

REFERENCES

Arthur, J., & Case-Halferty, A. (2008). Review of the book *They Say/I Say*. *Composition Forum, 18*. Retrieved from http://compositionforum.com/issue/18/they-say-i-say-review.php

Atwan, R. (1998). Foreword. In Atwan, R. (Ed.), *The best American essays 1998* (pp. xi–xiii). New York, NY: Houghton Mifflin.

Barnard, I. (2010). The ruse of clarity. *College Composition and Communication, 61*(3), 434–451.

Bartholomae, D. (1985). Inventing the university. In Rose, M. (Ed.), *When a writer can't write: Studies in writer's block and other composing-process problems* (pp. 134–165). New York, NY: Guilford.

Bawarshi, A. (2003). *Genre and the invention of the writer: Reconsidering the place of invention in composition*. Logan, UT: Utah State University Press.

Bennett, J. (2001). Liberal learning as conversation. *Liberal Education, 87*(2), 32–39.

Boler, M. (1999). *Feeling power: Emotions and education*. New York, NY: Routledge.

Bruffee, K. (1984). Collaborative learning and the "conversation of mankind". *College English, 46*(7), 635–652. doi:10.2307/376924

Bruffee, K. A. (1986). Kenneth A. Bruffee responds. *College English, 48*(1), 77–78. doi:10.2307/376589

Brummet, B. (1995). Speculations on the discovery of a Burkean blunder. *Rhetoric Review, 14*(1), 221–225. doi:10.1080/07350199509389061

Burdick, J., & Sandlin, J. (2010). Inquiry as answerability: Toward a methodology of discomfort in researching critical public pedagogies. *Qualitative Inquiry, 16*(5), 349–360. doi:10.1177/1077800409358878

Burke, K. (1941). *The philosophy of literary form*. Berkeley, CA: University of California Press.

Charteris-Black, J. (2004). *Corpus approaches to critical metaphor analysis*. New York, NY: Palgrave Macmillan. doi:10.1057/9780230000612

Converse. (2010). In J. Simpson (Ed.), *Oxford English Dictionary*. Retrieved from http://dictionary.oed.com

Devitt, A. (2007). Transferability and genres. In Keller, C., & Weisser, C. (Eds.), *The locations of composition* (pp. 215–227). Albany, NY: State University of New York Press.

Downs, D., & Wardle, E. (2007). Teaching about writing, righting misconceptions: (Re)Envisioning "First-year composition" as "introduction to writing studies". *College Composition and Communication, 58*(4), 552–585.

Elbow, P. (1987). Closing my eyes as i speak: An argument for ignoring audience. *College English, 49*(1), 50–69. doi:10.2307/377789

Elbow, P. (2006). The music of form: Rethinking organization in writing. *College Composition and Communication, 57*(4), 620–666.

Ellis, E. (2012). Back to the future? The pedagogical promise of the (multimedia) essay. In Whithaus, C., & Bowen, T. (Eds.), *Multimodal literacies and emerging genres in student compositions*. Pittsburgh, PA: University of Pittsburgh Press.

Eubanks, P. (1999). The story of conceptual metaphor: What motivates metaphoric mappings? *Poetics Today, 20*(3), 419–442.

Eubanks, P. (2001). Understanding metaphors for writing: In defense of the conduit metaphor. *College Composition and Communication, 53*(1), 92–118. doi:10.2307/359064

France, A. (1994). *Composition as a cultural practice*. Westport, CT: Bergin & Garvey.

Goatly, A. (2007). *Washing the brain: Metaphor and hidden ideology*. Philadelphia, PA: John Benjamins.

Graff, G. (2003). *Clueless in academe: How schooling obscures the life of the mind*. New Haven, CT: Yale University Press.

Graff, G., & Birkenstein, C. (2009). An immodest proposal for connecting high school and college. *College Composition and Communication, 61*(1), W409-416.

Graff, G., & Birkenstein, C. (2010). *They say / I say: The moves that matter in academic writing*. New York, NY: Norton.

Harris, J. (2006). *Rewriting: How to do things with texts*. Logan, UT: Utah State University Press.

Heilker, P. (1996). *The essay: Theory and pedagogy for an active form*. Urbana, IL: NCTE.

Heilker, P. (2006). Twenty years in: An essay in two parts. *College Composition and Communication, 58*(2), 182–212.

Hoy, P. (2001a). The disarming seduction of stories. *Writing on the Edge, 12*(1), 41–48.

Hoy, P. (2001b). The outreach of an idea. *Rhetoric Review, 20*, 351–358.

Hoy, P. (2001c). Requiem for the outline. *Writing on the Edge, 12*(2), 19–27.

Hoy, P. (2005). The art of essaying. *Rhetoric Review, 24*(3), 316–339. doi:10.1207/s15327981rr2403_5

Hoy, P. (2009). Healing conceptual blindness. *Rhetoric Review, 28*(3), 304–324. doi:10.1080/07350190902958933

Kirklighter, C. (2002). *Traversing the democratic borders of the essay*. Albany, NY: State University of New York Press.

Lakoff, G., & Johnson, M. (1980). Conceptual metaphor in everyday language. *The Journal of Philosophy, 77*(8), 453–486. doi:10.2307/2025464

Lakoff, G., & Turner, M. (1989). *More than cool reason: A field guide to poetic metaphor*. Chicago, IL: University of Chicago Press.

Lopate, P. (1997). *The art of the personal essay: An anthology from the classical era to the present*. New York, NY: Anchor Books.

NCTE Writing Study Group. (2004). *NCTE beliefs about the teaching of writing*. National Council of Teachers of English. Retrieved from http://www.ncte.org/positions/statements/writingbeliefs

Newkirk, T. (1989). *Critical thinking and writing: Reclaiming the essay*. Urbana, IL: NCTE.

Newkirk, T. (2005). Montaigne's revisions. *Rhetoric Review, 24*(3), 298–315. doi:10.1207/s15327981rr2403_4

Oakeshott, M. (1962). The voice of poetry in the conversation of mankind. In *Rationalism in politics and other essays* (pp. 197–247). London, UK: Methuen.

Olson, G. (1997). Publishing scholarship in rhetoric and composition: Joining the conversation. In Olson, G., & Taylor, T. (Eds.), *Publishing in rhetoric and composition* (pp. 19–33). Albany, NY: State University of New York Press.

Petraglia, J. (1991). Interrupting the conversation: The constructionist dialogue in composition. *JAC*, *11*(1), 37–55.

Pollan, M. (2006). *The omnivore's dilemma: A natural history of four meals*. New York, NY: Penguin.

Recchio, T. (1994). On the critical necessity of "essaying.". In Tobin, L., & Newkirk, T. (Eds.), *Taking stock: The writing process movement in the 90s* (pp. 219–235). Portsmouth, NH: Boynton/Cook.

Ritchie, D. (2003). Argument is war - Or is it a game of chess? Multiple meanings in the analysis of implicit metaphors. *Metaphor and Symbol*, *18*(2), 125–146. doi:10.1207/S15327868MS1802_4

Rundell, M. (2002). Metaphorically speaking. *English Teaching Professional*, *23*, 21–29.

Sawyer, R. (2001). *Creative conversations: Improvisation in everyday discourse*. Cresskill, NJ: Hampton.

Schlosser, E. (2001). *Fast food nation: The dark side of the all-American meal*. Boston, MA: Houghton.

Schmid, H., & Ungerer, F. (1996). *An introduction to cognitive linguistics*. New York, NY: Longman.

Seitz, J. (1991). Composition's misunderstanding of metaphor. *College Composition and Communication*, *42*(3), 288–298. doi:10.2307/358072

Semino, E. (2008). *Metaphor in discourse*. Cambridge, UK: Cambridge University Press.

Smit, D. (2004). *The end of composition studies*. Carbondale, IL: Southern Illinois University Press.

Snyder, D., & Dillow, S. (2010). *Digest of education statistics 2009*. Washington, DC: National Center for Education Statistics.

Spigelman, C. (2004). *Personally speaking: Experience as evidence in academic discourse*. Carbondale, IL: Southern Illinois University Press.

Stockwell, P. (2002). *Cognitive poetics: An introduction*. New York, NY: Routledge.

Thornbury, S., & Slade, D. (2006). *Conversation: From description to pedagogy*. Cambridge, UK: Cambridge University Press. doi:10.1017/CBO9780511733123

Trimbur, J. (1997). Consensus and difference in collaborative learning. In Villaneuva, V. (Ed.), *Cross-talk in comp theory* (pp. 439–456). Urbana, IL: NCTE.

Wardle, E. (2007). Understanding 'transfer' from FYC: Preliminary results of a longitudinal study. *WPA*, *31*(2), 65–85.

Warnock, T. (1986). Reading Kenneth Burke: Ways in, ways out, ways roundabout. *College English*, *48*(1), 62–75. doi:10.2307/376587

Winterowd, R. (1983). Dramatism in themes and poems. *College English*, *45*(6), 581–588. doi:10.2307/377144

Zembylas, M., & Boler, M. (2002). On the spirit of patriotism: Challenges of a "pedagogy of discomfort". *Teachers College Record*. Retrieved from http://www.tcrecord.org

ADDITIONAL READING

Adorno, T. (1991-1992). The Essay as Form. In Tiedemann, R. (Ed.), *Notes to Literature* (pp. 9–49). (Nicholsen, S. W., Trans.). New York: Columbia University Press.

Agger, B. (1990). *The Decline of Discourse: Reading, Writing, and Resistance in Postmodern Capitalism*. London: Falmer.

Anderson, C. (Ed.). (1989). *Literary Nonfiction: Theory, Criticism, Pedagogy*. Carbondale: Southern Illinois University Press.

Andrews, R. (2003). The End of the Essay? *Teaching in Higher Education, 8*(1), 117–128. doi:10.1080/1356251032000052366

Annas, P. (1985). Style as Politics: A Feminist Approach to the Teaching of Writing. *College English, 47*, 360–372. doi:10.2307/376958

Atwan, R. (1998). *Foreword. The Best American Essays 1998* (pp. xi–xiii). New York: Houghton Mifflin.

Bishop, W. (2003). Preaching What he Practices: Jim Corder's Irascible and Articulate Oeuvre. In Enos, T., & Miller, K. (Eds.), *Beyond Postprocess and Postmodernism: Essays on the Spaciousness of Rhetoric* (pp. 89–101). Mahwah, NJ: Lawrence Erlbaum.

Bloom, L. (1990). Why Don't we Write What we Teach? And Publish it? *Journal of Advanced Composition, 10*, 87–100.

Connors, R. (2000). Erasure of the Sentence. *College Composition and Communication, 52*(1), 96–128. doi:10.2307/358546

Corder, J. (1985). Argument as Emergence, Rhetoric as Love. *Rhetoric Review, 4*, 16–32. doi:10.1080/07350198509359100

Corder, J. (1991). Academic Jargon and Soul-Searching Drivel. *Rhetoric Review, 9*, 314–326. doi:10.1080/07350199109388936

D'Agata. J. (Ed.). (2003). *The Next American Essay*. Saint Paul: Graywolf Press.

D'Agata. J. (Ed.). (2009). *Lost Origins of the Essay*. Saint Paul: Graywolf Press. Ede, L. (2004). *Situating Composition: Composition Studies and the Politics of Location*. Carbondale: Sothern Illinois University Press.

Gage, J. (1995). Why Write? In Jolliffe, D., & Covino, W. (Eds.), *Rhetoric: Concepts, Definitions, Boundaries* (pp. 715–733). Boston: Allyn and Bacon.

Goleman, J. (2004). An "Immensely Simplified Task": Form in mModern Composition- Rhetoric. *College Composition and Communication, 69*, 51–71. doi:10.2307/4140680

Good, G. (1988). *The Observing Self: Rediscovering the Essay*. London: Routledge.

Hall, M. (1989). The Emergence of the Essay and the Idea of Discovery. In Butrym, A. (Ed.), *Essays on the Essay: Redefining the Genre* (pp. 253–270). Athens, GA: University of Georgia Press.

Joeres, B., Mittman, R., & Mittman, E. (Eds.). (1993). *The Politics of the Essay*. Bloomington: Indiana University Press.

Klaus, C. (2010). *The Made-up Self: Impersonation in the Personal Essay*. Iowa City: University of Iowa Press.

Lawrence, W. (2007). Debilitating Public Deliberation: Ronald Reagan's Use of the Conversation Metaphor. *The Southern Communication Journal, 72*(1), 37–54. doi:10.1080/10417940601174702

Limerick, P. (1993, October 31). Dancing with Professors: The Trouble with Academic Prose. *New York Times Book Review, 3*, 23-24.

Lynch, D., George, D., & Cooper, M. (1997). Moments of Argument: Agonistic Inquiry and Confrontational Cooperation. *College Composition and Communication, 48*, 61–85. doi:10.2307/358771

McNabb, R. (1999). Making All the Right Moves: Foucault, Journals, and the Authorization of Discourse. *Journal of Scholarly Publishing, 31*(1), 20–41.

McNabb, R. (2001). Making the Gesture: Graduate Student Submissions and the Expectation of Journal Referees. *Composition Studies, 29,* 9–26.

Miller, S. (2006). *Conversation: A History of a Declining Art.* New Haven: Yale University Press.

Newkirk, T. (1997). *The Performance of Self in Student Writing.* Portsmouth, NH: Boynton/Cook.

Pebworth, T. (1997). Not Being, but Passing: Defining the Early English Essay. *Studies in the Literary Imagination, 10,* 17–27.

Robillard, A. (2006). Young Scholars Affecting Composition: A Challenge to Disciplinary Citation Practices. *College English, 68,* 253–270. doi:10.2307/25472151

Spellmeyer, K. (2003). *Arts of Living: Reinventing the Humanities for the Twenty-first Century.* Albany: State University of New York Press.

KEY TERMS AND DEFINITIONS

Conceptual Metaphor: A metaphor that is rooted in or that influences human thought.

Conversation: Informal, interactive spoken communication.

Essay: A relatively short, structurally flexible piece of writing that often features a writer's intellectual explorations.

Metaphor: A figure of speech that compares one thing to something seemingly dissimilar.

Chapter 6
Tracing the Trope of Teaching as Transformation

Julie Myatt Barger
Middle Tennessee State University, USA

ABSTRACT

Transformation, or change on the part of the student, is the intended outcome of all learning situations, but at times this trope is taken too far. By considering how narratives of transformation too often fail to account for agency and complexity in student identity, this chapter answers Boler's call for interrogations of entrenched belief systems that inform educational practices. Taking American composition pedagogies as its example, the chapter calls attention to the limitations in pedagogies that render students "other" in the teacher's commitment to social change, proposing that portraying students as incomplete beings in need of transformation could reinforce misguided beliefs that hinder student/teacher interactions. The chapter then closes by encouraging educators to recognize student development as a process, and one that need not lead to beliefs that parallel those of the teacher.

NOT YET LIBERATED

Composition's Dependence upon Critical Pedagogies

It was not until the 1980s that journals in composition studies devoted sustained attention to feminist ideals (Kirsch, Maor, Massey, Nickoson-Massey, & Sheridan Rabideau, 2003, p. 5) and yet as early

as 1992, Gore called for new assessments of feminist praxis, noting that "Because of their roots in specific liberatory and emancipatory political projects, we might be least likely to question the claims to empowerment of the critical and feminist discourses" (p. 54). And yet, although few would argue that those engaging in radical pedagogies do so for questionable reasons, the fact that their outcomes may indeed be questionable should prompt us to interrogate these practices

DOI: 10.4018/978-1-61350-495-6.ch006

more closely - and interrogated they have been, quite thoroughly by this point. Despite their well-known critiques, these pedagogies continue to exert significant influence in composition theory and practice. Yoon (2005) argued that the large body of work criticizing these pedagogies notwithstanding, composition studies continues to cling to them:

Despite critiques of critical pedagogy's limitations [...], composition scholarship continues to show signs of its attachment to so-called emancipatory goals articulated by and attributed to critical pedagogy. Even if left with few concrete strategies to fulfill this vision, we seem to be, at the very least, reluctant to surrender these laudatory "social visions" of change, justice, transformation, and democracy. (p. 717)

Though Yoon's article focused on critical pedagogies' construction of teachers, not students, her observations reveal a need for renewed scrutiny where critical composition pedagogies are concerned. Taking up where Yoon left off, I study historically situated pedagogical accounts and their subsequent critiques to inquire into how feminist composition pedagogies (FCPs) construct students. Time and again, this inquiry revealed references to student transformation, and though methods for achieving it may have changed over the years, it remains present in writings informed by feminism's goals for teaching.

In the pages that follow, I focus on how both early FCPs and more recent accounts of service-learning initiatives rely on the trope of transformation. Some may consider it odd to connect feminist pedagogies with service-learning, yet as Kirsch et al. (2003) noted, "in recent years feminism has become 'mainstreamed' in composition studies" (p. 2), and thus we no longer encounter as many publications overtly labeled "feminist pedagogy," despite the fact that feminist ideals remain. Boler (1999), too, was concerned that feminist pedagogies and recognition of their contributions were

disappearing (pp. 108-109), and she called for inquiries into cases in which feminist methods are employed without being labeled as feminist (p. 112). Current composition scholarship concerned with bridging the gap between communities and universities proves a particularly rich site for contemporary references to feminist ideals. Thus, I answer Boler's call by turning to contemporary service-learning accounts to determine how the trope of transformation, a central tenet of FCPs, continues to play out in composition studies' narratives of student identity.

Throughout the chapter, I draw from various scholars' evaluations of critical pedagogies to illustrate how, in their attempt to promote the political agendas of feminism, many FCPs actually posited a limited conception of student identity, presenting all students as though they were in need of saving. The chapter further delineates how this entrenched conversion narrative has relied not only on a limited view of students but also on an exalted view of the feminist pedagogue's responsibilities. The publications cited herein range from some of composition studies' earliest feminist scholarship, dating back to the early 1970s, to works published as recently as 2007. By providing readers with these varied accounts, I trace both the trope of transformation and its attendant criticism as each relates to constructions of student identity, explaining how the concept of transformation has itself been transformed even as it continues to (in)form the ways teachers and students interact in the composition classroom.

"YOU SAY YOU WANT A REVOLUTION?": HOW FEMINIST PEDAGOGIES WANTED TO CHANGE THE WORLD

I take as my starting point Bauer's (1990/2003) "The Other 'F' Word" because Bauer, unlike many of her peers, stated explicitly her objective to convert students to the cause of feminism and recruit them for social action in spite of student resistance (pp. 352-353). Bauer observed, "When we ask students to identify with a political position offered in class or to identify with us as the most immediate representative of that political stance, we are asking them to give allegiance to an affinity or coalition politics that often competes with or negates other allegiances they have already formed," and she proposed that "we need to suggest something in the place of what we tear down when we ask students to resist cultural hegemony" (p. 355). What Bauer offered as the solution was, of course, feminism, which she identified as "a legitimate classroom strategy and rhetorical imperative," one which "offers a goal toward our students' *conversions* [italics added] to emancipatory critical action" (p. 355). Here Bauer stated a fact of which both we and our students are (often painfully) aware: teachers expect students to leave their classrooms different people than they were when they entered. For the act of learning to be complete, some change is necessary, but Bauer's claim that feminism should replace the paradigms students previously used to order their worlds demands further consideration. Bauer was far from alone in making such a claim, and let us turn now to her predecessors to learn how they employed this belief in the importance of making their mark on their students and sending students off to make their own mark on the world.

Before I continue outlining what I (and others who have gone before me) recognize as fissures and faults in feminist pedagogies' desire to convert students for their causes, I must first acknowledge that feminist pedagogies assume many forms. Indeed, Gail Hawisher (2003) reminds us that "there remain strong disagreements over what constitutes a feminist approach to teaching" (p. xvii), however she attempted to identify them by referring to their desired outcomes:

They seek to elicit in students a critical awareness of that which was once invisible - to provoke in students through reading, thinking, writing, and talk a sense of agency, a sense of possibility. They aim to forward, through teaching, a feminist agenda that probes the dominant discourses of sexism, gender preference, and increasingly in the 1980s and 1990s, racism and classism. (p. xvii)

Similarly, Ritchie and Boardman (1999/2003) identified three specific objectives recurrent in the role feminism has played in composition studies: understanding feminism as an "unspoken presence," striving for "inclusion and equality for women," and acting to "disrup[t] and critiqu[e]. . . hegemonic narratives" (p. 9).

In early FCPs, these goals are evident in an emphasis on personal writing; the thinking was that students could not change their circumstances until they felt authorized to contemplate them in writing. References to developing student voice are still common (see Moore, 2002), but early feminist pedagogues in particular strove to help students transform by developing their voices and speaking for themselves, a practice derived from the above-stated objectives of seeking inclusion and equality for women and disrupting hegemonic narratives. Bolker (1979/2003), describing two conscientious female students who expressed frustration with the "lack of personality . . ., sense of non-ownership, and . . . disappointment at not being able to make [themselves] heard" that they associated with their writing, proposed that "good girl[s]" constantly consider the reader to the detriment of their writing (p. 51). Evident in her description is the students' perceived lack of freedom to experiment, to explore, and to express themselves, the very practices feminists of the day were encouraging women to embrace. Bolker's pedagogy proposed to change female students who had previously been rewarded for complying with the system by allowing them to question it and to assert themselves by expressing their own opinions rather than what they thought others wished to hear. In doing so, the students would presumably become more aware of social structures and of their positioning within them and might thus realize that other, more empowering, subjectivities existed and were available to them. This knowledge could then eventually help them enact change in the world (see also: Annas, 1985/2003; Jackman, 1999; Lamb, 1991/2003; Moore, 2002; Qualley, 1994; Tedesco, 1991).

In order for students to find their own voices (a necessary step in the progression toward social change), feminist compositionists reasoned, they must develop a sense of agency, and so feminist pedagogues often promoted a dissolution of the boundaries existing between the private and the public by encouraging students to speak publicly of their own personal experiences and to learn from others' responses to them. Encouraging such writing is an attempt to help students come to consciousness, which Bauer (1990/2003) defines as "the recognition of the social signs we all internalize and inherit, inevitably against our will" (p. 358); the act of consciousness-raising was a reaction to patriarchy's attempts to dismiss women's claims of oppression on the basis that their assertions of struggle were "personal," and thus not indicative of widespread oppression. Thus the feminist response: the personal *is* political, and the feminist compositionist response of creating dialogic classrooms. Discussing private issues in the public realm was essential to early feminist composition pedagogues, who encouraged students to make connections between their own and others' life experiences as well as theory.

US AND THEM

How Liberatory Models of the Student as "Other" Thwart Feminist Goals

Many of the goals outlined above are admirable; however, they are not without their problems. Though Knoblauch (1991) characterized radical pedagogies as those concerned primarily with

students on the margins, that is not the case with FCPs, as they focused not only on the students residing in the liminal spaces of academic life, but on *all* students, seeking to recruit - or colonize? - them for the political agendas of feminism. To illustrate why I would use such strong language here, I cite Cushman's (1996/1999) observation that the distance between the academy and the community results in a "colonizing ideology" (p. 376). Next, I apply this notion to Bauer (1990/2003), who spoke of the "gap" (p. 356) separating students and teachers, who argued the need for students' "conversions" and for exposing students to the language of feminism in spite of "the social objections of others" (p. 359). Clearly, within Bauer's paradigm the distance between students and teachers was a given, and opposition rendered the cause of students' conversions to feminism not questionable but all the more worthwhile.

Yet, beginning around the late 1990s/early 2000s, goals like those espoused by Bauer garnered much attention from critical compositionists who determined that, regardless of how well-intentioned, these emancipatory goals often fell short when placed in the context of actual classroom teaching. Spigelman (2001), for one, cautioned that "while our liberatory classroom efforts are aimed at showing students how to resist domination in society, from the perspective of many students, it is our critical pedagogy that needs most to be resisted" (p. 337). After all, Spigelman continued, "our students do not come to us as disciples. Few wish to become like us. They arrive in our classrooms with their values already in place, values emerging out of family and community. But because they have been students for a very long time, they know that those who appear to embrace our views will receive our favor" (p. 338). Kopelson (2003) also noted that student resistance is nothing new (p. 116), but that composition's venture into cultural criticism resulted in a new form of resistance:

As composition theorizing and teaching have evolved in more cultural-studies-based or "critical" directions, student resistance has evolved from a rudimentary resistance to the writing course per se into resistance to the writing course as "inappropriately" politicized. Indeed, many of our students view the increasing pedagogical focus on "difference" as an intrusion of sorts, resenting and often actively rebelling against what they may experience as the "imposition" of race, class, gender, sexuality, or (more generally) cultural issues on to their "neutral" course of study (p. 117).

For the FCPs of the 1990s, all students were rendered others simply because they did not occupy the subject position of the teacher who subscribed to feminist ideals. In order for power structures to remain intact, those in control cannot contemplate the individuality of their subordinates; to do so would give the oppressed power and would thus jeopardize the cultural hegemony that benefits the oppressor. The same was true of FCPs because, as Gore (1992) explained, "The agent of empowerment . . . generally in critical pedagogy, is the teacher while the subject of empowerment is more than the individual student" (p. 57). Yes, as far as the critical pedagogies discussed here were concerned, the one in need of empowering was no longer the individual student, but *any* student failing to profess the teacher's politics.

Boler (1999) questioned whether the "problems" surrounding feminist pedagogy are "endemic to feminist pedagogy" or if they are instead "rooted in the deceptive binaries of Western language" (128), a question that highlights the need for further consideration of how expectations for teacher and student interaction influence pedagogy. Pedagogies appearing on the surface to disrupt the established order may in fact uphold it in their reliance upon inadequate conceptions of teacher and student identity. Students enter our classrooms bringing with them different backgrounds and different experiences, and though they may possess certain educational needs in

common, they are not all one and the same. This adherence to a limited conception of student identity is just one example of how difficult it is for radical pedagogies, including those adopted by feminist compositionists, to subvert the power structures they challenge. Davis (2000) offered the following observation of FCPs, noting that they:

typically offer themselves as alternatives, but they do so by inscribing themselves within a set of existing assumptions, within an already (phal) logocentric ordering system and its pedagogical imperative. In short, they enter the fight; they therefore assume the rules of that fight and end up protecting and perpetuating rather than dethroning the assumptions of the political and economic structures they mean to oppose. Feminist pedagogies, in this sense, operate as a symptom of, rather than a cure for, a much larger cultural/ pedagogical problem. (p. 211)

So, though feminist pedagogues sought to overturn current-traditional classroom practices, feminist calls for the development of student voice actually constructed students in a manner that enabled existing power structures to remain intact:

Paternalistic tendencies in critical and Anglo-American feminist education ultimately replace racist, classist, and sexist forms for students. Educators stand above their students, and guide them in their struggle for "personal empowerment" and "voice." The only call for change is on the part of the students. The only people who get "worked over" are the students. The only call is for student voice. Critical and feminist teachers, we are to assume, have already found and articulated theirs. (Orner, 1992, p. 87)

Orner and Davis made the case that by constructing students as flawed or incomplete beings, feminist pedagogues merely reinstated themselves in the position of the all-knowing teacher in possession of the answers.

The "answers" these feminist pedagogues believed themselves to possess were bound up in their political beliefs, indication of Davis' (2000) assertion that the teaching of composition is "*a seriously political business*" with composition courses "to the left and to the right . . . operat[ing] as prosthetic extensions of political agendas" (p. 210). Davis further cautioned that radical pedagogies and their feminist counterparts are far from harmless, that they "often camouflage pedagogical violence in their move from one mode of 'normalization' to another. Even so-called emancipatory pedagogical techniques function within a matrix of power, a covert carceral system, that aims to create useful subjects for particular political agendas" (p. 212). Feminist educators' very desires to help their students, to *free* them from their unenlightened pasts, are what lead to these acts of violence. Boler's (1999) question of "How can we really ever know the other save through a projection of the self?" is one that could very well be applied to FCPs, as is her subsequent query: "What is gained and/or lost by advocating as a cure for social injustice an empathetic identification that is more about me than you?" (p. 159). The radical teacher sees individual students only as members of the collective body of the unenlightened; in looking at them as people who represent an*other* position, the teacher relates to her students only in terms of their status as *others*, and in doing so validates her role as their savior.

This teacher-as-savior trope arises again and again in the scholarship under review, and it demands scrutiny even today, for it is founded on a juxtaposition of teachers and students that serves the teachers more than the students:

Having established that the agent of empowerment is usually the teacher, and that the subject (or object) of empowerment is Others, a distinction is immediately set up between "us" and "them" . . . As a given in any relationship which aims at empowerment, the agent becomes problematic when the us/them relationship is conceived as

requiring a focus only on "them". When the agent of empowerment assumes to be already empowered, and so apart from those who are to be empowered, arrogance can underlie claims of "what we can do for you." (Gore, 1992, p. 61)

Teachers subscribing to this model likely would not believe that they can learn from students, and thus students in their classes might not be granted opportunities to explore their own interests or exhibit their knowledge. Davis (2000) also commented on this pedagogy: "To be a good student is to be/come a beautiful mirror for the teacher. The pedagogue who encourages students to suppose s/he knows, to suppose that s/he can tell the truth about truth, makes them an implicit promise: that they too will know if they will only listen carefully and do what s/he asks" (p. 228). Certainly, we all ask students to trust in what we know when we make suggestions on students' papers, when we lecture about disciplinary conventions, when we introduce them to our readings of their ideas during conferences, but there is an important distinction to be made here: asking our students to do what we ask in terms of writing is one thing; asking them to subscribe to our beliefs is quite another. Boler (1999) reminded us of the need to look critically at our pedagogies, viewing them not merely in light of our own interests, but rather pausing to consider what versions of student identity they are predicated upon (see also Hairston, 1992/2003).

Difference, Dialogue, and the Desired Disruption of Limited Perspectives

FCPs often construct students not only as beings in need of (re)considering their own experiences, they propose that students need greater exposure to diversity. If one of the goals of feminist pedagogy is to confront essentialism and disrupt hegemonic narratives, then to replace predominant narratives with one singular, confining version of female experience would defeat the purpose. So feminist pedagogies often recommend having students explore their cultural values alongside those of others in hopes that students will understand that their experience is one among many (see Jarratt, 1991/2003; Osborn, 1991; Ritchie, 1990/2003). Lu (1998/2003) described how students revise their understandings of gender after reading about others' experiences and encountering multiple perspectives. An excerpt from one of her assignments illustrates this concept of embracing the unfamiliar to produce change:

Consider the extent to which your personal history might affect how you enact your yearning to eradicate oppression. What particular viewpoints and forces of which you have been a part can be used to advance your interest to combat which type(s) of oppression? Why? What particular "familiar" viewpoints and privileges must be surrendered for you to end which type(s) of oppression? Why? Which foreign ways of seeing and thinking might you need to make yourself vulnerable to? Why? (p. 442)

Accounts such as this were rooted in the teachers' estimation that students possessed limited experiences and needed exposure to alternate perspectives before they could see the world differently and change restrictive social structures.

TEACHER AS LIBERATOR

An Impossible (Yet Admittedly Appealing) Fiction

Despite their calls for dialogic classrooms, many feminist compositionists dismissed students' beliefs in favor of their own. Bauer (1990/2003) considered the classroom "a place to explore resistances and identifications" (p. 353), and she spoke of the need for welcoming "a multiplicity of voices into the cultural dialogue" (p. 354), and yet she also remarked that "students seem often quite unambiguously committed to 'the system'; their

ambivalence is buried deeply, already reconciled" (p. 354). Despite her tempered language, Bauer in essence considered students incapable of critical awareness. She further contended that "the gap of understanding between our students' experiences and our own . . . seems insurmountable" (p. 356).

Though I admit to holding Bauer (1990/2003) up as something of a straw woman, I acknowledge that she is not alone in possessing such views of students. Her statements are simply indicative of the extent to which an emancipatory model of teaching characterized composition pedagogy during the 1980s and 1990s. Walkerdine (1992) argued that "Women teachers became caught, trapped, inside a concept of nurturance which held them responsible for the freeing of each little individual, and therefore for the management of an idealist dream, an impossible fiction" (p. 16). Though many worthy objectives are evident in feminist pedagogies, critics have long questioned their reliance upon a construction of students as "others," and contemplating the reasons for the propagation of this narrative continues to be worthwhile even today. Aisenberg and Harrington (qtd. in Hunter, 1991) observed that "'the lure of teaching for many women is in the desire to reinvoke the transformational experience, their own experience of growth and change, for others . . . not, that is, simply an extension of the nonintellectual gifts of mothering transplanted to another, professional, scene, but something far more radical - women invoking change in others'" (p. 234). This desire to leave the world a better place than one found it is not unique to compositionists, but it has often been employed in our classrooms in ways that, though well-meaning, in reality may be detrimental to students. As those commenting on critical pedagogies would have it, we must pause to consider what students want from the classes we teach (see Smith, 1997; Spigelman, 2001). Hunter (1991) remarked: "How many of those of us who are feminists and composition teachers interact only with students eager to be transformed by the political agendas of feminist, or for that matter, even composition pedagogy?" (p. 230). Hunter and others contemplated why, if the students in our classes are resistant to our suggestions for how to improve their writing, we would think that students would be receptive to our attempts to persuade them politically. And yet, as evident in the FCPs cited here, that is exactly what many feminist compositionists set out to do.

Another common critique contends that teachers quite simply cannot ignore the socioeconomic contexts in which they and their students reside. Not unlike ourselves, our students strive for upward mobility, "seek[ing] not to resist but to *join* an elite which . . . makes up only about 20 percent of the US population" (Smith, 1997, p. 304). Knoblauch (1991) further acknowledged this when he questioned whether liberatory pedagogies were even plausible when "powerful self-interest, rooted in class advantage . . . works actively, if not consciously, against critical reflectiveness" (p. 15). He asked, "Does the moral commitment, and the political authority, of the critical teacher properly mandate a change in the consciousness of arguably disenfranchised students regardless of their own wishes, their own sense of what they might gain or lose from accommodating themselves to the dominant culture?" (1991, p. 15). Interesting that this consciousness-raising was undertaken without the students' express consent. Indeed these critical pedagogues (think Bauer, 1990/2003; Bolker, 1979/2003; and Howe, 1971/2003) who so emphasized agency were not concerned with whether their students were desirous of the kind of change they themselves sought. And Knoblauch's observations also raise questions about whether one can incite critical consciousness in another who is not receptive to this endeavor. Unfortunately, as this chapter has illustrated, FCPs too often placed the teacher in the role of liberator, students as those in need of saving. From Howe's admission that she longed to "rescue" her students to Bauer's reference to "conversion," FCPs over the years have relied on a dichotomy that elevates teachers above their

students, relegating students to a subject position not in their favor. And despite the many calls for the development of student voice, critiques of radical pedagogy illustrate the movement's propensity for valuing the teacher's voice above students'. As Mullin (1994) asserted: "If there is only one feminist voice in the classroom, the voice of Author-ity, then we risk erasing the feminine we claim to seek" (p. 23). And yet, this approach to teaching can clearly be found in the accounts studied here.

STILL SEARCHING FOR A SAFE SPACE?

The Exclusionary Nature of Feminist Composition Pedagogies

Feminist pedagogies long proposed that their classrooms offered students a "safe space," a place free from prejudice and gender inequality, where students could express their beliefs without fear of censure or retaliation. And yet scholars such as Davis (2000) and Orner (1992) critiqued FCP claims that the feminist classroom offered any such protection, noting that "the affirmation of student voice in the critical and Anglo-American feminist classroom is not automatic" (Orner, p. 87), and "this space is safe and/or equalizing only for those willing to operate within the lines of the 'new feminist epistemology' elaborated by the feminist pedagogue" (Davis, p. 220). Thus pedagogies like those outlined here prompt the question: how can we proclaim that our classrooms are "safe" for any of our students when we enter them fully intending for our students to leave as persons changed? Moreover, the very language often employed to present the classroom as a refuge for students serves as a dismissal of their abilities, as it characterizes students as victims in need of rescuing. Regardless of the location, if students are constructed as victims, their autonomy remains in jeopardy. Davis further argued that in the feminist composition classroom, "Difference is celebrated only inasmuch as it can be brought into line with whatever style of 'feminist transformation' this subject (who is) supposed to know [the teacher, in other words] envisions" (p. 221). In this model the teacher remains the authority figure, the one holding the answers, and though she may espouse theories accepting of diversity, her adherence to feminisms could possibly result in the dismissal of alternative viewpoints, rendering the classroom anything but a site of safety for students possessing those particular beliefs. Cushman (1996/1999) argued that this dismissal of certain beliefs is predicated on the teacher's identity and her inability to understand students more than on any actual student deficiency, and she linked this lack of insight to teachers' separation from the world outside the academy:

In some fundamental sense, the discursive posturing we so frequently hear would not be able to legitimize itself, if it didn't diminish others in its wake. The label of false consciousness, then, reveals more about the speaker's limited access to students and communities, than it reveals about the level of people's critical abilities. (p. 387)

This perceived divide between the university and the community, along with the realization that the classroom can no longer be considered a protected site, prompted a move away from scholarship privileging the supposed safe space of the classroom in favor of community engagement.

TRANSFORMATION REVISED

Service-Learning as the Student Agency and Social Action of Today

I turn now to service-learning pedagogies to illustrate how they have, since the decline of feminist composition scholarship, taken up the banner for the cause of transformation. Accounts of recent service-learning initiatives possess striking similarities to the FCPs described above. These recent efforts to engage students in community action perpetuate the trope of transformation, albeit in a slightly different form than that which has long since been criticized as a problematic component of critical pedagogies. In their collaboratively-written article Webb, Cole, and Skeen (2007) reflected on their own foray into service-learning, with Webb, the teacher of graduate students, identifying her goal as "rais[ing] students' awareness about the intersections between the theories we read and systemic patriarchy, and, possibly, encourag[ing] them to become active, ongoing participants in the organizations they worked with" (p. 239). Here we see that service-learning values engaging students in critical thinking and social action as a response to patriarchy and other oppressive structures much in the way that the FCPs discussed previously did. This emphasis on social action, whether in early FCPs or today's service-learning pedagogies, is indicative of the continued reliance upon the trope of transformation, evident in the following statement discussing connections between community service-learning and composition: "Both faculty and student participants report *radical transformations* [emphasis added] of their experiences and understandings of education and its relation to communities outside the campus" (Adler-Kassner qtd. in Himley, 2004, p. 1). Similarly, Reynolds (2004) noted that "Advocates of service learning will testify to the transformative nature of these alignments - that students are changed and enlightened" (p. 114).

Both FCPs and service-learning pedagogies speak of transformation in ways that support Yoon's (2005) previously invoked observation of our hesitancy to abandon these "laudatory 'social visions' of change, justice, transformation, and democracy" (p. 717). Thus, service-learning functions as a continuation of the goals outlined in early FCPs. It is not only a method of instruction that allows students to compare their experiences with others and thus engage in critical consciousness; by placing students in the community, it also purports to address the final goal of FCPs: social change. Webb et al. (2007) wrote that after students volunteered at a local community organization, they were assigned a reflective essay in which they contemplated "how their participation might transform the institutional situations in which they volunteered" (p. 239). Here we see that, like earlier FCPs, feminist service-learning initiatives still emphasize transformation - except this time students, not teachers, are the agents of change. This shift from constructing students as beings in need of saving to individuals capable of serving their communities does seem an improvement, yet one wonders if the trope of transformation continues to foster unrealistic expectations.

One area in which service-learning departs from some of the unrealistic expectations common to FCPs is in regard to the "safe space" of the classroom, as service-learning advocates seek to remove students from the security the classroom supposedly offers. Of course, this move away from the classroom also enables students to participate in the final goal of FCPs: social action. This marks a move away from the construction of the classroom as the site of transformation that Cushman (1996/1999) described when she remarked that "Some critical theorists believe that the primary means of effecting social change is to translate activism into liberatory classroom pedagogies" (p. 372). Service-learning thus seems a response to Cushman's proposal that composition scholars can accomplish social change outside the university, which she articulated by drawing from Edward Schiappa's assertion: "'Pedagogy that enacts cultural critique is important but it is not enough. . . . We should not allow ourselves the easy out of believing that being 'political' in the classroom is a substitute for our direct civic participation'" (as cited in Cushman, 1996/1999, p. 372). And of course engaging in one's own civic participation is also not enough; teachers wanting students to place their experiences in dialogue with oth-

ers' further desire for their students this form of experiential learning through civic participation. Reynolds (2004) stated that:

As composition scholars and practitioners advocate leaving behind familiar terrain in order to understand cultural difference and the complex conditions related to research and learning, a growing trend has emerged in higher education to send students out of the classroom, in various ways, in order to position the learner as an outsider, a foreigner, an other - a positioning that, in its discomfort, often stimulates reflection. (p. 113)

Though different schools of thinking exist in regard to whom service-learning positions as "knower," this model, at least on the surface, constructs students more positively than earlier FCPs that depict the teacher as all-knowing and students as cultural dupes. Of course, one could make the case that in transferring agency to students, the teacher renders students complicit in a system that constructs those outside the academic community as other (Himley, 2004; Spigelman, 2001). Webb et al. (2007) discussed how early service-learning initiatives positioned the student as knower and those in the community as other, while more recent forays into community service "share feminism's goal of building reciprocal relationships between the university and the community in a way that complicates the relationship between 'knower' and 'other'" (pp. 238-239). The model of social action described by Cushman (1996/1999, p. 380) and others writing about the benefits of service-learning presupposes a very different relationship between teacher and student/other than do earlier incarnations of feminist composition pedagogies. Service-learning pedagogies construct students as knowledgeable beings capable of enacting change in the world. Here students need not first walk through the proverbial footbath of FCPs to be disinfected from the hegemonic culture that has ordered their thoughts (see Bloom, 1996);

rather, students are viewed as persons who already sense problems in their communities and wish to address the problems and improve communities by becoming active, involved citizens.

TRADING TRANSFORMATION FOR A MUTUAL EXPLORATION OF STUDENT IDENTITY

A Recommendation

As Ritchie (1990/2003) noted, not all of our students will be transformed during the course of a semester. Indeed, many of our students take what are for them quite large leaps when they place their experiences in context with others'. To expect them to transform and adopt the political agenda of feminism as Bauer (1990/2003) would have it is quite simply asking too much. In her reading of Bauer's pedagogy, Anderson (1997) called our attention to the predicament facing such radical teachers when "the desirable positions they construct seem incompatible with the ideological images, values, and symbols occupied by their opponents" (p. 205), in this case, students. Furthermore, Anderson proposed that Bauer "undercuts identification when she offers students only a stark choice between positions she casts as incompatible. Students who want to move from one to the other must leap a wide gulf" (1997, p. 205). Anderson's reading of Bauer is evidence that we must admit to ourselves that our classrooms are not always spaces that prompt radical transformation in the ways that we and others might expect them to be. This desire for what Newkirk (2004) described as "the turn" in our students may be more detrimental than productive, a notion seconded by Spigelman:

Students do not passively accept our version of the ethical or the good - even when our version is reproduced on the pages of their compositions. Although they may ape our pieties, they may not

internalize our hopes for a better world. Thus, classroom power relationships, not conversion, may effect a change in views for the duration of the class without having a lasting impact. (2001, p. 338)

Clearly, introducing students to strategies that will help them resist and define themselves in opposition to patriarchal culture is not misguided, but critics of liberatory pedagogies encourage us to consider how far these goals should extend. Some scholars ask: Wouldn't helping students develop their abilities as rhetoricians, helping them become better writers and more effective communicators, even if their opinions differ from the teacher's, be a more effective means of ensuring equality and diversity? (See Logan, 1998/2003). Like so many other composition teachers who consider themselves responsible for "foster[ing] the attitudes and values of a just society" (Spigelman, 2001, p. 329), I am not yet ready to defer to student writing that erases difference, privileges heteronormativity, or denigrates people from races, classes, genders, sexual orientations, or belief systems other than the writer's own. And yet, like Spigelman and so many other of the teacher/scholars I have quoted herein, I recognize limitations in overly-politicized approaches to teaching.

DISRUPTING THE BINARIES THAT LIMIT STUDENT/ TEACHER INTERACTION

This chapter has outlined the narratives of student identity promoted by feminist composition pedagogies privileging student transformation. The accounts discussed are far from monolithic, with individual scholars privileging their own particular objectives for students that at times depart from the goals held by their feminist colleagues, and latter writers promoting goals that differ from their predecessors'. Webb et al. (2007) essay is a prime example of how feminist pedagogies exist on a continuum of sorts, with earlier models constructing students as other and relying heavily on the teacher as students' savior, whereas later models such as service-learning programs based in feminist methodologies grant students more agency and acknowledge the need to question the teacher's authority. They caution that anyone seeking to engage students in service projects informed by feminism

must reflect on how best to create a classroom environment in which students can use their own experiences to problematize and interrogate the perceived split between their roles as students and their "other" lives outside the academy. We may want to create an activist, change-based classroom, but we must recognize that we continually negotiate the tensions between empowering students and imposing our ideologies on them. In the very act of inviting students to define themselves, we run the risk of defining them through the lenses of our own agendas. (p. 239)

Unlike some of the other pedagogical accounts this chapter takes as its focus, Webb et al. exhibit both an awareness of the role their own feminist-located desire for change (in students and society) plays in their teaching and a recognition of the related need for teacher reflexivity.

Regardless of our disciplinary allegiances, our teaching should encourage reflexivity and find us attempting to disrupt the binaries by which we and students order our worlds, understanding that argument - and even identity - is more complex than us-and-them constructions allow. And yet just as we attempt to aid students in replacing these binaries with more nuanced understandings of difference, we must continue to remind ourselves not to expect students to see the world just as we do (not that "we" can even - or should necessarily - arrive at such a consensus). Instead, teachers should cultivate Welch's (2002) understanding of students' "back-and-forthness" between "present and past, connection and separation, 'they' and

'I'" in their own attempts to work with students toward creating "a much more responsible and responsive construction of mutuality" (p. 245), a pedagogical strategy akin to Qualley's (1994) discussion of her own endeavors to help students "negotiate the thickets of 'multiplicity,' 'ambiguity,' and 'complexity'" over time (p. 25). For Welch and Qualley, student identity is not fixed; rather, students are to be considered persons in process, engaged in multiplicitous and changing understandings of themselves and others.

In models of teaching like that Bauer (1990/2003) described, such a reading of student identity as in process, rather than incomplete, is jeopardized by the teacher's desire for the student to adopt the teacher's politics, and in seeking this objective for students, the teacher fails to acknowledge the many steps involved in a journey such as that she herself took toward developing her current political perspective. If, as Boler insisted, "emotions are inseparable from actions and relations, from lived experience" (p. 2) then feminist composition pedagogues - and indeed any teachers - seeking to liberate students from their supposedly flawed belief systems are failing to account for their students' own lived experience, whether past or future. This insistence that students adopt the teacher's politics also fails to acknowledge that the teacher's present politics were likely not those she possessed at a young age; rather, her lived experience undoubtedly led her to revise her worldviews over time, a growth process that we should remember and allow for when considering students' beliefs.

Boler acknowledged the value of student resistance and called for "creative spaces to develop flexible and creative modes of resistance involving emotional breadth and exploration that are not prescriptive" and which "involve the educator as well as the student undertaking the risky process of change" (p. 4). Boler asserted: "It cannot be up to the educator . . . to push a particular path of action" (p. 196); she, like Qualley and Welch, called instead for "mutual exploration" in which the teacher is not savior, but rather students are co-collaborators with the teacher, knowing all the while that they will not be evaluated on whether or how they elect to transform (p. 199). This approach to critical-consciousness could prevent the temporary adoption of the teacher's views that some identify as the result of overly-prescriptive critical pedagogies. And, as Davis (2000) proposed, we must "remain suspicious of any pedagogical imperative that does not admit that the solidification of identity ('self-consciousness' about who one *is*) functions as a manifestation of 'domination and exploitation'" (p. 250). As the critiques cited herein illustrate, pedagogies that adhere to traditional power relations and privilege radical student transformation possess the potential to devolve into forms of domination and exploitation. Thus, regardless of the labels we assign them, we must continue to scrutinize our pedagogies for how in employing this trope they construct and constrict student identity.

REFERENCES

Anderson, V. (1997). Confrontational teaching and rhetorical practice. *College Composition and Communication, 48*(2), 197–214. doi:10.2307/358666

Annas, P. J. (2003). Style as politics: A feminist approach to the teaching of writing. In Kirsch, G. E. (Eds.), *Feminism and composition: A critical sourcebook* (pp. 61–72). Boston, MA: Bedford. doi:10.2307/376958

Bauer, D. M. (2003). The other 'F' word: The feminist in the classroom. In Kirsch, G. E. (Eds.), *Feminism and composition: A critical sourcebook* (pp. 351–362). Boston, MA: Bedford.

Bloom, L. Z. (1996). Freshman composition as a middle class enterprise. *College English, 58*(6), 654–675. doi:10.2307/378392

Boler, M. (1999). *Feeling power: Emotions and education*. New York, NY: Routledge.

Bolker, J. (2003). Teaching Griselda to write. In Kirsch, G. E., et al. (Eds.), *Feminism and composition: A critical sourcebook*. (pp. 49-52). Boston, MA: Bedford. (Reprinted from *College English,* 1979, 40(8), pp. 906-908).

Cushman, E. (1999). The rhetorician as an agent of social change. In Ede, L. S. (Ed.), *On writing research: The Braddock essays* (pp. 372–389). Boston, MA: Bedford. doi:10.2307/358271

Davis, D. (2000). *Breaking up (at) totality: A rhetoric of laughter*. Carbondale, IL: Southern Illinois University Press.

Gore, J. (1992). What *can* 'we' do for 'you'?: Struggling over empowerment in critical and feminist pedagogy. In Luke, C., & Gore, J. (Eds.), *Feminisms and critical pedagogy* (pp. 54–73). New York, NY: Routledge.

Hairston, M. (2003). Diversity, ideology, and teaching writing. In Villanueva, V. (Ed.), *Cross-talk in comp theory: A reader* (2nd ed., pp. 697–713). Urbana, IL: National Council of Teachers of English.

Hawisher, G. E. (2003). Forwarding a feminist agenda in writing studies. In Kirsch, G. E. (Eds.), *Feminism and composition: A critical sourcebook* (pp. xv–xx). Boston, MA: Bedford.

Himley, M. (2004). Facing (up to) 'the stranger' in community service learning. *College Composition and Communication, 55*(3), 416–438. doi:10.2307/4140694

Howe, F. (2003). Identity and expression: A writing course for women. In Kirsch, G. E. (Eds.), *Feminism and composition: A critical sourcebook* (pp. 33–42). Boston, MA: Bedford. doi:10.2307/375624

Hunter, S. (1991). A woman's place *is* in the composition classroom: Pedagogy, gender, and difference. *Rhetoric Review, 9*(2), 230–245. doi:10.1080/07350199109388930

Hurlbert, C. M., & Blitz, M. (Eds.). (1991). *Composition and resistance*. Portsmouth, NH: Boynton/Cook.

Jackman, M. K. (1999). When the personal becomes professional: Stories from reentry adult women learners about family, work, and school. *Composition Studies, 27*(2), 53–67.

Jarratt, S. (2003). Feminism and composition: The case for conflict. In Kirsch, G. E. (Eds.), *Feminism and composition: A critical sourcebook* (pp. 263–280). Boston, MA: Bedford.

Kirsch, G. E., Maor, F. S., Massey, L., Nickoson-Massey, L., & Sheridan-Rabideau, M. P. (Eds.). (2003). *Feminism and composition: A critical sourcebook*. Boston, MA: Bedford.

Knoblauch, C. H. (1991). Critical teaching and dominant culture. In Hurlbert, C. M., & Blitz, M. (Eds.), *Composition and resistance* (pp. 12–21). Portsmouth, NH: Boynton/Cook.

Kopelson, K. (2003). Rhetoric on the edge of cunning; Or, the performance of neutrality (re)considered as a composition pedagogy for student resistance. *College Composition and Communication, 55*(1), 115–146. doi:10.2307/3594203

Lamb, C. E. (2003). Beyond argument in feminist composition. In Kirsch, G. E. (Eds.), *Feminism and composition: A critical sourcebook* (pp. 281–293). Boston, MA: Bedford.

Logan, S. W. (2003). "When and where I enter:" Race, gender, and composition studies. In Kirsch, G. E. (Eds.), *Feminism and composition: A critical sourcebook* (pp. 425–435). Boston, MA: Bedford.

Lu, M. (2003). Reading and writing differences: The problematic of experience. In Kirsch, G. E. (Eds.), *Feminism and composition: A critical sourcebook* (pp. 436–446). Boston, MA: Bedford.

Luke, C., & Gore, J. (Eds.). (1992). *Feminisms and critical pedagogy*. New York, NY: Routledge.

Moore, C. (2002). Why feminists can't stop talking about voice. *Composition Studies, 30*(2), 11–25.

Mullin, J. A. (1994). Feminist theory, feminist pedagogy: The gap between what we say and what we do. *Composition Studies, 22*(1), 14–24.

Newkirk, T. (2004). The dogma of transformation. *College Composition and Communication, 56*(2), 251–271. doi:10.2307/4140649

Orner, M. (1992). Interrupting the calls for student voice in 'liberatory' education: A feminist poststructuralist perspective. In Luke, C., & Gore, J. (Eds.), *Feminisms and critical pedagogy* (pp. 74–89). New York, NY: Routledge.

Osborn, S. (1991). "Revision/re-vision:" A feminist writing class. *Rhetoric Review, 9*(2), 258–273. doi:10.1080/07350199109388932

Qualley, D. J. (1994). Being two places at once: Feminism and the development of "both/and" perspectives. In Sullivan, P. A., & Qualley, D. J. (Eds.), *Pedagogy in the age of politics: Writing and reading (in) the academy* (pp. 25–42). Urbana, IL: National Council of Teachers of English.

Reynolds, N. (2004). *Geographies of writing: Inhabiting places and encountering difference*. Carbondale, IL: Southern Illinois University Press.

Ritchie, J. S. (2003). Confronting the "essential" problem: Reconnecting feminist theory and pedagogy. In Kirsch, G. E. (Eds.), *Feminism and composition: A critical sourcebook* (pp. 79–102). Boston, MA: Bedford.

Ritchie, J. S., & Boardman, K. (2003). Feminism in composition: Inclusion, metonymy, and disruption. In Kirsch, G. E. (Eds.), *Feminism and composition: A critical sourcebook* (pp. 7–26). Boston, MA: Bedford. doi:10.2307/358482

Spigelman, C. (2001). What role virtue? *JAC, 21*(2), 321–348.

Tedesco, J. (1991). Women's ways of knowing/women's ways of composing. *Rhetoric Review*, *9*(2), 246–256. doi:10.1080/07350199109388931

Villanueva, V. (Ed.). (2003). *Cross-talk in comp theory: A reader* (2nd ed.). Urbana, IL: National Council of Teachers of English.

Walkerdine, V. (1992). Progressive pedagogy and political struggle. In Luke, C., & Gore, J. (Eds.), *Feminisms and critical pedagogy* (pp. 15–24). New York, NY: Routledge.

Webb, P., Cole, K., & Skeen, T. (Eds.). (2007). Feminist social projects: Building bridges between communities and universities. *College English*, *69*(3), 238–259.

Welch, N. (2002). "And now that I know them:" Composing mutuality in a service learning course. *College Composition and Communication*, *54*(2), 243–263. doi:10.2307/1512148

Yoon, H. K. (2005). Affecting the transformative intellectual: Questioning "noble" sentiments in critical pedagogy and composition. *JAC*, *25*(4), 717–759.

ADDITIONAL READING

Adler-Kassner, L. (2008). *Activist WPA: The Changing Stories about Writing and Writers*. Logan, UT: Utah State University Press.

Adler-Kassner, L., Crooks, R., & Watters, A. (Eds.). (1997). *Writing the Community: Concepts and Models For Service-Learning in Composition*. Washington, DC: American Association for Higher Education.

Alexander, J. (2008). *Literacy, Pedagogy, Sexuality: Theory and Practice For Composition Studies*. Logan, UT: Utah State University Press.

Bloom, L. Z. (1992). *College English*, *54*(7), 818–825. doi:10.2307/378261

Bridwell-Bowles, L. (1992). Discourse and Diversity: Experimental Writing Within the Academy. *College Composition and Communication*, *43*(3), 349–368. doi:10.2307/358227

Coogan, D. (2006). Service Learning and Social Change: The Case For Materialist Rhetoric. *College Composition and Communication*, *57*(4), 667–693.

Crowley, S. (1998). *Composition in the University: Historical and Polemical Essays*. Pittsburgh, PA: University of Pittsburgh Press.

Crowley, S. (2006). *Toward a Civil Discourse: Rhetoric and Fundamentalism*. Pittsburgh, PA: University of Pittsburgh Press.

Deans, T. (2000). *Writing Partnerships: Service-Learning in Composition*. Urbana, IL: National Council of Teachers of English.

Ellsworth, E. (1992). Why Doesn't This Feel Empowering? Working Through the Repressive Myths of Critical Pedagogy. In Luke, C., & Gore, J. (Eds.), *Feminisms and Critical Pedagogy* (pp. 90–119). New York, NY: Routledge.

Ervin, E. (2006). Rhetorical Situations and the Straits of Inappropriateness: Teaching Feminist Activism. *Rhetoric Review*, *25*(3), 316–333. doi:10.1207/s15327981rr2503_5

Fishman, S. M., & McCarthy, L. P. (1996). Teaching for Student Change: A Deweyan Alternative to Radical Pedagogy. *College Composition and Communication*, *47*(3), 342–366. doi:10.2307/358293

Flower, L. (2008). *Community Literacy and the Rhetoric of Public Engagement*. Carbondale, IL: Southern Illinois University Press.

Gibson, M., Marinara, M., & Meem, D. (2000)... *College Composition and Communication*, *52*(1), 69–95. doi:10.2307/358545

Julier, L. (2001). Community-Service Pedagogy. In Tate, G., Rupiper, A., & Schick, K. (Eds.), *A Guide to Composition Pedagogies* (pp. 132–148). New York, NY: Oxford University Press.

Lazere, D. (1992). Back to Basics: A Force For Oppression or Liberation. *College English, 54*(1), 7–21. doi:10.2307/377555

Lunsford, A. A. (1999). Rhetoric, Feminism, and the Politics of Textual Ownership. *College English, 61*(5), 529–544. doi:10.2307/378972

Malinowitz, H. (1995). *Textual Orientations: Lesbian and Gay Students and the Making of Discourse Communities*. Portsmouth, NH: Boynton/Cook.

Mathieu, P. (2005). *Tactics of Hope: The Public Turn in English Composition*. Portsmouth, NH: Boynton/Cook.

Micciche, L. R. (2007). *Doing Emotion: Rhetoric, Writing Teaching*. Portsmouth, NH: Boynton/Cook.

Newkirk, T. (1997). *The Performance of Self in Student Writing*. Portsmouth, NH: Boynton/Cook.

Newkirk, T. (2004). The Dogma of Transformation. *College Composition and Communication, 56*, 251–271. doi:10.2307/4140649

Payne, M. (2000). *Bodily Discourses: When Students Write about Abuse and Eating Disorders*. Portsmouth, NH: Boynton/Cook.

Robillard, A. (2006). Young Scholars Affecting Composition: A Challenge to Disciplinary Citation Practices. *College English, 68*(3), 253–270. doi:10.2307/25472151

Robillard, A. (2006). Young Scholars Affecting Composition: A Challenge to Disciplinary Citation Practices. *College English, 68*(3), 253–270. doi:10.2307/25472151

Royster, J. J. (2003). A View From a Bridge: Afrafeminist Ideologies and Rhetorical Studies. In G. E. Kirsch, et al. (Eds.), *Feminism and Composition: A Critical Sourcebook*. (pp. 206-233). Boston, MA: Bedford. (Reprinted from *Traces of a Stream: Literacy and Social Change Among African American women*, 2000, Pittsburgh, U of Pittsburgh P).

Spigelman, C. (2004). Politics, Rhetoric, and Service-Learning. *WPA: Writing Program Administration, 28*(1-2), 95–114.

Stenberg, S. J., & Whealy, D. A. (2009). Chaos is the Poetry: From Outcomes to Inquiry in Service-Learning Pedagogy. *College Composition and Communication, 60*(4), 683–706.

Tobin, L. (2004). *Reading Student Writing: Confessions, Meditations, and Rants*. Portsmouth, NH: Boynton/Cook.

Weisser, C. (2002). *Moving Beyond Academic Discourse: Composition Studies and the Public Sphere*. Carbondale, IL: Southern Illinois University Press.

Welch, N. (2008). *Living Room: Teaching Public Writing in a Privatized World*. Portsmouth, NH: Boynton/Cook.

Williams, B. T. (2006). *Identity Papers: Literacy and Power in Higher Education*. Logan, UT: Utah State University Press.

Williams, B. T., & Zenger, A. (2007). *Popular Culture and Representations of Literacy*. New York, NY: Routledge.

Wood, W. J. (1998). Overlapping Discourses in a Film Writing Course. *College English, 60*(3), 278–300. doi:10.2307/378558

Zawacki, T. M. (1992). Recomposing as a woman - an essay in different voices. *College Composition and Communication, 43*(1), 32–38. doi:10.2307/357363

KEY TERMS AND DEFINITIONS

Agency: One's ability to think for him or herself and act to further his/her own goals. An individual asserting agency is aware of his or her capabilities and acts on them.

Composition: A field of study unique to the American educational system. Composition scholars study writing in various contexts, including educational settings, but the vast majority of research in composition concerns itself with writing at the university level.

Feminist Composition Pedagogy (FCP): An approach to teaching writing that privileges women's experiences and contributions to history by: introducing students to texts written by and about women, having students write about and reflect on their own experiences, and encouraging students to look critically at accepted or unquestioned social structures and practices. A primary goal of such a pedagogy is for students to understand how social structures shape the opportunities available to them so that students will possess strategies for changing social practices that confine or limit them.

Mutual Exploration: An act of learning in which both students and teachers seek to understand the beliefs they possess and how said beliefs influence their understanding(s) of the world and their role(s) in it. In this model, teachers alone do not hold the answers, and instead of expecting students to arrive at a predetermined point of development, teachers recognize that both they and their students can benefit from considering the binaries that shape, and possibly limit, their worlds.

Service-Learning: A form of teaching that engages students in acts of community service. Often, in composition classes, students are charged with writing public documents for, about, or with local community agencies or organizations and are then required to reflect on the experience.

Transformation: The intended outcome of all learning situations: change on the part of the student. At its most basic form, transformation involves the acquisition of skills a student did not possess previously, but for many educators, complete transformation requires social awareness resulting in students' desire to enact change in the world.

Chapter 7
Web 2.0 and Conscientização:
Digital Students and Critical Reflection on and in Multimedia

Heidi Skurat Harris
Eastern Oregon University, USA

ABSTRACT

This chapter introduces multiliteracy as an extension of traditional notions of critical pedagogy that uphold student reflection in and about their world through dialogue as a crucial component of becoming a truly literate human. Students immersed in digital media should be encouraged to investigate and create multimedia in the 21ˢᵗ century classroom. However, instructors not familiar with digital media can find opening their classrooms to digital texts a risk to their professional identities. Just as true education should help students challenge, resist, and modify their perceptions of reality, educators must constantly disrupt their own classrooms to experience true conscientização, or consciousness of consciousness along with students.

INTRODUCTION

New media and digital technology are invigorating twenty-first century classrooms. Students, particularly those labelled "Generation Y" come to our classroom "wired" in a Web 2.0 world where they function on Facebook, Twitter, del.icio.us,

DOI: 10.4018/978-1-61350-495-6.ch007

and YouTube simultaneously. However, educators, particularly those trained at universities that value primarily traditional print media, may not be inclined to use or value the use of new media or digital technology in the classroom. Writing instructors in particular may see introducing students to the conventions of the academy using the print media as their primary concern. When wired students meet these "weird" educators, the collision of the two worlds can cause tension and hostility. The educators bemoan students who would rather tweet and text than read and write; the students tune out, turn off, or "text-out" of classes they find dull and uninviting.

This chapter poses multiliteracy in the critical classroom as a means of encouraging students to explore reality by inviting them to become critically multiliterate. First, the chapter provides background on the ways that multimedia and critical pedagogy intersect in the classroom. Second, I argue that engaging in multiliteracy mirrors Paulo Freire's original work with Brazillian peasants. Just as Freire's work began with the analysis of cultural themes portrayed in photographs and visual representations of students' immediate surroundings, so, too, can twenty-first century students and instructors be challenged to investigate generative themes in their communities and cultures through the new media and digital technologies they often take for granted in their everyday lives. Finally, the chapter provides one example of how using multimedia can challenge students and educators to explore their often fragile identities in the classroom to become students/teachers along with teachers/students.

BACKGROUND

Twenty-first century educators can promote multiliteracy using the tenants of critical pedagogy. Critical pedagogy began with the methods and practices first espoused by Paulo Freire's *Pedagogy of the Oppressed,* particularly the concept of education as *conscientização,* or "consciousness of consciousness." Although practitioners over the last thirty years have interpreted Freire's original pedagogy in a plethora of ways, the majority of those interpretations focus on counteracting the deficiencies of the "banking system" of education, a system that sees students as blank slates or empty repositories to be passively filled with knowledge (see Giroux, 2001; Lee, 2000; Shor, 1980; Thelin & Tassoni, 2000).

Multiliteracy is one means of counteracting the banking system. When students are actively engaged with new media in a networked environment, they engage in dialogue, the centrepiece of Freire's pedagogy. Freire (1998) admonishes those who minimized dialogue as a part as educational practice:

How can I dialogue if I consider myself a member of the in-group of "pure" men, the owners of truth and knowledge, for whom all non-members are "these people" or "the great unwashed"? How can I dialogue if I start from the premise that naming the world is the task of an elite and that the presence of people in history is a sign of deterioration, thus to be avoided? (p. 71)

Exploring the digital world through multimedia can bring all together in naming reality through socially-constructed means, such as folksonomy. Thus, multiliteracy allows educators and students to move beyond simply using digital media as a means of transmitting "truth and knowledge" toward effectively navigating, managing, and transmitting through digital media use (see Hawisher & Selfe, 1999; Kress, 2003; Selber, 2004; Wysocki, Johnson-Eilola, Selfe, & Sirc, 2004,).

Several composition theorists have investigated the intersections of critical pedagogy and multiliteracy. Barbara Blake Duffelmeyer (2002) questioned how critical pedagogy and classroom technologies can work together to "provide an occasion for students to reflect on and articulate their relationship to digital technology, the forces that influenced the formation of that relationship, and the ways that they might develop some agency within the parameters of that relationship" (p. 358). Stuart Selber (2004) calls for students to be trained functionally, rhetorically, and critically in the use and consumption of technology. Functional multiliteracy is defined as "the skills associated with writing and communication processes as teachers have come to understand them in a digital age" (p. 44). Critical multiliteracy then "recognizes and then challenges the values of the status quo. Instead of reproducing the existing social and political order . . . it strives to both expose biases and provides an assemblage of cultural practices that in a democratic spirit, might lead to the production of positive social change" (p. 81). Finally, Selber defines rhetorical multiliteracy as "the thoughtful integration of functional and critical abilities in the design and evaluation of computer interfaces" (p. 145). In short, students must move beyond simply using digital media into critiquing their relationships to that media and creating their own digital media in order to fully become multiliterate citizens.

This chapter extends these theoretical perspectives by showing how exploration, reflection, and action through critical multiliteracy disrupts the traditional print-based "banking methods" of post-secondary education. Incorporating a critical multiliteracy approach closely replicates the original intent of Freire's vision, using images to encourage students and educators alike to question their culture and act on the structures that seek to repress them.

CRITICAL PEDAGOGY AND MULTI-MEDIA: REMIX AND REFLECTION

Critical pedagogy challenges the banking system Paulo Freire exposes in *Pedagogy of the Oppressed*. Freire (1998) calls to educators to "help the oppressed see themselves as women and men engaged in the ontological and historical vocation of becoming more fully human" (p. 48). The premise of critical classrooms operates by asking students and instructors to focus on their perception of themselves and their realities, and in doing so, to develop a consciousness of consciousness allowing them to engage in and change those realities.

Critical pedagogy's origins are in the informal educational systems of rural Brazil. Freire's initial work with Brazillian peasants focused not on memorizing words to develop literacy but on investigating the themes behind images that the peasants would find common. These images provided a conduit to a literate world as the peasants identified elements of the images and developed a vocabulary that could enable praxis through reflection and action. Freire writes, "within the word we find two dimensions, reflection and action, in such radical interaction that if one is sacrificed - even in part - the other immediately suffers. There is no true word that is not at the same time a *praxis*. Thus, to speak a true word is to transform the world" (*Pedagogy,* p. 68). Freire worked with people entrenched in a reality with which they passively struggled but did not feel enabled to change (Freire, 1987). Freire saw images as the pathway to helping the illiterate see how and where they could change their realities, not just to encounter and learn print text as a means of internalizing a power system already in place.

While Freire's work with peasants brought literacy education to communities, the American system of post-secondary education brings individual students from their home communities to a new, highly bureaucratic system of power with its own privileged methods of communication. From the late nineteenth- and early twentieth-century, print media has been the focus of knowledge and education, particularly in English departments where the bulk of literacy education often occurs (Dunn, 2001). Selfe (2009) states that "since the late nineteenth century, writing has assumed such a dominant and central position in our professional thinking that its role as a major instructional focus goes virtually uncontested, accepted as common sense" (p. 619). Students are texted through various levels of academia through standardized tests that revolve around print literacy. Educators proceed through the ranks of education in similar ways, through written examinations, tenure and promotion review of their scholarly publications in primarily print media.

In classrooms based on nineteenth- and twentieth-century literacy practices, students tend to most frequently read, discuss, and write *about* print media. Articles and books written by scholars and vetted through the process of peer review reinforce the primary messages of the banking system which validates and transmits information. Textbooks replace a student's consciousness (or perceived lack thereof) with that of the authority in lieu of encouraging students to develop their own consciousness of consciousness. Instead of beginning with the image that leads to the word that can then instigate reflection and action in Freire's system, the words of others are transmitted, paraphrased, summarized, and quoted. The "word" resides in the textbook, the words, reflections, and actions of others acting upon and within their realities. Academic texts print the voices of published writers, are vetted by scholars who write about theorized versions of gender, race, or class. Using these print-based texts gives lip-service to *conscientização,* transmitting peer-reviewed and academically-published print media instead of studying the word, reflections, and actions of the students themselves.

Often, students will reject these texts. As Villaneueva (1991) and Lee (2000) assert, students presented with readings that place them in the position of the "oppressed" will not necessarily accept that designation. Hendrix & Jacobson (2000) classroom gives an example of how students enact rejection of scholarly text. Students in a first-year English class were asked to read Mike Rose's *Lives on the Boundary*, Victor Villanueva's *Bootstraps*, and texts by bell hooks, Ira Shor, and Sapphire. The instructors assumed their first-year students in Lawrence, Kansas would identify with the readings and write about their struggles against a hegemonic system of educational repression. However, the reaction from students was rebellion; as one student writes, "the books that we had to read were quite boring and not very interesting - so

it was hard to write about them" and "it was very difficult to know what the teachers expected from us … it seemed as if there was a patronizing tone" (p. 53). Hendrix and Jacobson identify that the text selection and tone of the course could be seen as demeaning by "students coming to college with hopes of escaping their working-class identities in favor of elitist aims" and offend students who read that "working-class students. . . would learn nothing if teachers focused on where they, the students, came from" (p. 54). In reflection, they write, "this reminds us briefly of the importance of contextualization: far from starting our course from the level at which students perceived reality … we had already constructed an understanding for them; we had assumed their engagement with education issues without asking them what the nature of their engagement might be" (p. 54).

Disrupting this pattern of transmitting the words and realities of others through reading and writing in lieu of reflection and action requires reimagining the "radical interaction" of Freire's vision, shifting focus from basic literacy to multiliteracy. As Freire dialogued with Brazillian workers through discussion of images to develop literacy, so must we dialogue with 21st century students so that educators and students alike develop multiliteracy. Honoring students' ways of knowing and communicating, embedded and tacit in their realities, disrupts the notion that higher education's purpose is indoctrination and encourages a multiliteracy that empowers students to use technology for personal and social change.

Print Media and the Limitations of the Banking Method

The banking method relies on the binary of the knowledgeable teacher and submissive students or, if not explicitly constructed in terms of authority and submission, in the teacher as the bearer of knowledge and the student as receiver of knowledge. This dichotomy is reflected in the print media honored in the college classroom. Printed text codifies knowledge that which is peer-reviewed, vetted, and verified by scholars and experts and collected in libraries. In the classroom, print media are often considered more important or scholarly. Educators might construct research assignments that limit the number or type of electronic sources that can be used. Materials such as Wikipedia that demonstrate collective knowledge are dismissed out of hand, and peer-reviewed databases are taught in many cases as the only reliable academic sources. While peer-reviewed sources do, indeed, carry weight in academia, the majority of students will not be pursuing careers in academia. Limiting "knowledge" to these sources reinforces the knowledge-bearer, knowledge-seeker binary - reducing or eliminating true dialogic education. In addition, students rarely encounter their experiences or realities reflected in these peer-reviewed texts, further subjugating their experiences as the "unwashed."

In critical classrooms, students might read about or investigate the limited situations that construct their realities, and they might even be encouraged to use digital media in doing so. However, the results of their investigations are usually communicated within the walls of the classroom via the traditional essay. Essays, both exploratory and academic, are the "natural" forms of communication of a very limited amount of human experience primarily in the academy or in print-texts. Few of our students will pursue lives or livelihoods that rely on communicating in essay form. While peer-reviewed texts do carry weight in academia, this audience is one few students will become or engage beyond their years of formal post-secondary education.

Asking students to investigate the multi-faceted nature of twenty-first century realities and then communicate the nature of those realities through print media encourages small rebellions just as students enacted in the classrooms of Hendrix and Jacobson. Students refuse to practice authentic revision strategies. In some cases, student essays provide lists of quoted sources without contem-

plation or connection. A quote is dropped into a half-formed paragraph with no synthesis. Paraphrases or summaries of texts change words with thesaurus-like accuracy. Students neither absorb nor digest information but rather take in and immediately - and sometimes violently - regurgitate that information onto a page. The reductionist nature of text, the linearity and one-directional nature of the print-based medium, remove something of the passion and humanity that occurs in multimodal communication, particularly for students whose communication patterns outside the classroom are primarily multimodal. And, because Freire's call is for educators to help others and themselves become more human, any method of communication that limits the possibilities of that humanity is, by nature, antithetical to the premise and promise of critical pedagogy. Just as Freire's students were parts of a system in which they had been denied agency, asking students to use only a limited amount of their communication potential denies their agency, impeding the "vocation of becoming more fully human" (Freire, 1980, p. 48).

Educators who heed Freire's call by recognizing the limiting nature of print communication incorporate digital media and Web 2.0 technologies as ways to encourage students to engage in learning and interact with authentic audiences through digital forms of print communication. However, recent studies indicate that students increasingly resist media such as blogs or other primarily text-based media in digital form. A recent Pew Internet and American Life study shows only 15% of internet users aged 14-29 maintain a blog in 2009, down from 24% who blogged in 2007, in spite of the fact that young adults continue to use the internet as a primary means of accessing information and communicating with others (Lenhart, Purcell, Smith, & Zichuhr, 2010). According to Rideout, Foher, and Roberts (2010), the three most popular computer activities were accessing social networking sites, playing online games, and viewing videos on sites such as YouTube (p. 21). One reason for the shift from Blogger to

Facebook might be the nature of networking and community building through social media that is not necessarily present in other digital forms, highlighting the desire for connection, community, and dialogue students bring to our classrooms and that print-media does not always allow.

Multiliteracy in the Critical Classroom as Disruption of the Banking Method

Incorporating multiliteracy in the critical classroom not only operates to encourage dialogue and connection. It also operates as one form of Boler's pedagogy of discomfort where both students and instructors question their identities as participants in a system where technology exerts power and influence. As Boler (1999) states, "cultural identities and 'selves' are founded on vastly frail identities. National identities rest on complex fictions and investments; student identities are invested as well in the dominant paradigm. Students and educators may feel a sense of threat to our precarious identities as we learn to bear witness" (p. 195). To "bear witness" is to develop a "consciousness of consciousness," to explore and understand our place in and complacency with the current, dominant paradigm. Digital media forms work both to promote those dominant paradigms in which our identity is invested and to allow an outlet for us to question those dominant paradigms through the very media that, to an extent, sustains those paradigms.

Centering digital media as a generative theme in the classroom can counter what Shor (1980) claims is the tendency for students to "repeat the quick messages they had learned in school or from the media, bypassing a general discussion on the human power to make culture because they are already preoccupied with the question of power, although not in a crucial or liberating way" (p. 61). Social media and other forms of instant information exchange give the illusion of power through access. However, because those same media require investment, students both are both used by this technology just as they are use it. When individuals tap into media as complacent consumers, they participate in the "complex fictions" of power through information exchange. Asking students to investigate those exchanges using digital media, multimedia, and Web 2.0 platforms and then "bearing witness" of the results of their investigation using those same digital and multimedia allows students to both question dominant paradigms and take action through interaction in those paradigms.

To do so, however, poses a risk to student identities, a risk that educators must share in a truly critical multiliterate classroom. Selber (2004) admits that "teachers who espouse critical approaches, then, are generally interested in preparing students to be social critics rather than indoctrinated consumers of material culture. However, many teachers themselves have not been adequately prepared to think critically about computers" (p. 172). The critical classroom focused on dialogue and digital communication is the relationship between action, language, and reflection, all three surrounding a "point of encounter" at which "there are neither utter ignoramuses nor perfect sages; there are only people who are attempting, together, to learn more than they now know" (Freire, 1998, p. 71). In addition to offering students the opportunity to investigate, express, and reflect using a variety of media, the critical educator must be simultaneously investigating, expressing, and reflecting herself using the same media: sharing the results of her investigation, modeling her choices of media, and reflecting alongside students using those modes of communication most vital to her personal expression. This simultaneous investigation, action, and reflection reinforces Boler's insistence that "the educator's own beliefs and assumptions are by no means immune to the process of questioning and 'shattering'" (p. 188). Even educators familiar with multimedia and Web 2.0 technologies can question their beliefs and assumptions about digital media using multimedia and digital media to do so.

Questioning and "shattering" professional selves carries obvious risk for educators, particularly in academic cultures where a "rhetoric of excellence" is in practice (Reid, 2007, p. 185). As post-secondary institutions seek to tighten their cash-strapped belts, educators are naturally encouraged to maintain teaching excellence, to be increasingly proficient in the classroom, not to risk their professional identities to expose potential failures and weaknesses. As Duffelmeyer (2002) indicates in her work with teaching assistants attempting to implement critical pedagogies, the nature of the process as ongoing and unfinished can be threatening. She states, "critical composition pedagogy's possibilities in a multiliteracy environment…reminds us to regard critical composition pedagogy as a process that an instructor develops, not as a finished condition that can then be imparted to one's students" (p. 35). If pedagogy is never "finished," and is constantly changing as it is questioned and shattered, then proving competency in the classroom can be a challenge.

Educators asking students to take risks with expressing their identities and themes through multi-media must investigate and express using those same forms of media themselves, reflecting on their media use and sharing those projects with others in the same ways that they ask students to represent their identities in digital forms. And instructors must be willing to critically reflect on those instances when their expectations for student engagement through media are shattered or when students perform acts of resistance in the classroom in spite of the instructor's invitation to investigate, explore, reflect and reconfigure student reality digitally. As Freire (1980) points out, the instructor must not see herself as a fully-formed individual leading others into enlightenment. She must

constantly re-form [her] reflections in the reflection of the students. The students—no longer docile listeners—are now critical co-investigators in dialogue with the teacher. The teacher presents

the material to the students for their consideration, and re-considers her earlier considerations as the students express their own (p. 81).

The self-reflective practitioner explores her own multimedia use in the same ways as students. When an instructor asks students to question or shatter their own realities and form *conscientização* without simultaneously doing the same, the classroom can easily devolve to the binary of student/learner and teacher/knowledge-bearer.

While most educators can agree that they hope that students will be engaged in their learning, and even agree that incorporating multimedia study into the classroom is one way to encourage engagement, putting theory into practice is challenging. Therefore, what follows is an illustration of one multiliterate critical classroom investigating the theme of "multitasking."

MULTILITERACY IN PRACTICE

The multiliterate critical classroom engages learners, both teacher/student and students/teachers, in authentic *praxis* - or the interplay of word, reflection, and action - beginning with multimedia. Learners first identify key words and patterns to form a language to define and describe multiliteracy. Then, learners reflect on their own multiliterate practices and those of their peers and community using their shared language. The end result of the study and reflection is action as learners empower themselves to both understand their role in a digital world and act as agents in that world.

For this illustration, the learners investigate the theme of multitasking, one that is certainly immediate and relevant for both instructors and students in the 21st century classroom. Students can are tempted to check Facebook, send a quick text, and pursue other forms of digital distraction in the classroom any time that cell phones or laptops are present. Educators claim that students are distracted from learning by these pursuits, and students claim that they are able to multitask and still learn. Thus, using multitasking as a generative theme in the classroom places at the center of inquiry a concern of immediate importance.

To begin exploration, learners would collect media about multitasking, compiling videos, websites, and other sources about multitasking. One way that they might work to collect sources is through tagging, or "folksonomy" sites, such as Delicious (http://delicious.com), to connect with others who might be collecting similar materials outside the classroom. Tagging sources and following the tags of others online who have tagged those same sources allow learners to network, a practice with which 21st century students are very familiar. This allows students to begin the exploration in the familiar both thematically and practically.

Next, learners would begin reviewing the sources to note terms or elements consistent throughout those sources and to begin developing a shared vocabulary to use for further multiliterate exploration. For example, they might watch videos that deal with research on multitasking, such as the *Frontline* series "Digital Nation" from PBS. org. Instructors and students would first watch to take notes on content, identifying the primary points made by the speakers in each video. On a second viewing, teachers and students would be asked to note *whom* was allowed the privilege of speaking in each video and whose voices were not heard. Finally, a third viewing of the video would be completed in order to note camera angles, transitions, *mis-en-scene*, and other editing choices that contributed to the overall message. Learners then explore digital media to "consider carefully what is actually present on the page, screen, and in visual forms, not what they assume is there and what they assume it means" (Duffelmeyer, 2002, p. 44). Exploring unearths assumptions all learners hold about the theme, making ordinary multimedia consumption extraordinary.

Learners then work with the concepts they build in dialogue with each other to reflect on the media they consume and their own multitasking practices. Where the initial stage of data collection operated in a realm in which students are familiar, the reflection process can be where the instructor brings her strengths and knowledge to the classroom. Michael Wesch (2008) highlights how this co-exploration can lead instructors and students to a shared consciousness through combined strengths:

[Students] may know all about YouTube and Facebook and how to navigate these things to entertain themselves, but they know nothing about how to use these things to learn and for critical thought and more than anything, they rarely know how to use these things to create something interesting and new.

Thus, where students may be stronger in finding online media or networking, educators are stronger in guiding reflection, critical thought and purposeful, rhetorical use of texts, sometimes but not always including digital media. The equal footing of shared knowledge can be disconcerting at first for the educator who is unfamiliar with digital media. With this discomfort comes disruption for the educator, who can welcome this uncertainty just as she asks students to embrace the new and rocky footing of critical dialogue and expression. By acknowledging her discomfort with this disruption and by using her familiarity with critical thinking methods, she models a way for the students to both use their knowledge of digital and multimedia and also navigate their discomfort with unfamiliar conventions and terms. In this way, all learners can take the risks that can lead them to question the paradigms that shape their identities.

As a penultimate step, learners compose using the same multimedia they investigate. These compositions embody Reid's (2007) concept of "rip/mix/burn," or an "understanding of writing enabled by new insights into cognition and generated through the development of cybernetics and digital media" (p. 157). Just as students would traditionally be asked to compose research papers or essays pulling from a variety of print texts, students and educators in the classroom that implements multimedia investigation compose videos, Prezi projects (see http://www.prezi.com), or other digital projects that "rip" multiple pieces of media and remix them to form something new. In the process, learners can investigate such ideas as copyright, ownership, identity, and socially-constructed knowledge. In tandem with digital media production, learners should be asked to reflect on their processes of creation, both outlining the steps they took to create their productions and focusing on how those steps reflect their own ideas about self, identity, and how those are projected in the projects they created.

Finally, learners use their multiliteracy to take action. Learners might post their creations to YouTube or a similar site that allows for them to open dialogue with others about the issues raised in their projects. They might implement new practices, such as "multitasking breaks" where they practice working consistently for 15-30 minutes before allowing themselves a "Facebook break" to begin to take back power from those technologies that exert power over them. At a minimum, learners become more aware of how multitasking and digital media exert power over their lives and become agents of change to make technology work with and not against them.

Of course, not all learners exploring themes through digital and multimedia will find the experience life-changing. Some will struggle navigating the technology; others will find any investigation of everyday life too risky. Some students will sidestep critical exploration of themes or complete "fun" multimedia projects instead completing real, complex investigations. However, the space provided for students to communicate important

elements of their world wakes students from what Boler calls "inscribed habits of (in)attention," in some cases, giving opportunity for students to "witness," through "tracing genealogies of particular emotional investments" and capture a moment of their history for further exploration (1999, p.186).

Solutions and Recommendations

Becoming agents in exploring digital media in the classroom and communicating in forms that make the ordinary extraordinary and challenge conceptions of consciousness can be risky for both students and educators. However, continuing to ignore the digital revolution for the sake of textual traditions precludes the possibility to engage students in radical education and reinforces tacit power relations in the classroom. Multiliteracy in the classroom, as Reid (2007) contends, "set[s] aside the common complaints of student discipline or literacy or maturity to examine the aporia of the virtual-actual that lies beneath them" (p. 184). *Aporia* is the concept of reaching an impasse at which point we have true doubt about the perplexing issue before us. Educators are perplexed by student apathy and resistance to reading and writing: the fundamentals of academia they hold so dear. Students are perplexed when they disconnect from communities where they practice agency in order to enter new communities where they forfeit agency in the name of empowerment.

The only solution is to begin slowly, admit limitation, and embrace the aporia of the digital revolution. Those dedicated to education as Freire envisioned, as the ontological vocation of becoming more fully human, must recognize that print-based education can be just as dehumanizing for students as digital media can be for them. All people can and do make and maintain real and lasting connections through digital and social media that allow them to create and maintain a virtual presence as real in their Second Lives as in their "real" lives. Ignoring this reality risks reverting to the primacy of the banking model where we hold our textbooks as shields to defend ourselves against the windmills of digital technology in our minds.

FUTURE RESEARCH DIRECTIONS

Research on student multiliteracy and digital media use could provide valuable insight to assist instructors in not only better incorporating digital technologies in the classroom but also helping students see the cultural and personal ramifications of the acceleration new media promotes. Areas for continued research include:

- The intersections of critical pedagogy and multiliteracy, particularly how student media use influences an individual's experience in the classroom (see Skurat Harris, 2009).
- How students conceptualize digital audiences, particularly in their use of Web 2.0 technologies, and how those audiences do or do not replicate traditional notions of social structure.
- How new media in the classroom changes the focus of learning from ingesting and regurgitating data and facts to learning how to access, control, and communicate facts (see Wesch, 2009).
- Instructor and student concerns and hesitancy incorporating new media and multiliteracy work in the classroom
- The possibilities of thematic investigations of multimedia and Web 2.0 use in the classroom in a variety of disciplines.

Any of these research directions will allow us to better address a wide range of concerns with multimedia use and multiliteracy in 21st century classrooms.

CONCLUSION

While twenty-first century learners come wired to our classrooms, educators are often ardent defenders of traditional print-based literacy, reinforcing the notion that only information vetted by experts and codified in traditional forms is worthy of study. However, critical pedagogy informs us that the true nature of education is not in memorizing understanding words but in using those words to connect individuals in larger social structures where we can fight the complicity of oppressive paradigms. The classroom need not relegate students to the status of receptacles for knowledge. Incorporating digital technology and encouraging students and educators alike to become multiliterate disrupts oppressive systems by creating communities of co-learners invested in and in control of their own realities.

REFERENCES

Boler, M. (1999). *Feeling power: Emotions and education*. New York, NY: Routledge.

Duffelmeyer, B. (2002). Critical work in first-year composition: Computers, pedagogy, and research. *Pedagogy: Critical Approaches to Teaching Literature, Language, Composition, and Culture, 2*(3), 357–374. doi:10.1215/15314200-2-3-357

Dunn, P. (2001). *Talking, sketching, moving: Multiple literacies in the teaching of writing*. New Hampshire: Boynton/Cook.

Freire, P. (1998). *Pedagogy of the oppressed. 20ᵗʰ Anniversary Edition. (Trans.) Myra Bergman Ramos*. New York, NY: Continuum.

Giroux, H. (1992). *Border crossings: Cultural workers and the politics of education*. New York, NY: Routledge.

Giroux, H. (2001). *Theory and resistance in education: Toward a pedagogy for the opposition.* Westport, CT: Bergin & Garvey.

Hawisher, G., & Selfe, C. (Eds.). (1999). *Passions, pedagogies, and twenty-first century technologies.* Logan, UT: Utah State University Press.

Hendrix, S., & Jacobsen, E. (2000). What happened in English 101? In Tassoni, J., & Thelin, W. (Eds.), *Blundering for a change: Errors and expectations in critical pedagogy* (pp. 51–67). Portsmouth, NH: Boynton/Cook.

Kress, G. (2003). *Literacy in a new media age.* London, UK: Routledge. doi:10.4324/9780203164754

LeCourt, D. (1998). Critical pedagogy in the computer classroom: Politicizing the writing space. *Computers and Composition, 15,* 275–295. doi:10.1016/S8755-4615(98)90002-0

Lee, A. (2000). *Compositing critical pedagogies: Teaching writing as revision.* Urbana, IL: National Council of Teachers of English.

Lenhart, A., Purcell, K., Smith, A., & Zickuhr, K. (2010). *Social media and young adults.* Pew Internet and American Life Project. Retrieved from http://www.pewinternet.org/Reports/2010/Social-Media-and-Young-Adults.aspx

Reid, A. (2007). *The two virtuals: New media and composition.* West Lafayette, IN: Parlor Press.

Rideout, V., Foher, U., & Roberts, D. (2010). *Generation M²: Media in the lives of 8 to 18-year-olds.* Kaiser Family Foundation Study. Retrieved from http://www.kff.org/entmedia/upload/8010.pdf

Selber, S. (2004). *Multi-literacies for a digital age.* Carbondale, IL: Southern Illinois University Press.

Self, C. (2009). The movement of air, the breathing of meaning: Aurality and multimodal composing. *College Composition and Communication, 60,* 616–663.

Selfe, C., & Hawisher, G. (2004). *Literate lives in the information age: Narratives of literacy from the United States.* Mahwah, NJ: Lawrence Erlbaum Associates.

Shor, I. (1980). *Critical teaching and everyday life.* Boston, MA: South End Press.

Shor, I. (Ed.). (1987). *Freire for the classroom: A sourcebook for liberatory teaching.* Portsmouth, NH: Boynton/Cook.

Shor, I. (1992). *Empowering education: Critical teaching for social change.* Chicago, IL: University of Chicago Press.

Skurat Harris, H. (2009). *Digital students in the democratic classroom: Using technology to enhance critical pedagogy in the first-year composition classroom.* Unpublished doctoral dissertation, Ball State University.

Tassoni, J., & Thelin, W. (Eds.). (2000). *Blundering for a change: Errors and expectations in critical pedagogy.* Portsmouth, NH: Boynton/Cook.

Villanueva, V. (1991). Considerations for American Freireistas. In Richard Bullock, R., & Trimbur, J. (Eds.), *The politics of writing instruction: Postsecondary* (pp. 247–263). Portsmouth, NH: Boynton/Cook.

Wesch, M. (2008, June 17). *A portal to media literacy.* Presented at the University of Manitoba, June 17, 2008. Retrieved September 24, 2008 from http://www.youtube.com/watch?v=J4yApagnr0s

Wesch, M. (2009, January 7). From knowledgeable to knowledge-able: Learning in new media environments. In *Academic Commons* retrieved June 29, 2010 from http://www.academiccommons.org/commons/essay/knowledgable-knowledge-able.

Wysocki, A. F., Johnson-Eilola, J., Selfe, C., & Sirc, G. (2004). *Writing new media: Theory and applications for expanding the teaching of composition.* Logan, UT: Utah State University Press.

ADDITIONAL READING

Barton, M., & Cummings, R. (Eds.). (2008). *Wiki Writing: Collaborative Learning in the College Classroom*. Ann Arbor, MI: Digital Culture Books.

Duffelmeyer, B. (2000). Critical Computer Literacy: Computers in First-Year Composition as Topic and Environment. *Computers and Composition, 17,* 289–307. doi:10.1016/S8755-4615(00)00036-0

Duffelmeyer, B. (2001). Using Digital Technology to Augment a Critical Literacy Approach to First-Year Composition. In Muffoletto, R. (Ed.), *Education and Technology: Critical and Reflective Practices* (pp. 241–258). Cresskill, N.J.: Hampton.

Duffelmeyer, B., & Ellertson, A. (2005) Critical Visual Literacy: Multimodal Communication Across the Curriculum. In *Across the Disciplines: Interdisciplinary Perspectives on Language, Learning, and Academic Writing* retrieved June 30, 2010 from http://wac.colostate.edu/atd/visual/index.cfm.

Freire, P. (1998). *Pedagogy of Freedom: Ethics, Democracy and Civic Courage. (Trans.). Patrick Clarke.* Lanham, MD: Rowman and Littlefield.

George, A. (2001). Critical Pedagogy: Dreaming of Democracy. In Tate, G., Rupiper, A., & Schick, K. (Eds.), *A Guide to Composition Pedagogies* (pp. 92–112). New York: Oxford University Press.

Gerben, C. (2009). "Putting 2.0 and Two Together: What Web 2.0 Can Teach Composition about Collaborative Learning. *Computers and Composition Online.* Retrieved from http://candcblog.org/Gerben/.

Gooding, J. (2008). Web 2.0: A Vehicle for Transforming Education. *International Journal of Information and Communication Technology Education, 4*(2), 44–53. doi:10.4018/jicte.2008040104

Gore, J. (1993). *The Struggle for Pedagogies.* London: Routledge.

Haas, C. (1996). *Writing Technology: Studies on the Materiality of Literacy.* Mahwah, NJ: Erlbaum.

Handa, C. (2004). *Visual Rhetoric in a Digital World: A Critical Sourcebook.* Boston, MA: Bedford/St. Martin's.

Hawisher, G., Selfe, C., Moraski, B., & Pearson, M. (2004). Becoming Literate in the Information Age: Cultural Ecologies and the Literacies of Technology. *College Composition and Communication, 55*(4), 642–692. doi:10.2307/4140666

Hocks, M., & Kendrick, M. (Eds.). (2003). *Eloquent Images: Word and Image in the Age of New Media.* Cambridge, MA: Massachusetts Institute of Technology Press.

Jackson, B., & Wallin, J. (2009). Rediscovering the "Back-and-Forthness" of Rhetoric in the Age of YouTube. *College Composition and Communication, 61*(2), W374–W396.

Lutkewitte, C. (2009). Web 2.0 Technologies in First-Year Writing. *Computers and Composition Online.* Retrieved from http://www.bgsu.edu/cconline/Web2.0/default.htm.

McLaren, P. (2002). Critical Pedagogy: A Look at the Major Concepts. In Antonia Darder, A., Torres, R. D., & Baltodano, M. (Eds.), *The Critical Pedagogy Reader* (pp. 69–96). London: Routledge.

McLaren, P., & Hammer, R. (1999). Media Knowledges, Warrior Citizenry, and Postmodern Literacies. In Giroux, H., Lankshear, C., McLaren, P., & Peters, M. (Eds.), *Counternarratives: Cultural Studies and Critical Poedagogies in Postmodern Spaces* (pp. 81–115). New York: Routledge.

Nicotra, J. (2009). "Folksonomy" and the Restructuring of Writing Space. *College Composition and Communication, 61,* W259–W276.

Selber, S. (2004). Technological Dramas: A Meta-Discourse Heuristic for Critical Literacy. *Computers and Composition*, *21*, 171–195. doi:10.1016/j.compcom.2004.04.001

Selfe, C. (1999). *Technology and Literacy in the Twenty-First Century: The Perils of not Paying Attention*. Carbondale, IL: Southern Illinois University Press.

Takayoshi, P. (1996). Writing the Culture of Computers: Students as Technology Critics in Cultural Studies Classes. *Teaching English in the Two-Year College*, *23*(3), 198–204.

Tulley, C. (2009). Taking a Traditional Composition Program 'Multimodal': Web 2.0 and Institutional Change at a Small Liberal Arts Institution. *Computers and Composition Online*. Retrieved from http://www.bgsu.edu/cconline/Tulley09/.

Turnley, M. (2005). Contextualized Design: Teaching Critical Approaches to Web Authoring Through Redesign Projects. *Computers and Composition*, *22*, 131–148. doi:10.1016/j.compcom.2005.02.007

Westbrook, S. (2006). Visual Rhetoric in a Culture of Fear: Impediments to Multimedia Production. *College English*, *68*(5), 457–480. doi:10.2307/25472166

Wolff, W., Fitzpatrick, K., & Youssef, R. (2009). Rethinking Usability for Web 2.0 and Beyond. *Currents in Electronic Literacy*. Retrieved at http://currents.cwrl.utexas.edu/2009WolffFitzpatrickYoussef.

KEY TERMS AND DEFINITIONS

21ˢᵗ Century Learners: Students who have grown up with digital technologies as a part of their everyday life and who increasingly expect and thrive in environments infused with those technologies.

Banking System: The metaphor originally used by Paulo Freire in the book *Pedagogy of the Oppressed* to describe educational systems that view students as passive recipients of knowledge and teachers as those giving knowledge to the students.

Conscientização: Brazilian term meaning "consciousness of consciousness," or the ability of an individual to have an understanding that s/he is a participant in the construction of his/her reality.

Critical Pedagogy: A group of teaching methods whose primary focus is personal liberation through raising conscious awareness of the individual's place in reality. The end result of this individual consciousness is collective social change as the individual becomes more aware of how she is connected to others and under the power and influence of repressive political forces.

Digital (New) Media: Any form or combination of print, video, film, images, sound or other data that is primarily disseminated or accessed through computers or other digital technologies.

Generation Y: The generation born generally between the late 1970s and 2000. This group is characterized primarily by their familiarity with digital technologies.

Generative Themes: A topic of concern or importance in the Freirian model of literacy. The generative theme determines the words that participants will use in their investigation of the culture around them.

Glogs: A Web 2.0 technology that allows students to create multimedia "posters" that are then posted for access online at http://www.glogster.com.

Multimedia: A single form of media that combines a variety of individual forms (for example, a video that uses text, images, and sound).

Multiliteracy: The ability to understand and communicate effectively in a variety of media, including but not limited to print/text, video, audio, and images.

Praxis: The creation of reality through the use of words, reflection, and action in a cyclical process (words create realities, humans reflect on that reality and take action to shape it through the words they use).

Rip/Mix/Burn: A process of copying, quoting, or borrowing materials (rip) that a user then remakes into his or her own composition (mix), and compressing and disseminating those materials to others (burn) who then rip them to begin new compositions.

Web 2.0: Web applications that facilitate communication, interaction, and sharing on the internet as opposed to sites that allow only for the passive viewing of information.

Chapter 8
"I'm not Always Laughing at the Jokes":
Humor as a Force for Disruption

Julie Faulkner
RMIT University, Australia

Bronwyn T. Williams
University of Louisville, USA

ABSTRACT

Humor in popular culture plays with our perceptions and sense of dislocation. The inherently ambiguous logic of humor allows for multiple interpretations of social phenomena, and constructs the world as arbitrary, multiple, and tenuous (Mulkay, 1988). At the same time, humor is one of the central elements of much of what young people find appealing in popular culture. Exploring the potential of humor to interrogate cultural assumptions, Australian and American students participated in a cross-cultural television study. The student cohorts then communicated on line, developing their reading of the sitcom in a cross-cultural forum. Their responses highlight the disruption to accepted patterns of social order that the play upon form, or parody, delivers. Through exploring 'insider' and 'outsider' readings of a television parody, this chapter explores how humorous conventions function to reflexively position readers, and thus invite critical readings of popular and engaging texts. It also examines broader questions of the role of the US in producing and distributing popular culture, and how readers might find creative and critical ways to deal with culturally disparate world views.

INTRODUCTION

Although engaging students with popular culture texts continues to gain slow acceptance in literacy education, it remains a disruptive act in the classroom. The cultural status of popular culture texts, as easy to understand, pleasurable, and reliant on emotion and narrative, often runs run counter to standardized, dominant views of academic discourse. In addition, popular culture in the classroom also disrupts dominant pedagogical practices by engaging with texts in which students feel more ownership and expertise. It

DOI: 10.4018/978-1-61350-495-6.ch008

changes the relationship of who understands and interprets texts and engages student involvement and investment. Yet the use of popular culture can still address important issues about audience, interpretation, authorship and context.

Humor in popular culture, in particular, plays with our perceptions and sense of dislocation. The serendipitous 'logic' of humor allows for openness of interpretation and an understanding of the contingency of ways of knowing. At the same time, humor is one of the central elements of much of what young people find appealing in popular culture. Exploring the potential of humor to interrogate cultural assumptions, Australian and American students participated in a cross-cultural television study. They viewed an Australian sitcom, *Kath and Kim,* asking to what extent a knowledge of the sitcom's cultural norms was fundamental to an appreciation of the intended humor of the series. The student cohorts then communicated on line, developing their reading of the sitcom in a cross-cultural forum. Their responses highlight the disruption to accepted patterns of social order that the play upon form, or parody, delivers.

The study then asks how humor and popular culture could work in literacy classrooms as a disruptive pedagogy. The culturally contextualised nature of a local situation comedy works to suggest that accepted patterns have no necessity (Douglas, 1975) and that knowledge in this sense is always contingent. Juxtaposition, exaggeration or adopting an unexpected point of view in comedy throw 'natural' practices into relief, disrupting accepted patterns of social order, Through exploring 'insider' and 'outsider' readings of a television parody, this chapter will explore how humorous conventions function to reflexively position readers, and thus invite critical readings of popular and engaging texts. It will also examine broader questions of the role of the US in producing and distributing popular culture, and how readers might find creative and critical ways to deal with culturally disparate world views.

As literacy educators, we chose to use the collaborative ethos of online discussions of popular culture to explore concepts of literacy and context in cross-cultural settings with students. We felt confident that when given the opportunity to discuss, question, and debate television programs with students in another country, the students in our classes would engage in collaborative meaning making that would encourage them think about issues of reading texts across cultural boundaries.

Humor, because of its strong reliance on cultural context, seemed a particularly fruitful choice to challenge students to think about how cultural context influences literacy practices. Although the form of the sitcom might be familiar to both sets of students, the contexts for the humor within the form would require students to work together to make meaning, highlighting for them the situated nature of the text. At the same time, discussing sitcoms would offer a low-stakes conversation embedded in texts and forms with which they could feel confident and comfortable in their interaction. Moreover, appreciation of comedy depends to a large extent on levels of cultural understanding – how do semiotic elements such as language, accents, issues, stereotypes, class-based and regional references and even local production styles influence the ways we respond to comedy, particularly satire made for television? Collette (2006) highlights the role of television as a powerful mediator of 'a postmodern world … of surfaces and appearance' (p. 861). By having students have to confront and negotiate meanings with students from other cultures, this project disrupted students' ideas of textual stability and forced them confront culturally situated nature of all texts. Humor – parody in this case - offered us many possibilities for extending levels of critical thinking.

WHY DO WE LAUGH?

Freud (1960) saw the 'frivolousness' of humor as a relief from self-discipline; a release from the seriousness of our everyday lives. Bakhtin (1981) labelled the power of laughter to overturn the existing social order as 'carnivalesque'.

Theorising humor from cultural studies perspectives, Kellner (1995) argues that pleasure is learned. We learn what to enjoy and what we should avoid. Building on the work of Goffman, Billig (2008) argues that humor carries a social control function: a 'learnt rhetorical device that functions to discipline children – and the adults they become – into persons who observe everyday codes that govern social behaviour' (p. 88). If satire functions largely as a weapon, it raises the question of how it might subvert or reinforce such mechanisms, a question which will be addressed later in this chapter.

Every text grows from, and reflects its own cultural context. Capacity to respond to the text is dependent upon our existing cultural knowledge, or the social and political reference points in our everyday lives. Awareness of the elements which constitute the fabric of our lives is necessary if we are to realise the ways that humor plays with our perceptions of identity or dislocation. The inherently ambiguous logic of humor allows for multiple interpretations of social phenomena (Mulkay, 1988). For theorists like Mulkay, the world is constructed, arbitrary, multiple and tenuous.

The cultural anthropologist, Mary Douglas (1975), in writing about jokes as a form of humor, highlights the disruption to accepted patterns of social order that the play upon form, or joke, delivers. It is the clash of disparate elements, she argues, which questions the dominant ordering of experience and makes the viewer, through laughter, aware that

the accepted pattern has no necessity. [The joke's] excitement lies in the suggestion that any particular ordering of experience may be arbitrary

and subjective. It is frivolous in that it produces no real alternative, only an exhilarating sense of freedom from form in general. (p. 96)

Laughter may be exhilarating but might also produce a more ambivalent, uncomfortable response. Learning to inhabit more ambiguous, indeterminate spaces is the goal of 'pedagogies of discomfort', pedagogies which enable learners to recognize what they have been taught to see or not to see (Boler, 1999; Zembylas & Boler, 2002). 'Natural' practices are thrown into relief through comedy, via juxtaposition, exaggeration or adopting an unexpected point of view.

Using these reflexive notions of humor's capacity to build commonalities as well as to disrupt accepted patterns of social order, we designed our cross-cultural study around two 'local' television sitcoms. Both were popular among their target audiences and offered rich material for discovering how far, and in what ways, group references might be shared and reflected upon. Because so much popular culture circulates on a global scale today, yet humor is so dependent on local cultural contexts, sitcoms provide particularly intriguing texts to examine the ways in which people make meaning of texts that cross, or fail to cross-cultural borders.

The culturally situated nature of humor offers a reminder of the limitations of the concept of 'global popular culture". Certainly the technological advances of recent years, the same ones that have given rise to the practices of convergence culture, have allowed movies, television, music, video games all to cross-cultural boundaries with relative ease. It is also true that young people around the world often draw on popular culture that originates somewhere else in the world in their cultural choices and ways that it allows them to express their identities. Consequently it is not necessarily surprising to see the same kind of clothing or same song or same catchphrase from a movie popular in countries that are oceans apart. At the same time, however, it is important to remember that texts that circulate globally are still read and employed locally. Local uses of any text are always specific to those contexts, and therefore are not always predictable. Hip hop, for example, has as a musical form and a culture spread across the world. Yet hip hop has been adapted by local youth to express ideas about local conditions, and so often becomes less comprehensible to youth in other cultures. 'The creation of new styles may involve elements of imitation, but the imitation acquires a new meaning as a result of the person who appropriates it and the context in which it occurs' (de Block & Rydin, 2006, p. 300). Such local responses to 'global' popular culture offer creative opportunities, but also tensions and contested readings. Within our own cultures we often look to popular culture as common cultural touchstones which are understandable to all in the society. When popular culture texts are read in different contexts, however, our expectations of common understanding of the movie or television program can be resisted or denied.

Television sitcoms also often cross cultural borders, but are read in ways specific to local cultural contexts. The form may be familiar, but the common cultural touchstones that provide the context for interpretation are different. Because we draw on different intertextual backgrounds to make meaning of the program, our readings may be very different from those in another culture. When trying to understand a sitcom and humor from another culture, our intertextual connections also invariably include our perceptions of and power relationships with the country in which the program was created. Thus the laughter of the people across the ocean may puzzle, or even offend us.

Using reflexive notions of humor's capacity to build commonalities as well as to disrupt accepted patterns of social order, we designed our cross-cultural study around an Australian and a U.S. television sitcom. Both were popular among

their target audiences and offered rich material for discovering how far, and in what ways, group references might be shared and reflected upon.

THE STUDY

To explore aspects of humor in a cross-cultural context, Julie Faulkner, as the Australian researcher and Bronwyn Williams, American counterpart, exchanged recordings of sitcoms which originated in Australia and the US respectively. As far as possible, we chose programs which we assumed the respective overseas cohorts knew little or nothing of. *Kath and Kim* is a satirical view of Australian life in the aspirational suburbs of Melbourne. Originally commissioned by the government broadcaster at prime time, its success gained the show a commercial sale for its fourth season. *Kath and Kim* focuses on a parent-child relationship, a relationship lacking by conventional *Father Knows Best* standards. The central characters verge on the comically grotesque as they strive to be what they are not. The series was extraordinarily successful by Australian television standards, although failed miserably in its American version, both in Australia and the U.S.

Arrested Development is a US sitcom about another dysfunctional family. The patriarch, head of an apparently successful business, is jailed for embezzlement, leaving his grasping wife, one ambitious and two eccentric sons, materialistic daughter and their various dependents to fend for themselves. The pace of the series is fast, editing slick and script construction tight. It attracted a strong cult audience but was cancelled after three seasons on the FOX network.

For the study, the viewers of these sitcoms numbered approximately 12-15 students, and were, in Australia, Graduate Diploma of Education English method students. In the United States the students were postgraduate Master's and Doctoral students enrolled in a course on Popular Culture and Literacy. Students were asked to view several episodes of their relevant series and respond to an initial question about what they found, or failed to find funny. Each distinct cohort then met face-to-face to discuss their responses collectively. They then entered an online forum where they joined a threaded discussion with their international partners, which continued over a period of approximately two weeks.

Obviously the identity of these students provided both limitations and opportunities for the project. The students in the courses were strong readers and writers and adept at the conventions of academic conversations. They were comfortable reflecting on their answers and making connections between theory and practice. They were also able to discuss what pedagogical uses they might see for such an exercise with their students. Such abilities would provide us with strong insights into the texts and their cultural contexts, but also would not be what we would expect from a group comprised of secondary or university students less familiar with the conventions of academic discourse. Still, many of the interpretive moves made by both the Australian and U.S. students were similar to those made by different groups in other research (Morley 1992; Buckingham and Sefton-Green 1994; Lembo 2000), if at a different level of sophistication. For these reasons the research provided a productive and intriguing starting insight into how humor and popular culture could provide a useful intervention into a literacy classroom.

The face to face and digital discussion between Julie, Bronwyn and participating students were collected as data. Responses were analysed around themes raised by the discussants themselves. Using MacLachlan and Reid's framing theory (1984), we explored the extent to which laughter might be related to contextual knowledge based on media representations and further, what this knowledge might hold for literacy learning. Ma-

cLachlan and Reid suggest framing curriculum and reading responses to texts within extratextual, circumtextual, intertextural and intratextural approaches. Extratextual knowledge involves the understandings that the reader brings to the text, circumtextual elements describe what sits around the text to influence the reader, while intertextual framing brings related texts to enhance appreciation of the original. Intratextual framing seeks to identify generic conventions within the text.

WHAT DO WE NEED TO KNOW IN ORDER TO GET THE JOKE?

Intratextual references in a comparison between Australian and American television programs include sociolinguistic features, such as accent and vocabulary. No Australian student made any comment about these aspects in relation to *Arrested Development*. Kath and Kim's Australian accents are broad ('look at moie') and, for an Australian audience, are locatable within certain socioeconomic and regional strata. The characters use many mixed metaphors and malapropisms, usually in their attempts to sound, as one character remarks, more 'effluent'. Like *Arrested Development*, much humor flows from the interplay between the verbal and visual. While some of the humor works broadly within western conventions of farce, other jokes depend on local cultural knowledge. Kim, for example, takes a cantaloupe from the fridge, whining 'Well, Brett and I just can't elope!' The joke depends on reading the fruit in her hand as a 'canteloupe' rather than a 'rockmelon', although this term is not used universally, nor even throughout Australia, so the joke is diffused. The US cohort expressed no difficulty with Kath and Kim's accents. One student asked the meaning of 'a cushman', 'a little b.' and 'trim little p.i's'. Australian students were able to identify a 'cushman' as a 'cushion (soft) man' and explain 'b.' as a 'noice' abbreviation of 'bitch'. However, 'p.i's' remained unexplained until it was realised that it was most likely referred to 'p. a's.' (personal assistants) in a Kath and Kim nasal accent.

Students occasionally raised issues of cultural knowledge. *Kath and Kim* typically ends with a 'mother and daughter' moment sitting in the back yard. In one instance, Kath and Kim are leafing through gossip magazines and it is mentioned by Kim that she wished Nicole Kidman were featured more often on the cover. Rebecca from Australia comments that this postscript is only funny (in a sarcastic sense) if you have stood in Australian supermarkets containing ubiquitous images of Nicole Kidman on magazines. Similarly, Kath and her new husband, Kel, are trapped inside the airport in one episode and spend their time duty free shopping. A camera shot has them riding up the escalator in matching Coogee jumpers, but again, this is only funny if the viewer is familiar with the range of Australiana in duty free shops, knowing that most Australians would never buy the too-obvious products. Such examples, however, when raised by Australians, received the American response: 'it's hard to know what didn't come through to American viewers because we obviously wouldn't miss what we didn't know we didn't catch, (if that makes sense)' (Cynthia). Cynthia's reflexive stance raises the question of what levels of prior cultural knowledge are necessary to understand what it is you don't know.

As expected students in both countries used their familiarity with the genre of sitcoms to try to make sense of the program imported from outside their culture. Many of the students began their discussions by comparing elements of the new program with other programs with which they were more familiar.

Fiona, an Australian student, said:

I didn't know anything about Arrested Development when I first viewed it as part of this experiment, but I did come to it expecting one of two things to occur. One would be that it was a formulaic American sitcom (à la Friends, Will and Grace,

etc) or that it would be witty, insightful, and satiric with a fairly large slice of the outrageous (à la The Simpsons, South Park). I was pleased to find it was more the second expectation than the first.

This comment was echoed by her classmate, Tony, who said, 'I discovered that I 'got' all the jokes in *Arrested Development*, in the same way that I laughed at the comedy in *Seinfeld* and the *The Simpsons*.' What was interesting to note was that the Australian students, in making interpretive comparisons about *Arrested Development*, made most of their references to other programs from the U.S. such as *The Simpsons, Will and Grace,* or *The Gilmore Girls.* Yet it is noteworthy that in making such references, the Australian students usually moved quickly from how they had drawn on other sitcoms to frame their interpretations of *Arrested Development* to using such comparisons to justify their responses to the sitcom, or to make other evaluative comments. The Australian students could also, of course, discuss other programs that originated in Australia, but when they did so most of these comments were addressed to their Australian classmates; there was no expectation that the U.S. students would share the cultural reference. In this way the Australian students connected the text from the global market to their local intertextual connections and adopted the meanings of the U.S. program to their own local needs.

By contrast many of the U.S. students' initial comments indicated that they were drawing on other sitcoms to make meaning out of the places they found *Kath and Kim* confusing, rather than to justify their critical judgments. Such evaluative comments came later in the conversations. Most of the U.S. students drew on other U.S. programs for comparisons and explicitly mentioned how narrow they understood their range of Australian popular cultural references to be. They noted that Australian popular culture in the U.S. was largely limited to *The Crocodile Hunter, Outback Jack,* and the *Crocodile Dundee* and *Mad Max* movies.

(There was also some common ground in a few well-known British sitcoms that had played in both Australia and the U.S such as *Absolutely Fabulous, Fawlty Towers,* and *The Office.*) Consequently the U.S. students attempted to find genre connections between *Kath and Kim* and U.S. produced sitcoms with which they were familiar. As they made the connections they tried to explain how the shows were stylistically similar. Dan's comment about *Kath and Kim* was typical:

I found it a lot like The Simpsons. It relied a lot on having a certain set of cultural knowledge. There was lots of fast cutting, lots of irony. And there was just this brutal honesty about a dysfunctional family. There was this sense that it was telling a kind of exaggerated truth about family relationships.

Other U.S. programs to which the U.S. students compared *Kath and Kim* included *The Gilmore Girls, Married with Children, Roseanne,* and *South Park.* For the U.S. students the intertextual connections were already familiar to the Australians, and they quickly realized they did not have to elaborate with descriptions of the programs.

That the students drew on familiar texts to try find similarities in a text with which they were struggling is not a radical insight. Good critical readers, and these students were good readers, make such interpretive moves all the time with all kinds of texts. Good readers of television, and these students, like most people in the culture, were good readers of television, make the same moves with television programs. What is potentially useful in the literacy classroom is that students who are not strong readers, but who can make such interpretive moves with the television programs they feel comfortable watching and discussing, can be taught strategies for making such connections when reading print texts for school (Williams 2002).

The students' use of what MacLachlan and Reid (1994) call 'intertextual framing", or how the text relates to different but similar texts, is

particularly interesting in this cross-cultural context. Clearly the Australian students, with a more comprehensive knowledge of both U.S. and Australia television programs and genres, had an advantage in making meaning from both sitcoms and engaging in a wide range of comparisons.

There is a clear sense in many of their comments that the Australian students felt they understood U.S. popular culture and, by extension, had some sense of the contexts in which humor worked in sitcoms. As Tony said, 'We Australians have been importing U.S. culture for many decades now. Another view might be that we are victims of U.S. cultural imperialism. Whichever is more correct, we have an understanding of how U.S. TV and comedy works and have learned to understand what is funny on an imported U.S. TV production.' Fiona noted the difference in confidence level that the two sets of students displayed in their comments, and argued that the cause was the difference of cultural positioning in the U.S. and Australia in terms of relationships with the rest of the world:

I would like to suggest that the Australians participating in this experiment have been forced to adopt (based on the fact that we derive our English heritage from Britain and share with our Commonwealth family similar experiences of making sense of the world from a colonial perspective, in addition to the cultural imperialism coming from the U.S. for as long as I've been alive) a different and perhaps broader range of literacies than our American counterparts and therefore have been able to get more out of our experience with Arrested Development than Americans have with Kath and Kim. I would suggest that we have International Literacy Competencies.

The Australian students were keenly aware of the relations between their culture and the U.S. in terms of economic and cultural power. Although not directly part of this study, it is worth noting that the Australian students, while noting their position in relation to the power of the U.S., did not comment on their own positions of privilege and power in relation to other cultures in less economically powerful countries. Their confidence in their ability to accurately read the U.S. sitcoms because of their familiarity with similar texts raises a further question, however. This question would ask what they might be reading differently from the U.S. students because of the different intertextual connections they would make from their lived experiences in a different local context.

By contrast, for the U.S. students, their readings and comparisons were more hedged and marked by more frequent concerns about what they might not have understood while watching *Kath and Kim*. A number of the students asked questions about the program and questions about Australian culture in general. Such acknowledgments of confusion or misreadings were infrequent among the Australian students. By and large the Australians did not question what they were missing, or blame cultural myopia for potential misreadings.

James, a U.S. student, blamed his occasional confusion about *Kath and Kim* on his 'cultural ignorance' and said, 'What I mean is, would some of the jokes not translate at all? What didn't we get because we're American? I just feel as if I'd have to know a lot more about Australia before I really understood the show.'

SATIRE: DISRUPTIVE OR SELF-SATISFIED?

Questions persist around the belittling nature of satire as a humorous form and, therefore, the limitations of its potential to disrupt for change. Misson (1997) asserts that a powerful social purpose of humor is to create solidarity. Collective laughter asserts common values, and humor thus serves as an 'embedded, interactive and referential' process within a group (Fine & de Soucey, 2005, p. 1).

However, what might the affinity group be laughing at, exactly? Colletta (2009) argues that popular culture uses a kind of irony that is self-referential and postmodern. It is an irony

which claims our interpretations of reality impose form on the meaning of life: reality is constructed rather than perceived or understood, and it does not exist separately from its construction. Awareness of construction has replaced awareness of meaning ... A postmodern audience is made conscious of the constructed nature of meaning and its own participation in the appearance of things, which results in the self-referential irony that characterizes much of our cultural output today. (p. 856)

Satire as a form of popular culture has the capacity to encourage change, but this capacity is undermined by the irony of cynical knowingness. Collette claims that it is this ' smirky' irony which both engages us, yet subverts our political engagement. The sometimes aggressively derisive elements that pervade *Kath and Kim* leave some readers uncomfortable. Both US and Australian viewers identified unease while watching the Australian program, *Kath and Kim*. While laughing at the broadly stereotypical nature of the characters, the students articulated some disquiet over their amusement. James began to feel ill at ease about the ideological assumptions of the show: 'Something about the premise of the show made me think that I was laughing (and I did laugh – it's a funny show) at the expense of the characters' social status.'

Several US participants were not clear whether Kath and Kim represented the working or middle class and vacillated between categories. Similarly, a Sydney radio interviewer linked Kath and Kim to 'westies' or western suburbs, blue collar Australians. (In fact, the Melbourne location of *Kath and Kim* is in the more upwardly-mobile south east). Students were similarly unclear where, exactly, the program was positioning them as viewers. Cynthia writes 'I am not sure I can separate my pleasure from my politics' and asks 'are we supposed to feel sympathy for the characters or with the characters or feel derision for them and their urge to be 'effluent'?'

Neither set of students, however, had problems identifying the class status of the characters in *Arrested Development*, an affluent family trying to maintain its tenuous grip on wealth in the face of legal problems. A number of the U.S. students talked of feeling less comfortable with *Kath and Kim*, a show that poked fun at characters who were less educated and in a less powerful position in the culture than poking fun at the wealthy characters of *Arrested Development*. Stephanie suggested this could be connected to how audience members identified with the characters and that *Arrested Development's* characters 'are not of the class that most of the audience is. But *Kath and Kim* is this middle-class family that is probably not so far in where they live and what they do from a lot of people who watch'. Others suggested that the difference had more to do with the cinema verité style of production of *Kath and Kim*. Again, however, the U.S. students were more cautious in their statements about this aspect of *Kath and Kim* and seemed particularly concerned to not offend their Australian counterparts in making generalizations about social class that might be considered offensive and posed more questions in their posts.

The Australian students, conversely, seemed not to have the same hesitation to criticize U.S. culture. At the same time the Australian students were able to point out that part of the humor the U.S. students were missing were the aspirations for social mobility of the main characters in *Kath and Kim*, which lead to malaprops and other jokes. Rebecca argued that '*Kath and Kim* isn't poking fun at the lower middle classes, but challenging the idealized versions of suburban bliss that we have been living with for decades through soap operas like *Neighbours*.' An observation such as

Rebecca's comes from an awareness of the traditions and context within which *Kath and Kim* sits. Stripped from its context, *Kath and Kim* might look like a cheap shot, but an argument is made here for a more complex range of responses to the content. Susi noted also that the humor involved in *Kath and Kim* was not simply straightforward ridicule. She said, 'I understand it is in our culture to 'take the piss' out of ourselves and I'm sure we would all agree that *Kath and Kim* are try-hards, but this mocking of people from the 'burbs' and then in the same light almost celebrating them, for me seemed to be ironic and contradictory'.

Discomfort, however, was not limited to the American audience. Susana, an Australian, was overseas when popularity over *Kath and Kim* reached its height. Urged by friends to view the show, she felt 'embarrassed and surprised that so many people were embracing it'. Susana attempts to articulate her own viewing stance, or the awkward multiple stances which *Kath and Kim* work her into: 'Sure we would all agree that Kath and Kim are try hards, but this mocking of people from the 'burbs' and then in the same light almost celebrating them, for me seemed to be ironic and/or contradictory.'

Magda Szubanski, who plays Sharon, Kim's friend, in *Kath and Kim,* raised the theme of satire, suburbanity, and cultural identity in an interview in *Preview,* the weekend magazine of *The Age* Melbourne newspaper. She credited Barry Humphries' character, Edna Everage, as an intertextual reference, one which has paved the way for *Kath and Kim:*

I think [Humphreys] was first to understand how our suburbanity is our single most defining characteristic. The suburbs are our cultural magnetic north. We can never be anywhere but in relation to them; fearing and loving them, running away from them or to them. Kath and Kim follows along the trail he blazed, sitting proudly, if somewhat uncomfortably, smack bang in the fault line of love and hate that generates so much energy. (p. 6)

Phrases in the data such as 'mocking', 'derision', 'uncomfortably', and 'laughing at' reflect a concern that the satire could exist as an 'independent system of order' (Collette 2009 p. 857), working only to further itself. For humor to work, Freud (1960) noted, in relation to jokes, the need to identify with the teller of the joke, as well as an emotional distancing from the object of the humorous attack. One student (Fiona) found the 'tackiness and inappropriateness, the insensitivity and self-absorption of Portia de Rossi's character from *Arrested Development'* very similar to Kim from *Kath and Kim.* Fiona, an Australian, continues to comment that it is the degree to which characterization is extended that allows us to accept *Kath and Kim* as satire:

I think the nastiness of the characters and their inability to see their truly appalling behaviour for what it is that has enabled Turner and Riley [the writers] to present Australian audiences with a portrait of our worst characteristics in a way which is palatable. I think no one here would ever admit to being even a little like Kath or Kim, yet I recall after seeing Kim with her tacky acrylic nails, unsightly bulges and pathetic attempts to pursue the latest suburban trends, I stopped going to the nail salon and I swear I never even considered a G-string or ugg boots!

The extent to which Fiona is self-parodying is not clear in the print conversation, but she points to exaggeration as well as the satirical elements of the familiar, raised earlier in this chapter. The degree to which individual viewers recognize themselves in textual representations directly influences the 'palatability' factor and consequently, the allowance for laughter. In the second series of *Kath and Kim* (not viewed by the US cohort), Jane Turner and Gina Riley, as writers, producers and lead actors introduced two new characters to the narrative, Trude and Prue. These characters worked in an upmarket homeware store, and spoke scathingly in plum-in-mouth tones about regular shoppers such as Kath and Kim. Trude and Prue's names, hair, speech and attitudes offered an 'affluent' concession to the 'wannabe' stereotypes of Kath and Kim, perhaps in response to class criticism. We could now laugh (if we can muster enough distance) at our own snobbery, not just at their foibles. The paired opposites might also reflect aspects of ambivalence in national self-image, as Szubanski noted above in relation to Humphries' Edna Everage.

Discussions around textual relationships to cultural context - incongruities, ambivalence and ambiguity - offer robust ways of thinking about how we consume popular media. Collette (2009) notes that 'satire, through its irony, complicates and problematizes the way we see things and therefore it can challenge viewers in unexpected ways' (p. 864). To move readers from engagement to an awareness of how things might be seen (and thus acted upon) differently, teachers need to harness surprise and dislocation. 'Why do we laugh?' could be the pivotal question in accepting, as Douglas (1975) asserted 'that the accepted pattern has no necessity' (p. 96). Mobilizing the potential for disruption in constructive ways, therefore, depends on the capacity to move from Douglas's 'exhilarating sense of freedom from form' (p. 96) and Misson's (1997) collective laughter. To see beyond pastiche and self-reflexivity, readers need to consider that any particular ordering of experience may be arbitrary and subjective, and consider alternative possibilities. In this de-centering and destabilising process, we argue that in an educational context, the teacher's role to encourage deliberation of alternative realities is vital.

IMPLICATIONS FOR CROSS-CULTURAL COMMUNICATION

The intriguing results from this limited study offer several implications for teaching issues of genre and culture in the writing classroom. Perhaps most obvious is the value of connecting students across cultures. Whether for graduate students or first-year university students, the opportunities for cross-cultural conversation offered by online communication is a thrilling pedagogical development that needs to be used more frequently. The conversations that took place in each of our classes after the online conversation revealed how exciting and provocative the students found the exchange. The discussions also illustrated how students' attitudes evolved and how learning happened on both sides.

We realize we were fortunate in having had the opportunity to meet at a conference and, back in our respective countries, to be able to create this project. Engaging in this kind of cross-cultural teaching does not require such serendipitous events, however. In fact, the same kinds of online technologies that allow for the kinds of activities we describe here, can also be used to contact teachers in other countries. Social networking sites such as Facebook, have pages for organizations of literacy educators that allow individuals to contact other teachers for a variety of purposes. The Facebook page for the International Reading Association, for example, has more than 6,000 teachers linked to it from nations around the world including Indonesia, Australia, the United Kingdom, South Africa, the Philippines, Mexico, Egypt, the U.S., India, and many others. On the page there are discussion forums where a teacher can ask for help or, certainly, put out a request for partners to engage in online, cross-cultural teaching opportunities. Other literacy education organizations, including sites for teachers in individual countries, have similar pages on social networking sites or have their own websites through which one can make contact with other teachers. It is also the case that, since we conducted our research, it is much easier to share popular culture materials across borders. Instead of having sent DVDs across the ocean, it is now possible for students to access popular culture, from movies to television programs to

publications, online that they can then discuss questions of audience, authorship, and meaning. The key to such encounters is not the medium or even the specific program or film, but is setting up a situation in which students have to discuss their readings of texts from another culture with students from that culture.

Such conversations do not have to be limited to discussing popular culture. Still, popular culture does offer a set of high-engagement texts that students will regard as low-stakes even as they can be used to discuss important questions of genre, audience, narrative, and culture. The development of participatory popular culture means that increasingly the students who enter our classroom will be have experiences with this kind of online discussion of popular culture. On fan forums about television programs, for example, much of the content revolves around interpretive questions about the texts. People post summaries, questions, ideas, suppositions, predictions or spoilers for upcoming episodes, covering the smallest detail to the most sweeping theories and ranging in tone from humor to sober reflection. This approach to discussion of television programs, for example, creates a collaborative ethos in the online community. The confidence of forum participants in their ability to read, question, and make meaning from what they see stands in stark contrast to the often much more tentative interpretive moves the same students may make in the classroom. Jenkins (2006) speculates that fan forums are particular popular among university students where they can 'exercise their growing competencies in a space where there are not yet prescribed experts and well-mapped disciplines' (p. 52). As literacy educators we can use the collaborative ethos of online discussions of popular culture to explore with students concepts of literacy and context in cross-cultural settings.

The familiarity of popular culture forms, particularly in the way they circulate across borders, offers useful opportunities for students to discuss issues of genre and interpretation. If it is not possible to set up a collaborative project with another class in another country, it is at least possible for students to visit online fan forums and discussions from other countries or that have an international membership. On such forums students can see how individuals have to learn the rhetorical and discursive conventions (Williams, 2009) and see how such conventions are negotiated across cultures. Rather than disparage popular culture to our students we need to recognize the powerful cultural and rhetorical work students engage in with popular culture every day. When we discuss popular culture texts with students, respectfully, and also provide them with a critical vocabulary to frame the discussion, we can connect their readings and rhetorical knowledge of popular culture with that of academically privileged print texts (Williams, 2001; Williams, 2002; Alvermann, Moon, & Hagood, 1999; Faulkner, 2003). Introducing popular culture from outside students' home culture offers distinctive opportunities to engage students in discussions around how they interpret texts, including how they draw on intertextual and intratextual elements to work through their confusion and make meaning for themselves. Students can be encouraged to examine the cultural assumptions they make when reading each text, as well as how they draw on cultural knowledge and references in all their reading and writing. In our classes the different cultural positions of the two cohorts offered different opportunities. For the U.S. students there was the opportunity to struggle with an unusual text in a familiar genre that helped them think about genre conventions and audience expectations. For the Australian students there was the opportunity to pay attention to the texts with which one chooses to make comparisons and to consider how culture shapes audience response.

CONCLUSION

The global circulation of popular culture is a fact for our students that influences their daily lives. The flow of music, movies, television programs, video games, and web sites across cultures offer 'an ever-expanding sense of possibility – as well as terror and constraint – as modern humanity cultivates new interests, needs, desires, and fears in the landscape of new media'(McCarthy et al., 2003, p. 455). As teachers we have an obligation to engage students in reading and writing with and about these media so that they may live critically in a world simultaneously familiar and strange. While the 'fears' may speak to educators who have emerged from pre-digital, cultural heritage-based education, the 'strangeness' may resonate with learners attempting to connect with these worlds.

Using new media and popular texts challenges teachers to leave traditionally safe spaces; they become learners in the learners' worlds. However, this process occurs in an educational context, where learners come expecting to read such worlds with a guide. Understandings of textual relationships, identity representation and, cultural constructs lie more comfortably within the literacy educator's reach. A critical approach to humor and parody, however, holds the potential to disrupt such positions for both teacher and learners, asking us who we are as we laugh at, then contest, less secure interpretations of ourselves.

REFERENCES

Alvermann, D., Moon, J., & Hagood, M. (1999). *Popular culture in the classroom: Teaching and researching critical media literacy*. Chicago, IL: National Reading Conference.

Bakhtin, M. (1981). *The dialogic imagination* (Holquist, M., Ed.). Austin, TX: University of Texas Press.

Billing, M. (2008). Review: Laughter and ridicule: Towards a social critique of humor. *European Journal of Communication, 23*(1), 87–116.

Boler, M. (1999). *Feeling power: Emotions and education*. London, UK: Routledge.

Buckingham, D., & Sefton-Green, J. (1994). *Cultural studies goes to school*. London, UK: Taylor and Francis.

Collette, L. (2009). Political satire and postmodern irony in the age of Stephen Colbert and Jon Stewart. *Journal of Popular Culture, 5*(42), 856–874. doi:10.1111/j.1540-5931.2009.00711.x

De Block, L., & Rydin, I. (2006). Digital rapping in media productions: Intercultural communication through youth culture. In Buckingham, D., & Willett, R. (Eds.), *Digital generations: Children, young people, and new media* (pp. 295–312). Mahwah, NJ: Lawrence Erlbaum.

Douglas, M. (1975). *Implicit meanings: Essays in anthropology*. London, UK: Routledge and Kegan Paul.

Faulkner, J. (2003). Like you have a bubble inside of you that just wants to pop: Popular culture, pleasure and the English classroom. *English Teaching: Practice and Critique, 2*(2), 47–56.

Fine, G., & de Soucey, M. (2005). Joking cultures: Humor themes as social regulation in group life. *Humor: International Journal of Humor Research, 18*(1), 1–22. doi:10.1515/humr.2005.18.1.1

Freud, S. (1960). *Jokes and their relationship to the unconscious. The Standard Editions* (Strachey, J., Trans.). New York, NY: Norton.

Jenkins, H. (2006). *Convergence culture: Where old and new media collide*. New York, NY: New York University Press.

Kellner, D. (1995). *Media culture*. London, UK: Routledge. doi:10.4324/9780203205808

Lembo, R. (2000). *Thinking through television*. Cambridge, UK: Cambridge University Press. doi:10.1017/CBO9780511489488

MacLachlan, G., & Reid, I. (1994). *Framing and interpretation. Carlton, Australuia*. Melbourne University Press.

McCarthy, C., Giardina, M., Harewood, S., & Park, J.-K. (2003). Contesting culture: Identity and curriculum dilemmas in the age of globalization, postcolonialism, and multiplicity. *Harvard Educational Review, 73*(3), 449–465.

Misson, R. (1997). Only joking: Being critical and keeping sense of humor. Paper presented at SAETA Conference, Adelaide, October.

Morley, D. (1992). *Television, audiences, and cultural studies*. London, UK: Routledge.

Mulkay, M. (1988). *On humor: Its nature and its place in modern society*. Oxford, UK: Blackwell.

Szubanski, M. (2005, August 5). Fears of a clown interview by B. Hallett. *The Age, Preview Magazine,* 4-6

Williams, B. T. (2001). Reflections on a shimmering screen: Television's relationship to writing pedagogies. *The Writing Instructor 2.0.*

Williams, B. T. (2002). *Tuned in: Television and the teaching of writing*. Portsmouth, NH: Boynton/Cook.

Williams, B. T. (2009). *Shimmering literacies: Popular culture and reading and writing online*. London, UK: Peter Lang.

Zembylas, M., & Boler, M. (2002). *Teachers college record*. Retrieved from http://www.tcrecord.org/library

ADDITIONAL READING

Alvermann, D. E. (Ed.). (2010). *Adolescents' Online Literacies: Connecting Classrooms, Digital Media, and Popular Culture*. London: Peter Lang.

Beach, R., & O'Brien, D. G. (2008). Teaching Popular-Culture Texts in the Classroom. In Coiro, J., Knobel, M., Lankshear, C., & Leu, D. J. (Eds.), *Handbook of Research on New Literacies* (pp. 775–804). New York: Lawrence Erlbaum.

Black, R. W. (2008). *Adolescents and Online Fan Fiction*. London: Peter Lang.

Buckingham, D., & Willett, R. (2006). *Digital Generations: Children, Young People, and New Media*. Mahwah, N.J: Lawrence Erlbaum Associates, Publishers.

Burn, A. (2009). *Making New Media: Creative Production and Digital Literacies*. London: Peter Lang.

Bury, R. (2005). *Cyberspaces of Their Own: Female Fandoms Online*. New York: Peter Lang.

Cole, D. R., & Pullen, D. L. (Eds.). (2010). *Multiliteracies in Motion: Current Theory and Practice*. London: Routledge.

Dolby, N., & Rizvi, F. (Eds.). (2008). *Youth Moves: Identities and Education in Global Perspective*. London: Routledge.

Gee, J. P. (2004). *Situated Language and Learning: A Critique of Traditional Schooling*. London: Routledge.

Grazian, D. (2010). *Mix it up: Popular Culture, Mass Media and Society*. New York: W. W. Norton & Company, Inc.

Ito, M. (2006). Japanese Media Mixes and Amateur Cultural Exchange. In Buckingham, D., & Willett, R. (Eds.), *Digital Generations: Children, Young People, and New Media* (pp. 49–66). Mahwah, NJ: Lawrence Erlbaum.

Knobel, M., & Lankshear, C. (Eds.). (2007). *A New Literacies Sampler*. New York: Peter Lang.

Papen, U. (2007). *Literacy and Globalization: Reading and Writing in Times of Social and Cultural Change*. London: Routledge.

Selfe, C. L., & Hawisher, G. E. (2004). *Literate Lives in the Information Age: Narratives on Literacy from the United States*. Mahwah, NJ: Lawrence Erlbaum Associates.

Yancey, K. B. (2004). Made Not Only in Words: Composition in a New Key. *College Composition and Communication, 56*, 297–328. doi:10.2307/4140651

Chapter 9
Disrupting Disruption:
Invitational Pedagogy as a Response to Student Resistance

A. Abby Knoblauch
Kansas State University, USA

ABSTRACT

As educators look for productive ways to encourage students to disrupt their deeply held beliefs, they often turn toward liberatory pedagogies. Such pedagogical practices, however, often provoke student resistance to what is seen as attempts at indoctrination to liberal politics. This chapter explores responses to student resistance, especially Kopelson's (2003) performance of neutrality, and posits instead a pedagogical practice based in the theory of invitational rhetoric, one that asks instructors to (attempt to) relinquish their intent to persuade students. This invitational pedagogy provides a strategy to reduce nonproductive student resistance while allowing for critical inquiry within the college writing classroom.

INTRODUCTION

Early in the first chapter of her 1999 book *Feeling Power: Emotions and Education*, Megan Boler notes that the classroom is a space that links education and parenting, explaining that both realms are often fraught with struggles for control and autonomy, struggles that many educators label as resistance. In fact, taking the parent-teacher anal-

ogy further, Boler argues that sometimes students "may resist the educator's suggestions, no matter what that suggestion is," simply (although it is hardly simple) to assert some form of power. The "parental cliché, 'Do what I say because I know what's best for you,'" she believes, "is in part an invitation for the young person to rebel and say 'No, I'll decide what's best for me!'" (p. 4). In other words, Boler reads a teacher's assertion of authority as an invitation for student resistance.

DOI: 10.4018/978-1-61350-495-6.ch009

It is difficult to imagine *inviting* student resistance in this way, at least consciously. Many educators would say that they encourage disagreement, but this particular form of resistance—disagreeing solely to refuse agreement—seems less welcome. And yet, this sort of resistance can be quite common, especially in classrooms in which students are asked to interrogate their preconceived notions, deeply held beliefs, or adherence to dominant ideological values. In this chapter, I will begin by briefly discussing forms of resistance within the context of critical or liberatory pedagogies, especially within college composition classrooms[1]. Next, I will analyze Kopelson's notion of a "performance of neutrality" as one response to student resistance, exploring reasons for an attempt at teacher neutrality and the problems with this performative pedagogy. I will then offer communications scholars Foss and Griffin's (1995) proposal for *invitational rhetoric* as a more productive theory on which to base pedagogical practice, particularly when attempting to interrogate dominant cultural ideologies. Finally, I will connect what I call an *invitational pedagogy* to Boler's notion of a "pedagogy of discomfort" (1995), suggesting that while emotional discomfort is inevitable and even productive, an invitational pedagogy can reduce resistance sometimes sparked by feelings of threat and keep open the lines of communication. In brief, this chapter asks that we disrupt our own ideas of disruptive pedagogies, arguing that sometimes the most radical pedagogy is one that neither directly challenges students, nor performs neutrality, but instead attempts to avoid an intent to persuade in favor of an invitation to understanding.

BACKGROUND

The issue of student resistance in the classroom has garnered a surfeit of responses, in part due to the slippery nature of the term "resistance" itself.

Resistance to authority can connote positively, as is the case in much resistance theory, based largely on Freire's landmark work *Pedagogy of the oppressed* (2003/1970) in which Freire details his literacy work in Latin America as a form of resistance against an oppressive social structure. Proponents of critical composition pedagogies (also often termed liberatory, emancipatory, or radical pedagogies), primarily drawing on the work of scholars such as Freire, Giroux (1983, 1988), and Shor (1980), also see resistance as productive. Bizzell (1991), hooks (1994), Kennedy (1999), and Pratt (1991), for example, write about resistance in terms of liberation from hegemonic structures. But, as Welsh (2001) points out, "legitimate" resistance is often imagined as students recognizing and working against dominant ideologies (p. 556-7). When students defy instructors' efforts to unveil the false consciousness under which the students are assumed to be operating, however, such resistance is deemed less productive (or, more optimistically, simply a step toward more legitimate resistance of hegemony).

None of this is to say that liberatory or radical pedagogies are inherently problematic. Indeed, I am attracted toward their primary goals. I cannot but hope that one result of a university education is a student's heightened ability—and even desire—to challenge his or her deeply held beliefs. There are, however, a number of teacher-scholars who reject such approaches, particularly within the composition classroom. Critics of liberatory pedagogies have long lamented what they see as attempts at indoctrination in such classrooms—a troubling form of persuasion in which students feel pressured to adopt the politics or viewpoints of the instructor. Perhaps the most (in)famous of such critiques is Hairston's (1992) scathing characterization of radical pedagogy as one that "puts dogma before diversity, politics before craft, ideology before critical thinking, and the social goals of the teacher before the educational needs of the students" (p. 180). Fulkerson (2005), too, voices concerns over the drive toward political conversion in what he calls critical cultural studies classrooms.

In his 1998 article "The arts of complicity," Miller echoes many of these critiques, but also draws attention to the seductive appeal of critical pedagogies, asking "If we aren't in the business of liberation, uplift, and movement, however slow, towards a better social world, what is it we're doing in our classrooms?" (p. 12). But his sub-section heading "Everybody get in line: liberation and the obedient response," highlights concerns about indoctrination, or even student performance of indoctrination. In attempting to incorporate tenets of radical pedagogy into his own classrooms, Miller found that many students "resisted the 'politicization' of the classroom; those who didn't seemed overly eager to ventriloquize sentiments they didn't believe or understand" (p. 11). In other words, as a young man at the video store recently explained to me, as a student, you need only to deduce what groups the professors love and/or hate in order to succeed. Once you figure that out, he explained, you can write papers that reflect the professor's viewpoint and get an A. Unknowingly, this young man encapsulated one of the primary critiques of liberatory pedagogies. This is hardly the kind of critical thinking toward which most of us are striving.

Understandably, practitioners of critical pedagogy disagree with such representations of their classrooms. Wood (1993), for example, holds that liberatory instructors work *against* indoctrination and dogmatic teaching, attempting instead to "empower students and give them genuine voices of resistance" (p. 250). Stenberg (2006) paints a complex picture of liberatory classrooms, voicing concerns but ultimately arguing that the true liberatory composition teacher values critical inquiry, not a predetermined critical goal. And it should be noted that liberatory classrooms, like all classrooms, are complex, shifting, and dynamic. Yet a number of scholars (including Gorzelsky, 2009; and Welsh, 2001) continue to draw atten-

tion to students' resistance to critical or liberatory pedagogies based primarily on issues of power and conversion in college writing classrooms. It seems that despite more nuanced forms of critical pedagogies, many students are still responding negatively to instructors who voice their political viewpoints in the classroom, undermining the liberatory goals of such courses.

Despite these concerns, by 1995 Dennis Lynch had already noted (apprehensively) that within composition studies the question had become "not, should teachers bring their politics into the classroom, but, how should teachers and students together approach, resist, negotiate, affirm, transform, make use of, etc., the political relations and commitments that circumscribe and define the writing classroom and its activities?" (p. 351). I would argue that Lynch's anxiety is still somewhat misplaced, or at least misarticulated, as no classroom is void of politics. The instructor brings her political beliefs into the classroom, as do the students, whether she intends to or not. Whereas some teacher-scholars (such as Hairston, 1992; Lynch, 1995; and Soles, 1998) would prefer to avoid overt treatment of "political relations and commitments" (Lynch, 1995, p. 351), radical teacher-scholars hold that the composition classroom is precisely the place to address such issues. *How* teachers and students address those issues is still the topic of much scholarly discussion, in part because actual classroom practices vary so greatly.

The concerns surrounding critical pedagogies that I have noted revolve around the crossing of boundaries: the lines between education and indoctrination, critical thinking and conversion, resistance and reproduction, even the classroom and the public sphere. In all of these border disputes one can hear echoes of two primary issues: authority and resistance. Given that instructors have the authority to validate or refuse a student's response to any text, students often read such teacherly responses as attempts to convince students of the teacher's perspective. Karen Kopelson explores one common instructor response to such resistance: what she calls "a performance of neutrality." I will explore why Kopelson (and others) might gravitate toward performative pedagogy, discuss some of the concerns I have with this performance, and then offer an alternative pedagogical approach that I believe addresses many of the problems inherent in a performance of neutrality.

DISRUPTING STUDENT RESISTANCE

A Problematic Performance

As Kopelson explains, the move toward critical pedagogies and the attendant focus on human difference in the college writing classroom has sparked a shift in the forms of student resistance. Drawing on the work of Johnson (1994), Kopelson notes that instead of simply resisting the universality of the college writing requirement, students now see the more politicized college writing course as "an intrusion of sorts, resenting and often actively rebelling against what they may experience as the 'imposition' of race, class, gender, sexuality, or (more generally) cultural issues onto their 'neutral' course of study" (p. 117). This is especially true in geographical areas where socially liberal ideologies are seen as contributing to the decline of "traditional" values. In these cases, student resistance can be read as "protective": of self, of family, of communal values (Kopelson, p. 119).

Of course, asking most students to rethink any deeply held belief can result in classroom disruption, whether that's outward resistance, student silence, or passive aggressive behaviors. It is easier to understand this disruption when we imagine the positionalities of the students in a first-year writing course, however, particularly at schools such as the Midwestern state university at which I teach. Often hailing from small towns in relative geographical isolation, many of these students are, for the first time, away from home, away from their families, away from everything that they've known. Not only have their surroundings changed, but they are suddenly being asked to question their political beliefs, their understandings of the world, sometimes even the implications of their religious faiths. Regardless of from where our students hail, many of their beliefs are rooted in family, church, and community—sources of knowledge that many students are, understandably, uncomfortable critiquing. Student resistance to more politically charged classrooms, then, can be read as loyalty to family and community, as well as a fear of shattering those few things that students, now attempting to navigate new communities and experiences, hold as comforting certainties. It is hardly surprising that the disruption of these beliefs might cause resistance to the curriculum and the instructor.

The form that this resistance takes can be a result not only of the student's personal and social histories, but also of student (and teacher) expectations based on the teacher's age, gender, sexual orientation, race, ethnicity, able-bodiedness, or socio-economic class. In other words, student resistance can be informed by geography; personal, family, state, and larger social histories; as well as the students' and teacher's social positionalities. As Kopelson points out, "overtly 'critical' pedagogical approaches may be especially ineffective, and even counter-productive, for the teacher-subject who is immediate *read* by the students" as Other, as a member of a marginalized group (p. 118). While some teacher-scholars such as hooks, Jarratt, and Pratt call for overtly politicized classroom spaces in which students are directly challenged and made uncomfortable, the visibility of the teacher's social positionality in relation to the students' can make such pedagogical approaches especially problematic. When an older white male walks into the classroom, for example, for many students he immediately embodies the role of teacher. He is the one-who-knows and therefore may be more easily viewed as someone who has the authority to challenge students. But if the instructor does not conform to images of traditional authority—is young, female, transgendered, does not identify as heterosexual, and/or is non-white, for example—the instructor is often read as attempting to forward a personal activist agenda and is dismissed as biased.

Because many teacher-scholars in composition and rhetoric agree with Boler that "the obligation of educators is not to guarantee a space that is free from hostility—an impossible and sanitizing task—but rather, to challenge oneself and one's students to critically analyze any statements made in a classroom, especially statements that are rooted in dominant ideological values that subordinate on the basis of race, gender, class, or sexual orientation" (p. 4), Kopelson suggests that we develop pedagogies that are "sneakier," performing a stance of neutrality even if such neutrality is impossible or even undesirable (p. 121). She sees this performance as a "self-conscious masquerade that serves an overarching and more insurgent political agenda," (p. 123). It "feigns itself, *perverts* itself, in the service of other—disturbing and disruptive—goals" (p. 123, emphasis in original). When the instructor performs political neutrality, Kopelson argues, students are less likely to charge bias and may, then, focus more critically on texts and ideas they might ignore if they believed the instructor had a personal stake in them.

Kopelson notes that the risks of performing political neutrality include self-erasure of difference and the reinscription of assumptions about dominant culture and authority (p. 139). Yet she reminds us that all identities and pedagogies are a form of performance and that this is but one possible pedagogical practice to help combat student resistance to human difference-based curricula. I echo Kopelson's concerns about the attempted self-erasure of difference, even if that erasure is but a performance. I can see the potential liberatory move of that momentary (and strategic) denial of political positionality, but I wonder, too, about the implications of such denial itself. As hooks

reminds us, "the person who is most powerful has the privilege of denying their body" (p. 137). Scholars need to pay attention, then, to who is asked to deny the body, or the body politic, and who is not. Of course "asking" assumes a form of agency, the privilege to accept or refuse the invitation to deny. Kopelson might argue that given the strength of student resistance to challenging conservative values, especially when the instructor embodies the very "difference" the course is addressing, the choice is always already loaded. But I am persuaded by Banks who argues that when we act as if bodies do not matter, we run the risk of (falsely) assuming that "any *body* can stand in for another" (2003, p. 38, emphasis in original). Furthermore, while all identities may be performative, some identities are more easily performed than others. Kopelson seems rather certain that such a performance of neutrality is possible, and I do not want to dismiss her experience, but some identities are, literally, written on the body. While those marked as "other" might be able to perform practices associated with more traditional authority (lecturing, for example), this does not necessarily erase their perceived "otherness."

Still, we cannot avoid the difficulties inherent in asking students to question their views on human difference, especially when the instructor embodies one of more of those markers of "difference." For those instructors for whom a performance of neutrality seems problematic or even impossible, I offer Foss and Griffin's 1995 theory of invitational rhetoric as a basis for pedagogical practice that disrupts conventional notions of authority while allowing space to interrogate both students' and instructors' belief systems.

An Overview of Invitational Rhetoric

In their article, "Beyond persuasion," Foss and Griffin argue that Western rhetoric's historical association with persuasion reflects patriarchal values of dominance and change, functioning from within a "power-over" framework in which the rhetor determines self-worth by attempting to control the lives or viewpoints of the listener(s). Objecting to this (mis)use of power and to the conflation of rhetoric with persuasion, Foss and Griffin propose invitational rhetoric as one alternative. They define invitational rhetoric as a theory rooted in the feminist principles of equality, immanent value, and self-determination where immanent value refers to the idea that all beings are worthy as they are, and self-determination reflects the belief that individuals are the experts on their own lives (p. 4). Based in these principles, a rhetor practicing invitational rhetoric does not desire to change or persuade the listener because the listener, not the rhetor, is seen as the best authority on his or her life.

A rhetoric based in these principles is one that challenges the primacy of persuasion. If one begins with the premise that listeners and rhetor are equals, that listeners need not be changed, and that listeners are the experts on their own lives, then change can no longer be the primary goal of this form of rhetoric. Instead, the goal of invitational rhetoric is better understanding of all viewpoints offered and of the individuals who hold those viewpoints. Within an invitational framework, the rhetor offers her perspectives, thereby inviting the audience to see the world as the rhetor does and, in turn, the rhetor listens to all perspectives offered. She "does not judge or denigrate others' perspectives but is open to and tries to appreciate and validate those perspectives, even if they differ dramatically from the rhetor's own" (p. 5). Ideally, all audience members respond in kind, listening to the rhetor's perspective and then offering their own. In this ideal situation, rhetor and audience approach each other as equals within a framework of mutual respect in order to come to a better understanding of all possible facets of the issue at hand as well as of the participants themselves. In short, then, invitational rhetoric is a rhetoric of understanding, one in which the rhetor invites the listener(s) to enter her world

without attempting to persuade the listener(s) to adhere to the rhetor's beliefs[2].

Perhaps the key word in this brief overview of invitational rhetoric, particularly when one imagines it in a classroom, is "ideally." *Ideally* the listener accepts the rhetor's invitation. *Ideally* differences are examined in an environment of mutual respect. *Ideally* the rhetor does not seek to persuade the listener. And *ideally* all participants are treated equally. But of course we know that the classroom environment is not ideal. The classroom—any classroom—is rife with unequal power dynamics; people are silenced, sometimes unintentionally and sometimes intentionally; and respect for classmates, instructors, and even students is not always present. Additionally, it is difficult to imagine avoiding the desire to persuade, especially when faced with vast political chasms and with those who espouse racist, sexist, homophobic, or otherwise disturbing social or political values. Why, then, do I offer invitational rhetoric as a potential site for strategies of productive disruption? Because despite its challenges, a pedagogy based in invitational rhetoric provides instructors with a framework from within which they can challenge viewpoints without inducing a sense of threat (and therefore resistance) in students whose views differ from the instructor's. Additionally, from within an invitational frame, instructors need not silence their own beliefs or profess a neutrality they do not actually feel.

Invitational Pedagogy and a Pedagogy of Discomfort

There are many similarities between what I am calling an invitational pedagogy and what Boler calls a pedagogy of discomfort. Boler notes that "a pedagogy of discomfort is not a demand to take one particular road or action. The purpose is not to enforce a particular political agenda, or to evaluate students on what agenda they choose to carry out, if any" (p. 179). The goal of a pedagogy of discomfort is for all involved—teachers and students—to "explore beliefs and values; to examine when visual 'habits' and emotional selectivity have become rigid and immune to flexibility; and to identify when and how our habits harm ourselves and others" (p. 185) [3]. Such language echoes Foss and Griffin's notion of equality and self-determination. Boler goes on to explain, however, that while "an ethical pedagogy would seem to require listening with equal attention to all views and perspectives," some of those perspectives "are difficult, even dangerous" (p. 179). Attempting to really listen to racist views, for example, can indeed be difficult, and validating such views by listening for understanding could be dangerous. Similarly, asking students who hold such views to interrogate them can produce nonproductive forms of classroom resistance. Yet failing to engage such viewpoints is also problematic and, as Boler notes, "any pedagogy or curricula potentially evokes resistance, fear, and anger," but we, as educators, need to find ways to make such responses more productive and self-reflexive, using often-uncomfortable emotions to spark change and/or action (p. 183). An invitational pedagogy recognizes the resistance, fear, and anger inherent in most attempts to interrogate deeply-held beliefs, perhaps especially those that Boler (and myself) would label harmful or dangerous, but explicitly removing the pressure of change or conversion from the pedagogical equation can actually reduce student feelings of threat and defensiveness.

Some scholars find this concept problematic. Fulkerson (1996), for example, worries that invitational rhetoric's emphasis on the equal offering of perspectives makes real social and political change difficult, if not impossible, as people are not asked to abandon racist or homophobic views. Yet I would argue that more direct attempts at persuasion do not necessarily succeed in changing ingrained racist or homophobic beliefs either. As Foss, Griffin, and Foss (1997) explain, "trying to understand a racist's or a misogynist's position and inviting that individual to consider alternative perspectives [. . .] is one approach to interacting with such individuals—one that is no less viable or predictive of change than is persuasion" (p. 123). Foss, Griffin, and Foss advocate trying to understand racist or sexist views and, in an invitational format, hope that the listener will also try to understand the views of the rhetor who is (presumably) not (or less) racist or sexist. In other words, because an invitational rhetor attempts to create a safe space in which multiple viewpoints can be heard, thereby reducing the feelings of threat and defensiveness in the listener, there is an increased chance that the audience member might at least hear such alternatives. And within such invitational frameworks, rhetor or listener *may* be moved to change his or her view, even if this is not the primary goal of the rhetor and even if such change does not happen immediately. In other words, directly confronting racist or homophobic views seems rarely to lead the desired change; perhaps attempting to listen with understanding can create an environment in which the person holding racist views might consider alternatives.

Within the classroom environment, attempting to let go of the intent to persuade can be incredibly useful, if incredibly difficult (and even, perhaps, ultimately impossible). Of course, as a teacher who identifies herself as a feminist, I would be lying if I said that I did not hope to change sexist, homophobic, racist, or classist viewpoints. I do. My attempts at persuasion, however, have rarely been successful within the classroom. When students are asked to question those things of which they have always been certain—belief-systems that may be rooted in familial structures, home communities, and religious faiths—they can feel as if they are being asked to *change* their beliefs and therefore often respond with defensiveness, further entrenching themselves into the safety of these communal ways of thinking. When students believed I was trying to "convert" them, they resisted that conversion. An oppositional approach simply did not work in such instances. At best, it often felt as though the "good" students were simply parroting back to me what they believed I wanted to hear, a form of mimesis that Boyd (1999) critiques.

Yet when I began to let go of the intent to persuade my students and made my invitational approach transparent to students, they were less likely to immediately retreat into defensiveness. This is not to say that simply explaining an invitational approach eliminates student resistance; it is, however, to say that making students aware of invitational rhetoric as a classroom practice provides strategies for both instructors and students when faced with moments of emotional or psychological distress. Maher (2002) agrees, noting that one tactic to avoid students feeling as though their "ways of being" are "demonized" by the instructor (p. 86) is what Maher calls an "invitational interaction" (p. 87). Although different from the invitational pedagogy I am describing here, Maher acknowledges that the first step in creating a more productive classroom environment is explicitly naming the pedagogical framework from within which the instructor is working (p. 87). What, then, might this pedagogy look like?

An invitational pedagogy proceeds from the most basic tenets of invitational rhetoric. First, persuasion is not the instructor's primary goal. This is different from a performance of neutrality in that the instructor need not pretend to be apolitical. Instead, the instructor acknowledges her own political opinions, as well as the cultural logics that inform her claims[4]. Such a move is hardly radical, but to do so without the intent to persuade students of the superiority of the instructor's viewpoints is more difficult than it sounds. Of course the instructor believes her viewpoints are (mostly) correct—that is why she holds those views. But when students sense an intent to persuade, many respond in kind; such a cyclical process could lead to better understanding, but it is more likely to lead to resistance. When students are attempting to win what they see as an argument, they are less likely to listen for understanding, and less likely to remain open to the possibility of change.

Working from within an invitational mindset can also help produce the conditions of safety and value forwarded by Foss and Griffin. When students feel as though they are not being recruited to the liberal agenda, when they feel that they are being heard and valued, they tend not to feel as though their ways of knowing and being are threatened. As psychotherapist Carl Rogers (1970) explained, the largest barrier to effective communication is a sense of threat. Working to reduce that feeling of threat and judgment between interlocutors is, according to Rogers, the only way toward understanding, negotiation, and effective communication. Invitational rhetoric and a pedagogy based on its intent to understand rather than persuade is one way in which to reduce a sense of threat in students, thereby reducing their resistance and increasing the likelihood that they will at least attempt to hear alternative views.

An invitational pedagogy, then, is an *explicit* attempt by an instructor to critically engage students without an intent to persuade them of a particular political or social position. While change may happen, change is not the primary goal. Within such a framework, both students and instructor can offer any perspective, challenge any perspective, and yet must adopt none. Additionally, the instructor herself must be open to the possibility of change, sharing that vulnerability with students. Central to this pedagogy is also an understanding of the theory of invitational rhetoric by both instructor and students so that all participants have a common language and framework (offering of perspectives, intent to persuade, self-determination, immanent value, etc.). Additionally, students should be reminded regularly of the instructor's intent to work from within an invitational frame, especially within moments of discomfort or resistance. Finally, instructors should understand that an invitational approach is not a panacea. Like all classroom practice, no single pedagogical strategy works in all situations. But being explicit with students about the improbability of conversion within the classroom, despite the instructor's beliefs or desires, helps to create the conditions of safety and value that reduce feelings of threat and defensiveness.

I want to be clear in that I am not advocating an "I'm okay, you're okay" approach to discomfort wherein racist or sexist beliefs are simply "validated" by the instructor. Nor am I implying that instructors can completely relinquish their desire to persuade students to work toward social equality; certainly we should be working toward a more egalitarian society. What I am questioning is the viability of expecting students who were raised within familial or communal structures that have reinforced and perpetuated social inequality to abandon those cultural logics within one or two semesters. Many would say that instructors working within a critical pedagogy are asking only that students *question* their beliefs, not necessarily change them. But when students imagine that there is a correct answer to this form of questioning, one that contradicts their communal ways of knowing, they often interpret this as the instructor forcing a liberal ideology upon them. It then becomes easier for students to dismiss the entire course as an attempt at indoctrination.

Critics such as Fulkerson and Condit (1997) would respond that the sense of threat can never truly be eliminated because of the unequal power relations at play within the university. And they would be correct: I hold the gradebook and therefore savvy students might feel pressure to reproduce my political views. In the face of such power-dynamics, instructors must attempt—as they do on an almost daily basis—to evaluate students on the quality of their work and not the content of their views. While sometimes difficult, it is hardly a new struggle. Kopelson might argue that a performance of neutrality would better subvert students' desire to echo the professor; yet, as a woman discussing gender, many students simply assume I am a feminist. As a professor in the humanities, most students assume I am socially liberal. Despite any attempt to perform political neutrality, students make assumptions about

instructors, just as instructors make assumptions about students. Additionally, performing a political neutrality can be particularly problematic for instructors who students view as a biased "Other." And given the persistence of student resistance to liberatory pedagogies, it seems clear that more blatant forms of oppositional classroom practice are not always leading to the kinds of results hoped for by instructors. Simply *not* addressing issues of inequality also seems an untenable alternative for those instructors dedicated to social justice. An invitational pedagogy, however, provides a way for instructors and students to work toward understanding, particularly when persuasion is not possible. Being explicit with students about the improbability of persuasion can reduce the sense of threat that impedes effective communication and may at least open the possibility of disrupting, or at least questioning, students' adherence to dominant ideologies in a way that more traditional approaches often cannot.

FUTURE RESEARCH DIRECTIONS

Given the radical nature of invitational rhetoric, coupled with the interesting potential of this rhetorical theory as pedagogical practice, the scholarly engagement with this topic seems surprisingly limited. Ryan and Natalle (2001) argue that invitational rhetoric has not garnered much response primarily because it lacks theoretical grounding; I contend that invitational rhetoric has not received much attention, particularly in the fields of rhetoric and composition and particularly in relation to pedagogy, because there has been little discussion about how to operationalize such a theory in the classroom. There are a few exceptions, but most are within communication studies (Bone, Griffin, & Scholz, 2008; Glenn, 2004; Lozano-Reich & Cloud, 2009; Novak & Bonnie, 2009; Pollock et al, 1996). Thus far, there are no book-length studies in publication and few discussions at all within the realm of composition and rhetoric.

Much work is still being done in response to student resistance—too much, in fact, to even begin to list; this fact alone points to the need for a new area of investigation into issues of authority and power in the classroom. As educators struggle to find more productive ways to work toward social equality, to push students toward new and sometimes uncomfortable ways of thinking, they might look toward feminist rhetorical theories (Banks, 2003; Glenn, 2004; Hindman, 2002; Micciche, 2007; Ratcliff, 2005) in order to inform their praxis. Because feminist rhetorical theories are particularly concerned with issues of authority, power, language, and social equality, and because all classrooms are loci of language, power, and social identities, feminist rhetorical theories provide rich terrain from which to theorize and construct pedagogical practice. Ritchie and Ronald (2006) offer one such resource in their book *Teaching Rhetorica*, but much more work is necessary in this area so that we might reduce our students' resistance not simply to our own political leanings, but toward critical questioning and critique in general.

CONCLUSION

An invitational pedagogy that explicitly attempts to remove the intent to persuade, even if the desire to persuade is ultimately unavoidable, can help diminish student resistance to what is often viewed as a desire to convert them to liberal politics. Such praxis can be especially useful for instructors who, by the visibility of their gender, race, sexual orientation, size, age, or able-bodiedness, do not perform what many students see as the role of authority. In such situations, when the teacher in the room is seen as "Other," invitational pedagogy allows teachers to acknowledge their own worldviews while simultaneously disrupting the charge of bias that students sometimes level against instructors who do not identify with dominant social positionalities. In working toward understanding and listening rather than persuasion and conversion, instructors and students have a better chance of reducing the sense of antagonism that can result from more traditional liberatory pedagogies. Furthermore, an invitational pedagogy disrupts the belief that the most effective critical approach is, in fact, the most critical. When students are invited to understand a variety of viewpoints, including their own, without being asked to adopt any, they are less likely feel the need to defend the communities from which these viewpoints have stemmed. Invitational rhetoric and a pedagogical practice constructed from its basic tenets re-imagines the classroom space as one in which all viewpoints can be voiced, all viewpoints can be challenged, and no viewpoints must be adopted. It therefore expands the possibilities for critical examination of all belief systems, including the instructor's. Such a move, for students, might be the most disruptive pedagogy of all.

REFERENCES

Banks, W. (2003). Written through the body: Disruptions and "personal" writing. *College English*, *66*, 21–40. doi:10.2307/3594232

Bizzell, P. (1991). Classroom authority and critical pedagogy. *American Literary History*, *3*, 847–863. doi:10.1093/alh/3.4.847

Boler, M. (1999). *Feeling power: Emotions and education*. New York, NY: Routledge.

Bone, J. E., Griffin, C. L., & Scholz, T. M. L. (2008). Beyond traditional conceptualizations of rhetoric: Invitational rhetoric and a move toward civility. *Western Journal of Communication*, *72*, 434–462. doi:10.1080/10570310802446098

Boyd, R. (1999). Reading student resistance: The case of the missing other. *JAC*, *19*, 589–605.

Condit, M. C. (1997). In praise of eloquent diversity: Gender and rhetoric as public persuasion. *Women's Studies in Communications, 20*, 91–116.

Foss, S. K., & Griffin, C. L. (1995). Beyond persuasion: A proposal for an invitational rhetoric. *Communication Monographs, 62*, 2–18. doi:10.1080/03637759509376345

Foss, S. K., Griffin, C. L., & Foss, K. (1997). Transforming rhetoric through feminist reconstruction: A response to the gender diversity perspective. *Women's Studies in Communications, 20*, 117–135.

Freire, P. (2003). *Pedagogy of the oppressed* (M. B. Ramos, Trans.). 30th Anniversary edition. New York, NY: Continuum International Publishing, Inc. (Original work published 1970).

Fulkerson, R. (1996). Transcending our conception of argument in light of feminist critiques. *Argumentation and Advocacy, 32*, 199–217.

Fulkerson, R. (2005). Composition at the turn of the twenty-first century. *College Composition and Communication, 56*, 654–687.

Giroux, H. A. (1983). *Theory and resistance in education: A pedagogy for the opposition*. South Hadley, MA: Bergin & Garvey Publishers.

Giroux, H. A. (1988). *Schooling and the struggle for public life: Critical pedagogy in the modern age*. Minneapolis, MN: University of Minnesota Press.

Glenn, C. (2004). *Unspoken: A rhetoric of silence*. Carbondale, IL: Southern Illinois University Press.

Gorzelsky, G. (2009). Working boundaries: From student resistance to student agency. *College Composition and Communication, 61*, 64–84.

Hairston, M. (1992). Diversity, ideology, and teaching writing. *College Composition and Communication, 43*, 179–193. doi:10.2307/357563

Hindman, J. E. (2002). Writing an important body of scholarship: A proposal for an embodied rhetoric of professional practice. *JAC, 22*, 93–118.

hooks, b. (1994). *Teaching to transgress: Education as the practice of freedom*. New York, NY: Routledge.

Jarratt, S. (1991). Feminism and composition: The case for conflict. In Harkin, P., & Schilb, J. (Eds.), *Contending with words: Composition and rhetoric in a postmodern age* (pp. 105–123). New York, NY: Modern Language Association.

Johnson, C. (1994). Participatory rhetoric and the teacher as racial/gendered subject. *College English, 56*, 409–419. doi:10.2307/378335

Kennedy, K. (1999). Cynic rhetoric: The ethics and tactics of resistance. *Rhetoric Review, 18*(1), 26–45. doi:10.1080/07350199909359254

Kopelson, K. (2003). Rhetoric on the edge of cunning: Or, the performance of neutrality (re) considered as a composition pedagogy for student resistance. *College Composition and Communication, 55*, 115–146. doi:10.2307/3594203

Lozano-Reich, N., & Cloud, D. (2009). The uncivil tongue: Invitational rhetoric and the problem of inequality. *Western Journal of Communication, 73*, 220–226. doi:10.1080/10570310902856105

Lynch, D. (1995). Teaching rhetorical values and the question of student autonomy. *Rhetoric Review, 13*, 350–370. doi:10.1080/07350199509359192

MacDonald, A. A., & Sánchez-Casal, S. (Eds.). (2002). *Twenty-first century feminist classrooms: Pedagogies of identity and difference*. New York, NY: Palgrave MacMillan.

Maher, J. (2002). Invitational interaction: A process for reconciling the teacher/student contradiction. *Rocky Mountain Review, Spring*, 85-93.

Micciche, L. (2007). *Doing emotion: Rhetoric, writing, teaching*. Portsmouth, NH: Boynton/Cook.

Miller, R. (1998). The arts of complicity: Pragmatism and the culture of schooling. *College English, 61*, 10–28. doi:10.2307/379055

Novak, D., & Bonnie, B. (2009). Offering invitational rhetoric in communication courses. *Communication Teacher, 23*, 11–14. doi:10.1080/17404620802593013

Pollock, M. A., Artz, L., Frey, L. R., Barnett Pearce, W., & Murphy, B. A. O. (1996). Navigating between Scylla and Charybdis: Continuing the dialogue on communication and social justice. *Communication Studies, 47*, 142–151. doi:10.1080/10510979609368470

Pratt, M. L. (1991). Arts of the contact zone. *Profession, 91*, 33–40.

Ratcliffe, K. (2005). *Rhetorical listening: Identification, gender, whiteness*. Carbondale, IL: Southern Illinois University Press.

Ritchie, J., & Ronald, K. (Eds.). (2006). *Teaching rhetorica: Theory, pedagogy, practice*. Portsmouth, NH: Boynton/Cook.

Rogers, C. (1970). Communication: Its blocking and its facilitation. In Young, R. E., Becker, A. L., & Pike, K. L. (Eds.), *Rhetoric: Discovery and change* (pp. 284–286). New York, NY: Harcourt, Brace, & World Inc.

Ryan, K., & Natalle, E. (2001). Fusing horizons: Standpoint hermeneutics and invitational rhetoric. *Rhetoric Society Quarterly, 31*, 69–90. doi:10.1080/02773940109391200

Shor, I. (1980). *Critical teaching and everyday life*. Boston, MA: South End Press.

Soles, D. (1998). Problems with confrontational teaching. *College Composition and Communication, 49*, 267–269. doi:10.2307/358936

Stenberg, S. J. (2006). Liberation theology and liberatory pedagogies: Renewing the dialogue. *College English, 68*, 271–290. doi:10.2307/25472152

Welsh, S. (2001). Resistance theory and illegitimate reproduction. *College Composition and Communication, 52*, 553–573. doi:10.2307/358697

Wood, R. G. (1993). Responses to Maxine Hairston "diversity, ideology, and teaching writing" and reply. *College Composition and Communication, 44*, 248–256. doi:10.2307/358843

ADDITIONAL READING

Cohee, G., Däumer, E., Kemp, T., Krebs, P., Lafky, S., & Runzo, S. (Eds.). (1998). *The feminist teacher anthology: Pedagogies and classroom strategies*. New York, NY: Teachers College.

Ellsworth, E. (1989). Why doesn't this feel empowering? Working through the repressive myths of critical pedagogy. *Harvard Educational Review, 59*, 297–324.

Fleckenstein, K. (2003). *Embodied literacies: Imageword and a poetics of teaching*. Carbondale, IL: Southern Illinois University Press.

Foss, K., Foss, S., & Griffin, C. (1999). *Feminist rhetorical theories*. Thousand Oaks, CA: SAGE Publications.

Foss, K., Foss, S., & Trapp, R. (1985). *Contemporary perspectives on rhetoric*. Prospect Heights, IL: Waveland Press.

Freedman, D., & Stoddard Holmes, M. (Eds.). (2003). *The teacher's body: Embodiment, authority, and identity in the academy*. Albany, NY: State University of New York Press.

Glenn, C. (2002). Silence: A rhetorical art for resisting discipline(s). *JAC, 22*, 261–291.

Kill, M. (2006). Acknowledging the rough edges of resistance: Negotiation of identities for first-year composition. *College Composition and Communication, 58*, 213–235.

Luke, C., & Gore, J. (Eds.). (1992). *Feminisms and critical pedagogy.* New York, NY: Routledge.

Maher, F., & Thompson Tetreault, M. K. (2001). *The feminist classroom: Dynamics of gender, race, and privilege.* Lanham, MD: Rowman & Littlefield Publishers.

Maybery, M., & Cronan Rose, E. (Eds.). (1999). *Meeting the challenge: Innovative feminist pedagogies in action.* New York, NY: Routledge.

Probyn, E. (1990). Travels in the postmodern: Making sense of the local. In Nicholson, L. (Ed.), *Feminism/Postmodernism* (pp. 176–189). New York, New York: Routledge.

Ratcliffe, K. (1999). Rhetorical listening: A trope for interpretive invention and a 'code of cross-cultural conduct.' *College Composition and Communication, 51*, 195–224. doi:10.2307/359039

Weiss, G., & Fern Haber, H. (Eds.). (1999). *Perspectives on embodiment: The intersections of nature and culture.* New York, New York: Routledge.

West, T. (1996). Beyond dissensus: Exploring the heuristic value of conflict. *Rhetoric Review, 15*, 142–155. doi:10.1080/07350199609359211

Westbrook, B. E. (2002). Debating both sides: What nineteenth-century college literary societies can teach us about critical pedagogies. *Rhetoric Review, 21*, 339–356. doi:10.1207/S15327981RR2104_2

ENDNOTES

[1] I have often chosen to use the term "college composition classrooms" (or sometimes "college writing classes") throughout this chapter to refer to introductory writing courses at the university level. While approaches to these courses vary greatly, most are some form of introduction to college-level writing. I should also note that, in the U.S., the first-year writing course is typically a universal requirement: all students must earn the course credit before graduation.

[2] Foss and Griffin note that persuasion may happen, but it is not the rhetor's goal. Change, they explain, happens constantly as entities interact with one another. It is with the *desire* or *intent* to change or persuade that Foss and Griffin take issue.

[3] There are also similarities between an invitational pedagogy and forms of liberatory pedagogies. In fact, an invitational pedagogy might be seen as one strategy for enacting the goals of a liberatory classroom. For those liberatory instructors for whom change is the primary goal, however, invitational pedagogy would differ quite dramatically, both in practice and objective.

[4] Ratcliffe defines cultural logics as "a belief system or way of reasoning that is shared within a culture – for example, even though not all Green party members think exactly alike, certain tenets associated with the Green party form a recognizable Green cultural logic" (p. 10).

Chapter 10
Negotiating Disruption in Visual Arts Education

Jennifer Elsden-Clifton
RMIT University, Australia

ABSTRACT

The visual arts has a long tradition of providing a space for artists to take up disruptive practices such a, challenging what is known, questioning and exploiting cultural codes, and providing alternative social practices. This chapter is interested in how visual arts students take up these disruptive possibilities within the complexity of secondary schools; a space historically characterised by hierarchal power, surveillance, and institutionalized structure. This chapter draws upon interviews with art teachers to examine the discourses surrounding their observations of 'disruptive' art created in their classrooms. In particular, the author focuses on the stories of two students who through their artwork explored and transgressed normalised notions of sexualities and bodies, which was signalled to be problematic within the school context by the teachers. This discussion explores how teachers, students, and the general school community respond and negotiate the tension and discomfort that can arise from 'disruptive' art.

INTRODUCTION

According to hooks (1995) '[a]rt should be ... a place where boundaries can be transgressed, where visionary insights can be revealed within the context of the everyday, the familiar, the mundane' (p. 138). However, it is important to examine how

these disruptive possibilities might be constructed and dealt with within schools. How is transgression and visionary insights situated within the structures of education which is traditionally constructed by relations hierarchical structures that police bodies, behaviors and identities into normalised notions (Foucault, 1977). Elsewhere, I have explored how visual arts education has the potential to provide a space for students to take

DOI: 10.4018/978-1-61350-495-6.ch010

up the possibilities that hooks (1995) outlines and have argued that for some students the art classroom is one of the few schooling spaces that allow them to take up particular lines of flight into 'difficult' territories (Deleuze & Guattari, 1987, p. 277). However, the art classroom still exists within a school setting, which is defined by specific social and cultural structures. This chapter therefore, explores teachers' impressions of the tension and discomfort around disruptive students' art work and how the schooling community 'take up', view and respond to the art. To frame this discussion, I will draw on the concepts of transgression, bodies and sexualities within a feminist poststructuralist premise and Boler's (1999) notion of 'pedagogy of discomfort' to acknowledge, and frame, the difficulties around disruption within schooling spaces.

As a feminist poststructuralist researcher and educator, I feel it is important to acknowledge that 'difficult' art does arise. In this chapter, I draw upon interviews with three Australian secondary visual art teachers, Amy, Beth and Charlotte, about discomfort and disruption in the visual arts. I then narrow my research to examine the stories, discourses and repercussions that Charlotte outlines in relation to two of her students – Eloni and Francesca. In particular, these case studies draw upon the tensions and issues around students disrupting normalised notions of sexualities and bodies, which were signalled by the teacher to be problematic within the school context. First, I explore the discourses around an incident in which a Eloni, a male student was 'othered' as homosexual due to his interest in feminine art forms. Through the teacher's recollection of the incident, I outline how he was othered by his passion for fashion and costumes and placed in oppositions to his brother's 'ideal' or 'normal' model of masculinity and heterosexuality. Secondly, I discuss the responses around Francesca's art that explored the flows and intensities of female bodies. However, as I outline, such a public display of excessive female bodies and sexualities caused chaos and contro-

versy within the art classroom; as it blurred the public/private boundary where female bodies are usually positioned and it disrupted the traditional power relations between teachers and students. The purpose of this discussion of the teachers' discourses around students' art is twofold, first, to highlight the potential of the visual arts as a space within education to disrupt, challenge and seek alternative ways of seeing, but also to acknowledge the difficultly of doing so for those within schooling spaces.

THE DISRUPTIVE POSSIBILITIES OF ARTS EDUCATION

Eisner's (1972) work is productive to frame disruption within arts education. He notes that the visual arts:

call to our attention the seemingly trivial aspects of our experience, thus enabling us to find new value in them. The artist's eye finds delight and significance in the suggestive subtlety of the reminiscences and places of our existence. The work of art displays these insights, makes them vivid, and reawakens our awareness to what we have learned not to see. Thus, art is the archenemy of the humdrum, the mundane. (Eisner 1972, p. 16)

Thus, drawing upon Eisner (1972) I see disruption within the arts in terms of challenging what is known, seeing things in new ways and questioning the mundane. Indeed, throughout art history, there are many examples of artists and art movements that have sought to use the visual arts as a means of protest and activism, to question and exploit cultural codes, and to mobilize and promote alternative social practices. For instance, the political artist Alfredo Jaar epitomises this tradition when he states '[s]ometimes art is less a thing to look at than a way to see (2003, n.p.). As he explains:

I think as artists we are privileged, and we should use that privilege. Who out there is asking questions? Who questions the systems of our lives, and how? (Jaar, 1998, cited in Bricker Balken, 1999, p. 39)

These disruptive possibilities also transfer into visual arts education. Using art as a medium for disruption has been brought to the fore by many recent researchers such as Eisner (2001) and Freedman (2000), although one of the earlier and more notable contributions to this field is John Dewey (1934) in *Art as Experience*. Dewey (1934) believed that art is a form of experience that vivifies life and can contribute to an individual's sense of self and emotional fulfillment. For Dewey (1934), art is intrinsically valuable because it is an effective form of communication that 'breaks through the barriers that divide human beings, which are impermeable in ordinary association' (p. 244).

Freedman (2000) extends this view and outlines that 'students make art to express not only things about themselves, but about their surroundings, their social context, the things that act upon them' (p. 323). From this perspective, art can be a disruptive medium within education as it can provide spaces for students to challenge, question and explore their social and cultural worlds. In doing so, students may use imagination and creativity as a means of exploring new possibilities and ways of being. Elsewhere, I have discussed how students have taken up these possibilities in their art to question and exploit cultural codes, challenge traditional or stereotypical assumptions of identity or subjectivity, and promote alternative discourses that work towards the acknowledgement of difference (Elsden-Clifton, 2006). However, in this chapter I want to explore the tension around students taking up these disruptive possibilities within schools; a space historically characterized by hierarchic power, surveillance and institutionalised structure.

Foucault (1977) noted that schools were constructed by relations of power, control and resistance which are constructed by a complex hierarchical structure that polices bodies, behaviors and identities. These power struggles/relationships have been constructed through a myriad of binaries that places students as the unruly, negative term in need of control and regulation, and the teacher/system as the position of power. The aim of these disciplinary mechanisms is the attempt to generate 'docile bodies': a notion that Foucault (1977) defines as a body 'that may be subjected, used, transformed and improved' (p. 136). Within schooling contexts, the body is a site of manipulation and control. For instance, this can be seen in the struggle over the body through mechanisms such as uniforms, movement and desk arrangements. However, rather than seeing the 'disciplined body' as passive, docile or having little agency; Foucault provides a more active view. He believes that bodies have the potential to protest, rebel, critique and take up alternative becoming because of the shifting points resistance (Foucault, 1977).

Nevertheless, resistance and participation in disruptive practices can be difficult and risky (Grosz, 1994). Challenging an established set of values and conventions that has been internalised and institutionalised takes a great deal of support, collaboration and negotiation, and students, teachers and schools all have different investments in maintaining these dominant discourses. Thus, I turn to feminist poststructuralist theory as a means of exploring the theory around bodies and sexualities, but also to examine the tension that is evoked when students resist and disrupt the dominant discourses in schooling spaces.

POSTSTRUCTURALIST PERSPECTIVES

In line with the framework's theoretical premise of multiple truths, there is no one 'true' or fixed definition of poststructuralism. In my research, I have used Builema and Smelik's (1993) notion of poststructuralism which 'rejects the structuralist view that unchanging, fundamental and universal structures lie at the basis of the world of phenomena, texts, social systems' and instead 'focuses on problematising structures by studying their discursive construction, their function and their power' (p. 193). This definition enables me to look differently at the discursive and non–discursive spaces of art education and to open up what seems natural or normal in these sites to alternative understandings or possibilities (Adams St Pierre, 2000). In this chapter I draw upon two key aspects of feminist poststructuralism by specifically looking at how bodies and sexuality are positioned and constructed, and secondly, the using the potential of Boler's (1999) framework of a 'pedagogy of discomfort' to acknowledge, and frame the difficulties around disruption within schooling spaces.

Seeing the body as a text, which emits signs, is a feature of post-structuralism (Grosz, 1994). Indeed, for Foucault, the body was central to the understanding of self, because subjectivities are 'classified in terms of their bodies and their bodily function' (Danaher, Schirato, & Webb, 2000, p. 124). This view is also supported by Grosz (1994) who believes that all the effects of subjectivity and all the significant facets and complexities of subjects can be adequately explained using the subject's body as a framework (Grosz, 1994, p. vii). From this perspective, bodies can be understood as texts involved in power relations that invest them, mark them, train them, torture them, force them to carry out tasks, to perform ceremonies and to emit signs (Foucault, 1977). In other words, bodies have been inscribed socially with a language that determines hierarchal positions, subjectivities, and lived experiences (Grosz, 1994).

In my research, the body of students and teachers in schooling spaces can be seen not as passive but as actively shaped by (as well as shapers of) a system of meaning, signification and representation (Grosz, 1994). However, this fluidity of bodies and sexualities can also be problematic for education. Indeed, traditionally bodies, sexualities and education share a volatile, controversial and highly politicised relationship (Epstein & Johnson, 1998). This somewhat limiting relationship is driven by education's need to control, regulate and police sexualities and bodies into appropriate positions or models. As such, bodies and sexualities become a site of control in schools and traditionally when students or teachers disrupt or transgress these dominant positions it has been fraught with controversy, or met with resounding silences or condemnation (Epstein & Johnson, 1998).

Despite these mechanisms of discipline, sexuality and bodies are able to seep through these domains of control into the conversations, interactions, art classrooms, art pieces, visual diaries and other educational spaces. Sexuality has this ability to do so, as according to Grosz (1994), it is fluid, excessive and uncontrollable and refuses to stay within its predesignated regions (p. viii). Thus, in this chapter, I explore how the teachers' discourses around students' art evokes this 'excessive' notion of sexuality and bodies that seeks out alternative regions and crosses boundaries. However, as I demonstrate, in disrupting these redesigned regions and established values, it can be a difficult and risky space for teachers and students. It is therefore, productive to frame this discussion through Boler's (1999) 'pedagogy of discomfort'.

Boler's (1999) framework for exploring and transforming the education field, which she refers to as a 'pedagogy of discomfort', involves two stages (p. 175). First, a pedagogy of discomfort involves 'inviting educators and students to engage in critical inquiry regarding values and cherished beliefs and to examine constructed self–images in relation to how one has learned to perceive others' (Boler, 1999, p. 176f.). In other words, a pedagogy of discomfort 'aims to invite students and educators to examine how our modes of seeing have been shaped specifically by the dominant culture of the historical moment' (Boler, 1999,

p. 179). As well as questioning the dominant modes of thinking and seeing, the second stage of a pedagogy of discomfort calls for action and change (Boler, 1999).

This two pronged approach resonates with a feminist poststructuralist approach. Within this framework there is a commitment to the dual focus of firstly, the 'serious questioning of patriarchal adherence to the following: universal concepts of truth and methods of verifying truth; objectivity; a disembodied, rational sexually indifferent subject and the explanation of women's specificity in terms that are inherently masculine' (Grosz, 1986, cited in Wearing, 1996, p. 37). Secondly, transforming these sites to assemble and mobilize counter discourses that may problematize power, value difference and promote marginalized narratives.

In this chapter, I have drawn upon these frameworks to construct the my understandings of the notion of 'disruption' and 'discomfort', which I see as a way of describing and exploring how students and teachers: move past the dominant discourses circulating in education that attempt to control and discipline subjectivities; take up opportunities to consider the social and historical construction of their subjectivities; critically discuss the construction of their subjectivities by power relations; and mobilize spaces for alternative discourses that promote otherwise marginalized narratives in education (Boler, 1999).

Within this framework, however, Boler (1999) acknowledges that educators who take up these possibilities as agents of change 'undoubtedly face the treacherous ghosts of the other's fears and terrors, which in turn evoke one's own demons' (1999). As I will demonstrate in later sections of this chapter, sexualities and bodies that disrupt normalized notions in schools often resulted in teachers and students experiencing 'defensive anger, fear of change, and fears of losing our personal and cultural identities' (p. 176). Albers (1999) reinforces this view of discomfort but specifically locates it within visual arts education:

[e]ducators must not ignore the propensity of the visual arts to make visible ideologies that position some groups as more privileged than others. By acknowledging that 'difficult' art-works will arise, we can begin to openly discuss such issues ... we can forward art as a powerful way to instigate changes in students' beliefs about themselves and others. (p. 11)

Therefore, in my discussion of the two narratives, I have adopted a poststructuralist premise, as it allows my research to explore how students have used bodies and sexualities as a means of disruption. Also through the work of Boler (1999), I am able to examine the tension, ambiguity and discomfort that this creates within a schooling setting.

RESEARCH SPACES

This research stems from a larger project which involved collecting and analyzing the art and visual journals created by 126 senior art students (Years 11 and 12) across three Queensland secondary schools in Australia (Elsden-Clifton, 2004). The three schools were chosen based on representing a variety of locations across the state (rural and metropolitan) and different contexts (state and religious affiliated schools, large and small schools). I also conducted interviews with the three senior art teachers about their personal philosophies to teaching art education. As a means of providing further context for these texts, I spent one term in the schools undertaking observations of the school and classrooms.

This chapter however, focuses on the interviews that I conducted with the three female secondary art teachers, Amy, Beth and Charlotte who were teaching secondary senior art within these schools at the time. Each of these teachers had varying experiences and worked in different contexts. Amy had been teaching for nine years and taught at a state school in the outer suburbs of a large metropolitan city. This school had a large student population of almost 1400, with over 100 teachers. The school is situated on a major train line and many of the students travel to this school from outlying areas or other suburbs. This school predominantly services students from low socio–economic areas. The second teacher I worked with was Beth, who was a relatively new teacher; she had been teaching for two years in a rural Catholic affiliated school that caters for approximately 350 students, who reside in the predominantely mining township or surrounding farming areas. This chapter draws primarily on the interview I conducted with Charlotte. Charlotte taught secondary art, in a preschool to year 12 catholic school in a suburb of a major metropolitan city. As with the other teachers, Charlotte fulfills a number of roles within the school and education structures, as she outlined:

Creative Arts Co-ordinator, firstly, is my main role I suppose, as of this year.. . I am responsible for teaching art from Year 9 to Year 11 this year, last year I taught Year 12. I'm teaching Year 8 graphics. I'm a PC [pastoral care] teacher as well; I'm responsible for a Year 11 and 12 home class. And my last role I suppose is I'm a commit- tee member of the curriculum review committee. (Charlotte, School C)

Due to Charlotte's multiple roles, such as Arts Coordinator, Pastoral Care responsibilities and home class role, she had contact with the students she is referring to in the study beyond the art classroom, therefore, productively for this chapter, she was able to articulate the impact/reac- tions/repercussions of disruptive art work beyond visual arts education into other areas of the school (such as other teachers, different year levels). The students referred to in this study were in Year 11 and 12 (approximately 16-18 years old). Pseud- onyms were used to protect their identities. In the Queensland school system, students in these year levels are usually 16-17 years old. The students in the study were working within the board registered Visual Arts Senior Syllabus (board registered art counts towards an Overall Position – a final school exit score – which has more of a theoretical focus than non-board registered art). Elsewhere, I have drawn upon students' art work and visual journals as a way of exploring the possibilities of art education and students' engagement with transformative processes (Elsden-Clifton, 2004) as I find this a productive way of including students' voices and lived experiences into my research. In this chapter however, I am only using the teacher interviews, as they were recalling stories about former students.

The interviews I conducted with the three teachers were semi-structured, which provided an open framework that allowed for focused, conversational, two-way communication (Cohen, Manion & Morrison, 2000; Denzin & Lincoln, 2000). These interviews were then transcribed, and critiqued using a discourse analysis framework. Within poststructuralism, the term 'discourse' encapsulates more than just linguistic meaning: it is a social practice through which people are inducted into ways of valuing, stances and points of view which reflect and produce the interests of a group (Morgan, 2002). As such, the value of discourse analysis is that it makes available to educators 'a more fluid and complex understand- ing of the ways in which students are constructed' (Baxter, 2002, p. 6) in different classroom contexts. From this perspective, in my research the teachers, students and schools were situated within an array of intersections, networks, relations of power and discourses. In undertaking my discourse analysis, I focused on my specific research interests of investigating: how do students use bodies and sexualities as a medium for disruption? What are the possibilities for using disruptive pedagogy to explore multiple discourses of bodies and sexuali- ties? What emotions are evoked around disrup- tion? How do the visual arts provide a space for students to take up difficult lines of flight? How does the schooling community react to students disrupting traditional discourses of schooling?

VOLATILE BODIES AND SEXUALITIES

The teachers in my research utilized the pedagogical tool of disruption in various ways in their classrooms. From my observations of their classes and curriculum documents, the teachers (to different extents and in different contexts) worked to challenge the dominant discourses within art education, fostered difference in the art classroom and encouraged students to explore notions of subjectivity, society and culture. These characteristics emerged in the interviews. For instance, Charlotte noted 'I try to purposely look at artworks that will confront them and provoke comment' (School C) as a way of questioning and challenging students' beliefs and viewpoints.

Disruption was also evident in the curriculum documents that framed their art classrooms. The teachers had created learning experiences that specifically encouraged students to question and instigate a search for meaning and understanding about themselves and their subjectivities. For instance in School B, students in Year 12 complete a unit of work titled *Looking Beyond the Self*. In this unit students are 'required to find new sources for inspiration that go beyond their current understandings of the world around them' (School B, 2002, p. 11). Through this unit students are to 'push their notions of artistic practice' and to continue to explore the nature of art as a 'powerful mode of communication' and strategy of transformation (School B, 2002, p. 11).

However, the teachers also acknowledged that by disrupting the visual arts space, it can also evoke uncomfortable emotions and discomfort. As Beth (School B) outlined, 'I think in art you do give the kids opportunities to explore how they

are feeling, even if that is depressed and dark and strung out and on the edge kind of thing'. This was reinforced by Amy who noted:

Sometimes people will say that [students' art] is really depressing and that is because the emotions of a teenager are traditionally up and down, all over the place and they get caught up in relationships. Primarily because they are finding their way and so an adult will come along and see all of these doom and gloom pictures and say 'Oh that's really depressing'. Whereas art teachers are used to it so we know, we don't worry about it at all as we know it is kids just expressing their ideas. (Amy, School A)

Although Amy felt this was 'kids just expressing their ideas'; this disruption sits within the wider schooling space, and thus, discomfort and controversy can arise. Thus, in the next section, I explore Charlotte's recollections of two students whose art work transgressed the dominant discourses of sexualities and bodies in her school context that evoked resistance, controversy, confusion and/or anger (Boler, 1999).

Bodies that Challenge

Within the educational context, the mechanisms of discipline and binaristic thought have constructed a centre and a margin; which shapes the definitions of normalcy in students' and teachers' behavior, dress, bodies and sexuality. Within schools, the dominant roles of masculinity are assigned to male bodies which includes such ideals as conflict, hardness and competition (Denborough, 1996). This model of masculinity also has implications for male sexuality which is constructed as heterosexual, active and a source of power (Denborough, 1996). When male sexed bodies do not meet this definition of masculinity, they are traditionally labeled and marginalised — such as the case of Eloni.

When asked about art that has addressed issues such as sexuality, Charlotte recalled Eloni's art, which explored the female form. As she explains:

We had a kid, Eloni, who was an Islander kid. He had an older brother who was a football player. The kids loved [Eloni's brother] ... and he was a bit of a player, a bit of a ladies' man. And Eloni was just totally different again. People would meet him and say he's definitely homosexual, but he just didn't think about it. . .[h]e created the most beautiful costumes from feathers and beads and traditional Samoan costumes – the boys in the class did not bat an eyelid, that was just Eloni. Whereas other people said 'What's Eloni making that for?' you know 'Eloni's brother was a footy player, what's Eloni making this for?' 'What would Eloni's brother think?' and that came from the male members of staff. Again like mostly the PE [physical education] people that had a lot to do with his brother. His work provoked a lot of comment in terms of that. (Charlotte, School C)

In Charlotte's recollection, she explains how, although Eloni does not identify himself as homosexual he is positioned this way because the art he creates does not meet the dominant readings of masculinity. As such, his non–macho behaviour – or exploration of traditionally feminine art forms – is seen as 'weakness, softness and inferiority' and used it as evidence of Eloni's homosexuality (Lees, 1987, cited in Epstein & Johnson, 1998, p. 168). These judgemental comments about Eloni's non–masculine behaviour and art pieces became a way of controlling and policing his sexuality and the models of masculinity he was likely to adopt.

The process of marginalising the bodies and sexualities that do not fit the dominant model is also influenced by the binary of sameness/difference, and generated related categories of difference and otherness. Eloni's positioning as Other is reinforced by the comparison between him and his brother. In other words, Eloni becomes the Other against which the 'normal' is defined. In this case the 'normal' sexual and gender roles for males are defined and demonstrated by his brother who was a 'football player', popular and a 'bit of a ladies' man'. These were used to illustrate how 'abnormal' Eloni was through his interest in 'beautiful costumes' made from 'feathers and beads' and his interest in fashion (Charlotte, School C). Eloni's performance of masculinity falls outside the 'charmed circle' which his brother represents (Epstein & Johnson, 1998, p. 36). Instead, Eloni's sexuality and sexed body are unrecognised or misrecognised as homosexual and othered.

Eloni's divergence from these traditional gender and sexual norms has been treated negatively and divisively by the teaching staff — in this case a male physical education teacher. Through his art, Eloni challenged some of the cherished assumptions held by these teachers. In doing so, these teachers may have felt a threat to their own sexual identity, or a need to defend their investments in the values of the dominant masculine and active culture, evoking resistance, fear and anger. Thus, in a need to control or rein in the excessive and to reinforce the dominant, the teachers judged, policed and critiqued Eloni's alternative version of masculinity as a way of addressing their discomfort and confusion caused by the Other in the classroom. However, it is not only the male body that can cause discomfort in the classroom — female bodies can also create controversy and argument.

The Flows and Intensities of Female Bodies

In Eloni's example, the blurring of binaries such as masculine/feminine, active/passive and heterosexual/homosexual led to the othering or marginalization of his subjectivities. In a similar instance, Francesca's art blurred the binaries that attempt to contain and control female bodies (public/private, active/passive) and, in doing so, also created controversy and comment by students and other teachers.

Francesca's art is interesting in light of Grosz's (1994) theory, which she outlined in *Volatile Bodies*. Grosz (1994) argues that female bodies are positioned into limited and marginalised ways, as they are seen as: fluid and excessive; made up of intensities and flows; out of control; constructed by matter, substances and inscriptions; plagued by leakages, weaknesses and changes; and in opposition to the clean and proper body: the obedient, law abiding, social body (Grosz, 1994). However, in Grosz's theory, she sets out to explore how these traditionally limiting notions can be reconceptualized to transform the construction of female bodies and subjectivities. This is a similar premise adopted by Francesca's art that explored the specificities of the female body. In this art piece, Francesca explores many of the traditionally negative aspects assigned to the female body including blood, hair, breasts, a connection to earth and dirt, changes and fluidity (Grosz, 1994). This was seen in Charlotte's explanation of the painting:

Well, it's massive and it's blue, it has mountains and in between the mountains there are three torn away images of her torso – her neck to her stomach. With her hands in two covering her breasts and the other one I think is just covering her stomach. And then there's a figure down at the bottom that's lying down under the mountain — it's almost integrated into the mountains; you have to look really, really hard to see it. (Charlotte, School C)

In Francesca's art she explored the various cycles of bodily flow and in doing so illustrated the uncontrollable and fluid nature of the female body. In this art piece, the female body is able to flow with and in the breeze and seep beyond the outside of the body and integrate with the mountains. As such, it represents a body 'outside' its designated areas. This art piece also displays the specificities of female bodies such as blood, breasts and bodies in a classroom space (a space which typically seeks to edit out and control these characteristics). Indeed, this public display of these normally silenced issues caused discomfort and controversy, as seen in Charlotte's comments about other students' reactions to this painting:

Francesca's painting had three photos of her breasts on it, which the kids, the Year 9 boys in particular, couldn't cope with, and in the end we had to turn the painting around they were making that much — you know, stress about it. And it wasn't even a sexual painting; it was basically a self–portrait really. (Charlotte, School C)

Further Charlotte outlined that Francesca's art piece:

. . .definitely sparked some comment from other kids and teachers. Negative in terms of 'What the hell is she trying to say?' and you just say, 'Well look at the painting for more than two seconds before you say that, like really look at it' and it's massive and it does take a while to get around the whole thing. But positive in terms of 'Wow, she must feel very comfortable with herself to do that, to put herself out there, to express herself in this way'. (Charlotte, School C)

This painting explored many of the concerns or discomforts surrounding female bodies, such as, the disgust of the unknown female body: 'What the hell is she trying to say?' (Charlotte, School C). It also seeks to represent what Grosz (1994) refers to as the 'unspecifiable that permeates, lurks, lingers, and at times leaks out of the body' (p. 194) through the display of a student's unshaved (and, therefore, unclean) body. The uncovered female breast is also controversial; Grosz (1994) believes that this is because the breast represents the fluidity and indeterminacy of the female body, which needs to be confined, constrained and solidified. As noted by the teacher, when the female body seeps through the domains of control as it has done in this art piece, it can cause concern, conflict and controversy in the classroom. In this example, the female body on display was so confronting that 'in the end [the teacher] had to turn the painting around' (Charlotte, School C).

There are a number of other issues about female bodies that are emphasized in this art piece that students, teachers and other viewers could find difficult — in particular, the connection between female bodies and body fluid such as blood. As Charlotte explained in the painting:

[T]here's a big red window frame with big black night sky out with a red, very textured, very thickly textured red curtain coming in, blowing in the breeze. And that to me just represents blood for some reason, obviously, because it's red probably. (Charlotte, School C)

For the teacher, the flow of the red rich curtains represented the flow of blood from the female body. However, the association with blood is not traditionally seen as positive. As Grosz (1994) argues, menstruation is associated with blood, an injury or wound, and a mess that does not dry invisibly, but leaks and is uncontrollable. Indeed, the 'idea of soiling oneself, of dirt, of the very dirt produced by the body itself, staining the subject' (Grosz, 1994, p. 205) is an uncomfortable and negative notion towards female bodies.

However, in this painting, Francesca publicly acknowledged the flows and specificities of the body. In doing so, she brought into visibility the flesh and blood of the body and emphasized its materiality. Despite the transformative potential of doing so, it is a very difficult issue for others to understand or revel within, especially within traditional schooling spaces. This was seen in the following comments about other teachers' responses to the painting:

And it's quite funny, because some of the male teachers that come in were very confronted by it, you know, even the other art teacher. She asked her to take photos of her and she refused, she got another kid to take the photos of her. Which in this day and age, you never know, that could have issues or repercussions later on down the track. But I just think that's a bit, I don't know I've never been in that situation. (Charlotte, School C)

As seen in the comments made by Charlotte, viewing 'difficult' art can be an issue. However, in this instance, the viewing of this art piece is complicated by the power relationships which structure the 'gaze'; it raises questions of who is watching and who is being watched and broaches the issue of the power relationship between the observer and the observed. In this case, the gaze is framed by a tension between institutional standards which determines what is appropriate in terms of teachers viewing students' bodies. For teachers — who are bound by professional standards and regulated by a hierarchy of power — the gaze of a student's partly naked public body can be particularly uncomfortable. Interwoven with this complexity, there is also a tension between an educational focus on encouraging students' self–expression and the institutional imperatives in relation to bodies.

Francesca's art piece explores the body's complexity as a leaking, uncontrollable and seeping assemblage. Nevertheless, the fluidity of the body in this image disrupts some viewers as it 'attests to the permeability of the body, its necessary dependence on an outside, its liability to collapse into this outside. . .to the perilous divisions between the body's inside and its outside' (Grosz, 1994, p. 193). For Francesca and Eloni, the visual arts provided a space for them to question, explore and disrupt the dominant specificities of bodies and sexualities. However, as seen through the teacher comments it evoked a mired of discomfort and controversy, as this disruption was situated within a schooling context.

ART AS A DISRUPTIVE PROCESS

In this chapter, I have explored teachers' stories and discourses about disruptive students' art. In particular, I have focused on how two students have used the complexity of bodies and sexualities as a means of disruption, but also through the work of Boler (1999) I am able to examine the tension, ambiguity and discomfort that this creates within a schooling setting. As seen in the overview of the literature, schools can be a limiting space to take up alternative discourses of sexualities of bodies. This is because schools have traditionally operated within a hierarchal structure that seeks to control bodies and sexualities into normalized ideals. As seen through the examples of Francesca and Eloni, when students disrupt these normalised notions it is met with fear, controversy and discomfort. Nevertheless, I agree with Boler (1999, p. 198) that learning to live 'with ambiguity, discomfort, and uncertainty' in our classrooms is a worthy educational ideal. Therefore, this chapter drew upon feminist poststructuralist theory as a means of exploring the tension that is evoked when students resist and disrupt the dominant discourses of bodies and sexualities in schooling spaces. In doing so, it explores the potential of the visual arts as a space within education to disrupt, challenge and seek alternative ways of seeing and acknowledge the difficultly surrounding disruption in a schooling context.

Through this process, my research aims to advocate for arts' importance in schools and contribute to the literature that seeks to assist teachers and schools to recognize the impact and role art education has on the ongoing creation and negotiation of identity and subjectivity. It also sets out to acknowledge the difficult work that teachers carry out to encourage students to challenge our values and modes of seeing and thinking. This research also highlights how teachers take up the difficult task of negotiating discomfort. However, as seen through this chapter, it is through the actions and support of these teachers, that students were similarly able to disrupt normalised notions of sexualities of bodies in school and more widely society. Therefore, this chapter contributes to a continuing dialogue around the disruptive possibilities of education to provide spaces for students and teachers to challenge marginalization and contest traditional notions of bodies and sexualities which, despite the discomfort and difficulties, I believe are worthy educational goals.

REFERENCES

Adams St Pierre, E. (2000). Poststructural feminism in education: An overview. *Qualitative Studies in Education*, *13*(5), 477–515. doi:10.1080/09518390050156422

Albers, P. M. (1999). Art education and the possibility of social change. *Art Education*, *52*(4), 6–11. doi:10.2307/3193767

Baxter, J. (2002). A juggling act: A feminist poststructuralist analysis of girls' and boys' talk in the secondary classroom. *Gender and Education*, *14*(1), 5–19. doi:10.1080/09540250120098843

Boler, M. (1999). *Feeling power: Emotions and education*. London, UK: Routledge.

Bricker Balken, D. (1999). *Alfredo Jaar: Lament of the images*. Cambridge, MA: Massachusetts Institute of Technology.

Buikema, R., & Smelik, A. (Eds.). (1993). *Women's studies and culture: A feminist introduction*. London, UK: Zed Books.

Cohen, L., Manion, L., & Morrison, K. (2000). *Research methods in education* (5th ed.). New York, NY: Routledge. doi:10.4324/9780203224342

Danaher, G. R., Schirato, T., & Webb, J. (2000). *Understanding Foucault*. St Leonards, Australia: Allen & Unwin.

Deleuze, G., & Guattari, F. (1987). *Thousand plateaus: Capitalism and schizophrenia*. Minneapolis, MN: University of Minnesota Press.

Denborough, D. (1996). Power and partnership? Challenging the sexual construction of schooling. In Laskey, L., & Beavis, C. (Eds.), *Schooling & sexualities: Teaching for a positive sexuality* (pp. 1–10). Geelong, Australia: Deakin Centre for Education and Change, Deakin University.

Denzin, N. K., & Lincoln, Y. S. (Eds.). (2000). *Handbook of qualitative research* (2nd ed.). Thousand Oaks, CA: Sage.

Dewey, J. (1934). *Art as experience*. New York, NY: Minton, Balch & Company.

Eisner, E. W. (1972). *Educating artistic vision*. New York, NY: Macmillan.

Eisner, E. W. (2001). Should we create new aims for art education? *Art Education, 54*(5), 6–10. doi:10.2307/3193929

Elsden-Clifton, J (2004). Negotiating the transformative waters: Students exploring their subjectivity in art. *International Journal of Education through Arts, 1*(1), 43-51.

Elsden-Clifton, J. (2006). Constructing "Thirdspaces": Migrant students and the visual arts. *Studies in Learning, Evaluation. Innovation and Development, 3*(1), 1–11.

Epstein, D., & Johnson, R. (1998). *Schooling sexualities*. Buckingham, UK: Open University Press.

Foucault, M. (1977). *Discipline and punish: The birth of the prison*. London, UK: Penguin Books.

Freedman, K. (2000). Social perspectives on art education in the US: Teaching visual culture in a democracy. *Studies in Art Education, 41*(4), 314–329. doi:10.2307/1320676

Grosz, E. (1994). *Volatile bodies: Toward a corporeal feminism*. St Leonards, Australia: Allen & Unwin.

hooks, b. (1995). *Art on my mind: Visual politics*. New York, NY: The New Press.

Jaar, A. (2003). *Alfredojaar.net*. Retrieved 4 January, 2004, from www.alfredojaar.net

Morgan, W. (2002). *'Here be monsters': Emergent discourses of hybrid identity in students' hypertexual constructions*. Paper presented at the Australian Association for Research in Education, Brisbane, QLD. Retrieved March 23, 2005, from http://www.aare.edu.au/indexpap.htm

School B. (2002). *Work program*.

Wearing, B. (1996). *Gender: The pain and pleasure of difference*. Melbourne, Australia: Longman.

Chapter 11
Setting the Stage for Professionalism:
Disrupting the Student Identity

Lynn Hanson
Francis Marion University, USA

Meredith A. Love
Francis Marion University, USA

ABSTRACT

This chapter discusses the problem of professional writing students transitioning from an academic environment to a work environment. Even the best students struggle in their upper-level courses as instructors expect a higher level of professionalism from their more advanced students. The authors argue that the conflict between the "student" identity and the "professional" identity should be made explicit in the writing classroom. Students can learn to develop and perform new professional roles by employing a theatrical approach, a disruptive innovation that adopts Constantin Stanislavsky's system to the professional writing classroom. Although the approach begins as role-playing, the emphasis is on becoming the professional self. Specific assignments, projects, and student survey responses are discussed.

INTRODUCTION

Despite all of their efforts, training and good intentions, some of our most capable students struggle in our upper-level professional writing courses. They often struggle to meet our expectations because they approach their work as students when we prefer that they take a professional stance.

Our undergraduates' tendency to identify themselves as "students" is understandable but limiting. The traditional educational experience binds students to chairs, focuses their gaze on the chalkboard and teacher and requires them to complete assignments and tests in order to demonstrate knowledge. The experience requires reading, listening, watching, taking notes from texts and experts and repeating information from

DOI: 10.4018/978-1-61350-495-6.ch011

the endless data dumps that constitute traditional teaching methods. In short, through rote practicing and passively receiving "knowledge deposits" from teachers, only one major role is rehearsed and embodied for 12 or more years — the role of the student (Freire, 2005).

When teaching professional writing courses, however, we expect students to imagine a context beyond the classroom where they are motivated as professionals to take more responsibility for their work. For students to become effective professional communicators, we believe they must practice writing in the role of the "professional" and that teachers must create assignments that give students the opportunity to perform this new role and develop a professional identity.[1] In this way we attempt to compress the space between the classroom and the workplace, thus disrupting the traditional educational model and the comfort its familiarity brings.

Learning to write in a professional context is comparable in some ways to the acquisition of literacy that Freire discusses in his work. He writes, "Acquiring literacy does not involve memorizing sentences, words, or syllables ... but rather an attitude of creation and re-creation, a self-transformation producing a stance of intervention in one's own context" (1996, p. 48). Students in our courses are often uncomfortable with the realization that professional communication requires them to create a professional character and embody it believably.

This chapter explains how the field of professional writing addresses the student-workplace transition problem, how the problem manifests itself in our classrooms and how explicit instruction in character development and performance — a "disruptive innovation" in which we apply theatrical principles to writing studies — can create both discomfort and confidence for transitioning writers.

BACKGROUND

For decades, professional writing researchers have struggled with the problem of student transition, knowing that students must be taught much more than the "basics" of writing in order to be successful in the workplace (Anson & Forsberg, 1990). As Paré (2002) has noted, "Some of the most common writing-course exhortations could be disastrous if followed in the workplace: avoid the passive voice, write clearly ... This advice ... might well cause serious problems for the worker operating as a member of the community" (p. 64), especially one in which workplace politics require carefully studied communications. There is little argument over the fact that professional writing must adhere to a standard of "correctness," but what to teach in the classroom in order to best prepare students for their work as effective members of the workplace community is still a matter of debate.

In traditional educational models, college students in upper-level, discipline-specific courses learn the critical knowledge of the field and adopt the modes of thinking of its members. To become a true member of the disciplinary community, however, students must learn more than the "domain content" of a discipline (Geisler, 1994). They must learn the "rhetorical processes" of that discipline, or how that content is communicated. In other words, when the rhetorical processes are not explicated to students, the knowledge of a discipline and the actual *doing* of a discipline remain separate. As a result, many students become frustrated when their writing (which may be a perfectly fine student performance) is deemed unacceptable in their more advanced courses (Geisler, 1994).

In a professional writing program, the domain content might include the particulars of rhetorical theory, knowledge of genres, familiarity with copyediting skills and an understanding of the relationship between text and graphics and audience, for example. Most students can master the domain content of these courses, but when asked to write "professionally," their self-perceptions and their behaviors as "students" get in the way. Beaufort (1999) notes that in the workplace, employees write as members of the institution or community rather than as individuals (p. 5). While a novice "writes from a personal point of view," "focuses on generic audience and matters of correctness," and "takes pride in authorship," an expert writer "writes from [an] institutional point of view," "focuses on specific audience needs and social context," and uses writing skills for "institutional goals" (Beaufort, 1999, p. 75). To help students gain a better understanding of the rhetorical processes of the workplace, researchers have advocated involving "oldtimers" or experienced members of the profession (Adam, 2000; Le Maistre & Paré, 2006) in mentoring relationships or in research that informs teachers in the field about the processes of reading and writing on the job.

Another common approach to this problem is the case study. However, many argue that case studies and in-class exercises are examples of "simulation" writing in which students are not *really* writing to actual colleagues or clients but instead write "as though" they are these characters (Blakeslee, 2001; Freedman & Adam, 2000; Freedman, Adam, & Smart, 1994). Freedman and Adam recommend that teachers resist the rhetorical allure of such assignments because the *actual* purpose of these assignments is to demonstrate knowledge and the *actual* audience is the instructor (pp. 134-135); in other words, these assignments simply ask students to reiterate (and thus reinforce) their student role. Freedman and Adam instead advocate "practicum writing" that is action oriented where students are partnered with businesses and contribute to the conversations happening in that community, thus engaging in "real-world action" (p. 139).

Other scholars have critiqued the case study approach on the grounds that it does not fully represent the complexity of writing in the workplace. Helle, Tynjälä, and Vesterinen (2006) make a distinction between "problem-based" learning which includes case studies that require students to apply their knowledge to solve a problem and what they call "project-based" learning. Project-based learning involves a situation where students *produce* something as concrete as possible" (p. 196).

By advocating assignments in which students contribute to an institution or a particular project, all of these researchers seem to implicitly agree that students need practice writing "in a character" other than "the student." To this end, students need to understand the processes for *getting in character* in much the same way aspiring actors do. In fact, directorial advice to actors grounded in Constantin Stanislavsky's (1946) "system"[2] of method acting applies equally well to students embarking on their careers. This system maintains that, at any given moment, a person embodying a specified role — such as that of the *professional* — must fully understand the motives and contexts that generate the role.[3]

CREATING A NEW SCENE AND A NEW ROLE

Perhaps the problem of student-workplace transition can be diminished by disrupting the traditions of assignments, ways of learning and the roles we play in academia. The adoption of a professional identity requires the development of motivation and the acceptance of responsibility. Simply adding workplace tasks to the classroom is not sufficient. While case studies and classroom-community collaborations disrupt the traditional classroom, the more fundamental notion of identity must be disrupted.

By the time students arrive in our classrooms, they have been trapped in type-cast roles for many years and their "student" performances are often stilted, predictable and passive—not altogether helpful as preparation for the professional world. There is, of course, virtue to performing the student, to taking in information, increasing one's knowledge-base and, as David Bartholomae (1997) has put it, "inventing the university" by imitating the academic modes of thinking and writing. Although criticizing students for passivity is tempting, their passive behaviors are well-learned and well-taught—they are "expert students" (Le Maistre & Paré, 2006; Paré & Le Maistre 2006). And some students are, to some degree, aware of their role as performers and attempt in their writing to adopt the character of the academic or the scholar. As readers of these texts, writing instructors often overlook their performative nature, forgetting that "complex negotiations of identity" often "lie beneath the surface of what may appear at first to be 'inadequate' academic writing" (Ivanič, 1998, p. 343).

Paulo Freire describes the educational system as a narrative in which the teacher imparts "reality as if it were motionless, static, compartmentalized, and predictable" (2005, p.92) through which "Education thus becomes an act of depositing" (2005, p. 92). As students are "filled" with these knowledge deposits, they are kept in a passive position where they are invited to merely accept the world as it is rather than imagine their power to intervene in the world. Freire's solution is "problem-posing" education in which the teacher and the student engage in a dialogue to discover the answers to real world problems. In this equation "Problem-posing education affirms [people] as beings in the process of *becoming*—as unfinished, uncompleted beings" in a similarly "unfinished reality" (2005, p. 100)

Persuading students to see themselves as professionals-in-the-making is challenging, requiring both students and professors to resist familiar patterns of interactions and don new personas. Rather than passive receivers of information and instruction, students must learn to act like confident, independent professionals if they are to *be* confident, able professionals. Likewise, professors who typically impart knowledge and facilitate classroom exercises must learn to play CEO and managerial roles, which require more decision-making, less coaching, and less prodding. Even more complicated, professors must be keenly aware of students' needs and must know when to break role as CEOs and become teachers again.

Developing Motivation

In Shakespeare's *Henry IV*, the perpetually irresponsible Prince Hal declares he will "throw off" his "loose behavior," reform his faults, and redeem his character (Act I, scene 2)[4] at an hour when a prince is truly needed. Likewise, many students postpone becoming professionals until they are actually in professional positions. Like Hal, they seem to assume that when they are new employees in the right time and place, they will accelerate their learning curves, orient themselves swiftly, and become competent team players who make significant contributions to their organizations. Hal does indeed cast off his cloak of incompetence and rise to protect the unity of England from the rebels. He emerges as a leader, inspiring admiration on both sides, and revealing a greater character previously untapped. Unfortunately, too few undergraduates are really princes, and too few are motivated by the possibility of future success — or failure.

Anson and Forsberg, in their study of student interns, observe that "In order to write at all, in order to produce texts that become transactionally real, writers must be able to adopt a persona appropriate to their position in the workplace, acceptable to themselves, their superiors, and other eventual audiences of their work" (1990, p. 207). To spur undergraduates to adopt their professional roles sooner, the familiar academic environment must be disrupted. Professors can achieve this by integrating projects that serve clients outside the university and replicate workplace scenarios inside the classroom, thereby conflating academic life and professional life. In this simulated context, students can learn to do what professionals do because "real work" demands a higher level of motivation and performance.

Similar to actors learning how to become distinct characters, students must learn how to create and perform a professional character. Preparation begins with questions like these: "What does the situation demand from the characters? Who are you in this scene and what action is required from you?"

Much like audience analysis, standard content taught in most professional writing courses, the questions include a component of self-analysis. Current textbooks prompt students who write workplace communiqués to articulate their personal and professional goals before beginning the task.[5] Advancing the process further, Stanislavsky's system suggests even deeper character analysis, clarifying not only the external circumstances, but the intellectual and emotional life of the assigned character (1961, p. 25):

This is a difficult and important psychological moment in the whole period of preparation. It requires exceptional attention. This moment is what we in actor's jargon call the state of "I am,"...the point where I begin to feel myself in the thick of things, where I begin to coalesce with all the circumstances suggested...begin to have the right to be part of them. This right is not won immediately, it is achieved gradually. (1961, p. 26)

For students in client-based projects, this process requires actively merging the current self with a projected future self in a professional position, with supervisors and co-workers and daily efforts that serve their organizations. In this context, Stanislavsky's "magic *if*" question proves especially useful: "What would I do if...?" Designed to help actors understand the complications and motives of the characters they will play

on stage, the question can be asked repeatedly.[6] Guided by their answers moment by moment, both actors and students can improvise their responses "in character." In doing so, students begin taking on the actions and responsibilities they will soon assume as professionals.

And it's hard work. Preparing for a role using Stanislavsky's system takes active engagement of imagination with a sustained focus. The next phase in his system, actually embodying a role, takes an even greater act of will.

Accepting Responsibility

Not surprisingly, many students resist the process. Consequently, the discomfort of shedding the student skin for the professional one should be a central topic in advanced professional writing courses—or any other courses that cast students in professional roles in workplace situations.

Paulo Freire (1996) notes that "Responsibility cannot be acquired intellectually, but only through experience" (p. 16). Teachers can give students this experience by setting a stage and initiating a scene that requires students' participation as actors, as agents who are compelled to participate and thoughtfully contribute to the situation at hand.

Warming Up

In our courses, we work through an assignment sequence that eases students into a full-scale professional performance. Early in a semester, students study the roles they'll soon perform by reading the types of writing that professionals produce. At this point they can still be students and professors can facilitate their learning in the usual ways.

In addition, professors can lead brainstorming sessions in which students list the appropriate, recurring role behaviors that high-quality, competent professionals exhibit. Detailed descriptions and class discussion of each trait can reinforce their images of the professional and flesh out the character traits that students must create for themselves and ultimately perform.

Their "rehearsals" include problem-solving exercises and role-playing exercises that encourage students to function in scenarios that simulate workplace practices. These exercises posit potential workplace conflicts and ask students to respond in writing as professionals would. Scenarios might include correcting an accounting mistake, announcing a price hike, or answering customer complaints.

Simulating the Profession: Meredith's Vacation E-Mail Exercise

Simulations can be powerful intellectual low-stakes exercises that give students a chance to develop and rehearse their professional characters. Although they cannot "stand in" for work experience and its contextual complications, these assignments serve as rehearsal for the on-stage performances they will give later in the semester.

To help students understand the value of persuasion in the workplace, I recently used an exercise from our textbook, *Successful Writing at Work* (Kolin, 2008). The exercise asked students to rewrite an e-mail from an employee to a supervisor requesting vacation time during the company's busiest time of the year. The flawed sample required revision in several areas including tone and organization.

In class, students read over the original e-mail and were asked to comment on the needs of the author and her relationship with her audience, who is likely to be reluctant to grant her request. In the voice of the employee, students composed their revisions and sent them to an online drop box.

I then extended the original assignment by compiling several responses into one document and presenting them to the students with the following instructions:

You are the supervisor. Your busiest time of the year is usually in February. It is now December, and you have received an e-mail from one of your employees requesting vacation time. Read each e-mail message and choose which type of action you will take in response:

- *Grant the vacation time*
- *Decline the request for vacation time*
- *Demote the employee*
- *Fire the employee*

Students rated each message and then reported their suggested actions to the entire class. When I first assigned this exercise I was pleasantly surprised by the students' enthusiasm. They were invested in the role of the employee in part because it was a situation they could envision in their future (who doesn't like to ponder a vacation?). And during the discussion about their decisions, students were enthralled with the power of a supervisor who could make or break an employee's vacation plans. In short, they cared, they participated, they argued for their stance, they were passionate about their choices to grant or decline a vacation, demote or fire the employee for her poor communication skills.

Going beyond the initial role-playing, this exercise highlighted the practical importance of writing on the job and the effect it can have on the writer's professional life *and* personal life. As students observed how their peers (and their peers-as-supervisor) responded to their work, they also gained new understanding about the fundamental role writing plays in the work community. And although I had taken the students' names off their e-mail revisions, those who were "fired" for poor writing skills may have felt the uncomfortable sting of rebuke. This disruption of the usual paper progression signalled the consequences of the work we were doing together and disrupted the passivity of the student role.

Students who actively address the challenges inherent in simulations like this and in case studies engage in rehearsal strategies like Stanislavsky's "magic *'if.'*" Just as actors exist in multiple worlds simultaneously — as themselves in their own lives, as actors on a stage, and as characters in a playwright's imagined world, students also cultivate these necessary multiple identities: as themselves in their own lives, as students in a classroom, and as professionals in a textbook workplace. As Erving Goffman (1959) observes, the self "does not derive from the possessor, but from the whole scene of his action, being generated by that attitude of local events ....The self, then, as a performed character ... is a dramatic effect arising diffusely from a scene that is presented" (pp. 252-253). The self and the roles we take on, are performances. To effectively merge the actual self with the projected self and manifest both in believable actions,[7] Stanislavsky (1924) advises actors to analyze the "given circumstances" (p. 67) and ask themselves: "If this were real, how would I react? What would I do?" (p. 95) and then begin to do it.

When Students and Professors Take the Stage: Lynn's Advanced Business Writing Assignment

Just like acting exercises, simulations and case studies function as rehearsals (not replacements) for the work students will do beyond college. But simulations can only go so far. The products of such assignments end at school — the student turns in the work, it is evaluated then returned to the student with a grade or evaluative comment. As Freedman and Adam (2000) show, the professor is still the primary audience for the documents students write, and the assignment grade is the student's largest reward, realities that keep the experience on an academic stage and perpetuate the typical academic roles for professors and students.

In our classrooms, we have found that students benefit when they are given the opportunity to perform as professionals whose texts have a real life in a living, breathing context with human actors and consequences. Thus aligned with the approaches described by Blakeslee (2001) and Helle, Tynjälä, and Vesterinen (2006), assignments in the Francis Marion University Professional Writing Program frequently incorporate client-based projects in upper-level courses, a process that requires expanding roles for both students and professors, greater visibility and higher stakes.

Setting the stage for these projects begins with revisioning a class full of students as an office full of workers and establishing a writing service as a business. While teachers in a traditional classroom frequently function like stage directors — explicating texts, coaching actors, calling for special effects and managing the action — the directing role for client-based projects calls for additional labors and personas. In addition to serving as the course facilitator, the professor must function like the CEO and first-line manager of the small writing service.

The professor's planning entails finding appropriate clients who need documents, coordinating client timeframes with class schedules and determining methods for students to work as professional writers who meet each client's documentation needs.

Although professors are adept at planning and scheduling learning experiences, some will be less comfortable asserting that students will deliver usable products to clients. Typically some students will rise to the occasion, and some will not. But no one wants to fail in public, a risk that clearly raises stress levels for both teachers and students.

For example, in a recent course in Advanced Business Communication, the major projects of the semester revolved around real local clients with specific documentation needs, and a major student goal was to cultivate greater independence from the professor who usually directs the daily

153

workload. The course recasts the professor as the CEO of a small documentation company and the students as new hires who must prove their worth within the next three months in order to keep their jobs.

On the first day of class, students liked the idea, understanding that soon "the CEO" would introduce them to their assigned clients. Then as probationary employees, they would set about clarifying each client's needs and determining how to meet those needs. Students believed the "real work" would be meaningful, and they viewed it as an opportunity to apply their knowledge and skills in the most active and engaged way possible, just as they would on the job.

After meeting the first client for the semester, the class continued exploring what it means to act like a professional. The professor encouraged students to "get in character" and accordingly shifted into the CEO role. The ensuing workplace dialogue went something like this:

Professor/CEO: *"So we've met our client and toured the facility. During the trip, we received more information about what the client actually wants. We even discussed some potential ideas. So now: What should you do?"*

Students/Professional Writers: [Long pause.] *"We don't know."*

Professor/CEO: *"Okay. Given the reality that you don't know what to do, as a new hire, what should you do?"*

Students/Professional Writers: *"Ask you?"*

Professor/CEO: [Gently reminding] *"Well, I'm the CEO. Do you really want me to discover how little you learned in college, not to mention last week's new employee orientation?"*

Students/Professional Writers: *"No."*

Professor/CEO: *"So what other options do you have?"*

Students/Professional Writers: [Blank stares.]

In essence, the stage was set, the parameters were clearly defined, and the professor asked, "What would you do if I were not here to tell you what to do?"

Ideally, students would begin to act like professionals. They would draw on their memories of projects facilitated by their teachers, emulate them by making a list of action items and set up a schedule for collaboration (modeled after the processes they had followed in previous courses). They would be able to initiate their own projects, implement them and follow through with internal quality reviews before presenting their work to clients.

But this is the moment of disruption when students are asked to accept full responsibility for their work. They must step into the roles of competent team players who can clarify project goals, generate new ideas, develop processes for implementation, establish timelines of internal checkpoints, solve problems, ensure quality and help to lead a team without dominating it. It's a tall order and a big part.

Traditional students with limited work experience are likely to be the most stunned. "We're students," they say. "We don't know what to do." But even mature, non-traditional students with years of full-time work can be stymied by the full impact of the challenge. "*You're* the teacher," they say. "*You* tell us." The disruption in roles is too stark for comfort, the contrast too great. Students who typically take orders cannot immediately step into professional characters who take decisive action in the service of their organizations.

The challenge to do so elicits fear, doubt, and sometimes anger when students weary of floundering. "Why can't you just give us the answer and then we'll do it?" they say.

"Because we're cultivating independence this semester. Here's the situation in our office. I'm the CEO and I'm on the phone in the next room, calling more clients. You're supposed to be smart and capable. Come up with a plan to get the work done."

Frankly, the disruption was trying for everyone, with (1) frustrated students in uncharted territory, clamoring for a teacher, and (2) a frustrated teacher, withholding answers and prompting students to act like professionals.

OVERCOMING OBSTACLES

The obstacles to role creation and performance are substantial. Changing a role requires changing a context. Schooling tends to keep students in a safe place. The traditional student role is like the spectator role that Boler describes, a privileged position of "distance and separation" with the prerogative "to remain in the 'anonymous' spectating crowd and abdicate any possible responsibility" (Boler, 1999, p. 184).

Like so many others on the brink of change, students resist donning an unfamiliar role, especially in the moments when a curtain is rising on the professional arena. Boler's "pedagogy of discomfort," however, requires "students and educators to examine how our modes of seeing have been shaped specifically by the dominant culture" (p. 179) — in our case, the dominant culture of schooling.

We are not suggesting that students simply move from one dominant discourse community to another (from school to work). Social theories of language suggest that there is no truly stable discourse community and no pure linguistic self (Bakhtin, 1986). Consequently, all discursive roles are conglomerates. Temporarily setting aside the student role in our classes in order to develop a professional role serves to *expand* students' repertoires and helps them develop a kind of rhetorical flexibility. As Boler puts it, "An ethical aim of a pedagogy of discomfort is willingly to inhabit a more ambiguous and flexible sense of self" (1999, p.176).

Playing opposite their students, professors also are accustomed to their long-term roles as lecturers and imparters of knowledge. With aca-demic traditions so comfortably entrenched, any transitions toward change will have to begin at the professor's level. The task can begin, as Freire suggests, by shifting from the wisdom-imparting educator to "the problem-posing educator [who] constantly re-forms his reflections in the reflection of the students" (2005, p. 98). Here again, Stanislavsky's "magic *'if'*" can be a useful teaching tool for educators and students alike. As teachers change their roles, they prompt students with cues to change along with them. As in the use of case studies, "The students — no longer docile listeners — are now critical co-investigators in dialogue with the teacher" (Freire, 2005, p. 98).

An even greater obstacle to disrupting traditional academic roles is that most students know nothing about acting and its prerequisite steps of character development. Furthermore, professors familiar with Stanislavsky's contributions are typically in disciplines like fine arts or literature.

In fact, introducing disruption places greater demands on *both* students and professors. The familiar classroom setting is refashioned as an unfamiliar workplace. Students recognize the heightened performance standards even as they feel unprepared to meet them. Professors must learn and present new content beyond established course parameters. They also must play dual roles as teachers and CEOs, stepping in and out of both characters at will. The effect is a classroom environment that potentially can become filled with tension, resentment, and negativity.

Two student surveys administered at the end of the most recent client-based project provide some perspectives on the experience, with some of the most telling responses coming from the written comments.[8]

When asked about their level of preparation for client projects, four said they were not at all prepared:[9]

"Nothing prepared me for this project. I felt like I was a deer in the headlights."

"When I first started this class, nothing prepared me for our client projects. This was something new to me."

"I really had not had any experience prior to this project."

"Nothing could have truly prepared me for this situation. I had to work through everything one step at a time with the pretense that this was going to be how I would work through dealing with clients for the rest of my life. I would have liked to have more chances to interact with the clients over an extended time. But, this is how we learn in the safety net of college."

Interestingly, students did not perceive their negative experiences as irrelevant ones.[10] When asked to rank their levels of agreement with positively-worded statements, 37% strongly agreed, 53% agreed, and 9% were neutral. Only 1 person strongly disagreed with a statement but qualified the rating with a positive explanation.[11]

THE PAYOFF? IT WORKS.

In the post-project survey, written comments remained similarly positive. While some students acknowledged the frequent discomfort in the course, most indicated that they had indeed learned a great deal and felt better prepared to enter the job market.

"The activity changed my knowledge of working on a professional level. I've never had a class that has challenged me so much and I feel like it'll put me ahead of other graduates entering the workforce."

"I think this experience is a good transition before joining the workforce. It has enhanced my knowledge of working for a client to better prepare for future employers.

"I now hold myself to a higher standard."

"Yes the class definitely taught me a lot of real workplace experience — otherwise harder to gain in most college courses."

"I learned a lot about myself doing this project. I can push myself really hard to accomplish my goals."

"I will be able to offer a lot to a future employer because I've been through this process ... It let me know that things won't come as easy as they have before and that I have to think differently to earn successful results. This process has given me experience to solve problems that I've never thought of before. As much as I disliked this class, I've probably learned the most in this one class than I have the whole time I've been in college."

"I now have experience in professional writing for real life clients which gives me an edge over most other writers who have only had classroom experience as opposed to being exposed to what work would be like in the real world. I am grateful for the experience."

Although we cannot pinpoint which exercises, assignments, conversations, or feedback enabled students to finally own their professional roles, and we do not know the exact moment when they recognized their embodiment of that professional character, we do know that, at some point, this transition did begin. From the assessment measures used so far, student feedback like this seems to indicate that the payoff for disrupting traditional roles is worth the trouble.

CLASSROOM RECOMMENDATIONS

Naturally, with each experience and assessment, professors can gain new insights, adjust their methods and assignments, and enhance the learning opportunity for future students. To date, our client-based projects have rendered a number of guidelines that others can adapt, as needed. These include:

- Providing an appropriate amount of class time to conduct a character analysis of the chosen professional character and determine what motivates that character
- Creating opportunities for students to meet and ask questions of the clients and decision makers in the workplace
- Asking students to reflect upon the relationship between their chosen character and the multiple contexts for the documents they create
- Devoting some time for instruction on small group communication and group management
- Modeling the processes for collaborative writing early in the semester by facilitating a mini-project to establish classroom-workplace policies developed by all students
- Discussing how probationary employment status and termination processes will work in the classroom context
- Scheduling special "class times" distinct from professional work times, to allow students and professors to break role, return to familiar patterns of interaction, and review course content through instruction
- Requiring debriefing reports from each participant, perhaps as a final exam.

As professors integrate client-based projects in post-secondary courses, academic exercises are replaced with very real client expectations, an innovation which disrupts students' expectations of the academic environment, their life-long habits as knowledge recipients, and their comfort with conventional student roles and identities. By challenging students with real work and real problems, professors shepherd them through

practicing, to actually doing, to ultimately becoming professionals. This process is the source of the discomfort: increasing the expectations of academic performance to include professional behaviours and quality products.

Our assessments show that using surveys before and after these client-based projects can render data on the perceived value to students and identify areas that professors can further enhance. Future studies that include larger pools will produce even more refinements, as will tracking alumni and soliciting feedback when hind-sight is greater.

In addition, research into Stanislavsky's system and its evolution[12] will be especially useful to professors who direct students in developing their professionalism. Most specifically, professors need guidance on the application of Stanislavsky's rehearsal and acting techniques in a "new market" and a clearer understanding of how pretending gives way to becoming and being.

At a time when global competition for jobs is on the rise, conflating workplace settings and roles with those of the classroom can accelerate our students' readiness and therefore ability to vie for professional positions. The sooner they become professionals, the smoother their transition to the workplace. Furthermore, we suspect that students who have worked through the discomfort of self-reflection—and the risks of creating and performing new selves in the classroom—may even prove to be more astute and productive colleagues.

REFERENCES

Adam, C. (2000). What do we learn from readers? Factors in determining successful transitions between academic and workplace writing. In Dias, P., & Paré, A. (Eds.), *Transitions: Writing in academic and workplace settings* (pp. 167–182). Cresskill, NJ: Hampton Press.

Anson, C. M., & Forsberg, L. L. (1990). Moving beyond the academic community: Transitional stages in professional writing. *Written Communication, 7*(2), 200–231. doi:10.1177/0741088390007002002

Bakhtin, M. M. (1986). *Speech genres and other late essays.* (V.W. McGee Trans) (Emerson, C., & Holquist, M., Eds.). Austin, TX: University of Texas Press.

Bartholomae, D. (1997). Inventing the university. In Villanueva, V. (Ed.), *Cross-talk in comp theory: A reader* (pp. 589–620). Urbana, IL: NCTE.

Beaufort, A. (1999). *Writing in the real world: Making the transition from school to work.* New York, NY: Teachers College Press.

Benedetti, J. (1982). The progress of an idea. In *Stanislavsky: An introduction* (pp. 72–75). New York, NY: Theatre Arts Books.

Benedetti, J. (1998). *Stanislavsky and the actor.* New York, NY: Routledge/Theatre Arts Books.

Blakeslee, A. M. (2001). Bridging the workplace and the academy: Teaching professional genres through classroom-workplace collaborations. *Technical Communication Quarterly, 10*(2), 169–192. doi:10.1207/s15427625tcq1002_4

Boler, M. (1999). *Feeling power: Emotions and education.* New York, NY: Routledge.

Dias, P., Freedman, A., Medway, P., & Paré, A. (1999). *Worlds apart: Acting and writing in academic and workplace contexts.* Mahwah, NJ: Lawrence Erlbaum Associates.

Dias, P., & Paré, A. (Eds.). (2000). *Transitions: Writing in academic and workplace settings.* Cresskill, NJ: Hampton Press, Inc.

Freedman, A., & Adam, C. (2000). Bridging the gap: University-based writing that is more than simulation. In Dias, P., & Paré, A. (Eds.), *Transitions: Writing in academic and workplace settings* (pp. 129–144). Cresskill, NJ: Hampton Press.

Freedman, A., Adam, C., & Smart, G. (1994). Wearing suits to class: Simulating genres and simulations as genre. *Written Communication, 11*(2), 193–226. doi:10.1177/0741088394011002002

Freeland, R. (2000, September 15). The practical path, too, can be high-minded. *The Chronicle of Higher Education, 47*(3), B11.

Freire, P. (1996). *Education for critical consciousness.* New York, NY: Continuum. (Original work published 1969)

Freire, P. (2005). The banking concept of education. In Johnson, T. R. (Ed.), *Teaching composition: Background readings* (pp. 91–103). Boston, MA: Bedford/St. Martin's.

Geisler, C. (1994). *Academic literacy and the nature of expertise: reading, writing, and knowing in academic philosophy.* Hillsdale, NJ: Lawrence Erlbaum Associates.

Goffman, E. (1959). *The presentation of self in everyday life.* New York, NY: Doubleday.

Guffey, M. (2008). *Business communication: Process and product* (8th ed.). Mason, OH: South-Western Cengage Learning.

Helle, L., Tynjälä, P., & Vesterinen, P. (2006). Work-related project as a learning environment. In Tynjälä, P., Välimaa, J., & Boulton-Lewis, G. (Eds.), *Higher education and working life—Collaborations, confrontations, and challenges* (pp. 195–208). Oxford, UK: Elsevier.

Honan, W. (1999, March 10). Small liberal arts colleges facing questions on focus. *The New York Times.* Retrieved from http://www.nytimes.com

Ivanič, R. (1998). *Writing and identity: The discoursal construction of identity in academic writing.* Amsterdam, The Netherlands: John Benjamins Publishing Company.

Kolin, P. (2008). *Successful writing at work: Concise* (2nd ed.). Boston, MA: Houghton Mifflin Harcourt Publishing Company.

Le Maistre, C., & Paré, A. (2006). A typology of the knowledge demonstrated by beginning professionals. In Tynjälä, P., Välimaa, J., & Boulton-Lewis, G. (Eds.), *Higher education and working life—Collaborations, confrontations, and challenges* (pp. 103–113). Oxford, UK: Elsevier.

Locker, M., & Kienzler, D. (2008). *Business and administrative communication* (8th ed.). New York, NY: McGraw-Hill Irwin.

Merlin, B. (2007). *The complete Stanislavsky toolkit*. London, UK: Nick Hern.

Moore, S. (1974). *The Stanislavski system: The professional training of an actor* (Rev. ed.). New York, NY: Viking Press.

Paré, A. (2002). Keeping writing in its place: A participatory action approach to workplace communication. In Mirel, B., & Spilka, R. (Eds.), *Reshaping technical communication: New directions and challenges for the 21st century* (pp. 57–79). Mahwah, NJ: Lawrence-Erlbaum Associates.

Paré, A., & Le Maistre, C. (2006). Active learning in the workplace: Transforming individuals and institutions. *Journal of Education and Work, 19*(4), 363–381. doi:10.1080/13639080600867141

Stanislavsky, C. (1946). *An actor prepares* (Hapgood, E. R., Trans.). New York, NY: Theatre Arts.

Stanislavsky, C. (1946). *Building a character* (Hapgood, E. R., Trans.). New York, NY: Theatre Arts.

Stanislavsky, C. (1961). *Creating a role (E.R. Hapgood* (Popper, H., Trans. Ed.). New York, NY: Theatre Arts.

Stanislavsky, C. (1963). *An actor's handbook* (Hapgood, E. R. (Trans. Ed.)). New York, NY: Theatre Arts Books.

Stanislavsky, C. (1968). *Stanislavsky's legacy* (Hapgood, E. R. (Trans. Ed.)). 2nd ed.). New York, NY: Theatre Arts.

Strasberg, L. (1987). *A dream of passion: The development of the method* (Morphos, E., Ed.). Boston, MA: Little, Brown.

KEY TERMS AND DEFINITIONS

Client-based Projects: Academic assignments in which students provide actual services to local clients. In professional writing courses, for example, students produce high-quality, usable documents.

Magic "*if*": A fundamental component of Constantin Stanislavsky's proposed system for actors engaging in character development and rehearsal, derived from the preliminary question: "*What if I were in this situation?*" and followed by "How would I feel? What would I do?"

Practicum Writing: Advocated by Freedman and Adam (2000) as action-oriented writing in which students are partnered with businesses and contribute to the conversations happening in that community, thus engaging in "real-world action" (p. 139). Similar to client-based projects.

Problem-based Learning: Projects such as those described by Helle, Tynjälä, and Vesterinen (2006) that require students to work together to apply their knowledge to solve a problem while the instructor acts as a facilitator.

Problem-posing Education: Occurs when teachers and students engage in dialogue to ask questions and discover answers to real world problems together. Advocated by Freire (2005) as an alternative to the "banking" system of education.

Project-based Learning: Distinguished from problem-based learning by Helle, Tynjälä, and Vesterinen (2006) as academic assignments that require students to "*produce* something as concrete as possible" (p. 196).

Stanislavsky System: A process devised by Constantin Stanislavsky for theatre actors preparing for performance. The process includes intellectual, imaginative exercises and analysis, paired with systematic physical manifestations in order to believably convey a character's internal and external realities.

ENDNOTES

1. Although scholars have long argued that a liberal arts education is distinctly different from job training, some courses such as business writing and professional communication in departments of English seem to require conflating the two. The course titles themselves breach the divide. For a brief overview of perspectives on the appropriate focus of a liberal arts education, see William Honan's *New York Times* summary of the 1999 winter issue of *Daedalus*, the quarterly journal of the American Academy of Arts and Sciences, which centers entirely on that topic. See also Richard Freeland's article "The Practical Path, Too, Can Be High-Minded."

2. See also Lee Strasberg's modification of Stanislavsky's system, which became the basis for American "Method" acting.

3. See Stanislavsky (1936) *An Actor Prepares* and (1949) *Building a Character.* See also Merlin (2007), and Benedetti (1998).

4. When this loose behavior I throw off
   And pay the debt I never promised...
   Like bright metal on a sullen ground,
   My reformation, glittering o'er my fault,
   Shall show more goodly and attract more eyes
   Than that which hath no foil to set it off.
   I'll so offend, to make offence a skill;
   Redeeming time when men think least I will.

5. See Guffey (2008), Kolin (2008), and Locker (2008) for examples.

6. Sonia Moore (1974) explains that an actor who employs the "magic *if*" "does not have to force himself to believe that he is such a person in such circumstances. *If* is a supposition, and it does not imply or assert anything that exists. Through it an actor can create problems for himself, and his effort to solve them will lead him naturally to inner and external actions. *If* is a powerful stimulus to imagination, thought, and logical action.... Correctly executed logical action will stir the actor's inner mechanism of emotions" (p. 28).

7. In actions that "denote" both "truly." See Hamlet's speech on "actions that a man might play" (Act 1, scene 2) and his advice to the traveling players (Act 3, scene 2) in Shakespeare's masterpiece.

8. Eleven students completed both, with one survey comprised of 10 items to rank, ranging from strongly disagree to strongly agree (1 – 5). All items were stated so that higher numbers would typically signal the most positive responses. The other survey required students to write short responses to each of three questions.

9. Another four students said they *were* prepared by preliminary class activities; two said they were prepared by previous courses; and one claimed preparation through previous work experience.

10. Out of 25 written comments on the rating survey, only one was negative and one had negative implications. A common problem in collaborative projects was clearly articulated by one student who wrote, "Some people do not work at the same pace or ability." Another more subtly acknowledged "I was very aware of the people whose value system differed from my own."

11. "Most of the people that I worked with had the same goals as me, doing quality work and pleasing the client."

12. See also Jean Benedetti (1982) and Lee Strasberg (1987).

Chapter 12
Pre–Service Learning and the (Gentle) Disruption of Emerging Teaching Identity

Mia O'Brien
The University of Queensland, Australia

Shelley Dole
The University of Queensland, Australia

ABSTRACT

The application of 'identity' to analyses of teaching is not new. However in this chapter, the authors propose that the construct has as yet unexploited potential to refresh current theories about teacher learning. They discuss how notions of identity, when integrated with social learning theory, might offer fresh insights for both research and practice. And the authors illustrate this proposition by drawing on data collected from our own pre-service teacher education students as they navigate initial encounters with numeracy (with Dole) and the arts (with O'Brien). In these courses, the authors are concerned with limiting views of self that pre-service teachers can bring to their learning of these two curriculum areas. Such views predominantly stem from pre-service teachers' personal beliefs about the nature of these subjects, as well as confidence in their own ability 'to do' maths and/or art. Informed by Boler's (1999) pedagogy of discomfort, the authors deliberately, but gently move to facilitate the 'disruption' of these beliefs, values, and theories about 'self' as teacher. Located in supportive communal spaces within courses related to each subject, they authors design "collectivized engagement" (p. 176), as well as scaffolded learning and assessment that seek to engage but soften fears about "losing personal and cultural identities" (p. 176). There is evidence to suggest that this gentle disruption of beliefs and negative self-concepts assists in the eventual renegotiation of the students' emerging views of self-as-teacher.

DOI: 10.4018/978-1-61350-495-6.ch012

INTRODUCTION

In teacher education who one is and who one becomes as a teacher is a highly valued yet often implicit aspect of pre-service teacher learning. Students come to teaching with naïve conceptions about the profession, drawn from comparatively limited personal life experience (Lortie, 1975). Learning to teach can thus entail a shift from an initially simplistic view of self as teacher to the relatively sophisticated 'designated identity' that authentic teaching practice requires (Sfard & Prusack, 2005, p. 14). This shift can prove challenging on many levels but particularly so as personal boundaries and existing views of 'self' are renegotiated (Geijsel & Meijers, 2005; Korthagen & Vasalos, 2005). Indeed it is suggested that learning to teach entails the 'whole person' (Sfard & Prusak, 2005) in negotiation of a professional identity (Beauchamp & Thomas, 2009; Britzman, 2003; Korthagen 2004) within complex social settings through iterative stages of social interaction and personal reflection (Mayer, 1999; Walkington, 2005). The lens of teacher identity and its related constructs brings into view new and important ways of understanding teaching and learning to teach (Akkerman & Meijer, 2011; Beauchamp & Thomas, 2009).

Interest in the theoretical value and analytical affordances of teacher identity in educational research has flourished in the past two decades. The term was initially employed to broaden competency-based views of teaching to include conceptions of teaching as being a 'certain kind of person' (Gee, 2001); and in turn to emphasize how that entails the construction of particular ideas about 'how to be' teacher (Sachs, 2005). The use of identity as a theoretical and analytical construct within the field has varied widely. Ethnomethodological perspectives describe identity in terms of the narratives that teachers create to describe their teaching lives (Connelly & Clandinin, 1999) or the collections of stories and narratives about self that are in themselves identities (Sfard & Prusak, 2005). As a psychological construct, identity refers to the meanings, concepts and theories that people hold about themselves, which include conceptions of one's attributes, qualities, beliefs, characteristics and abilities (Collis, 2001; Stets & Burke, 2003). The sociocultural view situates identity within the appropriation of knowledge and practices that enable participation in socially derived meaning systems, relationships and communal activities (such as teaching) - that in turn inform us how to act, how to understand, and how to be (Olsen, 2008; Sachs, 2005). It is the psychological and sociocultural dimensions of identity formation that are of the most interest to us in this discussion.

TEACHER IDENTITY AND PRE-SERVICE TEACHER LEARNING

The sociocultural perspective that we employ views learning as a process of socialization, the appropriation of socially and culturally valued practices (Lortie, 1975; Kumpulainen & Renshaw, 2007; Wenger, 1998). Here we are keen to maintain what Eraut (2010) describes as a productive 'tension' between individual and social perspectives. To achieve this we draw from psychology and social learning theory for our discussion of identity in the context of pre-service teacher education. In this view learning to teach may be considered a process of becoming a teacher - an experience of identity development and formation (Britzman, 2003; Danielewicz, 2001; Mayer, 1999; Olsen, 2008). This process reaches beyond knowledge and skills. It requires the cultivation of a sense of self-identity and purpose (Mayer, 1999). As such individuals seek to "define themselves and [be] viewed by others as teachers" (Danielewicz, 2001, p. 4); and to appropriate valid forms of communicative practices and meanings relevant to the teaching community (Forbes & Davies, 2008; Wenger, 1998). The notion of 'self-in-practice' has origins in sociology and symbolic interactionism and views social behaviour as a reciprocal relationship between self and society (Stryker & Burke, 2006). There are some compelling parallels between identity theory (Hoggs, Terry & White, 1995; Stets & Burke, 2003) and social theories of learning (Wenger, 1998; Werstch, 1991) that together draw our attention to important aspects of becoming a teacher.

Identity is an evolving yet coherent concept of 'self' that people hold about themselves; which is consciously, unconsciously and iteratively constructed and reconstructed in interaction with cultural contexts, social institutions, local communities and people with which the self lives, learns and functions. An overall identity comprises multiple constituent identities, described by some as a 'series of categories or processes' by which individuals specify who they are and where they locate themselves relative to other people. They entail the meanings these imply for oneself as a group member, as a role holder, or as an individual within various social contexts (Ragins, 2009). These theories about who one is can be articulated as both personal identities and social identities (Bandura, 2001). Personal identities refer to the idiosyncratic traits, characteristics, talents, skills, beliefs, emotions, concerns, goals and various conceptions of self that comprise an individual's sense of 'self' and often transcend any alignment to specific social settings (Owens, 2006; Oyserman, 2001).

Social identities on the other hand, are strongly contextualized and include the traits, characteristics, goals and behaviours linked to specific social roles or groups to which one seeks to be a member (Hoggs et al, 1995; Stets & Burke, 2003). Social identities can be broad and demographically oriented (relating to race, gender, political affiliations and so on) or more narrowly focused upon a specific role (such as being a mother, a musician, an accountant) (Ragins, 2009). Teaching or being a 'teacher' is thus a role identity as it relates to the application of oneself to a specific role, and so requires the categorisation of one's self as the occupant of a particular role (Collier, 2001; Stets &

Burke, 2003). This categorization process entails the incorporation of meanings and expectations related to that role and its performance into the 'self' in ways that guide future behaviour, participation and plans. Recent research within identity theory points to the significant place of an individual's resources in the enactment of, and sustained communicative interactions required by, effective social participation and group membership (Burke, 1980; Freese & Burke, 1994). In other words, role identity appears to lean substantially on attributes that are considered situational specific, such as the capabilities and expertise, forms of knowing, and practices that align with those that are valued within particular contexts relevant to that role.

The Place of Identity in Learning

Inherent within the notion of 'becoming' is learning - and as we signalled earlier, social learning theories (Lave & Wenger, 1991; Lortie, 1975; Wenger, 1998; Werstch, 1991) provide a unique account of identity in learning. Here identity and identity formation are at the centre of the learning process. Social learning theories are concerned with the situated, reflexive and participatory nature of individual experience. Wenger (1998) frames identity as the concept that "serves as a pivot between the social and the individual" (p. 145) in that an identity is constituted through particular practices that have meaning within specific social groups or communities. That is, becoming a member of a community requires us to develop the knowledge, knowing and ability to participate legitimately in the community (in its shared enterprise, mutuality of engagement, and negotiated repertoires). In turn this evokes a process of transformation. As participants we negotiate new meanings, and develop new ways of knowing, acting, and being, which are realized within who we are and what we can do - a transformation that entails an "experience of identity" (Wenger, 1998, p. 215). Learning is viewed as a matter of negotiating forms of engagement with and contribution to the practices of a specific community and as such is considered to entail an experience of identity development. This view is congruent with aspects of psychology's emphasis on the relationship between people's (multiple) identities and particular behavioural roles they play within society. There are parallels across both perspectives as each highlights the process of self-categorisation, capability development, and identity formation via the negotiation of individual communicative activity and connectedness to group membership and role enactment.

RESEARCH APPROACH AND DESIGN

Sociocultural theories have been described as a variable and "loose cluster of complementary, sometimes competing, contributions from social psychology, social anthropology, sociolinguistics, and philosophy, that focus on the self in practice" (Olsen, 2008, p. 4). Our theoretical and analytical focus is on the student's emerging sense of self-identity and purpose (Mayer, 1999), of how they "define themselves and [seek to be] viewed by others as teachers" (Danielewicz, 2001, p. 4); and on their gradual appropriation of valid forms of communicative practices and negotiated meanings relevant to the teaching community (Forbes & Davies, 2008; Wenger, 1998), albeit within the context of sometimes unsettling personal views of self (Korthagen & Vasalos, 2005).

This action research study was undertaken in our respective courses (Numeracy and Arts) that run in parallel during the first year of the pre-service teacher education program. We took on the role of teacher-researcher. This enabled us to make close observations of students within our courses, to make field notes and annotations to our course materials on student responses to various learning experiences and activities, and to collaborate on the design of learning activities and teaching strategies. Data also included the collection of assessment tasks to provide insights into students' interpretations of key ideas within each course as well as their perceptions of themselves as teachers.

Learning to Teach Mathematics: Fear, Self-Efficacy, and Shifting Curricular Role Identity

In pre-service primary mathematics education courses, many students enter with fear and anxiety about their own capacity to 'do mathematics' and little confidence in their ability to teach mathematics. Indeed, when asked to nominate a color that encapsulates their feelings about mathematics, the three dominant colours are black (for fear, anxiety); red (for anger, frustration); or grey (for confusing, a mist). Such feelings typically stem from a strong belief that mathematics is a confusing, disconnected body of rule-governed knowledge. Pre-service teachers' own, prior lived experiences of school mathematics can be held accountable for this state of affairs, and without a deliberate attempt to disrupt these feelings towards mathematics, their enacted teaching practices as beginning teachers, will mirror those experienced when they were learners of mathematics. Regrettably, there is ample evidence to suggest that this occurs regardless of the mathematics education experienced by pre-service teachers (e.g., Foss & Kleinsasser, 1996; Kagan, 1992; Zeverbergen, 2005).

The aspiration in mathematics curriculum courses is for students to rediscover mathematics topics from a new perspective, where their prior mathematics knowledge is reawakened. It is a delicate balance of immersion in mathematical investigations to trigger mathematical thinking and avoid feelings of inadequacy. This requires continual monitoring of pre-service teachers as they engage in hands-on, visual and tactile experiences to ensure that meaning and success is being facilitated. Concrete materials to embody the concepts of focus are used to assist internalization and development of meaningful, mental representations of mathematical ideas. As they engage in such carefully orchestrated mathematical learning experiences they begin to see meaning in their disjointed mathematical knowledge and experience a sense of enjoyment in 'doing mathematics'. In this way, good teaching of mathematics is modeled and hence mathematical pedagogical knowledge for teaching is promoted. The following illustrative example describes how students revisit the mathematical topic of volume.

To reacquaint pre-service teachers with volume, they are asked to define it. Typically they state in parrot-fashion, the formula: LxWxH. Through prompting and being asked to think whether particular objects have volume, they may suggest that it is how much something holds (a slight confusion between volume and capacity). Eventually, they will agree that it means the amount of space something takes up, and immediately see meaning in this definition compared to the formula that was initially put forward. Students are then tasked to find their own volume, which they do in groups, crouching in a corner of the room with their peers measuring their approximate length, width and height. They multiply the measures, and because their length measures were in centimetres, they are surprised by the magnitude of their calculated volume (72 000 cm³ with measures of 60 cm x 30 cm x 40 cm). They are then asked to calculate how many of 'them' could fit into a phone box of 1 500 000 cubic centimetres. They perform some divisions and determine that there are quite a few of 'them' that will fit into the phone box. They compare the measure to that of their friends and then decide to find out if their whole group would be able to fit into the phone box. They construct a skeletal model of a cubic metre out of metre rulers and consider the size of one cubic centimetre in relation to the cubic metre. When they perform the calculations, after determining that each metre stick is 100 centimetres long, they are again surprised when they realise that there are one million cubic centimetres in a cubic metre.

But as a result of this series of activities, they have a greater understanding of measurements for volume, and an appreciation of the number of cubic centimetres in a cubic metre, the actual size of a cubic metre, and also a new approach to teaching volume that differs from how they were taught, which typically went something like this: The teacher draws a picture of a 3-dimensional cubic shape on the board and labels the three sides indicating the length, width and height of the object. The teacher writes the formula: V= LxWxH and substitutes the given values for length, width and height into the formula. The resulting measure is then written and the cubic symbol is provided to indicate that the volume has been determined. The teacher states that because the length, width and height are given in centimetres, the resulting volume is cubic centimetres. The students then practice calculations, and for an extra challenge, one of the exercises includes a side length in centimetres when the other two lengths are in metres. This tricks those students who do not, or can not, convert between units of measure. Students' memories of learning volume are about textbook exercises and application of a formula.

The gentle disruptive approach outlined above is not atypical in terms of pre-service teacher education programs, with many mathematics teacher educators identifying with such methods (e.g., Dole & Beswick, 2002; Zevenbergen, 2005). The approach provides models of effective and inclusive mathematics instruction to ensure maximum student participation and understanding. It is an opportunity for pre-service teachers to unlearn the drill and practice methods of their schooling (Ball, 1990) and to realise the limitations of their formulaic knowledge when applied in real situations. The approach simultaneously models good teaching practice and enables pre-service teachers to revisit their own mathematics knowledge and make connections and meaning between the isolated facts and procedures that they remember of their mathematics learning during their schooling years. The anticipated flow-on effect is that pre-service teachers use such approaches when they are teaching mathematics in their classrooms, and their students work in collaborative groups to solve rich tasks, developing shared conceptual understanding. Rather than drill and practice exercises, and the development of skills in order to solve applied problems, students are developing skills as well as conceptual understanding through problem solving.

Combined with immersion experiences of learning and revisiting mathematics knowledge in new and active ways, course assessment tasks can encourage deeper reflection about issues in mathematics education. An example of such a task is for pre-service teachers to select from a list of contentious issues (for example, that calculators should be banned in primary schools; that standards are falling and we must go 'back to the basics', that streaming is an effective school mathematics teaching practice), write their feelings about the issue, then read up on this issue by referring to relevant and reputable literature. They also seek others' opinions on the topic, and write a reflection about what they have found out. Responses are refreshingly honest. The majority of students readily admit to agreeing with the issue in the first instance but there is a visible shift in response as they move through the task. One student wrote: *I initially thought that calculators are a lazy way of doing mathematics, but after reading about how Year 1 students 'discovered' negative numbers using the calculator, I can see the value of the calculator as a teaching tool. I think that I am more balanced in my view as a result of this assignment.* (Melissa, pre-service teacher).

To further impact pre-service teachers' beliefs about mathematics, they are required to locate an investigative mathematics task and develop an assessment rubric. They then implement their task with some students and analyse their responses using the assessment rubric. Pre-service teachers write about the unanticipated ways their student solved the problem: *I was amazed by the approach taken by the student. It wasn't the way I would solve*

the problem, but it worked! (Nicole, pre-service teacher). They also see the value of a rubric to capture the complexity of learning mathematics and the value of collaborative tasks: *It is through the requirement placed on an individual by peers, in a group setting that can be seen as a positive in building learning.* (Mal, pre-service teacher).

By experiencing hands-on learning, creating investigative learning tasks and assessing such tasks, pre-service teachers are continually confronting their own images of teachers of mathematics. Commenting on an assignment, John wrote: *Essentially, this assessment piece realises something which I firmly believe about learning, that is, students should not be considered successful by memorising obsolete or irrelevant mathematical principles, but rather, they should be assessed on their ability to think through a task that requires problem solving, and to do so in a group setting.* Clearly, for John, the coursework of his pre-service mathematics teacher education program reinforced his notions of what good mathematics teaching is all about. The course possibly affirmed his ideas and beliefs about mathematics learning and gave him greater confidence to enact teaching approaches that matched his beliefs.

Can pre-service education courses impact on and transform mathematical teaching approaches? The following comment on end-of-course evaluation forms suggests that the gentle disruptive approach can bring about such change: *This course has changed my perspective of teaching and my life as I have seen first hand, the effects great teaching can have on other people. I entered the course cringing at the fact that I would have to participate in Maths concepts on a weekly basis as I had flashbacks of failing Year 8 maths. By the end of the course, I had changed my teaching preference from English/SOSE to Maths/ Science as I was shown that a topic many people fear, can be presented in a interesting way and be a lot of fun. I want to make a difference to students' lives like this. As a first year teacher, I look forward to my Maths lessons over any other KLA.*

Learning to Teach the Arts: Self-Consciousness, Indifference and Shifting Conceptions of Teaching Identity

In pre-service teacher education programs, courses that prepare students for 'teaching the arts' appear to elicit both extreme self-consciousness and indifference in equal measure. While this looks very different to 'fear' within mathematics, it can have the same effect on students: a bullish resistance to the subject area and hard to shift views of self-as-teacher. The students within the arts education course are no different. At the beginning of each semester a small minority of students thrill excitedly at the prospect of showcasing an existing 'talent' (often an area of art, music or drama developed throughout their school lives). But the majority are divided into one of two remaining camps: the 'I'm no good at art' camp or the 'but it's not *really* a serious academic subject so why bother?' camp (the latter being supplemented by the 'Art is for babies and I only want to teach *middle years*' sub-group).

As with mathematics, arts education students constantly rehearse negative self-stereotyping. In the first week of each semester students are asked to reflect on their personal experiences of the arts in school, and work in small groups to share their current views on teaching within the arts. Each group designs a poster to capture their collective thoughts, using words, phrases, icons and any kind of visual representation they deem adequate to this task. The result is usually a plethora of simply rendered stick figures holding expressively sad, worried faces, with text that reflects commonly shared themes of apprehension, self-consciousness, dread and dismay.

Many fear that their inexperience in the arts will be a disadvantage and that embarrassment and shame will surely follow (since they assume they will be made to draw, act, play music or dance in public). Paradoxically, countering these fears with consistent reassurances that the quality of their own work is not assessed, rather their understanding of the *nature* and *potential* of the arts to facilitate learning, fosters an equally onerous assumption. Many believe that the arts is thus non-academic and the course will 'be an easy pass' (overheard student comment). The minority of students who consider themselves to be 'talented' view the arts as a potential area of future specialization; while the majority offset waning confidence and fear of embarrassment with rationalizations that the arts are of low importance. The educative potential and pedagogical purpose of Arts within classrooms is thus not foremost in students' minds.

This pervading self-consciousness and indifference cannot be overlooked in the design of arts courses. To tackle these fears head on, our course was designed to gently disrupt these emerging teaching self-concepts as well as to disrupt the erroneous assumptions on which they were based. First, it aimed to reconstitute students' previous (potentially negative) personal experiences of the arts via weekly workshops that develop skills, knowledge, know-how, and extended practical experiences within each strand of the Arts. This recognises the potential for hands-on experiences to both strengthen pre-service teachers' self-image as artists and to consolidate their understanding of the role of the arts in learning (Davies, 2008). Second, it promoted the evidence based pedagogical potential of the arts as an important field of thinking, knowing, expression and social/cultural communication in its own right (Greene, 2000) *and* as an integrative window to other curriculum areas. The first aim placed the renewal of students' personal experience of the arts at the centre of the learning frame; and the second focused their attention on the role of the arts within teaching and learning more generally.

The workshops were designed within a 'process' rather than 'product' based philosophy. That is, activities emphasized learning achieved through arts-based processes rather than the quality of arts produced (Sinclair, Jenneret & O'Toole, 2009). Along with Davies (2008) we felt that such activities would enable students to undertake closely scaffolded experiences of being both students and teachers within key arts strands. Our intention was for the students to work 'artistically' without having to be 'artists'. Rather, techniques, skills and knowledge were fostered, and students were able to practice in well-supported hands-on environments. They learned to play drums in music workshops; use charcoal, pencil, inks, and dyes in visual arts workshops; engage in freeze-frames, role-plays and various other process drama activities within drama workshops and so on. Each workshop closed with debriefing sessions in which tutors complemented analyses of student experiences with discussion/reveals of teaching intentions and approach. This was particularly powerful in reinforcing the potential of all pre-service students to teach within the arts (since many process-based workshops required limited artistic ability on the part of the tutors). The students were required to make regular entries into folios linking weekly learning experiences to emerging principles and concepts within the arts. The following extracts are indicative of the kinds of shifts in perception that a high proportion of students experienced throughout the course. These extracts are from entries made in the first half of semester and reflect changes of attitude and confidence:

Every week I begin to notice why teaching through the arts is important! ...I can't draw or paint very well, but I know that encouraging arts in the classroom would be a great learning tool to teach children (Female student).

I'm not very confident with drama and improvisation so I was quite hesitant at the beginning of the lesson today. However, as the lesson progressed I became more confident to have a go (Male student).

The first thing that we learnt was that drama and theater are different which is something I never really knew. This made me think that it's probably

theater that I am scared of not drama. Drama focuses on the process whereas theater focuses on the product (Female student).

As the course unfolded, students developed a greater understanding of and appreciation for the potential of the arts for learning, and hence could see themselves more confidently as arts teachers. In these extracts we see that students have become more open to incorporating arts within their future practice:

Us singing as a group took on a bit of a symbolic meaning for me, the transformation of me being a bit skeptical and apprehensive of an arts subject, to singing in front of an audience now assured in myself about the importance of the arts and it's benefits it provides in the classroom. (Male student)

After having an entire term studying arts and education I have begun to realize that art is definitely not just a time filler, but in fact a way to teach the children through many different and interesting forms and there is tons of evidence that states that learning through drama helps develop oracy skills as well (Female student).

Whilst doing that assignment, I learnt more about the arts than I have in my entire life. It was a great assignment to complete, it was fun and interesting and beneficial for my learning. It was at that point that I realized how much of an effect teaching through the arts within education could have on children. I began to incorporate what I knew from this course into others, through the forms of theorists like Vygotsky (Female student).

Assessment in the course was designed to enable students to manage a dual focus (their personal experience of the arts and on the role of the arts in learning and teaching) explicitly and concurrently. Within the folio a template provided simple prompts to elicit self-analysis of engagement, reflections on individual and group learning, and scaffolded extrapolations of those analyses towards more general discussions about what and how students might learn the arts. As the weeks unfolded, lectures and other learning materials supplemented these experiences with detailed elaborations about learning in and through the arts. Together, these course elements (lectures, hands-on arts-based workshops, assessment and targeted learning resources) were specifically designed to tackle the pervading lack of confidence and indifference. Somewhat tongue-in-cheek, we made our intentions to change these ways of thinking explicit by promoting a 'course mantra' each week: *start with the arts*. These extracts (which include references to this mantra) are drawn from some students' final entries:

I will be the first to admit, as a first year university student, I was a little skeptical of the arts in education and the importance it held. I harbour feelings of fun from my primary education experience, enjoying working with clay and a few rudimentary computer programs working with art. But can I remember it helping me develop as a student? Ticking important boxes of acquired learning and skills? No, I can't remember that, as being a student, all I wanted to do was have fun. So it has taken a university course to open my eyes regarding the arts. This course has been very enjoyable, practical and useful in me going on as a student. This course has taken an unusual route, that is, chucking us all in the deep end and asking us to 'start with the arts', to express ourselves when most haven't really done that through the medium of the arts in quite a few years. (Male student)

I am in no way a beautiful, vibrant butterfly yet - I haven't finished learning about the arts. I have, however, had the guidance to become one in time. I have developed my skills, my knowledge, and my enthusiasm for the arts. I will most likely keep maturing in my cocoon for some time, discovering

more and more about the arts each day, until I feel prepared to emerge as a butterfly and share my knowledge and skills with the young "caterpillars" in my class. (Female student)

By "starting with the arts" I am ensuring that students receive the opportunity that I did not. Developing a deep appreciation for the arts and continuing to accumulate skills and techniques along the way will strengthen my journey to becoming a teacher who views the arts as being equally as important as any other key learning area. (Male student)

Not all students experienced such significant changes of perception, and there were certainly a number of more neutrally worded entries. However the interesting point here (and of the previous case study) is the very salient presence of students' identities or views of self-as-teacher within their experiences of learning to teach; and the potential of disruptive pedagogies in the formation and re-negotiation of teaching identities. As Boler (1999) has argued, the path of learning is one fraught with difficult challenges that engage people's hearts and views of self, not simply their minds.

DISCUSSION

Facilitating Identity Formation within Teacher Education

Initially our pedagogies of discomfort took the form of course aims, learning activities and assessment tasks designed to challenge negative perceptions and beliefs. Fear in mathematics, lack of confidence in both mathematics and the arts. Both are significant as they entail unhelpful self-images that are in turn projected negatively onto important and exciting areas of learning. Innovative teaching requires the willingness to take risks and large doses of creativity. Both require confidence and high self-efficacy. Fear and trepidation can drive teachers to revert to the transmissive teaching practices they experienced as students themselves (as documented in the mathematics education case study) or to place a low priority on the subject area disregarding its educative potential altogether (as discussed in the arts education case study).

To counter this we designed and implemented highly experiential activities that enabled students to explicitly challenge these negative beliefs and to renegotiate unhelpful self-images. We were informed by the theoretical views outlined earlier. That is, on the one hand that individuals learn in social and cultural settings, through active processes of engagement. Thus our attention as teacher educators was to the potential of teaching, as Eraut (2010) has proposed, to engage students in the kinds of authentic and iterative practices that gradually enlighten understandings of key concepts and principles in expansive ways. We were also keen to consider the feeling and power dimensions of learning that Boler (1999) speaks of. And importantly, we employed a 'role identity' frame to illuminate the centrality of identity, self-concept and self-in-practice in learning that Wenger (1998) and others have outlined.

This initially intuitive approach was based on our now explicit emerging theory: that learning to teach entails a complex and multidimensional process of identity formation and negotiation. We are not simply elaborating students' knowledge of mathematics, of arts, of science, or of teaching and learning practice. Rather, we are engaging them in direct examination of who they are and will be as teachers, of how they see themselves as teachers. Our pedagogies of discomfort aimed to scaffold gradual reformulation (perhaps transformation) of these views in light of deeper pedagogical understandings. The significance of our approach is evident in the students' self-reports. Students of both mathematics education courses and arts education courses reported shifts in their beliefs about the nature of the curriculum area as well as changes in their views of themselves as teachers.

Given the central place of identity within students' experiences of learning to teach, our question then is to the value of 'disruption' as a concept for teacher learning.

Disruption within Teacher Learning and Teacher Education Pedagogies

Many students choose teaching for altruistic yet naïve reasons. Data collected within our program reinforces this trend. In a recent survey 51% of our first year students chose teaching because they want to 'make a difference' to children's lives and 42% because they love children. Moreover, questions in which students described themselves as teachers elicited greater detail and richer responses than questions related to reasons for choosing teaching. Students have particular views of themselves as teachers. While these views are based precariously on narrow life experiences (Lortie, 1975), they are a vital starting point. They will inevitably shift and elaborate as students: encounter cultural and social norms within teacher education and school settings; develop deeper understandings of curricular domains and pedagogical practices; and experiences of actual classroom practice. This demanding transition appears similar to (albeit more complex than) Sfard and Prusack's (2005) theorized gap between one's actual identity and designated identity, a gap that seems better navigated explicitly than implicitly. In which case, pedagogies of disruption as applied to teacher learning may find value with the inclusion of identity and transformation as related theoretical constructs. We humbly propose that teacher learning when considered through the lens of Boler's (1999) pedagogy of disruption includes a process of consistently gentle renegotiation of self-as-teacher and of identity. This is an area of promising future research.

On the other hand, we propose disruption to be a most suitable concept for discussing teacher education. The theoretical framing reviewed here argues strongly for a social view of learning, and enthusiastically for pedagogies that model innovative teaching through practices appropriate to adult learners. The implications for teaching are captured succinctly by Kalantzis and Cope (2004), who argue that there are two vital conditions for learning: i) engagement of a person's *identity* in ways that ii) *broaden* that person's *existing horizons of knowledge and capability*. Together with Boler's (1999) framing of learning as power and feeling, and Wenger's (1998) learning as identity renegotiation and transformation further insights into teacher learning can be made. If we accept the proposition that learning to teach entails a complex process of identity formation, then it follows that our students ought to be engaged in the kinds of experiences that consider, challenge and reformulate existing beliefs towards more expansive theories of self-as-teacher.

We feel that teacher education pedagogies are yet to fully implement these principles, despite the rhetoric of teaching philosophies and research agendas. Instead, pre-service teacher education students continue to be exposed to hours of transmissive teaching and numerous in-authentically framed assessment requirements. Disruption, we feel (at the present moment) would be usefully deployed towards teacher education pedagogies as well as to pre-service teacher learning.

REFERENCES

Akkerman, S. F., & Meijer, P. C. (2011). A dialogical approach to conceptualizing teacher identity. *Teaching and Teacher Education, 27*(2), 308–319. doi:10.1016/j.tate.2010.08.013

Ball, D. (1990). The mathematical knowledge that prospective teachers bring to teacher education. *The Elementary School Journal, 90*, 449–466. doi:10.1086/461626

Bandura, A. (2001). Social cognitive theory: An agentic perspective. *Annual Review of Psychology, 52*, 1–26. doi:10.1146/annurev.psych.52.1.1

Beauchamp, C., & Thomas, L. (2009). Understanding teacher identity: An overview of issues in the literature and implications for teacher education. *Cambridge Journal of Education, 39*(2), 175–189. doi:10.1080/03057640902902252

Boler, M. (1999). *Feeling power: Emotions and education*. New York, NY: Routledge.

Britzman, D. (2003). *Practice makes practice: A critical study of learning to teach*. Albany, NY: State University of New York Press.

Burke, P. J. (1980). The self: Measurement implications from a symbolic interactionist perspective. *Social Psychology Quarterly, 43*, 18–29. doi:10.2307/3033745

Collier, P. (2001). A differentiated model of role identity acquisition. *Symbolic Interaction, 24*(2), 217–235. doi:10.1525/si.2001.24.2.217

Connelly, F. M., & Clandinin, D. J. (1999). Borders of space and time. In Connelly, F. M., & Clandinin, D. J. (Eds.), *Shaping a professional identity: Stories of educational practice* (pp. 103–113). New York, NY: Teachers College Press.

Danielewicz, J. (2001). *Teaching selves: Identity, pedagogy, and teacher education*. Albany, NY: State University of New York Press.

Davies, D. (2008). Enhancing the role of the arts in primary pre-service teacher education. *Teaching and Teacher Education, 20*(3), 630–638.

Dole, S., & Beswick, K. (2002). Maths anxiety self-assessment as a quality assurance measure. In B. Barton, K. Irwin, M. Pfannkuch & M. Thomas (Eds.), *Proceedings of the Twenty-Fifth Annual Conference of the Mathematics Education Research Group of Australasia* (pp. 236-243). Aukland, New Zealand: MERGA.

Eraut, M. (2010). Knowledge, working practices, and learning. In Billet, S. (Ed.), *Learning through practice* (pp. 37–58). Dordrecht, The Netherlands: Springer. doi:10.1007/978-90-481-3939-2_3

Forbes, C., & Davis, E. (2008). The development of pre-service elementary teachers' curricular role identity for science teaching. *Science Education, 92*(5), 909–940. doi:10.1002/sce.20265

Foss, D. H., & Kleinsasser, R. C. (1996). Pre-service elementary teachers' views of pedagogical and mathematical content knowledge. *Teaching and Teacher Education, 12*(4), 429–442. doi:10.1016/0742-051X(95)00049-P

Freese, L., & Burke, P. J. (1994). Persons, identities, and social interaction. In Markovsky, B., Heimer, K., & O'Brien, J. (Eds.), *Advances in group processes* (pp. 1–24). Greenwich, CT: JAI.

Gee, J. P. (2001). Identity as an analytic lens for research in education. *Review of Research in Education, 25*, 99–125.

Geijsel, F., & Meijers, F. (2005). Identity learning: The core process of educational change. *Educational Studies, 31*(4), 419–430. doi:10.1080/03055690500237488

Greene, M. (2000). *Releasing the imagination: Essays on education, the arts and social change.* New York, NY: Jossey-Bass.

Hoggs, M., Terry, D., & White, K. (1995). A tale of two theories: A critical comparison of identity theory with social identity theory. *Social Psychology Quarterly, 58*, 255–269. doi:10.2307/2787127

Kagan, D. M. (1992). Implications of research on teacher beliefs. *The Psychologist, 27*(1), 65–90.

Kalantzis, M., & Cope, B. (2004). Designs for learning. *eLearning and Digital Media, 1*(1), 38-98. Retrieved from http://www.wwwords.co.uk/elea/content/pdfs/1/issue1_1.asp

Korthagen, F. (2004). In search of the essence of a good teacher: Towards a more holistic approach in teacher education. *Teaching and Teacher Education, 20*(1), 77–97. doi:10.1016/j.tate.2003.10.002

Korthagen, F., & Vasalos, A. (2005). Levels in reflection: Core reflection as a means to enhance professional development. *Teachers and Teaching: Theory and Practice, 11*(1), 47–71. doi:10.1080/1354060042000337093

Kumpulainen, K., & Renshaw, P. (2007). Cultures of learning. *International Journal of Educational Research, 46*(3-4), 109–115. doi:10.1016/j.ijer.2007.09.009

Lave, J., & Wenger, E. (1991). *Situated learning: Legitimate peripheral participation.* Cambridge, Uk: Cambridge University Press.

Lortie, D. (1975). *Schoolteacher: A sociological study.* London, UK: University of Chicago Press.

Mayer, D. (1999). *Building teaching identities: Implications for pre-service teacher education.* Paper presented at the Australian Association for Research in Education, December 1999, Melbourne, Australia. Retrieved from http://www.aare.edu.au/99pap/may99385.htm

Olsen, B. (2008). Introducing teacher identity and this volume. *Teacher Education Quarterly,* (Summer): 3–6.

Owens, T. (2006). Self and identity. In Delamanter, J. (Ed.), *Handbook of social psychology* (pp. 205–233). New York, NY: Springer. doi:10.1007/0-387-36921-X_9

Oyserman, D. (2001). Self-concept and identity. In Tesser, A., & Schwarz, N. (Eds.), *The Blackwell handbook of social psychology* (pp. 499–517). Malden, MA: Blackwell.

Ragins, B. (2009). Positive identities in action: A model of mentoring self structures and the motivation to mentor. In Roberts, L., & Dutton, J. (Eds.), *Exploring positive identities and organisations: Building a theoretical and research foundation.* New York, NY: Psychology Press.

Sachs, J. (2005). Teacher education and the development of professional identity: Learning to be a teacher. In Denicolo, P., & Kompf, M. (Eds.), *Connecting policy and practice: Challenges for teaching and learning in schools and universities* (pp. 5–21). Oxford, UK: Routledge.

Sfard, A., & Prusak, A. (2005). Telling identities: In search of an analytic tool for investigating learning as culturally shaped activity. *Educational Researcher*, *34*(4), 14–22. doi:10.3102/0013189X034004014

Sinclair, C., Jenneret, C., & O'Toole, J. (2009). *Education in the arts: Teaching and learning in the contemporary curriculum*. South Melbourne, Australia: Oxford University Press.

Stets, J., & Burke, P. (2003). A sociological approach to self and identity. In Leary, M. R., & Tangney, J. P. (Eds.), *Handbook of self and identity* (pp. 128–152). New York, NY: Guilford Press.

Stryker, P., & Burke, P. (2006). The past, present and future of an identity theory. *Social Psychology Quarterly*, *63*, 284–297. doi:10.2307/2695840

Walkington, J. (2005). Becoming a teacher: Encouraging development of teacher identity through reflective practice. *Asia-Pacific Journal of Teacher Education*, *33*(1), 53–64. doi:10.1080/1359866052000341124

Wenger, E. (1998). *Communities of practice: Learning, meaning, and identity*. Cambridge, UK: Cambridge University Press.

Werstch, J. (1991). *Voices of the mind: A sociocultural approach to mediated action*. Cambridge, MA: Harvard University Press.

Zevengergen, R. (2005). Primary preservice teachers' understanding of volume: The impact of course and practicum experiences. *Mathematics Education Research Journal*, *17*(1), 3–23. doi:10.1007/BF03217407

KEY TERMS AND DEFINITIONS

Beliefs: A complex and interrelated system of personal and professional knowledge that serve as implicit theories that in turn inform and guide interpretation, experience and action.

Connected Mathematics: Mathematical understanding of the big ideas of mathematics as a rich conceptual schema; beyond isolated mathematical facts and rules.

Curriculum: The formal and informal areas of knowledge presented and encountered whilst learning.

Gentle Disruptive Pedagogy: The provision of learning activities that entice attention to ineffective knowledge and beliefs, participation without fear of inadequacy, and the renegotiation of knowledge and beliefs in ways that simultaneously model good pedagogy for teacher professional learning.

Identity: A complex and overlapping suite of personal and professional characteristics, beliefs, experiences, abilities and values that comprise one's theory of self.

Knowledge for Teaching: The specialist knowledge of teachers that differentiates good teachers from the ordinary citizen on the street.

Mathematics Anxiety: The irrational and mental paralysis that occurs when one is required to undertake any tasks involving mathematics.

Chapter 13

The Emotional Labor of Imagining Otherwise:
Undoing the Mastery Model of Mathematics Teacher Identity

Elizabeth de Freitas
Adelphi University, USA

ABSTRACT

The concept of emotional resistance is often used to describe student reluctance to grapple with difficult facts regarding inequity and injustice, especially if the students themselves are implicated in these facts by way of their privilege or advantage. Many successful students are reluctant to acknowledge how they are tacitly invested in a governing hegemonic system that has afforded them particular socio-cultural and economic status. Dorsey (2002), for instance, follows her largely white students' resistance to anti-racist pedagogy through a series of stages - discovery, dismay, denial, and dismissal - all of which indicate their reluctance to realize how their own positioning is enabled through hegemonic systems of oppression. Similarly, Boler and Zembylas (2003) note that students often refuse to recognize "race/ethnicity" differences as significant contributing factors of social capital, arguing for a benign tolerance of difference or denying difference as a significant factor.

INTRODUCTION

Students who invest in this resistance often do so with a great deal of emotional attachment to neo-liberal beliefs about merit-based success and status. In the context of school mathematics, where persistent misconceptions about intrinsic ability and merit-based mastery continue to dominate, the need to trouble these beliefs is all the more pronounced. Mathematics teachers function as pivotal agents in re-inscribing these beliefs through classroom discourse and through the enactment of particular professional identities.

DOI: 10.4018/978-1-61350-495-6.ch013

In this paper, I argue that identity work with pre-service mathematics teachers remains a crucial method for disrupting these patterns, and I offer evidence from a critical literacy course for pre-service mathematics teachers to show how this identity work unfolds.

MATHEMATICS TEACHER IDENTITY AND LANGUAGE

Rodriguez and Kitchen (2005) suggest that reluctance to see success in school mathematics through a sociocultural lens may be related to a sense of entitlement – granted and validated through previous school success – and may be the source of pre-service teachers' resistance to using mathematics as a social justice advocacy tool. This sense of entitlement, according to Rodriguez and Kitchen, is "a potential reason why they may resist efforts to prepare them to teach for diversity" (p. 35). I want to suggest that what is at stake in this apparent entitlement is a deep-seated fear of ambiguity and a deep-seated belief in and desire for the transparency of language. Indeed, I argue that many mathematics students – and here I am speaking of those who have already declared their intention to become mathematics teachers - are drawn to mathematics precisely because of their uncomfortable relationship with ambiguity in language. I am using the term "language" to refer to both the everyday language that students and teachers use to speak their identity, and through which their identity is spoken, and the esoteric discourse of school mathematics – a discourse which is highly symbolic, impersonal, acontextual, instrumental, and atemporal.

The everyday and the esoteric intersect in school mathematics discourse, since everyday language is used to frame mathematical activity. Moreover, the two are overlaid in word problems which enlist everyday language to describe application contexts, and one can find small words in even the most abstract mathematical statements

- such as "and", "of", "but", "at", "or" – which take on highly precise logical meaning once embedded in the esoteric discourse. It is important to note that the esoteric discourse, despite its rhetorical style of impersonal abstraction, also *speaks* an identity that is constituted in the bodies that deploy this discourse. Elsewhere, I have named this an "identity of mastery" (de Freitas, 2008a, 2009), and have argued that classrooms dominated by procedural facility tasks – in which teachers model algorithms and students mimic them – contribute to the entrenchment of this kind of teacher identity.

My pre-service mathematics teachers often think of language in purely functional terms, as though it were exhaustively determined by way of its function or purpose in conveying an unfettered intended meaning. In the survey that I distribute on the first day of the course, I ask them about their reading and writing habits, and their reasons for studying mathematics. The vast majority state unapologetically that they hate reading and writing and that they have chosen mathematics partially to avoid writing papers. They are disinclined to enjoy what Roland Barthes called the "decentration" of language, which marks, in his terms, the supplementarity or impertinent overflow of language in the face of our attempts to pin it to reality. More than other pre-service teachers in other disciplines, many in mathematics are frustrated by readings that use unfamiliar vocabulary and demand a nuanced or contradictory truth (Wallowitz, 2009).

A sentence, however, is "never saturable" with meaning, but rather "catalyzable, to use the accepted term, by successive fillings according to a theoretically infinite process: the center is infinitely displaceable" (Barthes, 1985, p. 103). According to Barthes, there is always play in the language apparatus – always some wiggle room in the tiny crevices and joints, where one witnesses the slippage of meaning. And thankfully it is this irresolvable asignifiying play in language that brooks all our attempts to use it as an entirely deterministic instrument of control.

For many of my mathematics students, however, it is precisely this ambiguity or supplementarity that undermines their functional use of language. They want to use language as a tool to relate to the world through certainty and completion. They hate the fact that language cannot complete them; they are threatened by the refusal of language to be accurate and functional. For if language is not merely a tool serving to accurately mark their subjectivity, then it becomes something dangerously *other*. There is something dirty about this dilution of functionality, something too close to bliss or joy about the play of language; this play of infinite variation, of difference without end, deeply disturbs them:

Language is a blissful enjoyment of fabrication and function. It is related to a psychoanalysis of pleasure, and at the same time a dynamics of function among its elements, which is both restrictive and supple. Language could also be called a stereophony (Barthes, 1985, p. 104).

EMOTIONAL ATTACHMENTS

Asking pre-service teachers to critique their mastery of the subject in terms of their own power and privilege can trigger anger and fear. Naming one's own privilege is always a difficult and self-disturbing affair. Such critique troubles the comforting notion that one's achievements are due entirely to one's own efforts. Developing a critical capacity to assess one's attachment to an identity is both a cognitive and emotional labor that disturbs the very ground one stands on. Pre-service teacher resistance to politicizing mathematics education entails a highly emotional defense of the mastery identity: "The emotional investment in a mastery identity may itself be a hindrance in learning to teach for diversity." (de Freitas, 2008, p. 44).

In this chapter, I argue that we need to focus more closely on the way pre-service mathematics teachers conceive of language – the way they

position themselves in relation to everyday language and the way they construe mathematics as outside of language – if we are to truly trouble the mastery identity that dominates and confines the capacity to imagine otherwise in the mathematics classroom. My hope is that such an approach might offer pre-service teachers a way to become more responsive to their students' diverse identities, and perhaps more importantly, to become more aware of how identity is leveraged in classrooms.

In mathematics classrooms where students are "wrong" more often than not, "ambiguity is feared; it is a source of discomfort to those forced to live in a culture defined by simple binary oppositions" (Boler & Zembylas, 2003, p. 122). And yet ambiguity is always a part of language, and always an incredibly creative site where variation, disruption and multiplicity flourish. Only when we recognize, and indeed embrace, the ambiguity in language do we begin to trace the rhetorical structure of meaning, and begin to imagine otherwise. Ambiguity points to the ungroundedness of meaning – it marks the play of signs, marks the disruptive wiggle within signification, marks the lack of transparency of all language. As such, ambiguity troubles the power of language to accurately describe reality. If language fails to map one-to-one onto the world, it becomes a material object like any other, and not a reliable system of signification. This dethroning of language as a coherent and closed sign system through which one accesses reality is highly disturbing to those who trusted its capacity to represent their authentic identity. The inherent ambiguity of language thus threatens our attachment to the notion of a coherent identity grounded in free will and self determination. In admitting the ambiguity of language, one must admit the inherent ambiguity in identity, and doing so demands that we sustain a high level of discomfort.

Focus on the emotional resistance to that discomfort allows us to first trouble the assumption that the individual is the site and source of emotion. Countering the liberal individualism that is so often the source of 'inscribed habits of inattention' (Boler 1997), Boler and Zembylas argue that emotions be seen as a 'collective and collaborative terrain' (Boler 1999, p. 6) or part of a system of 'emotional capital' (Zembylas 2007, p. 450). Once we see that emotions are socially organized and governed, we begin to trouble the common-sense assumption that they reflect our true coherent selves; we begin to see how our resistance is an emotional investment in collective norms (de Freitas & McAuley, 2008, p. 430).

The emotional labor entailed in interrogating one's emotional attachment to a particular identity is difficult work and requires time for practical and reflective action (Boler & Zembylas, 2003). Along with the difficult act of naming such attachment comes the need for linguistic and theoretical tools for disrupting the particularities of the identity as a social construct. The collective nature of pre-service teacher emotional attachment to the mastery identity must be made public so as to become contestable, for it is only through the active troubling of rigid confining social constructs that "difference is introduced into history" (p. 132). Of course, it is essential that a pedagogy of discomfort generate more than simple vulnerability (in recognizing the ambiguity inherent in identity), and proceed to mobilize "assemblages of vulnerability and hope, labor and passion, anger and self-discovery" (p. 132).

In triggering pre-service teacher commitment to action, a pedagogy of discomfort recognizes and problematizes "unconscious complicity with hegemony" (ibid., p. 111) while opening up spaces and freeing resources (in this chapter, those resources are discourse analytic tools), so that difference might be seen as a source of creativity, and ambiguity not feared. Such an approach "forces us to produce new narratives that erode the biases we so often ascribe to others, and to ourselves not least" (ibid., p. 129). If emotional investments and refusals are a means of defending particular ideological positions, my hope is that pre-service teachers will learn to interrogate

their emotional investment in a mastery identity by unpacking their beliefs about the transparency of language. The link between the emotional investment in mastery and the desire for linguistic transparency springs from the unique semiotic and social facets of mathematics discourse. In the context of mathematics education, the need to decouple attachments to liberal individualism (attachments to humanist notions of the subject, agency and language), and to own some part of one's capitulation and submission to a hegemonic discourse, is daunting and yet extremely important, given that the discipline functions severely as a "critical filter" in schools.

CRITICAL LITERACY IN MATHEMATICS

The course on critical literacy in mathematics education aims to introduce pre-service teachers to a variety of strategies for disrupting dominant discursive patterns of neo-liberalism. The course begins with discussions about the difference between critical literacy and functional literacy. Functional literacy is defined in terms of basic reading skills necessary for decoding texts according to the implicit rules of legitimate meaning making in the given community (Stevens & Bean, 2007). Any text produced within and for an institution must by necessity serve particular goals – both explicit and implicit - and one can "read off" many of these goals from the text once one has internalized the rules of meaning making. Reading functionally always involves a capitulation to the text, as though the text commanded the reader to submit to its rule. Functional literacy thus represents an extremely valuable way of reproducing cultural capital and contributing to the continuance of normalizing practices. In an esoteric discourse like mathematics, functional literacy is extremely challenging since the rules for meaningfully combining signs and generating legitimate text are highly coded. Written mathematics texts are composed of multiple semiotic systems, such as symbolic and numeric notation, written language, graphs and visual displays (Schleppegrell, 2007). Written mathematical English is marked with distinct grammatical patterns, such as dense noun phrases, technical jargon, few material or physical verbs, and the predominance of the verbs "to have" and "to be" to mark attributive clauses (irreversible) and identifying clauses (reversible) (Morgan, 2006). For instance, "A prime number is an integer that has no integral factors but itself and one" can be reversed around the "is" ("An integer that has no integral factors but itself and one is a prime number), but cannot be reversed around "has". Students regularly verbalize mathematics with material and physical verbs, but written mathematics erases this materiality and situatedness. Consider how students will typically verbalize in terms of actions, "Take a number, multiply it by 2 and add 2, then cube it, then subtract two times the number cubed to get 8", but the "proper" tense-free written form is "The difference of the cubes of two consecutive even numbers is 8". The latter is a dense noun phrase that has eliminated all the action. The process of becoming a successful mathematics student involves simultaneously mastering and submitting to these grammatical patterns. Since the verbs "to be" and "to have" function centrally but differently in different languages, English language learners in English classrooms face particular challenges (Adler, 2001; Moschkovich, 2007)

In contrast to functional literacy, critical literacy is defined as a disposition and set of strategies for decoding and interrogating texts whereby one interprets texts through a political lens, and broadens the notion of "reading" to include situated forms of meaning-making in relation to local and global power relations. Critical literacy is all about interrogating the text, authors, and the reader assumptions, and searching a text for the silences embedded within it. Although it is usually easier for students to imagine performing this sort of reading with the media, internet, music or even history and English textbooks, it is more challenging for students to imagine that *mathematics* texts might be interrogated in this way. Bringing critical literacy to mathematics means asking students to think critically about truth claims of all kinds. My students are quick to embrace a "multiple perspectives" position about texts that involve everyday language, comfortably acknowledging that linguistic meaning is "in the eye of the beholder". This concept of multiple perspectives, however, is in large part neo-liberal in that it continues to validate the individual over the collective; the vast majority of students fail to pursue the social ramifications of a theory of language that posits language as constitutive of collective meaning. The watered down relativism that often emerges at the outset of discussions around critical literacy is often an easy way to avoid the discomfort associated with difference. This stumbling block in the development of the course objectives has erupted each of the eleven times I have taught the course. The readings that help overcome this obstacle are frequently the ones from within the students' discipline, in particular the work of Rico Gutstein on critical mathematics education:

Critical literacy means to approach knowledge critically and skeptically, see relationships between ideas, look for underlying explanations for phenomena, and question whose interests are served and who benefits. Being critically literate also means to examine one's own and others' lives in relationship to sociopolitical and cultural-historical contexts (Gutstein, 2006, p. 5).

Rethinking mathematics: Teaching Social Justice by the Numbers (Gutstein & Peterson, 2005) and *Reading and Writing the World with Mathematics* (Gutstein, 2006) offer the students' concrete examples of how they might use mathematics to interrogate common injustices (for instance, quantifying the number and distribution of liquor stores in different SES neighborhoods or looking for statistical evidence of racial profiling in police highway patrol).

Online discussions about these readings are student led and student monitored. I bring highlights and issues from the discussion into the face-to-face class meetings, but I don't write anything in the online forum. The forum is a live-site, where students are expected to post reflections grounded in the readings, and to query others' posts with "difficult probing questions". Discussion often returns to the role of word problems or applications in mathematics, and how these kinds of problems assume a particular "normal" for students, ignoring the rampant differences in the lived experiences of all students. I find in these postings a complex matrix of beliefs regarding language and mathematics. For instance, after reading an article about a classroom where a teacher responds to a student query about the meaning of the expression "still water" in a word problem about rowing with "I'm not talking about reality" (Gellert & Jablonka, 2009), one of my pre-service teachers wrote "I kind of don't blame the teacher either because it is hard to explain. If the people who create word problems can stay away from this type of word choice then they should. It will be easier for both the students and the teachers." Later on, the same student again expresses her belief in language as a tool for accurately *representing* reality, as though language could function entirely "realistically" as a transparent index: "Teachers should try to find word problems that relate to outside of school, but in a realistic way." Another student echoes these sentiments: "This just further reiterates the fact that we need to make word problems clear, and be able to relate to all students in our classrooms." And another "Word problems connect the math taught to real life situations. But are the situations in the words problems really real? I believe that the situations in the word problems might be real for some people." These comments indicate both a form of relativism and an incredible faith that language – if properly cleaned up - can ultimately reach the "really real" and represent it unproblematically.

As we continue to explore critical literacy in the course, and unpack the ways that texts address readers in particular ways, many of my students grapple with the difference between "neutral" mathematical problems and "controversial" applications. Although we discuss the need to critique the concept of "neutrality", they continue to find themselves trapped in a tacit binary between pure language-less mathematics and the messy world of everyday language. One of my PowerPoint slideshows includes the very direct pronouncements:

- Appearing "neutral" can in fact create more injustice than showing one's affiliations and beliefs. If you say to your students that you are neutral about the rights of gay students to attend prom with their dates, then you are ACTUALLY supporting the status quo.
- Claiming "neutrality" often coincides with a dangerous silence on important issues.
- Are "numbers" neutral? Do we ever encounter numbers in some "pure innocent" way, or are they always embedded in human ways of making sense of them, and thus always enmeshed in politics?

The third bullet point above gives them the most trouble. When considering, for instance, the social justice activities found in *Rethinking Mathematics: Teaching Social Justice by the Numbers* (Gutstein & Peterson, 2005), three students discuss how to balance "neutral" problems with "controversial" problems, and reveal both their anxiety about a world filled with ambiguity and controversy, and their beliefs and desires for a pure language of description, exemplified in their desire for "real real-life problems". Note that S2 (who displayed almost no resistance to naming school mathematics as a critical filter contributing to social and economic injustice) believes that we can improve our word problems and make them "more inclusive", while also wanting to explore some math "without bringing in societal issues". Based on their other online contributions, one can see that both S1 and S3 are asking leading questions, trying to ensure that there remains some innocent space where pure mathematics might dwell. S3 (who displayed a great deal of resistance to social justice math) here reveals her anxiety that excessive attempts to attend to controversy and inequity through mathematics will swallow up its pure neutrality:

S1: *I agree with you on how "neutral" problems can exclude some students. Do you think we should eliminate "neutral" problems altogether or do you think there is a way to make real-world problems without excluding others?*

S2: *In response to your question, I don't think that "neutral" problems need to be eliminated altogether, I just think they need to be alternated so that they are more inclusive and represent different lifestyles ...I really think that the real real-life problems described in the articles are a great way to get students involved in and thinking about the community around them, but I don't think that necessarily means getting rid of "neutral" problems altogether, just as long as they are revised to be more inclusive.*

S3: *Since society is changing everyday, it becomes harder to find math word problems that are not controversial. However, do you think it is more important to discuss those controversial issues or to make sure the students understand the mathematical concepts behind the word problems?*

S2: *I definitely believe in the importance of both discussing controversial issues and understanding mathematical concepts. Discussing controversial issues allows for students to become aware of injustices in society, think critically, form their own opinions, and even correct these injustices. Not only that, but it shows students that math does in fact serve*

a purpose outside of the mathematical or classroom context and can make math more interesting for them. Though, at the same time, as someone who loves math, I would definitely like for my students to understand mathematical concepts and believe that math is important even without bringing in societal issues. However, if students do not see math in this same light, using math in the context of controversial issues can help students see the importance of understanding mathematical contexts in order to examine injustices.

One can see in this exchange how the students are beginning to embrace a critical literacy perspective, but are constrained by the collective assumption that mathematics (as a language or semiotic system) is somehow context free and ahistorical. And yet research on "real world" word problems has shown that student inclination to decode a problem in terms of the rules of school mathematics and not in terms of their reality impacts hugely on their performance in standardized testing (Cooper, 1998a, 1998b, 2001). Studies of working class students in the UK indicated that they were more inclined to interpret word problems "realistically" and to thereby miss the coded mathematical meanings embedded in the text (Cooper & Dunne, 2004).

Working class children were more likely to attempt to solve the tasks by using their everyday knowledge while service class children demonstrated an understanding of word problems as, in fact, being artificial although apparently 'real' (Gellert & Jablonka, 2009, p. 41)

Thus there are no neutral word problems. Most of my pre-service mathematics teachers, however, consistently blame the specific wording instead of recognizing the inherent ambiguity in language. Some do realize that the ambiguity in a word problem can be leveraged to serve particular people, but most resist the notion that ambiguity is inherent in language. In discussing another article about a classroom where African American students differently interpreted a word problem about bus costs and work schedules, and then failed to answer questions correctly on a test (Tate, 2005), one of my pre-service teachers wrote: "I think the bus question they talked about was way too open ended because everyone doesn't work five days a week. What if you work six or seven days a week? Or the bus is your only way of transportation and you use it for things other than work." The article by William Tate argues that school mathematics is a white discipline that fails to address African American students' experiences. The pre-service teacher quoted above – like almost all of my white male students – was highly resistant to the argument in this article, preferring to blame the "way too open" wording, and arguing that "these problems are consistent with almost all lower class students no matter the racial background." His attempt to erase the racism in the texts, and embrace a color-blind philosophy, is highly correlative with his belief in language as something that can be cleaned of ambiguity. Moreover, this kind of resistance to openness and ambiguity is precisely what leads pre-service teachers to resist the reform movement towards more inquiry pedagogy, and entrenches their commitment to a mastery identity and "one-correct-answer" style of teaching.

PEDAGOGICAL POSSIBILITIES FOR DISRUPTION

In this last section I want to briefly discuss two of the course assignments that have been very successful in helping pre-service teachers begin to think differently about language in mathematics classrooms. My hope is that through these assignments, students begin to recognize, interrogate and transform the "linguistic habitus" (Bourdieu, 1999, p. 506) that characterizes membership in school mathematics. Each assignment tackles

the issue of how mathematical ability or competence is "inseparable from the practical mastery of a usage of language and the practical mastery of situations in which this usage of language is socially acceptable" (p. 502).

1. Analyzing Textbooks for Tacit Forms of Address

Through the use of image and text, each textbook addresses and positions readers in particular socio-economic and cultural locations. For instance, textbook problems frequently ask the reader to maximize profit, thereby addressing the reader as a capitalist whose interest is economic gain. Fairclough (2003) claims that our school texts are saturated with "new liberalism" which he defines as "a political project for facilitating the re-structuring and re-scaling of social relations in accordance with the demands of an unrestrained global capitalism." (p.4). Pre-service teachers in the critical literacy course are asked to examine their math textbooks for evidence that this is true: does the text address readers as capitalists first, before it addresses them as citizens? Fairclough argues that a process of internalization – what is often called "inculcation" - occurs when we are addressed by texts in ways that position us within society. We are "inculcated" into particular cultural identities when we are addressed through particular forms of language. On the other hand, if we do not recognize ourselves in the form of address, we may "resist" the meaning of the text, and refuse to engage it. Pre-service teachers are asked to study textbooks to see which subject positions are built into the form of address: urban, consumer, capitalist, community worker, environmentalist, politically engaged, male/female, wealthy, young, US citizen, able bodies, white. Students are asked to look for evidence of what sorts of "identities" are validated through the language and imagery of the text.

Each mathematics text uses grammatical forms to address the reader in terms of varying degrees of agency. "Agency" refers to the "agent of action" who can be named, implied or mystified in statements that describe action. For instance, O'halloran (2005) studies television news stories where agency is mystified or weakly implied, as in "Eleven foreigners were shot dead when police opened fire on a rioting crowd ..." in which the grammatical form is passive and structured to minimize the responsibility of the police. In the case of mathematics texts, one can identify an array of grammatical forms that imply different kinds of agency. Consider this list of examples:

- No agency (statements without a subject for the action: "What is the probability that a rolled die will come up a 1?").
- Passive agency (statements that prioritize an action, but fail to specify a subject: "When a die is rolled, what is the power that a 1 will come up?")
- Regulated agency (Statements that recognize the reader as the subject of the action ("When you roll a die, what is the probability that it will come up a 1?".
- Shared agency (Statements that abstract the subject to the collective, "When someone rolls a die, what is the probability that it will come up a 1?"
- Authoring agency (statements that recognize the reader as uniquely inventive "How would you use probability to decide whether a 1 is likely to occur when you roll a die?")

Students are asked to examine the problems in the textbooks for grammatical evidence of these different forms of agency. Doing so begins to open the text up for a more careful critical reading. Students begin to see that there are particular linguistic patterns and ways of addressing the reader that might be made different.

2. Classroom Discourse Analysis

Veel (1999) points to the correlation between discursive patterns unique to mathematics classrooms and the larger institutional agenda of inculcation and cultural reproduction, noting that: "There is a kind of synchronicity – a conspiracy if you like – between classification, instructional discourse, regulative discourse and language that is noticeably stronger than in other subject areas." (p. 206).

In this assignment, students are asked to observe a classroom on three different occasions, and to look for discursive patterns using a code developed in advance. They are asked to record the gender, physical location, ethnicity, etc of the speaker and note who speaks, when they speak, and what they say. Some pre-service teachers record the ratio of teacher talk to student talk, the type of questions (content or process, on task or off task, conceptual or procedural, yes/no versus why/when/what if), the frequency with which the teacher corrects students or praises students (and the different ways she/he does so), the frequency of teacher talk that frames the difficulty of the tasks (such as "This one is an easy one", etc) or how often they refer to tests, and in what manner. This is basically a "counting" activity by which the students collect data on classroom discursive patterns. After they collect the data, they use graphing software to represent their findings, and they reflect on these graphical representations and on the contingencies of the context that might have contributed to the patterns in the data.

Pre-service teachers are regularly surprised by the patterns that they uncover. The exercise of looking closely at repetition of word-use helps them begin to think differently about how they might choose different words. For instance, they are overwhelmed by the dominance of regulative discourse in the classrooms, and shocked by how often teachers frame the mathematical activity with statements about final exams or state tests or difficulty. The assignment also helps them look more closely at gender and ethnicity patterns, recording not simply the speaker's identity, but simultaneously the nature of the speech act (self-initiated or called on, procedural or conceptual, "I" statement or "we" statement, etc). One pre-service teacher chose to record the frequency of "waste words", which she defined as those words that weren't needed, such as "like, um, you know". This focus allowed her to study the way these words function – often called "hedges" – as important parts of classroom discourse, whereby students and teacher locate themselves in terms of their commitment to the epistemic authority of what they are saying.

One student reflected: "This assignment made me really focus on the dynamics of dialogue in the classroom. It made me realize the importance of engaging every student as much as possible. As a teacher we already know the subject inside and out, but that is only a part of the job. The real purpose of a teacher is to captivate students in mathematical discussions and have them make the knowledge we present them, their own."

CONCLUSION: TEACHER POWER

Webb (2009) studies the way that teachers interact with power as a way to negotiate the political nature and "micropolitics" of their work. "One way to control teachers is to keep them ignorant about their power." (Webb, 2009, p. 1). He argues that teacher power cuts two ways, since it might be used to sustain and defend the status quo or it might be used to resist oppression and demand change. In either case, power must be traced by studying the daily and yearly social practices of interaction whereby people are produced and inscribed with identity.

Power is not simply a matter of coercion and repression whereby one group dominates another. Power resides in the ordinary everyday practices that constitute our lives, and as such we are complicit in its operation. At this molecular level of interaction, the "power economy" maps itself onto our bodies and serves the interests of the elite. But this is not the only way that power works. Power also needs to be thought through in terms of investments in desire, investments that sometimes go against the grain of one's interests. Power is thus both consolidated and dispersed, and sometimes there is a tension between these (dis)locations of power in that a subject position might be the site of a consolidated power (white male math teacher) while also being the site of innumerable other provisional investments, some of which might run counter to the power claims of the more consolidated identity. This poststructuralist approach honors the multiplicity of power, and traces the power differential across these multiplicities. Power is a "highly variegated substance" (Buchanan, 2008, p. 24). Tactics from critical literacy help all of us learn how to refuse to be hailed, recognized and constituted by the dominant culture's forms of address, and offer directions for interrupting and altering the dominant cultural message. These tactics undo the claim to universal unity on behalf of the dominant culture, and expose the mechanisms of cultural production whereby concepts like mathematical competency are generated. In some sense, these tactics demand that we map the power differentials across our identities, and trace the way power insinuates itself into our use of language.

In this chapter I have explored pre-service teachers' beliefs about language and mathematics, beliefs that are inextricably tied to their emotional investment in a particular concept of mathematical competency and identity. My hope is that some of the work they are doing in critical literacy is troubling these beliefs, and causing them to become uncomfortable with the ways that their beliefs serve particular neo-liberal agendas of individualism. The assignments offer the pre-service teachers a few tools for owning and leveraging their power in the classroom, and a means for beginning to imagine an otherwise education.

REFERENCES

Adler, J. (2001). *Teaching mathematics in multilingual classrooms*. Dordrecht, The Netherlands: Kluwer.

Barthes, R. (1985). *The grain of the voice: Interviews 1962-1980*. (L. Coverdale, Trans.). New York, NY: Hill and Wang (Division of Farrar, Strauss and Giroux).

Boler, M. (1997). Taming the labile other. In S. Laird (Ed.), *Philosophy of education society 1997* (pp. 258–270). Champaign, IL: Philosophy of Education Society.

Boler, M. (1999). *Feeling power: Emotions and education*. New York, NY: Routledge.

Boler, M., & Zembylas, M. (2003). Discomforting truths: The emotional terrain of understanding difference. In Trifonas, P. (Ed.), *Pedagogies of difference: Rethinking education for social change* (pp. 110–136). New York, NY: Routledge/Falmer.

Bourdieu, P. (1999). Language and symbolic power. In Jaworski, A., & Coupland, N. (Eds.), *The discourse reader* (pp. 502–513). New York, NY: Routledge.

Buchanan, I. (2008). *Deleuze and Guattari's anti-Oedipus*. London, UK: Continuum International Publishing Group.

Cooper, B. (1998a). Assessing national curriculum mathematics in England: Exploring children's interpretation of key stage 2 tests in clinical interviews. *Educational Studies in Mathematics, 35*(1), 19–49. doi:10.1023/A:1002945216595

Cooper, B. (1998b). Using Bernstein and Bourdieu to understand children's difficulties with 'realistic' mathematics testing: An exploratory study. *International Journal of Qualitative Studies in Education, 11*(4), 511–532. doi:10.1080/095183998236421

Cooper, B. (2001). Social class and 'real life' mathematics assessments. In Gates, P. (Ed.), *Issues in mathematics teaching* (pp. 245–258). New York, NY: Routledge/Falmer.

Cooper, B., & Dunne, M. (2004). Constructing the 'legitimate' goal of a 'realistic' maths item: A comparison of 10-11 and 13-14 year olds. In B. Allen & S. Johnston-Wilder (Eds.), *Mathematics education: Exploring the culture of learning* (pp. 69-90). New York, NY: Routledge/Falmer.

de Freitas, E. (2008a). Troubling teacher identity: Preparing mathematics teachers to teach for diversity. *Teaching Education, 19*(1), 43–55. doi:10.1080/10476210701860024

de Freitas, E. (2008b,). Critical mathematics education: Recognizing the ethical dimension of problem solving. *International Electronic Journal of Mathematics Education, 3*(2), 79–95. Retrieved from www.iejme.com

de Freitas, E. (2009). Analyzing procedural and narrative discourse in the mathematics classroom: The splitting of teacher identity. In Brown, T. (Ed.), *The psychology of mathematics education: A psychoanalytic displacement*. Rotterdam, The Netherlands: Sense Publisher.

de Freitas, E., & McAuley, A. (2008). Teaching for diversity by troubling whiteness: Strategies for isolated white communities. *Race, Ethnicity and Education, 11*(4), 429–442. doi:10.1080/13613320802479018

Dorsey, A. (2002). 'White girls' and 'strong black women': Reflections on a decade of teaching black history at predominantly white institutions. In Macdonald, A. A., & Sanchez-Casal, S. (Eds.), *Feminist classrooms: Pedagogies of identity and difference* (pp. 203–232). New York, NY: Palgrave Macmillan.

Fairclough, N. (1992). *Discourse and social change*. Cambridge, UK: Polity Press.

Fairclough, N. (2003). *Analyzing discourse: Textual analysis for social research*. New York, NY: Routledge.

Gellert, U., & Jablonka, E. (2009). "I am not talking about reality": Word problems and the intricacies of producing legitimate text. In Verschaffel, L., Greer, B., Van Dooren, W., & Mukhopadhyay, S. (Eds.), *Words and worlds: Modeling verbal descriptions of situations*. Rotterdam, The Netherlands: Sense Publishers.

Gutstein, E. (2006). *Reading and writing the world with mathematics: Toward a pedagogy for social justice*. New York, NY: Routledge.

Gutstein, E. (2008). Building political relationships with students: An aspect of social justice pedagogy. In de Freitas, E., & Nolan, K. (Eds.), *Opening the research text: Insights and in(ter)ventions into mathematics education*. New York, NY: Springer Verlag. doi:10.1007/978-0-387-75464-2_8

Gutstein, E., & Peterson, B. (2005). *Rethinking mathematics: Teaching social justice by the numbers*. Milwaukee, WI: Rethinking Schools.

Morgan, C. (2006). What does social semiotics have to offer mathematics education research? *Educational Studies in Mathematics, 61*(1-2), 219–245. doi:10.1007/s10649-006-5477-x

Moschkovich, J. (2007). Using two languages when learning mathematics. *Educational Studies in Mathematics, 64*(2), 121–144. doi:10.1007/s10649-005-9005-1

O'Halloran, K. L. (1999). Towards a systemic functional analysis of multisemiotic mathematics texts. *Semiotica, 124*(1/2), 1–29. doi:10.1515/semi.1999.124.1-2.1

O'Halloran, K. L. (2003). Educational implications of mathematics as a multisemiotic discourse. In Anderson, M., Saenz-ludlow, A., Zellweger, S., & Cifarelli, V. (Eds.), *Educational perspectives on mathematics as semiosis: From thinking to interpreting to knowing* (pp. 185–214). Ottawa, Canada: Legas Publishing.

O'Halloran, K. L. (2005). *Mathematical discourse: Language, symbolism and visual images*. London, UK: Continuum.

Rodriguez, A. J., & Kitchen, R. S. (Eds.). (2005). *Preparing mathematics and science teachers for diverse classrooms: Promising strategies for transformative pedagogy*. Mahwah, NJ: Lawrence Erlbaum Associates, Publishers.

Schleppegrell, M. (2007). The linguistic challenges of mathematical teaching and learning: A research review. *Reading & Writing Quarterly, 23*(2), 139–159. doi:10.1080/10573560601158461

Stevens, L. P., & Bean, L. P. (2007). *Critical literacy: Context, research and practice in the K-12 classroom*. New York, NY: Sage Publications.

Tate, W. F. (2005). Race, retrenchment, and the reform of school mathematics. In Gutstein, E., & Peterson, B. (Eds.), *Rethinking mathematics: Teaching social justice by the numbers* (pp. 31–40). Milwaukee, WI: Rethinking Schools.

Veel, R. (1999). Language, knowledge, and authority in school mathematics. In Christie, F. (Ed.), *Pedagogy and the shaping of consciousness* (pp. 185–216). London, UK: Cassell.

Wallowitz, L. (2009). *Critical literacy as resistance: Teaching for social justice across the secondary curriculum*. Peter Lang Publishers.

Webb, T. (2009). *Teacher assemblage*. Rotterdam, The Netherlands: Sense Publisher.

Zembylas, M. (2007). Emotional capital and education: Theoretical insights from Bourdieu. *British Journal of Educational Studies, 55*(4), 443–463. doi:10.1111/j.1467-8527.2007.00390.x

Chapter 14

"Are you Married?":
Exploring the Boundaries of Sexual Taboos in the ESL Classroom

Greg Curran
Victoria University, Australia

ABSTRACT

Within the adult English as a Second Language (ESL) classroom, heterosexuality is presumed perhaps more so than in other formal education settings. Curricula and everyday classroom exchanges reinforce its normative status with teachers wary of offending 'cultural sensibilities' and putting themselves in the spotlight. In this chapter however, the author argues that taboo topics can attract student interest. Further, the positioning of ESL students as able to discuss and work through 'sensitive' issues, within a classroom community that values positive, respectful interactions, may lead to more productive engagement around sexual diversity issues.

INTRODUCTION

Student:	*Are you married?*
Greg:	*No I'm not, but I do have a partner.*
Student:	*What's her name?*
Greg:	[thinking]...

DOI: 10.4018/978-1-61350-495-6.ch014

Are you married? Although this question is often asked, the package of acceptable, intelligible answers within the adult English as a Second Language (ESL) classroom is limited. With heterosexuality presumed, the notion that there might be gay, lesbian, or bisexual students and teachers is, most of the time, unthinkable. Moreover, monosexuality rather than multisexuality is the expectation, and it is rarely challenged (Nelson, 2006, 2009). Queer teachers and students regularly side-step questions or topics that might mean 'giving themselves away' (Curran, 2002; Evans, 2002; Rofes, 2005). This chapter explores moments where I strategically intervene to disrupt - at least temporarily - the heteronormativity of the English as a Second Language classroom (also see Curran, 2006).

This chapter's style can best be described as a reflexive practitioner account. As critical incidents took place (in my class), reflective notes and insights were written, then discussed and debated with critical friends. Throughout these conversations, I engaged with poststructural and queer informed educational texts (Britzman, 1995, 1998; Evans, 2002; Kumashiro, 2009; Nelson, 2009; Rasmussen, Rofes, & Talburt, 2004) as I sought to construct an analysis that resonated with contemporary understandings of queer issues. That being said, this chapter is subjective, necessarily influenced by my life-history, the various and shifting components of my identities, and my interest in queer theory and gay rights (Jarman, 1993; Jennings, 1994; Jagose, 1996; Rofes, 1998; Warner, 1999; Willett, 2000). It is but one perspective on what took place in my classroom. As a white, Anglo-Celtic, able-bodied gay man, I can't speak for all queers. What I notice and respond to - and how I analyse the data must therefore be viewed as partial (see Ellwood, 2006).

Teaching queerly in adult ESL classes within heteronormative university landscapes is challenging. Gaining funding for queer research projects can be difficult let alone finding willing research participants from Non-English Speaking Backgrounds (Nelson, 2009). Students may be supportive of queer issues on a one-to-one basis, as I have regularly found, yet they may be reluctant to participate in a formal queer research project due to the tensions that could arise with their peers in the classroom and wider community. Thus, I sought to take action 'in the now', responding to the issues that were arising in my class, bringing to the surface thoughts, ideas and values that would likely remain unquestioned,

or unexamined in other mainstream ESL classrooms. In so doing, I was aware of the need to act ethically, in care of my students, particularly in respect to their confidentiality. I have therefore kept details of my class, the time period, and the students themselves at a general level. I have also withheld information that may render a student's identity obvious.

This chapter is written with the goal of engaging classroom teachers. As someone who straddles the practitioner/academic boundary in the Further Education sector, I want to draw in those teachers who position academic writing as inaccessible, and not connected to the 'real' world of their classrooms. Eric Rofes, a queer education-focused writer, was a key influence in this regard. His first person accounts (Rofes, 2005) of teacher identity, being 'out' (open about his sexuality), and the politics of queerness in the classroom are direct, partial and messy, without clear-cut answers. Informed by theory, in an understated manner, they resonated powerfully for me both as a teacher, and a gay man schooled in queer activist, first person, confrontational challenging of norm texts (Rofes, 1999; Savage, 2006; Soldatow & Tsiolkas, 1996). In the manner of Rofes then, I seek to foreground the classroom incidents in this chapter, whilst weaving in theory in an unobtrusive manner. I also centre myself, within the text, so as to provide a point of identification and engagement for teachers.

To be or not to be 'out' in the classroom. It's a question that's often raised and pondered in education-focused texts (Curran, 2002; Jennings, 1994; Rofes, 1999, 2005). Does being out constitute an overstepping of professional boundaries; a pushing of a personal bandwagon or agenda? These questions are somewhat problematic in the traditionally heteronormative environs of ESL classrooms. Why for example, do some teachers seek to keep their sexuality private whilst most teachers make no such attempt to do so? It is not uncommon for teachers to talk about their partners and their family in the classroom setting without feeling the need to justify such practices. School curricula, resources and structures also regularly reinforce heterosexuality and heterosexual relationships as the norm (Bickmore, 1999; Dalley & Campbell, 2006; Letts, 1999; Rasmussen, 2004; see also Young, 1990).

This chapter then centres around how to deal with students' assumptions of heterosexuality, how to work with their reactions to discussions of queer topics, and ultimately, how to turn these moments of surprise, disbelief and awkwardness into a teaching opportunity. This chapter is structured as a series of narratives focused on a teaching experience where I was confronted by a student asking 'are you married?' Preceding each narrative is a brief outline of the strategies that I experimented with in order to find an effective way to disrupt the assumption of heterosexuality. Following the narratives, I critically reflect on the teaching experience. In the final section of this chapter, I identify some limitations of my approach.

NARRATIVE SCENE 1

We are always getting to know each other in adult ESL classrooms. Ongoing enrolment means that there's always someone new in the class. On this occasion, my class comprised refugees and migrants from Myanmar, Lebanon, China, India, Iraq and Japan who were studying for an English language certificate. They generally described themselves as being either Christian or Muslim and regularly referred to, or invoked, their religious belief systems in class. A number of their home countries have severe anti-gay laws. I had been teaching the class for a number of months when the marriage question was asked by a new student:

Student: *Are you married?*
Greg: *No I'm not, but I do have a partner.*
Student: *What's her name?*

Greg [*thinks: Do I, don't I? Do I change the topic? Do I avoid answering?*]

Feeling a sense of responsibility to queers and the queer community – tips the balance towards further disclosure.

Greg: *My partner's not a she. I have a male partner.*
Silence; awkward, drawn-out silence.
She sits back, bewildered.
Red faced, awkward, perhaps embarrassed.
She scrambles to process his responses;
to the routine line of questions surrounding marriage.

This moment is a mix of emotions for me. There's the sense that I've done it. I have faced the question and haven't avoided nor changed the subject. At the same time, I feel annoyed and frustrated. No sooner do I disrupt the initial presumption – then there are further heteronormative presumptions to unsettle. Aware that my language choice was critical, and not having a thought-out response, I decide to leave it there. I needed to work out some strategies to address these issues with the class the following week.

Reflecting

No matter how many times I am asked, the awkwardness, the tension, the dryness of mouth and the pounding heart are always there. I have previously documented my experience responding to the marriage question in an English for Academic Purposes class (Curran, 2006). This time there was one major difference, I was in a senior teaching position.

As senior member of staff, I was concerned about the possible loss of status within the broader refugee and migrant community, as well as within our student population. Would I be respected if I was known to be gay? The issues of same-sex attraction never came up in the various meetings and forums I attended for Culturally and Linguistically Diverse (CALD) communities. And whilst I was 'out' to staff, I didn't regularly mention it in my day to day work. Cultural diversity, culture shock, and the tackling of discrimination were regular topics within my sphere of English as a Second Language teaching but I had rarely heard these concepts being extended to same-sex attraction or homophobia.

'Cultural sensitivity' - the notion of being aware and respectful of ethnic cultures, values, and practices - was often invoked as a reason to tone down or not discuss queer-related topics in my field of education. This somewhat limited view of cultural sensitivity rests on a number of unspoken and contested assumptions: that ethnic cultures are homogenous and unchanging in respect to their opposition to homosexuality; and that anti-gay religious beliefs should be respected and not challenged. Tatchell (2007) argues that traditional notions of multiculturalism and cultural sensitivity are often deployed against women's rights and gay rights. He refers to a "...tainted hierarchy of oppression", arguing that "race and religion now rule" at the expense of the rights of women and gays. Similarly, Pallotta-Chiarolli (2003, 2005b) argues that racism is usually seen as 'safe' and 'appropriate' to challenge within classrooms while homophobia is generally positioned as 'unsafe' and 'inappropriate' to challenge. She refers to the 'ethnic excuse' whereby educators argue that "... any anti-homophobia work will upset the parents, be seen as racist, and ...against the promotion of multiculturalism" (Pallotta-Chiarolli, 2005b, P. 120). Pallotta-Chiarolli argues that such assumptions could be seen as racist. The anti-gay discourses of some community leaders are not, she suggests, representative of entire ethnic communities.

I knew this backdrop to queer issues in classrooms. I knew the points of anxiety. I knew how it got to me. And I knew the dangers of reacting in the moment – although it was extremely enticing

to do so. I wanted to step back from the 'are you married?' question and critically examine the *ways of being* made possible through particular 'getting to know you' questions (Kumashiro, 2009). The focus then would be directed at everyday language practices (see Moites-Lopes, 2006). At the same time, it was important to take advantage of this opportunity, to introduce students to the language around sexuality – knowing that it almost certainly wouldn't have been taught in their previous English classes.

My thinking around how to proceed was heavily influenced by my PhD thesis on queer youth (Curran, 2002). Of significance here, was a poststructural understanding of identity as dynamic, rather than fixed, and as being shaped through discourse rather than emanating from an essential self (Davies, 1999; Jagose, 1996). This notion of fluidity along with the notion that we actively create 'who we are' through discourse underpins the strategies I describe in this chapter.

In adopting a discursive pedagogical approach, I recognised the need to pay close attention to how I might frame the issues as well as the participants. Drawing on my prior teaching experience, as well as a substantial knowledge base about working with queer issues, I anticipated likely student reactions to the various discourses I would deploy. I also identified discourses that would likely resonate with the students, inviting their interest. My main consideration here was how to position students and myself for productive engagement with these issues.

Knowing that traditional 'getting to know you' discourses tend to work to shut out queer possibilities, I knew that one line of teacher response would be inadequate. I had to prepare multiple responses or lines of disruption to ensure that the discussion space was kept open, not shut down or hijacked for anti-gay rhetoric. The task here became one of "...engaging the limits of [students'] thought" (Britzman, 1995, P. 156). I determined that success would be more likely if I positioned the students as having the agency and maturity to deal with queer issues. I wanted to depart from the traditional deficit constructions of ESL learners as unable to cope and likely to react negatively. My reasons for such were twofold – firstly, students can tend to live up to their teacher's expectations – be they traditional, limiting or expansive. Secondly, deficit positionings of minority groups like refugees or migrants often lead to more narrow teaching interventions which do little to unsettle normalcy (Curran, 2002; see also Jennings & MacGillivray, 2007 and Rofes, 2004) and its "immanent exclusions" (Britzman, 1998, P. 80).

Having now gauged how the classroom situation might play out, I began to determine the strategies I would use for the first part of the lesson.

NARRATIVE SCENE 2A

Strategising

The lesson would need to proceed through a series of stages. The first stage would be devoted to framing. I would commence by highlighting a common student discourse pertaining to sexuality - 'we never talk about this topic' - to justify a focus on this topic and to gain their interest. Secondly, I would position the students as willing and sensitive, respectful participants. Third, I would offer a strategy that would enable them to negotiate the lesson.

The Classroom Narrative

Today we're going to talk about some topics that many teachers don't discuss. Many students tell me we never talk about these topics in our classes or our community but they're always really interested.

Many teachers don't think you can talk about these topics in English classes. They think that you'll get upset and annoyed. But I think you'll be fine. I know you respect each other's differences. We

help and support each other in our classroom community. We don't have to agree with each other but we do respect each other.

If you feel a bit uncomfortable or tense...feel it but keep listening. I know it might feel difficult but keep listening. I know you'll be okay if you just keep with us.

Reflecting

Initially, I use absence as a marketing or selling point for the lessons. I position myself as different to other teachers, as someone who would teach what other teachers avoided. These lessons were therefore a rare opportunity to learn about taboo concepts – yet I don't name the issues – I want to heighten the interest.

This initial framing approach is an attempt to gain 'buy-in' from the students through the invoking of specific discourses that would likely resonate with them – absence and taboo. It was also an effort to mark out a space for the discussion, and provide some sense of the context. Prior experience had taught me that launching into queer issues without sufficient background, framing or contextualisation often leads to hostile reactions (Curran, 2006, 2002; Curran, Chiarolli, & Pallotta-Chiarolli, 2009).

Having crafted a context for our discussions, my next task was to minimise the opportunities for anti-gay discourses. Queer focused lessons can at times tend to become reactive endeavours with the teacher attempting to justify what they are doing against a range of fundamentalist religious discourses. Knowing that such discourses had the potential to derail the lessons, I positioned the students as open and sensitive to the forthcoming discussion as indicated in the discourse, *'I think you'll be fine. I know you respect each other.'*

This discourse was an attempt to position the students as different - as not like teachers generally expected them to be. Framing what they could be,

I talked them up - positioning them as having the necessary qualities to rise above negativity and hostility - as being able to discuss this topic in a supportive, respectful manner.

At the same time, I acknowledged that some students may have difficulties with the content. In an effort to keep them engaged, I suggested a strategy that might help them to navigate through the lesson.

Teachers commonly presume that students will react negatively to queer content, assuming that they will have battle through the lesson and face a range of repercussions afterwards (Curran, 2002; Curran, Chiarolli, & Pallotta-Chiarolli, 2009; Martino & Pallotta-Chiarolli, 2005). Such thoughts lead to many teachers avoiding queer topics. Others may go ahead with a lesson, yet their deficit conceptualisation of students constrains what they do, and students tend to behave in the negative manner that teachers expected. Laying out the shape of the lesson upfront and positioning the students as able to navigate their way through such has, in my experience, led to much more positive engagement.

NARRATIVE SCENE 2B

Strategizing

In the next stage of the lesson, I set about building the theoretical framework for the discussion to follow. Key here was providing an expansive space for inclusive discourses whilst limiting the space for anti-gay religious discourse. The strategy involved departing from traditional Equal Opportunity approaches. Instead, I focused on the underpinning to law and government in Australia - through a discussion of secular and religious-based societies.

The Classroom Narrative

The class begins with the key vocabulary and concepts written on the board.

- Secular society
- Religious society
- Separation of Church and State

As a class, we discuss what each term or concept means. I then pose two broad questions seeking to identify how secularism might impact on everyday practices:

- How might secularism impact on institutions like our university?
- How might secularism affect laws such as Equal Opportunity?

Next we moved onto a comparison of secular and faith-based societies.

Students spoke about their experiences of living in a faith-based country and compared that to living in Australia. Commonly they spoke of the increased freedom in Australia, the fact that they were treated better here, were protected under law, and had status as women. Importantly, they also commented on their persecution at the hands of other religious groups in their home countries. They argued that that didn't happen in Australia.

These discussions provided me with an opportunity to link secularism to students' improved living conditions. They also enabled a focus on the limits of organised religion – in a secular society - in terms of government, laws and everyday life. Relating this back to the classroom, we examined what secularism might mean in respect to discussions of 'sensitive' topics like women's rights. This was an effort by me to contain student reactions – particularly in respect to their expectations and judgements of other people's behaviour according to their religious beliefs. It was also an effort to ensure that no one religious view predominated in the discussion.

Reflecting

Religion is often a key issue at play when queer issues are raised or surface in education settings (Curran, 2002; Martino & Pallotta-Chiarolli, 2003; Pallotta-Chiarolli, 2005b). This part of the lesson focused on containing the influence of fundamentalist anti-gay discourse. On a previous occasion I had started teaching about Equal Opportunity with a definition of the term and then outlined the various aspects of identity protected by it. This approach, however, turned out to be problematic. It didn't provide the necessary bulwark against anti-gay discourses. Whilst most students are keen to know their rights in a new country (see AMES, 2009), there is often a hierarchy of rights. In a context where teachers are concerned about being 'culturally sensitive', it is seen as okay and morally 'right' for example, to celebrate ethnic and religious diversity as well as discuss and challenge racism and religious discrimination. There is much less support for sexual diversity. Consequently, queer issues are usually absent from education settings and teachers generally fail to intervene against homophobia (Hillier, Turner, & Mitchell, 2005).

Using a conventional Human Rights or Equal Opportunity approach then to support a focus on gay issues is somewhat problematic. Teachers are working against a dominant culture in which gay rights and discrimination are viewed as less worthy of attention than ethnic and religious rights. It's not as simple as listing all the attributes protected by Equal Opportunity and expecting them to be viewed or treated in the same way. Quite clearly, within the dominant culture, it is evident that gays and lesbians are not of equal value or importance. Students are well aware of such and have an array of dominant discourses to draw upon

if a teacher were to break the silence surrounding queer perspectives.

Seeking to take a different approach, I focused upon secularism and the separation of Church and State as the foundation of Australia's system of government and law. In setting these parameters, I was drawing upon institutional discourse that supported restricting the influence of particular religious views whilst also expanding the space for pro-diversity discourse.

NARRATIVE SCENE 2C

Strategising

Having framed the discussion, set the theoretical framework, and positioned the students as able to engage in constructive, respectful manner – the foundation was laid for a critical inquiry approach to language use (Nelson, 2009). This approach of unpacking of what we say and do involved actively disrupting the taken for granted language practices of students - like asking 'are you married?' Such normative questions, lines of inquiry and responses largely pass by unnoticed and un-examined in mainstream contexts since they reflect – for the most part – mainstream values and belief structures.

This reflective teaching approach is readily intelligible and keenly embraced by ESL students since there is much interest in how and why language is used in particular ways. Here it involves asking general questions, and continually drilling down into the responses that students give. It also requires voicing the 'taboo' responses that students are reluctant to voice themselves, as well as encouraging students to interact with such taboos.

The Classroom Narrative

The lesson segment begins with the 'getting to know you' focus that prompted this teaching intervention.

Greg: *When we meet someone new what do we generally ask them? What do we ask so that we can get to know new people?*

Students responded with the following questions:

- *What's your name*
- *Where do you come from?*
- *Where do you live?*
- *Are you married?*
- *Do you have children? How old are they? What are their names?*
- *What do you want to do in Australia?*

Greg: *What questions are people happy to answer? Why? What questions make some people uncomfortable? Why?*

The next section of the lesson, involves zeroing in on 'taboo' topics.

Greg: *Some people might be uncomfortable answering, 'how old are you?' or 'what's your religion?' Why might these questions make them uncomfortable?*

In discussing likely reasons, students indicated that a person's reaction may depend on their location. This lead to a passionate exchange about the link between geographic location and our sense of identity or 'who we are' at any moment in time. Many students discussed how their persona varied from their home country to Australia.

Greg: *Some people might not want to answer, 'are you married?' 'Why might they be uncomfortable answering this question?'*

Students indicated that people may not wish to answer this question because they are divorced or separated, their husband or wife is dead or they don't want to get married.

Greg: *What answers can people give to the question, 'are you married?'*

Students responded:

- *Yes*
- *No*

Using sentence stems, I encouraged students to elaborate further:

Greg: *No I'm not married but I....*

Students identified different forms of relationships such as girlfriend and boyfriend. For example, *'No I'm not married but I have a girlfriend.'*

I then introduced two new terms, *domestic* and *de-facto partner*, before posing the question: *Why might people be uncomfortable talking about these different forms of relationships?*

Students identified a number of factors that would make some people wary of disclosing their relationship status yet didn't mention sexuality as an issue.

Greg: *What would you say if someone said, 'no I'm not married but I have a partner'*

Students indicated they would like to know the partner's name and assumed they were heterosexual.

Greg: *Let's consider the possibilities: If I'm male, I might have a....*
Students: *girlfriend*
Greg: *I might also have a....*
Students: *boyfriend*
Greg: *So when you ask a question, you need to remember that people are different. If I'm male I might not have a girlfriend, I might have a boyfriend. If I'm female, I might not have a boyfriend, I might have a girlfriend.*

Introducing the concept of presumption, I highlighted the presumptions that they were making, and suggested that they be cautious in respect to asking questions:

When you ask a question, you need to be ready because sometimes people might give you an answer that you don't expect or agree with. You need to be respectful of people's differences. You might not agree with people but you can be respectful.

Following this advice, we returned to specific 'getting to know you' questions and identified some responses that you might not expect. For example, we felt it would be unusual to hear someone to say they're an atheist or to indicate that they are gay or lesbian.

At this point, I steered the discussion towards gender and sexuality-related labels:

Now many students tell me they never get the chance to discuss such these things so tell me if this is not useful. Would you be interested if I went through the different words to describe sexuality? Maybe you know all the words, so tell me if this is not useful.

Students were uniform in their view that I continue and so I listed the various sexual and gender identity labels on the whiteboard. Many students indicated that they were not familiar with the different terms for homosexual or heterosexual. They were also especially interested to know which slang words were appropriate and inappropriate – in particular contexts.

Reflecting

At the start of this segment, I sought to stay broad rather than zeroing in on the 'are you married?' question. This enabled us to see how a range of people are excluded through everyday practices. It also afforded some protection from the possible charge that I was just pushing gay content.

With the knowledge that our language choices potentially open up or close down possibilities for others (Kumashiro, 2009), I asked students to identify inclusive and exclusive questions. A common pattern began to emerge. My attempts to disrupt normative practices were generally met with normative responses. Students self-censored – or failed to mention – questions that were likely to be seen as 'inappropriate' in mainstream contexts. This is not surprising since individuals within a classroom – along with the education setting itself – are inextricably linked to, and influenced by, broader societal and institutional structures (Evans, 2002). Faced with this absence, I needed to ask the taboo questions that they hadn't.

Modelling a critical inquiry approach, I asked students to explain why questions about religion might make some people uncomfortable. Here I was moving towards a focus on the 'are you married' question – which no-one had mentioned. Again this absence was not unexpected. Responses to gay content in the classroom are impacted upon by legal and religious frameworks, along with popular culture which underpin the privileging of heterosexuality and the relegating of homosexuality to the margins –as of little consequence – and not to be talked about (Curran, 2002; Evans, 2002; Pascoe 2007). Disrupting the normative line of responses therefore required giving voice to the questions students were reluctant to ask, and the responses they wouldn't give. It meant continually narrowing questions to bring them closer to the taboo topics. Still the heteronormative presumptions continued, no-one wanted to be the first to speak of queer possibilities. The resistance and silence was intense. Eventually I decided to take a back to basics approach, asking students to identify the partner possibilities for a male and female (male – female, male or both; female – male, female or both).

As we moved towards the latter stages of the lesson, I sought to draw the students back to the original 'getting to know you' questions. I problematised the questions, as well as the assumptions students were tending to make. Given the level of positive engagement, and the strong foundation built, I decided to make the most of this opportunity. We began a discussion about gender and sexual identity labels. Through my prior experience, I was concerned that such a focus might trigger a negative outburst. So I reinvoked the discourse of silence around sexuality issues:

Many students tell me they never get the chance to discuss such things. But tell me if this is not useful. Maybe you know all these words.

This was a moment that you don't forget as a teacher. There was complete interest as students keenly noted down the various sexuality and gender-related labels we raised and asked a range of questions about such. It seemed like there was an enormous chasm to fill - students wanted to make the most of this opportunity to find out new vocabulary or to confirm what they did know. There was no ready sign of discomfort or of students wanting to move on. They were keen to remain talking about queer labels even as our teaching day drew to a close. It was like a hunger that couldn't be satisfied.

LIMITATIONS

Traditional approaches to queer issues in schools tend to rely on positioning gays as existing outside the classroom – with teachers referring to gays in the outside world. Such practices contribute to the invisibility of queers and reinscribe the heteronormative space of the classroom and school (see Curran, 2002). The approach I have described in this chapter would be improved by disrupting the invisibility of queers in the education setting in a more explicit manner.

My focus on the question 'are you married' was motivated – in part – by my desire for students to recognise that there could be gay people in our class – who would feel excluded by such a ques-

tion. Yet this wasn't made explicit to the students. Nor did I explain that the teaching sessions were inspired by *my* being asked 'Are you married?' I could also have highlighted that there could be students with gay family members or friends, or that some heterosexual students could have found some of the questions problematic in respect to their relationship types.

REFERENCES

AMES. (2009). *It's your right: Human rights, everyone, everywhere, everyday.* Canberra, Australia: Commonwealth of Australia.

Bickmore, K. (1999). Why discuss sexuality in elementary school? In Letts, W. J., & Sears, J. T. (Eds.), *Queering elementary education: Advancing the dialogue about sexualities and schooling* (pp. 15–25). Lanham, MD: Rowman & Littlefield.

Britzman, D. P. (1995). Is there a queer pedagogy? Or stop reading straight. *Educational Theory*, *45*(2), 151–165. doi:10.1111/j.1741-5446.1995.00151.x

Britzman, D. P. (1998). *Lost subjects, contested objects: Towards a psychoanalytic inquiry of learning.* Albany, NY: State University of New York Press.

Curran, G. (2002). *Young queers getting together: Moving beyond isolation and loneliness.* (Unpublished PhD Thesis). Melbourne, Australia: University of Melbourne.

Curran, G. (2006). Challenging sexual norms and assumptions in an ESL classroom: Rethinking my teaching practice. *Journal of Language, Identity, and Education*, *5*(1), 85–96. doi:10.1207/s15327701jlie0501_6

Curran, G., Chiarolli, S., & Pallotta-Chiarolli, M. (2009). The C words: Clitories, childhood and challenging compulsory heterosexuality discourses with pre-service primary teachers. *Sex Education: Sexuality, Society and Learning, 9*(2), 155–168.

Dalley, P., & Campbell, M. D. (2006). Constructing and contesting discourses of heteronormativity: An ethnographic study of youth in a Francophone high school in Canada. *Journal of Language, Identity, and Education, 5*(1), 11–29. doi:10.1207/s15327701jlie0501_2

Davies, B. (1999). *A body of writing: 1990-1999.* Oxford, UK: Rowman & Littlefield.

Ellwood, C. (2006). On coming out and coming undone: Sexualities and reflexivities in language education. *Journal of Language, Identity, and Education, 5*, 67–84. doi:10.1207/s15327701jlie0501_5

Evans, K. (2002). *Negotiating the self: Identity, sexuality and emotion in learning to teach.* New York, NY: RoutledgeFalmer.

Hillier, L., Turner, A., & Mitchell, A. (2005). *Writing themselves in again: 6 years on - The 2nd national report on the sexuality, health and well-being of same-sex attracted young people in Australia.* Melbourne, Australia: Australian Research Centre in Sex, Health and Society, La Trobe University.

Jagose, A. (1996). *Queer theory: An introduction.* New York, NY: NYU Press.

Jarman, D. (1993). *At your own risk. A saint's testament.* London, NY: Vintage.

Jennings, K. (1994). *One teacher in 10. Gay and lesbian educators tell their stories.* Los Angeles, CA: Alyson Publications.

Jennings, T., & MacGillivray, I. K. (2007). Coming out and the new victim narrative. *Journal of Curriculum and Pedagogy, 4*(2), 54–58. doi:10.1080/15505170.2007.10411644

Kumashiro, K. (2009). *Against common sense: Teaching and learning towards social justice* (revised edition). New York, NY: Routledge.

Letts, W. J. (1999). How to make boys and girls in the classroom: The heteronormative nature of elementary school science . In Letts, W. J., & Sears, J. T. (Eds.), *Queering elementary education: Advancing the dialogue about sexualities and schooling* (pp. 97–110). Lanham, MD: Rowman & Littlefield.

Martino, W., & Pallotta-Chiarolli, M. (2003). *So what's a boy: Addressing issues of masculinity and schooling.* Maidenhead, UK: Open University Press.

Martino, W., & Pallotta-Chiarolli, M. (2005). *Being normal is the only way to be.* Sydney, Australia: University of New South Wales Press.

Moites-Lopes, L. P. (2006). Queering literacy teaching: Analyzing gay themed discourses in a fifth grade class in Brazil. *Journal of Language, Identity, and Education, 5*(1), 31–50. doi:10.1207/s15327701jlie0501_3

Nelson, C. D. (2005). Teaching of ESL . In Sears, J. T. (Ed.), *Youth, education and sexualities: An international encyclopedia* (pp. 299–303). Westport, CT: Greenwood Press.

Nelson, C. D. (2006). Queer inquiry in language education. *Journal of Language, Identity, and Education, 5*(1), 1–9. doi:10.1207/s15327701jlie0501_1

Nelson, C. D. (2009). *Sexual identities in English language education: Classroom conversations.* New York, NY: Routledge.

Pallotta-Chiarolli, M. (1998). *Cultural diversity and men who have sex with men.* Sydney, Australia: National Centre in HIV Social Research, Macquarie University.

Pallotta-Chiarolli, M. (2003). *Girls talk: Young women speak their hearts and minds.* Sydney, Australia: Finch Publishing.

Pallotta-Chiarolli, M. (2005). Ethnic identities. In Sears, J. T. (Ed.), *Youth, education, and sexualities: An international encyclopedia* (pp. 303–306). Westport, CT: Greenwood Press.

Pallotta-Chiarolli, M. (2005b). *When our children come out: How to support gay, lesbian, bisexual and transgendered young people.* Lane Cove, Australia: Finch Publishing.

Pascoe, C. (2007). *Dude you're a fag: Masculinity and sexuality in high school.* Berkeley, CA: University of California Press.

Rasmussen, M. L. (2004). Safety and subversion: The production of sexualities and genders in school spaces. In Rasmussen, M. L., Rofes, E., & Talburt, S. (Eds.), *Youth and sexualities: Pleasure, subversion, and insubordination in and out of schools* (pp. 131–152). New York, NY: Palgrave MacMillan.

Rasmussen, M. L., Rofes, E., & Talburt, S. (2004). *Youth and sexualities: Pleasure, subversion and insubordination in and out of schools.* New York, NY: Palgrave MacMillan.

Rofes, E. (1998). *Dry bones breathe: Gay men creating post-AIDS identities and cultures.* Binghamton, NY: The Harrington Park Press.

Rofes, E. (1999). What happens when the kids grow up? The long-term impact of an openly gay teacher on eight students' lives. In Letts, W. J., & Sears, J. T. (Eds.), *Queering elementary education: Advancing the dialogue about sexualities and schooling* (pp. 83–93). Lanham, MD: Rowman & Littlefield.

Rofes, E. (2004). Martyr-Target-Victim: Interrogating narratives of persecution and suffering among queer youth. In Rasmussen, M. L., Rofes, E., & Talburt, S. (Eds.), *Youth and sexualities: Pleasure, subversion and insubordination in and out of schools* (pp. 41–62). New York, NY: Palgrave MacMillan.

Rofes, E. (2005). *A radical rethinking of sexuality & schooling: Status quo or status queer.* Lanham, MD: Rowman & Littlefield.

Savage, D. (2006). *The commitment: Love, sex, marriage and my family.* New York, NY: Plume.

Soldatow, S., & Tsiolkas, C. (1996). *Jump cuts: An autobiography.* Milsons Point, Australia: Random House.

Tatchell, P. (2007, Spring). *Their multiculturalism and ours.* Retrieved May 7, 2010, from http://dissentmagazine.org/democratiya/article_pdfs/d8Tatchell.pdf

Warner, M. (1999). *The trouble with normal: Sex, politics and ethics of queer life.* New York, NY: The Free Press.

Willett, G. (2000). *Living out loud: A history of gay and lesbian activism in Australia.* St Leonards, Australia: Allen & Unwin.

Young, I. M. (1990). *Justice and the politics of difference.* Princeton, NJ: Princeton University Press.

Chapter 15
Disruptive Relation(ship)s:
Romantic Love as Critical Praxis

Rick Carpenter
Valdosta State University, USA

ABSTRACT

Historically, Western culture has maintained lines of strict demarcation between what is deemed personal and social, often with one eschewed and the other privileged. Doing so risks cutting ourselves off from useful avenues of inquiry, reflection, and, ultimately, transformation. Romantic love represents an especially effective entry point into a critical examination of the personal and its relationship to the social. Interrogating the personal/social binary can serve to problematize romantic love and destabilize cultural mechanisms of self-construction, along with the various attending epistemologies employed to "naturalize" distinctions of numerous kinds. As a critical methodology, romantic love facilitates a shifting of perspective from either/or to both/and, a move that can open transformative possibilities even as it challenges cherished beliefs, complicates reductive thinking, and explodes inequitable hierarchies.

INTRODUCTION

Whenever a celebrity or politician's infidelity makes the news, the entire sordid affair is attributed to "original sin," to weakness of character, as witnessed quite prominently during the scandal involving Tiger Woods. Seldom, if ever, however, is anything said about the complex relationship in the West between sex and love, let alone about love itself. Yet, if love is "the creator's greatest gift to humanity," if "true love" is required in order for one to be "complete," why, then, did Tiger "cheat" on his wife? And if all he wanted was to "play the field" and "sow his wild oats," why did he get married in the first place? And why to a Swedish model?

DOI: 10.4018/978-1-61350-495-6.ch015

Despite their amalgamation in the present milieu, romantic love is traditionally viewed as somehow apart from and above sexual desire. One of the dominating features of Western hegemonic logic is the creation and maintenance of binary oppositions that function to define and legitimize one in relation to (and at the expense of) the Other: male/female, straight/gay, civilized/uncivilized, Christian/heathen, white/non-white, capitalism/communism. Similarly, romantic love serves as a legitimizing agent of the status quo; rather than being viewed as an outcome of historical processes, romantic love is seen as something outside history and culture, a pure, "natural" force or state more akin to gravity than to any sort of ideological apparatus. Romantic love's privileged status as something so universal as to be beyond question is greatly strengthened by its relegation to the personal side of the personal/social binary.

Theorists, feminists most prominently, have pointed out that sexuality has been, in a similar fashion, anchored to private spaces despite its near omnipresence in the public realm. Barred from "proper" public discussion, discourses about sexuality - and sexuality *as* discourse - are, as a result, more easily regulated and controlled in order to effectuate and perpetuate power structures that depend upon sexuality as an exclusionary tool. While I applaud these critical insights into sexuality and the private sphere, and readily recognize the importance of such work in helping to secure a more just and equitable future, I want here to broaden the scope of critique to encompass the personal without collapsing it into either the private or the social. I maintain that in the process of challenging divisions between private and public, we have a tendency to reinforce, inadvertently, bifurcations between personal and social, with the social privileged and the personal ignored, dismissed, or even denied.

Certainly, attempts to unmask the unspoken and frequently unseen ways in which powerful public discourses permeate the supposedly private world of the individual contribute much to liberatory politics and pedagogies. But what of the personal? Even well-meaning advocates for social justice often attach a seemingly obligatory "merely" to any reference to the personal. Please do not mistake me: I understand the need to critique the personal. As critical and cultural theorists have pointed out, power is most effectively operationalized through the insidious process of masking its origin and replacing history with nature, whereby the social, the contingent, and the ideological are made to seem natural or universal. Consequently, nonconformity and resistance are privatized and pathologized, with "blame" placed upon the individual rather than upon institutions or ideologies. As a teacher who strives to empower students through a liberatory pedagogy, I subscribe to a constructivist approach to education that emphasizes the dialogic and culturally contextualized nature of teaching, learning, self, and reality.

Still, I don't want to toss the proverbial baby out with the bath water. To deny the personal risks eliminating the possibility of individual agency and transformation. However, to dichotomize the personal and the social is to fall prey to the same hermeneutical snare proffered by regimes of power that maintain the status quo through the deployment of binary oppositions (such as the private/public distinction).

Romantic love, I assert, represents an especially effective entry point into a critical examination of the personal and its relationship to the social, as well as, by extension, the often hidden ideologies and histories that construct and underpin our daily lives and identities. Learning to think critically involves the concomitant examination of the relationship between received knowledge and previously unknown perspectives and epistemologies, between habituated beliefs and practices and radically new and possibly frightening views and actions. As educators dedicated to progressive social change, we want our students to learn about the wider world and their places within it, and in so doing, to recognize and then analyze the multiplicity of connections between themselves and others. Framed in this manner, one could say we are trying to foster in students a developed understanding and appreciation of socio-cultural situatedness, including the role of institutions, ideologies, and discourse communities in constructing both knowledge and identity. Thus, when we speak of analyzing a semiotic system, reading a text, or composing a sophisticated critique, what we have in mind, I would argue, entails, broadly stated, a process of *relating*, of seeing - and hopefully building - relationships.

Romantic love is uniquely positioned as a scene for conducting a critical examination of relationships. Perceived as perhaps the very paragon of the personal, romantic love, crucially, nonetheless depends upon at least one other person - another/ an Other - for one to "complete" oneself. This tension between the intensely personal and the intimately collective (itself a contradictory relation) problematizes romantic love and destabilizes cultural mechanisms of self-construction, along with the various attending epistemologies employed to "naturalize" distinctions of numerous kinds. The idea that something so seemingly natural and personal as romantic love is a matter of culture and power rather than of destiny and biology is a notion so novel, so astounding to most people (students and teachers alike) that it borders upon heretical. And, of course, it *is* heresy (but that's the point).

In this chapter I argue that romantic love, as socio-historical concept, can be put to productive use within a variety of educational settings to help foster students' capacity for critical inquiry by disrupting received notions of self (and other) that work to limit ways of thinking, knowing, and being in the world. Scholars and educators have long examined sexuality as a complex nexus of cultural, political, and psychological forces that far exceeds mere biological drives, recognizing sexuality as a potentially subversive site to disrupt heteronormative/phallogocentric norms and hierarchies. My aim here is to extend such analyses from *eros* to Eros, from sexual desire to

sexual love. Doing so is not simply a lateral or perfunctory shift of focus. Instead, I believe that romantic love's pervasive and influential role in Western constructions of self, its ubiquitous yet multifaceted presence in our daily lives, makes it an especially useful site for analyzing and critiquing not only a wide range of cultural constructs but, importantly, culture as construct, including hegemonic forces and structures of power. What is more, utilizing romantic love as a methodology for interrogating the traditional bifurcation of personal and social allows us to shift perspective—our own as well as that of our students—from *either/or* to *both/and*, a move that can open transformative possibilities even as it challenges cherished beliefs, complicates reductive thinking, and explodes inequitable hierarchies.[1]

THE PERSONAL-SOCIAL MATRIX: THINKING CRITICALLY, THINKING RELATIONALLY

I came to view romantic love as a potentially useful pedagogical tool after reflecting upon the centricity of relational thinking to critical theory and, more specifically, American composition studies, both largely characterized by, among other things, an attention to social justice through analyses of the discourses of - and *to* - power. As a field, education, of course, also shares this attention, with scholar-teachers actively working to develop and advance theories and pedagogies directly related to such concerns as diversity, access, and empowerment. Regardless of disciplinary background or area of expertise, those committed to social justice generally seek connections over divisions and are distrustful of binaries and dichotomies.

Many who wish to move beyond debilitating dichotomies - especially concerning the personal and the social - have come to resist the *either/ or* logic of binary thinking by simply refusing to choose between the two given terms, electing instead to perpetually delay or deny resolution.

In "Social Constructionism and Expressivism: Contradictions and Connections," Neal (1993) asks, "How can the fundamental difference - the individual point of view in conflict with the social perspective - ever be reconciled?" (p. 47). As one possible answer, she suggests we "acknowledge and accept contradictions while enjoying the benefits of the connections" (47). Similarly, Burnham (1993) asserts that expressive rhetoric is social in nature and, as such, offers a "paradoxical but productive view of *the relationship between* the individual and the group" (p. 154; emphasis mine). Hindman (2001) emphasizes not productive paradox but productive tension in reconciling conflicting conceptions of self. In "Making Writing Matter: Using the 'Personal' to Recover(y) an Essential(ist) Tension in Academic Discourse," Hindman argues that "by refusing to delimit this conflict as a binary opposition that must be resolved, by instead holding that tension, we can critically, professionally affirm both the social basis of our professional discourse and our material agency as individual writers" (p. 89). For her, any attempt to dispel competing versions of how the self is constructed will prove to be futile. Better (i.e., more productive), in other words, to see versions of self not in opposition but rather in relation to one another.

I want to suggest that no resolution is needed if the personal and social are not viewed in paradoxical terms. I have come to conceive of the personal as not simply located within or adjacent to the social but rather as social itself. Put more succinctly, the personal *is* social, for we experience the social in ways conditioned by our own individual - and overdetermined - matrices. But then, in a sense, the social is personal as well, culture and society being nothing more (nor less) than the accumulation of traditions - past, present, future - beget by individuals. This is not to suggest some mythic progenitor of modern culture or life (though of course many belief systems are predicated upon such mythopoeia); rather, I only mean to call attention to the constituent subjects

of any collective, and the dynamic nature of that collective.

The social and the personal have no meaning as isolated terms; the two define each other relationally. I am reminded of Saussurean linguistics - the necessity of difference, the insubordination of language - as well as Bakhtinian dialogism. While it is pointless to discuss the personal without reference to the social, the inverse also holds true. In this regard, I imagine the social and the personal as interlaced - a grid or lattice perhaps. As a socially constructed individual, I embody the social in ways unique to myself, having traveled singular pathways along the matrix. Again, I do not mean to imply a completely relativistic construct of reality where no (lower-case) truths may exist. It is on such grounds that expressivists and other advocates of the personal have been traditionally attacked. I do mean to imply, however, that there are patterns to the grid. Anomalies. Waves. Fluctuations.

What I am variously calling a grid, lattice, or matrix, Smith (1990), borrowing from Jeffner Allen, calls "sinuous webs of intersubjectivity" (p. 15). In placing the body alongside discourse upon the web, Smith is drawing from those French feminists, such as Irigaray, Cixous, and Kristeva, who seek to empower women by empowering their bodies. However, Smith pointedly attempts to avoid the essentializing - or re-essentializing - potential a (re)turn to the body entails by stressing the multiplicity of subjectivities and, importantly, the personal agency afforded by these (discursive) subjectivities, so that "[e]ach of us, in our manifold positions in discursive fields, inhabits margins and centers *simultaneously* (p. 16; emphasis mine). The self is not so much shattered as dispersed, the one becoming the many, the personal the social.

Recognizing the empowering possibility of the personal within the social - or more appropriately, the personal-as-social - recalls certain aspects of a Foucauldian theory of power. According to Foucault, we are produced by power even as we resist it, for though we are subjugated by authority, we ourselves also and simultaneously author(ize). In fact, power and resistance, argues Foucault (1980), mutually constitute each other (p. 142). Collapsing the power/resistance binary complicates our notions of social relations and ourselves/our-selves. We see that patterns along the personal-social matrix originate, manifest, flow, alter, disenfranchise, and empower in myriad sites and ways, often simultaneously and congruently, and possibly at micro and/or macro levels.

In the process, we understand more fully the personal-social matrix. Because the individual can exercise power at the same time that power is exercised upon her or him - what Smith (1988) refers to as simultaneous marginality and centricity - the subject/self is both divorced from as well as always already a part of larger social and cultural constructs. Further, since power is everywhere and "power relations are the necessary precondition for the establishment of social relations" (McNay, 1992, p. 67), the subject, for good or ill, is always defined in relation to others; however, as it is more accurate to speak of subjectivities rather than of a singular subject, the defining "other" does not necessarily have to become the Other - the Other to the (white-bourgeois-Christian-heterosexual-male) One. The relational self is-but-is-not subject and object, personal and social, authority and unauthorized. Essentializing and hierarchical binaries are too simplistic to describe the complex fluidity of the self, who occupies a multiplicity of categories. Still, whatever the coordinates along the matrix, the self exists always in social relations.

In short, similar to the wave-particle duality of light, our identities - indeed, our realities - are simultaneously personally and socially constructed. Recognition of the personal-social matrix, the nexus of our experiences as teacher-learners and as human beings, holds vast potential that we are only just beginning to explore. As we have learned, we are all affected by such mechanisms as racism, patriarchy, and heteronormativity on very personal, individual levels of experience and comprehension even as we share commonalities with others. Therefore, my theoretical and pedagogical approach to critical literacy now looks beyond simply dismantling the Cartesian "I." My goals have broadened with experience: I want students to recognize the specific, local forms of personal individuality produced by political discourse as well as to connect their private selves to larger cultural forces without subsequently denying the existence or validity of those private selves (or rather, selves-in-process). In short, I strive to help students become more critical and intellectual by first helping them to think more relationally. In working to accomplish these goals, I've learned the efficacy of beginning where many of my students begin - with love.

THE HEART OF THE MATTER: FROM SHARED TO RELATIONAL SELF

The young are embarked upon two quests: to find love and to find themselves. The fact that they instinctively recognize the interrelatedness of the two while academics often fail to do so just illustrates how much more our students know than we acknowledge or realize. Indeed, recognition of romantic love's influential role in Western identity construction is nothing new; erotic/romantic love has long been viewed as a technology of self-definition (Ackerman, 1994; Carson, 1986; Lacan, 1978; Grosz, 1994; Wagoner, 1997). It is precisely romantic love's pervasive and continued contribution to Western perceptions of self that makes it especially relevant to liberatory teaching. If critical literacy is understood as "social action through language use that develops us as agents inside a larger culture" (Shor, 1999), then romantic love, I would argue, can be productively read as a type of literacy itself - a grand narrative or master trope through which we continually define and re-define ourselves *in relation to* others.

Within the traditional conception of romantic love first codified by Plato and still dominant today - what Singer (1984) terms the West's foundational model - love involves a melding of two souls into one. As such, the self is considered fundamentally incomplete, a notion with significant ramifications. An incomplete self must be viewed as fixed and invariable; otherwise, a multiplicity of ways in addition to a soul mate might be found to provide the incomplete self with what it needs. An outcome of this model is that in spite of the required Other, a relationship must necessarily collapse into a singularity that has difficulty seeing beyond itself, much as a massive aging star inevitably becomes a black hole from which not even light can escape. For what the lover seeks is not a relationship *per se* but rather him- or herself; the self, as Carson (1986) discusses, "forms at the edge of desire" (p. 39). "By virtue of consciousness," writes Sartre (1956), "the Other is for me simultaneously the one who has stolen my being from me and the one who causes 'there to be' a being which is my being" (p. 475). In other words, the self formed via love depends upon a particular person necessarily outside itself for its very existence and yet seeks in the very process of self-formation to deny this requisite dependency by subsuming the other person into the newly formed "complete" or melded self - an effort that must itself necessarily fail inasmuch as the self would be incomplete, would not "be," without the independent presence of the other person. As a result, the self is dependent upon and yet isolated from - and in conflict with - the Other.

An outgrowth of this dependency-conflict model is an emphasis on the individual. "Romantic love," Solomon (1990) explains in *Love: Emotion, Myth, and Metaphor*, "is strictly personal in that its roles are defined entirely in face-to-face confrontation, with a particular person" (p. 135). According to Coontz (2005), romantic love's connection to individualism began with Enlightenment notions of self-fulfillment and the pursuit of happiness. For Solomon, such a conjoining comes as no surprise since romantic love *requires* a philosophical and political emphasis on the individual for its very existence: "Only in a society with an enormously powerful ideology of the individual, in which the 'alienation' of the individual from the larger society is not only tolerated but even encouraged and celebrated, can the phenomenon of romantic love be conceivable" (p. 136). According to Solomon, romantic love is opposed to the larger world, preferring instead to construct a private, smaller world of its own.

Though, of course, love is not solely about one individual; love involves another. Solomon refers to this connection of self-and-other as the *shared self*: "a self that is conceived and developed together" (p. 142), "a self defined with, in and through a particular other person" (p. 148). Amid the confusion of our lives, "we look for a context that is small enough, manageable enough, yet powerful enough, for us to define ourselves, our 'real' selves - we think wishfully - and what could be smaller or more manageable than the tiniest possible interpersonal world, namely, a world of only two people. And so, in love, we define ourselves and define each other" (p. 143). The shared self can be understood, then, as a shared determination of self in an indeterminate world. Put another way, we construct our identities through interpersonal relations, and most of those relations - with strangers, with family, with the boss - are beyond our control; as a consequence, romantic love becomes a way to choose the self we want from the multiplicity of roles we play and identities we possess in any given day. After all, a shared self is a self shared through mutual agreement with someone else, someone who presumably shares "our most treasured self-images, which we can then define as 'my real self,' even against the consensus of all the facts and the opinions of all the world, as well as against our own uncertainties" (Solomon, p. 155).

An analysis of the shared self functions well as a method for cultural critique because the shared self is always already at odds with itself. If self-consciousness is defined by the struggle to reconcile what we are with what we aren't (but would like to be), romantic love is the strategic (and ultimately doomed) struggle to define ourselves by controlling how others define us. Love is the tension between being-for-others and recovering one's being from others. Within this tension is Burnham's productive paradox. "[T]he ostensible aim of the lover is in principle self-contradictory," explains Wagoner (1997). "The lover seeks to recover his [sic] being by totally absorbing the freedom of the other, but if he is successful in this, the beloved is no longer 'other.' The beloved would no longer be separate enough to provide the sense of distinct identity that the self craves. In other words, if love achieves unity, it fails" (p. 103). With unity denied or at the very least perpetually deferred, the shared self is but a convenient (and elaborate!) fiction designed to maintain the illusion of the individual's separation from society.

The need to maintain this illusion helps explain why romantic love is essentially and axiomatically associated with personal and private roles. It also helps explain why romantic love can be so effectively employed to instantiate what Boler (1999) terms a "pedagogy of discomfort" (p. 176). In my own teaching experience, students and teachers alike find a critical interrogation of romantic love to be even more discomforting than questions of race and sexuality, the two topics Boler cites as causing the most discomfort (p. 176). Engaging the private can be uncomfortable enough; critiquing the personal can be downright disturbing, and no wonder. As Solomon (1990) explains, "Romantic love has utterly nothing to do with, and no concern for, social roles, a fact which is obvious in our literature, as princes fall in love with showgirls and empresses take as lovers their gardeners or mad monks from Siberia" (p. 158). Roles are indeed learned from society, but love (and by extension, identity) is felt and perceived at the personal level alone: "we cannot possibly imagine our lives or our conceptions of ourselves, much [less] the phenomenon of romantic love" without the "all-important" distinction between

personal and public roles (pp. 158-159). Social roles are transformed through love into personal roles. Roles that were once dependent upon cultural definitions and measurements become dependent upon the views and judgment of just one other individual: the lover. Public is rendered private. Romantic love, then, can be viewed as a dialectical struggle between the romantic ideal of shared unity and the cultural demand for individual autonomy and identity. The shared self, the self transformed in love, emerges - but never quite escapes - from this struggle.

Beliefs (and resistance) notwithstanding, love and identity are both social *and* personal constructs. Outside points of view are only seemingly irrelevant to the shared self that emerges in love. Being that nothing is completely beyond cultural influence, outside points of view are not only relevant, they're requisite. The shared self, then, is a rhetorical fiction, similar to the "real true" self it seeks to create and maintain. Whatever self we share with another we simultaneously share with many others, including our own multiplicity of selves-in-process.

LOVE COMES WALKIN' IN: PEDAGOGICAL POSSIBILITIES

In this section, I wish to situate the foregoing discussion of romantic love and the relational self more explicitly within classroom practices and, specifically, my own teaching experiences. Trained and positioned in the field of rhetoric and composition, I teach writing courses at the post-secondary level. More specifically, much of my teaching experience has been rooted in first-year composition, though I also teach a variety of other writing courses at both the undergraduate and graduate level. That said, I hope to show that romantic love, as either content or interpretive lens, has broad applicability and need not be the sole or even the central focus of any particular course, lesson, activity, or assignment. After all, the goal is not for students to become "experts" on romantic love as scholarly subject. While a course devoted entirely to the study of romantic love would no doubt be of value, my interest lies elsewhere, in the myriad and complex ways in which romantic love reflects, connects, and/or undergirds relations across innumerable structures of knowledge and power. In other words, because romantic love plays such a crucial role in identity construction (at least in the West), its sphere of influence extends far indeed, making its relevance as an academic topic and educational tool equally as wide. Put yet another way, what isn't touched to at least some degree by love?

Accordingly, my goal is to complicate students' ideas about romantic love in order to complicate as well their thinking about a variety of relationships and (inter)connections, including the notion of *relation* (and the relative) itself. Certainly, other tools and areas of inquiry could and have been fruitfully employed both within education and beyond.[2] I only mean to assert here that romantic love represents an additional implement in the educator's toolbox, and an especially sharp and useful one at that.

The courses I teach are frequently informed by cultural studies, particularly popular culture studies. In the case of first-year composition, I explicitly structure the course around such a perspective. I have chosen to design my courses in this manner because I feel a critical examination of popular culture invites my students both to locate themselves and to see beyond their own perspectives and lives. In this, I share Boler's (1999) vision of education "as a means to challenge rigid patterns of thinking that perpetuate injustice and instead encourage flexible analytic skills, which include the ability to self-reflectively evaluate the complex *relations* of power and emotion" (p. 156; emphasis mine). Related, to write critically means, for me, to think not only critically but also - or consequently - relationally, to recognize and make connections between and among. Doing so, however, is no simple or easy enterprise

when identity itself is historically predicated and defined along lines of difference. It becomes a matter of self-preservation (literally) to maintain culturally inscribed distinctions between I (us) and you (them).

In demonstrating the way in which identities are seen as learned from society but rendered personal and private through the mechanism of romantic love, Solomon (1990) points the way toward a pedagogy of relations that I see as an outgrowth and particularized instantiation of Boler's pedagogy of discomfort, a methodology for critically interrogating, among other reductive binaries, the personal/social dichotomy. Recall that the shared self is founded upon a conception of self as fundamentally incomplete and isolated, forever yearning for its complementary other half. Under this paradigm, roles learned from social contexts that hold any relevance whatsoever to the romantic relationship - and what roles don't? - are seen as transformed by the loving relationship into new, personal(ized) ones, thereby remaking the social into the personal and recasting the public into the private. From this stems many relevant and unfortunate consequences. Things learned from the culture can be "made," or rather re-made, into things personal and private in an epistemological process that echoes that of love - lover/beloved transfigured into victim/villain or superior/inferior while maintaining the same architecture of design. Prejudice and inequity become personal preferences or consequences rather than systemic products. Likewise, other perspectives and ways-of-being can be - indeed, have to be, if one's identity construct is to be uncritically maintained - dismissed out of hand as pertaining to the ever-ambiguous "someone else," to the "not me." The customs of a different culture, for instance, can be essentialized as "just them."

Not surprisingly, many students enter my classroom holding the view that race, gender, politics, class, religion, disability, and other social constructs are unproblematic matters of individual biology or personal choice. Himley (1997) makes a similar observation in regards to a course she teaches on the rhetoric of AIDS: "[D]espite over a decade of safer sex PSAs and other information, most of my students continue to locate themselves outside of the crisis through reproducing us/them binaries" (p. 127). Cheu, in an article co-authored with Brueggemann, White, Dunn, & Heifferson (2001), echoes this same point in regards to disability, asserting that the "categorizing of disability as a 'personal problem' is one of the major barriers to understanding disability as a societal construction" (p. 388). Whenever I've assigned texts that challenge notions of identity permanence or complacency, such as Mairs's (1990) "Carnal Acts," which vividly describes how multiple sclerosis has affected the author's life and sense of self,[3] or Hamilton's (1995) "Evil Woman? Bad Mother? Single Parent! Escaping the Epithets," my students have generally responded sympathetically to what they perceive as the writer's plight or struggle. Some students are also empathetic, stating, as one student recently did, that they can "relate" to what the writer "has been through." At first glance, such a response from students seems desirable. However, as Schneider (2005) warns, such textual readings are, in fact, detrimental to education. She asserts that educators, in wanting to create multicultural pedagogies, inadvertently foster narcissistic reading practices in students by encouraging them to identify with texts in ways that can nurture racism because these practices tend to collapse difference.

In learning to heed Schneider's warning, I have extended her critique to other teaching and learning practices. What I take from her argument is that students frequently ignore or invalidate difference in one of two ways: by dismissing it as simply "not me," or by refiguring it so that it conforms to an already known and stabilized "me." In the context of my argument here, we can say that, in either case, the social is egocentrically personalized. The difficulty in getting students to see beyond themselves is that, as Schneider points out, what they most frequently, easily, and

sometimes exclusively see is, in fact, themselves. Schneider traces the problem to consumer culture and misguided teaching practices; I believe the nearly ubiquitous presence of romantic love is also a major contributing factor (which is precisely why romantic love needs to be confronted and complicated). Romantic love too seeks to collapse difference into the singular. However, as discussed earlier, love nevertheless depends upon the continued existence and recognition of difference, an Other through which to define oneself. It is this inherent tension that makes love a productive pedagogical tool. Inserted into the classroom, these tensions can work to destabilize the fixity of beliefs.

In addition to texts such as Mairs's and Hamilton's, I now also include texts that challenge, in a variety of ways, conventional ideas about romantic love, such as a *National Geographic* article by Slater (2006) that reports on studies showing romantic love to be a biochemical reaction that evolved because it increases our species' chances of survival, or Nehring's (2005) review of Diana Shader Smith's *Undressing Infidelity: Why More Wives Are Unfaithful*, in which Nehring presents an account of marriage as cultural construct. Such texts highlight the fact that romantic love overflows with contradictions: supposedly universal and yet intensely intimate, personal yet social, private yet public, eternal yet fleeting, powerful yet fragile. Of course, other identity markers and constructs may very well be equally as complex and contradictory. Still, romantic love is especially useful because of its visibility, as both a presence in daily life and a concept with obvious strains and internal pressures. Consequently, simply bringing romantic love into the classroom and treating it as a subject worthy of serious academic inquiry, as something that can, in fact, be studied, can by itself contribute much to enacting a pedagogy of discomfort "by inviting educators and students to engage in critical inquiry regarding values and cherished beliefs, and to examine constructed self-images in relation to how one has learned to perceive others" (Boler, 1999, p. 176).

Historicizing romantic love has been one way in which I have invited such critical inquiry. Most of my students come into the classroom already well versed in the language, codes, and rituals of romantic love. In spite of this, they are often surprised, even shocked, to learn that romantic love itself has a history. For them, love has always been seen (or unseen) as a taken-for-granted fact, something akin to (and just as immutable as) the laws of thermodynamics. Providing my students with opportunities to explore and analyze the history and evolving nature of romantic love in the West has been an extremely effective method for introducing them to notions of contingency, situatedness, and a social constructivist epistemology.

Let me be clear: I do not teach a course on or about romantic love. Neither does romantic love dominate any of the courses I teach, including first-year composition. And, given that each class and context is different and unique, I do not follow, and thus cannot reproduce here, a prescribed curriculum or detailed plan on Love as Critical Praxis. Let me instead illustrate my use of romantic love as a pedagogy of relations by describing a series of discussions and moments that occurred recently in a course I was teaching. I had assigned an essay by Mayer (2009), "The New Sexual Stone Age," in which she argues that popular music has witnessed a return to rampant chauvinism. Mayer's contrasting of popular music's regressive attitudes with the more progressive trends of other cultural products and institutions caught my students' attention, particular her use of the term *return*. During a class discussion on the essay, several students began to discuss and debate the history not only of popular music but also, importantly, of sexism and chauvinism in America. This discussion carried over into the next class, at which time I widened the scope of the conversation by connecting our present discussion with a prior reading on gender roles. As a result of this rather productive discussion, I decided to

assign a writing project that asked students to research and compare marriage, broadly conceived, within Western cultures during two different times or eras, such as, say, the present and the sixteenth century. Crucially, I pushed them to look beyond customs, laws, and codes to consider the differing ways of feeling (and thus of thinking and being) engendered by the respective cultural conventions and societal regulations. To facilitate a widening of perspective, I incorporated in-class activities and mini-assignments that asked them to examine attitudes and beliefs about love and marriage in Eastern cultures.

For many students, this project led to illuminating lines of inquiry and unanticipated discoveries, as numerous students expressed in the reflective piece that accompanied the research paper. For instance, Andy,[4] who had decided to compare contemporary views toward love and marriage in the United States with those of the 1960s because he is a fan of *Mad Men*,[5] used the reflective essay as an opportunity to cast his gaze both far wider and far closer to home:

You know, this assignment made me think a lot about my dad, who was born and raised in the 60s. He's always been the disciplinarian of the family and can be kind of harsh sometimes. And maybe cold too. Like he can't be bothered or something. Thing is, I hadn't really thought too much before now about how he's that way not just with us [the children] but also with mom too. And so I'm thinking now, how's their marriage? Because it's not the kind of marriage I'd want for myself. But maybe my dad's a product of his time. You know, the 1960s. Which makes me a product of my time too, I guess. So what kind of marriage do I want anyway? What kind of man am I if I'm not like my dad?

I read Andy's reflective statements as movement toward a more relational mode of thinking. He is not displaying the kind of narcissism discussed by Schneider (2005), and not just because this part of the project required him to practice self-reflection. Rather, he has taken what he's learned about the 1960s and applied it faithfully to his own personal experiences. More importantly, he is connecting his own personal experiences with those of others, past and present, and in the process beginning to situate himself within the larger world.

That romantic love has a history and that it has changed over the course of that history in response to cultural alterations and pressures is not something most students have previously considered, and to begin to do so requires a widened perspective of the world and one's place within it, a move that can seem quite threatening. One inevitably comes up against the paradox that is love: "Am I still a self if I do not find myself in another - that is, am I lost or incomplete? And am I still myself if I do find myself in another - that is, have I given up my own individuality?" (Wagoner, 1997, p. 3). Questioning one's sense of self is frightening, but then, love always is, isn't it?

CONCLUSION; OR, WHY I STILL LOVE YOU

As is readily apparent, epistemological concerns reside at the heart of my pedagogy. Reality, of course, is not simply "out there" waiting to be directly transcribed. However, neither does it reside solely within the individual. Rather, one's knowledge of reality should rely upon an integration of both the external and the internal (the social/public *and* the personal/private). The materiality of this epistemological stance I have called the relational self, and the relational self is most palpable, visible, apparent, and influential in regards to romantic love.

By critiquing romantic love and the personal/social dichotomy upon which it stands, we can come to read and deconstruct the fiction of the shared self and thereby complicate notions of identity, power, and discourse. In the process, we

can learn, as Boler (1999) suggests, "to inhabit a more ambiguous sense of self," one that "acknowledges [the] profound interconnections with others, and how emotions, beliefs, and actions are collaboratively co-implicated" (p. 187). It is for this reason that I have come to view romantic love as a useful and potentially subversive pedagogical tool. Learning to read and analyze romantic love entails learning to complicate the concept of *relationship* itself, an enterprise that in turn can help students to think more critically as they come to see relations of all kinds (including those associated with power and identity) as inherently social and dialogic. The process can be discomforting, for them and for me. But eventually, one comes to find that, in learning to recognize, analyze, invent, and construct a wide array of relations and connections, little is lost and quite a bit gained.

REFERENCES

Ackerman, D. (1994). *A natural history of love*. New York, NY: Random House.

Boler, M. (1999). *Feeling power: Emotions and education*. New York, NY: Routledge.

Brueggemann, B. J., White, L. F., Dunn, P. A., Heifferon, B. A., & Cheu, J. (2001). Becoming visible: Lessons in disability. *College Composition and Communication, 52*(3), 368–398. doi:10.2307/358624

Burnham, C. (1993). Expressive rhetoric: A source study. In Enos, T., & Brown, S. C. (Eds.), *Defining the new rhetorics: Essays on twentieth-century rhetoric* (pp. 154–170). Newbury Park, CA: Sage.

Carson, A. (1986). *Eros the bittersweet: An essay*. Princeton, NJ: Princeton University Press.

Coontz, S. (2005). *Marriage, a history: From obedience to intimacy, or how love conquered marriage*. New York, NY: Viking.

Foucault, M. (1980). *Power/knowledge: Selected interviews and other writings, 1972-1977 (C. Gordon* (Gordon, C. (Trans. Eds.)). New York, NY: Pantheon Books.

Grosz, E. (1994). Refiguring lesbian desire. In Doan, L. (Ed.), *The lesbian postmodern* (pp. 67–84). New York, NY: Columbia University Press.

Hamilton, S. J. (1995). Evil woman? Bad mother? Single parent! Escaping the epithets. In *My name's not Susie: A life transformed by literacy* (pp. 79–90). Portsmouth, NH: Boynton/Cook.

Himley, M. (1997). The classroom as city. In Himley, M., Le Fave, K., Larson, A., & Yadlon, S.Political Moments Study Group (Eds.), *Political moments in the classroom* (pp. 119–130). Portsmouth, NH: Boynton/Cook.

Hindman, J. (2001). Making writing matter: Using "the personal" to recover(y) an essential(ist) tension in academic discourse. *College English, 64*(1), 88–108. doi:10.2307/1350111

Lacan, J. (1978). *The four fundamental concepts of psycho-analysis (J.-A. Miller* (Sheridan, A. (Trans. Ed.)). New York, NY: Norton.

Mairs, N. (1990). Carnal acts. In *Carnal acts: Essays* (pp. 81–96). Boston, MA: Beacon.

Mayer, A. (2009). The new sexual stone age. In Maasik, S., & Solomon, J. (Eds.), *Signs of life in the USA: Readings on popular culture for writers* (6th ed., pp. 312–314). Boston, MA: Bedford/St. Martin's. (Original work published 2001)

McNay, L. (1992). *Foucault and feminism: Power, gender, and the self.* Boston, MA: Northeastern University Press.

Neal, M. (1993). Social constructionism and expressivism: Contradictions and connections. *Composition Studies: Freshman English News, 21*(1), 42–48.

Nehring, C. (2005). Fidelity with a wandering eye [Review of the book *Undressing infidelity: Why more wives are unfaithful,* by Diane Shader Smith]. *Atlantic (Boston, Mass.), 296*(1), 135–141.

Sartre, J.-P. (1956). *Being and nothingness: An essay on phenomenological ontology* (Barnes, H. E., Trans.). New York, NY: Washington Square Press.

Schneider, B. (2005). Uncommon ground: Narcissistic reading and material racism. *Pedagogy, 5*(2), 195–212.

Shor, I. (1999). What is critical literacy? *Journal of Pedagogy, Pluralism, and Practice, 1*(4). Retrieved June 29, 2010, from http://www.lesley.edu/journals/jppp/4/shor.html

Singer, I. (1984). Courtly and romantic: *Vol. 2. The nature of love.* Chicago. IL: Chicago University Press.

Slater, L. (2006). True love. *National Geographic, 209*(2), 32–49.

Smith, P. (1988). *Discerning the subject.* Minneapolis, MN: University of Minnesota Press.

Smith, S. (1990). Self, subject, and resistance: Marginalities and twentieth-century autobiographical practice. *Tulsa Studies in Womens Literature, 9*(1), 11–24. doi:10.2307/464178

Solomon, R. (1990). *Love: Emotion, myth, and metaphor.* Buffalo, NY: Prometheus Books.

Wagoner, R. (1997). *The meanings of love: An introduction to philosophy of love.* Westport, CT: Praeger.

ADDITIONAL READING

Banks, W. P. (2003). Written Through the Body: Disruptions and "Personal" Writing. *College English, 66*(1), 21–40. doi:10.2307/3594232

Bean, J. (2003). Manufacturing Emotions: Tactical Resistance in the Narratives of Working Class Students. In Jacob, D., & Micciche, L. R. (Eds.), *A Way to Move: Rhetorics of Emotion and Composition Studies* (pp. 101–112). Portsmouth, NH: Boynton/Cook.

Bell, J. S. (1997). *Literacy, Culture, and Identity*. New York: Peter Lang.

Berlant, L., & Warner, M. (1998). Sex in Public. *Critical Inquiry, 24*(2), 547–566. doi:10.1086/448884

Bishop, W. (1992). I-Witnessing in Composition: Turning Ethnographic Data into Narratives. *Rhetoric Review, 11*(1), 147–158. doi:10.1080/07350199209388993

Bordo, S. (1993). *Unbearable Weight: Feminism, Western Culture, and the Body*. Berkeley, CA: University of California Press.

Corder, J. W. (1985). Argument as Emergence, Rhetoric as Love. *Rhetoric Review, 4*(1), 16–32. doi:10.1080/07350198509359100

Giddens, A. (1992). *The Transformation of Intimacy: Sexuality, Love, and Eroticism in Modern Societies*. Stanford, CA: Stanford University Press.

Halperin, D. M. (1990). *One Hundred Years of Homosexuality and Other Essays on Greek Love*. New York: Routledge.

Hindman, J. (2002). Writing an Important Body of Scholarship: A Proposal for Embodied Rhetoric of Professional Practice. *JAC, 22*(1), 93–118.

Holstein, J. A., & Gubrium, J. F. (2000). *The Self We Live By: Narrating Identity in a Postmodern World*. New York: Oxford University Press.

Kipnis, L. (1998). Adultery. *Critical Inquiry, 24*(2), 289–327. doi:10.1086/448876

Kirtley, S. (2003). What's Love Got to Do With it?: Eros in the Writing Classroom. In Jacob, D., & Micciche, L. R. (Eds.), *A Way to Move: Rhetorics of Emotion and Composition Studies* (pp. 56–66). Portsmouth, NH: Boynton/Cook.

Lacan, J. (1978). *The Four Fundamental Concepts of Psycho-Analysis (J.-A. Miller* (Sheridan, A. (Trans. Ed.)). New York: Norton.

Linton, S. (1998). *Claiming Disability: Knowledge and Identity*. New York, NY: New York University Press.

McLaren, P. (1988). Schooling the Postmodern Body: Critical Pedagogy and the Politics of Enfleshment. *Journal of Education, 170*(3), 53–83.

Newkirk, T. (1997). *The Performance of Self in Student Writing*. Portsmouth, NH: Boynton/Cook.

Orner, M., Miller, J., & Ellsworth, E. (1996). Excessive Moments and Educational Discourses that Try to Contain Them. *Educational Theory, 46*(1), 71–91. doi:10.1111/j.1741-5446.1996.00071.x

Ronald, K., & Roskelly, H. (2002). Embodied Voice: Peter Elbow's Physical Rhetoric. In Belanoff, P., Dickson, M., Fontaine, S. I., & Moran, C. (Eds.), *Writing with Elbow* (pp. 210–222). Logan, UT: Utah State University Press.

Sedgwick, E. K. (2003). *Touching Feeling: Affect, Pedagogy, Performativity*. Durham, NC: Duke University Press.

Spigelman, C. (2001). Argument and Evidence in the Case of the Personal. *College English, 64*(1), 63–87. doi:10.2307/1350110

Stenberg, S. J. (2002). Embodied Classrooms, Embodied Knowledges: Re-thinking the Mind/Body Split. *Composition Studies, 30*(2), 43–60.

Stewart, R. (2001). Teaching Critical Thinking in First-Year Composition: Sometimes More Is More. *Teaching English in the Two-Year College, 29*(2), 162–171.

Vickers, N. J. (1993). Lyric in the Video Decade. *Discourse: Theoretical Studies in Media and Culture, 16,* 6–27.

Welch, N. (1993). One Student's Many Voices: Reading, Writing, and Responding with Bakhtin. *JAC, 13*(2), 493–502.

Yancey, K. B. (1998). *Reflection in the Writing Classroom.* Logan, UT: Utah State University Press.

KEY TERMS AND DEFINITIONS

Cartesian Dualism: The idea, as put forth by René Descartes, that the mind and body are distinct and separate.

Dialogic: Concept developed by Russian philosopher Mikhail Bakhtin to denote, among other things, the manner in which any utterance gains its meaning through its use in relation to a number of factors, including context, audience, and prior utterances.

Epistemology: Branch of philosophy concerned with the nature of human knowledge.

Hegemony: The dominance of one group over others; as developed by Antonio Gramsci and others, hegemony refers to the way in which dominant groups maintain their dominance not only by direct force but also by persuading subordinate groups to consent to the ideas and values of the dominant groups.

Heteronormativity: Short for normative heterosexuality; societal rules that force individuals to conform to heterosexual identity constructs (such as traditional masculine and feminine gender roles).

Social Constructionism: The view that social phenomena, including what we perceive as reality, are not natural givens but rather human creations or inventions.

Subject: Term employed by poststructuralists to emphasize the fact that individuals do not possess innate, stable identities; instead, individuals are subjected to external forces that render them products rather than sources of meaning.

ENDNOTES

[1] I wish to thank the anonymous reviewers for their insightful comments on an earlier version of this essay. I also want to thank Julie Myatt for helping me to clarify and develop my argument.

[2] Queer and disability studies come readily to mind.

[3] For an in-depth discussion of how Mairs's essay can challenge students, see the section authored by Heifferon (pp. 382-387) in Brueggemann, White, Dunn, Heifferon, & Cheu (2001).

[4] A pseudonym.

[5] *Mad Men*, a popular television program in the U.S., is set in the early 1960s.

Chapter 16
Performing Dissident Thinking through Writing:
Using the Proprioceptive Question to Break out of the Classroom

Kaitlin A. Briggs
University of Southern Maine, USA

ABSTRACT

Theoretically informed by Julia Kristeva's linkage of political dissidence with thinking, this chapter explores a deconstructive tool used to develop dissident thinking through writing in the post-secondary classroom: the "Proprioceptive Question," a central feature of Metcalf and Simon's Proprioceptive Writing™(2002). After this method's fundamentals are addressed, the devaluing of subjectivity throughout schooling, as played out through literacy learning, is surveyed. Analysis of the Proprioceptive Question in terms of its discursive components and examples of its academic uses follow in order to understand what makes this question such a powerful method for developing subjective engagement in the university setting. Just as dissidents separate from existing regimes to organize their opposition, this chapter concludes that student writers via the Proprioceptive Question create space between themselves and their thought content to challenge their own ideas. Thus the question serves as a form of political intervention, a disruptive pedagogical practice.

PRELUDE

The notion of *the dissident* was formulated in the post-World War II era behind the Iron Curtain, where Soviet bloc intellectuals, critics, and particularly writers - the most famous being Solzhenitsyn

- often *disappeared*, some placed under house arrest, others forced into psychiatric facilities and labor camps or permanently exiled, stripped of citizenship. These dissidents wrote in opposition to regime writers whose work supported the "ideological state apparatus" (Althusser, 1971). In the 1960s, as they took to the streets, American

DOI: 10.4018/978-1-61350-495-6.ch016

and European university students adopted the "*dissident function*"- a term later used by Bulgarian theorist and psychoanalyst Julia Kristeva (1986a, p. 294). Against these cross-cultural backdrops, Kristeva published her 1977 essay "A New Type of Intellectual: The Dissident" in which she remarks that: "true dissidence today is perhaps simply what it has always been: *thought*" (p. 299).

In the post Berlin Wall era, as the age of information technology has taken root with a rapidity and pervasiveness few could foresee, Western student dissidence has progressively dissipated, along with the Soviet dissident writer/regime writer binary and the harsh realities it produced. Yet Kristeva's coupling of dissidence and thinking has relevance particularly for educational settings in our new century's second decade. It is thinking - dissident thinking versus regime thinking - that must now provide opposition, engage cultural criticism, and structure a path to new social and political formations. Deleuze and Guattari (1987), for example, in their critique of Western, "arborescent" thought (p. 15) articulate an alternative reality based on "nomad thought" (Massumi, 1987, p. xii) with its rhizomatic outcroppings and "lines of flight" arriving and departing (Deleuze & Guattari, 1987, p. 3). An elaboration of Foucault's "outside thought" (Massumi, 1987, p. xiii), uncultivated nomadic thought travels without restriction in and around existing trees of thought, accepted knowledge, and dominant cultural values.

Teachers as cultural workers (Friere, 1998) are charged with developing engaged, participatory, democratic citizens who can ask questions and think nomadically but who must also be prepared to master appropriate skills in order to enter the free market, global economy where *out-of-the-box* thinking may be highly valued. However, teaching critical, nomadic thinking is easier said than done. Educators may ask: what does critical, nomadic, outsider, or dissident thinking look like in practice? And can it even be taught in school, a place where students learn skills but

also a place defined by norms and the need to conform? Teachers as cultural workers, teaching for transformative learning (O'Sullivan, Morrell, & O'Connor, 2002), may value dissident thinking, but it remains nonetheless elusive, an abstraction, perhaps an impossibility to teach and to enact.

This chapter explores critical, in-class language practice as a way to crack through that impossibility, in particular an adaptation of Metcalf and Simon's (2002) process writing method, Proprioceptive Writing™, for the post-secondary classroom. This writing method centers on the use of a deconstructive tool, the *Proprioceptive Question*, as a way for writers to explore and contest meaning and to activate dissident thinking - in writing. In her essay, Kristeva describes three types of dissidents (1986, p. 295). The first reflects those Soviet bloc dissident writers who constitute opposition within a system, but who, Kristeva explains, are insiders nonetheless and thus caught in Hegel's master/slave binary because of that positioning. The psychoanalyst who counters religious practice forms the second type of dissident. But Kristeva's third type of dissident best speaks to conceptualizing a disruptive pedagogical writing practice: the experimental writer, who undermines "the law of symbolic language" (Moi, 1986, p. 292) to create new syntheses, however temporary or enduring, through which "the master discourses begin to drift and the simple rational coherence of cultural and institutional codes breaks down" (Kristeva, 1986a, p. 294).

Placing a word, not under Derridian erasure, but under and into question, the Proprioceptive Question (the PQ) serves to undermine language - one's own. By asking the PQ, writers align themselves with the interrogative form, rather than predominantly making declarative statements one after the other and accepting them as fact. Moreover, this realignment via the PQ positions writers to interrogate jargon as well as ideological and dogmatic traces in their own thinking and to challenge their most ingrained assumptions.

In what follows, I contextualize the Proprioceptive Question more broadly both in terms of *proprioception* and in terms of Proprioceptive Writing™ and the specifics of this writing practice. A term I have used elsewhere, the "subjective engagement" (Briggs, 2009, p. 111) enacted by student writers using the PQ interrupts a complex schooling history, a history in which subjectivity has predominantly been devalued. While it is true that thinking accompanies life from moment to moment in the ebb and flow of consciousness that makes us human, our thinking, through the processes of enculturation, is not naturally in a critical stance. Children learn early on to disregard their own thinking (Fox, 1990). This chapter surveys this devaluing of subjectivity, how it occurs through literacy learning, in particular writing, as schooling progresses. With this context set, using the PQ in the university classroom setting serves as an intervention in and a counterpoint to this history.

In order to understand what makes the Proprioceptive Question such a powerful method for engaging subjectivity and for performing dissident thinking, I follow this history by parsing it into its discursive components. The chapter concludes with an examination of the question's academic uses, including examples, as well as its political ramifications. When student writers use the PQ, space emerges between themselves and their thought content (Metcalf & Simon, 2002, p. 8). In that space, they become experimental writers; they become strangers to their "own country, language, sex, identity" (Kristeva, 1986a, p. 298) - to their own thinking. Thus their Proprioceptive Questions become political acts, and for those moments they embody the dissident function of the intellectual, as described by Kristeva.

A working premise of this chapter is that theoretical discussion of disruptive pedagogies should be countered with new applications that put into play the ideas they aspire to - content and form thus in concert, echoing one another - applications that are themselves disruptive. Thus, breaking with traditional academic conventions, I have organized this chapter disruptively. Rather than only discuss the Proprioceptive Question as a method for developing dissident thinking, I perform it in the text as a model so that readers can see it in action.

THE PERFORMANCE

The history of the term *proprioception* begins in 1906 with neurophysiologist Sir Charles Scott Sherrington (Sacks, 1990, p. 43). In the 1970s the term achieved some notoriety when American beat poet Charles Olson used it as a poem title (1974, p. 17). And a famous Oliver Sacks case - "The Disembodied Lady" - involved a woman who had no proprioception (1990, pp. 43-54). Recently, discussion of *proprioception* across disciplines has increased, particularly in the psychology literature (PsycINFO lists 450 references to proprioception since 2000) and in literary theory (see, for example, Altieri, 2003).

What do I mean by *proprioception*? Often referred to as the "sixth sense" (Sacks, 1990, p. 43), proprioception is a physiological reference. Attached to the muscles, the *proprioceptors* function together as an involuntary system that operates below our conscious awareness: "that continuous but unconscious sensory flow from the movable part of our body (muscles, tendons, joints), by which their position and tone and motion are continually monitored and adjusted" (Sacks, 1990, p. 43). Essential to our effective functioning, this system allows us to locate and relocate ourselves spatially and, for example, to shift, change, and move around an obstacle while walking down the street or to walk in pitch black darkness. But most importantly, it is through proprioception that we experience our bodies as *our own* (Sacks, 1990, p. 43).

What do I mean by *our own*? The word *proprioception* etymologically derives from the Latin, *proprius*, meaning "one's own" (*Random

House Dictionary, 1987, p. 1551). This owning, however, is not fixed, but fluid and ongoing, not something we possess as much as something we experience. Yet proprioception is not only physiological. Our thought flow also accompanies us - and is distinctly our own. Reflecting our own individual ideas, concerns, fantasies, questions, grievances, remembrances, our thinking is not random. As a writing-to-learn *modality*, Proprioceptive Writing™ taps into this thought flow.

What do I mean by *modality*? Different from other forms of process writing, such as stream of consciousness writing or Elbow's freewriting (1971), Proprioceptive Writing™ directs writers to focus on and listen to their emerging thinking as they write. This listening takes form through asking and writing out the Proprioceptive Question: "What do I mean by _____?" (Metcalf & Simon, 2002, p. 34). Writers first *interrupt* their thought flow; stop, ask, and write the Proprioceptive Question of a particular word or short phrase just used; then proceed to continue writing in response. For example, after this last sentence, I might stop, ask, and write, "What do I mean by *interrupt*?"

In its full blown form, Metcalf and Simon's writing method involves structured twenty minute, open-ended writing sessions, which writers then read out loud. Committed to the method's pedagogical possibilities, I conducted a teacher research study theorizing the method and modifying it for the public university setting (Briggs, 1996). Since completing that study, I have used it as a central component of my Honors Program courses at the University of Southern Maine, USA over the past fifteen years. These courses include "Thinking and Writing in Honors: Focus on the Essay," an interdisciplinary, alternative first year writing course, and the "Honors Thesis Workshop," a thesis preparation course for students in their final undergraduate year (see Briggs, 2010a). In practical terms, I have shortened the writing sessions, maintained the reading out loud component as an option when and where possible, but particularly

zeroed in on the Proprioceptive Question as an interactive, in-class, writing-to-learn tool used to connect texts read, students writing, and class discussion as well as to improve writing fluency. However, because critical thinking development is a stated objective in these courses, my primary motivation has been to strike at the heart of student *complacency.*

What do I mean by *complacency*? As honors students, they have generally learned to perform well in school, but I often find their work flat and mechanical, even robotic. Almost stereotypical, their thinking can lack originality. As university students, they want to sound smart; but, imitating academic discourse and characterized by a tendency toward over-inflated word choices and strings of prepositional phrases that can suffocate fresh ideas, this need to sound smart siphons off energy. Moreover, they are not always committed to their ideas. And without a personal stake in their ideas, from where will the motivation to revise their writing come? As a disruptive pedagogical practice, asking the Proprioceptive Question serves as a method for locating that personal stake and unlearning that detachment. I want to know what students actually think, not what they think they are *supposed to* be thinking.

What do I mean by *supposed to*? Students learn very early in school to disregard their own thinking - their subjective, personal, familial, and experiential knowledge - in favor of teacher-dictated, textually-based knowledge (Fox, 1990). This devaluing of subjectivity evolves as schooling progresses and follows the trajectory of literacy learning across the educational hierarchy.

Even though the dominant materiality of the computer screen as a text, as a textual surface, is rapidly transforming the structure of *the book* in Western post-modern culture, reading books still plays a significant role in children's early literacy. Children's storybooks at home and early readers in school function as central platforms for their literacy learning. Learning to read, however, means learning to obey authority, the authority of the text but also the authority of parents, teachers, and other adult figures who have access to the knowledge and codes needed to enter those texts, those worlds, and to read them correctly in terms of prescribed, accepted norms (Baker & Freebody, 1989).

In aggregate, a series of sub-literacies or micropractices that must be mastered comprise the coordination needed for early literacy. Adhering to a specific ordering, for example, books open at *the front* to set up page turning, right to left. Image and word pairings run in parallel, page to page, enacting the mathematical one-to-one correspondence principle. Correct rhythm and pacing are essential. Once the words have been decoded, line by line, top to bottom, left to right, a slight pause occurs, a break in the flow, as the page is then turned. Together these micropractices structure the narrative progression. In part they are a function of mechanics; but as children absorb and attend to these cues, the locus of authority shifts. In order to achieve in school, children must learn to defer to what the teacher tells them, to master these textual cues, and to background their own experiences, reactions, and emotions. Fox (1990) points out that "students learn through educational experience to exclude their social identities as a resource for learning and understanding" (p. 7), although white middle class children will generally experience the most compatibility between home and school (Heath, 1983). By pointing to the non-neutrality of these textual practices and teacherly, parental explanations, the "metacommentary" (Baker & Freebody, 1989, p. 164) accompanying children's early literacy experiences, Luke (1988, 1993) furthers this analysis by conceptualizing literacy as more than a skill, an ability, or competency and implicating it in the reproduction of dominant cultural values.

In the 1960s and 1970s, expressive writing pedagogies seemed to lay challenge to this devaluing of subjectivity in schooling. By engaging the writer, an increased sense of writing ownership would emerge, these pedagogies assumed, but they only partially took hold. In their landmark study, Britton, Burgess, Martin, McLeod, and Rosen (1975) use the term "expressive" to describe writing that is close to the self, reflective, and speculative (pp. 88-90). They report that by the time the students in their study finished secondary school, writing categorized as expressive sharply declined, virtually disappeared, and was progressively superseded by writing that recapitulated information (p. 165). But this reduction of the expressive raises a red flag because it is in the expressive mode that our most original, most insightful, thinking is found, albeit in nascent form. In analyzing this finding, Britton et al. (1975) explain that "curricular aims did not include the fostering of writing that reflects independent thinking; rather, attention was directed towards classificatory writing which reflects information in the form in which both teacher and textbook traditionally present it" (p. 197). Furthermore, expressive writing, though less structured and more informal, provides a crucial matrix for the development of other kinds of writing: ". . . in the emergence of any original thinking, there is an expressive stage in that thinking whether the writing is ultimately informative, poetic, or persuasive" (p. 30). This decline of the expressive as these students progressed through their schooling is *troublesome* and has been left relatively unanswered in the composition literature.

What do I mean by *troublesome*? Cleary's (1991) ethnography of American secondary school student writers later echoes Britton et al.'s findings. These student writers explain that their success in school depends on their grades. However, getting a good grade is a precarious enterprise that largely depends on how well they are able to psyche out and to reproduce what each teacher wants. A new class means a new teacher to study; thus this psyching out looms large in their approach to their writing assignments. For these student writers, over time their writing and their thinking become less theirs - and more the property of their teachers. By inserting a thinking subject, in-class, non-instrumental, exploratory process writing using the Proprioceptive Question interrupts this history and activates instead *subjective engagement* out on the page.

What do I mean by *subjective engagement*? Dissidence requires dissonance, not just letting everything sail smoothly by; it's disquieting. Dissidents sit not in objective relationship to the regimes they oppose; on the contrary, they are subjectively engaged; they resist because what occurs disturbs - it matters to them. They demonstrate that caring by *not* going along with, by differentiating themselves from, by establishing space between themselves and the existing party line. Similarly, highlighting a word by asking the Proprioceptive Question creates a break in the status quo, the flow, as writers call their own words into question. But to take up the dissident position in relationship to their own thinking, writers must become participants, activists, alert to their own regimes of thought. The more Proprioceptive Questions asked, however, the more emboldened writers become. The question operates as a banner, placard, manifesto, protest song configured by three critical discursive features that interact together to produce this subjective engagement: its use of the first person pronoun, its auditory emphasis and recursive gesturing, and its structure via the interrogative form as a prompt to explore meaning.

Nineteenth Century American writer Henry David Thoreau claimed that in fact the first person is always speaking or writing (Lopate, 1995, p. xxxi), but, depending on the genre, this reality is obscured. The first person pronoun in the Proprioceptive Question anchors the writer's subjectivity out on the page, going directly against the grain of the earlier training described. Another important moment in this earlier training occurs during middle school literacy lessons when students first learn to write *papers* and to tackle the analytical expository composition mode, historically synonymous with philosophical discourse, its infrequent personal referencing, and its tight argumentative line.

In my introductory, first year alternative writing course, one assignment involves writing a literacy narrative in which the students must reflect on their own history learning to read and write and consider what was significant in that process. Over fifteen years giving this assignment, some noteworthy patterns have emerged. One such pattern points to the many students who were instructed during middle school not to use "I" in their papers but interpreted this instruction quite literally, from a developmental point of view (Briggs, 2009, p. 111). Beyond simply editing out the "I," they interpreted their teachers' instructions to mean that they were neither to invest themselves nor involve their own interests and concerns in their writing assignments. And this interpretation may not have been wrong. Indeed, this imperative to avoid the first person (pronoun), rationalized as a function of mechanics or genre conventions, may reflect a deep-seated bias against subjectivity, the personal, and the possibility of emotional expression in the classroom as schooling progresses, particularly in post-secondary education (Boler, 1999, p. xviii).

Language is never neutral, always has a point of view. The use of the first person pronoun in the Proprioceptive Question claims that possibility of emotion, that non-neutrality, that point of view - but does so dynamically in order to investigate and contest rather than to reproduce meaning. Moreover, the PQ is very particularly structured. Similar as they may seem, for example, the question is not "What is meant by _____?" but rather "What do *I* mean by _____?" Structured in the passive voice, the former line of inquiry signals the need to background the writer's thinking, to foreground instead the thinking of others, and to consult the experts, the databases, or the dictionary; the latter signals the reverse: that the writer's *thinking presence* is summoned in order to define, unpack, and explore meaning.

What do I mean by *thinking presence*? An important feature of Proprioceptive Writing™ is the directive to "write what you hear" and to listen to what unfolds out on the page (Metcalf & Simon, 2002, pp. 32-34). With this auditory emphasis there exists an intimacy. I can see two people engaged in conversation from quite far away; but in order to hear their conversation, I need to be fairly close by; thus there exists a relationship between hearing and proximity. Belenky, Clinchy, Goldberger, and Tarule (1986) clarify that "Unlike the eye, the ear requires closeness between subject and object. Unlike seeing, speaking and listening suggest dialogue and interaction" (p. 18). But in asking the Proprioceptive Question, this closeness, dialogue, and interaction occur within the writer as an intra-subjective exchange that permeates its use - the self with the self - a speaking voice and a "listening presence" (Metcalf & Simon, 2002, p. 34). In this intra-subjective exchange intimacy occurs as a tri-partite process: first, the writer's thinking attention is attenuated *reflexively* toward words already written to investigate; second, a moment of connection occurs as the question is formulated and asked of a particular word; and third, moving forward, the question is actually written out on the page, and the writer continues on to explore the answer through more writing.

What do I mean by *reflexively*? As writers write in Proprioceptive Writing™, they ask the Proprioceptive Question not just of any word (or short phrase) but of a word already thought and written. In order to ask the PQ, a writer must have heard or noticed their own unfolding language. In this way asking the PQ is recursive, meaning that it loops back, most often to a word within the last two sentences, in order to move forward. This backward movement, what I call *recursive gesturing*, indicates that "I," as the writer, have noticed, actually heard, my own thinking, a critical feature of subjective engagement. To begin, I have students review what they have written and choose

language to investigate that, like an embossed design, sticks out, that they might underline or put in quotation marks. Sensory experience surrounding the words evokes a connection in the writer that includes a physiological component, accessing "the felt sense" (Gendlin, 1981), the nonverbal underside of language (see also Perl, 1988, pp. 114-115), a more generalized term for proprioception.

Perhaps most critically, the Proprioceptive Question functions as a prompt to enter a word via its felt sense. Metcalf and Simon (2002) explain that "the PQ is an attention-focusing tool. It helps you to amplify your thought, express it more accurately, and reflect on it more meaningfully" (p. 35). But this expressive and reflective amplification engages an intensely personal dimension, *uncomfortable* as that can sometimes be.

What do I mean by *uncomfortable*? Metcalf and Simon further clarify that

When you ask the PQ, you are inquiring into the psychological or emotional sense the word has for you. Certain words arouse memories, failings, attitudes in your consciousness; they are 'charged' for you by your experience ... The PQ enables you to unpack and investigate them ... (pp. 35-6)

Although we operate as if emotion and intellect are separated from one another, Vygotsky (1986) corrects this misconception by pointing out that in reality these two parts of us are mutually entangled: "every idea contains a transmuted affective attitude toward the bit of reality to which it refers" (p. 10). As a prompt to explore meaning, the Proprioceptive Question brings writers closer to their affective attitudes, that charged experience, what matters to them.

Meaning is individual but it is also cultural, part of shared reality. To fully grasp the function of the Proprioceptive Question as a prompt to explore meaning in a larger, cultural context, however, necessitates theoretical discussion about the nature of language: what it is and how it functions. Poststructuralist notions of language best illuminate the possibilities of the PQ as a deconstructive tool for engaging and critiquing, formulating and reformulating meaning. Kristeva considers language to be a "complex signifying *process* rather than a monolithic *system*" (Moi, 1985, p.152). In this linguistic terrain the production of meaning circulates and shifts relationally and contextually. Characterized by Derrida's open-ended, "free play of signifiers" (Moi, 1985, p. 9), this de-centered production and circulation of meaning can be anyone's game and makes language "appropriable" (p. 158), a particularly significant theoretical implication for students. Student writers generally have been trained to understand meaning as part of the monolithic system that Kristeva critiques. From their point of view, meaning already exists in the dictionary or their textbooks or on the internet and precludes them because it has already been established by experts, authority figures, parents, and teachers. Meaning exists as a thing that students passively receive, not a process they are positioned to engage. Oppositional to this training, using the PQ *repositions* writers/thinkers/students as cultural agents for whom meaning becomes "constructed, contested, incessantly perspectival and polyphonic" (Lather, 1991, p. xx).

What do I mean by *repositions*? The Proprioceptive Question performs many functions. In practical terms, it is a method for unpacking academic jargon and disciplinary terminology. In a blog post about his honors thesis, a student named Nigel, a philosophy major, asks the PQ and then writes in response:

What do I mean by *cybernetics*? *[emphasis added] I believe that this is a good question to ask myself at this early juncture ... To be frank though, I feel like I don't really know what this term is supposed to mean, so it is difficult to say what I am trying to get at with it. To be sure, I grasp the wiki-overview insofar as cybernetics is the study of regulatory systems. Yet, as with the closely-related systems theory, the interdisciplinarity of this field makes it difficult to figure out where one is supposed to learn its basics and its history, which is to say, there is no Cybernetics 101 in 2009.*

... Yet, perhaps I'm being evasive about all this. What I am trying to get at is that I am used to thinking of cybernetics as this relatively brief attempt to unite the sciences to articulate a kind of general ontology of relations, a theory built not on the study of atomistic units (literal atoms, organisms, words, singular human beings, etc.) but rather the processes and systems that these individuals emerge out of ...

Nigel first begins considering existing, accepted definitions of cybernetics, what it is "supposed to" mean. Engaging Deleuzian and Guattarian lines of flight away from his evolving text, this consideration sends him off to consult Wikipedia for a summary of the term and then to an overview of "systems theory," a parallel field. But Nigel arrives back into his own text with what may be a new insight: that cybernetics is an interdisciplinary field drawing from many areas, and thus as a fundamental field of knowledge, it may not exist. In the second paragraph, this insight launches Nigel into his own thinking, "what I'm trying to get at," where he then proceeds to articulate and to synthesize what he himself knows about cybernetics.

Nigel's blog post demonstrates the way that the Proprioceptive Question operates as a springboard into further thinking. It functions as a counterpoint to the abbreviated, high-speed communication occurring via technology, the collapsing of encoded content, the convergent thinking, utilized in text messaging and in forms such as Twitter. Conversely, slowing writers down, asking the PQ prompts divergent thinking and results in a fuller, more complete explanation.

When developing a syllabus for my "Honors Thesis Workshop" several years ago, I needed to flesh out further our program's distinct approach to thesis research, so I explored in writing:

*["**What do I mean by research?***"] Research is an organized, intentional study of a subject using a wide range of resources and methods. It's a progressive accumulation of information. But more than that, research is about entering the unknown and creating knowledge. And the demands of thesis research even fold in a more complex dimension. The word thesis is derived from the Greek word tithemi, meaning "I put, place or establish," so a thesis is a place where you take your stand. However, tithemi is a verb, not a noun, and specifically a verb constructed in the first person. It's not uncommon for beginning researchers to get overwhelmed with the abundance of information connected to their emerging topics. And it's easy to incorrectly focus the bulk of their energy on accumulating it. But thesis research isn't about gathering this material. It's about creating meaning. It's about being the author of your project. It's a back and forth process between author and material. The material per se isn't really what is important; what's important is the process of establishing your stand within it. (Briggs, 2010b, p. 2)*

Like Nigel, asking the Proprioceptive Question launches me into more in depth, sustained thinking. Although I left out the PQ itself, I was able to insert the material I generated in response to the question directly into the syllabus. As they approach revision, student writers often struggle with how to develop their ideas further. Choosing a significant word to explore by using the PQ, as

I did here, provides students with a productive strategy for expanding first drafts of their writing.

In pedagogical terms, asking the Proprioceptive Question also helps students connect with a text, linking their subjectivities to their objects of study, the personal with the academic. Upon reading Cynthia Ozick's short story/novella *The Shawl* about a mother and daughter relationship during and after the Holocaust, a student named Alex wrote in an in-class writing activity:

*. . . [This] is probably one of the most touching and devastating works I've ever read. I think that it has to do with being a parent. Having a child **transforms** [emphasis added] the entire being. Enriching and expanding yet constraining all at once. **What do I mean by transforms?** [emphasis added]. Before finding myself a mother I was a different person on most levels. I was highly confrontational while being a pacifist. I was more outgoing & self-assured. Now Cody brings doubt, fear & an enlarged sense of empathy into my being along with the other things that come with his being in my life. I never openly felt my fear as I do now. I hid it more, denied its existence. Now I fear. Fear for his safety, that I'm screwing up, doing it wrong. Fear promotes doubt & caution. Things I never heeded before. (Briggs, 1996, pp. 119-120)*

Connecting text read and student writing, the PQ brings Alex's subjectivity into the classroom and allows her to give "an account of [her]self" (Butler, 2008, p. 19). Students do attempt to bring what matters to them into their school assignments, but in post-secondary education, their professors, working at cross-purposes, often remain oblivious to these attempts (Herrington & Curtis, 2000). For Alex, reading Ozick's short story becomes a path to understanding her own experience as a mother and a single parent, but the key to being able to articulate that understanding occurs through writing. Furthermore, when Alex asks, "What do

I mean by transforms?" the question takes her into an array of emotions - doubt, fear, and empathy - a radical moment in the university setting, as Boler declares (1999). The PQ launches Alex's account. Meaning invites emotion; emotion brings students closer to what matters to them. And when that articulation occurs in the classroom, a disruptive pedagogical moment intrudes upon the normative order and flow.

CODA

Asking the Proprioceptive Question, then asking it again, looping back and forth, fragmenting the linearity of thought flow out on the page, strikes a path, like following Ariadne's thread, that forms itself as it progresses. When writers move in with the PQ, they crack through, interrupt, the smoothness, the seamlessness, of the writing surface. Kristeva calls for new "aesthetic practices" in order "to counter-balance the storage and uniformity of information by present-day mass media, data-bank systems and, in particular, modern communication technology" (1986b, p. 210). As an aesthetic practice, asking and answering the PQ in writing intersects process and product, evokes rather than dictates, and breaks down the material presented, not by topic and paragraph, but by proprioception, by felt sense, interrupting thought flow. These operate together to create a fragmented rather than a unitary text that works "against imposition of a monolithic direction of meaning" (Lather, 1991, p. 10). A moment of independence characterized by movement, the practice, like deconstruction, intervenes "on behalf of the exuberance of life against a too-avid fixing and freezing of things" (Cocks, cited in Lather, 1991, p. 83).

However, asking the Proprioceptive Question as an aesthetic, linguistic practice across all of its possible uses has political ramifications. As writers take up positions as thinkers out on the page, ask the PQ, formulate, explore, and argue

over meaning, they enter a battleground. Foucault (1981) describes "the conflicts, triumphs, injuries, dominations and enslavements that lie behind these words" (p. 216). Asking the PQ provides an entry point into this battleground, transforming writers/thinkers/students, like Nigel and Alex, into those who can break down language, contest dominant meanings, and press forward into new, unknown directions.

Unlike the former Soviet bloc and other contemporary totalitarian regimes that maintain social control through external, state-mandated measures, democracies achieve social control voluntarily, individually, and internally (Chomsky, 1989). Within the privacy of thought, democratic citizens will self-regulate, censor, and conform. Asking the Proprioceptive Question destabilizes that self-censorship. Etymologically, the word *dissident* derives from the Latin, *dissidēre*, "to sit apart" (*Random House Dictionary*, 1987, p. 570), so there is a sense of *space between* embedded in the word. Thus dissident thinking and Proprioceptive Writing™ share geographical properties. Asking the Proprioceptive Question provides the possibility of an always moving space between writer and thought content - and in that space, the beginnings of dissidence stir.

REFERENCES

Althusser, L. (1971). *Lenin and Philosophy and Other Essays*. New York, NY: Monthly Review Press.

Altieri, C. (2003). Reading Feelings in Literature and Painting. In *The Particulars of Rapture: An Aesthetics of the Affects* (pp. 231–254). Ithaca, NY: Cornell University Press.

Baker, C., & Freebody, P. (1989). *Children's First School Books*. Cambridge, MA: Basil Blackwell.

Belenky, M. F., Clinchy, B. M., Goldberger, N. R., & Tarule, J. M. (1986). *Women's Ways of Knowing: The Development of Self, Voice and Mind*. New York, NY: Basic Books.

Boler, M. (1999). *Feeling Power: Emotions and Education*. NY: Routledge.

Briggs, K. (1996). *The Individual as a Site of Struggle: Subjectivity, Writing, and the Gender Order*. Unpublished doctoral dissertation, University of Massachusetts, Amherst.

Briggs, K. (2009). Thesis as Rhizome: A New Vision for the Honors Thesis in the Twenty-First Century. *The Journal of the National Collegiate Honors Council, 10*(2), 103-114.

Briggs, K. (2010a). Individual Achievement in an Honors Research Community: Teaching Vygotsky's Zone of Proximal Development. *Honors in Practice, 6*, 61–68.

Briggs, K. (2010b). *The Honors Thesis Workshop*. Course syllabus, University of Southern Maine Honors Program, Portland, ME.

Britton, J., Burgess, T., Martin, N., McLeod, A., & Rosen, H. (1975). *The Development of Writing Abilities* (pp. 11–18). London, UK: Macmillan.

Butler, J. (2008). An Account of Oneself. In Davies, B. (Ed.), *Judith Butler in conversation: Analyzing the texts and talk of everyday life* (pp. 19–38). New York, NY: Routledge.

Chomsky, N. (1989). *Necessary Illusions: Thought Control in Democratic Societies*. Cambridge, MA: South End Press.

Cleary, L. M. (1991). *From the Other Side of the Desk*. Portsmouth, NH: Boynton/Cook Publishers.

Deleuze, G., & Guattari, F. (1987). *A Thousand Plateaus: Capitalism and Schizophrenia* (Massumi, B., Trans.). Minneapolis, MN: University of Minnesota Press.

Elbow, P. (1971). *Writing Without Teachers*. New York, NY: Oxford University Press.

Foucault, M. (1981). The Discourse on Language. In *The Archaeology of Knowledge* (pp. 215–237). New York, NY: Harper & Row Publishers.

Fox, T. (1990). *The Social Uses of Writing*. Norwood, NJ: Ablex Publishing Co.

Friere, P. (1998). *Teachers as Cultural Workers: Letters to Those who Dare Teach*. Boulder, CO: Westview Press.

Gendlin, E. T. (1981). *Focusing*. New York, NY: Bantam Books.

Heath, S. B. (1983). *Ways with Words: Language, Life and Work in Communities and Classrooms*. Cambridge, UK: Cambridge University Press.

Herrington, A., & Curtis, M. (2000). *Persons in Process: Four Stories of Writing and Personal Development in College*. Urbana, IL: National Council of Teachers of English.

Kristeva, J. (1986a). A New Type of Intellectual: The Dissident. In Moi, T. (Ed.), *The Kristeva reader* (pp. 292–300). New York, NY: Columbia University Press.

Kristeva, J. (1986b). Women's Time. In Moi, T. (Ed.), *The Kristeva reader* (pp. 187–213). New York, NY: Columbia University Press.

Lather, P. (1991). *Getting Smart: Feminist Research and Pedagogy with/in the Postmodern*. New York, NY: Routledge, Chapman & Hall, Inc.

Lopate, P. (Ed.). (1995). *The Art of the Personal Essay: An Anthology from the Classical Era to the Present*. New York, NY: Anchor Books/ Doubleday.

Luke, A. (1988). *Literacy, Textbooks and Ideology: Postwar Literacy Instruction and the Mythology of Dick and Jane*. Philadelphia, PA: The Falmer Press.

Luke, A. (1993). Stories of Social Regulation: The Micropolitics of Classroom Narrative. In Green, B. (Ed.), *The Insistence of the Letter: Literacy Studies and Curriculum Theorizing* (pp. 175–194). Pittsburgh, PA: University of Pittsburgh Press.

Massumi, B. (1987). Translator's foreword: Pleasures of Philosophy. In Deleuze, G., & Guattari, F. (Eds.), *A Thousand Plateaus: Capitalism and Schizophrenia* (pp. ix–xv). Minneapolis, MN: University of Minnesota Press.

Metcalf, L. T., & Simon, T. (2002). *Writing the Mind Alive*. New York, NY: Ballantine Books.

Moi, T. (1985). *Sexual/Textual Politics: Feminist Literary Theory*. New York, NY: Methuen & Co.

Moi, T. (1986). Editor's Introduction: A New Type of Intellectual: The Dissident. In Moi, T. (Ed.), *The Kristeva Reader* (p. 187). New York, NY: Columbia University Press.

O'Sullivan, E., Morrell, A., & O'Connor, M. A. (Eds.). (2002). *Expanding the Boundaries of Transformative Learning*. New York, NY: Palgrave.

Olson, C. (1974). *Additional Prose*. Bolinas, CA: Four Season Foundation.

Perl, S. (1988). Understanding Composing. In Tate, G., & Corbett, E. P. J. (Eds.), *The Writing Teacher's Sourcebook* (pp. 113–118). New York, NY: Oxford University Press.

Random House Dictionary of the English Language, 2nd ed., unabridged (1987). New York, NY: Random House, Inc.

Sacks, O. (1990). *The Man who Mistook his Wife for a Hat and Other Clinical Tales*. New York, NY: Harper Collins Publishers.

Vygotsky, L. (1986). *Thought and Language* (Kozulin, A., Trans.). Cambridge, MA: MIT Press.

ADDITIONAL READING

Achbar, M. (Ed.). (1994). *Manufacturing Consent: Noam Chomsky and the Media. The companion book to the award-winning film*. Cheektowaga, NY: Black Rose Books.

Berlin, J. (1987). *Rhetoric and Reality: Writing Instruction in American Colleges, 1900 – 1985*. Carbondale, IL: Southern Illinois University Press.

Denzin, N. K. (2003). *Performance Ethnography: Critical Pedagogy and the Politics of Culture*. Thousand Oaks, CA: Sage Publications.

Derrida, J. (1976). *Of Grammatology* (Spivak, G. C., Trans.). Baltimore, MD: Johns Hopkins University Press.

Derrida, J. (1978). *Writing and Difference* (Bass, A., Trans.). Chicago: University of Chicago Press.

Derrida, J. (1981). *Dissemination* (Johnson, B., Trans.). Chicago: University of Chicago Press.

DuPlessis, R. B. (1990). *The Pink Guitar: Writing as Feminist Practice*. NY: Routledge, Chapman & Hill.

Johnson, B. (1987). *Mallarmé as Mother. A World of Difference* (pp. 137–143). Baltimore, MD: Johns Hopkins University Press.

Keller, E. F., & Grontkowski, C. R. (1983). The Mind's Eye. In Harding, S., & Hintikka, M. (Eds.), *Discovering Reality* (pp. 207–224). Dordrecht, Holland: Reidel Publishing Co.

Kristeva, J. (1986). Revolution in Poetic Language. In Moi, T. (Ed.), *The Kristeva Reader* (pp. 89–136). NY: Columbia University Press.

Luke, A. (1992). The Body Literate: Discourse and Inscription in Early Literacy Training. *Linguistics and Education, 4*(1), 107–129. doi:10.1016/0898-5898(92)90021-N

Marks, E., & de Courtivron, I. (1980). *New French Feminisms*. Brighton: Harvester.

Petersen, E. B. (2008). Passionately Attached: Academic Subjects of Desire. In Davies, B. (Ed.), *Judith Butler in Conversation: Analyzing the Texts and Talk of Everyday Life* (pp. 55–67). NY: Routledge.

Said, E. W. (2004). *Humanism and Democratic Criticism*. NY: Columbia University Press.

KEY TERMS AND DEFINITIONS

Dissident: A critic of an existing political regime actively engaged in protest and resistance. The modern construction of the dissident developed in the Soviet bloc countries during the era after World War II and before the destruction of the Berlin Wall (1989).

Dissident Thinking: Thinking that turns back on itself by calling into question one's own words, phrases, images, or ideas, laying challenge to the internal regime.

Experimental Writing: As described by Kristeva: experimental writing was produced by avant-garde writers such as Mallarmé and constitutes its own form of dissidence. Like social and political structures, language also prescribes to rules and conventions. Experimental writing, like that of the French feminist school of writing that includes such writers as Irigaray, Cixous, and even Kristeva herself, who titled her famous dissertation "Revolution in Poetic Language," challenges these linguistic laws.

Proprioception: A physiological system through which we are able to move and locate ourselves spatially. This system functions unconsciously and was first identified by the Nobel Prize winning neurophysiologist Sir Charles Scott Sherrington in 1906.

Proprioceptive Writing™: A process writing method developed by Metcalf and Simon and presented in their book, *Writing the Mind Alive* (2002). Writers have twenty minute sessions in which they produce "writes" that are then read out loud. Metcalf and Simon place particular emphasis on hearing thought flow. Like the proprioceptive system itself, thought flow also shifts and changes, constantly adjusts, and is distinctly inscribed by the thinker.

Proprioceptive Question: The prompt used by Metcalf and Simon (2002) in their writing method: "What do I mean by _____?"

Subjective Engagement: Historically, objectivity and detachment have been cardinal academic values, but in post-positivistic research, the researcher's presence, influence, and potential bias must be accounted for and tracked. Subjective engagement points to the importance of involvement, personal stake, and desire in thinking, writing, studying, and even research.

Chapter 17
The Risk of Rhetorical Inquiry:
Practical Conditions for a Disruptive Pedagogy

Drew Kopp
Rowan University, USA

ABSTRACT

In this chapter, the author provides a theoretical outline for a practice of rhetorical inquiry in the college writing classroom, and focuses on three conditions that permit this inquiry to enact a "pedagogy of discomfort" (Boler, 1999). The first condition calls for pedagogues to amplify the performative dimension of language to disrupt what Dewey terms the "quest for certainty." Second, students and teachers work to reconfigure their current perspectives through undergoing dialogic encounters between incongruous perspectives. Third, these performative and dialogic encounters must reiterate with increasing complexity and within increasingly unfamiliar and complex contexts. After an extensive theoretical exposition of these three conditions for a disruptive pedagogy, the author presents a few illustrative instances in the college writing classroom.

INTRODUCTION

To have an experience [with language] is an activity of a human subject who, through one method or another, controls and manages and possesses that experience as his own. In contrast, to undergo an experience with language means that language strikes us, befalls us, overcomes us, overwhelms and, most importantly, transforms us. [...] Indeed, Heidegger calls the hermeneutical experience of language "the event of Appropriation," an event that occurs when words overcome and overwhelm and transform us. (Worsham, 1987, pp. 227-228)

DOI: 10.4018/978-1-61350-495-6.ch017

Building from Heidegger's (1971) view, Worsham argued to disrupt the drive to codify and systematize writing, and to persuade writing instructors to remain open to the inquiry language invites us to undergo. For Heidegger, to "undergo an experience with language … means to let ourselves be properly concerned by the claim of language by entering into and submitting to it" (p. 57). What would it mean to *submit* to and properly take up the *claim* language poses rather than merely pursue the conservative aim to master its complexities and codify it into handy simplicity? At the most immediate level, submitting to language's claim promises to disrupt the conservative norm that regards language as a mere conceptual tool to be understood prior to use. Furthermore, if we accept the invitation to undergo this experience, we confront a novel insight concerning the relationship between identity and language: despite commonplace understanding, we do not use language - not at all. Rather, language uses us.

I will extend Worsham's project while pursuing precisely what she questions by prescribing how writing instruction might work to disrupt the drive to control and master language. This frame includes three practical conditions that promote a rhetorical inquiry wherein both students and instructors challenge and disrupt the drive to pursue what Dewey (1929) calls the "quest for certainty" (p. 8). This inquiry promises to cultivate rhetorical agility sufficient to respond to problems that unfamiliar genres of activity pose to us, problems that challenge and displace the certainty we strive to possess about what we already know (Darwin, 2003; Fleming, 2003).

The rhetorical practices of *articulation, reconfiguration*, and *reiteration* comprise the three practical conditions for rhetorical inquiry:1

1.   *Articulating* or *amplifying* the often-overlooked performative dimension of language calls both speakers and addressees to acknowledge and take up the transformative claim language makes;

2.   *Reconfiguring* a perspective held with certainty occurs through undergoing a dialogic encounter with an equally compelling but incongruous perspective;

3.   *Reiterating* or *cross-appropriating* the first two conditions within a series of increasingly complex and unfamiliar contexts works to cultivate rhetorical intelligence.

Cultivating rhetorical intelligence calls for us to be receptive to the *anomalous* within everyday situations, and consequently, to allow the anomalous to challenge and disrupt conservative norms.

BACKGROUND

The most notable forebears of rhetorical inquiry are the Old Sophists of Ancient Athens, who attracted customers with tantalizing promises. By empowering students to practice making the weaker argument appear to be the stronger and to see themselves as the measure of all things, Protagoras promised his students they would develop the rhetorical power to maintain their personal lives such that they could act within the political arena - a promise Plato anxiously interrogated as ungrounded in real knowledge (Plato, 1961). This educational promise continued with the rhetorical education that was productive of Isocrates' rhetor seeking advantage; of Cicero's ideal, philosophical orator delighting, moving, and educating with eloquent wisdom; and of Vico's rhetor inventing from the topics of the *sensus communis* in order to bring *phronesis* - a practical, rhetorical wisdom - to bear on the course of civic life (Ijsseling, 1976; Atwill, 1998).

This line of pedagogic practice enacts an inquiry into everyday, situated rhetorical practice: After unraveling the view that understands human beings as substances to be known and mastered, rhetorical inquiry reveals us to be history-shaping beings participating with and contributing to others engaged in everyday situations (Spinosa et al,

1997). Indeed, according to Vanderstraeten and Biesta (2006), it is only through "participation in the social practices in which meaning is formed and transformed" that education is even possible, where "it is not the teacher who directly educates the student, but that it rather is *the situation itself in which both participate*" (p. 167). However, as Boler (1999) posited, when "educators and students engage in a collective self-reflection and develop accountability for how we see ourselves, and as we question cherished beliefs, we are likely to encounter such emotions as fear and anger" (p. 188). Why practice a "pedagogy of discomfort," as Boler defined it, if doing so risks bringing students and teachers to the limits of identity and thus triggering moments of anxiety? The rationale is emancipatory: in pushing the disruptive limits of rhetorical inquiry, both instructors and students practice inhabiting "morally ambiguous" selves with an enhanced ability to interrogate, disrupt, and most importantly, revise conservative norms.

Such acts of revision involve designing new practices to cope with anomalous problems conservative norms overlook and actively avoid, for acknowledging a problem requires us to reconfigure our perspective. Becoming morally ambiguous requires developing the "ability to recognize [to articulate and amplify] what it is that one doesn't want to know, and how one has developed emotional investments to protect oneself from this knowing" (Boler, p. 200). Perhaps we avoid knowing that, despite our emotional investments to the contrary, the conservative norms that reinforce our identities as "true" are indeed rhetorically and socially constructed, and that furthermore, our existence as subjects independent of the situations we are called to participate in depends on perspectives often dismissed as valueless. In calling us to see divergent viewpoints as worthy, rhetorical inquiry invites us to repeatedly relinquish the drive to be right about what we already know and to instead *become*

rhetorical—tolerant of profound uncertainty and empowered to perform with invented authority within indeterminate social situations.

THREE CONDITIONS FOR RHETORICAL INQUIRY

Amplifying the Claim Language Makes

The call to bear witness to the value of a divergent perspective involves a performative request, a claim disruptive in its challenge for both the speaker and the addressee to enter an inquiry that cannot be resolved with pat answers, formulae, or tips and techniques. Rather than merely pursue answers, rhetorical inquiry invites participants to respond appropriately to challenges each performative request generates. I mean *performative* in the specialized sense Austin (1962) introduced, wherein a speech act *performs* through the act of speech itself: it does what it says (e.g., to declare, promise, request, etc). Rather than bringing us to judge whether a particular statement is true or false (e.g., "the sun is shining"), speech acts confront us at the level of our social existence, and consequently, our response is necessary but risky (e.g., "your assignment is to write a rhetorical analysis of a commercial advertisement"). Because we can never predict how anyone (even ourselves) will respond to a speech act (Kent, 1993), any response serves to disrupt subject positions that depend on remaining aloof from unpredictable social situations.

Responses to performatives - called "uptakes" in Speech Act Theory - span from complete resistance to total willingness to respond even when lacking a certain prescription. At the former end of the spectrum, we "take up" the performative address as a threat to our identity, and at the later end we respond to the speech act as an invitation to innovate within the constraints of the genre (Freadman, 1994). For Lyotard (1985), to innovate, we must see that the "ability to judge does not hang upon the observance of criteria [conservative norms]"; indeed, behind the ability to evaluate a speech act and respond is the "power to invent criteria" that effectively disrupt the prescriptions conservative norms impose (p. 17). The performative constitutes new social realities that call forth uptakes from addressees of the speech act, which is what Lyotard (1984) emphasized as the distinguishing quality of performativity: an agonistic game where each

language partner, when a "move" pertaining to him is made, undergoes a "displacement," an alteration of some kind that not only affects him in his capacity as addressee and referent, but also as sender. These "moves" necessarily provoke "countermoves" - and everyone knows that a countermove that is merely reactional is not a "good" move. (p. 16)

Performative countermoves bring participants to undergo displacements - that is, disruptions. Merely reacting to a performative move is informed by conservative norms under threat; we look to the familiar in order to cope with an inexplicable anomaly disclosed to us through a performative request. "That is why," says Lyotard, "it is important to increase displacement in the games," for doing so makes unexpected and novel responses possible (p. 16).

First year student writers, for instance, when responding to a request to perform rhetorical analysis, often "take up" the unfamiliar genre *as* a genre they are already well-acquainted with, such as the five paragraph essay, the book report, e-mail, and texting, all of which are co-articulated with the genres of summary (what something means), narrative (what happened), and evaluative argumentation (good/bad, like/dislike, etc.). Since conservative norms guide

us to see and respond to unfamiliar requests in familiar terms, the pedagogue is then challenged with *continuously* disclosing the irreducible gap between student uptakes and the innovative moves the performative request calls for. Consequently, the instructor must set up a series of performative requests designed to generate breakdowns, where retreating to familiar practices - such as writing according to simplistic formulae or writing only when one already "knows" what to say - fall short. Instructors must also take up the uncomfortable emotions that emerge once students realize the extent to which their familiar ways of responding no longer serve as "good" moves. I argue that these responses derive from a culturally inherited conservative norm that commits us to preserve identity through maintaining certainty and a complacent self-satisfaction in prior knowledge.

The distanced and apathetic perspective from which we customarily regard the world - the conservative norm that works to limit our participation with others - is the legacy of Descartes, who doubted anything infected with uncertainty and probability until he found the one purity that could never succumb to doubt: the doubter. Bordo (1987) argued that as a central practice at the root of the Western quest for objectivity, the resulting Cartesian purity of self-knowledge has provided the root sense of the modern subject existing independent of situation, and from its advantageous ahistorical position, this Cartesian subject can pass judgments on the world by virtue of its indubitable self-certainty.

This experience of the self as separate ramifies into the most everyday understanding of the self and the world. According to Spinosa et al. (1997), we "can find Cartesianism going strong in our personal wills to be right, our individual sense that what others say in heat is not to be trusted," and in "our individual sense that we should be responsible for knowing the facts of the matter in any discussion we undertake" (p. 8). In other words, we avoid acting unless we have prior knowledge that will, as Dewey (1929) suggested, ensure clear-headed "security in the results of action" (p. 39). As a result, our Cartesianism often precludes taking actions whose results might undermine desires to remain safe and certain. "We wish," add Spinosa et al, "for the architect's plan of the whole before we build a building, write a book, begin a career, or raise a child" (p. 8). Of course, significant consequences result from this Cartesian posture. In avoiding the risk of actual pragmatic situations until we know how to perform "correctly," we sidestep the possibility of participating in and effecting history (p. 10).

Thus practitioners of rhetorical inquiry have long sought ways to open students to a more direct and intimate relationship with language in order to empower them to impact everyday life, whether in personal, professional, or civic spheres (Lanham, 1974; Halloran, 1975; Fleming, 2003). However, practitioners have always to cope with resistance at every turn (Kill, 2006), and not just in their students: "a routine habit," noted Dewey (1922), "when interfered with generates uneasiness, sets up a protest in favor of restoration and a sense of need of some expiatory act" (p. 75). Indeed, deviation from habitual practice is uncomfortable to the degree our cultural identities survive through the protective force of conservative norms: "We cling to ways of doing things that promote and perpetuate the concerns that constitute our cultural identities even when we are shown more effective ways of coping" (Spinosa, et al., p. 147), which for Bawarshi (2003) explains why "writers will resist certain genres that conflict in some way with their commitments" (p. 99). Amplifying the performative dimension of language thus serves as a key practical condition for a disruptive pedagogy, especially when the performative invites the Cartesian in us to enter dialogic encounters with genres and correlative perspectives that thwart attempts to retreat to the familiar and comfortable.

Reconfiguring Perspectives

Once we encounter the call to respond without certainty, we begin to undergo what Burke (1954) called a "conversion downward," which begins the rhetorical process of "perspective by incongruity" (p. 88). According to Burke, any perspective will seek to maintain its pious orientation by *converting downward* other perspectives that appear to be incongruous, effectively dismissing them as lacking merit or value. Here *piety* is the moral principle that guides the formation of interpretations which coordinate actions, determine meaningful relationships, and permit transference between situations, all toward conservatively justifying and maintaining an orientation's existence. Because piety supplies "a desire to round things out, to fit experiences together into a unified whole," and provides us with "*the sense of what properly goes with what*" (p. 74), as soon as a disorientation occurs by virtue of *perspective by incongruity* - when we take up a performative request - a corresponding disruptive affect (a dis-eased orientation) emerges.

The risky uptake would be for addressees to revise or reconfigure their orientations, beginning with the inclusion of the divergent orientation's point of view they originally dismissed. This inclusion necessitates a shift in subjectivity toward a morally ambiguous stance. Crowley (2006) noted that the acceptance "of one's opponents as legitimate adversaries requires a change in subjectivity, a change in orientation toward antagonistic discourse, and an attitudinal change toward those with whom one disagrees" (p. 22). Seeing enemies as adversaries reconfigures the contest between incongruous perspectives as valuable (rather than as something to avoid in order to preserve identity), where one actually values an opponent's way as worthy of honor. Such a shift in subjectivity brings us to *experience* our own position from the point of view of the opposing value, that is, we undergo a "perspective by incongruity."

It is rare, however, to undergo a conversion downward without resistance. In fact, key to rhetorical inquiry is to welcome even highly resistant responses, as each expression of resistance calls for the development of a rhetorical subjectivity practiced at bringing the speech acts of an external authority into relationship with the integrity of an internal perspective. Rhetorical subjectivity emerges during a dialogic encounter, where the piety of our "home" perspective governs our responses to a disruptive *authoritative discourse* through the filter of an *internally persuasive discourse*. I understand authoritative discourse and internally persuasive discourse in the manner that Bakhtin (1981) distinguished them, where every authoritative discourse has its own internally persuasive discourse that "shows up" when we encounter a significant challenge from an incongruous perspective - when an authoritative discourse addresses our own authoritative discourse. A sufficiently disruptive request threatens to convert downward the "home" authoritative discourse and its internally persuasive discourse. If the conversion is "successful," Bakhtin explained, the challenging discourse performs "no longer as information, directions, rules, models and so forth," ordinarily easily dismissed, but instead strives "to determine the very bases of our ideological interrelations with the world, the very basis of our behavior; it performs here as *authoritative discourse*, and [as a newly inscribed] *internally persuasive discourse*" (p. 342). Rather than merely *having* an experience of language, Cartesian subjectivity shifts toward ambiguity through *undergoing* an experience with language (a conversion downward), where we intentionally take what appears to be a weaker, dismissible argument, amplify it as worthy of esteem, and consequently reconfigure our perspective.

For example, on the very first day of class, in order to encounter rhetorical inquiry *as a practice* rather than as a mere subject of study, students read the course description from the syllabus. I request that they set aside the familiar practice of reading for information, and to instead investigate what kind of person the text *requests* them to become. Students discuss in small groups what emotional responses they had while reading, which then opens up a class discussion concerning what language *does* to affect mood and understanding (rhetorical analysis), rather than merely concerning what it *is* or what it *represents* (summary): in short, students practice relating to the syllabus as a performative speech act, which is quite far from regarding this document as worthy of a mere cursory glance.

A student might say, as an instance of internally persuasive discourse resisting this new genre of performance, "Since I don't know what 'pedagogy' means, I felt uncomfortable when I read that part of the course description. The language wants me to be smarter than I think I am." This response does not simply inscribe the student in a weak posture in relation to the authority of the instructor; this kind of response is closer to a Cartesian assertion dismissing whatever threatens self-certainty. The threat occurs as such *because* the addressee takes up the requests of the syllabus - to be willing to be challenged, to undergo surprises, to grow and develop beyond current expectations - *as* requiring the adoption of a position lacking authority, and conservative norms call for various degrees of resistance to such threats.

The responses of an internally persuasive Cartesian discourse then serve as performative speech acts of students that challenge the self-certainty of the instructor. Rather than dismissing such responses as resisting authority, the rhetorical pedagogue must innovate to include the response as the most obvious step to take within the structure of the course. Another similar anecdote is of a conversion downward I experienced when a first-year honors student quoted Jonathan Swift to attack my use of language in the syllabus as unnecessarily abstruse, claiming that lack of clarity disguised incompetence. I realized right away the necessity to avoid the urge to save face, and instead, I let the risky game of rhetorical analysis continue. Applauding the student's observation, I asked the class to investigate what the student's language invited *me* to become, as well as what it invited the other students to become, especially in relation to my role as the "teacher." The class discussion then turned toward the role language plays in shaping identity, and how it structures authority and power between teachers and students. The point here is that the disruptive effects of rhetorical inquiry reach all participants. Furthermore, the degree to which an instructor is unwilling to relinquish certainty - that is, authority - is the degree to which rhetorical inquiry will fail to disrupt. If students can bear witness to the unmasking of an instructor's authority and so enter into dialogic encounters that rhetorical inquiry calls for, it becomes possible to permit and even welcome the breakdowns posed by the problems rhetorical inquiry discloses through constant reiteration in each unfamiliar writing situation.

Reiterating Performative and Dialogic Encounters

While I promote and honor the exercise of familiar writing practices, I work to slowly take away the option for students to rely on these practices with each new iteration of the first two conditions: amplification of the performative dimension of language and the reconfiguration of perspective that ensues. In effect, through cross-appropriating and performing maneuvers such as juxtaposing incongruous perspectives as equally valuable, students work to continuously disclose increasingly difficult problems that common sense overlooks. Rather than resting in a state of mastery, participants in rhetorical inquiry continue to disclose previously unnoticed problems, and with each new problem, a disruptive breakdown announces itself. Rhetorical inquiry, then, is about developing sensitivity to problems revealed in moments of breakdown - when ways of coping with everyday situations fail - which then allows for the possibility of designing new ways of being that can cope

with recurrent breakdowns (Winograd & Flores, 1986, p. 69). The arrangement and reiterative progression of perspectives by incongruity then serves to unveil problems, what Freire (2003) calls *boundary situations*, and with sustained reiteration, a durable rhetorical subjectivity emerges.

A boundary situation announces itself when an "untested feasibility" posed by an incongruous authoritative discourse emerges as a new genre of activity, though it is one that Cartesian subjectivity initially resists because of the looming threat it poses of a reconfigurative conversion downward. Herein lies the core pedagogical principle I have taken from Gadamer (1977):

There is always a world already interpreted, already organized in its basic relations, into which experience steps as something new, upsetting what has led our expectations and undergoing reorganization itself in the upheaval. [...] Only the support of familiar and common understanding makes possible the venture into the alien, the lifting up of something out of the alien, and thus the broadening and enrichment of our own experience of the world. (p. 15)

This encounter between "experience" and the always already interpreted world (i.e., the world disclosed to us by conservative norms) is precisely the encounter with a boundary situation, a breakdown that threatens identity with an untested feasibility, which more often than not only occurs as a marginalized practice to be avoided and dismissed because of its potential disruptiveness. Indeed, Gadamer emphasized an approach to understanding "existence" as exceeding the boundaries of science and its tools: "Boundary situations," Gadamer summarized, "are those situations in human life in which the individual must choose and decide without being guided by the certain knowledge provided by [Cartesian] science," which in many ways accounts for the consistency of the familiar genre of practice writing students often work from (pp. 137-138). Given the urgency of those moments when boundary situations occur, one must make a rhetorical move even if based on indeterminate probability: The performative call is to experiment, even though it is impossible to predict the outcome. Gadamer reflected that "one has to undergo such extreme situations of decision and choice in his own existence, and precisely how one faces up to them, how one acts, for instance, when death is near, brings out - *existere* - what he himself really is" (p. 138). However, rather than "really is," I am saying that boundary situations, especially if arranged within a series, bring out what someone is *rhetorically*. Thus, when encountering the boundary of one's customary understanding of everyday situations, a call arises for the exercise of rhetorical intelligence (*phronesis*), not merely the assertion of knowledge (*episteme*). Rhetorical action in the risky realm of probability results in our existing, or "standing out," in ways that promise to broaden and enrich our experience of the world.

From this point of view, if a teacher or student merely reasserts the already understood basic relations when encountering a boundary situation - which in the end defies familiarity to the core - no learning, no growth would be possible. As a customary practice that mechanically downgrades another authoritative discourse, understanding the unfamiliar in terms of the familiar only serves to maintain certainty concerning what is already known and understood, and it attempts to circumvent an encounter with a boundary situation in order to preserve the identity of the Cartesian subject. This then provides the rationale for reiterating the conditions of rhetorical inquiry. For instance, the request to revise a piece of writing from the point of view of an incongruous perspective flies in the face of conservative norms that seek to reconfirm a writer's original point of view as "right" and in no need of change. On the other hand, if through the dialogic reiteration or cross-appropriation of the practices of rhetorical inquiry, *performed within a space arranged such that the challenge is more likely to be faced*, encounters

with a boundary situation will challenge familiar practices and so disrupt the identity derivative of those practices such that a series of responses becomes possible - the designing of practices, of "limit-acts" (Freire, p. 99) appropriate to the new genre of performance.

In reiterating a series of boundary situations, rhetorical inquiry invites the cultivation of a subjectivity who performs such limit acts as listening receptively to difference and "trying on" or testing untested feasibilities. But another boundary situation follows, wherein we are challenged with how to deal with the divide between what occurs as familiar and as disruptive problems. Despite the commitment to disrupt Cartesian subjectivity, rhetorical inquiry also calls on its practitioners to reiterate and so undergo a conversion downward such that we once again *honor* the drive for certainty, "the familiar and common understanding," as valuable, though this occurs from a perspective that "exists" between incongruous perspectives, namely, a morally ambiguous, rhetorical subjectivity. Consequently, an important limit act rhetorical inquiry calls for is a fusion of incongruous perspectives within any given dialogic encounter. Students should not discard "home" practices, as they are necessary to the dialogue of rhetorical inquiry of the course. Customary "home" practices will continue to play significant roles throughout each reiterating dialogic encounter, providing the crucial positions from which the practices of rhetorical inquiry may be performed. Attempts to permanently convert Cartesian subjectivity down ultimately stifle and shut down rhetorical inquiry, because doing so presupposes an unquestioned critical truth as unassailably dominant.

Employing the Request to Revise as a Disruptive Strategy

One way I practice rhetorical inquiry to effect the emergence of a series of boundary situations and untested feasibilities is to challenge the customary understanding most students have concerning the distinction between editing and revising. What we customarily do when we go to revise writing is actually *edit*, for the activity of editing presupposes and ultimately clarifies and preserves the perspective the piece of writing reflects. Embedded within this customary practical understanding is the tranquil mood that "revision as editing" reinforces: editing poses no threat to one's self-understanding. However, revision does - to the degree one undergoes a perspective by incongruity when practicing revision.

Structuring this move involves setting up effective ground rules whose practical meaning defies the drive for certainty, thereby allowing for experiences of revision at the level of subjectivity as the inquiry reiterates assignment by assignment. For instance, I *promise* my students from the beginning - and especially at moments when boundary situations appear - "all that is necessary to perform well is to show up, on time, having done the work." However, the pragmatic meaning of those practices, as the course unfolds, transforms in such a way that defies the customary expectations my students have about what it means to be in a writing course - expectations given by conservative norms. More specifically, I take advantage of the Cartesian manner of relating to language as descriptive of static states of reality, and then by degrees I amplify the performative nature of my *promise* cum *request* for my students to show up, on time, having done the work.

A common student expectation limits application of this promise to the classroom, which I continually work to challenge, arranging the sequence of reiterative steps such that it becomes increasingly difficult for students to wait until the "last minute" to get the work done on time. Given the practical value I place on in-class workshopping, drafts are due to group members on days prior to class to allow for time to read and prepare comments. Each new draft in an assignment sequence requires taking up a purpose and audience incongruous with prior drafts. Even the e-mails

sent with drafts attached must include specific reflective commentary addressed to the workshop group, sharing what the writer intended and what the writer thought they actually accomplished. Thus, students must perform writing practices nearly every day of the week that - however short - *matter* in at least two social dimensions: peer to peer and student to instructor. As a recipient of these preparatory e-mails, I provide specific coaching to individuals in my replies to the group of three to four students.

I also use a class-wide listserv to recap and advance class discussion, adding elements that anticipate the next moments of class. The listserv provides a vehicle for students to post provocations, questions, and even challenges to the course. As students begin to interpret the practical meaning of the requests to perform as a given assignment unfolds, they pose questions to the listserv and share ways to pursue assignments - so that the entire course may "listen in" to the performance of these "limit-acts" that test the untested feasibility just beyond the boundaries of the customary limit situation. Those students who participate in these communications advance the conversation in ways that allow themselves and others - showing up on time - to begin to design themselves as beings who own the course as it develops.

The Aim of Rhetorical Inquiry: Becoming Rhetorical

A subjectivity skilled in shifting positions between contesting though equally pious values has some experience of rhetorical inquiry, which is distinct from the educational results informed merely by conservative norms: ideological positions that Cartesian subjectivity preserves and protects relentlessly. Additionally, because it includes Cartesian subjectivity as a dialogic partner, rhetorical inquiry is also distinct, though related to, the practice of critical pedagogy. For if instructors interrogate and challenge cherished *truths* of students, revealing them to be socially constructed and provisional *views*, all the while holding themselves aloof from the inquiry, a critical pedagogy may be at hand, but it would not include the rhetorical dimension that calls for instructors to also submit to the unmasterable claim language makes. At the same time, when surrendering certainty in order to reiterate performative and dialogic encounters with language, rhetorical subjectivity must continue to acknowledge the value of Cartesian subjectivity. The drive for certainty and for the safety of the familiar does not simply go away, even with decades of postmodern critique of Enlightenment rationality (Davis, 2000, p. 7). As a result of sustained encounters with problem-posing breakdowns, wherein the familiar continues to be honored even as we undermine it, we develop sensitivities to new kinds of rhetorical practices, such as amplifying or articulating a marginalized value or practice as valuable, reconfiguring one's perspective in light of a dialogue with an incongruous one, and cross-appropriating or reiterating new practices into various areas of everyday life (Spinosa et al, 1997).

Thus, rather than ignoring or covering up disruptive problems, if we dwell with the anomalous quality of the problem, amplifying it and bringing it into relationship with lived social reality, it becomes possible for us to develop a skillful way of being human Spinosa et al called *history-making*, which we enact whenever we *articulate*, *reconfigure*, or *cross-appropriate*. And when we do, "the way in which we understand and deal with ourselves and with things" changes within a practical domain prior to reflective and theoretical judgment, thus allowing for sustained modes of activity that impact personal and civic domains of life (p. 2). Developing a rhetorical subjectivity, I say, can *begin* even in the "artificial" space of a college writing classroom, where students work, even if in minute ways, to reiterate the articulative practice of summary and the reconfigurative practice of rhetorical analysis.

Within the writing classroom, students practice articulation when summarizing the argument of a text: They work toward creating a set of statements that connect their "home" perspective to the at times quite complex arguments of an academic text. When students fail to summarize (when they project language not operative in the text, or argue with the text, or merely re-narrate the text), it is usually a reflex of reproducing what is already known or understood in advance, taking up an academic voice as they conceive it (Bartholomae & Petrosky, 1986). Rhetorical inquiry invites attention to the gap between what the conservative norm dictates, and the novel performance of articulation the original request called for: To honor the value of a text, no matter how much it diverges from our own orientation, or even if valuing the text requires our having to regard our values in a disruptive light. Thus, the practice of articulation may serve as the performative address of Cartesian subjectivity to undergo a perspective by incongruity, even if the text appears to express a perspective congruent with the student's.

In order for students to move into a dialogue between opposing but equally valued orientations, I have them practice articulating a summary of a text they will likely already value because it enforces a widespread conservative norm about good writing. A chapter titled "Structure and Meaning" from a popular book by screenwriting guru Robert McKee (1997) serves this function quite well. In the chapter, McKee appeals to an audience of aspiring screenwriters to take up his pious value, namely, that a writer who follows a single controlling idea will more likely create stories that allow audiences to experience aesthetic emotion, and hence, those esteemed writers will more likely achieve success. The piety of this orientation is clear, especially as it works to convert downward a divergent orientation that for some *unthinkable* reason values fragmentary tangents. Focusing on a single controlling idea, McKee instructs, allows writers to overcome a common problem, namely, when following inconsequential tangents, writers become distracted from the main idea, leading to the failure to write convincingly. I call this negative outcome the perspective's *context*, which provides the urgency for an audience to embrace the author's pious *purpose*, which is, in this case, informed by the Cartesian quest for certainty in a single idea that will ensure success. McKee's argument values the rhetorical practice of articulation: The practice of combining seemingly unrelated particulars into a coherent unity - that is, the creative act of summary, of creating similarity from difference, which is indeed what students practice with this text.

In the next pedagogic step, students read an equally persuasive text that converts McKee's pious value downward: Jane Gallop's "The Ethics of Reading: Close Encounters" (2000). Here the summative practice of articulating a unity suffers a conversion downward through a critical, reconfigurative practice that reveals a hidden flaw - Gallop's *context* - operative within the perspective that desires unity above all else. Such desire, according to Gallop, excludes and marginalizes by allowing prejudices to operate without question. Emerging as a new pious value for students is the practice of attending to the different, to the tangential, to the surprising - all that would challenge and disrupt our desire to find our own prejudices reaffirmed in a given text or experience. The critical practice of attending to difference, Gallop argues, not only permits us to learn, but it grants access to the ultimate potential of being human, Gallop's pious purpose: caring ethically for the other *as* different. Through articulating Gallop's argument, students confront the request to value the reconfigurative practice of critical reflection - an incongruous perspective that threatens the value embedded in McKee's drive to articulate unity.

There are multiple disruptive moments during this process of perspective by incongruity. First, because McKee's argument presupposes an audience of unskilled writers who, to some degree, fail to enact the Cartesian quest to write according to a single controlling idea, beginning college writers are pressured to silence their own "home" discourses in deference to McKee's unequivocal authority. As students begin to project McKee's value onto Gallop's text, that is, as they work to summarize a text that itself cogently argues against reducing any text to a single main idea, students encounter a boundary situation. Here they confront an orientation that indirectly requests that we regard McKee's value in a negative light, even to perhaps see him as a pompous, authoritarian windbag who takes himself entirely too seriously in preaching his singular principle behind successful writing. But at the same time, students also have access to the compelling value of McKee's argument and the negative light it casts on Gallop's, which if followed to the extreme, may indeed lead to a complete inability to act decisively, because there is no Truth, and consequently no solid identity within Gallop's perspective - at least when converted down into a negative context within McKee's incongruous perspective. To extend and deepen this dialogic moment, students work collaboratively to write a dialogue between McKee and Gallop analyzing and judging the qualities of a selected text. This kind of exercise brings students to invent an articulated space wherein each persuades the other to value as strong what might occur as the weaker argument. Figure 1 illustrates one way to visualize how these incongruous perspectives convert each other downward in order to project their own value's purpose as pious.

The infinity image in Figure 1 signifies the virtually endless looping of a dialogue, where the goal is never to "wipe out the enemy but to strengthen the weaker and neglected side" (Elbow, 1993, p. 75). Within the "middle" and constantly shifting perspective of rhetorical subjectivity, neither perspective has permanent hegemony because each constrains the other to fall in turn.

Figure 1. Incongruous perspectives of McKee and Gallop in dialogue

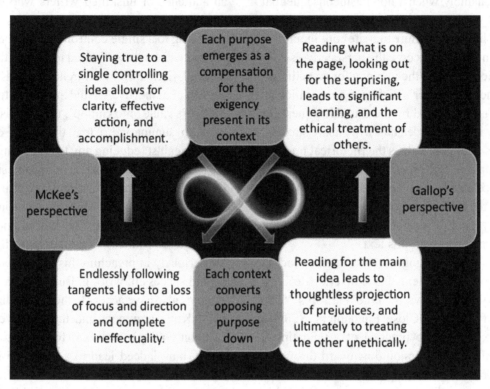

FUTURE RESEARCH DIRECTIONS

While undergoing perspectives by incongruity reiterated in increasingly unfamiliar writing situations, students and pedagogues together "ingest" divergent values, where each has their time in the sun and both suffer a conversion downward. Emotions inevitably emerge, from confusion to exhilarating bewilderment, especially as students confront and *undergo* the disruptive insight that no single orientation can be inherently true - the signature boundary situation rhetorical inquiry brings us to undergo repeatedly. Rather than trying to avoid or diffuse emotional reactions, pedagogues practicing rhetorical inquiry are to risk including emotion by amplifying the irreducible uncertainty present within the request to write, as every request to write, to respond to the other, invites us to exercise rhetorical intelligence: the ability to be receptive to difference even while maintaining integrity to the similar.

I offer this version of rhetorical inquiry and its conditions as a response to a perennial complaint: Disruptive pedagogies inevitably fail due to the dominating conservative forces of institutional structures (Worsham, 1991). Process pedagogy provides a salient example. Acting within the "new rhetoric" inaugurated during the latter half of the 20th century, advocates of the process movement saw a contradiction in so-called current-traditional writing pedagogy: Teaching toward product marginalized the valuable practices embedded in the processes of writing (Crowley, 1998). The field of rhetoric and composition emerged within North American institutions of higher education as key figures drew attention to this anomaly within the educational structures that had excised rhetoric, and in particular invention, from its curricula long ago. These efforts served to disrupt - to some degree - the conservative educational norms derivative of the Enlightenment project and Cartesian rationality.

However, despite the promise of process pedagogy, attempts to codify writing processes in order to better teach them permitted an unintended consequence: process pedagogy fell back into the very institutional structures advocates of process sought to disrupt (Kameen, 1980). The disruptive possibilities of rhetorical education have thus continued to remain inaccessible at a practical level; so goes the post-process critique, a project which has called for more attention to theoretical development in order to effect disruption of the hegemony of Cartesian rationality (Vitanza, 1991). Nevertheless, because it precludes any notion of resting upon a foundation, post-process offers a peculiar theoretical impasse: its critical direction does not allow for easy pedagogical application of its insights (Kastman Breuch, 2002). Consequently, in order to navigate this theoretical impasse, I offer this chapter's argument as a challenging request for pedagogues to risk their own certainty through experimenting with and studying the practical conditions of rhetorical inquiry.

CONCLUSION

While such an approach, on the surface, is not necessarily new - proponents of process and post-process pedagogies have all been seeking, in various ways, to guide students to engage with a critique of Enlightenment rationality toward liberatory aims (see Curry, 1993) - the dialogic approach of rhetorical inquiry is distinct, where the focus is on co-investigating the background practices that allow the world to show up in the style it does. It involves us considering the truly disruptive insight that our performance in the world, whether individually or as a community, is in a dance with how our orientations have us "take up" the claim language poses. Also different

is the focused approach to interrogate practices in a process that invites shifts in mood, and not just shifts in the understanding students develop while undergoing the cross-appropriation of rhetorical practices.

According to Alcorn (2002), both critical pedagogy and cultural studies seek to "change the subject," in both senses of the subject matter of the writing course and the subjectivity of participating students. But there are recalcitrant problems that produce breakdowns for each of these sets of pedagogical practices. Cultural studies (Berlin, 2003) relies on the premise that rational argumentation will produce shifts in subjectivity, while critical pedagogy relies heavily on authoritative persuasion (Bizzell, 1992). Alcorn claims that both overlook the passionate attachments of students: Rational argumentation and compelling authority may seem to produce shifts in subjectivity, but in the end prior passionate attachments "rule." Alcorn suggests instead a neo-Lacanian pedagogy that accounts for passionate attachment, and I claim that rhetorical inquiry does (see Rickert, 2007). Indeed, rhetorical inquiry presupposes as its primary premise that Cartesian subjectivity relentlessly seeks to maintain its tranquil hegemony through enacting what Boler (1999) called "inscribed habits of (in)attention," all in order to avoid irruptions of uncomfortable emotions such as fear and defensive anger (p. 186).

What rhetorical inquiry does is extend and complete the project of critical pedagogy by including the rhetorical dimension of human being, allowing for the Cartesian in us to undergo a dialogue with the indeterminacy of language. Consequently, the larger aim of the writing classroom is for students to continue practicing being rhetorical well beyond the course, for rhetorical subjectivity only persists and develops through reiterating the conditions of rhetorical inquiry in unfamiliar situations, which requires one to seek out and risk entering new genres while willingly embracing conversions downward of one's orientation.

REFERENCES

Alcorn, M. W. Jr. (2002). *Changing the subject in English class: Discourse and the constructions of desire*. Carbondale, IL: Southern Illinois U.P.

Atwill, J. (1998). *Rhetoric reclaimed: Aristotle and the liberal arts tradition*. Ithaca, NY: Cornell U.P.

Austin, J. L. (1962, 1975). *How to do things with words* (2nd ed., J.O. Urmson & M. Sbisà, Eds.). Cambridge, MA: Harvard U.P.

Bakhtin, M. M. (1981). *The dialogic imagination. (M. Holquist* (Emerson, C., & Holquist, M. (Trans. Eds.)). Austin, TX: University of Texas Press.

Bartholomae, D., & Petrosky, A. R. (1986). *Facts, artifacts and counterfacts: Theory and method for a reading and writing course*. Upper Montclair, NJ: Boynton/Cook.

Bawarshi, A. (2003). *Genre and the invention of the writer: Reconsidering the place of invention in composition*. Logan, UT: Utah State U.P.

Berlin, J. A. (2003). *Rhetorics poetics and cultures: Refiguring college English studies*. West Lafayette, IN: Parlor Press.

Bizzell, P. (1992). *Academic discourse and critical consciousness*. Pittsburgh, PA: U.P.

Boler, M. (1999). *Feeling power: Emotions and education*. New York, NY: Routledge.

Bordo, S. R. (1987). *The flight to objectivity: Essays on Cartesianism & culture*. Albany, NY: State University of New York Press.

Burke, K. (1984). *Permanence and change: An anatomy of purpose* (3rd ed.). Berkeley, CA: U. of California Press.

Crowley, S. (1998). *Composition in the university: Historical and polemical essays*. Pittsburgh, PA: U.P.

Crowley, S. (2006). *Toward a civil discourse: Rhetoric and fundamentalism*. Pittsburgh, PA: U.P.

Curry, J. B. (1993). A return to "converting the natives," or antifoundationalist faith in the composition class. *Rhetoric Review, 12*(1), 160–167. doi:10.1080/07350199309389031

Darwin, T. J. (2003). Pathos, pedagogy, and the familiar: Cultivating rhetorical intelligence. In Petraglia, J., & Bahri, D. (Eds.), *The realms of rhetoric: The prospects for rhetoric education* (pp. 23–37). Albany, NY: SUNY Press.

Davis, D. D. (2000). *Breaking up [at] totality: A rhetoric of laughter*. Carbondale, IL: Southern Illinois U.P.

Dewey, J. (1922). *Human nature and conduct: An introduction to social psychology*. New York, NY: Henry Holt and Company.

Dewey, J. (1929, 1960). *The quest for certainty*. New York, NY: Capricorn.

Elbow, P. (1993). Uses of binary thinking: Exploring seven productive oppositions. *JAC, 13*(1), 51–78.

Fleming, J. D. (2003). Becoming rhetorical: An education in the topics. In Petraglia, J., & Bahri, D. (Eds.), *The realms of rhetoric: The prospects for rhetoric education* (pp. 93–116). Albany, NY: SUNY Press.

Freadman, A. (1994). Anyone for tennis? In Freedman, A., & Medway, P. (Eds.), *Genre and the new rhetoric* (pp. 43–66). London, UK: Taylor and Francis.

Freire, P. (2003). *Pedagogy of the oppressed* (Ramos, M. B., Trans.). New York, NY: Continuum.

Gadamer, H.-G. (1977). *Philosophical hermeneutics*, (D. E. Linge, Trans.). Berkeley, CA: U.P.

Gallop, J. (2000). The ethics of reading: Close encounters. *Journal of Curriculum Theorizing, 16*(3), 7–17.

Halloran, S. M. (1975). On the end of rhetoric, classical and modern. *College English, 35*, 621–631. doi:10.2307/374944

Heidegger, M. (1971). The nature of language. In *On the way to language* (Hertz, P. D., Trans.). San Francisco, CA: HarperCollins.

Ijsseling, S. (1976). *Rhetoric and philosophy in conflict: An historical survey.* The Hague, The Netherlands: Martinus Nijhoff.

Kameen, P. (1980). Rewording the rhetoric of composition. *Pre/Text, 1*(1-2), 73-93.

Kastman Breuch, L.-A. M. (2002). Post-process "pedagogy": A philosophical exercise. *JAC, 22*(1), 119–150.

Kent, T. (1993). *Paralogic rhetoric: A theory of communicative interaction.* Lewisburg, PA: Bucknell U.P.

Kill, M. (2006). Acknowledging the rough edges of resistance: Negotiation of identities for first-year composition. *College Composition and Communication, 58*(2), 213–235.

Kopp, D. (2012). Cutting the Edge of the Will to Truth; Or How Post-Process Pedagogy is Biting its Own Tail. JAC: Rhetoric, Writing, Culture, Politics, 32.1.

Lanham, R. A. (1974). *Motives of eloquence: Literary rhetoric in the renaissance.* New Haven, CT: Yale U.P.

Lyotard, J.-F. (1984). *The postmodern condition: A report on knowledge* (Bennington, G., & Massumi, B., Trans.). Minneapolis, MN: U of Minnesota P.

Lyotard, J.-F., & Thébaud, J.-L. (1985). *Just gaming* (Godzich, W., Trans.). Minneapolis, MN: Minnesota U.P.

McKee, R. (1997). Structure and meaning. In *Story: Substance, structure, style, and the principles of screenwriting* (pp. 110–131). New York, NY: Harper Collins.

Plato,. (1961). Protagoras. In Hamilton, E., & Cairns, H. (Eds.), *The collected dialogues of Plato* (Guthrie, W. K. C., Trans.). New York, NY: Bollingen.

Rickert, T. J. (2007). *Acts of enjoyment: Rhetoric, Žižek, and the return of the subject.* Pittsburg, PA: University Press.

Spinosa, C., Flores, F., & Dreyfus, H. (1997). *Disclosing new worlds: Entrepreneurship, democratic action, and the cultivation of solidarity.* Cambridge, MA: MIT Press.

Vanderstraeten, R., & Biesta, G. (2006). How is education possible? Pragmatism, communication and the social organisation of education. *British Journal of Educational Studies, 54*(2), 160–174. doi:10.1111/j.1467-8527.2006.00338.x

Vitanza, V. (1991). Three countertheses: Or, a critical in(ter)vention into composition theories and pedagogies. In Harkin, P., & Schilb, J. (Eds.), *Contending with words: Composition and rhetoric in a postmodern age* (pp. 139–172). New York, NY: MLA.

Winograd, T., & Flores, F. (1986). *Understanding computers and cognition: A new foundation for design.* Boston, MA: Addison-Wesley.

Worsham, L. (1987). The question concerning invention: Hermeneutics and the genesis of writing. *Pre/Text, 8,* 197-244.

Worsham, L. (1991). Writing against writing: The predicament of *ecriture feminine* in composition studies. In Harkin, P., & Schilb, J. (Eds.), *Contending with words: Composition and rhetoric in a postmodern age* (pp. 82–104). New York, NY: MLA.

ADDITIONAL READING

Bakhtin, M. M. (1986). *Speech Genres and Other Late Essays. Vern W. McGee. (Trans.)* (Emerson, C., & Holquist, M., Trans.). Austin: University of Texas Press.

Ballif, M. (2001). *Seduction, Sophistry, and the Woman with the Rhetorical Figure*. Carbondale: Southern Illinois UP.

Bender, J., & Wellbery, D. E. (1990). Rhetoricality: On the Modernist Return of Rhetoric. In Bender, J., & Wellbery, D. E. (Eds.), *The Ends of Rhetoric: History, Theory, and Practice* (pp. 3–39). Stanford, CA: Stanford UP.

Billig, M. (1996). *Arguing and Thinking: a rhetorical approach to social psychology (revised edition)*. Cambridge: Cambridge University Press.

Bourdieu, P. (1977). *Outline of a Theory of Practice*. R. Nice (Trans.). Cambridge: UP.

Hawk, B. (2007). *A Counter-History of Composition: Toward Methodologies of Complexity*. Pittsburgh: University Press.

Heidegger, M. (1962). *Being and Time* (Macquarrie, J., & Robinson, E., Trans.). San Francisco: Harper & Row.

Hyde, B., & Bineham, J. L. (2000). From Debate to Dialogue: Toward a Pedagogy of Non-Polarized Public Discourse. *The Southern Communication Journal, 65*(2 & 3), 208–223. doi:10.1080/10417940009373168

Kameen, P. (2000). *Writing/Teaching: Essays Toward a Rhetoric of Pedagogy*. Pittsburgh: U.P.

Kopelson, K. (2003). Rhetoric on the Edge of Cunning; Or, the Performance of Neutrality (Re)Considered as a Composition Pedagogy for Student Resistance. *College Composition and Communication, 55*(1), 115–146. doi:10.2307/3594203

Neel, J. (1988). *Plato, Derrida, and Writing*. Carbondale and Edwardsville. Southern Illinois Press.

Nietzsche, F. (1999). On Truth and Lies in a Non-Moral Sense. In Breazeale, D. (Ed.), *Trans.), Philosophy and Truth: Selections from Nietzsche's Notebooks of the 1870's* (pp. 79–97). New Jersey: Humanity Books.

Polt, R. (1999). *Heidegger: an Introduction*. Ithaca, NY: Cornell University Press.

Rorty, R. (1979). *Philosophy and the Mirror of Nature*. Princeton, NJ: UP.

Seitz, J. (1992). A Rhetoric of Reading. In Andrews, R. (Ed.), *Rebirth of Rhetoric* (pp. 141–155). London: Routledge.

Vitanza, V. (1997). *Negation, Subjectivity, and the History of Rhetoric*. Albany: SUNY Press.

KEY TERMS AND DEFINITIONS

Anomaly: A problem that in any given situation defies commonsense understanding; acknowledgement of the anomalous challenges and disrupts conservative norms.

Articulation: A history-making practice wherein one brings forth (amplifies) a lost or displaced value/practice that permits incongruous perspectives to come together.

Boundary Situation: When, in the face of an anomaly, the conservative and familiar ways of coping with everyday life break down, thereby opening up opportunities for revision and the design of new practices.

Cartesian Subjectivity: The identity structuring tendency that enacts three related practices in any indeterminate situation: the drive to be right, to understand the unfamiliar in familiar terms, and to avoid an identity threatening risks.

Context: Within an argument, the negative value the argument uses to justify its purpose.

Conversion Downward: The downgrading of one's perspective when beginning to value an incongruous, divergent perspective.

Cross-appropriation (reiteration): A history-making practice that brings a value/practice original to one domain into another domain that does not already have the value/practice.

History-making Practices: A skillful way of being sensitive to anomalies such that it becomes possible to bring the anomaly into relationship with lived social reality (through the practices of articulation, reconfiguration, and cross-appropriation).

Performative Speech Acts: Speech that performs actions that in turn call for performative responses (uptakes); a way of relating to language as experiential rather than merely conceptual.

Perspective by Incongruity: The process of allowing oneself to experience one's perspective from within the value structure of an incongruous perspective.

Phronesis: The pragmatically wise stance wherein rhetorical subjectivity remains receptive to anomalies within a given situation in ways that permit the creative integration of one's commitments into the uncertain situation.

Piety: A moral principle that guides the formation of interpretations which then coordinate actions, determine meaningful relationships, and permit transference between situations, all toward conservatively justifying and maintaining an orientation's existence.

Purpose: The positive value that an argument promotes in any given situation.

Reconfiguration: A history-making practice where one makes a marginalized value/practice central, which then competes with the dominant value/practice.

Rhetoric: The study and performance of communicative acts that address specific audiences in order to resolve indeterminate social situations.

Rhetorical Inquiry: The practical investigation that discloses identity as socially constructed, thereby permitting for the revision of conservative norms and the design of new practices to cope with anomalies conservative norms customarily overlook.

Rhetorical Subjectivity: The subjectivity that emerges while undergoing reiterative dialogic encounters between incongruous perspectives; a subjectivity with some degree of tolerance for uncertainty and with some capacity to perform with authority in uncertain situations.

Uptake: When faced with the displacement a performative speech act poses, addressees respond according to how they "take up," or understand, the speech act.

ENDNOTE

[1] I am indebted to Spinosa, Flores, and Dreyfus (1997), who discuss the history-making practices of articulation, reconfiguration, and cross-appropriation, and the correlative ways of being we enact when performing these practices. The authors claim that a culture figure *articulates* a dispersed or lost value that contending views could share, allowing for solidarity to emerge; an entrepreneur *reconfigures* a commonplace perspective by amplifying some overlooked, but unique aspect therein that then competes with the original perspective; and a political activist *cross-appropriates* or reiterates practices from one arena of activity to another to effect social change. In each case, employing the practice brings members of a given community to undergo a transformation in their understanding of themselves and the world. However, rather than keep these practices entirely distinct, I articulate all three practices within a disruptive pedagogy to be productive of a rhetorical subjectivity who is both receptive to problems conservative norms overlook and at the same time willing to risk bringing one or all three of these practices to bear within the constraints of a particular situation. See also Kopp "Cutting the Edge of the Will to Truth" (*in press*).

Chapter 18
Teachers of Young Children:
Moving Students from Agents of Surveillance to Agents of Change

Susan Matoba Adler
University of Hawaii-West Oahu, USA

Jeanne Marie Iorio
University of Hawaii-West Oahu, USA

ABSTRACT

This chapter illustrates how an online early childhood teacher education program using Socratic inquiry methods inspires students to challenge habituated assumptions in the field. Academic pushdown, teacher identity, standardization, and developmentally appropriate practice are central assumptions in ECE that students challenge in their blogs and discussion board postings. The program goal is to empower students to become transformative intellectuals (Giroux, 1988) and ultimately agents of change. Student writing illustrates how students have begun the process of challenging assumptions, identifying multiple perspectives on critical issues, and articulating arguments based on self-reflection and critical analysis.

INTRODUCTION

The presence of questioning, interrogating power, and advocacy are central to our teaching practices. In many current teacher education programs, coursework is infected with standards and methodologies in response to federal mandates like *NCLB* and the conception of Highly Qualified

Teachers (HQT). HQT can punctuate the higher education classroom. For example, during a recent observation, we witnessed a professor spending over an hour telling an undergraduate class the specific content standards for a subject. Forty minutes were focused on telling how this knowledge, which she often referred to as "true" and "good," was paramount to teaching. A short time was spent with the undergraduates in small groups using a teacher-created chart to apply the

DOI: 10.4018/978-1-61350-495-6.ch018

teacher-generated knowledge of standards. Not once did we hear the professor ask the undergraduates to bring in their own experiences and lives in the world. At the beginning of the lesson, the professor stated her objective concretely, "The objective of this lesson is…." Then she completed the circle of rhetoric by stating, "The objective of this lesson was and we met this objective by…." Her choice in words and actions brought to life the structures as directed by accountability standards determined by our government through *No Child Left Behind* (http://www2.ed.gov/nclb/landing.jhtml). Following the lesson, we heard someone comment; "Now she can prepare highly qualified teachers." To us, all we could think is that this teacher candidate was an agent of surveillance.

Inspired by Foucault (1972; 1995), the concept of agent of surveillance emerged in opposition to inspiring agents of change, which is the desire we have in working with developing early childhood teachers. We see the current practice of *NCLB*, particularly the notion of creating HQT, as a policy that parallels Foucault's ideas of surveillance and technologies of power, particularly hierarchical observation, a "very efficient and effective form of super-vision" (Gallagher, 1999, p. 78). Standards and accountability act as these controlling instruments in order to inflict homogeneity and compliance, ensuring the habituated assumption of being a teacher and student is enacted. We observed that professor and shuddered as she was praised and given accolades for observance to constructed expectations, the essential elements of surveillance. These agents of surveillance walk the halls of many universities and are teaching future teachers to follow federal ideals and certainly not think about the communities and children who they serve.

Our path of disruption to early childhood practices based in standards, content, and rhetoric is to inspire agents of change within the early childhood undergraduate program. An agent of change is an advocate who is aware of policy, issues of social justice, and is supported to voice resistance and question existing policies and practices. Agents of change can be seen as advocates, "speaking on behalf of others, often from within existing political, social, and economic frames of reference" (Sumison, 2006, p. 3). In some cases, agents of change can also be activists "resisting and challenging those frames of references and the power bases that support them" (Kenny, 2004 in Sumison, 2006, p. 3).

ARTICULATED EARLY CHILDHOOD PROGRAM

Our early childhood teacher education Bachelors degree program, articulates with the university system Associates degree programs in Early Childhood Education based on a more mainstream perspective of early childhood focused mainly on child development. Our students are all practitioners working in the field of early childhood education In the Bachelor's degree program, we call for critiquing practice from theoretical and cultural perspectives, interrogating power within the workplace and community, and embracing advocacy so that teacher professionalism evolves as society changes. A culminating practicum for the Bachelors degree is 6-credit course which includes an action research project. In reality, the Associates degree maintains a more conservative norm of mainstream child development while the Bachelors degree expands with more progressive and liberal orientations to the field. This creates a tension for our students as we ask our students to disrupt what they know from their Associates program and begin to rethink practice from a critical framework.

The main format for our program is an online environment, moving away from the traditional in-person teaching configuration. Since our program services students on four islands, it is the first opportunity for many of our students to access further education beyond the Associate level. Through the use of an online platform supplied by the university and blogger.com, students engage with the readings and discussions based in a variety of texts. The process begins with each student writing a question in response to the readings and then writing an initial post to a blog or discussion board. Then, both the professor and peers respond back the initial post with more questions. These questions are meant to inspire deeper thinking and more questions rather than a specific answer. Our process is meant for the students to develop clarity and discomfort in order to evolve in their thought processes and teaching practices.

Students spend the first weeks of the course reviewing resources focused on Socratic ideals (including a colleague's paper on the Neo-Socratic method and the website http://socratesway.com/everyday.html) and the first posting on the discussion board or blog for the course is the students' interpretations of these ideas in relation to their experiences and beliefs. This experience begins the process of students becoming critical thinkers. One student shared in her posting:

....When we stop to analyze or critique something that is when we use our minds and develop our answers to what we believe in. We cannot always accept everything everyone says because to them, it means something and have created that thought because of an experience, and to say you agree but not look into the situation, you may never know what really is out there. Although professors are the ones that may know a lot of factual information on the topic of teaching, asking questions and wondering why something is the way it is allows you to have an understanding of why it is what it is instead of just accepting what they say without question because the professor may or may not be right depending on the situation.

Another student explains how the Socratic readings influence how he considers advocacy and teaching practices,

To be true advocates in the field of ECE, we all need look into ourselves and not be "sold" into one idea because it came from research or a text book. Besides the universal ECE shortcomings (wages, respect, gender equity) there are opportunities within our programs to advocate for or against something. Curriculum, training, reporting and assessment techniques are just a few aspects that differ from program to program. We need to get the facts and hear/tell the truth about how our programs can benefit or be hurt from the implementation of certain ideals.

Our choice to move beyond two-dimensional online practices like lectures and quizzes encourages our students to experience teaching as an engaging, experiential process. As they develop familiarity with the process, movement beyond static teaching techniques is a possibility, imagining and developing teaching practices based on critical theory and disruption of habituated assumptions so common in early childhood education.

HABITUATED ASSUMPTIONS AND TRANSFORMATIONS

Giroux (1988) explains that "the category of transformative intellectual suggests that teachers begin recognition of those manifestations of suffering that constitute historical memory as well as the immediate conditions of oppression" (p. 99). When students focus on pedagogy from a teacher or curriculum-centered view, they tend not to consider issues such as oppression, suffering, or risk factors. When they consider the *lived experiences* of individual children, their families, their cultures and languages, or their social economic status, then they tend to articulate human conditions affecting the children's lives.

Through our teaching framework, we challenge our students to think about what could be possible. As students describe looking at their selves in order to disrupt accepted curriculum practices or techniques, we are witness to their development as advocates. This advocacy is the beginning of a lifelong dialogue teachers should be engaging in as agents of change and is further illustrated as questions and reflections become the means for voice. Bringing these elements of discussion into action initiate teachers into creating "a better, fairer, more humane state of things." For example, in one blog, a student reflects on a reading from *Making Learning Visible* (2001), sharing her questions and beginning to deconstruct power ideas surrounding truth:

...This got me thinking about my own philosophy - it's something that has been in flux for the past few years, constantly being tweaked and refined as I take in and digest new information. I know I occasionally have a hard time accepting information that seems counter to what I've learned. Like Howard Gardner wrote about on page 337, learning new paradigms isn't always so easy. How do you un-think something you considered fact? Or, a bigger question could be, "What does it mean to know something?" This line of thinking takes me back to my philosophy classes discussing the concept of what is really truly real. Are your thoughts real? Are the things you can taste and touch (etc.) real? How can we ever really know the truth of life? Is there even such thing? And what, if anything, do these questions mean when working with young children?

This continues in her blog as she interrogating ideas of community, knowledge, and democracy,

...What is a democracy? What does it mean to live democratically? We hear people talking about these topics a lot in our country (at least I do, but that could be because I tend to watch the news a lot). Does democracy mean being able to make as much money as possible and spending it on whatever you want? Does it mean spending money on programs that help others because that benefits the whole of society? Does it just mean being able

to vote for your representatives? I know there are lots of varying degrees and differing points of view about democracy and democratic living. How could we talk about this with children? Does democracy mean fairness? What does it mean to be fair? Whose point of view are we looking at when we consider fairness?

The blog ends with a rethinking of the role of teacher, advocating for teachers to think deeply and philosophically, "I think now that we're discussing the idea of "big ideas" I have to dust off my old "philosophy" hat that I tend to keep tucked in the dark recesses under the bed. Teachers as philosophers - I could learn to like that idea."

Assumptions and Transformations in Early Childhood Education

Academic pushdown, teacher identity, standardization, and developmentally appropriate practice are central assumptions to the discussions in our program. Readings introducing these often "grand narratives" within early childhood education are offered to the students in order for the students to have a basic background to dispute. Alternative perspectives are also shared through the readings, presenting other ways to see these assumed practices. The hope is that inspiration for students to consider how their experiences can impact the disruption of a practiced pedagogy and move them from efficient practitioner to transformative intellectual (Giroux, 1988). In the following sections we will be sharing student blogs and discussion board postings highlighting student interrogation of the habituated assumptions in ECE (see Table 1).

Academic Pushdown in Early Childhood Education

Early childhood programs have become victims of academic push-down. Politicians, policymakers, and administrators are using academic push-down as a means to ready children for upper grades,

Table 1. Habituated assumptions and transformative practices in ECE

Habituated Assumptions in ECE	Transformative Practice in ECE
Academic push-down has diminished play in the ECE curriculum. NCLB has forced accountability for readiness skills.	Learning occurs through play and child initiated activities consistent with the child's home culture and community environments.
Early childhood teachers are primarily white, middle-class and motherly.	Early childhood teachers are diverse, racially, ethnically, linguistically and by gender.
Standardization of curriculum and assessment minimizes diversity and discounts oppressed population.	Teachers who are transformative intellectuals incorporate subjugated knowledge of oppressed populations in their curriculums.

placing childhood in the margin in the name of *No Child Left Behind (NCLB)*. Campbell (2008 in Pelo, 2008) shares the story of his own daughter's encounter in prekindergarten where the centers focused on literacy skills previously expected to be completed in the first grade are now part of the prekindergarten classroom. When Campbell brought the inappropriateness of the academic curriculum to the principal, she looked at Campbell, "rolled her eyes, and said calmly and confidently, "Well, it's not going to do them any harm" (Campbell, 2008 in Pelo, 2008, p. 58).

One might contend the principal's response as well as the push-down may relate to the need to complete Annual Yearly Progress (AYP), a component of *No Child Left Behind*. Yet, research indicates the failure of AYP to illustrate anything. Further, schools that may appear to be functioning well are not very different from those schools that are failing,

...AYP compares the current proficiency status of a school or district to a fixed annual target. According to this metric, schools report the percentage of students who are performing at or above the proficiency target for a given year. Thus AYP—as currently defined and used in most states—is not a measure that captures improvement, or gains in student achievement, from one year to the next (Linn, 2008 in Mintrop & Sunderman, 2009)

Part of the conversation of academic push-down, *NCLB*, and AYP is the concept of the early childhood aged child being "ready" to learn.

While attending a conference provided by the local department of education about the current early childhood programs, the attendees received a children's book by Rosemary Wells (2006) titled *My Shining Star: Raising a Child who is Ready to Learn*. In the pages of the text, the author shares a list of characteristics contributing to a child being ready to learn. Some of the elements offer basic life skills – honesty, respect, listening, trust – yet, among the list is reading and writing, implying the very academic push-down so prevalent in early childhood classrooms. The book ends with how the child will become shining star if the child embodies these characteristics as suggested by the text, again implying the academic push-down. When even children's texts are exemplifying the academic push-down, how can this injustice be disrupted?

NCLB has taken away the beauty of childhood, interpreting each child as the same, meeting the same standards, without regard to culture or context (Popkewitz & Brennan, 1998). Sameness continues as those with the power, politicians, policymakers, and administrators, impose academic push-down in hopes of ensuring, ironically, that no child is left behind. Ideas of push-down echo in children's texts, further pushing childhood to the margin and placing academic push-down as the norm.

One mid-September night, when I was tucking my 5-year-old son Eamonn in bed, the standardization madness came home to roost. With a quivering lip and tear-filled eyes, Eamonn told me he hated

school. He said he has to read baby books that didn't make sense and that he was in the "dummy group." Then he looked up at me and said, "I just want to read Frog and Toad." (Quinn, 2008 in Pelo, 2008)

The story of Eamonn is quite telling as he is sharing his own frustrations with the consequences of academic push-down and *NCLB*. As children share their stories of being forced into scripted curriculum, a product of *NCLB*, educators are positioned to listen and respond in order to interrupt these current classroom practices. How can teacher education programs inspire teachers to disrupt in order to see teaching from the perspective of the children and families they work with each day?

After engaging in the same readings as shared above, one student blogs her own frustration with societal expectations of academics and the bullying of her own son by his school's administration:

I find that explaining PLAY to anyone who has not been through an ECE program, to be difficult. Many of my friends have their children perform for me; "Tell Aunty what color this is." "Tell her how you spell your name." When reviewing my intake forms I find that ninety percent of parent's answers to, "What would you like your child to gain from this program" is phonics. When in public, I often hear my-child-can-do competitive conversations. It seems as though our society is so out of touch with the importance of play. There is a common misconception that sooner is always better.

....What will it take to turn this bus of academic bullying around? I fear for my son who used to love learning. Now I'm not so sure!

Another student discusses the victimization and rights of children from the academic push-down, referencing play and freedom:

Tests and standards hold too much weight in our schools. In fact, they are more important than the well-being of the child. What kind of logic is this? I don't understand why, when there is evidence to suggest otherwise and examples in other countries, parents and educators still insist on the earlier the better. I love Elkind's (1981/1988/2001) phrase "an assault on childhood". We are forcing our future generation to grow up too fast in a system that leads them to feel like they are failures. Imagine a future with no imagination, no creativity and little social skills. What kind of world are we creating?

....I believe that we in the early childhood field need to speak with one voice and advocate for play. Children should be allowed the freedom to play. It is their human right. It is their purpose. It is what they are supposed to do...what right do we have to take that away from them?

The student accounts depicted focus on how academics for young children are perceived as both pervasive and problematic. The pressure of testing has been pushed down to kindergarteners, even though "official" assessment to meet AYP technically starts at third grade (the end of the early childhood years). In chat discussions through the online teaching platform, students tell stories about their friends, trained in early childhood education, who have left public school elementary teaching because the job was becoming so standardized and focused on high stakes testing. They felt they had to develop teaching identities as technicians for testing, rather than creative, child-centered teachers. Spending time with these frustrations encourages the students to begin challenging the assumed practice of academic push-down, evident as the students advocate for children's rights and question administrative actions.

Identity of Early Childhood Teachers

The development of identity is part of the becoming process for each early childhood teacher. MacNaughton and Williams (2004) contend that education is a process rather than a place and therefore it is not the institutions that make interactions educational. Anyone, regardless of gender or cultural background can teach, anywhere, anytime.

Contrast this current perspective to one by Snyder in *Dauntless Women in Childhood Education 1856-1931* (1972) based on Froebel's *Mother Play* in which teaching young children in the kindergarten (nursery school) was women's work and mothers learned from the kindergarteners (teachers). She wrote about how the teaching force needed to change, moving towards a "more responsible social role" and the development of a more heterogeneous teachers (beyond the expected "Anglo-Saxon, middle class professional and business background, ardently Christian and Protestant") (p. 376).

Referring to the 19th century industrialization in American society, Cannella (1997) describes the feminization of early childhood practitioners, pointing out that women had few work opportunities outside the home. "As women were constructed as the moral foundation of the family and the instrument whose identity is inextricably tied to the child, teaching was declared the natural responsibility of women. In the name of motherhood, women were claimed to be the best suited to educate children" (p.141).

If we compare and contrast the previous quotes by Snyder and Cannella and pay attention to the historical context of their writing, we might conclude that early childhood teachers develop identity within practices of stereotyping, limited job opportunities (not to mention inequities in pay), and a myth that being maternal is somehow connected (and possibly a necessity) for teaching young children. Luckily, as MacNaughton and Williams describe the many ways of being a teacher, a door opens to the possibilities for many

types, backgrounds and genders of early childhood teachers. Within our teacher education program, the development of identity is part of inspiring agents of change.

Gender Identity of Early Childhood Teachers

The gendered view of the nurturing female early childhood teacher is considered the norm by many of our students. One female student shared:

We have a male assistant teacher that we just hired. I thought some of my parents might feel objected to the situation and worried how the children might take to him. But everyone is happy that we have him and he brings a different aspect to the profession than my past female co-workers.

This female teacher's statement plays into the societal expectation that teachers must be female and nurturing, evident in her statement discussing parental and student perspective. This is further illustrated in another female student's posting discussing males performing assumed female tasks is abnormal, "I believe it is important to have the male figure in our classroom, but because of the precautions and "scare" about abuse and molestation, rubbing backs etc. men don't want to run the risk of being in the classroom."

This student's blog outlined some of the main fears that both male and female teachers of young children face. Her phrase "don't want to run the risk…" emphasizes the fear of societal sanctions. Gender is often not readily challenged or critiqued and assumed conceptions of teacher identity are reinforced by the female students. The challenge comes from a male student,

I want to discuss an issue that hits close to home, gender equity in ECE. Being a male in this field isn't easy. People don't see males as the nurturing type and are quite confused as to what to think when their child has a male teacher. In this day

and age, the female plight towards equality has made great strides but male rights in ECE have been going backwards. Fear of lawsuits and accusations place fear in the hearts of male teachers and their administrators. Should male staff be allowed to change a child? Should they be allowed to be the last staff member alone with the children at closing time? Should children be allowed to sit on their laps? My answer to these questions is yes but I understand when administrators don't feel the same. It's difficult because a part of me wants to say, "If we give in and don't allow equality then views on this matter will never change" but at the same time, is the risk worth the reward? I would hate to be accused of or have any of my male staff accused of wrong doing especially if there are no other staff members present to justify our account of what did or did not take place. Yes, there are predators out there and statistically they are majority males but this type of prejudice is unfair. I do not want to work in fear. What can all of us do as advocates to change people's views on males in ECE? Is there any hope?

Through this student's posting, the females in the course began to see another side to their perspectives. One female student responded to this blog by recognizing the power of a male teacher in her own experiences as a student and a teacher,

Working with children I've learned that they respond to male figures better than us women teachers... ...Also as I grew up in school, a majority of the teachers I favored and most remembered were males. If we advocate more about how male teachers do have positive impacts on children, I do feel people will view this matter differently.

Another student identified the impact of having a male as a teacher on the students:

My first year of teaching I had about 9 boys in my classroom and out of that only 4 had positive fathers involved in their life. I think having a positive male figure in their life would be very beneficial and they have some references on how to be positive guy.

It is the early childhood professor's responsibility to challenge the habituated assumptions about gender relating to practice. As part of the blog process, one professor (Jeanne) posted these questions in response to the male student's blog in order to deepen the conversation for all students, male and female, in the course:

Your discussion about gender in early childhood education is so important. I wonder how much of the discrimination is related to societal assumptions about early childhood education. Have people in power (administrators, policymakers, etc) created a discourse in early childhood education depicting the expected early childhood teacher -- a female, nurturing, loves children? How can an administrator disrupt this discourse? Is it based in hiring, support, ensuring a space for male educators? Sometimes I wonder if it relates to the male children always seeing females as teachers? Has our profession become so female, males do not even consider teaching a suitable profession?

Through an active discussion between peers, Cannella's "feminization" of the field of ECE begins to be challenged. The experiences and perspectives of both the female and male teachers is part of the discussion, encouraging the development of a new perspective on what it means to be both male and female in the classroom. The professor's questions are meant as a challenge to the accepted ideals of identity from the viewpoint of gender and as a means of articulating identity beyond gender.

Racial/Ethnic Identity of Early Childhood Teachers

I (Susan) am an American of Asian heritage and phenotype, and as a teacher-educator of color, I have always been cognizant of how others (administrators, parents, students) saw me, ascribed identity to me. In the years of public school teaching I have been asked where I come from and why I speak English so well. There were also questions of how and where I was trained as a teacher from a mainly homogeneous central U.S. and Midwestern population. I had to reflect on my own identity, while thinking that I was no different from my students (a colorblind perspective). But once I studied multicultural education, I became cognizant of the need to address my identity in relationship to cultural diversity. Ooka Pang (2005) writes, "Identity is a core component of who we are" (pp. 41-42). Identity includes race, ethnicity and culture. Race is a sociopolitical construct, while ethnicity refers to cultural aspects of a particular ethnic heritage group. As immigrant groups come in contact with a host culture, or in the U.S. mainstream middle class European American culture, the ethnic identity may change as students acculturate. "The designation of American is generally reserved for those who are White and English-speaking," says multicultural education scholar, Nieto (2000). She continues, "Others, even if here for many generations, are still seen as separate" (p. 334). Identity also reflects one's worldview, which develops from one's family and community norms. Au (2007), in her article on culturally responsive instruction, points out that there are worldview differences between students in mainstream and multi-ethnic or diverse classrooms. A mainstream "American" worldview focuses on individual effort, competition, and personal achievement, while a diverse worldview is characterized by working with others, cooperation, well-being of the group, and interdependence (p.11).

Teachers on the U.S. mainland are predominantly white and middle class but in Hawaii, many teachers are of Asian heritage (mostly Japanese). To illustrate this diverse worldview, the following students describe themselves as racial/ethnic be-

ings within their home/community cultures and illustrate the diversity of Asian identities. One student wrote about her practice and cultural lens in regard to her identity:

Being in Hawaii, we do have to keep in mind that although a person is of Asian culture, does not mean that they are exactly like most, or any, other Asians. Take me, for example. I was born and raised in the Philippines. I exhibited the same behaviors as other Asians, such as avoiding eye-contact, kept personal matters within my family, and folded my arms across my chest. When I came to Hawaii and attended school, these behaviors suddenly became signs of defiance or disrespect. All I knew at the time was this is how I was raised and this is how we behaved in my home. Now there is this divide between the home and the school. What is appropriate at home is not always at school.

Whether we like it or not, we are all guilty of some kind of stereotyping or disrespect to another culture. Whether our intentions are good or bad is another thing. Just last week one of my children, a three-year-old boy who is Spanish, but speaks both English and Spanish, had difficulty playing in a group. He started to hit and yell so I thought it best to remove him from the classroom altogether, away from the noise, and took him outside where we could talk. I went down to his level and talked to him and the entire time he was not looking at me. Naturally, I took it as disrespectful so I firmly told him to look at me. When it dawned on me that this behavior was a part of his culture, I just felt like such an ass. I saw flashbacks of how he responded when his mother spoke to him and all times he did not make eye contact. He was not being disrespectful; rather, he was being respectful and doing what was natural when an adult spoke to him. I excused my behavior and apologized to him (yes, I know he's only three but he is a person and I respected him nonetheless).

Another student described her Japanese American identity:

I'm Japanese, but I feel like a fake Japanese. I don't speak Japanese, even though I tried to learn a number of times. I feel like sometimes people that are of a certain culture don't practice that culture is because their parents and family don't practice it. My parents don't speak Japanese so I feel like that is a small reason why I don't. We don't do some practices because we don't know how. Like pounding mochi, we don't do it, but my 2nd and 3rd cousins do. Their parents and grandparents passed down those practices to them, but if your parents don't know the practices, it might be a little hard for them to explain it to you if they really don't know about it themselves. I like that you're very passionate about your culture, but I feel like sometimes people might not practice their culture because maybe they are shame. Like I feel like my grandparents raised my parents more "American" than Japanese, because during the war, they felt like they didn't want their children to be picked on, so they tried to make them "American" so they might fit in better.

The students' postings describing their own racial/ethnic identities viewpoints challenged a conception of teachers as White and middle class. Identity is shaped by one's home culture which reflects a family's worldview. Although these student postings illustrated more specific cultural characteristics such as eye contact, the Asian influence was reflective of Au's diverse worldview. For example, the Filipino student spoke of how she was raised and "behaved at home" which is based upon worldview, the student from Japan spoke about interdependence between parent and child, which is shown by respect for adults, and the "fake" Japanese student spoke about "fitting in" to American norms, yet this is a strong Asian expectation. Further, as recognition of racial/ethnic identities as part of the course discussion, the identity and culture of the children and their teachers became important disputing the societal and habituated assumptions of a generic teacher.

Standardization versus Subjugated Knowledge

Our goal is to empower students to engage in "critical pedagogy" (Giroux's term). When students focus on pedagogy from a standardized, teacher or curriculum centered view, they tend *not* to consider issues such as oppression, suffering, or risk factors. When they consider individual children, families, or social economic status, then they tend to articulate human conditions affecting the children's lives. They become aware of subjugated knowledge of the oppressed. The concept of subjugated knowledge refers to what critical multiculturalists Kincheloe and Steinberg (1997) describe as the living body of knowledge open to different interpretations from the dominant society. It emerges from an understanding of the perspective of the powerless oppressed and is expressed as *subjugated knowledge* (p. 47) When students have been indoctrinated to accept a given norm of the dominant culture, they may find it challenging to see through the lens of those who are not part of that "norm". But when they choose to seriously consider teaching to meet the needs of all children, then, they must consider subjugated knowledge as well.

The following student started her discussion posting with a study from the text. As she critiqued it, she began to interrogate the educational consequences of oppression:

An issue that bothered me was the number of children who were qualified for special needs. The book mentions that the number increased 40% in the 10 year period from 1989-1999. This may not seem like a big percentage, although to me it feels like it is still big. I wonder what the percentage of children who were qualified for special needs now is like. From looking at the number of stu-dents who were put under in the different types of disability, it came to me in a shock. I wonder why it's so high the numbers. The disabilities that were mentioned were from hearing impairment to developmental delay. How are all these children qualified for special needs. What is making them have all these different disabilities? Could it be the fact that it's heritage? Are mothers who are pregnant not getting enough nutrition? Where are these mother coming from that produce these babies? I wonder where this study was done.

Another student expressed her understanding of the oppression of poverty through her own ex-periences and in response to the Diss and Buckley (2005) text,

A point raised in the Diss and Buckley textbook is the importance of understanding poverty (pg. 43). The authors talk about the effects of poverty on children in school. When limited financial resources must be spent on meeting basic needs for survival, those children don't get to have the extras that our materialistic society unfortunately places great value on. I experienced this as a child. Children can be very mean! I think this applies more to school-age, even older school-age, as was my own experience. Not fitting in at school and among peers has negative consequences not only on self-esteem but also on social skills. Children who don't fit in don't really have friends. There are no playdates or sleepovers; even if there are friends to ask over, parent(s) are working a lot and not able to supervise, especially in a single-parent home. Social skills go by the wayside when there is little opportunity to use them. Another negative effect, again especially in a single parent home where the parent id at work a lot, and then busy doing household chores when at home, is the lack of relationship between child(ren) and parent(s). I also experienced that; my mother hardly talked to me when I was a child because she was too busy managing life. Thankfully, even though I am now

a single rather poor mom, I have time to devote to my daughter. We read, talk, snuggle, play games, go places, we do a lot together and our relationship shows that. Although she is only in preschool so far, we are blessed that she doesn't have to face the negative effects of poverty on social skills that many children in poverty do face.

The previous student discussions on special needs children and families living in poverty il-lustrate both an understanding of the subjugated knowledge or the "view from below" as well as the causes and inequities faced by parents and children in these life circumstances. These stu-dents were trying to understand the perspectives of the oppressed in order to advocate for them, evident in sharing their own stories and develop-ing questions to consider. If teachers stuck to the lens of their own upbringing, they may not be able to develop the empathy and understanding of "others". The concept *subjugated knowledge* that Kincheloe and Steinberg (1997) present is key to students challenging, critiquing, and changing existing school policies and curriculum to meet needs of all children. A comprehension of these ideas offers our student a perspective necessary to acting as agents of change.

PRACTICING AS AGENTS OF CHANGE

The culminating event in our early childhood program is our students completing a senior practi-cum experience and an action research project. Action research includes action, thought, and inquiry through a cyclical and spiraling process. Teachers act as researchers, engaging with the daily classroom practices in order to rethink the possibilities within the act of teaching. Lewin (1946) coined the phrase action research noting this research would be a means for social change. This is further reflected in the work of Freire (1973) as he believed the community can take its own action positioning teachers as agents of change. Through action research, teachers can voice and add awareness of identity in developing their own understandings of teaching practice (Britzman, 2003) and realize issues of equity (Caro-Bruce, Flessner, Klekr, Zeichner (Eds.), 2007). The process offers both moments of reflection, doubt, and transformation – all part of being an agent of change.

One student's action research project contemplated this question: Will Openness in Teaching and Learning Help Empower Children's Learning Experiences? Previously, this student assumed it was the teacher creating the atmosphere and activities which offered opportunity to a holistic experience. Self-reflection upon videotaping herself teaching became an a-ha moment when she saw how she was manipulating the children into believing they were important in the curriculum, illustrating herself as a teacher with all the power. The change she immediately enacted was sharing power with the children and letting her own power go as the teacher. This student engaged as an agent of change and continues to explore these elements as both a graduate student and director/head teacher of a local program. Entering a classroom as an agent of change empowers each of our graduates to be positioned to create evolving teaching practices, not held to programmed methodologies or "bag of tricks" defined outside of the teaching context. Self-reflection and teacher identity as well as a strong knowledge base on different curriculums set the foundation for teachers as life-long learners. It is mutually beneficial for teachers and students.

CONCLUSION

Often we are held to established (state and national) content standards and student learning outcomes (as well as department/division and institutional learning outcomes) that syllabi become standard-ized and prescriptive. In order to entice students to think critically and examine multiple perspectives on issues, teacher educators need to have the freedom to be flexible and engage in meaningful discourse with students. Though we may write a student learning outcome as "to demonstrate critical thinking", how that is scaffolded or allowed to evolve naturally depends upon the instructor's ability to open the door to inquiry.

As teacher educators we have opened our students' minds to an early childhood program in which they reflect upon their practice, interrogate ideas, engage in critical thinking, and take and defend intellectual positions. Our goal has been to empower our students to become transformative intellectuals and ultimately agents of change. In this chapter we have identified four habituated assumptions in early childhood education and provided examples of student writing illustrating how they take positions, provide rationale and challenge established ideas. We then further this positioning by sharing our students engaging as agents of changes as they develop and practice action research, grappling with their own pedagogy in a systematic and meaningful way, while learning techniques of effective research. Our program framework inspires our students will continually engage in democratic practice and social justice.

REFERENCES

Au, K. (2007). Culturally responsive instruction: Application to multicultural classrooms. *Pedagogies: An International Journal, 2*(1), 1–18.

Campbell (2008). The scripted prescription: A cure for childhood. In A. Pelo (Ed.), *Rethinking early childhood education.* Wisconsin: Rethinking Schools.

Cannella, G. S. (1997). *Deconstructing early childhood education: Social justice and revolution.* New York, NY: Peter Lang.

Caro-Bruce, C., Flessner, R., Klehr, M., & Zeichner, K. (Eds.). (2007). *Creating equitable classrooms through action research*. Thousand Oaks, CA: Corwin Press.

Diss, R. E., & Buckley, P. K. (2005). *Developing family and community involvement skills through case studies and field experiences*. Upper Saddle River, NJ: Pearson Education, Inc.

Elkind, D. (1981/1988/2001). *The hurried child*. Reading, MA: Addison-Wesley.

Foucault, M. (1972). *The archaeology of knowledge*. New York, NY: Pantheon.

Foucault, M. (1995). *Discipline and punish: The birth of the prison*. New York, NY: Vintage.

Freire, P. (1970). *The pedagogy of the oppressed*. New York, NY: Seabury.

Freire, P. (1973). *Education for critical consciousness*. New York, NY: Continuum.

Gallagher, S. (1999). An exchange of gazes. In Kincheloe, J. L., Steinberg, S. R., & Villverde, L. E. (Eds.), *Rethinking intelligence* (pp. 69–83). New York, NY: Routledge.

Giroux, H. A. (1988). *Teachers as intellectuals. New York, NY*. Bergen: Garvey.

Greene, M. (1986). Reflection and passion in teaching. *Journal of Curriculum and Supervision, 2*, 68–81.

Grieshaber, S., & Cannella, G. (Eds.). (2001). *Embracing identities in early childhood education*. New York, NY: Teachers College Press.

Kessler, S., & Swadener, B. B. (Eds.). (1992). *Reconceptualizing the early childhood curriculum*. New York, NY: Teachers College Press.

Kincheloe, J., & Steinberg, S. (1997). *Changing multiculturalism*. Philadelphia, PA: Open University Press.

Lewin, K. (1946). Action research and minority problems. *Journal of Social Issues, 2,* 34-46.

MacNaughton, G., & Williams, G. (2004). *Teaching young children: Choices in theory and practice*. Australia: Pearson Education Australia.

Mintrop, H., & Sunderman, G. L. (2009). Predictable failure of federal sanctions-driven accountability for school improvement - And why we may retain it anyway. *Educational Researcher, 38*(5). doi:10.3102/0013189X09339055

Nieto, S. (2000). *Affirming diversity: The sociopolitical context of multicultural education*. New York, NY: Longman.

Pang, V. O. (2005). *Multicultural education: A caring-centered, reflective approach*. Boston, MA: McGraw Hill.

Peshkin, A. (1988). In search of subjectivity: One's own. *Educational Researcher, 17*(7), 17–22.

Popkewitz, T., & Brennan, M. (1998). *Foucault's challenge: Discourse, knowledge, and power in education*. New York, NY: Teachers College Press.

Project Zero & Reggio Children. (2001). *Making learning visible*. Reggio Emilia, Italy: Reggio Children.

Quinn (2008). I want to read *Frog and toad*. In A. Pelo (Ed.), *Rethinking EARLY CHILDHOOD EDUCATION*. Wisconsin: Rethinking Schools.

Robinson K. (2010, June, 26). Transform education? Yes, we must. *The Huffington Post*.

Snyder, A. (1972). *Dauntless women in childhood education 1856-1931*. Washington, DC: Association for Childhood Education International.

Sumsion, J. (2006). From Whitlam to economic rationalism and beyond: A conceptual framework for political activism in children's services. *Australian Journal of Early Childhood, 31*(1), 1–9.

Swadener, B. B., & Lubeck, S. (1995). *Children and families "at promise": Deconstructing the discourse of risk*. New York, NY: State University of New York Press.

Wells, R. (2006). *My shining star: Raising a child who is ready to learn*. New York, NY: Scholastic Press.

ADDITIONAL READING

Adler, S. (1998). *Mothering, Education, and Ethnicity*. New York: Routledge.

Ayers, W. (2010). *To Teach: The Journey of the Teacher*. New York: Teachers College Press.

Cannella, G. (1998). *Deconstructing Early Childhood Education: Social Justice and Revolution*. New York: Peter Lang.

Jipson, J. (Ed.). (1995). *Repositioning Feminism and Education: Perspectives on Educating for Social Change*. Santa Barbara, CA: Greenwood.

Mallory, B., & Mallory, B. N. (1994). *Diversity and Developmentally Appropriate Practices: Challenges for Early Childhood Education*. New York: Teachers College Press.

Chapter 19
Creating Tension:
Orchestrating Disruptive Pedagogies in a Virtual School Environment

Gloria Latham
RMIT University, Australia

ABSTRACT

This chapter will critically examine the disruptive pedagogies being employed during the initiation, transition, and extension phases of a virtual school culture and its impact upon the virtual school community, pre-service, and ultimately, in-service-teachers. Through the virtual, it is intended that pre-service teachers (who have a placement at this school of ideas) may be able to experience new ways of teaching and learning and, in turn, start to step away from their schooled pasts in order to reflect upon, critically assess and then enact needed change. As pre-service teachers are the potential creators of yet unchartered pedagogies, they are a vital resource. Provocation will be examined using an Action Research model.

INTRODUCTION

Teacher educators are responsible for preparing aspiring novices for the educational systems they will enter as well as challenging the norms of those systems by interrogating how well they meet the needs of substantially new kinds of learners requiring interdisciplinary, global, multimodal and project-based learning. These two roles of the teacher educator are often at odds with one another. It is the role of provocateur that this chapter addresses.

By creating Lathner Primary, a virtual school, it was our intention that the physical environment, the authentic learner-centred ideas and lecturers' face-to-face interrogation of the norms of teaching would assist in altering pre-service teachers' views of schools.

DOI: 10.4018/978-1-61350-495-6.ch019

BACKGROUND

Much has been written about changing mindsets and practices around an industrial model of teaching and learning that dispenses information and normalizes students, content and practices (Fullan, 2007, 2008; Darling-Hammond, 2009; Hargreaves & Shirley, 2009) While educators recognize and accept that today's learners are radically different and require learning that responds to the rapidly changing socio-cultural, technological and global conditions, little has altered in reality. Research also emphasises the centrality of the teacher in the learning process (Hattie, 2009; Darling-Hammond, 2009). Responsive teachers start by getting to know their student's strengths and learning styles, attitudes and interests and only then do they address mandated curriculum, programs and standards.

Teachers need to reconceptualize what schools can become so that today's learners explore, problem solve and design new knowledge within a range of learning communities. New kinds of responsive teachers reflect upon and then enact teaching and learning practices that do far more than merely replicate past practices that no longer serve learner needs. Rather, they create and implement innovative practices that reflect real world issues. Hargreaves and Fullan (1998) suggest that the teaching profession has not yet come of age. They question whether the next decade can 'develop its own visions of and commitments to educational and social change, instead of simply vetoing and reacting to the change agendas of others.' (p. 103)

New ways of learning 'outside' of formal schooling continue to bring about fundamental changes to the ways in which learners interact with others, and how identities are enlarged and strengthened by local and global connectedness. Linda Darling-Hammond's (1998) statement over a decade ago holds even greater credence today. Darling-Hammond says that 'today's schools face enormous challenges ... [they] are being asked

to educate the most diverse student body in our history to higher academic standards than ever before' (p. 6). Twenty-first century learners are accustomed to self-regulated learning, learning that provides choice in what they learn, where they learn and when they learn. These students are digital natives, "wired" as Prensky (2005) describes them. They have grown up with access to a wide range of digital technologies that allow them a range of social networks locally, nationally and globally, along with vast amounts of information at their fingertips.

While teachers are aware of the dramatic changes in 21st century learners there is often an inability to let go and, at times, a resistance to disrupt the norms of schooling so tightly ingrained in teachers, parents and students' consciousnesses. Judith Butler draws upon Foucault's (1969) work in the ways that linguistic constructions create our reality through the speech acts we participate in every day. While our reality is a social construction, teachers continue to perform these learned constructions. By embodying them, artificial conventions appear to be natural and necessary. They are, one might suggest, artificial habits of mind and they embed themselves in language, relationships and professional practices. They become powerful manifestations of our identities. Thus the task of re-culturing teachers and schooling, as Fullan (2001) recommends, is an enormous and often painstaking one.

Yet education is also the ideal platform to enact transformations through critical reflection; to provoke change to become as Boler (1999) argues, less encumbered by constraints. As well as building sustained innovations at Lathner Primary, we wanted to enact disruptive innovations so that systemic change could be realized. These disruptive innovations need to unsettle the comfort of known, routinized ways of thinking and behaving.

Adopting a pedagogy of discomfort is likely to produce fear of change and defensive anger (Boler, 1999). Such reactions should be interpreted as a defence of one's investments in dominant cultural values, but nevertheless, it is the task of the critical educator to interrogate habitual practices. A confrontational approach may be counterproductive in terms of shifting student perceptions about schooling, so we searched for more supported ways of guiding change. Boler refers to this as

a means of offering stability through ... rough terrain ... Through our capacity to shift our positionality and modes of seeing, we can allow ourselves to inhabit the 'old familiar' spaces and begin our process of inquiry by noticing where we are currently situated.' (p. 197)

Prior to facing the challenges Boler presents, it was necessary to better understand what was being asked of our pre-service teachers. Milstein (1993) and Marshak (1996) argue that change means loss, uncertainty and often grief as [the] teachers move into the unknown. From a very early age, children have been fed stories about schooling narrated by family members and friends, film and television, thus establishing patterns of knowing about what school is while paving a clear path of certainty. Additionally, over their many years of schooling, pre-service teachers have been inducted into the codes and linguistic practices of what it means to be a student, a teacher and of what it means to 'do school'. Selecting to become a teacher is often founded on these comfortable and learned practices. Then, when novice teachers go out on school placements, they are witness to many of these all too familiar linguistic and cultural practices, serving only to reaffirm their beliefs.

In acting as provocateurs, our small team of lecturers wanted to replace some of the old, no longer purposeful yet ingrained narratives of teaching and learning with new ones, while assisting our pre-service teachers to interrogate the usefulness of the cultural stories and the teacher identities they continue to proffer.

Drawing upon Clay Christensen's (2000) concepts of sustained and disruptive innovations, there was a need to start with more sustained

innovations that tinkered at the edges of known ways of teaching to better existing classroom practices before moving towards disruptive innovations that seek to totally dismantle, and then alter, existing practices. Sustained changes connect what learners already know to less familiar territory. Schlechty (2005) argues that a disruptive change, such as giving students autonomy, may require the role of teachers and the authority of that role to be redefined. 'While invention is the first occurrence of an idea for a new product or process, innovation is the first attempt to carry it out into practice' (Fagerberg, 2004, p. 2). It was our intent to use the potential of Information and Communication Technologies to play out what new kinds of learning look like, sound like, and feel like in a virtual school context. To this end, we created Lathner Primary: a school of ideas. Our pre-service teachers have a placement in this virtual school. Placing our pre-service teachers in this school offered them freedom to take risks while planning for virtual students, and they were provided a community of 'others' who were also experiencing the shock of the 'new'. They were also being part of a collective of courage.

At the same time we understood the need to encourage and support our novice teachers with ways to become 'comfortable' with the unknown and embrace uncertainty (Davis, Luce-Kapler & Sumara, 2000). We asked them to dismantle and critique the known while rebuilding and redefining new teacher identities and therefore new possibilities.

In order to monitor the effects of our provocation, we employed an Action Research methodology that involved the team of lecturers planning, acting, reflecting, evaluating, and initiating additions and improvements to our teaching which assisted in expanding and strengthening our virtual school over time (Kemmis & McTaggart, 1988; Burns, 1999). As a process-oriented collective approach, Action Research helped us to contextualize the research knowledge being assembled, and analyze it while making informed and systematic decisions about necessary change to our teaching and to the virtual school. This research approach allowed us to transform our practices in response to the needs of our learners. Therefore, through informed research, we were provoking our thinking as lecturers and enacting the needed changes we were asking of our pre-service teachers. In order to better understand the impact of our provocations and the learning gained from such a focus, we collected pre-service teachers' initial responses to the virtual school. We also held small group conversations with pre-service teachers, analysed their reflective journal assignments, online discussion forums, end of year evaluations and we also reflected upon and analyzed our teaching practices. These data sources provide rich qualitative information upon which to assess the effectiveness of our direction.

INITIATION: BUILDING LATHNER PRIMARY

The first iteration of Lathner Primary began as a virtual classroom a colleague and I developed on our Blackboard site for a literacy course. We built 25 Year 4/5 student portraits based on children we both knew and a class teacher we named Anna Jones. Our pre-service teachers worked in this virtual classroom, observed and planned curriculum. At the start of the semester we asked the novice teachers to apply for the pre-service position in Anna Jones's classroom, by addressing selection criteria. Once they were appointed to the position we asked them to document their reactions when they first entered the classroom, what surprised them, made them feel uncomfortable and what delighted them. From their responses we learned far more about their hopes and fears.

I had a look around the school before my interview. My first impression was that the school was badly in need of repair. It was housed in a sturdy brick building yet the school didn't stand tall... But as soon as I sat down for my interview I was surprised how fast my feelings about the school changed. I liked Brian Treadwell the principal, right away. He looked tired but there was a hopeful sparkle behind his eyes... This school might hold possibilities for me as a teacher. Here I might be able to enact some of my strong beliefs. (4th Year BEd student)

In tutorials we got our novice teachers to role-play life in this classroom and explore practices that were somewhat foreign to them. For instance, Anna Jones believes learners should be empowered to drive their learning. She does not believe in streaming students and creates individual learning plans to further independent study. Anna's teaching fosters integrated problem-based learning driven by students' open-ended authentic problems. She also takes the children far beyond the classroom allowing them to experience life from the source.

Initially, our provocation was focussed solely on the beliefs and practices of the class teacher. We deliberately created a teacher who understood and responded to the needs of 21st century learners. Yet we felt it was also important for Anna Jones to keep facing her traditional past; slipping back to old modes of operating while desiring needed change. We wanted pre-service teachers to see aspects of themselves in this teacher.

To encapsulate some depth in the representation of Anna Jones and her students, inner thoughts of the teacher were exposed in the teacher's professional journal. Anna's reflections were an attempt to help our novice teachers make sense of some of the questions, paradoxes, frustrations and insights Anna Jones is presented with daily.

From the pages of her professional journal, Anna Jones shares some of her learning needs.

I realise that most of the questions are coming from me lately – I'm slipping back a little as I try and take the students on to where I want them to go, not where they are interested in going. I don't feel I can always relinquish that control. Tomorrow I'm going to consciously try a different starting point from their questions, and see where that goes ...

We furthered this teacher's beliefs in lectures, tutorials, online and in her interactions with the pre-service teachers, other colleagues, parents and students.

Anna Jones is a teacher who questions her teaching. In the same respect, Anna asks our pre-service teachers to defend why they are proposing particular practices and content. Anna's questions were ones we wanted our novice teachers to start asking for themselves.

- Why am I teaching this now, in this way? How is this responsive teaching?
- What possibilities are open for differentiated learning?
- Who is being advantaged and who is being disadvantaged if I do it that way?
- What opportunities are provided for learners to take control of their learning?
- How will I know what learning has occurred?

Anna also shared her philosophical beliefs.

Ever since we instituted the Opening Windows Opening Doors Policy we started spending time in one another's classrooms. I love learning this way! When many of the teachers at a school believe in similar fundamental things, like child advocacy, learner-centred integrated learning it is possible to accomplish great things. We may not be blessed with a lot of resources in this school but we are blessed with a committed learning community. The children at the school have became accustomed to working with a range of adults from time to time observing cases, sharing some information or skill or just pitching in.

In the entry above, we planted seeds about the importance of learning about new ways of teaching within a professional learning community where ideas for effective change are exchanged and supported.

Our anecdotal research during this first phase of exploring how the virtual informs the real, indicated that in a safe environment where pre-service teachers are being encouraged to think outside the square, many began to question some of their long held beliefs about learning and teaching. Yet there were still a vast majority of pre-service teachers who longed for a 'normal' comfortable school with a 'normal' teacher just like the schools they attended when they were young.

To be honest my initial reaction isn't a positive one... I feel reluctant and hesitant to give it a go because it is unlike anything I have ever done before. I'm used to the "normal" way of doing things and tend to have trouble accepting change. However, like most new things I know that if I give it a shot and take to it with an open mind I will get a lot out it. (2nd Year BEd student)

In their initial reactions to the virtual school we asked our pre-service teachers about their level of comfort taking risks and what surprised them. Many admitted that they are not risk takers.

I have to say that the school was not what I expected. The cross between the reality of the outside of the school and the unrealistic components and designs of the classrooms really surprised me. I feel a bit nervous taking risks. I start to feel a sense of insecurity if things start to go wrong. (4th Year BEd student)

TRANSITION STAGE

During the next phase of the virtual school, we recognized the need to reduce the number of virtual children in Anna Jones's class (as virtual children are more difficult to get to know) and also add to each individual student's learning files. We also wanted to demonstrate how change occurs in the wider school community. We started building profiles of other staff members in the school (change resisters like Eileen Trigony and innovators like Richard Battersby). We strengthened the community in and around the school to give credence to the pedagogical and physical shifts in this school, and in Anna Jones's classroom in particular. Reading about change theory confirmed the notion that it is often in times when there is instability, threat, or new opportunities that change is sought. We began building narratives that positioned Lathner Primary School as having been a school under threat.

The School Infrastructure

We recognized the potential of a virtual environment to provoke new thinking. The Educational Media Group (EMG) at RMIT University was enlisted to make some of the dreams in our heads, realities, and to build a school away from its Blackboard site. This media group provides expertise in multimedia production, graphic design, web development, video production, photography, research and innovation to staff.

Many of the technical design concepts we requested were unfamiliar and uncomfortable to the designers as well. For instance there is no site map to guide viewers through the virtual school. We wanted visitors to get lost and encounter surprises along the way, rather than be directed in their journey. Maxine Greene's (1973) concept of 'teacher as stranger' was enacted to allow pre-service teachers' entry to an experience as anthropologists might encounter strange, unfamiliar surrounds. We wanted to allow novice teachers opportunities to become critically conscious of the cultural oddities they experience in order to question them and ultimately break with 'fixed, customary modes of seeing' (p. 8). We wanted even the familiar to be viewed differently.

The EMG group built the architecture for the virtual environment over a two year period. They used Flash-related technologies to enable the print on the classroom walls to appear and then reappear as another text over time as the user visits each room. This dynamic use of the environment encourages participants to revisit the rooms and make new discoveries.

Once inside, the visitors are disoriented, moving them far away from the comforts of the known. The pre-service teachers navigating the school encounter audio files, folders and filing cabinets in the office, staffroom and classrooms that open when they run their cursor over them. Inside these folders is a vast array of information about the background of the school, the teachers, the school's philosophy, history, the students, and current practices. Visitors to the site can open and read all teachers' professional journals to discover these teachers' ideas for planning, observations of children, inner thoughts, struggles and successes. Their professional journals also reveal ways in which these teachers are grappling with the complexities of day-to-day life in the classroom and in the school community. In some classrooms, the navigator can study student files, work samples, notes about students, and comments from parents. There is also a great deal of visual information provided on the walls of the school in the form of charts, welcome messages on computer screens, drawings and designs that give visitors a sense of what this school community values.

Surprises are designed to appear at every turn to create a virtual wonderland of new ideas. It is often difficult to determine where rooms are located, and whether visitors are upstairs or downstairs. Flying cupcakes with wings that flutter are heard in the Prep room, a cat named Stanley growls like a lion and appears at various unsuspected locations, vegetables grow in several locations as they are touched by the mouse, dinosaurs emerge from the walls, the staff room is in an idyllic outdoor setting, leaves blow and a trapdoor appears from a swirling staircase.

Learning to observe classroom practices is aided by elements of surprise. Adler (2008) defines surprise as recognizing an occurrence or event that is contrary to our expectations. These surprises motivate us to learn differently, to question the known. Laurel (1991) believes in the importance of surprise and reversal elements, stating that 'the discovery process becomes more interesting when the information found is not what the user might have expected' (p. 90). In the case of reversal or a surprise that reveals the opposite of what might have been expected, a learner's interest might be heightened, or a path might be changed. Laurel suggests that to focus solely on information delivery, we risk missing the opportunity to view web design as engagement and performance. Duffy (2003) asks us to turn surprises into questions. She believes that unexpected occurrences can stimulate *un*learning and raise questions that may in time alter existing mindsets (Latham, 2007).

Therefore, one of the ways we provoked students' thinking about schooling is through the learning environment we created at Lathner Primary. Our students often find their first virtual visit pleasurable, even though they experience difficulty navigating their way. They sit together at computers and delight in making discoveries in the halls, rooms and out of doors. Soon, however, reality hits that they must teach in this unconventional school. While they understand the importance of disrupting their taken for granted beliefs about teaching, they are terrified by the prospect of being out of control and uncomfortable. A few reactions follow:

Wow! This online form of learning in the form of Lathner Virtual School is one that I have never experienced before! I think it will be really beneficial for students who enjoy exploration. (2nd Year BEd student)

I was confused…I still haven't explored the school to its full potential but I realize I need to get lost and be open to new ideas and experiences. I know

I need to push myself and explore new knowledge and ways of doing things. However there is so much at risk; the children and their education, my professional reputation and employment. Too many times I have asked myself, 'What if?' Maybe I should be asking 'What if I don't? (4th Year BEd student)

While visiting the virtual environment, our students were learning about transformative teaching. Transformations are attempts to thoughtfully and critically shake up the norms of schooling. Transformative teacher professionals are those who are innovative creators of curriculum rather than blind followers of established curriculum. Transformative teachers live comfortably with uncertainty, are risk-takers and change agents. Through collaborative exchanges with other teachers, they take ownership of ideas. Mocklier (2004, p. 7) asserts that 'transformative teachers value divergent and risky thinking in themselves, their colleagues and their students, and in doing so assist students in the development of their own critical and transformative capacities.

EXTENSION PHASE: NEW SCHOOL NARRATIVES

Over the six years of the virtual school's existence we have continued to build new narratives around the school and invent and reinvent its history. These narratives seek to demonstrate how a failing school underwent difficult yet purposeful, responsive and effective change. We started small and based our directions on ongoing research. We often modified changes while expanding the content.

The history of the school established a context and need for change. Five years ago, Brian Treadwell, the principal, received a letter from the Department of Education expressing concern about the status of Lathner Primary. A letter of this nature was sent to all principals of what the government deemed *underperforming schools.*

The letter stated that the national test scores of students at Lathner had been falling well below average, attendance rates had steadily declined, there was a low teacher-to-student ratio and little community support demonstrated by declining student numbers. As well, an inspector's report undertaken of the school's structure, resources and grounds showed Lathner Primary to be unsatisfactory.

The directive stated that Lathner Primary had three years to turn its low performance status around. To this end they requested a detailed plan and budget that clearly outlined the steps that would be undertaken to make the necessary improvements. Failure to provide the required documentation within 90 days and/or failure to improve the quality of the school within the designated timeframe would result in the school's closure or in an immediate school merger.

Brian Treadwell had been expecting a letter of this nature for some time. He had been fighting hard to make small improvements in teaching and learning, well aware that the academic achievements of his students fell beneath the desired norms. While he had created a number of initiatives to try and better performance, there was little change. He told those present at an emergency meeting he called that, with regret, he could see no way out. Lathner, a once middle class predominantly Anglo Saxon population became a far more multicultural community with greater mobility, and quite varied economic levels. There were more rental properties than ever before and more families in financial need. There were also fewer children in the area and the population of Lather Primary was rapidly declining. So, this once stable and somewhat predictable school community was in the midst of a sizable change.

Along with these two major shifts, five teachers at the school retired or transferred schools. Two of these teachers admitted they had become unable to cope with the daily student demands. One long standing, highly traditional teacher remained at Lathner Primary. She would represent teachers who hold onto patterned ways of teaching. Mrs Trigony refuses to adopt the new pedagogies and holds tightly to her formal and highly disciplined teacher-centred approach. Yet we also did not want to polarize this teacher and paint her as a stereotype of the 'old guard'. Pre-service teachers learn to recognise more of the complexities involved with changing beliefs.

One of our pre-service teachers recognised herself in Eileen Trigony. In dialogue with the virtual teacher, Anna Jones, she said:

When I first met Eileen last term, I realised ... that this is what I'm like. Not to say Eileen isn't a wonderful teacher, but her teaching style has nothing to do with the philosophy of the school and the culture you create in your classroom that I now love so much. This got me thinking that I need to change and try a different approach to teaching to be better able to engage students to learn.

In folders in the virtual school we reveal that a new group of beginning teachers was hired along with one more experienced teacher, each bringing their unique orientations and personalities to teaching and learning and new challenges to existing staff. These teachers breathed new life and energy into a somewhat tired and troubled school. One of these new teachers was Anna Jones. At staff meetings Anna, in particular, kept asking questions, important questions about some of the existing and enduring beliefs and practices at the school. From this group of new teachers with current pedagogies and critical questioning came renewed energy for change in the principal and in several members of staff. We recently provided far more contextual information; biographies of the teachers at the school and new plans and exciting plans for change. Children at the school are working on a garden project and creating designs for a new play site at their school.

The principles of Lathner Primary have unfolded and continue to evolve. They embrace the following tenets:

- Leadership that manages and supports effective change;
- A shared meaning (theoretical underpinning) between all staff at the school, students and family members;
- Teachers who are learners, curious about the world;
- The creation of learning opportunities for 21st century learners that are student centred and purposeful;
- Collegiality, in the form of a professional teaching and learning community that creates the new direction undertaken;
- Evidence-based research documenting and defending student performance.

The school community started a process of bettering existing conditions. A series of sustained and disruptive innovations were planned, agreed upon and actualised, drawing staff and the wider community into ongoing communities of practice. They formulated and sent off a three year plan for Lathner Primary.

The Three Year Plan

By creating a school under threat we were creating the necessary conditions for change. The features of the plan follow. They were formulated by the entire school community.

- New Staff with 21st Century Mindsets
- Working Locally and Globally
- Making Teaching Public
- *From Behind Closed Doors and Screens:* Opening learning up far beyond the four walls of the classroom.
- Monitoring and Researching New Directions
- Bridging Towards the Future
- Learning in Learners' Hands
- *Securing Unified Commitment:* Opportunities for all stakeholders to be heard and for current staff not adhering

to the learning/teaching charter to transfer schools or retire.
- *Reculturing and Rebuilding:* Enhancing the School structural and improvements designed and agreed upon by the local community.
- Clear Channels of Communication

We began building Lather Primary Virtual School in order to see how the big ideas being touted about 21st century teaching and learning might play out in generative ways on the ground. The virtual school and its ideas continue to grow and change as the community surrounding it changes. We continue to work towards building greater capacity. This aligns itself to Lambert's (2002) notion of leadership. Lambert recognizes that leadership is about reciprocal and purposeful learning that allows participants in the community to construct meaning and knowledge together in order to forge shared meanings. From ongoing research, we continue to learn what our novice teachers and teacher graduates require and carefully consider any changes. We support our pre-service teachers' need to be co-constructing the virtual school in order to feel a sense of ownership with the place. They continue to contribute their expertise. They've enriched the virtual school by providing support advice for indigenous students and autistic students, initiating and running an inservice programme on thoughtful ways to use Web 2.0 technologies and have contributed new observations of students in the school for their learning files.

CONCLUSION

Of course there are limitations to creating a virtual experience. Although pre-service teachers can take risks in this school, it is not possible to give them a real sense of how these risks play out with respect to the individuals and their learning. As well, a virtual primary school can never mirror the moment-to-moment dynamics of an actual school environment. We also recognise that there will always be pre-service teachers who do not adhere to the philosophy of this virtual school and find it too difficult to change. There are also pre-service teachers who long to teach in the same comfortable ways in which they had been taught. While accepting the novice teachers' discomfort, we remain committed to acting as provocateurs. This act of revisiting a lived experience in a classroom is not possible in the actual classroom, yet returning to an experience virtually and viewing it over time through a range of lenses in the company of other novice teachers can promote disruptive critically reflective practice. Employing both sustained and disruptive innovations opens possibility to engender new beliefs and gently cracks the ingrained, and often seemingly impenetrable, culture of schooling.

REFERENCES

Adler, J. A. (2008). Surprise. *Educational Theory*, *58*(2), 149–173. doi:10.1111/j.1741-5446.2008.00282.x

Boler, M. (1999). *Feeling power: Emotions and education*. London, UK: Routledge.

Britzman, D. (1998). *Lost subjects, contested objects. Toward a psychoanalytic inquiry of learning*. Albany, NY: State University of New York Press.

Butler, J. (1997). *Excitable speech: A politics of the performative* (1st ed.). New York, NY: Routledge.

Christensen, C. (1997). *The innovator's dilemma: When new technologies can cause great firms to fail*. Boston, MA: Harvard Business School Press.

Darling-Hammond, L. (1998). Teachers and teaching: Testing policy hypotheses from a national commission report. *Educational Researcher*, *27*(1), 5–16.

Davis, B., Sumara, D., & Luce-Kapler, R. (2000). *Engaging minds: Learning and teaching in a complex world*. Mahwah, NJ: Laurence Eribaum.

Duffy, F. (2003). I think, therefore I am resistant to change: What we know - or think we know - is our biggest roadblock to learning. *Journal of Staff Development, 24*(1). Retrieved 11 December, 2010, from http://www.nsdc.org/library/publications/jsd/duffy241.cfm

Fagerberg, J. (2004). Innovation: A guide to the literature. In Fagerberg, J., Mowery, D. C., & Nelson, R. R. (Eds.), *The Oxford handbook of innovation* (pp. 1–26). Oxford University Press.

Foucault, M. (1969). *The archaeology of knowledge*. New York, NY: Routledge.

Fullan, M. (1991). *The new meaning of educational change*. New York, NY: Teachers College Press.

Fullan, M. (2001). *Leading in a culture of change*. San Francisco, CA: Jossey-Bass.

Greene, M. (1973). *Teacher as stranger: Educational philosophy for the modern age*. New York, NY: Wadsworth Publishing.

Hargreaves, A., & Fullan, M. (1998). *What's worth fighting for out there?* New York, NY: Teachers' College Press.

Hargreaves, A., & Shirley, D. (2009). *The fourth way: The inspirational future for educational change*. New York, NY: Sage.

Hattie, J. (2009). *Visible learning: A synthesis of over 800 meta-analyses relating to achievement*. Oxford, UK: Routledge.

Kemmis, S., & McTaggart, R. (1990). *The action-research planner*. Geelong, Australia: Deakin University.

Lambert, L. (2002). A framework for shared leadership. *Educational Leadership, 59*(8), 37–40.

Latham, G. (2007). *New learning: Building surprise through the virtual. E-Learning at RMIT.* Melbourne RMIT University.

Laurel, B. (1991). *Computers as theatre.* Reading, MA: Addison-Wesley Publishing Company.

Marshak, D. (1996). The emotional experience of school change: Resistance, loss, and grief. *NASSP Bulletin, 80*(577), 72–77. doi:10.1177/019263659608057713

Milstein, M. M. (1993). *Restructuring schools doing it right.* New York, NY: Corwin Press, Inc.

Prensky, M. (October, 2001). *Digital natives, digital immigrants.* Retrieved 9 October, 2009, from http://www.twitchspeed.com/site/Prensky%20 -%20Digital%20Natives,%20Digital%20Immigrants%20-%20Part1.htm

Schlechty, P. C. (2005). *Creating the capacity to support innovations.* Occasional Paper No. 2. Louisville, KY: Schlechty Centre.

Sumara, D. (1996). *Private readings in public: Schooling the literary imagination.* New York, NY: Peter Lang.

Chapter 20

Coevolving through Disrupted Discussions on Critical Thinking, Human Rights and Empathy

Susie Costello
RMIT University, Australia

ABSTRACT

This chapter considers how teaching and learning cross culturally inevitably disrupts or interrupts and disturbs teachers' and students' assumptions. Such educational confrontation can produce mind-opening opportunities or mind-numbing fear that can preclude learning. The teacher's challenge is to find a balance between harnessing disruption as an impetus for learning and creating a safe environment for constructive learning exchanges.

Six stories illustrate some of the frustration, confusion, and insight that can arise from mis-interpretation, acontextual teaching, and pedagogical assumptions. The author discusses personal and pedagogical discoveries that emerged during an international social work education program with refugee teachers, health, and community workers from Burma living in exile on the Thailand Burma border (the border). Tensions between East and Western philosophies and methods of teaching called for processes to indigenize the Australian model of social work to the local cultures.

The resulting exchanges of knowledge laid the ground for knowledge and cultural exchanges in interactive, unexpected educational processes.

DOI: 10.4018/978-1-61350-495-6.ch020

BACKGROUND

This chapter explores processes of teaching and learning in an international environment, using a case study of an educational program with people displaced from Burma, living in Thailand. Their lives shattered by violence, war and flight from their country, Burmese refugees in Thailand face continual disruptions to their security, cultures, languages, health and identity and have minimal access to education.

Twenty years ago, Dr. Cynthia Maung established the Mae Tao Clinic (MTC, 2010) to provide free medical services to refugees seeking health care unavailable inside their country of Burma. Responsive to emerging problems, the clinic offers multiple services in the border townships (orphanages, women's shelters, boarding houses) and inside Burma (jungle clinics, outreach backpack medical teams, jungle health and education programs). Dr. Cynthia recruited international assistance to train medics and health workers and, in 2007, sought training to increase workers' awareness of and skills to respond to *social* problems. This formed the basis of a social work education project conducted in 2007 by the author, an Australian social work educator and practitioner. The chapter considers the author's core dilemma of how to deliver a culturally-relevant, sustainable educational program as an outsider.

The understanding of social work education in Australia is very different from social work training on the Thailand Burma border. In Australia and the Western world, social work is known as a vocational discipline which derives historically from church, charity and the welfare state's provision of a financial safety net for people unable to provide for themselves, and laws and policies to provide safety. The content and methods of teaching are prescribed and monitored through accreditation by international and national associations (the International Federation of Social Workers and, in Australia, the Australian Association of Social Workers, AASW).

In Thailand, there are 16,000 refugees displaced from Burma in refugee camps along the border (TBBC, 2010) and thousands of others who live as unregistered refugees and migrants. There is no government support and basic health and other care is provided by local and international aid. Education is minimal and vocational training such as health or social work training is provided through initiatives such as Dr Cynthia's request, which brings international people who have the motivation, time and resources to do so. Courses are not accredited, legal frameworks are ambiguous and while Thailand's fledgling democracy has seen some governmental commitment to social welfare through the introduction of child protection legislation and policies, the role of social workers remains unfamiliar to most people.

The Stories

Offering a six week course on social work for Burmese refugees in Thailand confronted the assumptions, beliefs and practices of the educator and participants. On many occasions, cross cultural or linguistic confusions rendered everyone unclear about how to proceed. The teacher had to bumble along, looking for clues that did not translate and making it up as she went along. These uncomfortable moments, however, were often resolved in a flash of understanding that deepened cross cultural understandings. The following stories illustrate such disruptive moments, each of which exemplifies Prigogine and Stenger's (1984) concept of a 'bifurcation point', described as a pivotal point of 'stuckness' or 'not knowing', which marks a 'singular moment' of discovery (Gibney, 1987). Being disrupted from your comfort zone can stretch you intellectually and personally, offering insights previously not considered.

The following stories illustrate six points of disruption in cross cultural education. The first describes challenges of interpreting and translating. The second considers Eastern versus

Western philosophies of teaching while the third story explores differences in east west emotional responses. Examples of cultural conflict and discrimination comprise the fourth and fifth story, with the final story reminding us of the costs of change. The chapter concludes with reflections on the interrelatedness of disruption and discovery with recommendations for transferring these insights to universal teaching and learning practices.

Story 1: "What is Ethics?" Issues in Interpretation

Hugman (2010) suggests that those teaching social work internationally must first consider what to include as core values and ethics in the curriculum. In their program of social work education in Vietnam, Hugman, Nguyen and Nguyen's (2007) curriculum included human rights, ethics and empathy which are core to the International and Australian codes of ethics (IFSW, 2005; AASW, 2010), so these values were selected as starting points. Consultation with prospective participants indicated their interest in learning about these concepts but it became clear that there was no shared understanding of what these values meant or could apply in this context:

When we stopped for morning tea an hour into the session on ethics, I thought things were going well since everybody looked content. I asked the interpreter how it was going. He said 'Fine. Only one question: What is 'etics'?'

The sickening feeling as I wondered how he had been translating 'ethics' to the group constituted an early bifurcation point. At that moment, I had to step away from my customary ways of working with interpreters and reflect critically. Critical thinking is an attempt at reviewing your own biases, determinants, assumptions. It is a social process of mutual observation and learning (Pakman, 1995).

Two realizations emerged from this disruption: One, body language and nonverbal indicators differ in a cross cultural context; contented-looking facial expressions do not indicate their comprehension. Second, professional jargon is doubly unfamiliar to an interpreter. How presumptuous of me to assume he knew what ethics meant, when students in Australia often ask for clarification that ethics are what people consider correct or right. It made me wonder what else I did not know about communication in this context and how I could teach if my words were not being conveyed accurately.

As a result, regular times were established to go over content, language and concepts with the interpreter well in advance of the lesson. This was difficult to do, with the constant day to day adaptation of the content to fit the context and participants' needs, often right up until the last minute. It was through time spent negotiating how to work together, however, that we found our way through this stuck point. Asking the teacher for clarification of terms was framed as a cultural exchange, resourcing the teacher, rather than a situation where the interpreter would 'lose face' (Goodfellow, O'Neil and Smith, 1996). We worked out how the interpreter would let me know if he was unsure of the meaning.

The interpreter explained that while Burmese is the assigned common language in that setting, many newly arrived refugees from different ethnic nationalities did not yet speak it well, so their friends were translating the interpreter's Burmese translation of my English, into their own languages. This left great room for error. A group of workers involved in a newly established (December 2010) mental health coordination group on the border (Derina from Ireland, Julia from Australia, Liberty who is Karen from Burma and Whitney from USA) is in the process of developing a lexicon of words and phrases constantly being translated in psychosocial work with refugees and migrants. They are describing the literal translation in each of the languages, some of which are referred to in the following stories.

Navigating language was only the first hurdle. The next challenge was to introduce one of the social work values – human rights.

While Burmese refugees on the border have a strong sense of injustice about the way they have been treated by the military in Burma, and anger at the mistreatment of Burmese factory workers by the Thais, few generalized the notion of human rights to include the practical implementation of justice for all people. Women's and children's rights have been overlooked in refugees' fights for survival, with no clear policies, laws or interventions against violence, apart from a few initiatives, for example by Dr. Cynthia Maung and the Migrant Assistance Program (MAP, 2010). What risks are there in raising awareness of people's rights when there are inadequate systems to assert them? Is the Western notion of human rights a relevant concept for people committed to the traditional Asian values of *responsibility, social norms, family, stability, and relationships* fundamental to the collective harmony of Confucian philosophy (Yip 2004)?

Is it possible and safe to even talk about human rights on the Thailand Burma border, where people are astutely alert to the risks of speaking out to unknown people? Many are ex-political prisoners who retain fear of speaking out, having borne the consequences of doing so inside Burma. Why would anyone risk naming human rights abuses to an outsider who needed an interpreter to communicate?

Nussbaum (2000) offers a practical and ethical way around some of these questions. She suggests that rights-based initiatives should focus on *doing* things rather than just talking about seemingly unachievable concepts such as rights. By identifying problems of oppression, then finding ways (capabilities) to attain rights with and for those affected, people learning about human rights can see how they look and feel. Hugman (2010) suggests that where local and contextual

values conflict with universal values, it is useful to prioritize them as primary or secondary. Primary values are universal (such as human rights) and secondary values are local (such as ensuring people are not arrested by border police despite their rights to citizenship not being addressed). Hugman calls this 'ethical pluralism' (p. 133).

Prioritizing values as Hugman (2010) suggested, and heeding Nussbaum's (2000) idea of doing things rather than just talking about them, some decisions were made. First, it was right to teach the principles and practices of human rights, despite the lack of opportunity for them to be realized in the context on the border. Second, it should be done in ways that make sense in terms of local norms and culture, experientially, so that people have a vision of what having rights feels like. Third, there are lessons from others who have liberated silenced people, notably Freire (1973) and Boal (1979), three decades ago.

Boal's (1979) *Theatre of the Oppressed* emerged originally to give voice to peasants and workers in Chile about their oppressive social and political conditions. Freire (1973) and Boal (1979) used creative arts and drama with illiterate impoverished people to express their views and generate solutions. Through drama, people play out real life situations. The facilitator invites them to 'act' out suggestions for positive change. The key moment of transformation occurs when the facilitator invites members of the audience to step into the shoes of the 'actors' and play it differently. Experiencing and offering alternative responses from the outside, then stepping inside to try it out, participants and audience gain insight, empathy and shifts in thinking and beliefs (Boal, 1995).

A *Theatre of the oppressed* method was used in the project in Thailand by asking the participants first to list the problems confronting them. Small groups selected a problem each to enact in silent, still, drama scenes, while the other groups watched. One group depicted a woman being abused by her husband while their scared children crouched behind their mother. Another group acted refugees being locked up by Thai security guards and returned to Burma. A third group showed children being sold for unpaid labour and sex work.

In the next step, each group created an image of a resolution of their problem, again in silence. In the first group, the abused women was now being hugged and cared for by a loving husband in a scene of a happy family, (wishful thinking as most social workers know, particularly so in this context where violence against women does not register as illegal).

The transformational third step asked the group to act out another scene depicting one transitional step that could change the problem towards resolution. Members of the audience could step in and act out a suggestion.

After conferring together, the group created a scene where the community leader took the 'violent' man aside and admonished him for his violent behaviour, while the women sheltered the woman and children. This was an achievable community step. As Freire (1973) and Boal (1979) described, drama can liberate people's capacity to think critically, through silent action and communal problem-solving. Drama addressed several confronting issues: problems were defined by the group, rather than the teacher; silence avoided the need for interpreting, speaking out or discussion; and the act of developing a realistic transitional image demanded collaborative critical thinking where participants chose their own solutions to achieve human rights and responsibility.

The next step was to introduce the social worker's role in responding to emotional pain, as requested by Dr. Cynthia. Medical treatment was not helping people with loss, trauma, grief or mental illnesses.

Story 2. "Why Did You Make her Cry?" Disrupting Values – Empathy

Although human rights depend on the implementation of and access to laws, the values of compassion, patience, commitment and selflessness are also necessary for human rights practice (Hugman, 2010), along with ethics, humanity and empathy (Hugman, Nguyen, & Nguyen, 2007). Empathy is 'the ability to stand in another's shoes, to feel what it's like there and to care about making it better if it hurts' (Szalavitz & Perry, 2010, p.12). In Burmese translation, it is 'sar nar day' which means sharing the feeling of others. In Karen language, it is interpreted as 'heart echo'. Szalavitz and Perry argue that empathy determines brain development and survival. The infant's attachment experience determines well-being, mental health and relationships in adulthood. Empathic responses can assist recovery from abuse, neglect and trauma. This story describes experiences of learning about and trying to teach empathy as responses to people's social and emotional problems.

As part of a project to raise awareness and money for children needing expensive medical care, I interviewed their parents with a nurse acting as interpreter, and wrote about their stories on the clinic website. On one such occasion, a young Burmese mother cried as she told of her husband's death as they ran from soldiers and their burning village. I responded with concern for her situation. While we were talking, the nurse who was interpreting was giggling with another nurse. I glared at them. Afterwards, I asked them why they were laughing. 'Because', one said, the other nodding, 'You were making her cry by asking her those questions. We were trying to cheer her up'.

The nurses' response shocked me in its apparent lack of empathy for the mother. Their accusation of my improper behaviour left me feeling bewildered. I did not know how to judge whether I was being culturally inappropriate, if the nurses had compassion fatigue or if it was something else.

Nguyen and Bowles (1988) emphasize the need for empathic listening, moving slowly, with the right timing. My quick empathic response and judgement of the giggling nurses was probably mis-timed, yet Nguyen and Bowles say that 'a sure sign that Vietnamese clients are ready to talk about something is the rare occasion of them losing control and crying' (p. 45). That provides an opportunity for them to share their pain. Bang (1983) emphasizes the need for emotionally articulate Western workers to understand the importance of non-verbal communication in Asian cultures, but she is not referring to observing facial expressions. She means practical support, showing interest in people's extended family and stories and being honest and open in response to questions. These writers see empathy as a necessary part of the process of building trust and rapport in Asian cultures where open expression of emotions and problems is less common.

This was not the view of one of the clinic staff who provided counselling and assistance to people with mental health issues or who came to have their HIV status clarified.

It's easy to see people who are HIV positive as you know what to tell them - get plenty of sleep, eat good food, don't injure yourself... but what do you tell someone with a mental health problem?

The fact that the counsellors saw their role as 'telling' people (about, or to do something) indicated a culturally different interpretation of counselling from the empathic, meaning- making approach espoused in the social work program. Linguistically, there are at least two different interpretations of counselling in Burmese and Karen; one means consoling, another means giving advice. A directive, advice-giving approach is perhaps the most practical in the circumstances on the border where there are few medical resources for HIV positive people, and minimal understanding of psychiatric illnesses. There seemed to be no room for empathy, however, and no structural analysis of their problems.

In an exercise developed to explore 'empathy', the class studied a locally developed case scenario of a young Muslim Burmese woman, Ma Phyu, pregnant with her recently deceased HIV positive partner's child. Alone and without an income, she wanted an abortion, which is illegal and forbidden, and threatened suicide if she had to continue her pregnancy. The concept and practice of empathy was explained, then the participants were asked to identify and respond with empathy to an emotion Ma Phyu might be feeling. We went around the circle hearing from each person:

The first problem was that the 'emotion' that many described was 'crying'. This produced another one of those 'where do I go with this?' disruptive moments that had become quite common. I side-stepped a grammar lesson and moved on to their responses - the second problem. Their 'empathic' response to the woman crying was to say: 'Stop crying', There's no point crying', 'Crying isn't going to help' and, another suggestion further along the circle, which was at least different: 'No need to cry now. I am a social worker and will fix everything for you'. I gave up hoping they would say something empathic so modeled it myself, repetitively: 'you seem really sad'; 'the situation has made you really unhappy'; 'no wonder you are scared'……

When the 27th, 28th and 29th participant actually reflected the feeling they had identified and said something along the line modelled, it was difficult to tell if they understood how to show empathy or if it was 'empty verbalism' (Buckingham, 1993). Their unexpected responses were confronting. Their lack of empathy shocked me but, on reflection, made sense if viewed as a dissociative response to trauma that many had experienced in Burma.

As a way to find common understandings, next time the group considered the circumstantial and structural factors (social empathy) affecting Ma Phyu. This was followed by a role play demonstration of an empathic conversation with 'Ma Phyu', with the idea that watching a practical example would demystify the process of empathy. In this dramatization, the interpreter nurse who had made the pregnant widow laugh to 'cheer her up' in the earlier situation, volunteered to play the pregnant woman. The 'social worker' modelled an empowerment approach, identifying Ma Phyu's strengths in the face of structural and discriminatory barriers.

After the role play, participants said they were surprised that the pregnant woman was not just lying to get a service from the clinic and that she seemed to have a genuine problem. The nurse actor told the group that although she felt very sad 'being' the pregnant woman, she was pleased to be believed and gained hope from the options and support offered. Through the experience of 'stepping into the shoes of' the character, she said she felt sad for the woman and more inclined to believe people who came to the clinic with social problems.

The development of empathy in the refugee workers raised a reflective question: What effects would using an empathic approach have on workers, many of whom had suffered trauma? Conscious of the risks of imposing Western therapeutic approaches, the next stage sought to indigenize the educational program (Gray, 2005). Indigenization includes consultation with, respect for and inclusion of local and diverse people's knowledge, skills and case examples.

Story 3: "We'd Stone Her": Disruptive Values – Discrimination

The training programs comprised people from many ethnic nationalities from Burma and beyond: Arakan, British, Burmese, Canadian, Dashelay, Filippina, Karen, Mon, Pa O, Paulong, Tavoy and Thai. When forming small groups to respond to exercises, people grouped according to ethnic, or non-ethnic categories based on religion or the geographic area they came from. There was always a group of people who did not fit into any of the identified categories, so they became a group of

their own, different each time. Being flexible provided opportunities for self-selected cultural groups to share their village and cultural practices.

While the cultural diversity of participants had been acknowledged, there had been no reference to 'culturally specific ways of help-seeking behaviour and traditional ways of coping with emotional distress' (Miller, Kulkarni, & Kushner, 2006, p. 409). For example, Chan, Chan, and Ng (2006) draw on Eastern philosophies and concepts from traditional Chinese medicine to advocate restoring clients' mental strength through meditation, healing rituals, social support and philosophical teachings.

Miller and Rasco (2004) argue that mental health interventions for refugees should target the psychological consequences of their exposure to the violence and destruction of wartime experiences, as well as the distress they experience living in exile. They encourage attention to local beliefs and practices that culturally construct meanings.

These ideas motivated an exercise attempting to acknowledge local wisdom and practices, where, in cultural, ethnic or spiritual groups, participants could discuss how their traditional communities respond to some of the social problems they had identified: aggressive people, migrant workers, AIDS, HIV, alcoholism, mental illness, poverty, security, unwanted pregnancy and abandoned babies.

These are the notes from their responses:

- *People with HIV AIDS: You get it because you had sex with too many people. We don't dare to be close to them, we don't touch them, we look down on them, hate them, feel they are dirty, I know I shouldn't look down on them but in practice I can't be near them. We discriminate against them, don't eat with them. We can only give education how to prevent HIV.*

- *Unwanted pregnancy & abortion: We look down on them, say bad things about them, they are bad, they don't make friends, they are bad women. Nobody feel sorry for them. People think they have to take responsibility for self, we think they are guilty. We punish them, kick them out from the village, some are tied in rope and thrown with stone, but not in our village.*

- ***Mental illness:** If we see people with mental problems, we feel sorry for them; think they are foolish, but don't blame them. We think they are funny when they do crazy things. We don't think they have any value.*

So much for respecting local culture! Rather than discovering and including useful local responses, this exercise produced a range of discriminatory, excluding and inhumane ways of responding to vulnerable people. I was shocked and had difficulty managing my own emotional response to the inherent discrimination within the group. It is difficult respecting different cultural practices that do not sit comfortably with us (Laird, 1998). Blackwell (2005) describes the need for people working with refugees to be aware of their own defenses in preparation for being unprepared. A discussion with the group about our earlier role play with the pregnant woman drew some connections between their apparent empathy in that situation and general discriminatory behavior.

Story 4: "She's Not One of Us": Disruptive Values – Exclusion

Gravers (2007) argues that people from ethnic minorities on the Thailand Burma border harbor internalized hostilities from their former lives, which contribute to their sense of being 'victims'. They lose sight of the possibility that they can intervene and change the perspectives of those in power (hooks, 2003). The exercise described in the last story invited different ethnic groups to describe their community's responses to different social problems, as outlined in the last section. People could group in ethnic nationalities, or ac-

cording to religious, language, place or any other group identifier.

Within one group, I noticed some wriggling and tense body language, so, via the interpreter, asked what was going on. One of the women in the Burman group, Soe Soe, was objecting to another woman, Mi Yin, joining them because previously she was in another group, the Mons. Through the interpreter, she told us that last time she was with the Mons as her mother was Mon. Today she wanted to be with the Burmans, like her father. Soe Soe objected – no, you're Mon! You're not one of us!

Remembering that "(a)cts of acknowledgement [...] can serve a strong educative and transformative function" (Howard, 1999, p. 78), this issue was pursued in dialogue with the whole group:

Who else has two or more ethnic identities? A third of the group responded, including Soe Soe whose father is Chinese: 'but' she said, 'I'm not Chinese, I'm Burman like my mum'. This led to a theoretical discussion of the constructed nature and politics of ethnicity. What was it like for Mi Yin's Mon friends for her to want to leave them and join the Burman group? They felt hurt and insulted. What were the dilemmas for those with multiple ethnicities? Some told stories of confused loyalties, of not belonging and feeling embarrassed. People listened.

One man, however, celebrated his multiple ethnicities: 'I'm part of many groups, not just one'. He was a popular, funny member of the group and his viewpoint had an impact. We returned to what we knew about human rights. Do Min Yi and Soe Soe have the right to decide their ethnic allegiances? Do they have the right to change their mind?

At the end of this discussion, Soe Soe invited Min Yi into their group. Min Yi had a tearful conver-

sation with her Mon friends and then joined the Burman group for the rest of the exercise.

Laird (1998) describes culture as a fluid, contextual *performance*. Culture is intersectional in that no one fits only one category: a woman has a race, class, sexual orientation and age, each with contextually ascribed meanings. Culture is political in that people do not have equal voice in shaping their personal narratives. These narratives are embedded in larger social discourses that become known as 'truths'. They can be liberating and open possibilities, or subjugating and limit the range of possibilities for ourselves and lives. While Laird was not only referring to the literal performance of culture, a performance on the final day of the training program captured the liberatory possibilities of naming cultural differences in the way people did in this program:

When I returned from the lunch break, the room was alive with music and dancing. Each group was demonstrating their ethnic songs and dancing, teaching each other the moves, laughing at funny actions and hugging.

Pakman (1998) uses the term 'cultural borderlands' to refer to the socially constructed boundaries between cultures that are 'created, maintained, and perpetuated by discourses and daily micro-practices' (p. 23). Cultural borders are maintained through ongoing perceptions of difference and the potential for tension or enrichment. Pakman argues that merely training people to 'understand' 'other cultures' is condescending and risks differences being misconstrued according to one's own traditions. Rather, he suggests, cultural borderlands are opportunities for reflections together on the perception of the fluctuating, socially constructed hierarchies of differences. Our therapeutic role, says Pakman, is to create communication processes where we can reflect on ourselves and the world in which we live. 'Reflection is the process that, through differ-

ent means, allows people to see themselves and others through different eyes, stepping out of the restrictions they have set for themselves' (p. 29).

Critical reflection is central to transformative processes but must include emotion and intuition, space for deep listening to conversations that involve everyone, the use of narratives and questions and an ethical use of knowledge where the adult learners are coequals in the learning experience. Within this framework, disagreements can be seen as diverse 'pieces of a whole' brought together through collaboration and connection (Wiessner & Mezirow, 2000). Through reflection, dialogue and dance, the group embarked on a process of dismantling the 'frozen products of tradition that are maintained through ... the micro-politics of everyday experience' (Pakman, 1998, p. 25). What is it like for displaced people who experience such change?

Story 5: "I Cannot Go Back": The Dangers of Change

Transformative learning is often prompted by a disorienting dilemma, an experience that causes a person to question what he or she has previously believed to be unquestionable' (Wiessner & Mezirow, 2000, p. 333). The dilemma can be epochal (sudden) or cumulative (unfolding over time) and can be exciting, painful or both:

Ler Moo described his deep sadness at the sense of loss he'd experienced since he left his village in Karen state three years before. He now works in a senior position with an NGO, having been selected for an education program in leadership, human rights and critical thinking. Now, he said, he finds it almost impossible to go back to his village, not because of the dangers of travelling through land mine infested jungles but because, when he goes there, he no longer feels he belongs. His family and community now seem like peasants. He feels ashamed of their simple uncritical life. Yet that life existed for centuries, he said. Sons take over paddy farming from their fathers and grandfathers with a certainty that was now missing from his life. He feels his individual quest for education has disrupted a culture that he yearns for but no longer feels part of. He questioned the legitimacy of this process.

Ler Moo's critique exemplifies the disorienting dilemma that can occur in the move between traditional Eastern values of community and village egalitarianism, relational and familial obligations and identities and the commitment to harmony and solidarity (Milner & Quilty, 1996) and the individualistic, liberal-democratic traditions of the west. It is a circular argument, one that he found difficult, because despite his criticisms, he has chosen and benefited from his education. Ler Moo's dilemma exemplifies the 'masochistic ritual which underlies all great intellectual efforts in the West, [which is] a circle of intellectual torture' (Kowalski, 1999, p. 205). There are no simple answers to the dilemmas that emerge with greater learning and insight, and there is no going back.

CONCLUSION AND RECOMMENDATIONS

The final story seems a good way to end because it is unsettling and disruptive to assumptions that international education is useful, relevant or sustainable. Where people's lives are disrupted by their past, present and unknown futures, educators need to be wary of inflicting additional risks and pressures by imposing Western concepts and teaching methods. Deeply held culturally prescribed beliefs and assumptions are not easily challenged or changed, for neither the outsider teacher nor the host country learners.

Cross cultural learning occurs through a process of co-evolution of knowledge, which includes times of Not Knowing. Neither teacher nor students are fully aware of what they do not know and it can be intimidating and humiliating finding out. The international educator steps out of her or his comfort zone into linguistic, cultural and pedagogically unfamiliar territory, becoming a learner of new ways of thinking, speaking and listening.

Communication does not work in expected ways in an international context. Cues from body language need to be reinterpreted within the new cultural context and it is not straightforward to ask about nonverbal behaviours. Working with interpreters presents linguistic, ethical and professional challenges in the international context. Eastern notions of respect for the teacher and the risk of 'losing face' disrupt communication processes that seem natural in your home environment.

Attempting to teach from a Western educational philosophy based on critical thinking, discussion and democracy requires mutual adjustment for the teacher and students in the Asian context. The Western focus on rights, equality, individual autonomy, change and empowerment clash with Asian values of family obligation, responsibility and stability. Discussions of human rights and empathy may be conceptually and experientially unfamiliar and present risks for people expressing individual views.

The process of education can therefore create mind-opening opportunities and mind-numbing fear that precludes learning. The teacher's challenge is to create a safe environment for constructive learning exchanges, harnessing the discomfort of not knowing as an impetus for learning.

As with any social work experience, relationships provide the way through dilemmas. Through listening, laughter, warmth and honesty, connections can circumvent cultural boundaries. Drama and other nonverbal communication methods can provide ways for people to acknowledge cultural differences and ethnic hostilities that are difficult to articulate verbally. The resulting exchanges of knowledge lay the ground for knowledge and cultural exchange in interactive, transformational, unexpected educational processes.

REFERENCES

AASW. (2010). *Code of ethics* (3rd ed.). Australian Association of Social Workers. Retrieved 14 November, 2010, from http://www.aasw.asn.au/document/item/740/

Bang, S. (1983). *We come as a friend –Towards a Vietnamese model of social work*. Leeds, UK: Refugee Action.

Blackwell, D. (2005). *Counselling and psychotherapy with refugees*. Philadelphia, PA: Jessica Kingsley Publications.

Boal, A. (1979). *Theatre of the oppressed*. London, UK: Pluto Press.

Boal, A. (1995). *The rainbow of desire*. New York, NY: Routledge Press.

Buckingham, D. (1993). *Reading audiences: Young people and the media*. Manchester, UK: University Press.

Chan, C., Chan, T., & Ng, S. (2006). *The strength-focused and meaning oriented approach to resilience and transformation (SMART): A body-mind spirit approach to trauma management*. The Hawthorn Press.

Freire, P. (1973). *Education as the practice of freedom in education for critical consciousness*. New York, NY: Continuum.

Gibney, P. (1987). Co-evolving with anorectic families: Difference is a singular moment. *The Australian and New Zealand Journal of Family Therapy, 8*(2), 71–80.

Goodfellow, R., O'Neil, D., & Smith, P. (Eds.). (1996). *Saving face, losing face, in your face: A journey into the Western heart, mind and soul*. Oxford, UK: Butterworth Heinemann.

Gravers, M. (Ed.). (2007). *Exploring ethnic diversity in Burma*. Denmark: Nais Press.

Gray, M. (2005). Dilemmas of international social work: Paradoxical processes in indigenisation, universalism and imperialism. *International Journal of Social Welfare, 14*(3), 231–238. doi:10.1111/j.1468-2397.2005.00363.x

hooks, B. (2003). *Teaching community: A pedagogy of hope*. New York, NY: Routledge.

Howard, G. (1999). *We can't teach what we don't know: White teachers, multiracial schools*. New York, NY: Columbia Teachers College Press.

Hugman, R. (2010). *Understanding international social work: A critical analysis*. London, UK: Palgrave Macmillan.

Hugman, R., Nguyen, T. T. L., & Nguyen, T. H. (2007). Developing social work in Vietnam. *International Social Work, 50*(2), 197–211. doi:10.1177/0020872807073985

IFSW. (2005). *International federation of social workers*. Retrieved 6 November, 2010, from http://www.ifsw.org

Kowalski, S. (1999). Western education: Because it works… for now. In R. Goodfellow, O'Neil & P. Smith (Eds.), *Saving Face, losing face, in your face: A journey into the Western heart, mind and soul*. Oxford, UK: Butterworth Heinemann.

Laird, J. (1998). Theorizing culture: Narrative ideas and practice principles. In McGoldrick, M. (Ed.), *Revisioning family therapy: Culture, gender and clinical practice*. New York, NY: Guilford Press.

MAP. (2010). *Migrant assistance program, Thailand*. Retrieved 6 November, 2010, from www.mapfoundationcm.org/

Miller, K., Kulkarni, M., & Kushner, H. (2006). Beyond trauma-focused psychiatric epidemiology: Bridging research and practice with war affected populations. *The American Journal of Orthopsychiatry, 76*(4), 409–422. doi:10.1037/0002-9432.76.4.409

Miller, K., & Rasco, L. (2004). *The mental health of refugees: Ecological approaches to healing and adaptation*. New Jersey: Lawrence Erlbaum Associates.

Milner, A., & Quilty, M. (1996). *Australia in Asia: Comparing cultures*. Melbourne, Australia: Oxford University Press.

MTC. (2010). *Mae Tao Clinic*. Retrieved 15 November, 2010, from http://maetaoclinic.org/

Nguyen, T., & Bowles, W. (1988). Counselling Vietnamese refugee survivors of trauma: Points of entry for developing trust and rapport. *Australian Social Work, 59*(2), 41–47.

Nussbaum, M. (2000). *Women and human development*. Cambridge, UK: Cambridge University Press.

Pakman, M. (1995). Therapy in contexts of poverty and ethnic dissonance: Constructivism and social constructivism as methodologies for action. *Journal of Systemic Therapies, 14*(4), 64–71.

Pakman, M. (1998). Education and therapy in cultural borderlands: A call for critical social practices in human services. *Journal of Systemic Therapies, 17*(1), 18–30.

Prigogine, I., & Stengers, I. (1984). Order out of chaos: Man's new dialogue with nature. *International Journal of Technology and Human Interaction, 1*(3), 1–14.

Szalavitz, M., & Perry, B. (2010). *Born for love: Why empathy is essential- And endangered*. New York, NY: Harper Collins.

TBBC. (2010). *Thai Burma Border Consortium*. Retrieved 15 November, 2010, from http://www.tbbc.org/

Wiessner, C., & Mezirow, J. (2000). Theory building and the search for common ground. In Mezirow, (Eds.), *Learning as transformation: Critical perspectives on a theory in progress* (pp. 329–358). New York, NY: Jossey-Bass.

Yip, K. (2004). A Chinese cultural critique of the global qualifying standards for social work education. *Social Work Education, 23*(5), 597–612. doi:10.1080/0261547042000252316

KEY TERMS AND DEFINITIONS

Bifurcation: Splitting or division. A 'bifurcation point' is a moment of critical decision where through 'not knowing', a person must make certain choices and in so doing, discovers new ways of thinking.

Cultural Relativism: The view that human values vary according to different cultural perspectives, rather than being universal.

Displacement: The process where people are forced to move from their home or country because of war, persecution or environmental disasters.

Empathy: The ability to identify with, understand and care about another's feelings and situation.

Ethics: Relates to what is considered correct or right by a culture or group.

Indigenization: Includes consultation with, respect for and inclusion of local and diverse people's knowledge, skills and case examples.

Chapter 21

The New Public Management of Higher Education:
Teaching and Learning

Heather Brunskell-Evans
University of Greenwich, UK

ABSTRACT

This chapter explores the possibilities of Michel Foucault's philosophical-political writings for practicing a "pedagogy of discomfort" in Higher Education (HE). Foucault's method of genealogy and his concept of governmentality are used to reflect upon the dynamics of power underlying the government of HE in the United Kingdom, in particular the new modes of teaching and learning. The chapter has three inextricably entwined aims: it presents a genealogical history of the changing face of HE under the auspices of New Public Management (NPM) as a form of neo-liberal governmental disciplinary control; it describes the new modes of teaching and learning as examples of that control; and it argues that inherent in genealogical modes of analysis are possibilities and opportunities for educationists concerned with politically framed progressive action to develop pedagogical practices that disrupt or challenge the government of teaching and learning.

HIGHER EDUCATION AS THE OBJECT OF GOVERNMENTAL CONTROL

In contrast to the proposition that despite the rapidly altering context of technologies of communication since the 1980s current teachers working across a range of educational institutions still perpetuate conservative and outmoded models of teaching and learning, I argue, taking HE as an example, that university lecturers actively embrace emerging demands to develop new models of teaching and learning. However, rather than viewing the transformative changes in teaching and learning as redesigning future progressive possibilities for individual learning, I argue that the new pedagogical models, in adapting to the

DOI: 10.4018/978-1-61350-495-6.ch021

world of the future, are themselves instrumental in conveying and mobilizing conservative norms whilst replacing old ones. I suggest that Foucault's anti-humanist theoretical analysis of the liberal government of institutions provides a fruitful way to understand the politics of teaching and learning in the contemporary university. I propose that the new pedagogical practices be situated under the umbrella of New Public Management (NPM) of HE which, since the 1980s, can be seen as comprised of a number of technologies or strategies of governmentalization.

Governmentality

Foucault (1982, 1991) coined the neologism 'governmentality' to describe the structures of power in liberal democracies by which the conduct of individuals is orchestrated through mobilizing their self-organizing capacities so that they align their wants, aspirations, hopes and desires to the needs of the state. This orchestration occurs through various statutory and non-statutory institutions and the official knowledges which support them. The desired effect of the apparatuses and formal knowledges which make up governmentality is a population of subjects who voluntarily and willingly delegate their autonomy and responsibility to obedience to being governed in their conduct by a 'moral' force (the state and society) which is experienced as external to the self. Governmentality refers not only to ways of thinking about, and a set of practices for government, but also the colonization of the psyche which governmentality entails, where acts of obedience in relation to sets of truth seem normal and beyond contestation.

Foucault's aim in analyzing the strategies of governmental power in modern liberal democracies is not to ascertain the legitimacy or illegitimacy of power but to understand the nature of power. His genealogies of the prison and of sexuality (Foucault, 1977, 1978) describe the power that is exercised within liberal modes of governing as 'normalizing power'. The human

sciences (psychology, sociology, anthropology, and economics) formulate the axes of normal/abnormalcy for human functioning. Normalizing power produces human individuals as particular kinds of subjects who carry out self-regulation according to established norms for human behavior. The main characteristic of the power exercised in liberal democracy is thus not its negativity but its productivity and its constant exercise *through* us. Normalcy/abnormalcy is a specific form of 'reason' and is reproduced through institutions such as schools, universities, prisons and hospitals which deploy the truths of the human sciences for their functioning and modes of operation. As such, processes of 'subjectification' occur whereby human beings self-regulate and take up their places within the complex divisions of labor that the society requires.

In conclusion, governmentality involves the calculations, programs, strategies, reflections and tactics by which the state attempts to 'conduct the conduct' of individuals and groups of individuals in order to achieve social order. Self-surveillance around the concept of the norm does not emerge from direct control but is instigated through a range of cultural practices of moral endorsement, persuasion and enablement, right through to the formalized technical knowledges through which government is exercised. What makes power hold good in liberal democracy and what makes it accepted is precisely that it does not bear down upon us as a negative force but that it traverses us, induces specific pleasures in us and mobilizes us to govern ourselves as 'free' autonomous subjects. In contrast to the humanism of the liberal theory of individual autonomy, Foucault's anti-humanist thesis is that liberal government is dependent on the practices that have already rendered the individual obedient. Instead of understanding the human being as antecedent to power, genealogy traces the production of the human being an autonomous subject by the power/ knowledge relations of government. Discipline is inextricably linked with desires and values which find expression through forms of self-regulation freely created and embraced; individuals lose themselves in regimes of power/ knowledge but are paradoxically created as subjects by these same regimes.

Foucault's concept of governmentality does not describe one homogenous or blanket mode of liberal democratic government since governmental administrations shift according to historical and political circumstances. It makes available a way of theorizing and formulating specific analyses of local sites of government according to the central, component strategies of classic liberalism described above. What follows below is a genealogical way of conceptualizing how the contemporary neo-liberal state, HE and the economic are enmeshed and how tutors and students are thereby normatively disciplined.

New Public Management (NPM) of Higher Education

A History of the 'New' University in Three Acts

In the UK the Further and Higher Education Act 1992 advocated the expansion of HE by turning the 'old' polytechnic colleges into 'new' universities (Salter & Tapper, 1994). This expansion was combined with a governmental promotion of widening participation under the rubric of equity of opportunity for non-traditional students. Since then widening participation has become popularly understood as greater freedom to participate in and have access to the liberal democratic political framework. Alongside the widening participation agenda the Act also signifies a changed political relationship between the state and HE. Whereas the university had previously been understood as relatively autonomous, since 1992 it has been tied to the state across a whole range of issues, which ultimately involve its accountability to the needs of the economy and the production of a workforce with skills suited to the needs of the global market place (Salter & Tapper, 1994).

The twenty year period since 1992 has witnessed the formulation and implementation of two further HE acts: the Teaching and Higher Education Act 1998 and the Higher Education Act 2004 (Olssen, Codd, & O'Neill, 2004). Through the implementation of the three Acts the state has acquired consistent and incremental powers which, unlike any other historical period, has effected change on a vast scale and in a manner that determines the everyday practices of the academy, including teaching and learning. Moreover changes to HE in the UK can be seen to belong to a larger European project in which the distinction made between education and training is now beginning to disappear. A new model of HE is emerging which provide a 'seamlessness' between work and education: employability skills-based training; 'distance learning'; new qualification frameworks with 'flexible pathways'; credit transfers; and a push for ongoing improvement of outcomes as measured by student access, participation and retention (Olssen, Codd, & O'Neill, 2004).

New Public Management

A number of Foucauldian scholars (Clegg, 1998; Peters, Marshall, & Fitzsimons, 2000; Olssen, Codd, & O'Neill, 2004; Starkey & McKinlay, 1998) analyze the contemporary changes to HE by discussing NPM as a particular and specific neo-liberal governmental practice. The theory of NPM suggests that one of the features of the neo-liberal environment since the 1980s is the deregulation of the state and the tendency to define social, economic and political issues as problems to be solved through economic management.

A specific constellation of theories and models for management have been used as the legitimating basis and instrumental means by which public institutions and public policy have been redesigned. These theories are variants of classical liberal thought sharing many of its major presuppositions: subjects are economically self-interested; competitiveness in the market place is a mechanism for quality and efficiency; individuals are rational optimizers and are the best judges of their own interests and needs; government should rule 'from a distance' through concepts of choice, freedom, empowerment, and autonomy; and a 'flexible' or deregulated labor market provides equal opportunity for people to develop skills and optimize their life-goals. By regarding all purposively rational conduct as economic, and attributing to all subjects the fundamental faculty of choice, self-actualization is the key enterprise of the individual producer-consumer.

Although the ascendancy of social organization through NPM has taken place in the context of the ideology of neo-liberalism and globalization, it is manifested in discrete and local contexts. The most significant element is the decentralization of management control onto the individual institution and this is enabled by a new contractuarilsm (the doctrine of self-management) coupled with a new accountability and funding structures. NPM borrows a range of managerial notions from the private sector, such as an emphasis on organizational performance, efficiency and responsiveness to consumers. It introduces standardized, depersonalized practices, such as pre-set, evidence-based output measures and assessment programs which themselves find their origin in a longer tradition of scientific management. There is an elaboration of explicit standards and measures of performance in quantitative terms that set specific targets for personnel, an emphasis on economic rewards and sanctions, and a reconstruction of accountability relationships.

Although the decentralization of management control has often been accompanied by a disaggregation of large state bureaucracies into autonomous agencies and this is accompanied by a clarification of organizational objectives, the paradox of the discourse of greater rationalization, autonomy, individual choice and freedom however is that NPM promises government's greater social control through specific forms of normalization. Variations of managerialism constitute regulatory, supervisory and controlling mechanisms which aim at the 'standardization' and 'normalization' of the conduct of public service employees, and public service clients. Managerialism is a 'faceless' technology in which corporatist management practices involve individuals in implicating themselves in their own government, where self-government occurs at the intersection of technologies of discipline and technologies of self. Since 'obedience' is central to organizational control of 'free' subjects, any organization will normally attempt to construct the architectonic of some overall strategic practices of discipline. Such practices will not only be constraining, they will endorse and enable obedient wills and constitute organizationally approved forms of creativity and productivity through transitive processes (via rules, superiors etc.) and intransitive processes (via the acquisition by members of organizationally proper conduct).

New Public Management of Higher Education

In the context of the deregulated state NPM reforms have characterized public sector institutions in English speaking countries such as Australia, New Zealand, Canada, the United States, but also in other countries such as Germany and Japan. The concept of governmentality provides a powerful tool for understanding how, since the early 1990s, HE has been transformed through being tied to both the neo-liberal state and NPM, and how this is accomplished through the production of self-governing subjects who tailor their educational and life aspirations and desires to the requirements of the state (Peters, Marshall, & Fitzsimons, 2000; Olssen, Codd, & O'Neill, 2004).

Rather than represent a withdrawal of state power from HE, NPM strategies deploy a power which is increasingly pervasive since it functions to simultaneously centralize and individualize. A whole raft of changes have occurred coupled with a widening participation agenda: the development of interdisciplinary, experiential and workplace-based learning focused on a theory-practice dialogue; quality assurance; resource-maximizing organizational principles; and new funding models which encompass public and private partnerships. These reforms have worked to destabilize universities across numerous dimensions: it has impacted on the internal dynamics of management, teaching and learning; it has transformed the external dynamics of HE as a public good offered to serve public interests to a semi-private enterprise harnessed to the advantage of economic private interests. Taking the rationale of economic entrepreneurship as a model for the government of HE and for the 'empowerment' of students as citizens does not make individuals free from power, but induces individuals to turn themselves into the kinds of subjects necessary for government (Olssen, Codd, & O'Neill, 2004).

THE SELF-GOVERNMENT OF THE UNIVERSITY STUDENT AND TEACHER

I analyze the new models of learning and teaching as a local enacting of policy discourse informed by NPM of HE mobilized through forms of subjectification. The discourses of teaching and learning and the practices that are attached reshape subjectivity, and retune the relationship between the tutor and student according to the disciplinary requirements of the knowledge economy rather than the values of professional critical judgment and the classroom as a democratic learning environment.

The Self-Government of the University Student

The re-configuration of learners and the learning environment has been substantive in relation to the university as a market place involving greater co-ordination between HE and public and private

institutions. In the interests of brevity I take two examples here, that of widening participation and experiential work-based learning.

The Widening Participation Agenda

The widening participation agenda is mobilized by government within rhetoric of the greater equality of citizens and the mitigation of social exclusion. New policies have been implemented in the UK which charge universities with the task of achieving 40-50% of the population taking up university places after their compulsory education is complete. This injunction allegedly means greater participation in, access to, and equity in liberal democracy. However, as Burke & Jackson (2007) point out, HE policy is underpinned by specific neo-liberal assumptions about the characteristics of 'the individual' who will become educated: the individual is self-maximizing and self-interested individual, and is not gendered, raced or classed; there is an unproblematic connection made between the individual's personal investment in education (as if only by choice) and the rewards obtained in paid work (as if only by merit); and the individual consumes education as a product for instrumental purposes. The values of individual enterprise, risk-taking and competitiveness are mobilized through discourses that uphold the notion of a meritocratic society in which enterprising individuals grab the (presumed) equally available opportunities to improve their futures.

Despite the rhetoric of widening participation which suggests a more inclusive HE system, Burke and Jackson (2007) insist that mass HE has generated new inequalities and has deepened social stratification. Widening participation conceals structural, cultural, discursive and material mis-recognitions, ignoring the way that 'intelligence', 'ability' and 'potential' favor the interests of particular hegemonic groups and communities. For example, whist minority ethnic groups and women are now in the main well-represented, these groups are clustered around particular HE disciplines, where a hierarchical division has occurred between the traditional university and the 'new' university.

Experiential Work-Based Learning

As a result of the new configuration of the university, Burke and Jackson (2007) point out that, knowledge is increasingly evaluated for its pragmatic, utilitarian value rather than as an end in itself. Competency-based approaches to curriculum delivery and learning are driven by strong, externally defined standards that treat learning as a set of discrete outcomes which are not multidimensional. Changes to knowledge are driven, in part, by the needs of trans-national companies and related knowledge-based industries: partnerships between universities and industries are being formed and carefully nurtured; the boundaries between the academy, government and business have been loosened and re-formulated; and corporate interests play a more powerful role in determining the purpose of HE. Greater co-ordination and co-operation between public and private institutions has resulted in new funding models for higher education and, although it is still largely dependent on state funding, the university is expected to meet the requirements of the private sector economy. There are multiple linkages between the university and the different stakeholders in the economy and since universities are framed as a source of labor market training they are being increasingly encouraged to work with industry and commerce to generate knowledge, wealth and regional and national economies.

Olssen, Codd, & O'Neill (2004) agree and point out that the paradox of the discourses of widening participation, student choice and freedom is government's greater social control through 'normalization'. Notions such as 'flexible' learning are integral to neo-liberal work and management relations, and require malleable individuals who continually train and re-train to meet the changes to the economy and the knowledges required.

The notion of " 'flexibility' redesigns skills and human capital as the personal responsibility of the individual worker, enabling the structures of both the economy and state maximum ability to accommodate change" (2004, p. 189). Power "is concentrated, focused and implemented while not appearing to be centralized. In Foucauldian terms, flexibility represents a micro-technology of power that sustains relations of governmentality" (ibid).

The Self-Government of the University Lecturer

Universities as organizations are increasingly characterized by the institution of work measurements, such as the Research Assessment Exercises (RAE) and the Teaching Quality Assessments (TQA). These are 'practices instantly recognizable to any practitioner of Scientific Management' (Jackson & Carter, 1998, p. 62). In the interests of brevity I take one example here, that of TQA.

Teaching Quality Assessments

Morley (2003) argues that neo-liberal governmental technologies comprise a new form of power which systematically undoes and reconstructs the practices of professionalism in HE. Academic identity is no longer linked to one's academic discipline, but to league-table scores, quality assurance and managerialism. The irony is that whilst academics are increasingly expected to operate managerially (re-professionalization), they are also expected to consent to being led (de-professionalization). There are two salient features to de-professionalization: the beginnings of removal of discretionary power with regard to pedagogy; constraints imposed on teaching practice by having to meet bureaucratic criteria imposed by quality assurance agencies such as the TQA. Whist the rationale for externality is that it enhances quality and professionalism, the fact remains that quality assurance is the authoritative construction of norms, with limited opportunities for individuals to question their legitimacy and move beyond conventionally justified beliefs and values. Academics no longer legislate for what is correct knowledge, 'they are more likely to be interpreters of the workplace or consultants to knowledge workers such as teachers etc' (Morely, 2003, p. 92).

Burke and Jackson (2007) argue that the TQA claims to produce knowledge of the teacher on grounds which would be unacceptable within the rules of any discourse other than the discourse of control. Quality assurance regimes, designed to make judgments about the effectiveness of the teaching and learning for which teachers are responsible, effectively establish normalizing and standardizing practices for teachers. The TQA framework largely draws on quantitative methodologies to measure what is actually a qualitative problem. Understanding what 'quality' means would entail complex methodological approaches that would explore and scrutinize pedagogical relations and experiences. The current framework is unable to do this because it conceptualizes teaching as a toolkit for learning and reduces it to a 'how to': how to lecture, how to make a hand-out, how to create a power-point presentation, how to give feedback, how to use small groups, and so forth. These tools are assumed to be meaningful in themselves, rather than understanding that it is the pedagogical approach that makes the tools meaningful (or not). The NPM reforms of teaching can be seen to consist of regulatory, supervisory and controlling mechanisms with regard to our own practices and the kinds of knowledge/learning we provide for the students. University lecturers re-construct and enact neo-liberal policies: as teachers we teach students to learn to work, and to learn to learn, according to compliance to strong externally defined standards that treat learning as a set of discrete outcomes that are not multidimensional, and which individualizes responsibility for learning. As such the subjectification of the tutor is mobilized to effect the subjectification of the student.

The interlocking of the 'tutor-subject' and 'student-subject' shifts the purpose of learning onto a different terrain than that of critical thought. The 'tutor-subject' is subjectified both as a teacher who legitimizes certain practices and provides a framework for describing and creating practices scaffolded, by the language of accountability, standards, high performance and student employability that once belonged to the language of business. The idea of subjectification does not imply that human beings are 'cultural dupes' who blindly 'obey'. It is quite clear that on the one hand the individual (student or teacher) within the university is not a nexus point for relays of power that offers no impedance whatsoever. Universities are locales in which negotiation, contestation and willful struggle are a routine occurrence. On the other hand, although resistance is pervasive it also sits alongside our 'freely' mobilizing the new managerialism.

ETHICS: A PEDAGOGY OF DISCOMFORT

I have taught in HE in the UK for the past fifteen years and have witnessed the constant move to renounce or displace a previously held strong criterion for the purpose of HE, namely that of developing critical thought in the students. There is a culture of compliance to the neo-liberal policy discourses of HE, and I, like countless colleagues, perform within these regulatory frameworks. The contractual basis upon which I am employed is premised on my compliance to monitoring and accountability, organized through the new managerialism and established through measurable outputs, as described above. If I am to emancipate myself in some measure from this form of disciplinary control, what form might my emancipation take? If power is always present in that we mobilize it in our own thoughts, hopes, desires and ambitions how, as an individual tutor, can I resist my own subjectification as a 'tutor-subject' and provide an environment where I encourage critical engagement and resistance from 'student-subjects'?

One of my responsibilities as a university tutor is teaching undergraduates on an Education Studies Program. The Education Studies Program is comprised of the theories and practices that inform contemporary primary and secondary school education, for example knowledge of Special Educational Needs, children's learning styles, curricula, child mentoring techniques and so on. Although there are pockets of critical thought, on the whole the opportunity to develop critical pedagogies is constrained by the regulatory practices with regard to our roles as teachers and by an instrumental view of what the students need to know in order for them to become effective teachers. On the one hand as a teacher on this program I am placed within the governmental changes to HE and what constitutes knowledge and how it is learnt which I have to operate and mobilize. On the other hand I have found ways to circumvent this which affords a measure of escape from these constrictions.

Educational Thought and Social Theory

I teach an option course entitled Educational Thought and Social Theory for which I am wholly responsible with regard to curriculum content and delivery (although the course has been ratified by the university). Its broad sweep is the sociology of education and it traces the sociological history of liberal thought about education policy and practice since the inception of state education in the UK to the present. In teaching Educational Thought and Social Theory I attempt not to be incorporated into discursive practices that are in fundamental opposition to my own beliefs about the nature of scholarship and of best practice. I specifically take the 'new' modes of teaching and learning as an object of critical enquiry rather than an internalized modus operandi. I use genealogy to help perform a critical ontology of the teaching and learning

subjectivities created by the NPM of HE and as such I deploy 'a pedagogy of discomfort' (Boler, 1999, p. 176).

Sociology as an academic discipline has traditionally provided the forum in HE where critical thought can be specifically addressed and fostered. One of its purposes is to dislocate the idea of the 'free' individual with its own characteristics and capacities who exists anterior to society, and to demonstrate the social forces and power relations that operate on individuals in an 'undisclosed' way within the capitalist economies of liberal democracies and their institutions. Within the sociological canon, Foucault's thesis is radical in that it takes sociological perspectives themselves – for example Durkheimian, Weberian, and more contemporaneously Marxist – and demonstrates that whilst these theories are 'freeing' of thought in that they help us reflect upon ourselves as 'socialized' subjects they are simultaneously restrictive. Foucault points out that liberal theory which describes the capacities of 'intelligence', 'ability' and 'potential' as individual phenomena, and sociology, which describes these latter as social phenomena nevertheless perform a similar conceptual maneuver. They are both humanistic modes of thought founded on the idea that 'man' (sic) exists as a human subject. In contrast Foucault's genealogies, as we saw earlier, do not presume the human subject but strive to demonstrate the various ways that human beings are produced as particular kinds of subjects by governmental relations.

My university belongs to one side of the hierarchical divide between teaching and research universities which increasingly distinguishes universities in the UK. I teach in a 'new' university where there is a preponderance of 'non-traditional' or working class students who have either failed to get into 'elite' research (or Russell Group) universities, or who did not apply because of lack of academic qualifications. In discussion students often display trust and faith in the avowed governmental commitment to the widening participation agenda for social inclusion and citizenship, and to provision of the changing skills base necessary for them to participate in the global economy. They also often reveal that their experience of education prior to HE was often one of shame, humiliation, fear and anger. These negative feelings are tempered by the desire for the restitution of self-esteem through the HE experience and the joy and pleasure that this opportunity now affords them.

A pedagogy that deploys the anti-humanist thrust of genealogy can be very uncomfortable for such students. This critical view suggests that, as well as being emancipatory, in some senses the changes to HE in the past twenty years mobilize regulatory and disciplinary practices. A genealogical analysis of their own subjectivity invites the students to engage in a view of HE as a contemporary and historical site for social control, and in doing so, it asks them to understand their own educational past and current choices, hopes, values, desires and educational aspirations as the 'product' of governmentalization. This approach thus flies in the face of the neo-liberal discourses which frames students' understanding of their own participation in HE and of themselves as autonomous individuals who exist outside of power. Understanding one's self as the effect of disciplinary educational technologies rather than perceiving one's self as an independent agent who interacts with education requires not only a shift in intellectual understanding how power functions in liberal democracies but it has the potential to arouse strong anxieties, and even to undermine the student's sense of identity and autonomy.

The emotions aroused are not ignored in the class room but are taken, like the theories of governmentalization and of education, as an object of reflection. This requires gently fostering a non-judgmental atmosphere in which we collectively understand the fragilities of our own identities. Moreover as a tutor engaging in a pedagogy of discomfort I clarify for the students my own ethical responsibility to them. For example, whilst

demonstrating the disciplinary costs of subjection, I point out that genealogy can also provide support for the benefits of organizing and adopting liberal policies and subject positions, particularly where they may come to the conclusion that the adoption of such positions might well be beneficial to them. I point out that a genealogy of how freedom has become connected to their aspiration for university qualifications has not revealed this expression of freedom as a sham, but it has revealed how they have come to define and act towards themselves in terms of this notion of freedom. Genealogy demonstrates how the contemporary relationship between university qualifications and personal enhancement and career development has been historically put together, the practices which support it, and the techniques and relations of power that go up to make it.

THE DISSIDENCE OF INTELLECTUALS

What is the ethical purpose in deploying a pedagogy of discomfort?

A genealogical approach to ethics suggests abandoning the idea that we can emancipate ourselves by escaping from power. Genealogy does not describe a dichotomy between the exercise of power and its absence since individuals are never 'free' in the sense that we exist as autonomous individuals prior to or anterior to the power which is exercised over us. The idea of standing outside of power emerges from the liberal idea that the major mechanisms of political power are negative and bear down upon individual subjects to oppress them. Clearly power does function negatively by coalescing around certain groups to form hierarchical divisions, as witnessed by the preponderance at new universities of working class and minority ethnic students who (on the whole) have weak scholarly backgrounds. However in the genealogical view, as we have seen, the major mechanism of political power is that it is productive of subjectivity. This provides a new political imaginary of the modes of resistance needed if, as theorists working for progressive social and educational change, we are to challenge power in its various manifestations.

The freedom to resist power and to formulate ethical relations, unlike a traditional Marxist position, does not involve globalizing visions of overthrowing power, since this would be impossible, but the analysis of the micro-politics of power and how these that produce us as governable subjectivities at specific sites. Foucault argues that freedom is thought reflecting upon itself; ethics is the practice, on the basis of that reflection, of acting upon the self to conduct oneself, with others, 'differently'. As such freedom and ethics imply each other: A genealogical approach to emancipation forefronts a 'philosophical ethos' which "separates out from the contingency of that has made us what we are, the possibility of no longer being, doing or thinking what we are, do, or think … it is seeking to give new impetus … to the undefined work of freedom" (Foucault, 1994, pp. 315-316). This anti-humanist approach to freedom and ethical action fosters my particular pedagogy of discomfort and mirrors Boler's elaboration of a pedagogy of discomfort. She (1999, p. 176) argues a pedagogy of discomfort is 'both an invitation to inquiry as well as a call to action'.

In deploying genealogy to help create a critical ontology of the teaching and learning subjectivities created by the NPM of HE such an approach has an 'emancipatory effect' (Biesta, 2008, p. 202). Although this form of emancipation is not emancipation in the traditional sense where one tries to escape power, its emancipatory effect arises from the transgression of existing self-evidence so that other subject positions become available. Human beings cannot escape power, but what they can do is weigh up the costs and benefits of particular forms of subjectivity and decide collectively how to act at 'the limits of the self' or even transgress these limits at local sites of power. For the revolutionary educationist this vision of dissent may be depressing: it has no clear outcomes; it does not hold globalizing visions for revolution. I have found it hugely productive to work at the limit of myself in my pedagogical role, and of inducing the students to 'see' that this mode of freedom is available to them too. I understand my ethical task as examining those aspects of teaching and learning that appear to be both neutral and independent so that the powers that are exercised obscurely are unmasked. In doing so I hope not only to have carried out a critical ontology of myself as a teacher-subject with the hopes of transgressing its normalizing limit position but have facilitated the possibilities for students to transgress the limit position of their own student-subjectivities.

As an educator I induce the students to inquire both into the discursive processes by which current educational truths are constructed and how these intersect with politics and the discursive processes by which they, as student-subjects, are constructed. As such I attempt to wrest the students from 'blindly' conforming to the learning subjectivities they embrace and the kinds of educators they are being trained to become. I invite the students to question their beliefs and values and to ponder new ethical and moral dimensions for education and social organization. In doing so my minimal hope is that they examine the political processes they have undergone in becoming the students they have become, and this hope is largely borne out. Many of my students have recounted how, in electing to consider the complexity of ethical relations and how we are taught to 'see' and to 'be', genealogical self-reflection has transformed their thinking and their relationship to themselves. My major hope is that genealogical self-reflection will lead to a willingness to undergo a possible transformation of educational self-identity in relation to those others whom they will eventually teach. It is up to the students, however, to consider for themselves the costs and benefits of no longer being, doing or thinking what they are, do, or think, and whether they want to attempt to move beyond that limit-position in practice.

REFERENCES

Biesta, G. (2008). Encountering Foucault in life-long learning. In Fejes, A., & Nicoll, K. (Eds.), *Foucault and life-long learning*. London, UK: Routledge.

Boler, M. (1999). *Feeling power: Emotions and education*. New York, NY: Routledge.

Burbules, N., & Torres, C. (Eds.). (2000). *Globalisation and education: Critical perspectives*. London, UK: Routledge.

Burke, P. J., & Jackson, S. (2007). *Reconceptualising lifelong leaning: Feminist interventions*. Oxford, UK: Routledge.

Clegg, S. (1998). Foucault, power and organisations. In McKinlay, A., & Starkey, K. (Eds.), *Foucault, management and organisation theory*. London, UK: Sage.

Dreyfus, H. L., & Rabinow, P. (1982). *Michel Foucault: Beyond structuralism and hermeneutics*. New York, NY: Harvester Wheatsheaf.

Foucault, M. (1977). *Discipline and punish: The birth of the prison*. London, UK: Penguin.

Foucault, M. (1978). The history of sexuality: *Vol. 1. An introduction*. London, UK: Penguin.

Foucault, M. (1982). The subject and power. In Dreyfus, H. L., & Rabinow, P. (Eds.), *Foucault: Beyond structuralism and hermeneutics*. Chicago, IL: University of Chicago Press.

Foucault, M. (1991). Governmentality. In Burchell, G., Gordon, C., & Miller, P. (Eds.), *The Foucault effect: Studies in governmentality*. London, UK: Harvester Wheatsheaf.

Foucault, M. (1994). What is enlightenment? In Rabinow, P. (Ed.), *Michel Foucault: Ethics –Essential works of Foucault 1954-1984*. London, UK: Penguin.

Jackson, N., & Carter, P. (1998). Labour as dressage. In McKinlay, A., & Starkey, K. (Eds.), *Foucault, management and organisation theory*. London, UK: Sage.

McKinlay, A., & Starkey, K. (Eds.). (1998). *Foucault, management and organisation theory*. London, UK: Sage.

Morley, L. (2003). *Quality and power in higher education*. Berkshire, UK: SRHE and OUP.

Olssen, M., Codd, J., & O'Neill, A.-M. (2004). *Education policy: Globalisation, citizenship and democracy*. London, UK: Sage.

Peters, M., Marshall, J., & Fitzsimons, P. (2000). Managerialism and educational policy in a global context: Foucault, neoliberalism, and the doctrine of self-management. In Burbules, N., & Torress, C. (Eds.), *Globalisation and education: Critical perpectives*. London, UK: Routledge.

Salter, B., & Tapper, T. (1994). *The state and higher education*. Essex, UK: Woburn Press.

Starkey, K., & McKinlay, A. (1998). Deconstructing organisation-discipline and desire. In McKinlay, A., & Starkey, K. (Eds.), *Foucault, management and organisation theory*. London, UK: Sage.

Chapter 22
Disrupting the Utilitarian Paradigm:
Teachers Doing Curriculum Inquiry

Pamela Bolotin Joseph
University of Washington Bothell, USA

ABSTRACT

The purpose of this chapter is to explain the importance of curriculum inquiry for teacher change and the development of curriculum leaders. The author depicts the utilitarian or standardized management paradigm that dominates United States education and then explores the nature of curriculum inquiry, considering why such study helps educators become critically conscious of dominant assumptions and policies that influence their teaching and their schools. Drawing from reflections from "lived curriculum investigations," the chapter illustrates how teachers recognize, question, and challenge previously unexamined norms, and practices. Moreover, the author explains how reflection, transformative learning, affect, and experience support teacher change and why curriculum inquiry is a crucial component of teachers' identities as curriculum workers — educators who are transformative intellectuals and curriculum leaders. This chapter concludes with consideration of another type of curriculum inquiry, "curriculum worker portraits," to study the beliefs and practices of innovative educators.

INTRODUCTION

As a teacher educator working with experienced educators in graduate professional development programs during an era in which education for utilitarian purposes has been the primary rationale

DOI: 10.4018/978-1-61350-495-6.ch022

for schooling in the United States, I have sought to help teachers name and understand the commonplaces that surround them. My hope has been for educators who work in such environments to reject roles as technicians delivering a mandated curriculum, to challenge the dominant order of schooling, and to see themselves as "curriculum workers" — a designation within curriculum theory for reflective activist educators who have the insight, initiative, and courage to challenge the dominant order of schooling. In this chapter I will discuss the predominant utilitarian or "standardized management paradigm" (Henderson & Gornik, 2007), the nature of curriculum inquiry, and the role of curriculum inquiry in teacher change and the development of curriculum leaders. Also, I will depict teachers' insights from "lived curriculum investigations" of their classrooms and schools and how their investigations had become "disruptive pedagogies" (Boler, 1999) as teachers questioned the status quo, articulated awareness of the nature of schooling, posed moral questions about treating children as workers or products, and began to develop identities as curriculum workers. I conclude with discussion about the need to go beyond investigating the status quo to instead study the beliefs and practices of innovative educators who teach to their ideals even within the utilitarian educational climate.

THE UTILITARIAN PARADIGM

Critical curriculum scholars view contemporary education in the United States as characterized by the omnipresent utilitarian or "standardized management paradigm" (Henderson & Gornik, 2007) imbued with a top-down curriculum planning focused on "how best to improve student performance in standardized tests" and "methods such as memorization, drill, test preparation, and other related types of learning activities that it is believed help students perform well on standardized tests" (Heyer & Pifel, 2007, p. 569). Moreover, schooling to serve and emulate industry has led to a contraction of the curriculum so that the underlying mission of schooling has become passing standardized tests instead of the development of well-rounded individuals or informed citizens. As a result, there neither is interest in creating curriculum for students to study meaningful questions based on their curiosity about the world nor helping learners to imagine how they could change the world. Similarly, there is no debate within conventional schooling about the possibilities of education as a catalyst for the transformation of individuals or for social reform.

Such limited aims have had devastating consequences affecting children's educational experiences and creating inequality of school resources and opportunities. Likewise, curriculum – as an imaginative concept that attends to learners' experiences as well as the enduring consequences of education for individuals or society – does not enter contemporary political discussions focused on "accountability," "competition," and "achieving excellence." The situation has become a "nightmare that is the present state of pubic miseducation" (Pinar, 2004, p. 5).

In this paradigm, the curriculum is narrowed as high standards become equated with standardized curriculum — thus leading to standardized tests as the prime means of measuring student achievement of standards. Consequent outcomes are teaching to the test, curriculum fragmentation, scripted curriculum, disregard of content or goals deemed untestable, and diminishment of high-quality instruction. Critics note that *No Child Left Behind* legislation that influences all of public schooling actually makes it harder for states to improve the quality of teaching as tests are influenced by "a narrow view of what constitutes learning" (Darling-Hammond, 2007, p. 14) and do not assess for "higher-order thinking" (Neill, 2003, p. 225). "The mandated testing regimen require[es] teachers to reconfigure nearly every teaching or planning moment into a form of test preparation" (Symcox, 2009, p. 59) as "teaching to the test substitutes for deeper intellectual inquiry" (Sleeter, 2008, p. 148).

The standardized management paradigm also has serious ramifications for educators: narrowing of professional roles, demoralizing working conditions, and teachers' lack of authority for curriculum development. Administrators feel pressure to evaluate performance solely on test scores and to devalue teachers' nurturing of children and planning of innovative curriculum; thus the "standardized examination system becomes a powerful evaluative device in confining teachers' professional autonomy in teaching" (Wong, 2006, p. 29). Within such milieus, teachers "mourn the loss of their own and their students' creativity" (Hargreaves & Shirley, 2009, p. 2510) as the narrowed curriculum takes "the soul out of teachers and the joy out of teaching" (Kozol, 1997, p. 2). Ultimately, such an environment devalues teachers' academic expertise and dismisses the moral dimensions of teaching that encompass caring, nurturing, and attention to children's developmental or emotional needs.

Therefore, administrators and politicians may appreciate teachers only for their ability to increase test scores and not for the other important features of their work, including creative curriculum making. Such circumstances increasingly pressure teachers to think about themselves as technicians rather than educators.

Stripped of autonomy and intentionality, emptied of inner life, reduced to conglomerations of skills that are employed in environments in order to stimulate predetermined responses, teachers can easily be replaced by bureaucrats, mechanics, or machines. Reduced to information and metacognitive skills, the curriculum lends itself to teacher-proof scripts (Taubman, 2009, p. 194).

This current state of affairs refers to the deskilling of teachers (Apple, 1986) in which "educators lose their dynamic roles as curriculum workers when they no longer are allowed to create or modify curriculum" (Joseph, 2010, p. 283). Deskilling means that

[A]s teachers deliver curriculum rather than use their academic and pedagogical expertise, they will in fact lose some skills. Or, teachers may be

hired because they do not have strong knowledge and skills because they can be paid low salaries and will be compliant—readily following scripted curriculum and feeling dependent on the state or administration to give them curriculum. Moreover, teachers may accept their deskilled roles as the discourse of corporatism and managerialism becomes legitimized. (Joseph, 2010, pp. 283-285)

Critics of schooling note that as teachers become "more and more viewed as technicians called upon to implement classroom objectives that are tightly controlled and defined by others higher upon the administrative chain of command" (Purpel & Shapiro, 1995, p. 109), they continue to lose their authority as professionals.

Such a role increasingly precludes the involvement of teachers from any real authority for decision making in the school. It robs them of the opportunity to think creatively about how they teach or what it is that should be taught. And it denies them the moral and political significance of what they do.... The 'deskilled' teacher is required to teach with little consciousness or conscience about the fundamental values that he or she is trying to initiate in the classroom (Purpel & Shapiro, 1995, p. 109).

When federal and state mandates as well as school cultures continually reinforce the utilitarian worldview, it becomes increasingly difficult for educators to envision alternatives or to connect to the idealism that might have brought them into the teaching profession. Indeed, it becomes hard to even name the paradigm that envelopes them. To teach against the grain of the contemporary educational and political climate in the United States first requires that educators – who are enmeshed in the standardized management paradigm – be able to recognize, question, and challenge previously unexamined norms, beliefs, and habitual behaviors.

CURRICULUM INQUIRY

To transform educational aims and practices, educators need to be continually engaged in inquiry and introspection. As well, curriculum itself should be perceived as a dynamic process including in-depth examination of practices, interactions, values and visions as well as "an inward journey" (Slattery, 1995, p. 56) of personal reflection. It is "the purpose of curriculum...to engage the imagination" (Doll, 2000, p. xi) so that educators can reflect on their beliefs and actions and to engage in a vigorous discourse about moral and social visions for education. As follows, study of curriculum becomes a catalyst for moral and political deliberation within "complicated curricular conversations" (Henderson, 2001) and the desire for curriculum transformation.

Curriculum inquiry provides deep understanding of the norms, patterns, and structures that obstruct as well make curriculum transformation possible. Educators thus can make known common discourses, forces, structures, and hierarchies that remain unquestioned (Bowers, 2010; Greene, 1978).

Change in the culture of school requires examination and alteration of both thought and action in the context of the school.... All of the teachers, principal, and other staff members — examine what already exists and explore alternative explanations, meanings, and actions.... By promoting reflection in action – questioning everything and trying out many ideas in thought and action – culture is less likely to invisibly determine what goes on in school (Heckman, 1993, p. 270).

Naming of structures and forces brings about problem posing to understand the agendas for schools held by outside forces, to "transcend a belief that the system of schooling is neutral," and to gain "a historic sense of the roots of antidemocratic trends in curriculum" (Wood, 1990, pp. 101-102, 107). It is such scrutiny and attention that Greene (1978) encourages when she implores educators to shake off "indifference, a lack of care, an absence of concern" (p. 43) and "to make sense of what is happening... to be autonomous" (p. 44). It is by becoming "wide awake" can educators "develop the sense of agency required for living a moral life" (p. 44).

Through curriculum inquiry, educators learn to inquire into embedded metaphors, assumptions, and visions and to critique beliefs, goals, and practices; also, they examine and reflect on the norms and values that have direct and unforeseeable influences upon schooling. When teachers are engaged in curriculum inquiry by investigating and questioning the commonplace, they become "critically conscious of what is involved in the complex business of teaching and learning" (Greene, 1973, p. 11). "Becoming critically conscious means for teachers to engage with the world in an expansive yet disciplined way, to question their sense of reality as well as the forces that influence their lives and work" (Joseph, 2007, p. 283).

In the past decade, I have made curriculum inquiry a feature of an introductory graduate-level curriculum studies course that I teach yearly. I assigned "lived curriculum investigations" to help educators become aware of curriculum as lived or experienced (Aoki 1991; 1993) as opposed to a set of guidelines or objectives (Westbury, 2000). I wished for teachers to "make the commonplace problematic" (Pink, 1990, p. 139) by challenging the idea of curriculum as a singular reality and instead to consider curriculum as deeply influenced by culture, for example, to probe the belief systems that determine what is considered normal or alternative or simply unthinkable. Moreover, I wanted teachers to see how curricula enacted in classrooms and schools are created cultures and to not "accept the prevailing culture as normal or unalterable" (Joseph, 2007, p. 284). A further aim was to apply the concept of curricular orientations or cultures what teachers see in practice — to discern if curriculum continually changes in response to outside forces or exists as a congruent set of practices supported by visions or ideals.

The lived curriculum investigations required that teachers study their own classrooms and practices or – if they were currently not teaching – the work of another educator via observations and interviews. Although I modified the specific directions over time, overall the assignment featured two components: findings and analysis (or reflection). The findings section was based on the curricular commonplaces (Schwab, 1973; Connelly & Clandinin, 1988): learners, teachers, content, and milieu. Other elements of this section included curriculum planning and evaluation, beliefs about the purpose of education (Goodlad, 1994; Joseph et al., 2000) and the values explicitly or implicitly present in classrooms and schools (Jackson, Boostrom & Hansen, 1993). These are examples of questions for this assignment:

- *Students*
  - What are the beliefs about students' needs, development, competencies, motives, and interests?
  - How have these beliefs influenced practice?
- *Teachers*
  - What are the beliefs about the role of teachers?
  - How should they facilitate learning?
- *Content*
  - What constitutes the subject matter?
  - How is the subject matter organized?
- *Context*
  - What is the environment of the classroom? of the school?
  - How is instruction organized?
- *Planning*
  - What are the models of curriculum development?
  - Who plans the curriculum?
  - Who has the power to make decisions?
- *Evaluation*
  - How should students be assessed?
  - How is the worth or success of the curriculum determined?

- *Purposes*
  - What beliefs about "what schools are for" exist in the educational setting?
- *Values*
  - How are values conveyed in classrooms and schools?

In the analysis or reflection section, teachers might discuss the existence of an ad hoc curricular culture or if the culture of the classroom and school consistently reflects the school's explicitly stated purposes. Teachers also probed the hidden and null curriculum (Eisner, 1985) or how official curriculum might vary from curriculum taught, learned, and tested (Cuban; 1993). Furthermore, teachers considered social, political, and economic issues related to their interrogations. I also required that the analyses connect to course readings about dominant school structures and norms as well as progressive curricular orientations. In particular, teachers read heuristics about curriculum theory and about mainstream and alternative curricular cultures (see Joseph, Bravmann, Windschitl, Mikel & Green, 2000).

INTERROGATING THE UTILITARIAN PARADIGM

Lived Curriculum Investigations

When I first assigned the lived curriculum investigations, I was interested primarily in helping teachers to make sense of the dominant culture of schooling and to imagine alternatives to it. However, their vivid descriptions and poignant reflections prompted me early on to get permission to use the teachers' writings to study my own practice as a teacher educator — to learn if engagement in curriculum inquiry through the study of their own practices, classrooms, and schools indeed allowed teachers to discern and reflect on the culture that surrounds them and is, at the same time, self-created. And, on the whole, I found over time that curriculum inquiry investigations prompted serious reflection about teachers' work and their school cultures and in some cases cast light on how curriculum inquiry became a catalyst for transformative learning (see Joseph, 2007).

Pertaining to this chapter's emphasis on "disrupting pedagogies," I focus on the writing of the majority of teachers – from kindergarten teachers to community college instructors – who wrote about their growing awareness of the standardized management paradigm and how schools increasingly emphasized curriculum for the workplace, material success, competition, and achievement tests. In addition, when teachers examined customary practices and systems within these utilitarian contexts, they recognized contradictions between sanctioned practices and school missions or between their own ideals and school expectations.

These investigations cast light on how schooling for work permeates American culture. In fact, even children in both public and private schools had this view of schooling. For examples, two teachers studied a parochial school and discovered that all the students surveyed there viewed education only for the purpose of getting better jobs — despite the school's strong religious mission. Other teachers reported how their schools increasingly asked them to accelerate the academic learning of very young children or to teach to the state standardized test. In this climate, educators found it increasingly difficult to be holistic, creative educators sensitive to their pupils' needs and interests.

Various examples from lived curriculum papers illustrate how the utilitarian motif permeated classroom and school cultures and how these investigations provoked teachers' critical awareness, recognition of moral dilemmas, questioning, concern, and anguish:

Students are reminded throughout the entire school building that "learning is their job" and "always do your best".... Posts that declare,

"Winners never quit and quitters never win" and "Never give up" ... adorn the hallway.... Instead of nurturing students and fostering their love of learning, teachers are required to teach to the test.

In examining the different cultures, I realize the vision I have for my classroom is mainly vocationally-based and I don't like that at all. In special education, the culture of curriculum, although child-centered, is vocational. Even on the elementary level, we are thinking ahead to what the child will be doing for work. I am really calling into question whether my class is child-centered or not.

All of the [students that I surveyed] concluded that they want to follow the rules, or something to that effect. This began my thinking about [how] students really see school. If the only theme congruent with each student was the idea of behaving in class, I wonder what we are really teaching kids.... I am wondering if students are getting the wrong message about what is really important in school... Are we really wanting to turn them into life-long learners as we state in our [the school's] mission statement?

The focus of the mission statement ... ties to the new push for students who are a product rather than an individual. The irony of this statement is even more fascinating when realizing the stated objective of the school is to create life-long learners, yet the institutionalized and rigid curricula pushes leave little opportunity for students to even learn how to be students. Administration on a regular bases structure in-services and staff meetings around how to help students pass the [state standardized test].

The realization that the true gap in curricular cultures is based on economic status frustrates me.... Throughout this course I have envisioned how public schools are training "worker bees." However, the ultimate frustration is that the "queen bees" will be students that come from wealthy families and would have excelled in school and the job market no matter what their educational background, while their "worker bee" subjects were never even given the educational opportunity to develop skills and talents beyond basic work and survival.

I find I am constantly trying to balance what I believe makes sense and what I have observed excites children with the realities of the ways in which they will be assessed. The two, although not always, are often at odds. The place where the rub shows up most often is time — how much time can I allow kids to construct meaning, take a subject deeper, etc., before the panic sets in that they won't have been exposed to all the different tasks they will face on a standardized test.... As a teacher in a public system, am I morally obligated to promote something I see little long-term value in or am I morally obligated to teach in a way that is congruent with my beliefs about education?

Every time I looked at my students' work, I would ask them if it was quality work.... Did it look like quality work? Their coloring was expected to be inside the lines.... I would tell them that this wasn't what a first grade teacher would want to see. After all, they were going to be first graders.... It makes me nervous now to think that I was teaching the "factory model" instead of the way I truly wanted to teach!

When discussing her investigation in class that evening, the kindergarten teacher (in the above example) burst into tears saying, "This is not why I became a teacher!"

So, too, these investigations have led to profound inquiry about the effect of such schooling on young people and society. For instance, a teacher describing her public middle school's district-imposed standardized curriculum asked telling questions about the nature of learning and teaching:

Where do the interests of the individual enter into this type of curriculum? Where is the development of self and spirit or the focus on process seen in deliberating democracy? There is very little choice for the students.... They don't get to select reading books or different types of projects. The district is afraid of allowing students too much choice in the curriculum because then they couldn't ensure that all students were learning the same skills and covering the same material. [Yet] [t]he curriculum lacks the spontaneity of life that delights us, the freedom of choice that empowers us - both teachers and students - and the ability to meet students where they're at. There is a double message being sent. On the one hand, every teacher needs to deliver the same lessons at the same time to ensure the same high quality level of teaching. Will that ensure high quality teaching? What does high quality teaching look like? How else could it be achieved?

A teacher working in a private middle school with an elite student clientele wrote about his concerns for how his school might educate future leaders:

[My school] does not place serious value upon students gaining practice in challenging the established order or practicing democracy. In their embrace, then, of training for work and survival, while [our] students will learn the attributes "... of "good work" such as thoroughness, promptness, neatness, reliability, and punctuality"... they may also accept a ""bound" world in which the status quo is accepted...." In their pursuit of the canon, [our] students will learn to search for the "right" history rather than creating histories of their own... Is this the kind of leadership we hope and dream about for the future? an army of efficient, neat, task doers who do their best to please previous arbiters of right and wrong?

I cannot help wondering whether a better future demands a different kind of leadership — leaders that are able to make decisions predicated upon their own standards of justice; leaders that see the world not as a host of competitors (or poor people that need our "help"), but rather as an intricate web of mutually dependent organisms; leaders that are motivated to creatively construct new structures and solutions for the problems that surround them; leaders who seek to do better, and suspect that they can.

Both of the teachers in the above examples left their schools at the end of the year and were able to find positions in schools that appeared more conducive to realizing their ideals. Other teachers also found it untenable to continue working in environments resistant to change. For instance, two secondary teachers (taking my class in different years) became disheartened by their school's authoritarian nature and singular emphasis on competition. Inspired also by readings on critical pedagogy, both eventually decided that they could not teach for social justice at the school and found employment at informal education settings in which they could work as critical educators.

Moreover, educators began to make significant changes in their curriculum work, although not necessary during the class (during a 10-week quarter) but later in their graduate studies as they conducted action research projects to transform their teaching and their pupils' experiences. Some teachers began to talk with colleagues about making changes in curriculum and advocated for a more active role for teachers in the curriculum planning process. For example, one teacher who articulated her concerns about teaching numerous mandated curriculum packages eventually took leadership in having teachers create collaborative professional development opportunities. Others embraced constructivist, student-centered, democratic, or multicultural pedagogy.

BECOMING CURRICULUM WORKERS

Research on teacher development suggests four major avenues for teacher change: reflection, transformative learning, affect, and experience. Curriculum inquiry relates directly to the first three of these paths for helping educators go through of process of awareness and understanding leading to the strong desire for change — notwithstanding the importance of experience because for educators to become successful in new practices they need to have "intensive, multiple supports to encourage continual change" (Kent, 2004, p. 430) and collaborative and/or long-term inquiry-based efforts (Reiman & Peace, 2002, p. 55; Richardson & Placier, 2001, p. 921).

Studies of teacher change demonstrate the value of systematic inquiry for changing "beliefs, conceptions, and practices" (Richardson & Placier, 2001, p. 921). Boler (1999) refers to the reflection as a result of critical inquiry as "disrupting pedagogies" in which educators' "critical inquiry has brought them to a crossroads of determining for themselves what kinds of action make sense for them to take given their own ethical vision" leading to taking action and leadership (p. 198). As such, there are strong parallels with such teacher development and transformative learning theory (Mezirow, 1991) in which individuals change the way they "see themselves and their world" (Brown, 2004, p. 77) and modify their beliefs, attitudes, and emotions (Imel, 1998). In the process of transformative learning, individuals "engage in critical reflection on their experiences" (Mezirow, 1991, in Imel, 1998, p. 2) resulting in "perspective transformation." Several teacher educators (Cranton & King, 2003; McCallister, 2002) believe that transformative learning allows teachers to see alternatives "and thereby act differently in the world" (Cranton & King, 2003, p. 32) and should be an explicit goal of professional development.

Some researchers also attend to the role of affect as a catalyst for change and educational reform (van den Berg, 2002). Inquiry may lead individuals to understand the need to modify practices, but reflection in itself may not be enough to motivate educators to strongly desire change, for teachers to have an "inner desire to learn new strategies and practices" (Kent, 2004, p. 430). Similarly, Boler (1999) notes how affect accompanies reflection:

A pedagogy of discomfort does not intentionally seek to provoke, or cause anger or fear. However, as educators and students engage in collective self-reflection and develop accountability for how we see ourselves, and as we question cherished beliefs, we are likely to encounter such emotions as fear and anger — as well as joy, passion, new hopes and a sense of possibility.... (p. 188).

Certainly, the lived curriculum writing conveyed emotions – as Boler (1999) describes – as manifest in these teachers' searching questions: "Are we really wanting to turn them into life-long learners as we state in our mission statement?" "Am I morally obligated to promote something I see little long-term value in or am I morally obligated to teach in a way that is congruent with my beliefs about education?" "Is this the kind of leadership we hope and dream about for the future?" Such curriculum inquiry, reflecting educators' deeply felt existential quandaries, challenges individuals' purposes and school cultures.

Critical scholars see curriculum inquiry as part of the identity of educators whom Giroux (1985/2010) refers to as "transformative intellectuals." Becoming transformative intellectuals means an essential change of self-understanding as teachers move away from conceiving themselves as technicians, skills-developers, or knowledge imparters to "assuming their full potential as active, reflective scholars and practitioners" (Giroux, 1985/2010, p. 202). Others characterize identities of reflective activist educators as "curriculum workers" who have the insight, initiative, and courage to challenge the dominant order of schooling. Sears (2004) describes curriculum workers as "public moral intellectuals who work within an embryonic democracy unafraid of stirring controversy, stimulating critical analysis, challenging orthodoxy, pursuing collaboration, and searching for consensus" (p. 8). These identities include both the ability and habit of reflection and striving for progressive educational reform.

Curriculum workers actualize their ideals within their own classroom practices but do not work in isolation as they develop as leaders for curriculum transformation.

In their continually emerging leadership, curriculum workers give themselves over to a steadily deepening commitment to what a good education and worthy curriculum would mean in the lives of students now and in the future — to moral concerns for the lives of their own students. A later and broader focus of this concern for human well being is turned to the lives of students more generally, a more ethical sociopolitical focus that expands outward from the classroom to more distant school locales. (Joseph, Mikel, & Windschitl, 2011, p. 67)

Furthermore, curriculum leadership may be seen as an affective process encompassing existential doubt as well as moments of exciting possibility.

Becoming a curriculum leader itself calls for a significant leap of faith to a recast identity and professional orientation and thus emergent curriculum leadership has its existential side. When educators seek to institute the new meaning systems of recultured curriculum, they must embrace the new identities and orientations — always coming to moments in which personal histories and professional careers are in existential balance. As such, curriculum workers face moments when the

risk and unfamiliarity and exhilaration of reaching for possibilities of profound change – interim
steps toward their ultimate vision – hover around
the decision to engage lightly, heavily, or not at
all in curriculum transformation. (Joseph, Mikel,
& Windschitl, 2011, p. 66)

Clearly, when educators become curriculum
workers they assume complex and perhaps disquieting personal and professional identities that
continually encompass habits of inquiry, reflection, and agency.

TRANSCENDING THE UTILITARIAN PARADIGM

Curriculum Worker Portraits

Hence, in view of my students' critical consciousness in the lived curriculum investigations and
their willingness to confront their own beliefs and
practices and question their school environments,
I was quite surprised when I eventually encountered stunning resistance to the assignment and the
course readings. Several teachers – who worked
in a public school district whose raison d'être was
preparation for state standardized tests – became
increasingly hostile in the class; when not glaring
at me or the other students during discussions, they
openly expressed their opinions that progressive
alternatives to dominant curricula are unrealistic and ridiculously idealistic. They refused to
question the status quo or to consider how they
might modify practices or school culture. I cannot say if these individuals had become crushed
by the dominant paradigm, were overwhelmed
by hopelessness, or if they had truly identified
with the utilitarian purpose of education in their
schools. In any case, their behaviors sometimes
made the class climate feel uncomfortable and
the experience unnerved me. I began to question
if this assignment could be valuable for teachers

deeply enculturated into school cultures devoted
to the standardized management paradigm.

I decided to modify the assignment when
teaching the course the following year. I changed
the name of the curriculum inquiry assignment
from "Lived Curriculum Investigation" to "Curriculum Worker Portrait" and requested the study
of an innovative educator who is doing creative,
exciting curriculum work and not just teaching
for test preparation; teachers who felt that their
practices were innovative had the option of writing
a self-study. I based my decision on the rationale
that this approach could allow those socialized
into the standardized management paradigm to
consider progressive practices without having to
so utterly reject their own work — hopefully to
be open-minded rather than resistant. Yet, I was
concerned that the new version of the curriculum
inquiry assignment, the curriculum worker portrait, would not allow for crucial insight and affect.
Could teachers be able to disrupt the encompassing utilitarian paradigm surrounding them if they
did not intensely experience disequilibrium and
moral uncertainty?

Accordingly, in the classes I have taught in
more recent years that entailed curriculum worker
portraits, the inquiries have lacked the disruptive
quality of the lived curriculum investigations and
were less focused on political-economic critique.
On the other hand, the curriculum worker portraits
have not conveyed despair but instead illustrate
hopefulness. Certainly, the different tone in these
papers relates to the requirement to study educators who try to survive within this current climate
and want to teach according to their ideals, e.g., to
enact rich, creative, multi-disciplinary curriculum
to guide learners toward self-knowledge, caring
for others, and deep understanding of the world.

The portrait self-studies written by experienced
educators depicted how individuals working
within a standardized-testing environment seized
every opportunity possible to modify the mandated
curriculum; these teachers expressed frustration

with the current educational climate but also seem determined to hold on to their progressive identities. Clearly, these teachers who studied their own practices were aware of the utilitarian paradigm and reflected on the challenges that they had to overcome to create holistic or constructivist curriculum to the extent possible in a standards-based environment. Once more, my students who did not yet have their own classrooms learned about innovative educators' expert practices, leadership in creating non-traditional curriculum, passion for teaching, and beliefs about their pupils' intelligence and potential. In that sense, these curriculum worker portraits were inspirational.

CONCLUSION

I have found that by doing lived curriculum investigations – especially when there has been strong affective response that accompanies reflection – teachers reached the first stages of transformative learning: they experienced disequilibrium, questioned their beliefs and practices, and modified their assumptions. Moreover, a number of teachers eventually demonstrated the later stages of transformative learning — taking action and developing new identities as curriculum workers. Although only a minority of teachers fully experienced transformative learning during the class itself, their action research in following quarters speaks to their change in practices and often their desire to bring about more equitable educational opportunities for children. Even when teachers did not undergo major identity shifts nor become transformative curriculum leaders, they had, at the very least, seriously questioned "business as usual" in their classrooms and schools. However, as the utilitarian motive for education has become so ubiquitous in American schools and society, perhaps it is time to move beyond merely discerning the standardized management paradigm to finding models of educators who transcend it.

REFERENCES

Aoki, T. T. (1991). *Inspiriting curriculum and pedagogy: Talks to teachers*. Edmonton, Canada: Faculty of Education, Department of Secondary Education, University of Alberta.

Aoki, T. T. (1993). Legitimizing lived curriculum: Towards a curricular landscape of multiplicity. *Journal of Curriculum and Supervision, 8*(3), 255–268.

Apple, M. W. (1986). *Teachers and texts*. New York, NY: Routledge.

Boler, M. (1999). *Feeling power: Emotions and education*. New York, NY: Routledge.

Bowers, C. A. (2010). Understanding the connections between double bind thinking and the ecological crises: Implications for educational reform. *Journal of the American Association for the Advancement of Curriculum Studies, 6*. Retrieved March 10, 2010, from http://www.uwstout.edu/soe/jaaacs/vol6/Bowers.htm

Brown, K. M. (2004). Leadership for social justice and equity: Weaving a transformative framework and pedagogy. *Educational Administration Quarterly, 40*(1), 77–108. doi:10.1177/0013161X03259147

Connelly, F. M., & Clandinin, D. J. (1988). *Teachers as curriculum planners: Narratives of experience*. New York, NY: Teachers College Press.

Cranton, P., & King, P. (2003). Transformative learning as a professional development goal. *New Directions for Adult and Continuing Education, 98*, 31–38. doi:10.1002/ace.97

Cuban, L. (1993). The lure of curricular reform and its pitiful history. *Phi Delta Kappan, 75*(2), 182–185.

Darling-Hammond, L. (2007). Evaluating No Child Left Behind. *Nation (New York, N.Y.), 284*(20), 11–28.

Doll, M. A. (2000). *Like letters in running water: A mythopoetics of curriculum*. New York, NY: Routledge.

Eisner, E. W. (1985). *The educational imagination: On the design and evaluation of school programs*. New York, NY: Macmillan.

Giroux, H. (1985/2010). Teachers as transformative intellectuals. In Canestrari, A., & Marlow, B. (Eds.), *Education foundations: An anthology of critical readings* (pp. 197–204). Thousand Oaks, CA: Sage Publications.

Goodlad, J. I. (1994). *What schools are for* (2nd ed.). Bloomington, IN: Phi Delta Kappa.

Greene, M. (1973). *Teacher as stranger: Educational philosophy for the modern age*. Belmont, CA: Wadsworth.

Greene, M. (1978). *Landscapes of learning*. New York, NY: Teachers College Press.

Hargreaves, A., & Shirley, D. (2009). The persistence of presentism. *Teachers College Record*, *111*(11), 2505–2534.

Heckman, P. E. (1987). Understanding school culture. In Goodlad, J. (Ed.), *The ecology of school renewal: Eighty-sixth yearbook of the National Society for the Study of Education, part I* (pp. 63–78). Chicago, IL: University of Chicago Press.

Henderson, J. G. (2001). Deepening democratic curriculum work. *Educational Researcher*, *30*(9), 18–21. doi:10.3102/0013189X030009018

Henderson, J. G., & Gornik, R. (2007). *Transformative curriculum leadership* (3rd ed.). New York, NY: Prentice Hall.

Heyer, K. D., & Pifel, A. (2007). Extending the responsibilities for schools beyond the school door. *Policy Futures in Education*, *5*(4), 567–580. doi:10.2304/pfie.2007.5.4.567

Imel, S. (1998). *Transformative learning in adulthood. ERIC Digest No. 200*. Columbus, OH: ERIC Clearinghouse on Adult Career and Vocational Education.

Jackson, P. W., Boostrom, R. E., & Hansen, D. T. (1993). *The moral life of schools*. San Francisco, CA: Jossey-Bass.

Joseph, P. B. (2007). Seeing as strangers: Teachers' investigations of lived curriculum. *Journal of Curriculum Studies*, *39*(3), 283–302. doi:10.1080/00220270600818481

Joseph, P. B. (2010). Deskilling. In Kridel, C. (Ed.), *Encyclopedia of curriculum studies* (pp. 283–285). Thousand Oaks, CA: Sage Reference Publications.

Joseph, P. B., Bravmann, S. L., Windschitl, M. A., Mikel, E. R., & Green, N. S. (2000). *Cultures of curriculum*. New York, NY: Routledge.

Joseph, P. B., Mikel, E. R., & Windschitl, M. A. (2011). Reculturing curriculum. In Joseph, P. B. (Ed.), *Cultures of curriculum* (2nd ed., pp. 55–77). New York, NY: Routledge.

Kent, A. M. (2004). Improving teacher quality through professional development. *Education*, *24*(3), 427–435.

Kozol, J. (1997). *Race and class in public education*. Address Presented at the State University of New York at Albany, NY. October 17, 1997. Retrieved from http://www.alternativeradio.org/programs/KOZJ002.shtml

McCallister, C. (2002). Learning to let them learn: Yielding power to students in a literacy methods course. *English Education*, *34*(4), 281–301.

Mezirow, J. (1991). *Transformative dimensions of adult learning*. San Francisco, CA: Jossey-Bass.

Neill, M. (2003). Leaving children behind: How No Child Left Behind will fail our children. *Phi Delta Kappan*, *85*(3), 225–228.

Pinar, W. F. (2004). *What is curriculum theory?* New York, NY: Routledge.

Pink, W. T. (1990). Implementing curriculum inquiry: Theoretical and practical implications. In Sears, J. T., & Marshall, J. D. (Eds.), *Teaching and thinking about curriculum* (pp. 138–153). New York, NY: Teachers College Press.

Purpel, D. E., & Shapiro, S. (1995). *Beyond liberation and excellence: Reconstructing the public discourse on education.* Westport, CT: Bergin & Garvey.

Reiman, A. J., & Peace, S. D. (2002). Promoting teachers' moral reasoning and collaborative inquiry performance: A developmental role-taking and guide inquiry study. *Journal of Moral Education, 31*(1), 51–66. doi:10.1080/03057240120111436

Richardson, V., & Placier, P. (2001). Teacher change. In Richardson, V. (Ed.), *Handbook of research on teaching* (pp. 905–947). Washington, DC: American Educational Research Association.

Schwab, J. J. (1973). The practical 3: Translation into curriculum. *The School Review, 79,* 501–522. doi:10.1086/443100

Sears, J. T. (2004). The curriculum worker as a public moral intellectual. In Gaztambide-Fernandez, R. A., & Sears, J. T. (Eds.), *Curriculum work as a public moral enterprise* (pp. 1–13). Lanham, MD: Rowman & Littlefield.

Slattery, P. (1995). *Curriculum development in the postmodern era.* New York, NY: Garland.

Sleeter, C. E. (2008). Teaching for democracy in an age of corporatocracy. *Teachers College Record, 110*(1), 139–159.

Symcox, L. (2009). From "a nation at risk" to "No Child Left Behind:" 25 years of neoliberal reform in education. In J. Andrzejewski, Marta Baltodano, & L. Symcox (Eds.), *Social justice, peace, and environmental education: Transformative standards* (pp. 53-65). New York, NY: Routledge.

Taubman, P. (2009). *Teaching by numbers: Deconstructing the discourse of standards and accountability in education.* New York, NY: Routledge.

van den Berg, R. (2002). Teachers' meanings regarding educational practice. *Review of Educational Research, 72*(4), 577–625. doi:10.3102/00346543072004577

Westbury, I. (2000). Teaching as reflective practice: What might Didaktik teach curriculum? In Westbury, I., Hopmann, S., & Riquarts, K. (Eds.), *Teaching as a reflective practice: The German Didaktik tradition* (pp. 15–40). Mahwah, NJ: Lawrence Erlbaum.

Wong, J. L. N. (2006). Control and professional development: Are teachers being deskilled or reskilled within the context of decentralization? *Educational Studies, 32*(1), 17–37. doi:10.1080/03055690500415910

Wood, G. H. (1990). Teachers as curriculum workers. In Sears, J. T., & Marshall, J. D. (Eds.), *Teaching and thinking about curriculum: Critical inquiries* (pp. 97–109). New York, NY: Teachers College Press.

Compilation of References

AASW. (2010). *Code of ethics* (3rd ed.). Australian Association of Social Workers. Retrieved 14 November, 2010, from http://www.aasw.asn.au/document/item/740/

Ackerman, D. (1994). *A natural history of love*. New York, NY: Random House.

Adam, C. (2000). What do we learn from readers? Factors in determining successful transitions between academic and workplace writing. In Dias, P., & Paré, A. (Eds.), *Transitions: Writing in academic and workplace settings* (pp. 167–182). Cresskill, NJ: Hampton Press.

Adams St Pierre, E. (2000). Poststructural feminism in education: An overview. *Qualitative Studies in Education, 13*(5), 477–515. doi:10.1080/09518390050156422

Adler, J. (2001). *Teaching mathematics in multilingual classrooms*. Dordrecht, The Netherlands: Kluwer.

Adler, J. A. (2008). Surprise. *Educational Theory, 58*(2), 149–173. doi:10.1111/j.1741-5446.2008.00282.x

Akkerman, S. F., & Meijer, P. C. (2011). A dialogical approach to conceptualizing teacher identity. *Teaching and Teacher Education, 27*(2), 308–319. doi:10.1016/j.tate.2010.08.013

Albers, P. M. (1999). Art education and the possibility of social change. *Art Education, 52*(4), 6–11. doi:10.2307/3193767

Alcorn, M. W. Jr. (2002). *Changing the subject in English class: Discourse and the constructions of desire*. Carbondale, IL: Southern Illinois U.P.

Althusser, L. (1971). *Lenin and philosophy and other essays*. New York, NY: Monthly Review Press.

Altieri, C. (2003). Reading feelings in literature and painting. In *The particulars of rapture: An aesthetics of the affects* (pp. 231–254). Ithaca, NY: Cornell University Press.

Alvermann, D., Moon, J., & Hagood, M. (1999). *Popular culture in the classroom: Teaching and researching critical media literacy*. Chicago, IL: National Reading Conference.

AMES. (2009). *It's your right: Human rights, everyone, everywhere, everyday.* Canberra, Australia: Commonwealth of Australia.

Anderson, V. (1997). Confrontational teaching and rhetorical practice. *College Composition and Communication, 48*(2), 197–214. doi:10.2307/358666

Annas, P. J. (2003). Style as politics: A feminist approach to the teaching of writing. In Kirsch, G. E. (Eds.), *Feminism and composition: A critical sourcebook* (pp. 61–72). Boston, MA: Bedford. doi:10.2307/376958

Anson, C. M., & Forsberg, L. L. (1990). Moving beyond the academic community: Transitional stages in professional writing. *Written Communication, 7*(2), 200–231. doi:10.1177/0741088390007002002

Aoki, T. T. (1991). *Inspiriting curriculum and pedagogy: Talks to teachers*. Edmonton, Canada: Faculty of Education, Department of Secondary Education, University of Alberta.

Aoki, T. T. (1993). Legitimizing lived curriculum: Towards a curricular landscape of multiplicity. *Journal of Curriculum and Supervision, 8*(3), 255–268.

Apple, M. W. (1986). *Teachers and texts*. New York, NY: Routledge.

Argyris, C. (1993). *On organizational learning*. Cambridge, MA: Addison Wesley.

Argyris, C., & Schön, E. (1978). *Organizational learning.* Reading, MA: Addison Wesley.

Arthur, J., & Case-Halferty, A. (2008). Review of the book *They Say/I Say. Composition Forum, 18.* Retrieved from http://compositionforum.com/issue/18/they-say-i-say-review.php

Atwan, R. (1998). Foreword. In Atwan, R. (Ed.), *The best American essays 1998* (pp. xi–xiii). New York, NY: Houghton Mifflin.

Atwill, J. (1998). *Rhetoric reclaimed: Aristotle and the liberal arts tradition.* Ithaca, NY: Cornell U.P.

Au, K. (2007). Culturally responsive instruction: Application to multicultural classrooms. *Pedagogies: An International Journal, 2*(1), 1–18.

Austin, J. L. (1962, 1975). *How to do things with words* (2nd ed., J.O. Urmson & M. Sbisà, Eds.). Cambridge, MA: Harvard U.P.

Baker, C., & Freebody, P. (1989). *Children's first school books.* Cambridge, MA: Basil Blackwell.

Bakhtin, M. M. (1986). *Speech genres and other late essays (V.W. McGee Trans* (Emerson, C., & Holquist, M., Eds.). Austin, TX: University of Texas Press.

Bakhtin, M. M. (1981). *The dialogic imagination. (M. Holquist* (Emerson, C., & Holquist, M. (Trans. Eds.)). Austin, TX: University of Texas Press.

Ball, D. (1990). The mathematical knowledge that prospective teachers bring to teacher education. *The Elementary School Journal, 90,* 449–466. doi:10.1086/461626

Bandura, A. (2001). Social cognitive theory: An agentic perspective. *Annual Review of Psychology, 52,* 1–26. doi:10.1146/annurev.psych.52.1.1

Bang, S. (1983). *We come as a friend –Towards a Vietnamese model of social work.* Leeds, UK: Refugee Action.

Banks, W. (2003). Written through the body: Disruptions and "personal" writing. *College English, 66,* 21–40. doi:10.2307/3594232

Barnard, I. (2010). The ruse of clarity. *College Composition and Communication, 61*(3), 434–451.

Barnes, D. (1979). *From communication to curriculum.* New York, NY: Penguin Books.

Barthes, R. (1985). *The grain of the voice: Interviews 1962-1980.* (L. Coverdale, Trans.). New York, NY: Hill and Wang (Division of Farrar, Strauss and Giroux).

Bartholomae, D., & Petrosky, A. R. (1986). *Facts, artifacts and counterfacts: Theory and method for a reading and writing course.* Upper Montclair, NJ: Boynton/Cook.

Bartholomae, D. (1985). Inventing the university. In Rose, M. (Ed.), *When a writer can't write: Studies in writer's block and other composing-process problems* (pp. 134–165). New York, NY: Guilford.

Bartholomae, D. (1997). Inventing the university. In Villanueva, V. (Ed.), *Cross-talk in comp theory: A reader* (pp. 589–620). Urbana, IL: NCTE.

Bauer, D. M. (2003). The other 'F' word: The feminist in the classroom. In Kirsch, G. E. (Eds.), *Feminism and composition: A critical sourcebook* (pp. 351–362). Boston, MA: Bedford.

Bawarshi, A. (2003). *Genre and the invention of the writer: Reconsidering the place of invention in composition.* Logan, UT: Utah State University Press.

Baxter, J. (2002). A juggling act: A feminist poststructuralist analysis of girls' and boys' talk in the secondary classroom. *Gender and Education, 14*(1), 5–19. doi:10.1080/09540250120098843

Beauchamp, C., & Thomas, L. (2009). Understanding teacher identity: An overview of issues in the literature and implications for teacher education. *Cambridge Journal of Education, 39*(2), 175–189. doi:10.1080/03057640902902252

Beaufort, A. (1999). *Writing in the real world: Making the transition from school to work.* New York, NY: Teachers College Press.

Belenky, M. F., Clinchy, B. M., Goldberger, N. R., & Tarule, J. M. (1997). *Women's ways of knowing: The development of self, voice, and mind.* New York, NY: Basic Books.

Benedetti, J. (1982). The progress of an idea. In *Stanislavsky: An introduction* (pp. 72–75). New York, NY: Theatre Arts Books.

Benedetti, J. (1998). *Stanislavsky and the actor*. New York, NY: Routledge/Theatre Arts Books.

Bennett, J. (2001). Liberal learning as conversation. *Liberal Education, 87*(2), 32–39.

Berlin, J. A. (2003). *Rhetorics poetics and cultures: Refiguring college English studies*. West Lafayette, IN: Parlor Press.

Bickmore, K. (1999). Why discuss sexuality in elementary school? In Letts, W. J., & Sears, J. T. (Eds.), *Queering elementary education: Advancing the dialogue about sexualities and schooling* (pp. 15–25). Lanham, MD: Rowman & Littlefield.

Biesta, G. (2008). Encountering Foucault in life-long learning. In Fejes, A., & Nicoll, K. (Eds.), *Foucault and life-long learning*. London, UK: Routledge.

Billing, M. (2008). Review: Laughter and ridicule: Towards a social critique of humor. *European Journal of Communication, 23*(1), 87–116.

Bizzell, P. (1991). Classroom authority and critical pedagogy. *American Literary History, 3*, 847–863. doi:10.1093/alh/3.4.847

Bizzell, P. (1992). *Academic discourse and critical consciousness*. Pittsburgh, PA: U.P.

Blackwell, D. (2005). *Counselling and psychotherapy with refugees*. Philadelphia, PA: Jessica Kingsley Publications.

Blakeslee, A. M. (2001). Bridging the workplace and the academy: Teaching professional genres through classroom-workplace collaborations. *Technical Communication Quarterly, 10*(2), 169–192. doi:10.1207/s15427625tcq1002_4

Bloom, L. Z. (1996). Freshman composition as a middle class enterprise. *College English, 58*(6), 654–675. doi:10.2307/378392

Boal, A. (1979). *Theatre of the oppressed*. London, UK: Pluto Press.

Boal, A. (1995). *The rainbow of desire*. New York, NY: Routledge Press.

Boler, M. (1999). *Feeling power: Emotions and education*. New York, NY: Routledge.

Boler, M., & Zembylas, M. (2003). Discomforting truths: The emotional terrain of understanding difference. In Trifonas, P. (Ed.), *Pedagogies of difference: Rethinking education for social change* (pp. 110–136). New York, NY: Routledge/Falmer.

Boler, M. (1997). Taming the labile other. In S. Laird (Ed.), *Philosophy of education society 1997* (pp. 258–270). Champaign, IL: Philosophy of Education Society.

Bolker, J. (2003). Teaching Griselda to write. In Kirsch, G. E., et al. (Eds.), *Feminism and composition: A critical sourcebook*. (pp. 49-52). Boston, MA: Bedford. (Reprinted from *College English*, 1979, 40(8), pp. 906-908).

Bone, J. E., Griffin, C. L., & Scholz, T. M. L. (2008). Beyond traditional conceptualizations of rhetoric: Invitational rhetoric and a move toward civility. *Western Journal of Communication, 72*, 434–462. doi:10.1080/10570310802446098

Bordo, S. R. (1987). *The flight to objectivity: Essays on Cartesianism & culture*. Albany, NY: State University of New York Press.

Boud, D., & Walker, D. (1998). Promoting reflection in professional courses: The challenge of context. *Studies in Higher Education, 23*(2), 191–207. doi:10.1080/03075079812331380384

Bourdieu, P. (1999). Language and symbolic power. In Jaworski, A., & Coupland, N. (Eds.), *The discourse reader* (pp. 502–513). New York, NY: Routledge.

Bowers, C. A. (2010). Understanding the connections between double bind thinking and the ecological crises: Implications for educational reform. *Journal of the American Association for the Advancement of Curriculum Studies, 6*. Retrieved March 10, 2010, from http://www.uwstout.edu/soe/jaaacs/vol6/Bowers.htm

Boyd, R. (1999). Reading student resistance: The case of the missing other. *JAC, 19*, 589–605.

Bricker Balken, D. (1999). *Alfredo Jaar: Lament of the images*. Cambridge, MA: Massachusetts Institute of Technology.

Briggs, K. (2010a). Individual achievement in an honors research community: Teaching Vygotsky's zone of proximal development. *Honors in Practice, 6*, 61–68.

Briggs, K. (1996). *The individual as a site of struggle: Subjectivity, writing, and the gender order.* Unpublished doctoral dissertation, University of Massachusetts, Amherst.

Briggs, K. (2009). Thesis as rhizome: A new vision for the honors thesis in the twenty-first century. *The Journal of the National Collegiate Honors Council, 10*(2), 103-114.

Briggs, K. (2010b). *The honors thesis workshop.* Course syllabus, University of Southern Maine Honors Program, Portland, ME.

Britton, J., Burgess, T., Martin, N., McLeod, A., & Rosen, H. (1975). *The development of writing abilities* (pp. 11–18). London, UK: Macmillan.

Britzman, D. (1998). *Lost subjects, contested objects: Toward a psychoanalytic inquiry of learning.* Albany, NY: State University of New York Press.

Britzman, D. (2003). *Practice makes practice: A critical study of learning to teach.* Albany, NY: State University of New York Press.

Britzman, D. P. (1995). Is there a queer pedagogy? Or stop reading straight. *Educational Theory, 45*(2), 151–165. doi:10.1111/j.1741-5446.1995.00151.x

Britzman, D. P. (1998). *Lost subjects, contested objects: Towards a psychoanalytic inquiry of learning.* Albany, NY: State University of New York Press.

Brookfield, S. (1995). *On becoming a critically reflective teacher.* San Francisco, CA: Jossey Bass.

Brookfield, S. (2000). Transformative learning as ideology critique. In Mezirow, J. (Ed.), *Learning as transformation: Critical perspectives on theory as progress* (pp. 125–150). San Francisco, CA: Jossey Bass.

Brown, K. M. (2004). Leadership for social justice and equity: Weaving a transformative framework and pedagogy. *Educational Administration Quarterly, 40*(1), 77–108. doi:10.1177/0013161X03259147

Brown, L. M., & Gilligan, C. (1992). *Meeting at the crossroads: Women's psychology and girls' development.* New York, NY: Ballantine.

Brueggemann, B. J., White, L. F., Dunn, P. A., Heifferon, B. A., & Cheu, J. (2001). Becoming visible: Lessons in disability. *College Composition and Communication, 52*(3), 368–398. doi:10.2307/358624

Bruffee, K. (1984). Collaborative learning and the "conversation of mankind". *College English, 46*(7), 635–652. doi:10.2307/376924

Bruffee, K. A. (1986). Kenneth A. Bruffee responds. *College English, 48*(1), 77–78. doi:10.2307/376589

Brummet, B. (1995). Speculations on the discovery of a Burkean blunder. *Rhetoric Review, 14*(1), 221–225. doi:10.1080/07350199509389061

Bruner, J. (1996). *The culture of education.* Cambridge, MA: Harvard University Press.

Buchanan, I. (2008). *Deleuze and Guattari's anti-Oedipus.* London, UK: Continuum International Publishing Group.

Buckingham, D., & Sefton-Green, J. (1994). *Cultural studies goes to school.* London, UK: Taylor and Francis.

Buckingham, D. (1993). *Reading audiences: Young people and the media.* Manchester, UK: University Press.

Buechner, F. (1983). *Now and then: A memoir of vocation.* San Francisco, CA: Harper.

Buikema, R., & Smelik, A. (Eds.). (1993). *Women's studies and culture: A feminist introduction.* London, UK: Zed Books.

Burbules, N., & Torres, C. (Eds.). (2000). *Globalisation and education: Critical perspectives.* London, UK: Routledge.

Burdick, J., & Sandlin, J. (2010). Inquiry as answerability: Toward a methodology of discomfort in researching critical public pedagogies. *Qualitative Inquiry, 16*(5), 349–360. doi:10.1177/1077800409358878

Burke, K. (1941). *The philosophy of literary form.* Berkeley, CA: University of California Press.

Burke, P. J. (1980). The self: Measurement implications from a symbolic interactionist perspective. *Social Psychology Quarterly, 43*, 18–29. doi:10.2307/3033745

Burke, K. (1984). *Permanence and change: An anatomy of purpose* (3rd ed.). Berkeley, CA: U. of California Press.

Burke, P. J., & Jackson, S. (2007). *Reconceptualising lifelong leaning: Feminist interventions.* Oxford, UK: Routledge.

Burnham, C. (1993). Expressive rhetoric: A source study. In Enos, T., & Brown, S. C. (Eds.), *Defining the new rhetorics: Essays on twentieth-century rhetoric* (pp. 154–170). Newbury Park, CA: Sage.

Burton, F. R., & Seidl, B. (2002). Teacher researcher projects: From the elementary school teacher's perspective. In Flood, J., Lapp, D., Squire, J., & Jensen, J. M. (Eds.), *Handbook of research on teaching the English language arts* (2nd ed., pp. 225–231). Mahweh, NJ: Lawrence Erlbaum Associates.

Butler, J. (1997). *Excitable speech: A politics of the performative* (1st ed.). New York, NY: Routledge.

Butler, J. (2008). An account of oneself. In Davies, B. (Ed.), *Judith Butler in conversation: Analyzing the texts and talk of everyday life* (pp. 19–38). New York, NY: Routledge.

Campbell (2008). The scripted prescription: A cure for childhood. In A. Pelo (Ed.), *Rethinking early childhood education.* Wisconsin: Rethinking Schools.

Cannella, G. S. (1997). *Deconstructing early childhood education: Social justice and revolution.* New York, NY: Peter Lang.

Caro-Bruce, C., Flessner, R., Klehr, M., & Zeichner, K. (Eds.). (2007). *Creating equitable classrooms through action research.* Thousand Oaks, CA: Corwin Press.

Carson, A. (1986). *Eros the bittersweet: An essay.* Princeton, NJ: Princeton University Press.

Chan, C., Chan, T., & Ng, S. (2006). *The strength-focused and meaning oriented approach to resilience and transformation (SMART): A body-mind spirit approach to trauma management.* The Hawthorn Press.

Charteris-Black, J. (2004). *Corpus approaches to critical metaphor analysis.* New York, NY: Palgrave Macmillan. doi:10.1057/9780230000612

Chomsky, N. (1989). *Necessary illusions: Thought control in democratic societies.* Cambridge, MA: South End Press.

Christensen, C. (1997). *The innovator's dilemma: When new technologies can cause great firms to fail.* Boston, MA: Harvard Business School Press.

Clandinin, D. J. (1985). Personal practical knowledge: A study of teachers' classroom images. *Curriculum Inquiry, 15*(4), 361–385. doi:10.2307/1179683

Clarke, A. E. (2007). Feminisms, grounded theory, and situational analysis. In Hesse-Beber, S. (Ed.), *Handbook of feminist research: Theory and praxis* (pp. 345–370). Thousand Oaks, CA: Sage.

Cleary, L. M. (1991). *From the other side of the desk.* Portsmouth, NH: Boynton/Cook Publishers.

Clegg, S. (1998). Foucault, power and organisations. In McKinlay, A., & Starkey, K. (Eds.), *Foucault, management and organisation theory.* London, UK: Sage.

Cochran-Smith, M., & Lytle, S. L. (1999). Relationships of knowledge and practice: Teacher learning in communities. *Review of Research in Education, 24,* 249–305.

Cochran-Smith, M., & Lytle, S. L. (2009). *Inquiry as stance: Practitioner research for the next generation.* New York, NY: Teachers College Press.

Cohen, D. K., Raudenbush, S. W., & Ball, D. L. (2003). Resources, instruction and research. *Educational Evaluation and Policy Analysis, 25*(2), 119–142. doi:10.3102/01623737025002119

Cohen, L., Manion, L., & Morrison, K. (2000). *Research methods in education* (5th ed.). New York, NY: Routledge. doi:10.4324/9780203224342

Collette, L. (2009). Political satire and postmodern irony in the age of Stephen Colbert and Jon Stewart. *Journal of Popular Culture, 5*(42), 856–874. doi:10.1111/j.1540-5931.2009.00711.x

Collier, P. (2001). A differentiated model of role identity acquisition. *Symbolic Interaction, 24*(2), 217–235. doi:10.1525/si.2001.24.2.217

Collinson, V., & Cook, T. F. (2007). *Organizational learning: Improving learning, teaching, and leading in school systems.* Thousand Oaks, CA: Sage Publications.

Condit, M. C. (1997). In praise of eloquent diversity: Gender and rhetoric as public persuasion. *Women's Studies in Communications, 20,* 91–116.

Conle, C. (2003). An anatomy of narrative curricula. *Educational Researcher, 32*(3), 3–15. doi:10.3102/0013189X032003003

Connelly, F. M., & Clandinin, D. J. (1990). Stories of experience and narrative inquiry. *Educational Researcher, 19*(5), 2–14.

Connelly, F. M., & Clandinin, D. J. (1988). *Teachers as curriculum planners: Narratives of experience.* New York, NY: Teachers College Press.

Connelly, F. M., & Clandinin, D. J. (1999). Borders of space and time. In Connelly, F. M., & Clandinin, D. J. (Eds.), *Shaping a professional identity: Stories of educational practice* (pp. 103–113). New York, NY: Teachers College Press.

Converse. (2010). In J. Simpson (Ed.), *Oxford English Dictionary.* Retrieved from http://dictionary.oed.com

Coontz, S. (2005). *Marriage, a history: From obedience to intimacy, or how love conquered marriage.* New York, NY: Viking.

Cooper, B. (1998a). Assessing national curriculum mathematics in England: Exploring children's interpretation of key stage 2 tests in clinical interviews. *Educational Studies in Mathematics, 35*(1), 19–49. doi:10.1023/A:1002945216595

Cooper, B. (1998b). Using Bernstein and Bourdieu to understand children's difficulties with 'realistic' mathematics testing: An exploratory study. *International Journal of Qualitative Studies in Education, 11*(4), 511–532. doi:10.1080/095183998236421

Cooper, B. (2001). Social class and 'real life' mathematics assessments. In Gates, P. (Ed.), *Issues in mathematics teaching* (pp. 245–258). New York, NY: Routledge/Falmer.

Cooper, B., & Dunne, M. (2004). Constructing the 'legitimate' goal of a 'realistic' maths item: A comparison of 10-11 and 13-14 year olds. In B. Allen & S. Johnston-Wilder (Eds.), *Mathematics education: Exploring the culture of learning* (pp. 69-90). New York, NY: Routledge/Falmer.

Cranton, P. (1994). *Understanding and promoting transformative learning.* San Francisco, CA: Jossey Bass.

Cranton, P., & King, P. (2003). Transformative learning as a professional development goal. *New Directions for Adult and Continuing Education, 98,* 31–38. doi:10.1002/ace.97

Cranton, P. (2000). Individual differences and transformative learning. In Mezirow, J. (Ed.), *Learning as transformation* (pp. 181–204). San Francisco, CA: Jossey Bass.

Crispeels, J. H. (Ed.). (2004). *Learning to lead together: The promise and challenge of sharing leadership.* Thousand Oaks, CA: Sage.

Crowley, S. (1998). *Composition in the university: Historical and polemical essays.* Pittsburgh, PA: U.P.

Crowley, S. (2006). *Toward a civil discourse: Rhetoric and fundamentalism.* Pittsburgh, PA: U.P.

Cuban, L. (1993). The lure of curricular reform and its pitiful history. *Phi Delta Kappan, 75*(2), 182–185.

Cuoto, D. (2002). The anxiety of learning. *Harvard Business Review, 80*(3), 100–107.

Curran, G. (2006). Challenging sexual norms and assumptions in an ESL classroom: Rethinking my teaching practice. *Journal of Language, Identity, and Education, 5*(1), 85–96. doi:10.1207/s15327701jlie0501_6

Curran, G., Chiarolli, S., & Pallotta-Chiarolli, M. (2009). The C words: Clitories, childhood and challenging compulsory heterosexuality discourses with pre-service primary teachers. *Sex Education: Sexuality, Society and Learning, 9*(2), 155–168.

Curran, G. (2002). *Young queers getting together: Moving beyond isolation and loneliness.* (Unpublished PhD Thesis). Melbourne, Australia: University of Melbourne.

Curry, J. B. (1993). A return to "converting the natives," or antifoundationalist faith in the composition class. *Rhetoric Review, 12*(1), 160–167. doi:10.1080/07350199309389031

Cushman, E. (1999). The rhetorician as an agent of social change. In Ede, L. S. (Ed.), *On writing research: The Braddock essays* (pp. 372–389). Boston, MA: Bedford. doi:10.2307/358271

Dalley, P., & Campbell, M. D. (2006). Constructing and contesting discourses of heteronormativity: An ethnographic study of youth in a Francophone high school in Canada. *Journal of Language, Identity, and Education, 5*(1), 11–29. doi:10.1207/s15327701jlie0501_2

Danaher, G. R., Schirato, T., & Webb, J. (2000). *Understanding Foucault*. St Leonards, Australia: Allen & Unwin.

Danielewicz, J. (2001). *Teaching selves: Identity, pedagogy, and teacher education*. Albany, NY: State University of New York Press.

Darling-Hammond, L. (1998). Teachers and teaching: Testing policy hypotheses from a national commission report. *Educational Researcher, 27*(1), 5–16.

Darling-Hammond, L. (2007). Evaluating No Child Left Behind. *Nation (New York, N.Y.), 284*(20), 11–28.

Darwin, T. J. (2003). Pathos, pedagogy, and the familiar: Cultivating rhetorical intelligence. In Petraglia, J., & Bahri, D. (Eds.), *The realms of rhetoric: The prospects for rhetoric education* (pp. 23–37). Albany, NY: SUNY Press.

Davies, D. (2008). Enhancing the role of the arts in primary pre-service teacher education. *Teaching and Teacher Education, 20*(3), 630–638.

Davies, B. (1999). *A body of writing: 1990-1999*. Oxford, UK: Rowman & Littlefield.

Davis, D. (2000). *Breaking up (at) totality: A rhetoric of laughter*. Carbondale, IL: Southern Illinois University Press.

Davis, B., Sumara, D., & Luce-Kapler, R. (2000). *Engaging minds: Learning and teaching in a complex world*. Mahwah, NJ: Laurence Eribaum.

De Block, L., & Rydin, I. (2006). Digital rapping in media productions: Intercultural communication through youth culture. In Buckingham, D., & Willett, R. (Eds.), *Digital generations: Children, young people, and new media* (pp. 295–312). Mahwah, NJ: Lawrence Erlbaum.

de Freitas, E. (2008a). Troubling teacher identity: Preparing mathematics teachers to teach for diversity. *Teaching Education, 19*(1), 43–55. doi:10.1080/10476210701860024

de Freitas, E., & McAuley, A. (2008). Teaching for diversity by troubling whiteness: Strategies for isolated white communities. *Race, Ethnicity and Education, 11*(4), 429–442. doi:10.1080/13613320802479018

de Freitas, E. (2009). Analyzing procedural and narrative discourse in the mathematics classroom: The splitting of teacher identity. In Brown, T. (Ed.), *The psychology of mathematics education: A psychoanalytic displacement*. Rotterdam, The Netherlands: Sense Publisher.

de Freitas, E. (2008b,). Critical mathematics education: Recognizing the ethical dimension of problem solving. *International Electronic Journal of Mathematics Education, 3*(2), 79–95. Retrieved from www.iejme.com

Deleuze, G., & Guattari, F. (1987). *A thousand plateaus: Capitalism and schizophrenia* (Massumi, B., Trans.). Minneapolis, MN: University of Minnesota Press.

Denborough, D. (1996). Power and partnership? Challenging the sexual construction of schooling. In Laskey, L., & Beavis, C. (Eds.), *Schooling & sexualities: Teaching for a positive sexuality* (pp. 1–10). Geelong, Australia: Deakin Centre for Education and Change, Deakin University.

Denzin, N. K., & Lincoln, Y. S. (Eds.). (2000). *Handbook of qualitative research* (2nd ed.). Thousand Oaks, CA: Sage.

Devitt, A. (2007). Transferability and genres. In Keller, C., & Weisser, C. (Eds.), *The locations of composition* (pp. 215–227). Albany, NY: State University of New York Press.

Dewey, J. (1934). *Art as experience*. New York, NY: Minton, Balch & Company.

Dewey, J. (1922). *Human nature and conduct: An introduction to social psychology*. New York, NY: Henry Holt and Company.

Dewey, J. (1989). How we think. In Boydston, J. A. (Ed.), *John Dewey: The later works, 1925-1933* (*Vol. 8*, pp. 107–352). Carbondale, IL: Southern Illinois University Press. (Original work published 1933)

Dewey, J. (1929, 1960). *The quest for certainty*. New York, NY: Capricorn.

Dias, P., Freedman, A., Medway, P., & Paré, A. (1999). *Worlds apart: Acting and writing in academic and workplace contexts*. Mahwah, NJ: Lawrence Erlbaum Associates.

Dias, P., & Paré, A. (Eds.). (2000). *Transitions: Writing in academic and workplace settings*. Cresskill, NJ: Hampton Press, Inc.

Diss, R. E., & Buckley, P. K. (2005). *Developing family and community involvement skills through case studies and field experiences*. Upper Saddle River, NJ: Pearson Education, Inc.

Dole, S., & Beswick, K. (2002). Maths anxiety self-assessment as a quality assurance measure. In B. Barton, K. Irwin, M. Pfannkuch & M. Thomas (Eds.), *Proceedings of the Twenty-Fifth Annual Conference of the Mathematics Education Research Group of Australasia* (pp. 236-243). Aukland, New Zealand: MERGA.

Doll, M. A. (2000). *Like letters in running water: A mythopoetics of curriculum*. New York, NY: Routledge.

Dorsey, A. (2002). 'White girls' and 'strong black women': Reflections on a decade of teaching black history at predominantly white institutions. In Macdonald, A. A., & Sanchez-Casal, S. (Eds.), *Feminist classrooms: Pedagogies of identity and difference* (pp. 203–232). New York, NY: Palgrave Macmillan.

Douglas, M. (1975). *Implicit meanings: Essays in anthropology*. London, UK: Routledge and Kegan Paul.

Downs, D., & Wardle, E. (2007). Teaching about writing, righting misconceptions: (Re)Envisioning "First-year composition" as "introduction to writing studies". *College Composition and Communication, 58*(4), 552–585.

Drago-Severson, E. (2009). *Leading adult learning: Supporting adult development in our schools*. Thousand Oaks, CA: Corwin.

Dreyfus, H. L., & Rabinow, P. (1982). *Michel Foucault: Beyond structuralism and hermeneutics*. New York, NY: Harvester Wheatsheaf.

Duffelmeyer, B. (2002). Critical work in first-year composition: Computers, pedagogy, and research. *Pedagogy: Critical Approaches to Teaching Literature, Language, Composition, and Culture, 2*(3), 357–374. doi:10.1215/15314200-2-3-357

Duffy, F. (2003). I think, therefore I am resistant to change: What we know - or think we know - is our biggest roadblock to learning. *Journal of Staff Development, 24*(1). Retrieved 11 December, 2010, from http://www.nsdc.org/library/publications/jsd/duffy241.cfm

Dunn, P. (2001). *Talking, sketching, moving: Multiple literacies in the teaching of writing*. New Hampshire: Boynton/Cook.

Eisner, E. W. (1972). *Educating artistic vision*. New York, NY: Macmillan.

Eisner, E. W. (2001). Should we create new aims for art education? *Art Education, 54*(5), 6–10. doi:10.2307/3193929

Eisner, E. W. (1985). *The educational imagination: On the design and evaluation of school programs*. New York, NY: Macmillan.

Elbow, P. (1987). Closing my eyes as i speak: An argument for ignoring audience. *College English, 49*(1), 50–69. doi:10.2307/377789

Elbow, P. (2006). The music of form: Rethinking organization in writing. *College Composition and Communication, 57*(4), 620–666.

Elbow, P. (1971). *Writing without teachers*. New York, NY: Oxford University Press.

Elbow, P. (1993). Uses of binary thinking: Exploring seven productive oppositions. *JAC, 13*(1), 51–78.

Elkind, D. (1981/1988/2001). *The hurried child*. Reading, MA: Addison-Wesley.

Ellis, E. (2012). Back to the future? The pedagogical promise of the (multimedia) essay. In Whithaus, C., & Bowen, T. (Eds.), *Multimodal literacies and emerging genres in student compositions*. Pittsburgh, PA: University of Pittsburgh Press.

Ellwood, C. (2006). On coming out and coming undone: Sexualities and reflexivities in language education. *Journal of Language, Identity, and Education, 5*, 67–84. doi:10.1207/s15327701jlie0501_5

Elsden-Clifton, J. (2006). Constructing "Thirdspaces": Migrant students and the visual arts. *Studies in Learning, Evaluation. Innovation and Development, 3*(1), 1–11.

Elsden-Clifton, J (2004). Negotiating the transformative waters: Students exploring their subjectivity in art. *International Journal of Education through Arts, 1*(1), 43-51.

Epstein, D., & Johnson, R. (1998). *Schooling sexualities.* Buckingham, UK: Open University Press.

Eraut, M. (2010). Knowledge, working practices, and learning. In Billet, S. (Ed.), *Learning through practice* (pp. 37–58). Dordrecht, The Netherlands: Springer. doi:10.1007/978-90-481-3939-2_3

Eubanks, P. (1999). The story of conceptual metaphor: What motivates metaphoric mappings? *Poetics Today, 20*(3), 419–442.

Eubanks, P. (2001). Understanding metaphors for writing: In defense of the conduit metaphor. *College Composition and Communication, 53*(1), 92–118. doi:10.2307/359064

Evans, K. (2002). *Negotiating the self: Identity, sexuality and emotion in learning to teach.* New York, NY: RoutledgeFalmer.

Fagerberg, J. (2004). Innovation: A guide to the literature. In Fagerberg, J., Mowery, D. C., & Nelson, R. R. (Eds.), *The Oxford handbook of innovation* (pp. 1–26). Oxford University Press.

Fairclough, N. (1992). *Discourse and social change.* Cambridge, UK: Polity Press.

Fairclough, N. (2003). *Analyzing discourse: Textual analysis for social research.* New York, NY: Routledge.

Faulkner, J. (2003). Like you have a bubble inside of you that just wants to pop: Popular culture, pleasure and the English classroom. *English Teaching: Practice and Critique, 2*(2), 47–56.

Feiman-Nemser, S. (2006). Beit Midrash for teachers: An experiment in teacher preparation. *Journal of Jewish Education, 72*(3), 161–181. doi:10.1080/15244110600990148

Fine, G., & de Soucey, M. (2005). Joking cultures: Humor themes as social regulation in group life. *Humor: International Journal of Humor Research, 18*(1), 1–22. doi:10.1515/humr.2005.18.1.1

Fleming, J. D. (2003). Becoming rhetorical: An education in the topics. In Petraglia, J., & Bahri, D. (Eds.), *The realms of rhetoric: The prospects for rhetoric education* (pp. 93–116). Albany, NY: SUNY Press.

Forbes, C., & Davis, E. (2008). The development of pre-service elementary teachers' curricular role identity for science teaching. *Science Education, 92*(5), 909–940. doi:10.1002/sce.20265

Foss, S. K., & Griffin, C. L. (1995). Beyond persuasion: A proposal for an invitational rhetoric. *Communication Monographs, 62*, 2–18. doi:10.1080/03637759509376345

Foss, S. K., Griffin, C. L., & Foss, K. (1997). Transforming rhetoric through feminist reconstruction: A response to the gender diversity perspective. *Women's Studies in Communications, 20*, 117–135.

Foss, D. H., & Kleinsasser, R. C. (1996). Pre-service elementary teachers' views of pedagogical and mathematical content knowledge. *Teaching and Teacher Education, 12*(4), 429–442. doi:10.1016/0742-051X(95)00049-P

Foucault, M. (1981). The discourse on language. In *The archaeology of knowledge* (pp. 215–237). New York, NY: Harper & Row Publishers.

Foucault, M. (1972). *The archaeology of knowledge.* New York, NY: Pantheon.

Foucault, M. (1995). *Discipline and punish: The birth of the prison.* New York, NY: Vintage.

Foucault, M. (1978). The history of sexuality: *Vol. 1. An introduction.* London, UK: Penguin.

Foucault, M. (1991). Governmentality. In Burchell, G., Gordon, C., & Miller, P. (Eds.), *The Foucault effect: Studies in governmentality.* London, UK: Harvester Wheatsheaf.

Foucault, M. (1982). The subject and power. In Dreyfus, H. L., & Rabinow, P. (Eds.), *Foucault: Beyond structuralism and hermeneutics.* Chicago, IL: University of Chicago Press.

Foucault, M. (1980). *Power/knowledge: Selected interviews and other writings, 1972-1977 (C. Gordon* (Gordon, C. (Trans. Eds.)). New York, NY: Pantheon Books.

Foucault, M. (1994). What is enlightenment? In Rabinow, P. (Ed.), *Michel Foucault: Ethics –Essential works of Foucault 1954-1984*. London, UK: Penguin.

Fox, T. (1990). *The social uses of writing*. Norwood, NJ: Ablex Publishing Co.

France, A. (1994). *Composition as a cultural practice*. Westport, CT: Bergin & Garvey.

Freadman, A. (1994). Anyone for tennis? In Freedman, A., & Medway, P. (Eds.), *Genre and the new rhetoric* (pp. 43–66). London, UK: Taylor and Francis.

Freedman, K. (2000). Social perspectives on art education in the US: Teaching visual culture in a democracy. *Studies in Art Education, 41*(4), 314–329. doi:10.2307/1320676

Freedman, A., Adam, C., & Smart, G. (1994). Wearing suits to class: Simulating genres and simulations as genre. *Written Communication, 11*(2), 193–226. doi:10.1177/0741088394011002002

Freedman, A., & Adam, C. (2000). Bridging the gap: University-based writing that is more than simulation. In Dias, P., & Paré, A. (Eds.), *Transitions: Writing in academic and workplace settings* (pp. 129–144). Cresskill, NJ: Hampton Press.

Freeland, R. (2000, September 15). The practical path, too, can be high-minded. *The Chronicle of Higher Education, 47*(3), B11.

Freese, L., & Burke, P. J. (1994). Persons, identities, and social interaction. In Markovsky, B., Heimer, K., & O'Brien, J. (Eds.), *Advances in group processes* (pp. 1–24). Greenwich, CT: JAI.

Freire, P. (1993). *Pedagogy of the oppressed*. New York, NY: Continuum.

Freire, P., & Macedo, D. (1995). A dialogue: Culture, language, and race. *Harvard Educational Review, 65*(3), 377–402.

Freire, P. (1996). *Education for critical consciousness*. New York, NY: Continuum. (Original work published 1969)

Freire, P. (1973). *Education for critical consciousness*. New York, NY: Continuum.

Freire, P. (1973). *Education as the practice of freedom in education for critical consciousness*. New York, NY: Continuum.

Freire, P. (2005). The banking concept of education. In Johnson, T. R. (Ed.), *Teaching composition: Background readings* (pp. 91–103). Boston, MA: Bedford/St. Martin's.

Freire, P. (2003). *Pedagogy of the oppressed* (M. B. Ramos, Trans.). 30th Anniversary edition. New York, NY: Continuum International Publishing, Inc. (Original work published 1970).

Freud, S. (1960). *Jokes and their relationship to the unconscious. The Standard Editions* (Strachey, J., Trans.). New York, NY: Norton.

Friere, P. (1998). *Teachers as cultural workers: Letters to those who dare teach*. Boulder, CO: Westview Press.

Fulkerson, R. (1996). Transcending our conception of argument in light of feminist critiques. *Argumentation and Advocacy, 32*, 199–217.

Fulkerson, R. (2005). Composition at the turn of the twenty-first century. *College Composition and Communication, 56*, 654–687.

Fullan, M. (1991). *The new meaning of educational change*. New York, NY: Teachers College Press.

Fullan, M. (2001). *Leading in a culture of change*. San Francisco, CA: Jossey-Bass.

Fuller, F. F. (1969). Concerns of teachers: A developmental conceptualization. *American Educational Research Journal, 6*(2), 207–226.

Gadamer, H.-G. (1977). *Philosophical hermeneutics*, (D. E. Linge, Trans.). Berkeley, CA: U.P.

Gallagher, S. (1999). An exchange of gazes. In Kincheloe, J. L., Steinberg, S. R., & Villverde, L. E. (Eds.), *Rethinking intelligence* (pp. 69–83). New York, NY: Routledge.

Gallop, J. (2000). The ethics of reading: Close encounters. *Journal of Curriculum Theorizing, 16*(3), 7–17.

Gee, J. P. (2001). Identity as an analytic lens for research in education. *Review of Research in Education, 25*, 99–125.

Geijsel, F., & Meijers, F. (2005). Identity learning: The core process of educational change. *Educational Studies, 31*(4), 419–430. doi:10.1080/03055690500237488

Geisler, C. (1994). *Academic literacy and the nature of expertise: reading, writing, and knowing in academic philosophy.* Hillsdale, NJ: Lawrence Erlbaum Associates.

Gellert, U., & Jablonka, E. (2009). "I am not talking about reality": Word problems and the intricacies of producing legitimate text. In Verschaffel, L., Greer, B., Van Dooren, W., & Mukhopadhyay, S. (Eds.), *Words and worlds: Modeling verbal descriptions of situations.* Rotterdam, The Netherlands: Sense Publishers.

Gendlin, E. T. (1981). *Focusing.* New York, NY: Bantam Books.

Gibney, P. (1987). Co-evolving with anorectic families: Difference is a singular moment. *The Australian and New Zealand Journal of Family Therapy, 8*(2), 71–80.

Gilligan, C. (1982). *In a different voice: Psychological theory and women's development.* Cambridge, MA: Harvard University Press.

Gilligan, C., Spencer, R., Weinberg, M. K., & Bertsch, T. (2003). On the listening guide: A voice centered relational method. In Camic, P. M., Rhodes, J. E., & Yardley, L. (Eds.), *Qualitative research in psychology: Expanding perspectives in methodology and design* (pp. 157–172). Washington, DC: American Psychological Association. doi:10.1037/10595-009

Gilligan, C. (1996). The centrality of relationship in human development: A puzzle, some evidence, and a theory. In Noam, G. G., & Fischer, K. W. (Eds.), *Development and vulnerability in close relationships* (pp. 237–261). Mahwah, NJ: Lawrence Erlbaum Associates.

Giroux, H. (1992). *Border crossings: Cultural workers and the politics of education.* New York, NY: Routledge.

Giroux, H. (2001). *Theory and resistance in education: Toward a pedagogy for the opposition.* Westport, CT: Bergin & Garvey.

Giroux, H. A. (1983). *Theory and resistance in education: A pedagogy for the opposition.* South Hadley, MA: Bergin & Garvey Publishers.

Giroux, H. A. (1988). *Schooling and the struggle for public life: Critical pedagogy in the modern age.* Minneapolis, MN: University of Minnesota Press.

Giroux, H. A. (1988). *Teachers as intellectuals.* New York, NY. Bergen: Garvey.

Giroux, H. (1985/2010). Teachers as transformative intellectuals. In Canestrari, A., & Marlow, B. (Eds.), *Education foundations: An anthology of critical readings* (pp. 197–204). Thousand Oaks, CA: Sage Publications.

Glenn, C. (2004). *Unspoken: A rhetoric of silence.* Carbondale, IL: Southern Illinois University Press.

Goatly, A. (2007). *Washing the brain: Metaphor and hidden ideology.* Philadelphia, PA: John Benjamins.

Goffman, E. (1959). *The presentation of self in everyday life.* New York, NY: Doubleday.

Goodfellow, R., O'Neil, D., & Smith, P. (Eds.). (1996). *Saving face, losing face, in your face: A journey into the western heart, mind and soul.* Oxford, UK: Butterworth Heinemann.

Goodlad, J. I. (1994). *What schools are for* (2nd ed.). Bloomington, IN: Phi Delta Kappa.

Gore, J. (1992). What *can* 'we' do for 'you'?: Struggling over empowerment in critical and feminist pedagogy. In Luke, C., & Gore, J. (Eds.), *Feminisms and critical pedagogy* (pp. 54–73). New York, NY: Routledge.

Gorzelsky, G. (2009). Working boundaries: From student resistance to student agency. *College Composition and Communication, 61*, 64–84.

Graff, G. (2003). *Clueless in academe: How schooling obscures the life of the mind.* New Haven, CT: Yale University Press.

Graff, G., & Birkenstein, C. (2009). An immodest proposal for connecting high school and college. *College Composition and Communication, 61*(1), W409-416.

Graff, G., & Birkenstein, C. (2010). *They say / I say: The moves that matter in academic writing.* New York, NY: Norton.

Gravers, M. (Ed.). (2007). *Exploring ethnic diversity in Burma.* Denmark: Nais Press.

Gray, M. (2005). Dilemmas of international social work: Paradoxical processes in indigenisation, universalism and imperialism. *International Journal of Social Welfare, 14*(3), 231–238. doi:10.1111/j.1468-2397.2005.00363.x

Greene, M. (2000). *Releasing the imagination: Essays on education, the arts and social change.* New York, NY: Jossey-Bass.

Greene, M. (1986). Reflection and passion in teaching. *Journal of Curriculum and Supervision, 2,* 68–81.

Greene, M. (1973). *Teacher as stranger: Educational philosophy for the modern age.* New York, NY: Wadsworth Publishing.

Greene, M. (1978). *Landscapes of learning.* New York, NY: Teachers College Press.

Grieshaber, S., & Cannella, G. (Eds.). (2001). *Embracing identities in early childhood education.* New York, NY: Teachers College Press.

Grosz, E. (1994). *Volatile bodies: Toward a corporeal feminism.* St Leonards, Australia: Allen & Unwin.

Grosz, E. (1994). Refiguring lesbian desire. In Doan, L. (Ed.), *The lesbian postmodern* (pp. 67–84). New York, NY: Columbia University Press.

Guffey, M. (2008). *Business communication: Process and product* (8th ed.). Mason, OH: South-Western Cengage Learning.

Gutstein, E. (2006). *Reading and writing the world with mathematics: Toward a pedagogy for social justice.* New York, NY: Routledge.

Gutstein, E., & Peterson, B. (2005). *Rethinking mathematics: Teaching social justice by the numbers.* Milwaukee, WI: Rethinking Schools.

Gutstein, E. (2008). Building political relationships with students: An aspect of social justice pedagogy. In de Freitas, E., & Nolan, K. (Eds.), *Opening the research text: Insights and in(ter)ventions into mathematics education.* New York, NY: Springer Verlag. doi:10.1007/978-0-387-75464-2_8

Hairston, M. (2003). Diversity, ideology, and teaching writing. In Villanueva, V. (Ed.), *Cross-talk in comp theory: A reader* (2nd ed., pp. 697–713). Urbana, IL: National Council of Teachers of English.

Halloran, S. M. (1975). On the end of rhetoric, classical and modern. *College English, 35,* 621–631. doi:10.2307/374944

Hamilton, S. J. (1995). Evil woman? Bad mother? Single parent! Escaping the epithets. In *My name's not Susie: A life transformed by literacy* (pp. 79–90). Portsmouth, NH: Boynton/Cook.

Hargreaves, A., & Fullan, M. (1998). *What's worth fighting for out there?* New York, NY: Teachers' College Press.

Hargreaves, A., & Shirley, D. (2009). *The fourth way: The inspirational future for educational change.* New York, NY: Sage.

Hargreaves, A., & Shirley, D. (2009). The persistence of presentism. *Teachers College Record, 111*(11), 2505–2534.

Harris, J. (2006). *Rewriting: How to do things with texts.* Logan, UT: Utah State University Press.

Hattie, J. (2009). *Visible learning: A synthesis of over 800 meta-analyses relating to achievement.* Oxford, UK: Routledge.

Hawisher, G., & Selfe, C. (Eds.). (1999). *Passions, pedagogies, and twenty-first century technologies.* Logan, UT: Utah State University Press.

Hawisher, G. E. (2003). Forwarding a feminist agenda in writing studies. In Kirsch, G. E. (Eds.), *Feminism and composition: A critical sourcebook* (pp. xv–xx). Boston, MA: Bedford.

Hawkins, D. (1974/2002). I, thou, and it. In Hawkins, D. (Ed.), *The informed vision: Essays on learning and human nature* (pp. 48–62). New York, NY: Agathon Press.

Heath, S. B. (1983). *Ways with words: Language, life and work in communities and classrooms.* Cambridge, UK: Cambridge University Press.

Heckman, P. E. (1987). Understanding school culture. In Goodlad, J. (Ed.), *The ecology of school renewal: Eighty-sixth yearbook of the National Society for the Study of Education, part I* (pp. 63–78). Chicago, IL: University of Chicago Press.

Heidegger, M. (1971). The nature of language. In *On the way to language* (Hertz, P. D., Trans.). San Francisco, CA: HarperCollins.

Heilker, P. (1996). *The essay: Theory and pedagogy for an active form*. Urbana, IL: NCTE.

Heilker, P. (2006). Twenty years in: An essay in two parts. *College Composition and Communication, 58*(2), 182–212.

Helle, L., Tynjälä, P., & Vesterinen, P. (2006). Work-related project as a learning environment. In Tynjälä, P., Välimaa, J., & Boulton-Lewis, G. (Eds.), *Higher education and working life—Collaborations, confrontations, and challenges* (pp. 195–208). Oxford, UK: Elsevier.

Henderson, J. G. (2001). Deepening democratic curriculum work. *Educational Researcher, 30*(9), 18–21. doi:10.3102/0013189X030009018

Henderson, J. G., & Gornik, R. (2007). *Transformative curriculum leadership* (3rd ed.). New York, NY: Prentice Hall.

Hendrix, S., & Jacobsen, E. (2000). What happened in English 101? In Tassoni, J., & Thelin, W. (Eds.), *Blundering for a change: Errors and expectations in critical pedagogy* (pp. 51–67). Portsmouth, NH: Boynton/Cook.

Hensley, B. (2009). *Seeking safe spaces: The impact of campus climate on college choice*. Ph.D. dissertation, University of Cincinnati, United States -- Ohio. Retrieved February 25, 2011, from Dissertations & Theses @ University of Cincinnati. (Publication No. AAT 3371013).

Herrington, A., & Curtis, M. (2000). *Persons in process: Four stories of writing and personal development in college*. Urbana, IL: National Council of Teachers of English.

Hesse, K. (1997). *Out of the dust*. New York, NY: Scholastic.

Heyer, K. D., & Pifel, A. (2007). Extending the responsibilities for schools beyond the school door. *Policy Futures in Education, 5*(4), 567–580. doi:10.2304/pfie.2007.5.4.567

Hillier, L., Turner, A., & Mitchell, A. (2005). *Writing themselves in again: 6 years on - The 2nd national report on the sexuality, health and well-being of same-sex attracted young people in Australia*. Melbourne, Australia: Australian Research Centre in Sex, Health and Society, La Trobe University.

Himley, M. (2004). Facing (up to) 'the stranger' in community service learning. *College Composition and Communication, 55*(3), 416–438. doi:10.2307/4140694

Himley, M. (1997). The classroom as city. In Himley, M., Le Fave, K., Larson, A., & Yadlon, S.Political Moments Study Group (Eds.), *Political moments in the classroom* (pp. 119–130). Portsmouth, NH: Boynton/Cook.

Hindman, J. E. (2002). Writing an important body of scholarship: A proposal for an embodied rhetoric of professional practice. *JAC, 22*, 93–118.

Hindman, J. (2001). Making writing matter: Using "the personal" to recover(y) an essential(ist) tension in academic discourse. *College English, 64*(1), 88–108. doi:10.2307/1350111

Hoggs, M., Terry, D., & White, K. (1995). A tale of two theories: A critical comparison of identity theory with social identity theory. *Social Psychology Quarterly, 58*, 255–269. doi:10.2307/2787127

Holzer, E. (2002). Conceptions of the study of Jewish texts in teachers' professional development. *Religious Education (Chicago, Ill.), 97*(4), 377. doi:10.1080/00344080214723

Holzer, E. (2006). What connects "good" teaching, text study and Hevruta LEARNING? A conceptual argument. *Journal of Jewish Education, 72*(3), 183–204. doi:10.1080/15244110600990163

Honan, W. (1999, March 10). Small liberal arts colleges facing questions on focus. *The New York Times*. Retrieved from http://www.nytimes.com

hooks, b. (1994). *Teaching to transgress: Education as the practice of freedom*. London, UK: Routledge.

hooks, b. (1995). *Art on my mind: Visual politics*. New York, NY: The New Press.

hooks, b. (2003). *Teaching community: A pedagogy of hope*. New York, NY: Routledge.

Howard, G. (1999). *We can't teach what we don't know: White teachers, multiracial schools.* New York, NY: Columbia Teachers College Press.

Howe, F. (2003). Identity and expression: A writing course for women. In Kirsch, G. E. (Eds.), *Feminism and composition: A critical sourcebook* (pp. 33–42). Boston, MA: Bedford. doi:10.2307/375624

Hoy, P. (2001a). The disarming seduction of stories. *Writing on the Edge, 12*(1), 41–48.

Hoy, P. (2001b). The outreach of an idea. *Rhetoric Review, 20,* 351–358.

Hoy, P. (2001c). Requiem for the outline. *Writing on the Edge, 12*(2), 19–27.

Hoy, P. (2005). The art of essaying. *Rhetoric Review, 24*(3), 316–339. doi:10.1207/s15327981rr2403_5

Hoy, P. (2009). Healing conceptual blindness. *Rhetoric Review, 28*(3), 304–324. doi:10.1080/07350190902958933

Huebner, D. (1987). The vocation of teaching. In Bolin, F., & Falk, J. M. (Eds.), *Teacher renewal: Professional issues, personal choices* (pp. 17–29). New York, NY: Teachers College Press.

Hugman, R. (2010). *Understanding international social work: A critical analysis.* London, UK: Palgrave Macmillan.

Hugman, R., Nguyen, T. T. L., & Nguyen, T. H. (2007). Developing social work in Vietnam. *International Social Work, 50*(2), 197–211. doi:10.1177/0020872807073985

Hunter, S. (1991). A woman's place *is* in the composition classroom: Pedagogy, gender, and difference. *Rhetoric Review, 9*(2), 230–245. doi:10.1080/07350199109388930

Hurlbert, C. M., & Blitz, M. (Eds.). (1991). *Composition and resistance.* Portsmouth, NH: Boynton/Cook.

IFSW. (2005). *International federation of social workers.* Retrieved 6 November, 2010, from http://www.ifsw.org

Ijsseling, S. (1976). *Rhetoric and philosophy in conflict: An historical survey.* The Hague, The Netherlands: Martinus Nijhoff.

Imel, S. (1998). *Transformative learning in adulthood. ERIC Digest No. 200.* Columbus, OH: ERIC Clearinghouse on Adult Career and Vocational Education.

Ivanič, R. (1998). *Writing and identity: The discoursal construction of identity in academic writing.* Amsterdam, The Netherlands: John Benjamins Publishing Company.

Jaar, A. (2003). *Alfredojaar.net.* Retrieved 4 January, 2004, from www.alfredojaar.net

Jackman, M. K. (1999). When the personal becomes professional: Stories from reentry adult women learners about family, work, and school. *Composition Studies, 27*(2), 53–67.

Jackson, P. W., Boostrom, R. E., & Hansen, D. T. (1993). *The moral life of schools.* San Francisco, CA: Jossey-Bass.

Jackson, N., & Carter, P. (1998). Labour as dressage. In McKinlay, A., & Starkey, K. (Eds.), *Foucault, management and organisation theory.* London, UK: Sage.

Jagose, A. (1996). *Queer theory: An introduction.* New York, NY: NYU Press.

James, K., Mann, J., & Creasy, J. (2007). Leaders as learners: A case example of facilitating collaborative leadership learning for school leaders. *Management Learning, 38*(1), 79–94. doi:10.1177/1350507607073026

Jarman, D. (1993). *At your own risk. A saint's testament.* London, NY: Vintage.

Jarratt, S. (1991). Feminism and composition: The case for conflict. In Harkin, P., & Schilb, J. (Eds.), *Contending with words: Composition and rhetoric in a postmodern age* (pp. 105–123). New York, NY: Modern Language Association.

Jarratt, S. (2003). Feminism and composition: The case for conflict. In Kirsch, G. E. (Eds.), *Feminism and composition: A critical sourcebook* (pp. 263–280). Boston, MA: Bedford.

Jenkins, H. (2006). *Convergence culture: Where old and new media collide.* New York, NY: New York University Press.

Jennings, K. (1994). *One teacher in 10. Gay and lesbian educators tell their stories.* Los Angeles, CA: Alyson Publications.

Jennings, T., & MacGillivray, I. K. (2007). Coming out and the new victim narrative. *Journal of Curriculum and Pedagogy, 4*(2), 54–58. doi:10.1080/15505170.2007.10411644

Johnson, M. (1989). Embodied knowledge. *Curriculum Inquiry, 19*(4), 361–377. doi:10.2307/1179358

Johnson, C. (1994). Participatory rhetoric and the teacher as racial/gendered subject. *College English, 56,* 409–419. doi:10.2307/378335

Johnston, C. (1996). *Unlocking the will to learn.* Thousand Oaks, CA: Corwin Press, Sage Publications.

Johnston, C. (1998). *Accountability that counts: Making a difference for learners.* Retrieved on February 15, 2005, from http://www.letmelearn.org

Johnston, C., & Dainton, G. (1987). *Learning connections inventory.* Turnersville, NJ: Learning Connections Resources. Retrieved from http://lcrinfo.con/index/shtml

Jordan, J. V. (2008). Learning at the margin: New models of strength. *Women & Therapy, 31*(2-4), 189–208. doi:10.1080/02703140802146365

Jordan, J. V. (2004). Relational resilience. In Jordan, J. V., Walker, M., & Hartling, L. (Eds.), *The complexity of connection: Writings from the Stone Center's Jean Baker Miller Training Institute* (pp. 28–46). New York, NY: Guilford Press.

Joseph, P. B. (2007). Seeing as strangers: Teachers' investigations of lived curriculum. *Journal of Curriculum Studies, 39*(3), 283–302. doi:10.1080/00220270600818481

Joseph, P. B., Bravmann, S. L., Windschitl, M. A., Mikel, E. R., & Green, N. S. (2000). *Cultures of curriculum.* New York, NY: Routledge.

Joseph, P. B., Mikel, E. R., & Windschitl, M. A. (2011). Reculturing curriculum. In Joseph, P. B. (Ed.), *Cultures of curriculum* (2nd ed., pp. 55–77). New York, NY: Routledge.

Joseph, P. B. (2010). Deskilling. In Kridel, C. (Ed.), *Encyclopedia of curriculum studies* (pp. 283–285). Thousand Oaks, CA: Sage Reference Publications.

Kagan, D. M. (1992). Implications of research on teacher beliefs. *The Psychologist, 27*(1), 65–90.

Kalantzis, M., & Cope, B. (2004). Designs for learning. *eLearning and Digital Media, 1*(1), 38-98. Retrieved from http://www.wwwords.co.uk/elea/content/pdfs/1/issue1_1.asp

Kameen, P. (1980). Rewording the rhetoric of composition. *Pre/Text, 1*(1-2), 73-93.

Kastman Breuch, L.-A. M. (2002). Post-process "pedagogy": A philosophical exercise. *JAC, 22*(1), 119–150.

Kegan, R. (1982). *The evolving self.* Cambridge, MA: Harvard University Press.

Kegan, R. (1994). *In over our heads: The mental demands of modern life.* Cambridge, MA: Harvard University Press.

Kegan, R., & Lahey, L. L. (2009). *Immunity to change: How to overcome it and unlock the potential in yourself and your organization.* Cambridge, MA: Harvard Business Press.

Kellner, D. (1995). *Media culture.* London, UK: Routledge. doi:10.4324/9780203205808

Kemmis, S., & McTaggart, R. (1990). *The action-research planner.* Geelong, Australia: Deakin University.

Kennedy, M. M. (2006). Knowledge and vision in teaching. *Journal of Teacher Education, 57*(3), 205–211. doi:10.1177/0022487105285639

Kennedy, K. (1999). Cynic rhetoric: The ethics and tactics of resistance. *Rhetoric Review, 18*(1), 26–45. doi:10.1080/07350199909359254

Kent, O. (2008). *Interactive text study and the co-construction of meaning: Hevruta in the DeLeT Beit Midrash.* Boston: Brandeis University.

Kent, T. (1993). *Paralogic rhetoric: A theory of communicative interaction.* Lewisburg, PA: Bucknell U.P.

Kent, A. M. (2004). Improving teacher quality through professional development. *Education, 24*(3), 427–435.

Kessler, S., & Swadener, B. B. (Eds.). (1992). *Reconceptualizing the early childhood curriculum.* New York, NY: Teachers College Press.

Kill, M. (2006). Acknowledging the rough edges of resistance: Negotiation of identities for first-year composition. *College Composition and Communication, 58*(2), 213–235.

Kincheloe, J., & Steinberg, S. (1997). *Changing multiculturalism.* Philadelphia, PA: Open University Press.

Kirklighter, C. (2002). *Traversing the democratic borders of the essay*. Albany, NY: State University of New York Press.

Kirsch, G. E., Maor, F. S., Massey, L., Nickoson-Massey, L., & Sheridan-Rabideau, M. P. (Eds.). (2003). *Feminism and composition: A critical sourcebook*. Boston, MA: Bedford.

Knoblauch, C. H. (1991). Critical teaching and dominant culture. In Hurlbert, C. M., & Blitz, M. (Eds.), *Composition and resistance* (pp. 12–21). Portsmouth, NH: Boynton/Cook.

Kolin, P. (2008). *Successful writing at work: Concise* (2nd ed.). Boston, MA: Houghton Mifflin Harcourt Publishing Company.

Kopelson, K. (2003). Rhetoric on the edge of cunning; Or, the performance of neutrality (re)considered as a composition pedagogy for student resistance. *College Composition and Communication, 55*(1), 115–146. doi:10.2307/3594203

Kopp, D. (2011). Cutting the edge of the will to truth; Or how post-process pedagogy is biting its own tail. *JAC: Rhetoric, Writing, Culture. Politics, 31*.

Korthagen, F. (2004). In search of the essence of a good teacher: Towards a more holistic approach in teacher education. *Teaching and Teacher Education, 20*(1), 77–97. doi:10.1016/j.tate.2003.10.002

Korthagen, F., & Vasalos, A. (2005). Levels in reflection: Core reflection as a means to enhance professional development. *Teachers and Teaching: Theory and Practice, 11*(1), 47–71. doi:10.1080/1354060042000337093

Kowalski, S. (1999). Western education: Because it works… for now. In R. Goodfellow, O'Neil & P. Smith (Eds.), *Saving Face, losing face, in your face: A journey into the Western heart, mind and soul*. Oxford, UK: Butterworth Heinemann.

Kozol, J. (1991). *Savage inequalities: Children in America's schools*. New York, NY: Crown Publishers.

Kozol, J. (1997). *Race and class in public education*. Address Presented at the State University of New York at Albany, NY. October 17, 1997. Retrieved from http://www.alternativeradio.org/programs/KOZJ002.shtml

Kreisburg, S. (1992). *Transforming power: Domination, empowerment, and education*. Albany, NY: SUNY Press.

Kress, G. (2003). *Literacy in a new media age*. London, UK: Routledge. doi:10.4324/9780203164754

Kristeva, J. (1986a). A new type of intellectual: The dissident. In Moi, T. (Ed.), *The Kristeva reader* (pp. 292–300). New York, NY: Columbia University Press.

Kristeva, J. (1986b). Women's time. In Moi, T. (Ed.), *The Kristeva reader* (pp. 187–213). New York, NY: Columbia University Press.

Kumashiro, K. (2009). *Against common sense: Teaching and learning towards social justice* (revised edition). New York, NY: Routledge.

Kumpulainen, K., & Renshaw, P. (2007). Cultures of learning. *International Journal of Educational Research, 46*(3-4), 109–115. doi:10.1016/j.ijer.2007.09.009

Lacan, J. (1978). *The four fundamental concepts of psycho-analysis (J.-A. Miller* (Sheridan, A. (Trans. Ed.)). New York, NY: Norton.

Laird, J. (1998). Theorizing culture: Narrative ideas and practice principles. In McGoldrick, M. (Ed.), *Revisioning family therapy: Culture, gender and clinical practice*. New York, NY: Guilford Press.

Lakoff, G., & Johnson, M. (1980). Conceptual metaphor in everyday language. *The Journal of Philosophy, 77*(8), 453–486. doi:10.2307/2025464

Lakoff, G., & Turner, M. (1989). *More than cool reason: A field guide to poetic metaphor*. Chicago, IL: University of Chicago Press.

Lamb, C. E. (2003). Beyond argument in feminist composition. In Kirsch, G. E. (Eds.), *Feminism and composition: A critical sourcebook* (pp. 281–293). Boston, MA: Bedford.

Lambert, L. (2002). A framework for shared leadership. *Educational Leadership, 59*(8), 37–40.

Lanham, R. A. (1974). *Motives of eloquence: Literary rhetoric in the renaissance*. New Haven, CT: Yale U.P.

Latham, G. (2007). *New learning: Building surprise through the virtual. E-Learning at RMIT*. Melbourne RMIT University.

Lather, P. (1991). *Getting smart: Feminist research and pedagogy with/in the postmodern*. New York, NY: Routledge, Chapman & Hall, Inc.

Laurel, B. (1991). *Computers as theatre*. Reading, MA: Addison-Wesley Publishing Company.

Lave, J., & Wenger, E. (1991). *Situated learning: Legitimate peripheral participation*. Cambridge, Uk: Cambridge University Press.

Lawrence-Lightfoot, S. (2003). *The essential conversation: What parents and teachers can learn from each other*. New York: Ballantine Books.

Le Maistre, C., & Paré, A. (2006). A typology of the knowledge demonstrated by beginning professionals. In Tynjälä, P., Välimaa, J., & Boulton-Lewis, G. (Eds.), *Higher education and working life—Collaborations, confrontations, and challenges* (pp. 103–113). Oxford, UK: Elsevier.

LeCourt, D. (1998). Critical pedagogy in the computer classroom: Politicizing the writing space. *Computers and Composition, 15*, 275–295. doi:10.1016/S8755-4615(98)90002-0

Lee, A. (2000). *Compositing critical pedagogies: Teaching writing as revision*. Urbana, IL: National Council of Teachers of English.

Lembo, R. (2000). *Thinking through television*. Cambridge, UK: Cambridge University Press. doi:10.1017/CBO9780511489488

Lenhart, A., Purcell, K., Smith, A., & Zickuhr, K. (2010). *Social media and young adults*. Pew Internet and American Life Project. Retrieved from http://www.pewinternet.org/Reports/2010/Social-Media-and-Young-Adults.aspx

Letts, W. J. (1999). How to make boys and girls in the classroom: The heteronormative nature of elementary school science. In Letts, W. J., & Sears, J. T. (Eds.), *Queering elementary education: Advancing the dialogue about sexualities and schooling* (pp. 97–110). Lanham, MD: Rowman & Littlefield.

Lewin, K. (1946). Action research and minority problems. *Journal of Social Issues, 2*, 34-46.

Locker, M., & Kienzler, D. (2008). *Business and administrative communication* (8th ed.). New York, NY: McGraw-Hill Irwin.

Logan, S. W. (2003). "When and where I enter:" Race, gender, and composition studies. In Kirsch, G. E. (Eds.), *Feminism and composition: A critical sourcebook* (pp. 425–435). Boston, MA: Bedford.

Lopate, P. (Ed.). (1995). *The art of the personal essay: An anthology from the classical era to the present*. New York, NY: Anchor Books/Doubleday.

Lortie, D. C. (1975). *Schoolteacher: A sociological study*. Chicago, IL: University of Chicago Press.

Lozano-Reich, N., & Cloud, D. (2009). The uncivil tongue: Invitational rhetoric and the problem of inequality. *Western Journal of Communication, 73*, 220–226. doi:10.1080/10570310902856105

Lu, M. (2003). Reading and writing differences: The problematic of experience. In Kirsch, G. E. (Eds.), *Feminism and composition: A critical sourcebook* (pp. 436–446). Boston, MA: Bedford.

Luke, C., & Gore, J. (Eds.). (1992). *Feminisms and critical pedagogy*. New York, NY: Routledge.

Luke, A. (1988). *Literacy, textbooks and ideology: Postwar literacy instruction and the mythology of Dick and Jane*. Philadelphia, PA: The Falmer Press.

Luke, A. (1993). Stories of social regulation: The micropolitics of classroom narrative. In Green, B. (Ed.), *The insistence of the letter: Literacy studies and curriculum theorizing* (pp. 175–194). Pittsburgh, PA: University of Pittsburgh Press.

Lynch, D. (1995). Teaching rhetorical values and the question of student autonomy. *Rhetoric Review, 13*, 350–370. doi:10.1080/07350199509359192

Lyotard, J.-F. (1984). *The postmodern condition: A report on knowledge* (Bennington, G., & Massumi, B., Trans.). Minneapolis, MN: U of Minnesota P.

Lyotard, J.-F., & Thébaud, J.-L. (1985). *Just gaming* (Godzich, W., Trans.). Minneapolis, MN: Minnesota U.P.

MacDonald, A. A., & Sánchez-Casal, S. (Eds.). (2002). *Twenty-first century feminist classrooms: Pedagogies of identity and difference*. New York, NY: Palgrave MacMillan.

MacLachlan, G., & Reid, I. (1994). *Framing and interpretation. Carlton, Australuia*. Melbourne University Press.

MacNaughton, G., & Williams, G. (2004). *Teaching young children: Choices in theory and practice*. Australia: Pearson Education Australia.

Maher, F., & Thompson Tetreault, M. (2001). *The feminist classroom: Dynamics of gender, race, and privilege*. New York, NY: Rowman & Littlefield Publishers, Inc.

Maher, J. (2002). Invitational interaction: A process for reconciling the teacher/student contradiction. *Rocky Mountain Review, Spring*, 85-93.

Mairs, N. (1990). Carnal acts. In *Carnal acts: Essays* (pp. 81–96). Boston, MA: Beacon.

MAP. (2010). *Migrant assistance program, Thailand*. Retrieved 6 November, 2010, from www.mapfoundationcm.org/

Marris, P. (1975). *Loss & change*. New York, NY: Doubleday.

Marshak, D. (1996). The emotional experience of school change: Resistance, loss, and grief. *NASSP Bulletin, 80*(577), 72–77. doi:10.1177/019263659608057713

Martino, W., & Pallotta-Chiarolli, M. (2003). *So what's a boy: Addressing issues of masculinity and schooling*. Maidenhead, UK: Open University Press.

Martino, W., & Pallotta-Chiarolli, M. (2005). *Being normal is the only way to be*. Sydney, Australia: University of New South Wales Press.

Massumi, B. (1987). Translator's foreword: Pleasures of philosophy. In Deleuze, G., & Guattari, F. (Eds.), *A thousand plateaus: Capitalism and schizophrenia* (pp. ix–xv). Minneapolis, MN: University of Minnesota Press.

Maxwell, J. (2005). *Qualitative research design: An interactive approach* (2nd ed.). Thousand Oaks, CA: Sage.

Mayer, A. (2009). The new sexual stone age. In Maasik, S., & Solomon, J. (Eds.), *Signs of life in the USA: Readings on popular culture for writers* (6th ed., pp. 312–314). Boston, MA: Bedford/St. Martin's. (Original work published 2001)

Mayer, D. (1999). *Building teaching identities: Implications for pre-service teacher education*. Paper presented at the Australian Association for Research in Education, December 1999, Melbourne, Australia. Retrieved from http://www.aare.edu.au/99pap/may99385.htm

McCallister, C. (2002). Learning to let them learn: Yielding power to students in a literacy methods course. *English Education, 34*(4), 281–301.

McCarthy, C., Giardina, M., Harewood, S., & Park, J.-K. (2003). Contesting culture: Identity and curriculum dilemmas in the age of globalization, postcolonialism, and multiplicity. *Harvard Educational Review, 73*(3), 449–465.

McKee, R. (1997). Structure and meaning. In *Story: Substance, structure, style, and the principles of screenwriting* (pp. 110–131). New York, NY: Harper Collins.

McKinlay, A., & Starkey, K. (Eds.). (1998). *Foucault, management and organisation theory*. London, UK: Sage.

McNay, L. (1992). *Foucault and feminism: Power, gender, and the self*. Boston, MA: Northeastern University Press.

Merlin, B. (2007). *The complete Stanislavsky toolkit*. London, UK: Nick Hern.

Metcalf, L. T., & Simon, T. (2002). *Writing the mind alive*. New York, NY: Ballantine Books.

Mezirow, J. (1990). *Fostering critical reflection in adulthood: A guide to transformational and emancipatory practice*. San Francisco, CA: Jossey-Bass.

Mezirow, J. (1991). *Transformative dimensions of adult learning*. San Francisco, CA: Jossey-Bass.

Mezirow, J. (2000). *Learning as transformation: Critical perspectives on a theory in progress* (1st ed.). San Francisco: Jossey-Bass.

Mezirow, J. (1991). *Transformative dimensions of adult learning*. San Francisco, CA: Jossey-Bass.

Mezirow, J. (2000a). Learning to think like an adult. In Mezirow, J. (Ed.), *Learning as transformation* (pp. 3–34). San Francisco, CA: Jossey Bass.

Mezirow, J. (2000). Learning to think like an adult: Core concepts of transformation theory. In J. Mezirow & Assoc. (Eds.), *Learning as transformation: Critical perspectives on a theory in progress* (pp. 3-33). San Francisco, CA: Jossey-Bass.

Micciche, L. (2007). *Doing emotion: Rhetoric, writing, teaching*. Portsmouth, NH: Boynton/Cook.

Miller, J. B. (1976). *Toward a new psychology of women*. Boston, MA: Beacon Press.

Miller, J. B., & Stiver, I. P. (1997). *The healing connection: How women form relationships in therapy and in life*. Boston, MA: Beacon.

Miller, J. L. (1990). *Creating spaces and finding voices: Teachers collaborating for empowerment*. Albany, NY: State University of New York Press.

Miller, R. (1998). The arts of complicity: Pragmatism and the culture of schooling. *College English*, *61*, 10–28. doi:10.2307/379055

Miller, K., Kulkarni, M., & Kushner, H. (2006). Beyond trauma-focused psychiatric epidemiology: Bridging research and practice with war affected populations. *The American Journal of Orthopsychiatry*, *76*(4), 409–422. doi:10.1037/0002-9432.76.4.409

Miller, K., & Rasco, L. (2004). *The mental health of refugees: Ecological approaches to healing and adaptation*. New Jersey: Lawrence Erlbaum Associates.

Milner, A., & Quilty, M. (1996). *Australia in Asia: Comparing cultures*. Melbourne, Australia: Oxford University Press.

Milstein, M. M. (1993). *Restructuring schools doing it right*. New York, NY: Corwin Press, Inc.

Mintrop, H., & Sunderman, G. L. (2009). Predictable failure of federal sanctions-driven accountability for school improvement - And why we may retain it anyway. *Educational Researcher*, *38*(5). doi:10.3102/0013189X09339055

Misson, R. (1997). Only joking: Being critical and keeping sense of humor. Paper presented at SAETA Conference, Adelaide, October.

Moi, T. (1985). *Sexual/textual politics: Feminist literary theory*. New York, NY: Methuen & Co.

Moi, T. (1986). Editor's introduction: A new type of intellectual: The dissident. In Moi, T. (Ed.), *The Kristeva reader* (p. 187). New York, NY: Columbia University Press.

Moites-Lopes, L. P. (2006). Queering literacy teaching: Analyzing gay themed discourses in a fifth grade class in Brazil. *Journal of Language, Identity, and Education*, *5*(1), 31–50. doi:10.1207/s15327701jlie0501_3

Moore, C. (2002). Why feminists can't stop talking about voice. *Composition Studies*, *30*(2), 11–25.

Moore, S. (1974). *The Stanislavski system: The professional training of an actor* (Rev. ed.). New York, NY: Viking Press.

Morgan, C. (2006). What does social semiotics have to offer mathematics education research? *Educational Studies in Mathematics*, *61*(1-2), 219–245. doi:10.1007/s10649-006-5477-x

Morgan, W. (2002). *'Here be monsters': Emergent discourses of hybrid identity in students' hypertexual constructions*. Paper presented at the Australian Association for Research in Education, Brisbane, QLD. Retrieved March 23, 2005, from http://www.aare.edu.au/indexpap.htm

Morley, D. (1992). *Television, audiences, and cultural studies*. London, UK: Routledge.

Morley, L. (2003). *Quality and power in higher education*. Berkshire, UK: SRHE and OUP.

Moschkovich, J. (2007). Using two languages when learning mathematics. *Educational Studies in Mathematics*, *64*(2), 121–144. doi:10.1007/s10649-005-9005-1

MTC. (2010). *Mae Tao Clinic*. Retrieved 15 November, 2010, from http://maetaoclinic.org/

Mulkay, M. (1988). *On humor: Its nature and its place in modern society*. Oxford, UK: Blackwell.

Mullin, J. A. (1994). Feminist theory, feminist pedagogy: The gap between what we say and what we do. *Composition Studies*, *22*(1), 14–24.

NCTE Writing Study Group. (2004). *NCTE beliefs about the teaching of writing*. National Council of Teachers of English. Retrieved from http://www.ncte.org/positions/statements/writingbeliefs

Neal, M. (1993). Social constructionism and expressivism: Contradictions and connections. *Composition Studies: Freshman English News*, *21*(1), 42–48.

Nehring, C. (2005). Fidelity with a wandering eye [Review of the book *Undressing infidelity: Why more wives are unfaithful*, by Diane Shader Smith]. *Atlantic (Boston, Mass.)*, *296*(1), 135–141.

Neill, M. (2003). Leaving children behind: How No Child Left Behind will fail our children. *Phi Delta Kappan, 85*(3), 225–228.

Nelson, C. D. (2006). Queer inquiry in language education. *Journal of Language, Identity, and Education, 5*(1), 1–9. doi:10.1207/s15327701jlie0501_1

Nelson, C. D. (2009). *Sexual identities in English language education: Classroom conversations.* New York, NY: Routledge.

Nelson, C. D. (2005). Teaching of ESL. In Sears, J. T. (Ed.), *Youth, education and sexualities: An international encyclopedia* (pp. 299–303). Westport, CT: Greenwood Press.

Newkirk, T. (1989). *Critical thinking and writing: Reclaiming the essay.* Urbana, IL: NCTE.

Newkirk, T. (2005). Montaigne's revisions. *Rhetoric Review, 24*(3), 298–315. doi:10.1207/s15327981rr2403_4

Newkirk, T. (2004). The dogma of transformation. *College Composition and Communication, 56*(2), 251–271. doi:10.2307/4140649

Nguyen, T., & Bowles, W. (1988). Counselling Vietnamese refugee survivors of trauma: Points of entry for developing trust and rapport. *Australian Social Work, 59*(2), 41–47.

Nieto, S. (2000). *Affirming diversity: The sociopolitical context of multicultural education.* New York, NY: Longman.

Nieto, S. (2008). Nice is not enough: Defining caring for students of color. In Pollock, M. (Ed.), *Everyday antiracism: Getting real about change in school* (pp. 28–31). New York, NY: The New Press.

Novak, D., & Bonnie, B. (2009). Offering invitational rhetoric in communication courses. *Communication Teacher, 23*, 11–14. doi:10.1080/17404620802593013

Nussbaum, M. (2000). *Women and human development.* Cambridge, UK: Cambridge University Press.

O'Halloran, K. L. (1999). Towards a systemic functional analysis of multisemiotic mathematics texts. *Semiotica, 124*(1/2), 1–29. doi:10.1515/semi.1999.124.1-2.1

O'Halloran, K. L. (2005). *Mathematical discourse: Language, symbolism and visual images.* London, UK: Continuum.

O'Halloran, K. L. (2003). Educational implications of mathematics as a multisemiotic discourse. In Anderson, M., Saenz-ludlow, A., Zellweger, S., & Cifarelli, V. (Eds.), *Educational perspectives on mathematics as semiosis: From thinking to interpreting to knowing* (pp. 185–214). Ottawa, Canada: Legas Publishing.

O'Sullivan, E., Morrell, A., & O'Connor, M. A. (Eds.). (2002). *Expanding the boundaries of transformative learning.* New York, NY: Palgrave.

Oakeshott, M. (1962). The voice of poetry in the conversation of mankind. In *Rationalism in politics and other essays* (pp. 197–247). London, UK: Methuen.

Olsen, B. (2008). Introducing teacher identity and this volume. *Teacher Education Quarterly,* (Summer): 3–6.

Olson, C. (1974). *Additional prose.* Bolinas, CA: Four Season Foundation.

Olson, G. (1997). Publishing scholarship in rhetoric and composition: Joining the conversation. In Olson, G., & Taylor, T. (Eds.), *Publishing in rhetoric and composition* (pp. 19–33). Albany, NY: State University of New York Press.

Olssen, M., Codd, J., & O'Neill, A.-M. (2004). *Education policy: Globalisation, citizenship and democracy.* London, UK: Sage.

Orner, M. (1992). Interrupting the calls for student voice in 'liberatory' education: A feminist poststructuralist perspective. In Luke, C., & Gore, J. (Eds.), *Feminisms and critical pedagogy* (pp. 74–89). New York, NY: Routledge.

Osborn, S. (1991). "Revision/re-vision:" A feminist writing class. *Rhetoric Review, 9*(2), 258–273. doi:10.1080/07350199109388932

Osterman, K. F., & Kottkamp, R. B. (2004). *Reflective practice for educators: Professional development to improve student learning* (2nd ed.). Thousand Oaks, CA: Corwin Press.

Owens, T. (2006). Self and identity. In Delamanter, J. (Ed.), *Handbook of social psychology* (pp. 205–233). New York, NY: Springer. doi:10.1007/0-387-36921-X_9

Oyserman, D. (2001). Self-concept and identity. In Tesser, A., & Schwarz, N. (Eds.), *The Blackwell handbook of social psychology* (pp. 499–517). Malden, MA: Blackwell.

Pakman, M. (1995). Therapy in contexts of poverty and ethnic dissonance: Constructivism and social constructivism as methodologies for action. *Journal of Systemic Therapies*, *14*(4), 64–71.

Pakman, M. (1998). Education and therapy in cultural borderlands: A call for critical social practices in human services. *Journal of Systemic Therapies*, *17*(1), 18–30.

Pallotta-Chiarolli, M. (1998). *Cultural diversity and men who have sex with men*. Sydney, Australia: National Centre in HIV Social Research, Macquarie University.

Pallotta-Chiarolli, M. (2003). *Girls talk: Young women speak their hearts and minds*. Sydney, Australia: Finch Publishing.

Pallotta-Chiarolli, M. (2005b). *When our children come out: How to support gay, lesbian, bisexual and transgendered young people*. Lane Cove, Australia: Finch Publishing.

Pallotta-Chiarolli, M. (2005). Ethnic identities. In Sears, J. T. (Ed.), *Youth, education, and sexualities: An international encyclopedia* (pp. 303–306). Westport, CT: Greenwood Press.

Palmer, P. J. (2007). *The courage to teach: Exploring the inner landscape of a teacher's life*. San Francisco, CA: Jossey-Bass.

Pang, V. O. (2005). *Multicultural education: A caring-centered, reflective approach*. Boston, MA: McGraw Hill.

Paré, A., & Le Maistre, C. (2006). Active learning in the workplace: Transforming individuals and institutions. *Journal of Education and Work*, *19*(4), 363–381. doi:10.1080/13639080600867141

Paré, A. (2002). Keeping writing in its place: A participatory action approach to workplace communication. In Mirel, B., & Spilka, R. (Eds.), *Reshaping technical communication: New directions and challenges for the 21st century* (pp. 57–79). Mahwah, NJ: Lawrence-Erlbaum Associates.

Pascoe, C. (2007). *Dude you're a fag: Masculinity and sexuality in high school*. Berkeley, CA: University of California Press.

Perl, S. (1988). Understanding composing. In Tate, G., & Corbett, E. P. J. (Eds.), *The writing teacher's sourcebook* (pp. 113–118). New York, NY: Oxford University Press.

Peshkin, A. (1988). In search of subjectivity: One's own. *Educational Researcher*, *17*(7), 17–22.

Peters, M., Marshall, J., & Fitzsimons, P. (2000). Managerialism and educational policy in a global context: Foucault, neoliberalism, and the doctrine of self-management. In Burbules, N., & Torress, C. (Eds.), *Globalisation and education: Critical perpectives*. London, UK: Routledge.

Petraglia, J. (1991). Interrupting the conversation: The constructionist dialogue in composition. *JAC*, *11*(1), 37–55.

Pinar, W. F. (2004). *What is curriculum theory?* New York, NY: Routledge.

Pink, W. T. (1990). Implementing curriculum inquiry: Theoretical and practical implications. In Sears, J. T., & Marshall, J. D. (Eds.), *Teaching and thinking about curriculum* (pp. 138–153). New York, NY: Teachers College Press.

Plato,. (1961). Protagoras. In Hamilton, E., & Cairns, H. (Eds.), *The collected dialogues of Plato* (Guthrie, W. K. C., Trans.). New York, NY: Bollingen.

Pollan, M. (2006). *The omnivore's dilemma: A natural history of four meals*. New York, NY: Penguin.

Pollock, M. A., Artz, L., Frey, L. R., Barnett Pearce, W., & Murphy, B. A. O. (1996). Navigating between Scylla and Charybdis: Continuing the dialogue on communication and social justice. *Communication Studies*, *47*, 142–151. doi:10.1080/10510979609368470

Popkewitz, T., & Brennan, M. (1998). *Foucault's challenge: Discourse, knowledge, and power in education*. New York, NY: Teachers College Press.

Pratt, M. L. (1991). Arts of the contact zone. *Profession*, *91*, 33–40.

Prensky, M. (October, 2001). *Digital natives, digital immigrants*. Retrieved 9 October, 2009, from http://www.twitchspeed.com/site/Prensky%20-%20Digital%20Natives,%20Digital%20Immigrants%20-%20Part1.htm

Prigogine, I., & Stengers, I. (1984). Order out of chaos: Man's new dialogue with nature. *International Journal of Technology and Human Interaction, 1*(3), 1–14.

Project Zero & Reggio Children. (2001). *Making learning visible.* Reggio Emilia, Italy: Reggio Children.

Purpel, D. E., & Shapiro, S. (1995). *Beyond liberation and excellence: Reconstructing the public discourse on education.* Westport, CT: Bergin & Garvey.

Qualley, D. J. (1994). Being two places at once: Feminism and the development of "both/and" perspectives. In Sullivan, P. A., & Qualley, D. J. (Eds.), *Pedagogy in the age of politics: Writing and reading (in) the academy* (pp. 25–42). Urbana, IL: National Council of Teachers of English.

Quinn (2008). I want to read *Frog and toad.* In A. Pelo (Ed.), *Rethinking EARLY CHILDHOOD EDUCATION.* Wisconsin: Rethinking Schools.

Ragins, B. (2009). Positive identities in action: A model of mentoring self structures and the motivation to mentor. In Roberts, L., & Dutton, J. (Eds.), *Exploring positive identities and organisations: Building a theoretical and research foundation.* New York, NY: Psychology Press.

Raider-Roth, M. B. (2005). *Trusting what you know: The high stakes of classroom relationships.* San Francisco, CA: Jossey-Bass.

Raider-Roth, M. B., Albert, M. K., Bircann-Barkley, I., Gidseg, E., & Murray, T. (2008). Teaching boys: A relational puzzle. *Teachers College Record, 110*(2), 443–481.

Raider-Roth, M. B., & Holzer, E. (2009). Learning to be present: How *Hevruta* learning can activate teachers' relationships to self, other and text. *Journal of Jewish Education, 75*(3), 216–239. doi:10.1080/15244110903079045

Raider-Roth, M. B. (2010). Listening to the heartbeat of the classroom: Bringing the listening guide to teaching and learning. In Davis, P. C. (Ed.), *Enacting pleasure.* London, UK: Seagull Books.

Raider-Roth, M. B., Stieha, V., & Hensley, B. (2010a). *Rupture and repair in the relational triangle: Veteran teachers, professional development and collaborative text study.* Manuscript under review.

Raider-Roth, M. B., Stieha, V., & Hensley, B. (2010b). *Rupture and repair: Episodes of resistance and resilience in teachers' learning.* Paper presented at the 31st Annual Ethnography in Education Research Forum.

Random House Dictionary of the English Language, 2nd ed., unabridged (1987). New York, NY: Random House, Inc.

Rasmussen, M. L., Rofes, E., & Talburt, S. (2004). *Youth and sexualities: Pleasure, subversion and insubordination in and out of schools.* New York, NY: Palgrave MacMillan.

Rasmussen, M. L. (2004). Safety and subversion: The production of sexualities and genders in school spaces. In Rasmussen, M. L., Rofes, E., & Talburt, S. (Eds.), *Youth and sexualities: Pleasure, subversion, and insubordination in and out of schools* (pp. 131–152). New York, NY: Palgrave MacMillan.

Ratcliffe, K. (2005). *Rhetorical listening: Identification, gender, whiteness.* Carbondale, IL: Southern Illinois University Press.

Recchio, T. (1994). On the critical necessity of "essaying." In Tobin, L., & Newkirk, T. (Eds.), *Taking stock: The writing process movement in the 90s* (pp. 219–235). Portsmouth, NH: Boynton/Cook.

Reid, A. (2007). *The two virtuals: New media and composition.* West Lafayette, IN: Parlor Press.

Reiman, A. J., & Peace, S. D. (2002). Promoting teachers' moral reasoning and collaborative inquiry performance: A developmental role-taking and guide inquiry study. *Journal of Moral Education, 31*(1), 51–66. doi:10.1080/03057240120111436

Reynolds, N. (2004). *Geographies of writing: Inhabiting places and encountering difference.* Carbondale, IL: Southern Illinois University Press.

Richardson, V., & Placier, P. (2001). Teacher change. In Richardson, V. (Ed.), *Handbook of research on teaching* (pp. 905–947). Washington, DC: American Educational Research Association.

Rickert, T. J. (2007). *Acts of enjoyment: Rhetoric, Žižek, and the return of the subject.* Pittsburg, PA: University Press.

Rideout, V., Foher, U., & Roberts, D. (2010). *Generation M²: Media in the lives of 8 to 18-year-olds*. Kaiser Family Foundation Study. Retrieved from http://www.kff.org/entmedia/upload/8010.pdf

Ritchie, D. (2003). Argument is war - Or is it a game of chess? Multiple meanings in the analysis of implicit metaphors. *Metaphor and Symbol, 18*(2), 125–146. doi:10.1207/S15327868MS1802_4

Ritchie, J., & Ronald, K. (Eds.). (2006). *Teaching rhetorica: Theory, pedagogy, practice*. Portsmouth, NH: Boynton/Cook.

Ritchie, J. S. (2003). Confronting the "essential" problem: Reconnecting feminist theory and pedagogy. In Kirsch, G. E. (Eds.), *Feminism and composition: A critical sourcebook* (pp. 79–102). Boston, MA: Bedford.

Ritchie, J. S., & Boardman, K. (2003). Feminism in composition: Inclusion, metonymy, and disruption. In Kirsch, G. E. (Eds.), *Feminism and composition: A critical sourcebook* (pp. 7–26). Boston, MA: Bedford. doi:10.2307/358482

Robinson K. (2010, June, 26). Transform education? Yes, we must. *The Huffington Post*.

Rodriguez, A. J., & Kitchen, R. S. (Eds.). (2005). *Preparing mathematics and science teachers for diverse classrooms: Promising strategies for transformative pedagogy*. Mahwah, NJ: Lawrence Erlbaum Associates, Publishers.

Rofes, E. (1998). *Dry bones breathe: Gay men creating post-AIDS identities and cultures*. Binghamton, NY: The Harrington Park Press.

Rofes, E. (2005). *A radical rethinking of sexuality & schooling: Status quo or status queer*. Lanham, MD: Rowman & Littlefield.

Rofes, E. (1999). What happens when the kids grow up? The long-term impact of an openly gay teacher on eight students' lives. In Letts, W. J., & Sears, J. T. (Eds.), *Queering elementary education: Advancing the dialogue about sexualities and schooling* (pp. 83–93). Lanham, MD: Rowman & Littlefield.

Rofes, E. (2004). Martyr-Target-Victim: Interrogating narratives of persecution and suffering among queer youth. In Rasmussen, M. L., Rofes, E., & Talburt, S. (Eds.), *Youth and sexualities: Pleasure, subversion and insubordination in and out of schools* (pp. 41–62). New York, NY: Palgrave MacMillan.

Rogers, C. (1970). Communication: Its blocking and its facilitation. In Young, R. E., Becker, A. L., & Pike, K. L. (Eds.), *Rhetoric: Discovery and change* (pp. 284–286). New York, NY: Harcourt, Brace, & World Inc.

Rose, M. (1989). *Lives on the boundary: A moving account of the struggles and the achievements of America's educational underclass*. New York, NY: Penguin Books.

Rundell, M. (2002). Metaphorically speaking. *English Teaching Professional, 23*, 21–29.

Rusch, E., & Horsford, S. (2008, November). Unifying messy communities: Learning social justice in educational leadership classrooms. *Teacher Development, 12*(4), 353–367. doi:10.1080/13664530802579934

Rusch, E. A. (2004). Gender and race in leadership preparation: A constrained discourse. *Educational Administration Quarterly, 40*(1), 16–48. doi:10.1177/0013161X03259110

Rusch, E. (2004a, November). *Transformative learning: The foundation to transformative leadership*. Paper presented as part of symposium with D. Miller, K. Sernak, M. Scherr. University Council for Educational Administration, Fall Convention, Kansas City, MO.

Rusch, E. (2005, April). *Self knowledge that transforms*. Paper presented to the Annual Meeting of the American Educational Research Association. Montreal, CA.

Ryan, K., & Natalle, E. (2001). Fusing horizons: Standpoint hermeneutics and invitational rhetoric. *Rhetoric Society Quarterly, 31*, 69–90. doi:10.1080/02773940109391200

Sachs, J. (2005). Teacher education and the development of professional identity: Learning to be a teacher. In Denicolo, P., & Kompf, M. (Eds.), *Connecting policy and practice: Challenges for teaching and learning in schools and universities* (pp. 5–21). Oxford, UK: Routledge.

Sacks, O. (1990). *The man who mistook his wife for a hat and other clinical tales*. New York, NY: Harper Collins Publishers.

Salter, B., & Tapper, T. (1994). *The state and higher education*. Essex, UK: Woburn Press.

Sartre, J.-P. (1956). *Being and nothingness: An essay on phenomenological ontology* (Barnes, H. E., Trans.). New York, NY: Washington Square Press.

Savage, D. (2006). *The commitment: Love, sex, marriage and my family*. New York, NY: Plume.

Sawyer, R. (2001). *Creative conversations: Improvisation in everyday discourse*. Cresskill, NJ: Hampton.

Schlechty, P. C. (2005). *Creating the capacity to support innovations*. Occasional Paper No. 2. Louisville, KY: Schlechty Centre.

Schleppegrell, M. (2007). The linguistic challenges of mathematical teaching and learning: A research review. *Reading & Writing Quarterly, 23*(2), 139–159. doi:10.1080/10573560601158461

Schlosser, E. (2001). *Fast food nation: The dark side of the all-American meal*. Boston, MA: Houghton.

Schmid, H., & Ungerer, F. (1996). *An introduction to cognitive linguistics*. New York, NY: Longman.

Schneider, B. (2005). Uncommon ground: Narcissistic reading and material racism. *Pedagogy, 5*(2), 195–212.

Schön, D. (1983). *The reflective practitioner. City*. Basic Books.

Schön, E. (1987). *Educating the reflective practitioner*. San Francisco, CA: Jossey Bass.

School B. (2002). *Work program*.

School Reform Initiative. (2009). Retrieved December 5, 2009, from www.schoolreforminitiative.org

Schwab, J. J. (1973). The practical 3: Translation into curriculum. *The School Review, 79*, 501–522. doi:10.1086/443100

Sears, J. T. (2004). The curriculum worker as a public moral intellectual. In Gaztambide-Fernandez, R. A., & Sears, J. T. (Eds.), *Curriculum work as a public moral enterprise* (pp. 1–13). Lanham, MD: Rowman & Littlefield.

Seitz, J. (1991). Composition's misunderstanding of metaphor. *College Composition and Communication, 42*(3), 288–298. doi:10.2307/358072

Selber, S. (2004). *Multi-literacies for a digital age*. Carbondale, IL: Southern Illinois University Press.

Self, C. (2009). The movement of air, the breathing of meaning: Aurality and multimodal composing. *College Composition and Communication, 60*, 616–663.

Selfe, C., & Hawisher, G. (2004). *Literate lives in the information age: Narratives of literacy from the United States*. Mahwah, NJ: Lawrence Erlbaum Associates.

Semino, E. (2008). *Metaphor in discourse*. Cambridge, UK: Cambridge University Press.

Senge, P., Cambron-McCabe, N., Lucas, T., Smith, B., Dutton, J., & Kleiner, A. (2000). *Schools that learn: A fifth discipline fieldbook for educators, parents, and everyone who cares about education*. New York, NY: Doubleday.

Sfard, A., & Prusak, A. (2005). Telling identities: In search of an analytic tool for investigating learning as culturally shaped activity. *Educational Researcher, 34*(4), 14–22. doi:10.3102/0013189X034004014

Shohat, E. (1995). The struggle over representation: Casting, coalitions, and the politics of identification. In de la Campa, R., Kaplan, E. A., & Sprinkler, M. (Eds.), *Late emperial culture*. New York, NY: Vetso.

Shor, I. (1980). *Critical teaching and everyday life*. Boston, MA: South End Press.

Shor, I. (Ed.). (1987). *Freire for the classroom: A sourcebook for liberatory teaching*. Portsmouth, NH: Boynton/ Cook.

Shor, I. (1992). *Empowering education: Critical teaching for social change*. Chicago, IL: University of Chicago Press.

Shor, I. (1999). What is critical literacy? *Journal of Pedagogy, Pluralism, and Practice, 1*(4). Retrieved June 29, 2010, from http://www.lesley.edu/journals/jppp/4/shor.html

Silverburg, R., & Kottkamp, R. (2006). Language matters. *Journal of Research on Leadership Education, 1*(1). Retrieved on April 4, 2010 from http://www.ucea.org/jrle

Sinclair, C., Jenneret, C., & O'Toole, J. (2009). *Education in the arts: Teaching and learning in the contemporary curriculum*. South Melbourne, Australia: Oxford University Press.

Singer, I. (1984). Courtly and romantic: *Vol. 2. The nature of love. Chicago*. IL: Chicago University Press.

Skurat Harris, H. (2009). *Digital students in the democratic classroom: Using technology to enhance critical pedagogy in the first-year composition classroom.* Unpublished doctoral dissertation, Ball State University.

Slater, L. (2006). True love. *National Geographic, 209*(2), 32–49.

Slattery, P. (1995). *Curriculum development in the postmodern era*. New York, NY: Garland.

Sleeter, C. E. (2008). Teaching for democracy in an age of corporatocracy. *Teachers College Record, 110*(1), 139–159.

Smit, D. (2004). *The end of composition studies*. Carbondale, IL: Southern Illinois University Press.

Smith, P. (1988). *Discerning the subject*. Minneapolis, MN: University of Minnesota Press.

Smith, S. (1990). Self, subject, and resistance: Marginalities and twentieth-century autobiographical practice. *Tulsa Studies in Womens Literature, 9*(1), 11–24. doi:10.2307/464178

Snyder, D., & Dillow, S. (2010). *Digest of education statistics 2009*. Washington, DC: National Center for Education Statistics.

Snyder, A. (1972). *Dauntless women in childhood education 1856-1931*. Washington, DC: Association for Childhood Education International.

Soldatow, S., & Tsiolkas, C. (1996). *Jump cuts: An autobiography*. Milsons Point, Australia: Random House.

Soles, D. (1998). Problems with confrontational teaching. *College Composition and Communication, 49*, 267–269. doi:10.2307/358936

Solomon, R. (1990). *Love: Emotion, myth, and metaphor*. Buffalo, NY: Prometheus Books.

Spencer, R., Porche, M. V., & Tolman, D. L. (2003). We've come a long way -- Maybe: New challenges for gender equity in education. *Teachers College Record, 105*(9), 1774–1807. doi:10.1046/j.1467-9620.2003.00309.x

Spigelman, C. (2004). *Personally speaking: Experience as evidence in academic discourse*. Carbondale, IL: Southern Illinois University Press.

Spigelman, C. (2001). What role virtue? *JAC, 21*(2), 321–348.

Spinosa, C., Flores, F., & Dreyfus, H. (1997). *Disclosing new worlds: Entrepreneurship, democratic action, and the cultivation of solidarity*. Cambridge, MA: MIT Press.

Stanislavsky, C. (1946). *An actor prepares* (Hapgood, E. R., Trans.). New York, NY: Theatre Arts.

Stanislavsky, C. (1946). *Building a character* (Hapgood, E. R., Trans.). New York, NY: Theatre Arts.

Stanislavsky, C. (1963). *An actor's handbook* (Hapgood, E. R. (Trans. Ed.)). New York, NY: Theatre Arts Books.

Stanislavsky, C. (1968). *Stanislavsky's legacy* (Hapgood, E. R. (Trans. Ed.)). 2nd ed.). New York, NY: Theatre Arts.

Stanislavsky, C. (1961). *Creating a role (E.R. Hapgood* (Popper, H., Trans. Ed.). New York, NY: Theatre Arts.

Starkey, K., & McKinlay, A. (1998). Deconstructing organisation-discipline and desire. In McKinlay, A., & Starkey, K. (Eds.), *Foucault, management and organisation theory*. London, UK: Sage.

Stenberg, S. J. (2006). Liberation theology and liberatory pedagogies: Renewing the dialogue. *College English, 68*, 271–290. doi:10.2307/25472152

Stets, J., & Burke, P. (2003). A sociological approach to self and identity. In Leary, M. R., & Tangney, J. P. (Eds.), *Handbook of self and identity* (pp. 128–152). New York, NY: Guilford Press.

Stevens, L. P., & Bean, L. P. (2007). *Critical literacy: Context, research and practice in the K-12 classroom.* New York, NY: Sage Publications.

Stieha, V. (2010). *The relational Web in teaching and learning: Connections, disconnections and the central relational paradox in* schools. Ph.D. dissertation, University of Cincinnati, United States -- Ohio. Retrieved February 25, 2011, from Dissertations & Theses @ University of Cincinnati. (Publication No. AAT 3419997).

Stockwell, P. (2002). *Cognitive poetics: An introduction.* New York, NY: Routledge.

Strasberg, L. (1987). *A dream of passion: The development of the method* (Morphos, E., Ed.). Boston, MA: Little, Brown.

Stryker, P., & Burke, P. (2006). The past, present and future of an identity theory. *Social Psychology Quarterly, 63,* 284–297. doi:10.2307/2695840

Sumara, D. (1996). *Private readings in public: Schooling the literary imagination.* New York, NY: Peter Lang.

Sumsion, J. (2006). From Whitlam to economic rationalism and beyond: A conceptual framework for political activism in children's services. *Australian Journal of Early Childhood, 31*(1), 1–9.

Swadener, B. B., & Lubeck, S. (1995). *Children and families "at promise": Deconstructing the discourse of risk.* New York, NY: State University of New York Press.

Symcox, L. (2009). From "a nation at risk" to "No Child Left Behind:" 25 years of neoliberal reform in education. In J. Andrzejewski, Marta Baltodano, & L. Symcox (Eds.), *Social justice, peace, and environmental education: Transformative standards* (pp. 53-65). New York, NY: Routledge.

Szalavitz, M., & Perry, B. (2010). *Born for love: Why empathy is essential- And endangered.* New York, NY: Harper Collins.

Szubanski, M. (2005, August 5). Fears of a clown interview by B. Hallett. *The Age, Preview Magazine,* 4-6

Tappan, M. B. (2001). Interpretive psychology: Stories, circles and understanding lived experience. In Tolman, D. L., & Brydon-Miller, M. (Eds.), *From subjects to subjectivities: A Handbook of interpretive and participatory methods* (pp. 45–56). New York, NY: New York University Press. doi:10.1111/j.1540-4560.1997.tb02453.x

Tassoni, J., & Thelin, W. (Eds.). (2000). *Blundering for a change: Errors and expectations in critical pedagogy.* Portsmouth, NH: Boynton/Cook.

Tatchell, P. (2007, Spring). *Their multiculturalism and ours.* Retrieved May 7, 2010, from http://dissentmagazine.org/democratiya/article_pdfs/d8Tatchell.pdf

Tate, W. F. (2005). Race, retrenchment, and the reform of school mathematics. In Gutstein, E., & Peterson, B. (Eds.), *Rethinking mathematics: Teaching social justice by the numbers* (pp. 31–40). Milwaukee, WI: Rethinking Schools.

Taubman, P. (2009). *Teaching by numbers: Deconstructing the discourse of standards and accountability in education.* New York, NY: Routledge.

TBBC. (2010). *Thai Burma Border Consortium.* Retrieved 15 November, 2010, from http://www.tbbc.org/

Tedesco, J. (1991). Women's ways of knowing/women's ways of composing. *Rhetoric Review, 9*(2), 246–256. doi:10.1080/07350199109388931

Thompson-Grove, G. (January 2005). *A call to action.* Keynote Address (abridged) The 9th Annual NSRF Winter Meeting. Cambridge, MA.

Thornbury, S., & Slade, D. (2006). *Conversation: From description to pedagogy.* Cambridge, UK: Cambridge University Press. doi:10.1017/CBO9780511733123

Trimbur, J. (1997). Consensus and difference in collaborative learning. In Villaneuva, V. (Ed.), *Cross-talk in comp theory* (pp. 439–456). Urbana, IL: NCTE.

Tronick, E. Z., & Weinberg, M. K. (1997). Depressed mothers and infants: Failure to form dyadic states of consciousness. In Murray, L., & Cooper, P. (Eds.), *Postpartum depression and child development.* New York, NY: Guilford Press.

Turner, V. (1986). *The anthropology of performance.* Baltimore, MD: PAJ Publications.

van den Berg, R. (2002). Teachers' meanings regarding educational practice. *Review of Educational Research*, *72*(4), 577–625. doi:10.3102/00346543072004577

Van Gennep, A. (1909). *The rites of passage* (2004th ed.). London, UK: Routledge.

Vanderstraeten, R., & Biesta, G. (2006). How is education possible? Pragmatism, communication and the social organisation of education. *British Journal of Educational Studies*, *54*(2), 160–174. doi:10.1111/j.1467-8527.2006.00338.x

Veel, R. (1999). Language, knowledge, and authority in school mathematics. In Christie, F. (Ed.), *Pedagogy and the shaping of consciousness* (pp. 185–216). London, UK: Cassell.

Villanueva, V. (Ed.). (2003). *Cross-talk in comp theory: A reader* (2nd ed.). Urbana, IL: National Council of Teachers of English.

Villanueva, V. (1991). Considerations for American Freireistas. In Richard Bullock, R., & Trimbur, J. (Eds.), *The politics of writing instruction: Postsecondary* (pp. 247–263). Portsmouth, NH: Boynton/Cook.

Villegas, A. M., & Lucas, T. (2002). *Educating culturally responsive teachers: A coherent approach*. Albany, NY: State University of New York Press.

Vitanza, V. (1991). Three countertheses: Or, a critical in(ter)vention into composition theories and pedagogies. In Harkin, P., & Schilb, J. (Eds.), *Contending with words: Composition and rhetoric in a postmodern age* (pp. 139–172). New York, NY: MLA.

Vygotsky, L. (1986). *Thought and language* (Kozulin, A., Trans.). Cambridge, MA: MIT Press.

Wagoner, R. (1997). *The meanings of love: An introduction to philosophy of love*. Westport, CT: Praeger.

Walkerdine, V. (1992). Progressive pedagogy and political struggle. In Luke, C., & Gore, J. (Eds.), *Feminisms and critical pedagogy* (pp. 15–24). New York, NY: Routledge.

Walkington, J. (2005). Becoming a teacher: Encouraging development of teacher identity through reflective practice. *Asia-Pacific Journal of Teacher Education*, *33*(1), 53–64. doi:10.1080/1359866052000341124

Wallowitz, L. (2009). *Critical literacy as resistance: Teaching for social justice across the secondary curriculum*. Peter Lang Publishers.

Wardle, E. (2007). Understanding 'transfer' from FYC: Preliminary results of a longitudinal study. *WPA*, *31*(2), 65–85.

Warner, M. (1999). *The trouble with normal: Sex, politics and ethics of queer life*. New York, NY: The Free Press.

Warnock, T. (1986). Reading Kenneth Burke: Ways in, ways out, ways roundabout. *College English*, *48*(1), 62–75. doi:10.2307/376587

Wearing, B. (1996). *Gender: The pain and pleasure of difference*. Melbourne, Australia: Longman.

Webb, P., Cole, K., & Skeen, T. (Eds.). (2007). Feminist social projects: Building bridges between communities and universities. *College English*, *69*(3), 238–259.

Webb, T. (2009). *Teacher assemblage*. Rotterdam, The Netherlands: Sense Publisher.

Weick, K. E. (1969). *The social psychology of organizing*. Reading, MA: Addison-Wesley Pub. Co.

Weick, K. E. (1995). *Sensemaking in organizations*. Thousand Oaks, CA: Sage.

Welch, N. (2002). "And now that I know them:" Composing mutuality in a service learning course. *College Composition and Communication*, *54*(2), 243–263. doi:10.2307/1512148

Wells, R. (2006). *My shining star: Raising a child who is ready to learn*. New York, NY: Scholastic Press.

Welsh, S. (2001). Resistance theory and illegitimate reproduction. *College Composition and Communication*, *52*, 553–573. doi:10.2307/358697

Wenger, E. (1998). *Communities of practice: Learning, meaning, and identity*. Cambridge, UK: Cambridge University Press.

Werstch, J. (1991). *Voices of the mind: A sociocultural approach to mediated action*. Cambridge, MA: Harvard University Press.

Wesch, M. (2008, June 17). *A portal to media literacy.* Presented at the University of Manitoba, June 17, 2008. Retrieved September 24, 2008 from http://www.youtube.com/watch?v=J4yApagnr0s

Wesch, M. (2009, January 7). From knowledgeable to knowledge-able: Learning in new media environments. In *Academic Commons* retrieved June 29, 2010 from http://www.academiccommons.org/commons/essay/knowledgable-knowledge-able.

Westbury, I. (2000). Teaching as reflective practice: What might Didaktik teach curriculum? In Westbury, I., Hopmann, S., & Riquarts, K. (Eds.), *Teaching as a reflective practice: The German Didaktik tradition* (pp. 15–40). Mahwah, NJ: Lawrence Erlbaum.

Wiessner, C., & Mezirow, J. (2000). Theory building and the search for common ground. In Mezirow, (Eds.), *Learning as transformation: Critical perspectives on a theory in progress* (pp. 329–358). New York, NY: Jossey-Bass.

Willett, G. (2000). *Living out loud: A history of gay and lesbian activism in Australia.* St Leonards, Australia: Allen & Unwin.

Williams, B. T. (2002). *Tuned in: Television and the teaching of writing.* Portsmouth, NH: Boynton/Cook.

Williams, B. T. (2009). *Shimmering literacies: Popular culture and reading and writing online.* London, UK: Peter Lang.

Williams, B. T. (2001). Reflections on a shimmering screen: Television's relationship to writing pedagogies. *The Writing Instructor 2.0.*

Willinsky, J. (1989). Getting personal and practical with personal practical knowledge. *Curriculum Inquiry, 19*(3), 247–264. doi:10.2307/1179416

Wilson, D. E., & Ritchie, J. S. (1994). Resistance, revision, and representation: Narrative in teacher education. *English Education, 26*(3), 177–188.

Winograd, T., & Flores, F. (1986). *Understanding computers and cognition: A new foundation for design.* Boston, MA: Addison-Wesley.

Winterowd, R. (1983). Dramatism in themes and poems. *College English, 45*(6), 581–588. doi:10.2307/377144

Witherell, C., & Noddings, N. (1991). Prologue: An invitation to our readers. In Witherell, C., & Noddings, N. (Eds.), *Stories lives tell: Narrative and dialogue in education* (pp. 1–12). New York, NY: Teachers College Press.

Wong, J. L. N. (2006). Control and professional development: Are teachers being deskilled or reskilled within the context of decentralization? *Educational Studies, 32*(1), 17–37. doi:10.1080/03055690500415910

Wood, R. G. (1993). Responses to Maxine Hairston "diversity, ideology, and teaching writing" and reply. *College Composition and Communication, 44,* 248–256. doi:10.2307/358843

Wood, G. H. (1990). Teachers as curriculum workers. In Sears, J. T., & Marshall, J. D. (Eds.), *Teaching and thinking about curriculum: Critical inquiries* (pp. 97–109). New York, NY: Teachers College Press.

Worsham, L. (1991). Writing against writing: The predicament of *ecriture feminine* in composition studies. In Harkin, P., & Schilb, J. (Eds.), *Contending with words: Composition and rhetoric in a postmodern age* (pp. 82–104). New York, NY: MLA.

Worsham, L. (1987). The question concerning invention: Hermeneutics and the genesis of writing. *Pre/Text, 8,* 197-244.

Wysocki, A. F., Johnson-Eilola, J., Selfe, C., & Sirc, G. (2004). *Writing new media: Theory and applications for expanding the teaching of composition.* Logan, UT: Utah State University Press.

Yip, K. (2004). A Chinese cultural critique of the global qualifying standards for social work education. *Social Work Education, 23*(5), 597–612. doi:10.1080/0261547042000252316

Yoon, H. K. (2005). Affecting the transformative intellectual: Questioning "noble" sentiments in critical pedagogy and composition. *JAC, 25*(4), 717–759.

Young, I. M. (1990). *Justice and the politics of difference.* Princeton, NJ: Princeton University Press.

Zembylas, M. (2007). Emotional capital and education: Theoretical insights from Bourdieu. *British Journal of Educational Studies, 55*(4), 443–463. doi:10.1111/j.1467-8527.2007.00390.x

Zembylas, M., & Boler, M. (2002). On the spirit of patriotism: Challenges of a "pedagogy of discomfort". *Teachers College Record*. Retrieved from http://www.tcrecord.org

Zembylas, M., & Boler, M. (2002). *Teachers college record*. Retrieved from http://www.tcrecord.org/library

Zevengergen, R. (2005). Primary preservice teachers' understanding of volume: The impact of course and practicum experiences. *Mathematics Education Research Journal, 17*(1), 3–23. doi:10.1007/BF03217407

About the Contributors

Julie Faulkner is a Senior Lecturer in Education at RMIT University in Melbourne, Australia. Her research and publications have been in the areas of popular culture and literacy practices, multiliteracies, pedagogy, and questions around professional representation and identity. She has co-edited Learning to Teach: New Times, New Practices (Oxford University Press), currently preparing for second edition.

* * *

Susan Adams is the Project Alianza Director in the College of Education at Butler University where she teaches graduate courses for practicing middle and high school teachers. A former high school Spanish and ESL teacher and instructional coach, Susan is a doctoral candidate in Literacy, Culture, and Language in Education at Indiana University at the School of Education in Indianapolis. She is a national facilitator and Critical Friends Group Coach with the School Reform Initiative and a Teacher Consultant with the National Writing Project and a site leader of the Hoosier Writing Project. Her research interests include equity, teacher transformation, and ELL student writing development.

Susan Matoba Adler, PhD, is Associate Professor of Elementary and Early Childhood Education at the University of Hawai'i West Oahu. Dr. Adler was a former faculty member of the University of Illinois at Urbana-Champaign, the University of Michigan- Ann Arbor, and the University of Wisconsin-Madison. She was a Head Start Education Coordinator in Wisconsin, an Early Childhood Laboratory school teacher/director in North Carolina, and a public school elementary teacher in Colorado. Dr. Adler is author of Mothering, Education, and Ethnicity: The Transformation of Japanese American Culture (1998). Her research on Hmong education, the racial/ethnic socialization of Asian American children, and teacher epistemology has been published in many education professional texts and journals. She is currently Chair of the UHWO Division of Education and is working on two grants; one on the Hawaiian Internment site Honolulu and the other with kindergarten and Head Start teachers of Hawaiian and South Pacific children.

Julie Myatt Barger is an Assistant Professor of English at Middle Tennessee State University, where she teaches first-year composition, sophomore literature, and graduate courses in Composition. She also supervises the English Graduate Teaching Assistants, a demanding but rewarding responsibility. In addition to the connections between feminist pedagogies and service-learning initiatives, her research interests include teacher training, the performance of identity in writing and in student/teacher interactions, and ways in which online forums allow individuals to challenge problematic portrayals of particular identity groups in mainstream media stories. She is currently studying the implications President Barack Obama's Culture of Service has for university service-learning initiatives.

Kaitlin A. Briggs, Ed. D., is Associate Professor of Interdisciplinary Studies and Associate Director of Honors Writing and Thesis Research at the University of Southern Maine, USA. Her recent publications include "Individual Achievement in an Honors Research Community: Teaching Vygotsky's Zone of Proximal Development" in *Honors in Practice* (2010) and "Thesis as Rhizome: A New Vision for the Honors Thesis in the Twenty-First Century" in *Journal of the National Collegiate Honors Council* (2009). Started with a grant from the Sophia Smith Collection, Smith College, Northampton, MA (2006), her current research focuses on the seventy year diary of American composer and music educator Dorothy Smith Dushkin (1903-1992).

Heather Brunskell-Evans is a Senior Lecturer in Education Studies at The University of Greenwich, UK. Her theoretical background is in philosophy and sociology, particularly feminist philosophy and poststructuralist theory. Her current research branches into two areas. The first concerns the governmental restructuring of Higher Education, social policy, and neo-liberal politics. In particular she is completing work critically reflecting on the Educational Doctorate as a professional development qualification. The second area is research into the relationship between social forces, epistemology, and the science of climate change.

Rick Carpenter is Assistant Professor of English at Valdosta State University in Valdosta, Georgia, United States, where he teaches undergraduate and graduate courses in writing, rhetorical theory, new media, and composition pedagogy. His published work appears or is forthcoming in *M/C Journal: A Journal of Media and Culture, Computers and Composition,* and *New Media Literacies and Participatory Popular Culture Across Borders*. His research interests include genre theory, new media studies, disability studies, and identity construction.

Susie Costello is a Senior Lecturer in Social Work at RMIT University in Melbourne Australia. Her background is in social work practice in diverse fields including health, disability, psychiatry, child protection and family support services. In 2007, Susie lived in Thailand near the border of Burma and worked with health and community workers in setting up a basic social work education program. She worked with UNICEF in Burma contributing to the University of Yangon's social work diploma and in developing the beginning of a child protection system. She teaches courses in social work practice, advocacy, and culture. She can be contacted on susan.costello@rmit.edu.au

Greg Curran is Program Manager of Language & Literacy Programs at Victoria University (Melbourne, Australia). Previously, he taught English as a Second Language (ESL) in the Tertiary and Further Education (TAFE) and elementary school system. Greg also lectured in the fields of education and health promotion at a number of Victorian universities. Greg's academic interests include gender and sexual diversity, and the teaching of multimedia and work-integrated learning within adult ESL settings.

Elizabeth de Freitas is an Associate Professor at Adelphi University. Her research interests include mathematics education and cultural studies. She has published articles in *Educational Studies in Mathematics; Qualitative Inquiry; Race, Ethnicity and Education; Mathematics Teacher Education; The International Journal of Education and the Arts; Teaching Education; Language and Literacy; Gender and Education; The Journal of the Canadian Association for Curriculum Studies*; and *The Canadian Journal of Education*. She is also co-editor of the book Opening the research text: Critical insights and in(ter)ventions into mathematics education, published by Springer Verlag in 2008. Recent publications include the 2010 online Making mathematics public: Aesthetics as the distribution of the sensible available at http://ccfi.educ.ubc.ca/publication/insights/v13n01/articles/defreitas/abstract.html

Shelley Dole is a Senior Lecturer in Mathematics Education at The University of Queensland. She teaches in the Bachelor and Master of Education programs. She is an experienced classroom teacher of over ten years and has been a tertiary educator for fifteen years. Shelley's teaching focus is on promoting preservice teachers' confidence in their own ability to do and teach mathematics. She strives to engage students in rich investigative activities that serve to bring meaning to mathematics and simultaneously model good mathematics pedagogy. Shelley's research interests include students' mathematical learning difficulties; the development of proportional reasoning within the study of rational numbers; mental computation; numeracy across the curriculum; and teacher professional development. She is author of several books on teaching mathematics in schools.

Erik Ellis teaches in the Program in Writing and Rhetoric at Stanford University. He has a Ph.D. in Rhetoric, Composition, and the Teaching of English from the University of Arizona. His essay "Back to the Future?: The Pedagogical Promise of the (Multimedia) Essay" appears in the collection *Multimodal Literacies and Emerging Genres in Student Compositions*, edited by Carl Whithaus and Tracey Bowen.

Jennifer Elsden-Clifton is a Lecturer in the School of Education at RMIT University. As an experienced secondary school teacher and university educator, she teaches in teacher preparation programs in the areas of health education, professional issues in teaching, diversity, and curriculum. Jennifer is an experienced researcher in the areas of sexuality education, health education, visual arts education, and teacher education. An emerging research interest concerns beginning teachers.

Lynn Hanson is a Professor of English and Coordinator of the Professional Writing program at Francis Marion University in Florence, South Carolina. She teaches business and technical communication and directs the internship program for students in professional writing. For over 12 years, Dr. Hanson has developed experiential learning projects for classes and internships in which students produce usable documents for professional clients. While also serving as the coordinator of university accreditation from 2005 - 2008, Dr. Hanson hired undergraduates to assist with writing and editing compliance documentation. The quality of their work serves as a testament to experiential learning success.

Heidi Skurat Harris is currently an Assistant Professor of English and Writing for Eastern Oregon University in La Grande, OR. She earned her Ph.D. in Rhetoric and Composition with a Specialization in Computer-Mediated Instruction in May 2009 from Ball State University (BSU). Heidi holds an M.A. in Creative Writing from BSU, an M.A. in Writing (Rhetoric and Composition) from Missouri State

University (MSU), and a B.A. in English from College of the Ozarks. In her fourteen years of teaching experience, Heidi has taught courses in five different disciplines and at four types of higher-learning institutions, including a community college, three state universities, a private Christian university, and a proprietary online school. Among these institutions are Ozarks Technical Community College and Missouri State University, where she was a full-time English Instructor for four years prior to her doctoral studies. Teaching in varied contexts—traditional classrooms, computer-assisted classrooms, and online learning environments—gives Heidi a deep understanding of the benefits and barriers presented by technology. In addition to her position at EOU, Heidi is active in professional organizations. She recently served on the Executive Board for the Two-Year College Association--Midwest. She also is a member of the Conference on College Composition and Communication of the National Council of Teachers of English, where she has presented several panels, including one outlining the results of her dissertation on student use of the Blackboard CMS at CCCC 2010. Heidi currently teaches introduction to college-writing, advanced technical writing, exploratory and expository writing, and digital rhetoric at Eastern Oregon University.

Jeanne Marie Iorio, Ed.D., is an Assistant Professor in Early Childhood Education at the University of Hawai`i-West Oahu. As both an educator and artist, Jeanne Marie has intertwined the arts and education, focusing her research on child-adult conversations as aesthetic experiences. She is currently working on a documentary depicting the stories of LGBTI adults and their early childhood experiences. Her research interests include arts research methodologies, power differences between children and adults, preschool stories as documentation, action research, gender and early childhood, and democratic education. Jeanne Marie serves as the program co-chair for Critical Perspectives on Early Childhood SIG for the American Educational Research Association and the co-chair of University of Hawaii Commission on the Status of LGBTI Equality. She completed her doctoral work at Teachers College, Columbia University.

Pamela Bolotin Joseph is Senior Lecturer at University of Washington Bothell, USA. She is a scholar in the field of curriculum studies and has published on the topics of curriculum inquiry, curriculum leadership, the teaching profession, moral education, and the moral dimensions of teaching. She is editor and author of chapters in of Cultures of Curriculum, 2nd Edition (Routledge) and co-editor and author of chapters in Images of Schoolteachers in America (Routledge). She has published articles in *Asia-Pacific Journal of Teacher Education, Journal of Curriculum & Pedagogy, Journal of Curriculum Studies, Journal of Moral Education, Journal of Peace Education, Journal of Teacher Education, Phi Delta Kappan, Social Education,* and *Theory and Research in Social Education*. A former high school and middle-school teacher, Joseph has focused her career in higher education on helping teachers to develop expertise and identities as scholars, researchers, reflective practitioners, educational leaders, and activists.

Suzanne Knight is an Assistant Professor of English at The University of Michigan-Flint. She teaches both undergraduate methods courses and graduate courses that focus on pedagogical topics and issues in English language arts. In addition to narrative inquiry as both pedagogy and research methodology, her research interests include: English education, specifically the content that constitutes English education and the relationship between effective pedagogies in English language arts and English education; inter-disciplinary approaches to teacher education; teacher narratives, specifically as they relate to public perceptions of teachers and schooling, as well as larger discussions around educational policy; and theorizing the nature of spirituality in teaching.

Abby Knoblauch is an Assistant Professor of English at Kansas State University where she teaches undergraduate and graduate courses in expository writing, rhetorical and composition theories and histories, teacher development, and popular culture. Her primary interests include feminist rhetorical theories and "alternative" rhetorics, composition studies, teacher development, and popular culture and the teaching of writing. In addition to various reviews and teaching tips, she has published articles on composition history and pedagogies, and on Buffy the Vampire Slayer and rhetorical theory. She has also co-edited a book on teaching first-year writing courses. When not reading, writing, or teaching, she enjoys reading bad vampire novels and walking the Konza Prairie.

Drew Kopp, an assistant professor in the Writing Arts department at Rowan University, teaches both first-year college composition and upper level undergraduate courses within the Writing Arts major. In addition to theorizing how performative rhetorical pedagogies work to bring process and post-process writing pedagogies into dialogue, he also investigates how writing with new media (especially digital video) may both cultivate rhetorical intelligence and help shape public conversations concerning the nature and value of writing and writing instruction. Connecting both projects is a larger investigation into the historical conflicts between philosophy and rhetoric and the intersections of these conflicts with writing pedagogy. Dr. Kopp may be contacted at kopp@rowan.edu.

Gloria Latham is a Senior Lecturer in the School of Education, College of Design and Social Context at RMIT University. Gloria is the recipient of a 2009 Australian National Award (ALTC) for inspiring face to face teaching that supports and challenges knowledge creation while utilizing sustained innovative design and application of educational technologies. Her research interests include disruptive pedagogies and ongoing teacher research regarding teacher education, virtual schools, reflexive practice, journal writing and critical incidents to foster new understandings. Gloria's teaching approach supports and challenges knowledge creation while utilizing sustained and disruptive innovative design and the application of educational technologies. Gloria is editor of the text Learning to teach: New times, new practices now in its 2nd edition. A virtual school of ideas founded in 2003 and expanded each year, complements the text.

Meredith A. Love is Associate Professor of English and Composition Coordinator at Francis Marion University in Florence, SC where she teaches courses in composition, professional writing, composition pedagogy, and gender and rhetoric. Her work has been published in journals such as *College Composition and Communication, Feminist Teacher,* and *Composition Studies* and can also be found in the forthcoming book, Code Meshing as World English: Policy, Pedagogy, Performance, edited by Vershawn Ashanti Young and Aja Y. Martinez (NCTE Press). She is currently working on a quantitative research project examining measures of preparedness for college writing and on an article about popular responses to Barack Obama's performance of eloquence in the 2008 presidential campaign.

Mia O'Brien is a Lecturer in Pedagogy and in Arts Education at the University of Queensland. She teaches in the Bachelor of Education (Primary, Middle Years, and Secondary) programs. Experienced in classroom teaching, university teaching, classroom research, and professional development, Mia's teaching focus is on the facilitation of preservice teachers' emerging pedagogical identities and practice, and on the advocacy of arts-rich pedagogies. Mia is a qualitative researcher with interests in: teacher identity, pedagogical content knowledge, pedagogical reasoning, and arts-based pedagogies; and she has authored several book chapters and journal articles on these themes. She is also an enthusiastic amateur musician, visual artist, and singer-songwriter.

Ross Peterson-Veatch is the Associate Academic Dean at Goshen College, in Goshen, Indiana, USA, where he teaches undergraduate courses in Race and Culture. At Goshen he is also the Director of Curriculum, Teaching, and Faculty Development at the Center for Intercultural Teaching and Learning, and will begin in Fall of 2011 as director of the Master's program in Intercultural Leadership. He is a former high school Spanish and Social Studies teacher, instructional coach, and school transformation coach. He taught Spanish, Folklore, and Economics at Earlham College and Indiana University, and before coming to Goshen, was a faculty member in the Liberal Arts and Management Program at Indiana University Bloomington. He is a national facilitator and Critical Friends Group coach with the School Reform Initiative. His research interests include intercultural leadership, equity in education, transformative adult learning, and higher education administration.

Miriam B. Raider-Roth is an Associate Professor of Educational Studies and Urban Educational Leadership and the Director of the Center for Studies in Jewish Education and Culture at the University of Cincinnati. She received her Doctorate from the Harvard University Graduate School of Education. Her research focuses on the relational context of teaching and learning; children's and teachers' conceptions of their relationships in school; use of descriptive process in teacher professional development; action research, and feminist qualitative research methods. She is the author of *Trusting What You Know: The High Stakes of Classroom Relationships* (2005) and Learning to be Present: How *Hevruta* Learning Can Activate Teachers' Relationships to Self, Other and Text (with E. Holzer) (2009). She is currently studying how teachers' engagement with collaborative text study shapes their understanding of learning and teaching.

Edith A. Rusch is a Professor in the Department of Educational Leadership at the University of Nevada Las Vegas. Her research is grounded in concepts of democratic praxis and her publications interrogate the knowledge and skill base of academics to engage in diversity issues, social justice in leadership education, the disconnected K-16 pipeline, and how democratic praxis influences profound cultural change in educational setting. She is the editor of the *Journal of Research on Leadership Education,* and her publications have appeared in *Educational Administration Quarterly, Review of Higher Education, Journal of School Leadership, International Journal of Educational Management, Teacher Development, International Journal of School Reform,* and *the International Journal of Leadership in Education.* Her most recent publications include Changing hearts and minds: The quest for open talk about race in Educational Leadership and contributions to Breaking into the All Male Club: First Women in Educational Administration Departments (SUNY Press, 2009).

Vicki Stieha teaches graduate courses in the School of Education at the University of Cincinnati. As an educator and researcher committed to educational transformation, her research looks not only at the experiences of the individual, but also at the contexts that support and inhibit innovation and transformation. Her research has spanned the P-16 spectrum with particular interest in schooling in urban-metropolitan areas. Recent publications include Expectations and Experiences: The voice of a First-generation First-Year College Student and the Question of Student Persistence (2010) and The Relational Web in Teaching and Learning: Connections, Disconnections and the Central Relational Paradox in Schools (Doctoral dissertation, University of Cincinnati, 2010).

Bronwyn T. Williams is a Professor of English at the University of Louisville. He writes and teaches about issues of literacy, popular culture, digital media, pedagogy, and identity. His recent books include Shimmering Literacies: Popular Culture and Reading and Writing Online (Peter Lang); Popular Culture and Representations of Literacy (Routledge, with Amy Zenger); Identity Papers: Literacy and Power in Higher Education (Utah State); and Tuned In: Television and the Teaching of Writing (Boynton Cook).

Index